# CROWNING GLORY

## SILVER TORAH ORNAMENTS

### of The Jewish Museum, New York

# CROWNING GLORY

## Silver Torah Ornaments

### OF THE JEWISH MUSEUM, NEW YORK

BY

## Rafi Grafman

EDITED BY

## Vivian B. Mann

ༀༀༀༀༀ
ༀༀༀༀ
ༀༀ
ༀ
·

*Published by* THE JEWISH MUSEUM · NEW YORK *under the auspices of*
THE JEWISH THEOLOGICAL SEMINARY OF AMERICA
*in association with*
DAVID R. GODINE · PUBLISHER · BOSTON

*First published in 1996 by*
DAVID R. GODINE, *Publisher*
P. O. Box 9103
Lincoln, Massachusetts 01773

The Jewish Museum, Inc.
1109 Fifth Avenue
New York, New York 10128

ISBN: 1-56792-068-3

First Edition
Manufactured in the United States of America

# DONORS TO THE CATALOGUE

The Jewish Museum gratefully acknowledges the Roy J. Zuckerberg Family Foundation for its generous support of both this publication and the research that preceded it.

Additional funding was provided by income from the Dorot Foundation Publications Fund and by grants from the National Endowment for the Arts, a federal agency, The Lucius N. Littauer Foundation, the Samuel H. Kress Foundation, the Nathan and Louise Goldsmith Fund, and Elizabeth Cats.

# Table of Contents

❧

# Acknowledgments

❧

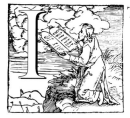T IS RARE that we have the opportuntity to pause and assess the results of a museum's collecting for ninety years. This catalogue of Torah ornaments, culled from one of the three largest collections of Jewish ceremonial art in the world, represents such a singular moment in the curatorial history of The Jewish Museum. Drawn from the universe of works created for ritual use in synagogues and homes, the objects used to protect, facilitate, and enhance the reading of the Torah (the Scroll inscribed with the first five Books of the Hebrew Bible) are among the most exquisitely and lovingly created.

The collection of silver Torah ornaments in The Jewish Museum is distinguished by its size, its comprehensive representation of numerous artistic styles and countries of origin, and by exceptional works from eastern Europe and Germany. In documenting and cataloguing these works, we have undertaken a project of enormous proportions. Our goal has been to make known, in image and text, over nine hundred Torah ornaments that were collected over a ninety year period.

Some of these works belong to the group of ceremonial objects given to The Jewish Theological Seminary of America in 1904 by Judge Mayer Sulzberger who hoped that his gift would be the beginning of a Jewish museum under Seminary auspices. Soon, larger, important collections were joined to the Sulzberger gifts: the Benguiat Family Collection in 1924, the donations of Dr. Harry G. Friedman, and the holdings of the Jewish Community of Danzig which arrived at the Seminary in July, 1939, just before the Second World War. After the museum's move to the Warburg Mansion site at 1109 Fifth Avenue, other gifts and collections were added so that today, The Jewish Museum possesses one of the largest collections of Torah ornaments in the world.

The process of surveying and analyzing a collection of this scope offers an opportunity to discover new information, to conduct new research, and to create new exhibition ideas. The works under consideration, while created mainly for use in synagogues, can be appreciated from a variety of perspectives. This collection, ranging from the 16th century to the present, represents hundreds of synagogues and communities located throughout the Jewish world and often serves as a reminder of populations lost in the Holocaust. The Torah Shields, Finials, Pointers, and Crowns form an eloquent reminder of the Jewish past and a source of knowledge about history. With its many illustrations of virtually all of the 925 objects in the collection, this catalogue comprises a new resource for scholars and silver collectors, particularly since the work of many important silversmiths is included.

The person responsible for initiating this project, Roy Zuckerberg, is himself a collector of silver. His combined interest in the medium and commitment to the collecting mission of The Jewish Museum inspired the curatorial staff to begin this project. His generosity made possible the photography of the works, and most importantly, it enabled the museum to hire Judaica expert, Rafi Grafman whose more than three years of work in the storerooms and archives of the museum, researching and cataloguing the collection, informs all aspects of this book. We are grateful to Mr. Zuckerberg for his inspiration and to Mr. Grafman for his acumen and diligence.

The timing of the work on the project was such that the collection needed to be studied simultaneously with its move out of the "old" Jewish Museum into storage, and its return to new storerooms in the renovated and expanded Museum, reopened in June of 1993. These conditions required exceptional patience of Mr. Grafman, and demanded careful administration by the Judaica Department of the Museum. Special thanks are due to Assistant Curators Diane Saltzman and Claudia Nahson who coordinated retrieval, polishing, photography, and publication of the works, to Visual Resources Archivist Barbara Treitel who organized all of the records of preexisting photographs and assisted in all aspects of the photography, to intern Gavriel Bellino who was responsible for the organization of new photographs, and to Research Assistant Sharon Wolfe, Associate Curator Susan L. Braunstein, and Lori Friedfertig and Deena Barth Fiedler, Administrative Assistants, all of the Judaica Department, who helped with diverse aspects of the project. Dr. Vivian Mann, Morris and Eva Feld Chair of the Judaica Department, supervised all of the research, photography and conservation, and also edited the book. She is to be congratulated for seeing the project through its many stages, and for her extensive and admirable knowledge of The Jewish Museum's collection and of comparative material. Without Dr. Mann's exceptional scholarly abilities, and her vision for a project of this scope, it would not have been accomplished. Additional appreciation is extended to Ward Mintz, the Museum's Assistant Director for Programs until July, 1994, who oversaw much of the project's development and was responsible for its integration into the larger project of reopening the Museum.

As is the case with an exhibition, an endeavor of this scope relies upon the cooperation of several departments and in this case thanks are due to Lynn Thommen, Deputy Director of Development, Donna Jeffrey, Comptroller, Claudette Donlon, Deputy Director of Administration until December, 1994, Geri Thomas, former Administrator for Exhibitions and Collections, Susan Palamara, Registrar, Lisa Mansfield, Assistant Registrar, Carolyn Nutovic, former Associate Registrar, and Julia Goldman, former Curatorial Assistant in the Department of Exhibitions and Collections. Finally, all those who worked on the project are grateful to the teams of volunteers who came day after day, week after week, to polish the silver prior to photography.

In the final stages, Scott-Martin Kosofsky of The Philidor Company, Boston, worked with Vivian Mann and Rafi Grafman to create a truly beautiful book. The vast majority of photographs were masterfully done especially for this volume by John Parnell. *Crowning Glory: Silver Torah Ornaments of The Jewish Museum New York* has been funded by Roy and Barbara Zuckerberg, the Dorot Foundation Publications Fund, the National Endowment for the Arts, The Lucius N. Littauer Foundation, the Samuel H. Kress Foundation, the Nathan and Louise Goldsmith Fund, and Elizabeth Cats.

Finally, thanks are extended to the Board of Trustees of The Jewish Museum, whose leadership has encouraged curatorial creativity, and to all of those people who donated objects, funds, and knowledge to build such an extraordinary collection in the ninety years since The Jewish Museum was established by The Jewish Theological Seminary of America. The collection of Torah Ornaments is one that resonates both in the world of decorative arts and in the universe of Jewish history, and serves as an incomparable source of pleasure and study.

JOAN ROSENBAUM
*Helen Goldsmith Menschel Director*

# Using the Catalogue

⌘

THE CATALOGUE is organized geographically and chronologically. Within this framework are also groupings by type (with the result that, occasionally, a Polish-made finial may be listed under a German type).

The object name is followed by The Jewish Museum accession number. Accession numbers prior to 1980 are prefixed by letters as follows: **D** = Danzig Collection, acquired in 1939; **F** = Dr. Harry G. Friedman Collection, acquired 1941–1965; **JM** = Jewish Museum, 1947–1979; **M** = The Rose and Benjamin Mintz Collection, acquired in 1952; **S** = The Jewish Theological Seminary Collection, acquired 1904–1946, which includes the earliest Jewish Museum objects as well as the Hadji Ephraim and Mordecai Benguiat Family Collection, acquired in 1924; "Unknown" objects, whose original accession number has been lost, bear a **U** prefix.

ILLUSTRATIONS: All the objects in the Catalogue are illustrated except for some duplicates or near duplicates.

PLACE OF ORIGIN generally refers to the location where the object was made. Where the city is known, no country has been given: many of the places referred to were in continuous political upheaval for most of the period represented. For example, Bratislava = Pressburg = Poszony has been, at one time or another, part of the Kingdom of Hungary, the Austro-Hungarian Empire or the Republic of Czechoslovakia.

DATES are based either on hallmarks and inscriptions, or on parallels and/or on technical considerations such as the character of repoussé or engraving.

MATERIALS AND TECHNIQUES: Only decorative techniques are given, after the respective material. CHASING refers to modelling with hammer and punches on the outer surface of the metal; REPOUSSÉ refers to modelling with hammer and punches on both surfaces. ENGRAVING removes metal with a burin, leaving a groove in the surface; ETCHING removes through the corrosive action of an acid, leaving a groove (which is not as sharp as an engraved line). DIE-STAMPING refers to mechanical patterns attained by pressing metal into a die, or by stamping its surface with a patterned punch. CASTING refers to any one of several processes by which molten metal is poured into a mold containing the negative form of the desired pattern. Where an entire object is cast in one piece, ornamentation may be integrated into the casting. Elements such as feet, handles, pendants, bells, and finials, are often cast for later attachment to a larger object. GILDING may cover an entire object, or may be partial ("parcel-gilt"). PARCEL-GILDING may be used to emphasize specific parts of a design, such as script or foliage, or may be limited to specific elements, such as bells or lions.

DIMENSIONS: In all cases, maximum dimensions are given, but do not include movable parts (such as loops, suspension chains, pendants, bells), unless otherwise noted. H = height; W = width; L =length; DIAM = diameter; all dimensions are in centimeters.

HALLMARKS: Concerning identifiable marks, references are to the standard works, abbreviated in accord with the Bibliography on p. 395. In the Scheffler volumes, the numbers are those of the marks, not of the silversmiths. The designation "var." following a reference signifies that the mark on the object is similar to, but not identical with, the mark in the published source. Hitherto unpublished marks are described briefly and appear in the plates of hallmark photographs on p. 367.

INSCRIPTIONS: Transcriptions of the Hebrew inscriptions are complete throughout, except for biblical and talmudic passages, whose sources are identified. The new Jewish Publication Society translation of the Bible (1985) has been used, sometimes modified. In transcribing the Hebrew Tetragrammaton, the letter *qof* substitutes for *heh*. Honorifics are generally left untranslated except where of particular significance; other Hebrew abbreviations and contractions are translated in full, and are enclosed by square brackets. The common Hebrew abbreviation ז״ל, literally "May his memory be blessed," has been translated throughout as "the late . . . ." Chronograms of Hebrew dates are either translated or their biblical source noted, and the year calculated with its Gregorian equivalent. Due to the limitations of printing, the wide range of marks used to denote abbreviations and "numerical" letters could not be reflected in the entries. Where no indication of a month is present, the Jewish year is designated as overlapping two Gregorian years, for example, 1994/95. Biblical names with common equivalents are written in English. Other transliterations are based on the system employed by the *Encyclopædia Judaica*.

BIBLIOGRAPHY: Only actual publications of the object are included. For the abbreviations of the sources in both the introduction and the entries, see the Bibliography on p. 395.

REMARKS: This rubric may contain further information on the object itself, on parallels, and on historical or geographical data concerning the piece. Occasionally there is also a discussion of the general type of object or of the maker.

The final section of the Catalogue includes items of dubious nature. They are arranged by type and Museum accession number, but have not been given Catalogue numbers. Cross-references to them are preceded by the abbreviation "No." (e.g. "No. F 5675"), to distinguish them from objects not included in the Catalogue (such as spice containers or Hanukkah lamps), which are referred to by accession number alone (e.g. "F 2707"). The objects of this final section are not indexed.

RAFI GRAFMAN

# Torah Ornaments before 1600

## *Vivian B. Mann*

ev

לזכרון אבי מורי ישעיהו יעקב אייזנברג ז״ל

One acts towards a kosher Torah Scroll with additional holiness and great honor …A *tik* [container] that was prepared for a Torah Scroll which was laid in it, textile wrappers, and the ark and the reader's desk … and also the chair prepared to rest the Torah Scroll on it, and it rested on it, all are implements of holiness … and the silver and gold *rimmonim* [finials], and the like, that are made for the beauty of the Torah Scroll, are implements of holiness …"

—MAIMONIDES, *Mishneh Torah,* Hilkhot Sefer Torah, 10:4

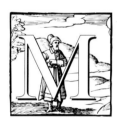

AIMONIDES' DISCUSSION of the sanctity of Torah cases, mantles, arks, reader's desks, chairs, and finials states that all are sacred because they come into physical contact with the holiest artifact of Judaism, the Torah Scroll.[1] All other types of Jewish ceremonial art, with the exception of *tefillin* and *mezuzot,*[2] are handmaidens of the performance of religious commandments, but do not have the inherent sanctity defined by Maimonides.

Torah ornaments, then, have a special status within Judaism. Given their revered position, we may be surprised to learn that the corpus of these ornaments has not been static, but has developed over time. This essay will describe the process of that development during the two periods for which few actual examples exist, antiquity and the Middle Ages.

The Torah Scroll is inscribed with the first five Books of the Hebrew Bible, traditionally believed to have been dictated by God to Moses during the forty days the great leader spent on Mount Sinai, and written down at a later date. Genesis, Exodus, Leviticus, Numbers, and Deuteronomy contain the early history of the Jewish people and the laws, precepts, and ethical norms they are commanded to follow.

Although worship was primarily sacrificial throughout the periods of the First and Second Temples (950 BCE –70 CE), biblical sources record the existence of Torah Scrolls used for study.[3] We know little of their appearance and appurtenances, however, until the beginning of our own era when the literary evidence of the Mishnah (redacted ca. 250 CE) and the Talmud (compiled by 500 CE) is supplemented by visual evidence found among the decoration of early synagogues and tombs, in the reliefs and paintings of Roman and Early Jewish and Christian art, and in later medieval works based on earlier models.

1. I wish to thank Professor Richard I. Cohen of the Hebrew University for all the constructive comments he made to an earlier version of this essay, and Rafi Grafman for his suggestions.

2. *Tefillin* are a pair of leather boxes containing passages from the Torah, written on parchment, whose wearing during morning prayers is based on the passage "Bind them as a sign on your hand and as a symbol on your foreheads." (Deut. 6:8, 11:12). *Mezuzot* are parchment scrolls bearing passages from Deuteronomy that are enclosed in protective cases affixed to the doorways of the house. The objects used to protect the *tefillin* and the *mezuzot* derive sanctity from them, as the appurtenances of the Torah derive holiness from the Scroll.

3. See, for example, Neḥemiah 8:1–9:3. For a comparison between the functions of the synagogue and the Temple see Rachel Hachlili, *Ancient Jewish Art and Archaeology in the Land of Israel,* Leiden, New York, Copenhagen, Cologne, 1988, pp. 138–39.

4. For example, Babylonian Talmud, Megillah, fol. 7a–b and fol. 14a, for the terms *mitpaḥat,* or wrapper, and *tevah,* or ark; fol. 26b for *tik.* According to Samuel Krauss, Talmudic references to beautiful silks as coverings for the Torah Scroll far outnumber references to *tikim* and arks. Silks were probably, therefore, the most widely used type of covering in antiquity. (*Synagogale Altertümer,* Berlin-Vienna, 1922, p. 384.)

5. Yigael Yadin, *Bar-Kokhba,* New York, 1971, p. 67. I want to thank Rafi Grafman for emphasizing the significance of this textile.

6. Mishnah, Kelim, 28:4.

7. For figured Coptic textiles, see G. Egger, "Koptische Wirkerei mit figuralen Darstellungen," *Christentum am Nil,* Recklinghausen, 1964, p. 243 ff.; Gary Vikan, "Joseph Iconography on Coptic Textiles," *Gesta,* XVIII (1979), pp. 99–108.

8. Robert G. Calkins, *Illuminated Books of the Middle Ages,* Ithaca, 1983, pp. 36, 53–57.

9. For a detailed reproduction, see Karl Katz, P. P. Kahane, and Magen Broshi, *From the Beginning,* London, 1968, pp. 116–17.

10. Veronika Gervers, "An Early Christian Curtain in the Royal Ontario Museum," *Studies in Textile History in Memory of Harold B. Burnham,* ed. by Veronika Gervers, Toronto, 1977, fig. 1. See also fig. 3, where the triangular motifs appear along the bottom border.

Given the Torah's exalted status within Judaism, its physical form has always been regarded as a sacred object to be protected and honored. The Talmud mentions protecting the Scroll by wrapping it in precious silks, by housing the Torah in a *tik,* or container, or by placing it within a *tevah,* or ark.[4]

During excavations of caves dating to the period of Bar Kokhba (ca. 135 CE), archaeologists recovered a textile that was used as a scroll wrapper (fig. 1).[5] It is a fragment of striped cloth. The Mishnah also mentions the use of silks with figurative decoration as wrappers for the Torah Scroll,[6] which may be an allusion to figured Coptic textiles; the earliest extant examples were found in Egypt and date to the late Roman period.[7] A parallel use of Coptic textiles to wrap sacred writings may have been the custom of Early Christians in Egypt, home to the monks who later spread Christianity to Ireland and Northumbria. Coptic textiles with crosses and interlace designs of the 3rd–4th centuries are thought to have been the models for carpet pages in the Insular Book of Durrow, the first Gospels with a coherent system of decoration (second half of the 7th century).[8] Its carpet pages were conceived as replacements for textiles, and served as inner bindings, marking off sections of the text. Textile wrappers are known to have been used in the 10th century on Christian and Islamic books, added evidence for their earlier employment to protect holy writings during the classical period, as was done for the Torah Scrolls.

The 6th-century mosaic floor of the Beit Shean synagogue demonstrates that Coptic textiles were esteemed enough to be used in association with the Torah. This mosaic features a Torah Shrine hung with a Coptic curtain.[9] Its rows of evenly-spaced motifs on a white background and the border of triangles are closely paralleled in a contemporaneous 6th-century curtain now in the Royal Ontario Museum, Toronto (acc. no. 910.125.32).[10]

No example of a *tik* or container for the Torah survives from the period of the Mishnah and the Talmud; however, Roman and early medieval manuscript illuminations depict authors writing, with a cylindrical container for scrolls beside them on the floor. A Roman example is the portrait of Virgil in the *Virgilius Romanus,* generally dated to the 5th–6th century (Vatican City, Vatican Library, Cod. lat. 3867, f. 3v; fig. 2).[11] A Carolingian continuation of the same iconography appears in a Gospel from Reims, dated 845–82 (New York, Morgan Library, M.728).[12] The portrait of Saint John on folio 141v shows the Evangelist holding a long, open scroll. Another, rolled scroll rests against a closed *tik* or *capsa.*

Despite the anachronistic representation in the Morgan manuscript, the Gospels were generally written in one codex or book by the 4th century. This different format required a box-shaped container; the earliest extant example is Irish and dated to the 7th century.[13] Like other aspects of Insular art, this form may reflect influences from Egypt, the home of many Irish and Northumbrian monks.[14] "The [Irish] practice of making cumdachs or containers for holy books ... reveals that these books were regarded as holy relics of the Word of God."[15]

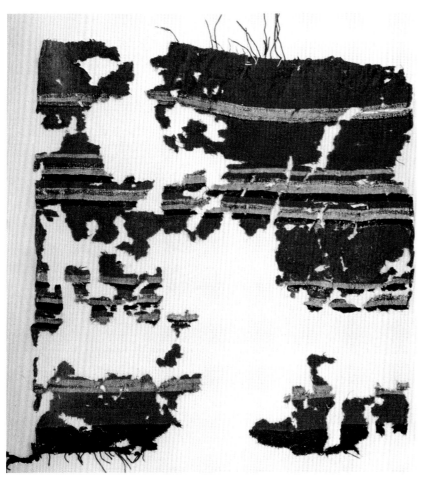

FIG. 1. Textile mantle from Cave of Letters

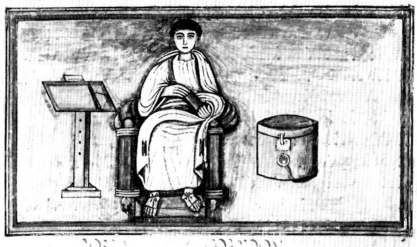

FIG. 2. *Virgilius Romanus,* 5th–6th century, Vatican City, Vatican Library, Cod. lat. 3867, fol. 3v

11. It has been suggested that the cloth-covered object near the legs of a prophet with open scroll painted on the west wall of the Dura Europos Synagogue before 256 CE is also a *tik.* (Joseph Gutmann, *The Jewish Sanctuary,* Leiden, 1983, p. 6 and pl. IV.)

12. The Morgan Library, *Medieval and Renaissance Manuscripts. Major Acquisitions of the Pierpont Morgan Library 1924–1974,* by William Voelkle, New York, 1974, no.3.

13. For examples of Irish book boxes, see New York, The Metropolitan Museum of Art, *Treasures of Early Irish Art 1500 B.C. to 1500 A.D.,* exhibition catalogue, 1977, cat. nos. 57–58, 65–66.

14. For examples of Insular art reflecting Coptic influence, see Martin Werner, "The Four Evangelist Symbols Page in the Book of Durrow," *Gesta,* VIII (1969), pp. 3–17.

15. Calkins, *Illuminated Books,* p. 60.

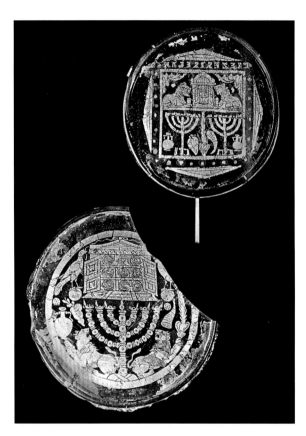

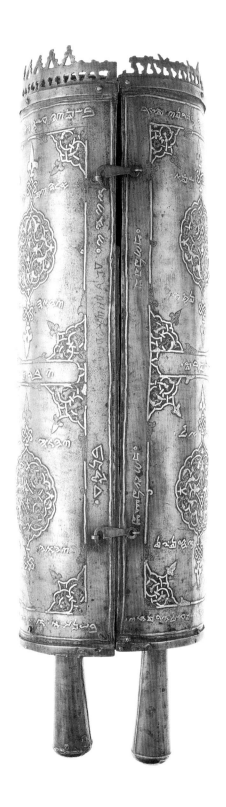

FIG. 3, *above.* Gold Glasses: cup bottoms with Torah Arks and implements, Rome, 4th century. Jerusalem, The Israel Museum, 66.36.14 (above); and 66.36.15 (below)

FIG. 4, *right.* Samaritan *tik,* 1568. New York, The Jewish Museum, S 21 (No. 899)

16.  New York, The Jewish Museum, *Gardens and Ghettos: The Art of Jewish Life in Italy,* ed. by Vivian B. Mann, exhibition catalogue, 1989, figs. 53, 66, 68–69. For a listing of representations in the decoration of ancient synagogues, see Hachlili, *Jewish Art and Archaeology in Late Antiquity,* pp. 167–87.

17.  New York, The Metropolitan Museum of Art, *The Age of Spirituality,* ed. by Kurt Weitzmann, exhibition catalogue, 1980, cat. nos. 382, 347–48, 388, and 396.

The third manner of storing Torah Scrolls mentioned in the Talmud, the ark, appears on gold glasses, funerary reliefs, and frescoes found in the Jewish catacombs of Rome (fig. 3), and on the mosaics, reliefs, and frescoes of ancient synagogues in Eretz Israel and the Diaspora.[16] The gold glass fragments were used, like those of Christians and pagans, to mark the graves of the deceased. Jewish examples are distinguished by their symbolic decoration, a departure from the portraiture favored by the other religious groups.[17] One of the most popular Jewish symbols is an open ark flanked by *menorot* and heraldic lions (a composition often found in the mosaic floors of ancient Israeli synagogues).[18] The interior of the open cabinet is fitted with divided shelves, each accommodating a single scroll wound about an *umbilicus*, the Roman term for the rod used to prevent damage to rolled parchment. Although the Jewish gold glass of Rome dates to the 4th century CE, the depictions of the ark recall a discussion in the Talmud between Rabba (d. 330) and Rabbi Joseph (d. 333). Both agreed that the Torah read on the Sabbath should be written on only one scroll (instead of on five individual scrolls as had been done previously).[19] It would appear that the scrolls depicted in the ancient Roman Torah Arks reflect an earlier way of writing the sacred text. In contrast, the representations of arks found in Ancient Israel have closed doors. This practice of placing the sacred Torah Scroll in an ark or chest recalls similar customs among other religions of the ancient world.[20]

When only a single Torah Scroll was written, the length of the text and, therefore, the length of the parchment, made it necessary to use two rods for support, one at each end of the scroll, which was then rolled toward the middle.[21] Based on literary allusions to the Torah as a source of life and the Tree of Life, the rods become known as *atzei ḥayyim*, "Trees of Life." They are mentioned in rabbinic literature and depicted in late medieval manuscripts, but only one pair survives from the Middle Ages.

According to the inscription integrated into their carved decoration, the extant wooden Torah staves belonged to Nathanael Trabot, who worked as a punctuator and copyist of Hebrew manuscripts during the last quarter of the 15th century and the early 16th.[22] He belonged to a family that had emigrated from France to Italy. Based on their style, the staves date to the late 15th century. The undulating leaf motif along the bottom band and the multiple-lancet windows above appear on a Gothic chalice of that period.[23]

Rabbi Solomon Luria (Jerusalem? 1534–1572 Safed), in a responsum dealing with heirs who wished to reclaim a Torah Scroll donated by their father, discussed the case of donors who reprised the silver rods and chains used to roll the Torah Scroll and keep it in place. This text indicates that some *atzei ḥayyim* had become expensive, decorative elements by the 16th century.[24] A miniature in the Ulm Maḥzor, dated before 1460, shows an open ark whose Torah Scrolls rest on thin, silver-colored rods, an illustration of Rabbi Luria's words.[25] Other depictions of *atzei ḥayyim* in medieval manuscripts are wood-colored and thicker, the ends of the staves carved in bulbous form to facilitate holding.[26]

18. For example, *Gardens and Ghettos,* fig. 67. See Hachlili, *Jewish Art and Archaeology in Late Antiquity,* pp. 361–62 for a listing of ancient synagogues in which this composition appears.

19. Babylonian Talmud, Gittin, 60a.

20. For example, Samaritans stored their holy text, the *markah,* in a *tevah,* an ark or chest. (Z. Ben-Ḥayyim, *Tībât Mårqe,* Jerusalem, 1988, p. 15.) I want to thank Richard Cohen for this reference.

21. Franz Landsberger, "The Origin of European Torah Decorations," *Beauty in Holiness,* ed. by Joseph Gutmann, New York, 1975, p. 89.

22. G. Green, "Texts and Studies in Italian Jewish History during the Sixteenth Century" (Ph.D. Diss., The Jewish Theological Seminary of America, 1974). On the staves, see *Gardens and Ghettos,* cat. no. 115 and fig. 180. They are now in the Gross Family Collection, Ramat Aviv.

23. Braunschweigisches Landesmuseum, Herzog Anton Ulrich-Museum and Dom am Burgplatz, *Stadt im Wandel,* exhibition catalogue, vol. 2, Braunschweig, 1985, no. 1130.

24. Solomon Luria, *She'alot u-Teshuvot ha-Maharshal,* Lemberg, 1859, no. 15.

25. Thérèse and Mendel Metzger, *Jewish Life in the Middle Ages,* Fribourg, 1982, fig. 98.

26. Metzger, *Jewish Life in the Middle Ages,* figs. 94, 97, 99, and 105.

27. Johannes Pedersen, *The Arabic Book,* trans. by Geoffrey French, ed. by Robert Hillenbrand, Princeton, 1984, pp. 106–07.

28. For illustrations of Samaritan *tikim* still in Israel, see Jacob Pinkerfeld, *Bishvilei Amanut Yehudit,* Merḥaviah, 1957, p. 111.

29. Robert T. Anderson, *Studies in Samaritan Manuscripts and Artifacts. The Chamberlain-Warren Collection.* The American Schools of Oriental Research, 1978, pp. 62–64.

30. Shlomo David Goitein, "The Synagogue Building and Its Furnishings according to the Records of the Cairo Genizah," *Eretz-Israel* 7(1964), 91.

31. Goitein, "The Synagogue Building and Its Furnishings," p. 95.

32. *The Kaufmann Haggadah. Facsimile Edition of Ms. 422 of the Kaufmann Collection in the Oriental Library of the Hungarian Academy of Sciences,* Budapest, 1957; Metzger, *Jewish Life in the Middle Ages,* fig. 95; Bezalel Narkiss, *Hebrew Illuminated Manuscripts in the British Isles,* Oxford and Jerusalem, 1982, cat. no. 13. Recently, Sharon Makover-Assaf and Daisy Raccah-Djivre described the Barcelona *tik* as painted or covered with a cloth ("The 'Flowering Vase' Torah Mantle from Morocco," *Israel Museum News,* XI (1993), p. 73). The rigidity of the form, however, argues against the depiction of a cloth; while the existence of inlaid mosque furniture from the 12th century through the 16th suggests that the same technique was used to decorate *tikim.* (See below, nn. 33-34 for illustrations.)

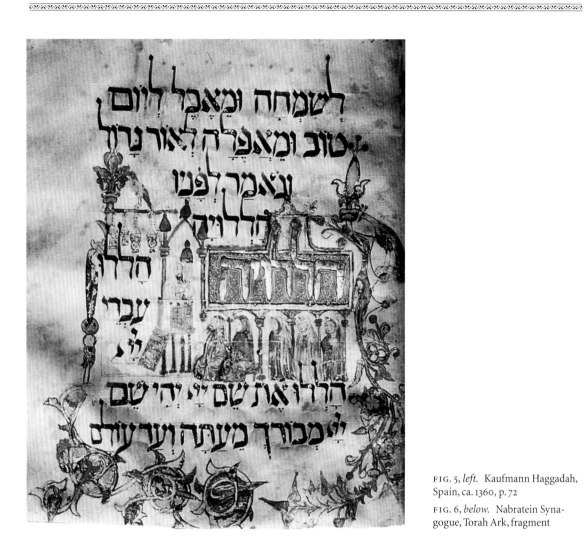

FIG. 5, *left.* Kaufmann Haggadah, Spain, ca. 1360, p. 72

FIG. 6, *below.* Nabratein Synagogue, Torah Ark, fragment

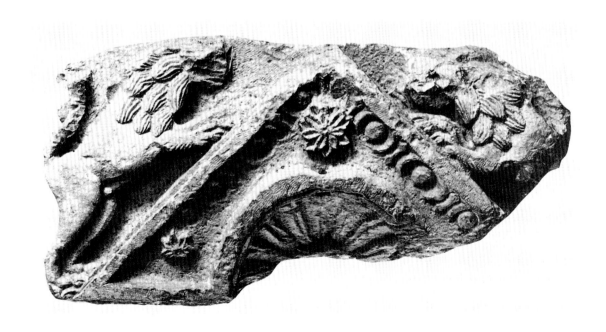

An early group of *atzei ḥayyim* are part of five Samaritan *tikim* dated to the 16th century. One *tik,* in the collection of The Jewish Museum, is of copper inlaid with silver Mamluk ornaments, and bears an inscription naming Rabbi Abi Uzzi son of Rabbi Joseph of Damascus and the date 1568 (No. 899; fig. 4). Its most prominent decorative motif is a Mamluk medallion ending in points which frames a field of fine tracery, offset against a plain ground. This style of decoration is similar to a Muslim book cover design which appeared ca. 1500[27] and may have been adapted from it. Three other *tikim* still belong to the Samaritan community of Israel,[28] and the final example is in the University of Michigan.[29]

Copper *tikim* are mentioned in a memo dated 1075 that was found in the Cairo Genizah listing the contents of the Jerusalemites' Synagogue in Fostat.[30] The remaining fifteen cases owned by the synagogue were of wood. A later document from the same synagogue dated 1159 lists among its possessions a *tik* of wood inlaid with silver, and another of pure silver.[31]

Although there are no depictions of *tikim* contemporaneous with the Genizah documents, two later miniatures in Spanish Haggadot of the 14th century include *tikim* with the same mix of Jewish function and Islamic decorative traditions as is found on the New York *tik*. Both the example in the Kaufmann Haggadah (Budapest, Hungarian Academy of Sciences, Ms.422, p. 72, fig. 5) and that in the Barcelona Haggadah (London, British Library, Ms. Add 14761, fol. 65v) are cylindrical cases with bulbous tops. The Barcelona *tik* appears to be inlaid with varicolored woods.[32] A *minbar* from Córdoba dated to the 12th century establishes the use of such techniques and decorative patterns on mosque furniture during the High Middle Ages;[33] while three 16th- and early 17th-century Koran cases, similar in form to the *tik* in the Kaufmann Haggadah, suggest their continued usage through the intervening centuries since the Kaufmann and Barcelona Haggadot were created.[34] The use of wood for *tikim* never disappeared in a variety of communities, although metal became the more common material.

Torah Scrolls wrapped in textiles and others in *tikim* and in arks or *tevot* were placed in shrines of various forms. Remains of wooden and stone examples have been found in early synagogues.[35] The two most interesting shrines were found at Dura-Europos (Syria), dated before 256, and at Nabratein (Galilee), dated before 354. The first is a niche whose gable encloses a shell-shaped shield, symbol of honor and sacredness in the ancient world.[36] Above are frescoes of biblical themes. All that remains of the Nabratein shrine is a fragmentary relief of confronted lions rampant along the curve of a shell that formed the top part of the structure (fig. 6).[37] It is an iconographic composition commonly found on shrines of the post-medieval period.[38]

Three late medieval shrines exist. The first is in fragments, a series of boards engraved with biblical passages and with the name of a 13th-century donor, which was found in the Cairo Genizah (The Jewish Museum, S727).[39] In the oldest extant medieval synagogue, the Altneushul in Prague dated ca. 1265, is a Gothic stone shrine carved into the back wall of the main

33. New York, The Metropolitan Museum of Art, *Al-Andalus: The Art of Islamic Spain,* ed. by Jerrilyn Dodds, exhibition catalogue, 1992, no. 115.

34. Istanbul, Topkapi Palace Museum, *The Anatolian Civilisations III. Seljuk/Ottoman,* exhibition catalogue, 1983, nos. E147, E149, and E151.

35. See Hachlili, *Jewish Art and Archaeology in Late Antiquity,* pp. 167–87 for a listing of excavated arks.

36. The niche at Dura has been widely published. See, for example, Erwin Goodenough, *Jewish Symbols in the Greco-Roman Period,* Princeton, 1964, vol. ix, pp. 65–77; vol.xi, illus. I. Hachlili, *Jewish Art and Archaeology in Late Antiquity,* pl. 27, passim.

37. Eric M. Meyers, James F. Strange, and Carol L. Meyers, "The Ark of Nabratein — A First Glance," *Biblical Archaeologist* (Fall, 1981), pp. 237–243.

38. For example, New York, The Jewish Museum, *The Jewish Museum,* ed. by Vivian B. Mann with Emily Bilski, 1993, fig. 31, an ark from Westheim bei Hassfurt, Bavaria, dated 18th century.

39. Stephen S. Kayser and Guido Schoenberger, *Jewish Ceremonial Art,* Philadelphia, 1955, no. 2.

40. Zdenka Munzer, *Die Altneusynagoge in Prag,* Prague, 1932.

41. The Jewish Museum, *Gardens and Ghettos,* fig. 93; Victor Klagsbald, *Catalogue raisonné de la collection juive du Musée de Cluny,* Paris, 1981, pp. 94–96.

42. Two of the texts which mention the controversy are: Joseph Caro, *Sh'elot u-Teshuvot Evkat Rukhal,* Jerusalem, 1950, no. 65; David ben Shlomo ibn Abi Zimra, *Sh'elot u-Teshuvot haRadbaz,* Warsaw, 1882, vol. IV, no. 1178. For a synopsis of the controversy, see Isaac Farkas Kahan, *Meḥkarim be-sifrut ha-teshuvot,* Jerusalem, 1973, pp. 355–56.

43. This case was published by David Kaufmann, "Art in the Synagogue," *Jewish Quarterly Review* IX(1897), pp. 254–69.

44. Maimonides, *Mishneh Torah. Hilkhot Sefer Torah,* ch. 10, section 2.

45. For example, ibn Abi Zimra, *She'elot u–Teshuvot ha-Radbaz,* vol. I, no. 80.

46. Maimonides, *Teshuvot ha-Rambam,* vol. II, ed. by Jehoshua Blau, Jerusalem, 1960, no. 165.

47. Krauss, *Synagogale Altertümer,* p. 391. The robbery of removable finials continued to be a problem in the later Middle Ages. For example, see Yom Tov ben Abraham Ishbili, *Sh'elot u–Teshuvot,* ed. by Joseph Kapah, Jerusalem, 1959, no. 159.

48. Avraham Grossman, *The Early Sages of Ashkenaz,* Jerusalem, 1981, 7, n. 25 (Hebrew). I wish to thank Richard Cohen for this reference.

49. Meir of Rothenberg, *She'alot u–Teshuvot,* Prague, 1608, no. 879.

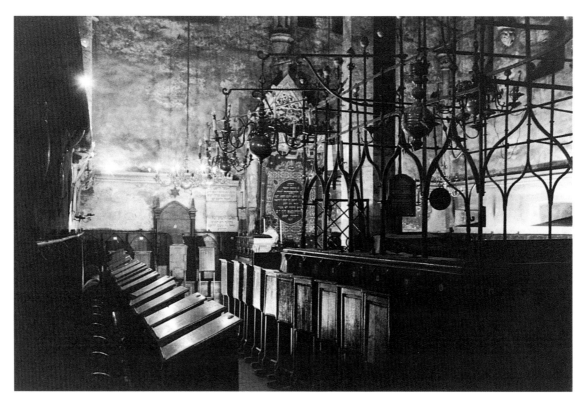

FIG. 7. Interior of the Altneushul, Prague

synagogue (fig. 7).[40] Its vegetal decoration matches that over the main portal. Still in Gothic style is the third extant medieval shrine, a wooden cabinet from Modena dated 1472, that is today in the Cluny Museum (Cl. 12237).[41] The front is divided into rows of squares each carved as an arcade of lancet windows surmounted by flamboyant tracery.

In the early 16th century, an incident in Candia, Crete, aroused the ire of rabbis all over the Mediterranean world.[42] Joseph Caro recounts the story of a powerful and wealthy congregant in Candia who sought to place a marble relief of his coat of arms, which included the crowned figure of a lion, above the Torah Shrine. He was forbidden to do so by the local rabbi, Elihu Capsali, who consulted not only Caro, but also David ibn Zimra of Egypt, Moses Trani of Safed and Meir Katzenellenbogen of Padua. They were unanimous in their condemnation of the decoration. The donor only desisted after governmental intervention. A similar case in southern Italy involved the placement of relief figures of lions at the base of a shrine.[43] Although paired lions have been found on ancient synagogues and became common on shrines of the 18th century on, their appearance in association with the Torah Ark, the focus of prayer in the synagogue, was deemed unacceptable in the 16th century.

Silks, *tikim,* and chests or arks were the three types of cover for the Torah Scroll in antiquity and the Middle Ages. According to Maimonides, these were "implements of holiness" (*tashmishei kedushah*) that had to be treated with proper decorum should they become damaged and unusable.[44] He accorded the same level of holiness to ornaments for the Torah

Scroll — for example, silver finials, although their purpose was merely aesthetic, rather than protective. The one difference between a scroll and its ornaments lay in the fact that the silver could be sold to buy a single book of the Bible or a Torah Scroll, while the scroll could not be sold. Other rabbis allowed the sale of ornaments for additional purposes: to support the poor or to redeem captives.[45] These texts, and others like a Maimonidean responsum concerning a drunk cantor who caused a finial to fall and break,[46] indicate that in the 12th century Torah Finials were removable objects, separate from the rods or *atzei ḥayyim*. It is unclear at what date this development occurred. Some of the earliest references are in Christian texts, one of Saint Severus and the other in the writings of Gregory of Tours dated 598, both of whom mention the robbery of a synagogue, but they are ambivalent about whether or not the ornaments were attached to the rods.[47] An 11th-century text of Rabbi Judah Cohen, who lived near Mainz, refers to commissioning a *tsipui zahav* for the top portion of a Torah Scroll.[48] The literal meaning of the phrase, a gold plating, probably refers to the gilding of the staves, rather than to the independent ornaments which became current a century later. It is important to note that plating the staves in precious metals continued even after the adoption of removable finials as attested to by the illumination in the Ulm Maḥzor, before 1460, cited above, and by a responsum of Meir of Rothenberg to a man who had commissioned gold plating and was cheated by the silversmith who supplied gilt silver.[49]

Later, the independence of the finials allowed them to be used for other purposes. A miniature in the Sister of the Golden Haggadah depicts the synagogue service prior to the Seder.[50] The reader stands on the almemor whose poles are adorned with piriform silver finials (fig. 8), similar to those on the Córdoba mosque almemor. This is a custom still followed in Italy, the former Ottoman Empire, and other countries of the Sephardi diaspora.[51] Rabbi Samuel de Medina, of Salonika (1506–89), records another usage: synagogues were decorated with finials on Sabbaths, holy days, and on festive personal occasions such as circumcisions and weddings.[52]

A detailed list of Torah Finials (*rimmonim*) occurs in the 1159 inventory of the Jerusalemite Synagogue in Cairo, mentioned earlier.[53] The list includes (as separate items) silver finials, others that were gilt, and two pairs of inlaid *rimmonim*. Four crowns for the Torah Scroll are also listed, one of silver, another of gilt silver, a third gilt, and the fourth, a silver crown with inlay. Their forms and decoration are unknown, however.

Aside from the Haggadah miniatures, the only complete picture of medieval *rimmonim* comes from a single extant pair used on Sicily that date to the late 15th century (fig. 9).[54] Now in the Cathedral Treasury of Palma de Majorca, where they are employed as verge or stave ends, the finials are tower forms in Mudejar style, overlaid with delicate filigree and inlaid with semiprecious stones.[55] They clearly demonstrate the use of a common artistic vocabulary by Jews, Christians, and Muslims on the Iberian peninsula during the Middle Ages. The

50. Narkiss, *Hebrew Illuminated Manuscripts in the British Isles,* cat. no. 12, fig. 187.

51. Mili Mitrani and Ersin Alok, *Anatolian Synagogues,* Istanbul, 1992, pp. 48–49, 146–47, 190–91.

52. Morris S. Goodblatt, *Jewish Life in Turkey in the XVIth Century as Reflected in the Legal Writings of Samuel De Medina,* New York, 1952, p. 64 and n. 28.

53. Goitein, "The Synagogue Building…," p. 91.

54. F. Cantera y J. M. Millas, *Las Inscripciones Hebraicas de España,* Madrid, 1956, p. 389–93. In the century after the Majorcan finials were created, another pair was made in Pest, then part of the Ottoman Empire. They are spherical in form, recalling the terms used in Spanish rabbinic texts, *rimmonim* (pomegranates) and *tapukhim* (apples), for Torah Finials. The Pest finials bear an inscription date of 1601/2 and a dedication to the Sephardic synagogue of Pest. (Alexander Scheiber, *Jewish Inscriptions in Hungary,* Budapest and Leiden, 1983, no. 153.)

55. For a comparison of the verge or stave ends and the *rimmonim,* see Braha Yaniv, "Nisayon le–Shikhzur Itzuvam shel Rimmonei Migdal mi-Morocco al-pi Degamim mi-Sefarad," *Pe'amim* 50 (1992), pp. 73–76. For similar verge heads of the period, see E. Arnaez, *Orfebrería Religiosa en la Provincia de Segovia hasta 1700,* Madrid, 1983, v. 1, p. 49, fig. 1; p. 79, fig. 32.

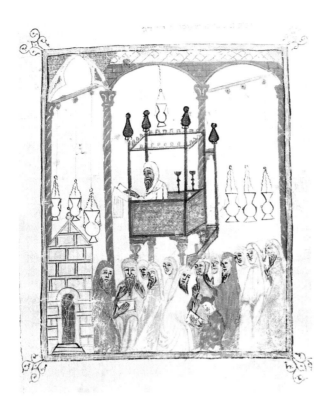

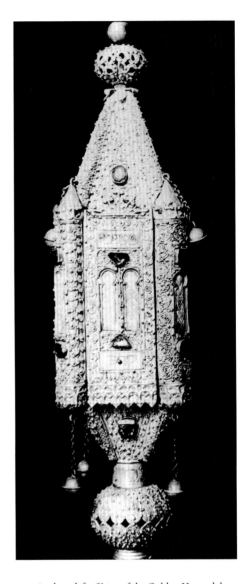

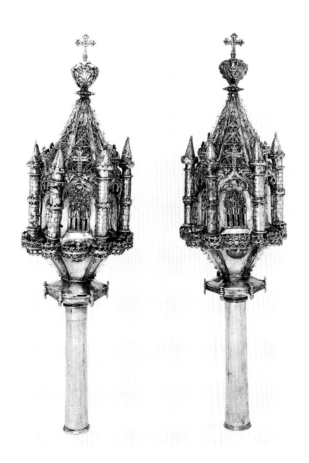

FIG. 8, *above left.* Sister of the Golden Haggadah, Spain, 1325–50, fol. 17v

FIG. 9, *above. Rimmon,* Spain, 15th century, Cathedral Treasury of Palma de Majorca

FIG. 10, *left.* Christian verge heads, Spain, 15th century, Victoria & Albert Museum, London

double arch of the towers is commonly found among the buildings of the Alhambra, and the *vermiculée* filigree has a long history in Spanish metalwork. It appears, for example, on the 12th-century Altar Frontal of Santo Domingo de Silos.[56] Translated into pen drawings, *vermiculée* filigree appears in a wide variety of manuscripts.[57] A number of tower-form verge heads were made for Spanish churches in the late 15th century (fig. 10). It is only the extensive Hebrew inscriptions which attest to the original use of the pair on Palma de Majorca.

The custom of using crowns to adorn the Torah Scroll may be even older than that of using *rimmonim*. Inscriptions indicate the deposit of honorific crowns, arms, and shields in ancient synagogues, a practice analogous to those followed by pagans who deposited trophies in temple treasuries.[58] By the 11th century, according to Hai ben Sherira (939–1038), one of the leading scholars of Babylonian Jewry, congregants were adorning their Torah Scrolls on the holiday of Simḥat Torah with crowns composed of silver, gold, myrtle, or women's jewelry which were subsequently returned to their owners and at other times with silver crowns.[59]

Documents of the 12th century attest to the existence of Torah Crowns in two areas of the Jewish world, Egypt and Spain. The 1159 inventory found in the Cairo Genizah of property given to the Palestinian Synagogue listed four crowns, each in a different type of metal.[60] It is interesting that earlier synagogue inventories found in the Genizah do not mention crowns. Early in the next century, Rabbi Abraham of Lunel urged a Spanish synagogue to commission a silver crown for the Torah, instead of using materials which were returned to their owners after use.[61]

Rabbi Abraham's request was also honored elsewhere in Spain. In a responsum, Rabbi Solomon ben Adret (1235–1310) recalled that when he was a child in Barcelona, it was customary to place Torah Crowns on the heads of young children and on the heads of those honored with readings (*aliyot*) during the celebration of the Simḥat Torah festival.[62] He saw nothing wrong with the practice which honored the Torah and, further, was a practice the donors of the crowns intended. His text indicates that Torah Crowns were used in Barcelona ca. 1335.

The most complete description of a medieval Torah Crown appears in a contract written on March 24, 1439, by leaders of the synagogue in Arles with the silversmith Robin Asard of Avignon.[63] The contract specifies an hexagonal crown of silver fitted with an internal copper support. Each angle of the hexagon was to be decorated with pillars adorned with the head of a lion from whose mouth emerged three chains bearing bells. The sides between the pillars were to appear as masonry portals topped by crenellations, so that the whole resembled the foundation of a fortress. Above this foundation rose six towers. All remaining surfaces of the crown were to be ornamented with "the most beautiful" gilt silver leaves that the silversmith could make. Five pillars like those on the new crown were to be attached to an old crown owned by the congregation. Members of the synagogue were responsible for supplying the

56. New York, The Metropolitan Museum of Art, *The Art of Medieval Spain A.D. 500–1200*, New York, 1993, cat. no. 134, there the older literature.

57. For example, New York, The Jewish Museum, *Convivencia: Jews Muslims, and Christians in Medieval Spain*, ed. by Vivian B. Mann, Thomas F. Glick, and Jerrilyn Dodds, exhibition catalogue, 1992, fig. 43.

58. Krauss, *Synagogale Altertümer*, p. 163.

59. Isaac ben Judah ibn Ghayyat (11th century), *Sha'are Simḥah*, Fürth, 1862, 117 ff. For a translation, see Franz Landsberger, "The Origin of European Torah Decorations," *Beauty in Holiness*, ed. Joseph Gutmann, n.p., 1970, pp. 94–95.

60. Goitein, "The Synagogue Building ...," pp. 90–95.

61. Abraham of Lunel, *Ha-Manhig*, Berlin, 1855, no. 59. A translation appears in Landsberger, "Origin of European Torah Decorations," pp. 95–96.

62. Solomon ben Adret, *Teshuvot u–She'alot le-ha-Rashba*, Rome, 1470, no. 73.

63. The text of the contract, drawn from French archival files, was first published in [Georges Stenne], *Collection de M. Strauss*, Poissy, 1878, viii-x.

64.  Peter Lasko, *Ars Sacra 800–1200,* Harmondsworth, 1972, pp. 178–79, 216, pls. 187, 246–47.

65.  For the inscription on the Aachen candelabrum, see Percy Ernst Schramm and Florentine Mutterich, *Denkmäle der Deutschen Könige und Kaiser,* Munich, 1962, no. 177.

66.  Asunción Blasco Martínez, "Pintores y Orfebres Judiós en Zaragoza (Siglo XIV)," *Aragón en la Edad Media,* Zaragoza, 1989, pp. 123–31.

67.  Ubieto Arteta, J. Delgado Echeverría, J. A. Frago Gracía, and M. del C. Lacarra Ducay, *Vidal Mayor: Estudios* (Huesca, 1984), there the older literature; Malibu, J. Paul Getty Museum, *The Vidal Mayor: Feudal Customs of Aragon,* exhibition brochure, 1990; New York, The Jewish Museum, *Convivencia,* no. 24.

68.  See Arteta et al., folios 114r, 180r, 243v, 175v; Mann, et al., *Convivencia,* figs. 1 and 24.

69.  Moses of Coucy, *Sefer Mitzvot Gadol,* ed. by Alter Pinhas Ferber, n.p., 1991.

70.  Solomon Grayzel, *The Church and the Jews in the Thirteenth Century,* ed. by Kenneth R. Stow, New York and Detroit, 1989, pp. 276, 280–82.

materials, and Asard was enjoined from working on the Jewish Sabbaths and holy days.

The Arles contract is significant, first of all, for the clause indicating Robin Asard's responsibility to refurbish an old crown owned by the synagogue with new iconographic elements, pillars with lions' heads and bells. The practice of refurbishing used Torah ornaments continues into the modern era. Second, the detailed account of the Arles synagogue commission suggests that the new Torah Crown resembled in form and concept a monumental type of church candelabrum commissioned for the Stiftskirche in Gross-Komburg, ca. 1130, and for the Palace Chapel at Aachen by Frederick Barbarossa in 1166.[64] These elaborate architectural compositions symbolized heavenly Jerusalem, a meaning underscored by accompanying inscriptions.[65] It was a suitable concept for the form and decoration of a crown to adorn the Torah Scroll.

Although the Arles contract is the only document to afford a glimpse of the complete appearance of a now lost Torah ornament of the Middle Ages, further documentary evidence for Jewish familiarity with Christian silver supports the thesis that Christians and Jews used the same vocabulary of forms.

Recent investigations of the state archives in Aragon and Zaragoza revealed documents naming Jewish painters and silversmiths active between 1316 and 1416.[66] In all regions of Spain whose medieval archives have been studied (Navarre and Toledo in addition to Aragon and Zaragoza), records show that silversmithing was a preferred profession among Jews. These Jewish artists worked for both the Jewish community and the Gentile, and were even hired by mainstream conservative institutions like the church. Contracts exist between Jewish artisans and Christian patrons, like the king, the archbishops, and the nobles, for the production of secular tableware and also for crosses and reliquaries. These Jewish silversmiths must have been using the same forms and decorative motifs as non-Jewish artisans for their wares to be sought by non-Jewish patrons.

Visual evidence for such activity appears in the *Vidal Mayor,* the law code of King James I of Aragon written in the second half of the 13th century and now in the J. Paul Getty Museum (Malibu, Ms. Ludwig XIV 6, 83.MQ.165).[67] Four of the recorded cases involve Jews. All are marked by illuminated initials. Jews are shown as silversmiths, as merchants of metalwork and cloth, as pawnbrokers (accepting metalwork as surety), and as litigants before the king in a case involving metalwork.[68]

Rabbinic sources from France and Germany attest to similar activities that would have afforded Jews firsthand knowledge of metalwork made for Christians. Rabbis Eliezer of Metz (12th century) and Moses of Coucy (13th century) both discuss Jewish trade in church silver, the result of pawnbroking.[69] Contemporaneous church decrees likewise attest to extreme discomfort with an economic activity that seems to have been commonly practiced.[70]

Although the medieval literary sources cited mention crowns and finials separately, as distinct ornaments, there exists one important piece of evidence that they were used together to adorn the Torah Scroll, at least by the 14th century. A miniature in the Sarajevo Haggadah (Sarajevo, National Museum), written and decorated in Barcelona in the second quarter of the 14th century, shows the congregation leaving the synagogue as the sexton closes the doors to the Torah Ark (fig. 11).[71] Within are three scrolls covered with fringed silk mantles and decorated with both crowns and finials, the finials projecting from the center of the straight-sided crowns. This usage was later followed in countries of the Sephardi diaspora: Italy, Holland, and the Ottoman Empire.[72] Rabbi Obadiah de Bertinoro, who visited Palermo in 1487, may refer to this practice in a letter to his father: "[The synagogue] contains rolls of the Law which are ornamented with crowns and pomegranates [*rimmonim*] of silver and precious stones."[73]

The two remaining types of ornament, shields and pointers, are both latecomers, inventions of the late 15th and 16th centuries. They may have arisen out of a confluence of Jewish needs and the development of Gentile silver forms that could be appropriated for Jewish purposes.

With the discovery of the Americas, larger amounts of silver were available in Europe. Its ownership was an aspect of personal or corporate display and expressed the power and wealth of its possessor. At the same time, this form of display was immensely practical, since in difficult times silverware could be melted to supply ready cash. New types of tableware and corporate emblems were created, and owners possessed greater numbers of silver pieces than heretofore.[74] This general affluence is reflected in inventories and the larger numbers of remaining examples. Jewish participation is indicated, in part, by the creation of new silver appointments for the Torah Scroll.

In the mid-15th century, Rabbi Israel ben Petaḥiah Isserlein (1390–1460) was asked if it were permissable to use the poles from which the Ark Curtain hung to make plates on which would be written the name of the lection to which the Torah Scroll was turned.[75] The question indicates that silver Torah Shields did not

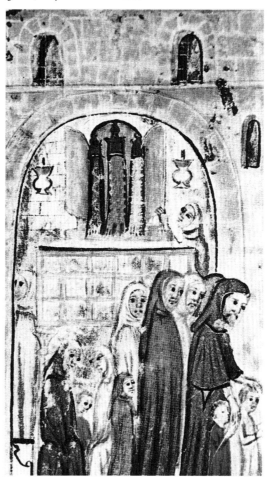

FIG. 11, Illumination showing Torah Ark, Sarajevo Haggadah, Sarajevo National Museum

71. On the Sarajevo Haggadah, see Cecil Roth, *The Sarajevo Haggadah,* Sarajevo, n.d.

72. *Gardens and Ghettos,* figs. 197 and 205; Jerusalem, Israel Museum, *Jews of the Ottoman Empire,* ed. by Esther Juhasz, exhibition catalogue, 1990, figs. 23 and 33; New York, Yeshiva University, *The Sephardic Journey,* exhibition catalogue, 1992, fig. 45.

73. Elkan Nathan Adler, ed., *Jewish Travellers in the Middle Ages,* New York, 1987, p. 211.

74. For example, see Manfred Meinz, "Ratssilber in niedersächsischen Städten," *Stadt im Wandel. Kunst und Kultur des Burgertums in Norddeutschland 1150–1650,* vol. 3, ed. by Cord Meckseper, exhibition catalogue, 1985, 661–65. In 1598, the city of Luneburg possessed nearly 300 pieces of City Council silver. For extant examples see *Stadt im Wandel,* vol. 2, pp. 986–1012.

75. Israel ben Petaḥiah Isserlein, *Sefer Terumat ha-Deshen,* New York, 1958, no. 225.

76. Antonius Margaritha, *Der Gantz Jüdisch Glaub,* Leipzig, 1705, pp. 267–68.

77. In an article published in 1979, Victor Klagsbald argued that two antique plaques with dedicatory inscriptions, one in his own collection and another in the London Jewish Museum, were early examples of Torah Shields. ("Un plaque de Torah antique," *Journal of Jewish Art,* VI (1979), pp. 127–32.) The function of most post-medieval shields, however, is to indicate the reading to which the scroll was turned. These shields often bear dedicatory inscriptions, but they are of secondary significance. East European examples bearing only dedicatory inscriptions refer to the birth of children and are shaped like functional shields. On the other hand, Romaniot communities have a tradition of engraved metal votive plaques that were affixed to synagogue furnishings like Torah Curtains. Since nothing in the dedicatory inscriptions published by Klagsbald refers to the Torah, and since the plaques are non-functional when compared to later Torah Shields, it seems much more plausible to see them as early examples of the later Romaniot plaques, especially since both stem from the Byzantine realm.

78. On Jewish ceremonial silver from Frankfurt, see Vivian B. Mann, "The Golden Age of Jewish Ceremonial Art in Frankfurt. Metalwork of the Eighteenth Century," *Leo Baeck Institute Yearbook XXXI* (1986), pp. 389–403.

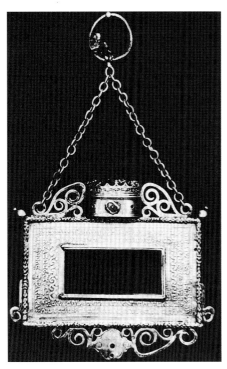

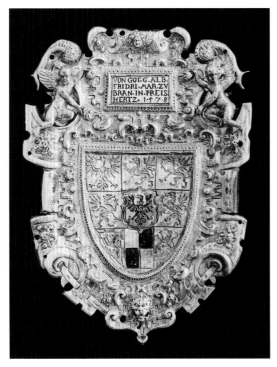

FIG. 12, *left,* Torah Shield, SIlver, Frankfurt 1587

FIG. 13, *right,* Coat of Arms shield of Johann Sigismund von Brandenburg, 1599. Berlin, Schloß Charlottenberg

yet exist. In his answer, Rabbi Isserlein remarked that such plates did nothing to beautify the appearance of the Torah Scroll. Approximately seventy years later, a convert's account of Jewish worship first published in Augsburg in 1530, Anthonius Margaritha's *Der Gantz Jüdisch Glaub,* records the hanging of silver plates with silver chains over the mantles of Torah Scrolls.[76] The plates bore inscriptions indicating which Scroll should be read and also the phrases "Crown of Torah" or *kodesh la-Shem* (dedicated to God). Margaritha's account is not specific enough to indicate whether the shields he saw were fitted with a box of interchangeable plaques engraved with the names of holy days, which would represent the mature version of the shield, widely used in the 18th and 19th centuries.[77]

The record of the Frankfurt Goldsmiths' Guild, *Probierbuch der Frankfurter Goldschmiedezunft für alle die zu Frankfurt in der Zeit von 1512–1576 hergestellten goldenen und silbernen Geräte* (Frankfurt, Stadtarchiv Ugb. C.30 D), has three entries dated mid-16th century that could signify Torah Shields.[78] In 1545, Rudolf Kolb made a *Judentafel,* a Jewish plaque, and in 1557, Karl von Sandt made a *Tabul Moisi darzu die 10 gepott gestochen* (a Moses plaque engraved with the Ten Commandments), and in 1563 Heinrich Heidelberger made two silver covers over a Jewish Torah Scroll.[79] A single extant example from the end of the 16th century satisfies the aesthetic requirements of Rabbi Isserlein. This silver shield from Bingen dated 1587 (fig. 12) is rectangular in form and has a relatively large rectangular opening for inscribed plaques that signified the reading to which the Scroll was turned.[80]

Once Rabbi Isserlein's injunction, that the plaque marking the reading should beautify the Scroll, was taken into account, several models could have been used for this new type of Judaica. One was the guild emblem: shield-shaped with a central motif and pendant elements; another was the Coat of Arms Shield of reigning nobles like that of Johann Sigismund von Brandenburg dated 1599 (Berlin, Schloss Charlottenberg; fig. 13). It was but a short step from these to the mature constructions of 17th- and 18th-century Torah Shields.[81]

There is no mention in early texts of the Mishnaic and Talmudic periods of a special rod or pointer used to follow the sacred text.[82] The injunction against touching the parchment with a "naked" hand was expressed in the Talmud by the phrase: Whoever touches a naked Torah will lie naked when buried.[83] The need for covering was presumably met by wrapping one's hand in silk or in one's prayer shawl, a custom still followed in the 16th century according to Margaritha.[84] The oldest pointer known was made in Ferrara in 1488 and is today in the Nahon Museum, Jerusalem.[85] It ends in a hand, the most popular terminal found on pointers for centuries to come. Archival sources indicate that in 1581, the Jewish community of Prague ordered pointers with hand terminals from Christian silversmiths attached to the imperial court who were considered far superior to the poorly-trained Jewish silversmiths.[86] None of these Prague pointers is extant. Rabbi Moses Isserles of Cracow (1525/30–1572) states that wooden pointers were also used during his lifetime; actual examples survive from subsequent centuries.[87] With the turn of the 17th century, silver Torah Pointers were made in larger numbers as were other types of silver ornaments.

✧

By the year 1600, then, a complete corpus of Torah ornaments existed (in addition to various textiles) including covers (silks, *tikim,* and arks), finials, crowns, shields, and pointers. Although their materials are often known, and a few examples remain, few texts or representations are detailed enough to allow knowledge of their forms and decorative elements. Still, the consideration of all types of evidence, literary sources, representations in various media, and the few extant examples, can create a fuller picture of medieval Torah ornaments than was known previously.

79. Wolfgang Scheffler, *Goldschmiedes Hessens,* Berlin-New York, 1976, pp. 92, 96, 106. Scheffler's transcription of the *Probierbuch* corrects older readings such as that found in Landsberger, "Origin of European Torah Ornaments," pp. 100–01. One of the citations accepted by Landsberger, a large silver plate made for a Jew by Jost Koch, seems too unspecific to consider a definite reference to a Torah Shield.

80. This shield was first published by Hava Lazar ("Du Nouveau dans l'art sacré juif," *L'Oeïl* 288/289 (1979), pp. 62–63.

81. See below, cat. nos. 2 ff.

82. Krauss, *Synagogale Altertümer,* p. 384, n.2.

83. Babylonian Talmud Megillah 32a.

84. Margaritha, *Jüdisch Glaub,* p. 268.

85. Dora Liscia Bemporad, "Jewish Ceremonial Art in the Era of the Ghettos," *Gardens and Ghettos,* p.111; Umberto Nahon, *Ornamenti di Sefer Tora,* Jerusalem, 1966, fig. 23.

86. Josef Hrasky, "La corporation juive d'orfèvrerie à Prague," *Judaica Bohemia* 2, 1 (1966), p. 26; Tobias Jacobovitz, "Die jüdischen Zunfte in Prag," *Jahrbuch der Gesellschaft für Geschichte der Juden in der Czechoslov. Republik* 8 (1936), p. 129.

87. Joseph Caro, *Shulḥan Arukh,* Oraḥ Ḥayyim, 154:6, commentary of R. Moses Isserles. For examples, see Vivian B. Mann, "Community Life," *The Precious Legacy. Treasures from the Czechoslovak State Collections,* ed. by David Altshuler, New York, 1984, cat. nos. 65–72, fig. 128; and nos. 529, 557, 682, 744, 764a, 889, 891a, 894, 896, 898, and 893 in the present volume.

THE COLLECTION OF

# Torah Ornaments

OF THE JEWISH MUSEUM

## *Rafi Grafman*

❧

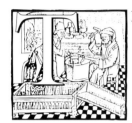HE JEWISH MUSEUM'S COLLECTION of Judaica is one of the three largest in the world. The other two are in Prague and Jerusalem. The New York museum's collection of Torah ornaments (other than textiles) include some two hundred eighty Torah Shields, nearly two hundred Torah Finials, seventy Torah Crowns and almost five hundred Torah Pointers, as well as forty other items such as Torah Cases. They are the subject of the present catalogue. As with any public collection which grew haphazardly, The Jewish Museum's collection is very strong in some areas and deficient in others. Thus, material from central and eastern Europe is very well represented, while that of the Jewish communities of North Africa, the Middle East, and the Balkans, is treated according to its proportion in the collection. The German silver objects, which comprise some of the finest Ashkenazi ritual art ever made, can now be documented in great detail, based on recent and more complete studies of hallmarks, an advantage not available to the previous generation of scholars at the Museum.

This review of the works in The Jewish Museum's collections is presented within a chronological-developmental framework. Little basic research has previously been done on ritual objects of these types, and no adequate typology has been published for any of them. Because only those objects of particular interest or significance could be noted here, only a fraction of the collection is directly discussed. However, all of the Museum's Torah ornaments are listed in the Catalogue section, which includes brief discussions of specific items and groups.

❧

### TORAH SHIELDS

The earliest Torah Shield in The Jewish Museum's collections bears a Hebrew date equivalent to 1669, and in form belongs to the earliest type of Torah Shields, which seems to have appeared in Germany during the mid-16th century.[1] The earliest extant Torah Shield, now in a private European collection, is dated 1587 and, though dedicated to the Jewish community in Bingen, was made in Frankfurt am Main.[2] The two other pieces made prior to The Jewish Museum's shield are one from Amsterdam, 1607 (made there by a silversmith from Emden, and apparently following a north German model), and another from Emden, 1639–40.[3]

What characterizes this group, including The Jewish Museum's No. 1, is a horizontal rectangular sheet of silver with a central rectangle intended to secure and display the current

1. No. 1, in the Catalogue. See also Vivian Mann's essay, above.

2. Lazar 1979. Reexamination of the hallmarks confirms the Frankfurt identification.

3. See, e.g., Belinfante 1991, p. 76 upper right; Emden 1992. The Hebrew dedication on the Emden shield specifically names it a *tas* (Mishnaic Hebrew meaning a bright sheet of metal), the first appearance of the word on the object itself.

*parashah* plaque (denoting the Torah reading). A crown is positioned at or on the upper edge and openwork strap or scroll ornamentation surrounds the rectangular sheet on three or even four sides. Generally, these shields are two-sided; that is, *parashah* plaques could be displayed on the front or on the back (in which case the shield would be turned around, back to front). The Jewish Museum's shield differs from this latter scheme in several respects. First, there is no outer ornamentation beyond the rectangular sheet. Moreover, the single *parashah* plaque is a fixed, raised rectangle, not a frame for removable plaques, as on the other early examples. This feature, however, would seem to be a direct outcome of the *raison d'être* of this particular shield: The inscription is essentially the same as those found on Torah Binders (*Wimpeln*) from the German Jewish sphere, and includes a newborn boy's name, his birth date, and a portion of the blessings for the circumcision ceremony. In this example, the *parashah* plaque reads "Holy Sabbath," but these two words also form part of the date of the child's birth, for he was born on the Sabbath, 9 Sivan, 5429 (= Saturday, 8 June 1669). Thus, plaques for other *parashiyot* would be out of place and superfluous here.

The Jewish Museum's early shield is of considerable interest in that it reflects not only the German-Jewish tradition of marking the reading, but also the tradition of dedicating an object by or in honor of a newly circumcised boy. In German-speaking lands, this tradition is often encountered in Torah Binders, but on Torah Shields it is very rare.

## *Galicia*

The tradition of a father's dedicating a small ornamental Torah Shield upon the circumcision of his son is well established, however, in the Galician-Ukrainian sphere, but shields there had no provision for denoting the *parashah* reading. They were intended solely to be dedicatory. The earliest dated Galician example appears to be contemporaneous with the earliest of the German group, and clearly displays the arched façade form so characteristic of eastern European Torah Shields in general.[4]

The Museum has a relatively extensive group of about thirty small Torah Shields from 18th- and 19th-century Galicia and the Ukraine which are in decided contrast to other, more ostentatious types of Torah Shields from this region. Generally, their craftsmanship is modest — and most (if not all) of the artisans were certainly Jewish.[5] The majority of the shields of this type give no indication that they were intended to mark Torah Scrolls for particular readings. Quite the contrary: the few which do incorporate plaques do so in the form of an immovable, rectangular, raised panel, usually bearing the Hebrew inscription *Shabbat* (or *Shabbat Qoddesh*). Thus, most of this group are ornamental — intended to enhance the beauty of the Torah (*hiddur mitzvah*). Often they also honor a donor or commemorate some other person or event, such as a birth.

Of The Jewish Museum's Torah Shields of this type, five bear no indication of their

4. This unpublished shield, in a private collection in New York, seems to bear a Hebrew date equivalent to 1579.

5. For material related to this group, see now Kantsedikas 1992 — which must be used with reservation concerning terminology, ascriptions, and dating.

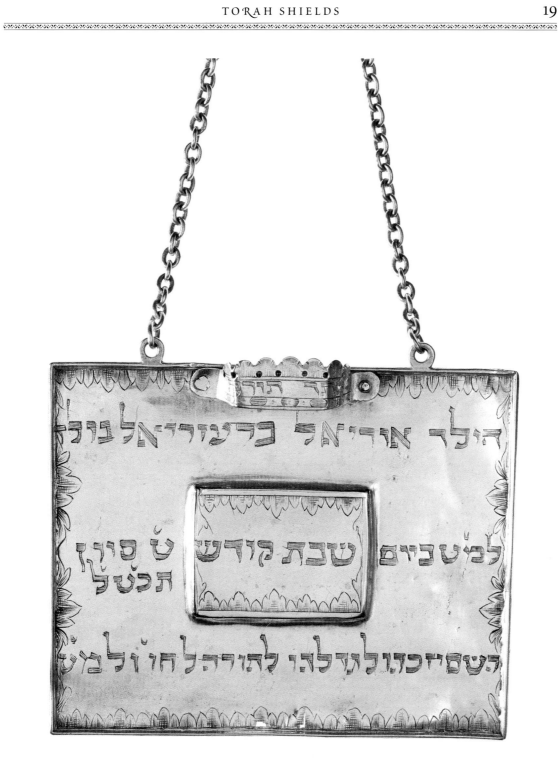

N.B. All objects illustrated
in this essay are in the
collection of The Jewish
Museum, New York

FIG. 1. Torah Shield,
Germany, 1669, Gift of
Dr. Harry G. Friedman,
F 2653 (No. 1)

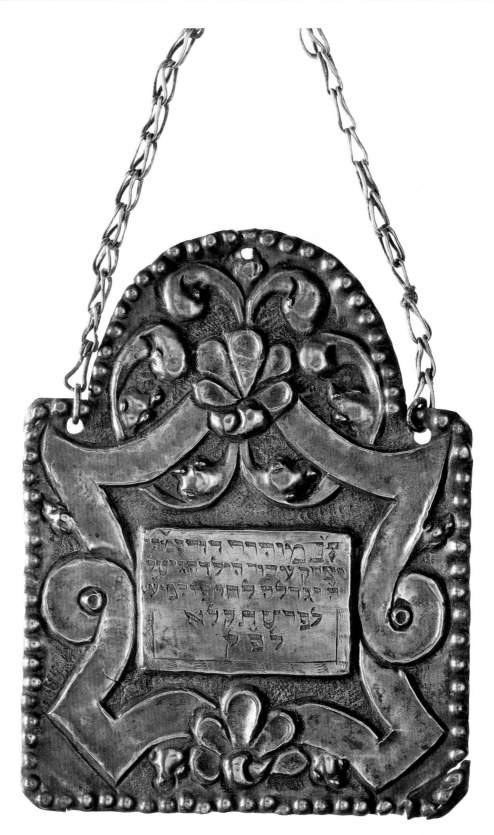

FIG. 2. Torah Shield, Galicia,
1770/71, The Rose and Benjamin Mintz Collection,
M 207 (No. 156)

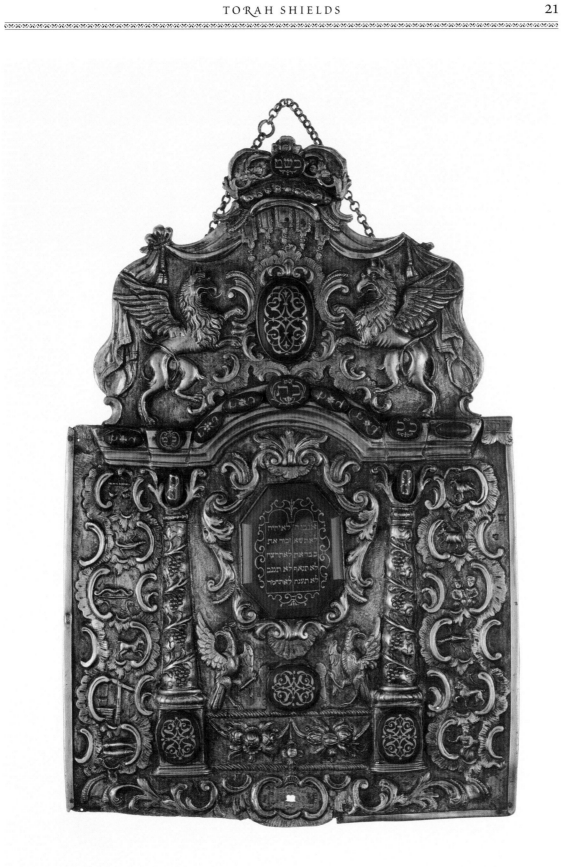

FIG. 3. Torah Shield,
Lvov(?), 1800/01, Gift of
Dr. Harry G. Friedman,
F 2280 (No. 174)

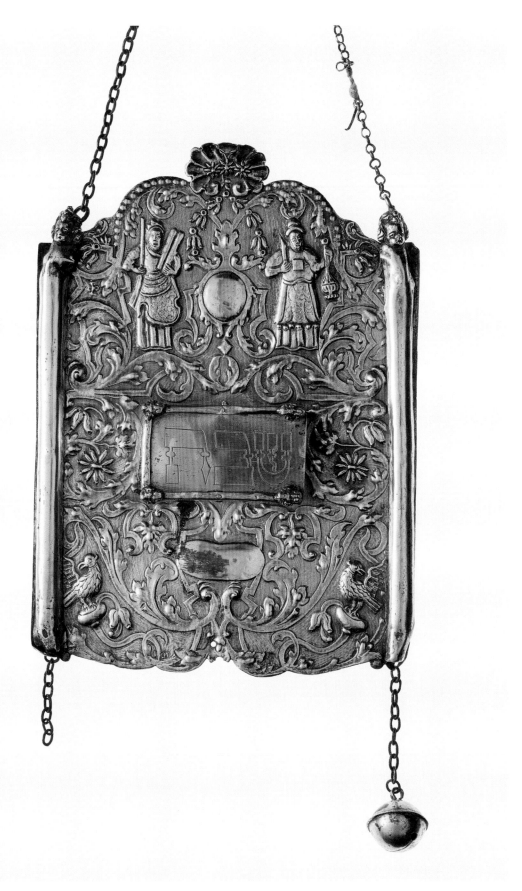

FIG. 4. Torah Shield, Galicia(?), early 18th century, Gift of Else Samson in memory of Rabbi Wilhelm Buchheim of Dortmund, 1993–146 (No. 172)

donors' identity, but only such phrases as *Keter Torah*, "Crown of the Torah," or *Qoddesh Le-Y.Y.*, "Holy unto the Lord." Several seem to have had inscriptions that were erased. As common on Jewish ceremonial silver from this region, many carry depictions of vases with symmetrical vines or floral motifs, often inhabited by birds. Sometimes Tablets of the Law are shown, and often these have applied crowns near the top. One (No. 154) has a gabled top, rather than the usual dome or arch. Another (No. 151) follows a rather stock form for shields: Tablets of the Law flanked by a pair of lions, but with a pair of priestly hands above, indicating it was donated by a *kohen* or priest. A third shield (No. 158) has both "Crown of the Torah" and "Holy unto the Lord" inscribed, with the date added.

Many of these small Torah Shields bear dedicatory inscriptions; the common formula is: "This was donated by (or 'belongs to') X son of Y in the year A." One shield (No. 177) has a rather long memorial inscription. Two shields (Nos. 147 and 148) are gifts "to the Holy Society of Tailors"; in both cases these mid-19th century inscriptions are written over earlier, erased dedications.

A shield with a long memorial inscription bears the name Moshe Segal (= *Segan leKohen*, "Assistant to a Priest") and the motif of a Levite pitcher and laver (No. 177); another (No. 144) gives the name "Joseph Katz" (Katz = *Kohen Tzeddeq*, "Priest of Righteousness"), and bears the priestly hands. One shield (No. 168) from the Danzig Collection at The Jewish Museum, was commissioned by the synagogue *gabbai* or treasurer. Pairs of tiny holes all around the edges of one Torah Shield (No. 161) indicate that it might have been sewn to a Torah mantle or an ark curtain.[6]

Three shields of this group come from the same community. One (No. 139) was originally inscribed "Belonging to X son of Y, in the year A," but at some time later it was given to the ". . . Burial Society of the Holy Congregation of Pisek."[7] A second shield (No. 155) also belonged to this society; as did the third (No. 160): " to the Burial Society of . . ."). The third also bears a more interesting formula, introducing us to another major subtype —Torah Shields commemorating the birth of a child. It reads: "This was donated by X son of Y, on behalf of his son, the boy Z. May the Lord raise him to the To(rah), to the *Ḥu(ppah)* (lit. marriage canopy) and to Good Deeds, in the year A." This text is adapted from the circumcision ceremony. Such shields were surely dedicated either at the time of the circumcision or, possibly, a year later, or on an occasion such as the first visit of the child to the synagogue. Thus they are a Galician analogue to the German-Bohemian Torah Wrappers, made from the swaddling cloths used at the circumcision ceremony.

Several shields of this type at The Jewish Museum are of further interest: One (No. 137) was dedicated by a father on behalf of "his sons X [and] Y. May the Lord raise them to the Torah"— possibly referring to a pair of twins. Two others (Nos. 146 and 156) are inscribed: "This was donated by X son of Y, on behalf of the girl (or 'his daughter') Z. May the Lord raise

6. A similar shield, at the Skirball Museum in Los Angeles, Inv. No. 7.7 from the late 18th century, has pairs of holes around the perimeter.

7. I wish to thank Bill Gross for his comments on the identification of the name Piesk as that of some fifty places in Poland and Belorussia (letter dated Dec. 11, 1992). He notes that there are "53 such shields [of this general type] in the Krakow National Museum, almost all are from Galicia or adjoining areas . . . . [and] more than 50 of this type in Kiev, a few in Lvov, in Warsaw, in Prague and a small group in the Israel Museum."

her to the marriage canopy and to Good Deeds, in the year A." Thus, though the girls were not blessed to be "raised to the Torah," they would receive honor and best wishes from their parents, an interesting variation of the usual practice.

## Early Germany

Returning to the early German Torah Shields of the baroque period, the sequence continues with a group of shields from various German communities, dated ca. 1680 through ca. 1720.[8] A rapid series of divergencies in form began in the late 17th century and led to the emergence of specific and regional types at the various centers of silver production, of which Augsburg was probably the most prolific. The sequence and dating of the Augsburg Torah Shields can now be established,[9] and the series there from ca. 1680 on, includes over sixty examples, serving as a reliable framework for discussing the development of the shield in Germany.

Early Torah Shields were decidedly horizontal in orientation — formal frames for the *parashah* plaques. A change occurred in the basic composition around 1680. The first evidence comes from Augsburg, a center of innovative silver design, where a new feature appeared on shields: a pair of columns flanking the plaque box. This introduced verticality into what had until then been an entirely horizontally-oriented rectangular design. The vertical element probably derives from the design of contemporaneous synagogue textiles.

The Torah silver of other cities in Germany showed similar developments at the very end of the 17th century. For example, in Nuremberg rectangular shields have an upper arch, a form possibly influenced by the small dedicatory Torah Shields of Galicia. The Nuremberg shields also have two twisted columns flanking the plaque box, with a small crown above. At Hamburg in the 1690's, the first of a series of large shields appears, with flanking columns forming the sides and three crowns across the upper part, often topped by a fourth.[10] In other locales, however, such as Frankfurt am Main, columns never became a popular motif, although they are found occasionally.

Perhaps under the influence of synagogue textile designs, a pair of heraldic lions, usually flanking a relatively large crown, appears in the late 1690's. Among the early examples is a fine shield from Augsburg, from ca. 1705, with large, flanking lions grasping the columns. It is identical in design to a shield at The Jewish Museum, made by Domenikus Saler in 1705 which, however, lacks the lions (No. 2).[11] These shields present a splendid mass of swirling leaves surrounding and integrating the iconographic motifs into one design. The Saler type shield would seem to have inspired the earliest of the Torah Shields made in the Weinolt workshop in Augsburg in 1705, now at The Jewish Museum (No. 3).[12] Large lions are a major feature of another elegant shield at The Jewish Museum (No. 12), undoubtedly made by Johann Adam Boller in Frankfurt, possibly as early as 1710.[13] This shield was copied in the 19th century, entirely in repoussé work, and the copy is also at The Jewish Museum (No. 13).

8. There are about twenty shields in this group, scattered in the literature; for the earliest, see Barnett 1976a, No. 136 (dedicated in 1682).

9. For an earlier attempt to analyze the Torah Shields from Augsburg, see Cohen 1978. We are now fortunate to be able to refer to Seling (published in 1980), as well as Ansbacher 1985; the former allows us to date Augsburg silver on a firm basis, while the latter considerably expanded the number of examples.

10. See Schleimann 1985, Figs. 841–43 (1709–18), 842 (1740), 843 (1728–32). The three or four crowns on these shields are especially typical of Hamburg and other north German cities.

11. For the shield with lions, see Ansbacher 1985, No. 2.5.

12. For the Weinolt shields see the remarks under No. 3.

13. For the initial identification of Boller as the maker of this shield, see Mann 1982, No. 67. A similar floral layout can be observed in several Torah Shields made by Johann Conrad Weiss of Nuremberg, at about the same time; cf., e.g., Stieglitz, No. 21.

Large lions were soon reduced to more modest proportions, almost invariably flanking and supporting a large, central crown in the upper part of the shield.

In the second decade of the 18th century, the architectural motif becomes more complex. What until then had been pairs of single, isolated columns gives way to pairs, or even doubled pairs, of supporting columns. The latter combination is the basis of the magnificent Torah Shield at The Jewish Museum (No. 6), made by Zacharias Wagner of Augsburg, in 1717–18.[14] A spirited Weinolt shield at The Jewish Museum (No. 4), made in 1730–32, presents a highly imaginative version of this scheme, depicted as an arbor for a grapevine.

Columns were not a popular motif on Torah Shields in Frankfurt am Main during the 18th century, but they do appear on one particular type of shield, all apparently made in the Schüler workshop, ca. 1730–32. The Jewish Museum possesses a fine example of this group (No. 15), made up of cast openwork elements framed by splendid, cast baroque ornaments. On the main panel, the central *parashah* plaque box is flanked by columns with a small crown above. A fragment by the same smith (No. 16) seems to fit atop this shield, with its inscribed medallion supported by two large lions. If so, the whole would have been suspended from a tripartite chain, with the fragment's hook at the top. Other shields of this group are similarly constructed, sometimes with various appliqués such as animals, angels, and rosettes. This group still reflects the older, 17th-century form and may have been fabricated hurriedly to replace Torah shields lost in the fire which swept through the Frankfurt Ghetto in 1711.[15]

A very unusual Torah Shield at The Jewish Museum (No. 19) represents a small group of Nuremberg shields. The Museum's piece, the earliest and finest of the group,[16] incorporates a unique device for indicating the *parashiyot*. Individual, interchangeable letters and symbols, which combine to spell the *parashah* to be read, replace the usual word plaques. The decorative motifs on this shield include a pair of unicorns, other animals, and foliage.

Small areas of lattice ground began appearing on Augsburg silver as early as the 1710's, but this motif became particularly common for proportionately larger areas only in the late 1720's. It reached its height of popularity in the 1730's and 1740's. A Weinolt Torah Shield at The Jewish Museum, made in 1732–33 (No. 5), displays a fine lattice with its characteristic central rosettes. This motif remained prominent on Torah Shields into the 20th century.[17] Several of the Weinolt shields have a baldachino at the top and this, too, was a long-lived motif. It appears prominently on two other shields at The Jewish Museum, both clearly derived from Augsburg prototypes of ca. 1735. One of them (No. 8), from mid-18th-century Nuremberg, probably ca. 1760, closely resembles another shield, from Oettingen, made by a silversmith whose initials were CIK (No. 9). Interestingly, two other identical shields by this same master are known, one of which bears a Hebrew date equivalent to 1773/74.[18]

In the 1730's, the rococo style appears on Augsburg silver, and silversmiths there were

14. And cf. Torah pointer No. 519, also by Wagner; and cf. a very similar Torah Shield at the Israel Museum (148/2) by Fassnacht, Cohen 1978, Fig. 11.

15. For a fuller treatment of this group of Torah shields, see Mann 1986, esp. pp. 393–95.

16. See also Skirball Museum, Los Angeles, No. 7.21; Gutmann 1964, color pl. III.

17. For the evolution of the lattice background motif in Augsburg, see Seling II, figs. 1034 (1712–15), 1001 (1716), 1076 (1729–30), 1066 (1731), 692 (1731), 929 (1735–40).

18. Israel Museum 148/75; the other is at the Jewish Museum in Augsburg; cf. Ansbacher 1984, No. 2.36.

soon producing Torah Shields which display full mastery over its intricacies, and their inge-nious spirit produced such masterpieces as the shield at The Jewish Museum which bears symbolic depictions of the appurtenances of Solomon's Temple (No. 7). It bears no hallmarks but was probably made in Nuremberg, according to its style and workmanship.[19] The Tem-ple appurtenances, and those of the Priests and Levites, have remained popular motifs on Torah shields ever since.

Another new motif introduced into Torah Shield design in the mid-18th century is a pair of tied and draped curtains, often suspended from a baldachino and usually flanking the two columns. This became an integral element of Augsburg and other Torah Shields from the end of the 18th century and later (see below). Biblical scenes also appear, as on a splendid Nurem-berg Torah Shield, probably from the 1720's that was once on loan to The Jewish Museum. Its scenes derive from an Amsterdam prayer book of 1717, while its shape is based on that of large domestic platters and trays of this period, which often depict biblical and mythological scenes.[20]

A specific biblical motif that first appears on Torah Shields in the mid-18th century is paired figures of Aaron the High Priest and Moses the Lawgiver. This scheme, which has a long and widespread history on Hebrew title pages, appears to have been used for the first time on shields at Breslau, where it is also commonly seen on the backwalls of Hanukkah lamps.[21] The earliest datable example of this type is The Jewish Museum's very dignified and elegant No. 42, made in 1731–37. Three other Jewish Museum shields, all of the early 20th cen-tury, are close adaptations of an early Breslau example with Moses and Aaron (Nos. 45–47).[22] The most outstanding of the Museum's Breslau shields, however, is No. 43, made around 1790, possibly by Johann Gottlob Boettiger. It closely resembles several other Breslau shields of this period, in which Aaron, wearing the High Priest's breastplate, is holding a censer, and Moses, two rays of light emitting from his head, is holding the Tablets of the Law. One interesting detail is the fact that Moses is shown wearing sandals, while Aaron is depicted barefoot. Moses's sandals are an oblique, symbolic reference to the biblical account that he removed them in the presence of the Lord, before the Burning Bush.[23]

This iconographic type spread to many locales where other figures were often included. Few examples can match The Jewish Museum's No. 125, apparently from Hermannstadt (Nagyszeben) in Transylvania, which features not only Moses and Aaron, but also David and Solomon, all with specific attributes, as well as the Ark of the Covenant and the Offering of Isaac.[24]

In the 1750's, a particular combination of Temple appurtenances appears as the central motif on many Augsburg Torah Shields: the Tablets of the Law resting on the *parashah* plaque box, now representative of the Ark of the Law. This combined motif, in vogue for many decades, seems to have been adopted from numerous Torah Shields from Nuremberg and the

19. See Kayser, No. 54, where it is noted that this shield was accompa-nied by Torah Pointer No. 520, bearing a Wurzburg hallmark.

20. See Kayser No. 52 and Grossman 1989, No. 12. For the domestic par-allels, see Seling II, e.g. Figs. 631–32.

21. Cf., e.g., Klagsbald 1982, No. 89. For title-pages with the Moses and Aaron motif see, e.g., Croft-Murray 1951, p. 67, fn. 71.

22. The prototype is Hintze 1929, No. 212, dated 1753.

23. And cf. No. 44, also bearing the figures of Moses and Aaron, from the second half of the 18th century.

24. For a shield from Prague, depicting Moses and Judith (an icono-graphically related com-bination of figures found on Hanukkah lamps) made on the backwall of a Hanukkah lamp, see Grotte 1915, p. 50, Fig. 23. For a photo-graph of a Torah Shield formerly in the Great Synagogue of Vilna, depicting Moses and Aaron with David between, see *Gazit* 6/8 (April 1944), p. 6 (Hebrew).

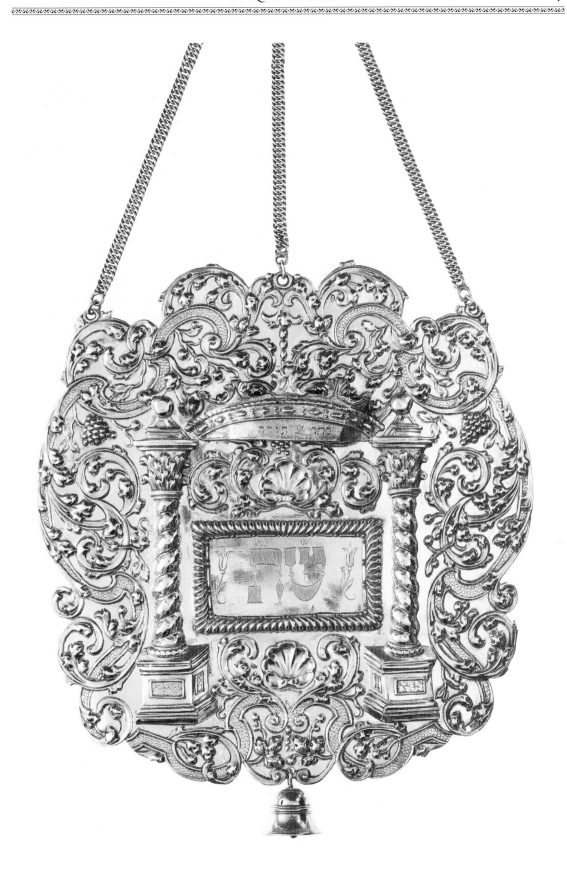

FIG. 5. Torah Shield, Augsburg, 1705, Successors of
Marx Weinolt, active
1700–1747, The Hadji
Ephraim and Mordecai
Benguiat Family Collec-
tion, S 34 (No. 3)

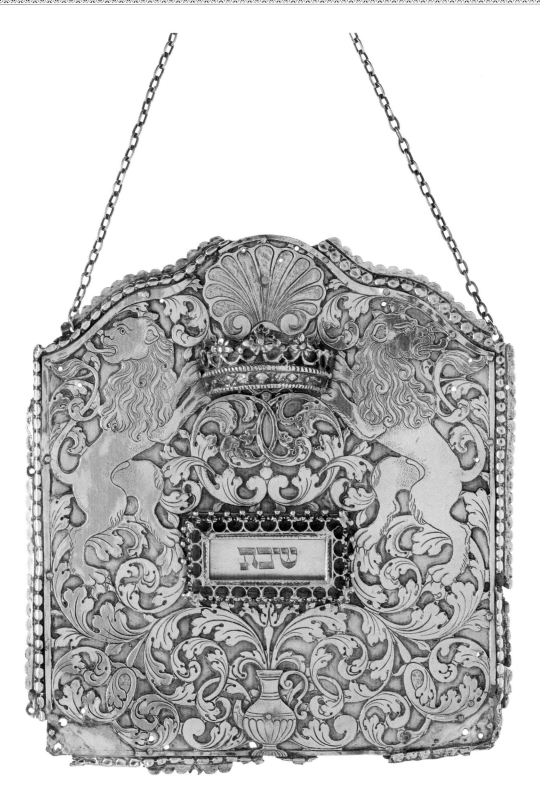

FIG. 6. Torah Shield,
Frankfurt am Main,
1709–25, Johann Adam
Boller(?), active 1706–32,
Jewish Cultural Recon-
struction, JM 28–52
(No. 12)

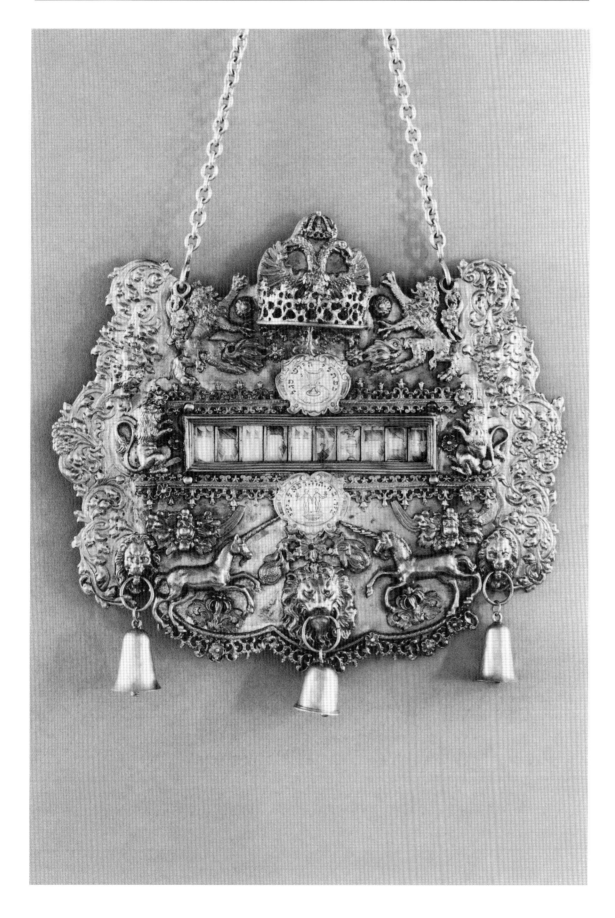

FIG. 7. Torah Shield, Nuremberg, early 18th century (ca. 1720), Gift of Dr. Harry G. Friedman, F 3686 (No. 19)

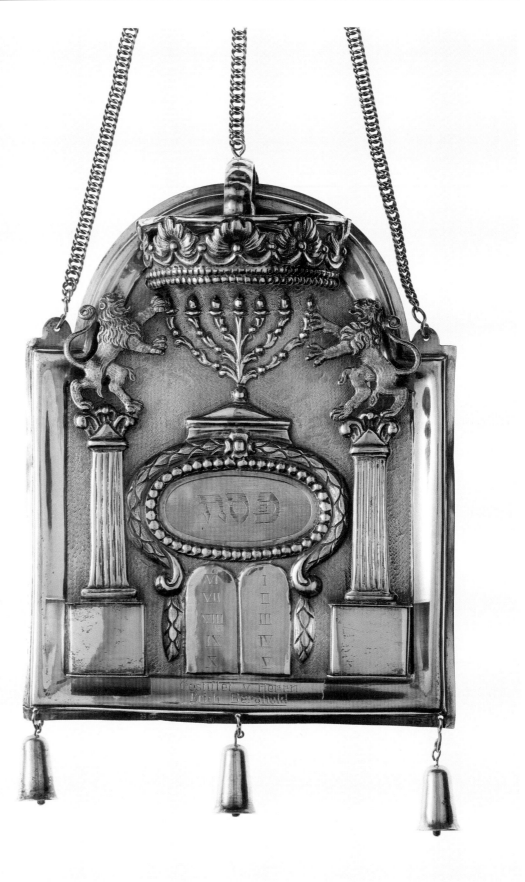

FIG. 8. Torah Shield,
Nuremberg, ca. 1800–
1804, Wolfgang Schubert,
active 1774–1803 or later,
Gift of the Jewish Com-
munity of Danzig, D 136
(No. 31)

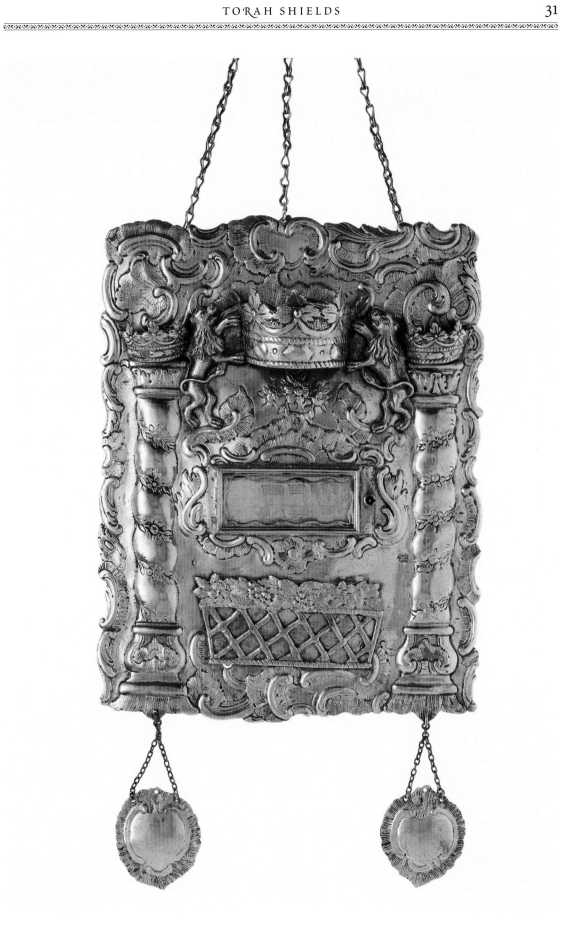

FIG. 9. Torah Shield, Berlin, ca. 1763–72, Joachim Hübener II, active ca. 1737–80, The Rose and Benjamin Mintz Collection, M 11 (No. 37)

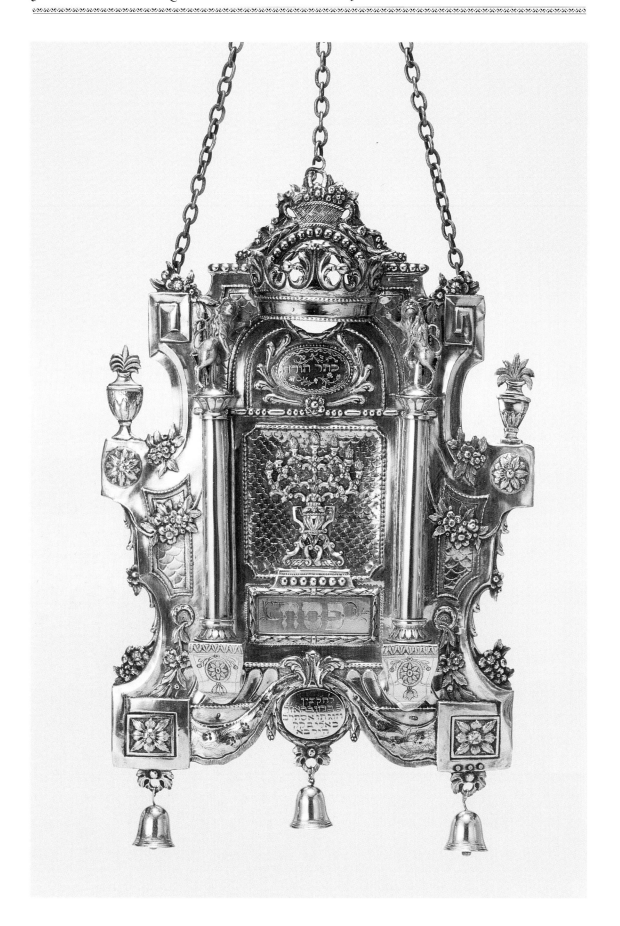

FIG. 10. Torah Shield,
Augsburg, 1808, Joseph
Anton Seethaler, active
1766–1811, Gift of Dr.
Harry G. Friedman, F 60b
(No. 55)

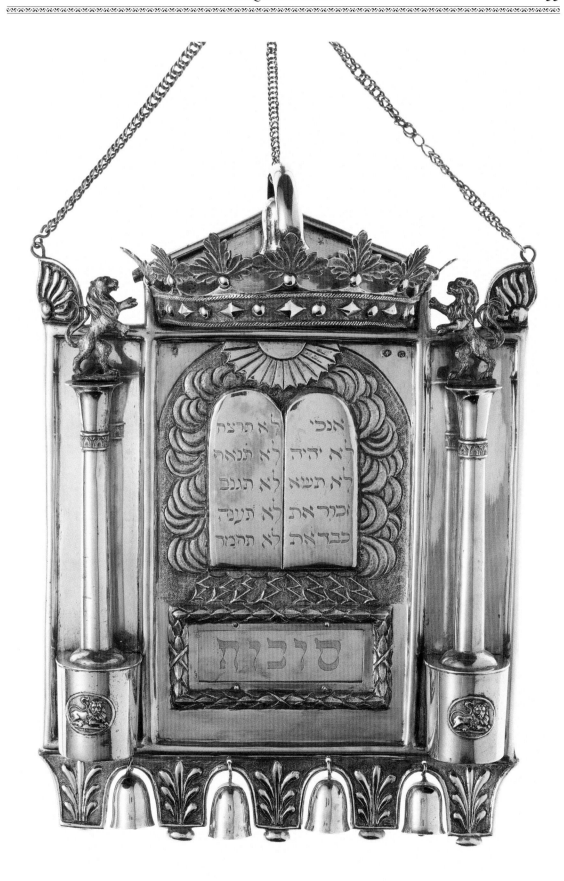

FIG. 11. Torah Shield,
Nuremberg, ca. 1840, Gift
of Dr. Harry G. Friedman,
F 1473 (No. 93)

25. For the Galician type of ornamental Torah Shields, see above. Their probable influence on the shape of German Shields is one facet of the interplay between east European and German Jewish customs and ritual art. For the arched form on amulets in Poland, cf. The Jewish Museum's M 103 and M 104; for a similar amulet integrated into a shield, see *Kings and Citizens*, No. 77.

26. Skirball 7.18 (Jeremias Zobel's mark appears only on the *parashah* plaques!); see, e.g., *Wüb*, No. 2.

27. Two other, very similar Hübener shields are known: Brooklyn Museum 49.228.2 and Christies' New York 1993, No. 455 (formerly Jewish Museum, F 3915). For another "square" Hübener shield, see Hintze 1929, No. 214.

28. *Wüb*, No. 24; Mann 1986, Fig. 6; also cf. Israel Museum 148/35, and Jacobs 1887, No. 1458, both by Herfurt. For an almost identical shield by Johann Jakob Leschhorn, dated 1784, see Ellenbogen 1988, No. 10.

29. The Jewish Museum possesses several of his pieces. See Nos. 450 and 523 in this catalogue.

30. See note 9, above. The general style of these Torah Shields, employing the usual corpus of decorative motifs of this period, can be seen not only in the matching Torah Finials (see below), but in several other types of Jewish ritual art, such as spice boxes (Jewish Museum, F 2117) and Hanukkah lamps (Jewish Museum, F 1536 made by Carl Bitzel in 1803).

adjacent town of Fürth. Often these Nuremberg shields had a specific shape, a square topped by an arch running almost the entire width. This Nuremberg form, which was popular for a long time, may derive from the ornamental Torah Shields so typical of Galicia and its vicinity.[25] The Jewish Museum possesses several excellent Nuremberg examples: one bearing a dedication dated 1746 (No. 21), fairly early for this classic shape; two others (No. 29 and 30), of the 1790's, and a fourth (No. 31), of 1800–04, all by Wolfgang Schubert, a prolific silversmith who made a considerable amount of Jewish silver. At nearby Fürth, today a suburb of Nuremberg, this was also the prevalent type, and the Museum has a fine example (No. 32), dating from 1797/98, that was on display at the pre-war Jewish Museum in Frankfurt.

Still another shape of Torah Shield in the mid-18th century is an irregular rectangle; the earliest example is apparently from Frankfurt am Main and dates to the late 1740's.[26] It may have evolved from earlier types like No. 14, made by Schedel who was probably using an earlier pattern from the Schüler workshop. The earliest example of this "square" type at The Jewish Museum, which dates to the 1760's (No. 37), is also the earliest of the Museum's three shields made by Joachim Hübener of Berlin. His two more elaborate Torah Shields, both in the Danzig Collection (Nos. 38 and 39), are from the first half of the 1770's.[27]

One of The Jewish Museum's finest masterpieces displays a new, unusual feature: the high positioning of its *parashah* plaque box. This is Rötger Herfurt's Torah Shield, an innovative piece of exceptional beauty dated 1761 (No. 17). The design of the upper portion of this Torah Shield, and others from the same workshop, appears to be closely related to that of the contemporaneous Frankfurt-type Hanukkah lamps.[28]

Another new form, appearing during the 1780's at Nuremberg, incorporates rococo elements. As can be seen on two examples at The Jewish Museum, both by the same silversmith (Nos. 23 and 24), the central elements are nearly the same as those on older Nuremberg shields. But while the columns are in a rather archaic, twisted style with sunken niches behind, reminiscent of the early 18th century, the outer frame resembles a rococo mirror or panel frame. An archaistic style characterizes a Nuremberg Torah Shield at The Jewish Museum (No. 28) made ca. 1770 by Samuel Beckensteiner, a prolific silversmith of Judaica.[29] The shield bears earlier forms: columns on plinths backed by niches and a "masonry" background; but in the very center are typical rococo flourishes — a rather bombastic blend of old and new.

## Later Germany

The Jewish Museum possesses a significant group of eight shields from Augsburg, dating from the end of the 18th century through the first several decades of the 19th. All uniformly reflect the early Empire tradition in which fine workmanship and clearly defined forms prevail.[30] The Torah Shields of this group were often made in sets along with matching Torah

Finials.[31] This model remained in fashion well into the 1860's, and was directly copied in other German cities[32] and influenced shields produced in other countries as well.

The forerunner of this group, The Jewish Museum's No. 49, was made in 1793–95 by Johann Matthias Lang.[33] The decorative scheme does not yet include all the elements characteristic of the group, but these are present on two Museum shields made in 1797–99 by Friedrich Anton Gutwein (Nos. 50 and 51).[34] The salient characteristics include: a pair of flanking columns topped by vases of flowers; a domed frame enclosing a *menorah* which stands on a base containing the Tablets of the Law which, in turn, stands on the *parashah* plaque box; a baldachino above, topped by a crown; knotted drapery on either side; and a broad, molded base with a central wreath medallion.

Subsequent shields made by Gutwein and others at Augsburg (including The Jewish Museum's No. 55) have the lions atop columns supporting the crown, which is now lower down, often projecting from the flat surface. Thus, there is a gradual tendency toward verticality. Later in the 19th century, some of the iconographic elements were dropped and new elements introduced. The basic decorative style also changed, but throughout the century the general schematic program remained the same.

The decorative motif of a domed frame enclosing several elements, found for several preceding decades on shields of other German cities, was new in Augsburg, and seems to derive from the typical Nuremberg shield.[35] This basic scheme, with the *menorah* motif above the Tablets of the Law on the plaque box, remained dominant on Augsburg shields and on those in many other cities copying them, even in the second half of the 19th century. An example is The Jewish Museum's Augsburg Torah Shield made by Magnus Unsinn in 1865 (No. 60).[36]

In Nuremberg, too, this scheme remained in vogue, although another type emerged that was initially influenced by the Empire style and, later, by the Biedermeier. The Jewish Museum has a series of such Torah Shields and an interesting subtype as well. They all have rather plain flanking columns with classical appliqué masques and rosettes, and lions supporting a crown (see, for example, No. 92, dated 1815).

The shields of the subtype, which appears in the late 1830's or early 1840's, mostly bear two new motifs: billowing clouds that surround central Tablets of the Law, with a radiant sun above and zigzag streaks of lightning below; and a series of cutout arches along the bottom enclosing bells, with palmettes or other classical motifs on the spandrels between. This type seems to have originated in Nuremberg, for The Jewish Museum has three examples from that city dated to the 1840's (Nos. 93–95). The type soon appeared in other German cities (e.g. No. 97, Altona, ca. 1860) and in the German Jewish community in New York (No. 96, 1861).

In Berlin, the new type was apparently introduced by August Gentzmer, who produced both shields following earlier designs (see Nos. 40 and 41) and several of the new type (including Nos. 65 and 67).[37] The new type shields were also made by the Müller family (No.

31. For the complementary types of Augsburg Torah Finials of this period see below, pp. 44. There are few if any original sets still intact.

32. For an example of a Torah Shield at a locale other than Augsburg, but modelled after an Augsburg type, see No. 9 from Oettingen.

33. For Lang, see Seling 2591 (R³ 985), Master 1782, died ca. 1806. Of his three known pieces of Jewish ceremonial art, two are at The Jewish Museum.

34. For Gutwein, see Seling 2455 (R³ 1005), Master 1759, died 1805. Six of his seventeen known pieces of Jewish ceremonial art are at The Jewish Museum.

35. For typical Nuremberg Torah Shields, see below, and Nos. 21 and 22. The Torah Shields of Fürth, adjacent to Nuremberg, follow the same form, e.g., No. 32, dated 1798.

36. For Unsinn, see Seling 2753, Master 1847; died 1889; The Jewish Museum also possesses a pair of Torah Finials made by Unsinn in 1866 (No. 273). For examples from other cities, see No. 78, made in Kassel (along with finials No. 313) in 1836; and No. 61, made in Ansbach (also as part of a set, with finials No. 296) later in the 19th century.

37. Bendt 1989, Fig. 42 (probably by Gentzmer).

64), a classic example, ca. 1802; and Nos. 72 and 63, from 1823/24 and 1829/30, respectively). A characteristic feature on these shields is the lattice background, not the lattice seen on Augsburg shields of the 1730's, but a simpler, linear grid. These Berlin examples are relatively uniform, with little deviation later in the 19th century, even when they were copied in eastern locales (for example in Danzig, Nos. 71 and 79). The Museum collection includes a half dozen or so Berlin shields of this type from later in the century,[38] and even one example (No. 88) probably made in Hanau or Frankfurt sometime early in the 20th century.

Finally, a small, specific group of Torah Shields should not be ignored — though they are a negative factor in the development of the form. In Germany, at the end of the 19th century, several centers of silver production began casting Jewish ritual objects including Torah Shields, often bearing false hallmarks of earlier periods. A good example, long catalogued as an 18th-century piece, is The Jewish Museum's No. 27, bearing a Nuremberg hallmark and the mark of the well-known silversmith G. N. Bierfreund. The intent of the manufacturers and dealers (including such reputable firms as the famous Posen family, which had shops in both Frankfurt am Main and Berlin) does not seem to have been deception. Rather, their pieces were products of the general "Historismus" trend. Many "nostalgia" items manufactured during this period are still confounding connoisseurs the world over.[39]

## Poland

A small group of shields from eastern Europe, represented at The Jewish Museum by two examples (Nos. 34 and 35), includes the earliest Polish shields with *parashah* plaques. They closely resemble the earliest Nuremberg type in form and style as well as in their fine workmanship, and may even be as early. Where they were actually made is not clear, but the type seems to be associated with the town of Lissa in the Poznan district. A recently acquired shield (No. 172) is similar in workmanship, and its decorative elements resemble those on No. 34, although its form is somewhat different. This group seems to form a link between Germany and Poland.

Many early Polish shields have no *parashah* plaques. They display a pair of flanking columns on plinths supporting an architrave. Between the columns there is often a dedicatory inscription, and above is a crown, usually supported by a pair of rampant lions or griffins. Germany is certainly the source of inspiration for these columned shields. Eventually myriad variations evolved, many of which are represented in The Jewish Museum collection. An elegant example is the Museum's No. 178, ca. 1800; an earlier, rococo example dated 1768/69 seems to have been made by a provincial Jewish silversmith (No. 167). One of the finest examples of this type is No. 174, made in Galicia (Lemberg or Brody) toward the end of the 18th century. This shield is of special interest, for it bears depictions of the twelve signs of the zodiac, presented in accord with the Jewish year. Another Jewish Museum shield of the

38. See shields Nos. 68, 75, 76, and 98 (Berlin), 73, 74, and 83–85 (Danzig). These are by various silversmiths, including Sonnabendt, Gebhardt, Kessner, and Reich. Other Berlin silversmiths (represented at The Jewish Museum by other works such as Torah Finials) also made shields of this type. They include Burcky, Vogel, and the prolific Eisolt.

39. And cf. Nos. 88–90.

late 19th century bears signs of the zodiac on columns flanking a filigree Torah ark which is supported by a pair of lions (No. 200).

A common variation of the Polish Torah Shields, apparently from Lublin, has openwork columns and other applied elements including birds and stags. There is a Torah Ark at the center and below, a cartouche of varying form, often inscribed. Fine examples of this type are the Jewish Museum's No. 192, dated 1838/39, and Nos. 190–191.[40]

The Museum collection includes eight examples of an elegant group of Warsaw Torah Shields. The most refined is No. 206, while No. 203 is partly in filigree, giving it a special charm. Though a few examples of this type have been ascribed to the very end of the 18th century, those at the Museum all seem to be of the second half of the 19th.[41] Other Warsaw types are well represented by the Museum's flowery No. 208, made in the 1850's by M. Swinarski, a silversmith who made much Judaica. Indeed, from the mid-19th century up to the World War II, large Warsaw workshops produced quantities of standardized Jewish ritual art.[42]

## Ukraine and Russia

Many types of Judaica, including Torah silver, were shared by the Ukraine, part of the Russian empire, and adjacent Galicia, part of the Austrian empire. While Jewish silversmithing is in evidence in Galicia in the 18th century (and possibly earlier), it seems to have developed in the Ukraine only after 1850 and in character was usually not as fine, especially the filigree. In workmanship, The Jewish Museum's No. 188, a shield in filigree, closely resembles the Hanukkah lamps from this region.[43] In form, it resembles shield No. 213, a sheet-silver shield with engraved ornamentation, bearing Russian hallmarks for 1865.

In Russia proper also, Judaica generally was made only from the mid-19th century on. The Jewish Museum has a half dozen Russian shields, largely from St. Petersburg and Moscow. The two earliest, made in Moscow in 1841 and 1842, are almost identical (Nos. 209 and 210). Their iconography is rather peculiar, centering on an obelisk topped by a star of David and flanked by a pair of rampant lions supporting a large crown, beneath the double-headed eagle of Russia. Another shield (No. 212) seems to have been made in Odessa in 1857; it resembles Polish examples, with a Torah Ark at the center flanked by a pair of columns, in turn flanked by griffins supporting a large crown above, with a pair of crouching lions below.

## East European Types in Western Lands

A fascinating aspect of the Polish-Russian Torah ornaments is their echo in lands of immigration — England and particularly the United States — around the turn of the century. At The Jewish Museum, a large group of this category includes one shield from England (No. 230) and several from the United States, many made in New York (for example, Nos. 218 and 219). Often bearing false Russian hallmarks[44] to make them acceptable to the new immi-

40. Similar pieces are Martyna 1993, Nos. 44 and 46.

41. A similar piece is in the Stieglitz Collection, No. 3 (with matching finials, No. 4); the hall-marks require further study.

42. Based on their names, 25 percent of the smiths listed in Lileyko after 1850 were Jewish.

43. For the problem of the dating and ascription of this shield, see the catalogue entry.

44. The most common "Russian" mark is that of the "84" standard which is much lower than sterling. The eagle (cf. Lileyko 90) also appears, as well as marks resembling the assayer's mark with date (cf. Lileyko 84–89), even with dates as late as 1903. In the Russian Empire the date marks were dropped in 1896; and cf., e.g., Postnikova 1974.

45. Cf., e.g., Juhasz 1990, illus. on pp. 52–57; *Sephardic Journey*, illus. on pp. 109, 204; for a representative exception, see Mann 1982, No. 202 = *JMNY* 1993, fig. 40b (=Grossman 1995, NMAH 154.990).

46. The matching pair of finials is presently at the Wolfson Museum at Heichal Shelomo in Jerusalem; they bear a dedication almost identical to those on the other pieces. See also n. 47, below.

47. A member of the Soriano family dedicated all three pieces of Torah ornaments in the set. At The Jewish Museum there is an ornamented *ketubbah* (S 142) from Rhodes dated 1830, made for Yosef son of Moshe Tarica, and Rivka daughter of Moshe *Soriano*. See *JMNY* 1993, p. 29, fig. 24 (color) = Juhasz 1990, p. 218, fig. 1.

48. See Levy 1989, pl. (16), lower, on right of photo (after Strumza 1936).

49. Though dedicated to the synagogue in New York, it was apparently made in Ioannina, as indicated by the inscription.

grants from eastern Europe, they are also marked with the Sterling standard. In design they closely copy Polish types, including some instances of filigree work, but the workmanship is somewhat different.

## The Austrian Empire

The style of the Torah Shields from the Austrian empire is based on that of the capital, Vienna. The Jewish Museum has no early shields from Vienna, but the basic form can be seen in two from Pressburg (Bratislava), made by Adam Renner in the 1810's (Nos. 133–34). Like Vienna shields, these exhibit first-rate workmanship and a sense of grandiosity. The same characteristics appear in the Vienna shields from later in the century, such as the Museum's Nos. 109 and 113, the latter in a flamboyant style.

## The Mediterranean

Torah Shields are generally an Ashkenazi phenomenon, particularly those with *parashah* plaques, but some appear in lands with Sephardi and Eastern Jewish communities. An interesting example of the small type of Torah Shield from Italy (there called *hatzi keter*, "demi-crown") is The Jewish Museum's No. 241, a small oval shield dedicated in 1707/08. This and other Italian type shields are still found in synagogues in the westernmost parts of the former Ottoman empire, a region with long commercial ties to Italy. Native Ottoman Torah Shields are almost always ornamental,[45] are generally round or oval, richly ornamented with floral motifs, and often bear dedicatory inscriptions. Many are in secondary use, having been adapted from objects such as fancy mirror backs. The Jewish Museum possesses a fine round example from the island of Rhodes, dated 1859/60 (No. 245). Its main motif, a large, spiralling rosette, matches the decoration on a Torah Crown (No. 500) and a pair of finials,[46] all originally one set. The dedication on the shield, almost identical with those on the crown and finials, calls the object a *tas* and records the name of the donor, "Michael Ḥayyim David Soriano son of Jacob," scion of a well-known Sephardi family in Rhodes.[47] Indeed, a photograph taken outside a Rhodes synagogue prior to World War II shows a Torah Scroll dressed in this very set of Torah ornaments, confirming their Rhodian provenance.[48]

Another Ottoman Torah Shield at The Jewish Museum (No. 246), made in Ioannina in northwest Greece, bears a sunburst pattern. It was made for the Ioannina community synagogue in New York in 1919. The Museum received it from that synagogue along with other Torah ornaments.[49]

## Varia

A late name for the Torah Shield, an alternative to *tas*, is *ḥoshen*, a reference to the High Priest's breastplate. This late usage led to the manufacture of a small number of Torah Shields

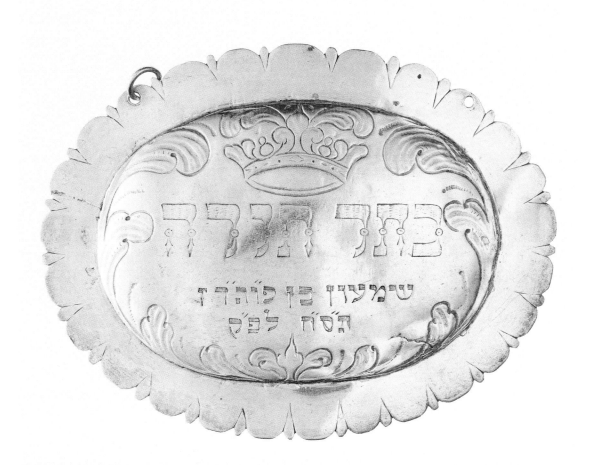

בתר תרדה

שמעון בן פה"ר
הס"ח לפ"ק

FIG. 12. Torah Shield, Italy,
1707/08 or 1847/8, Gift of
Dr. Harry G. Friedman,
F 4071 (No. 241)

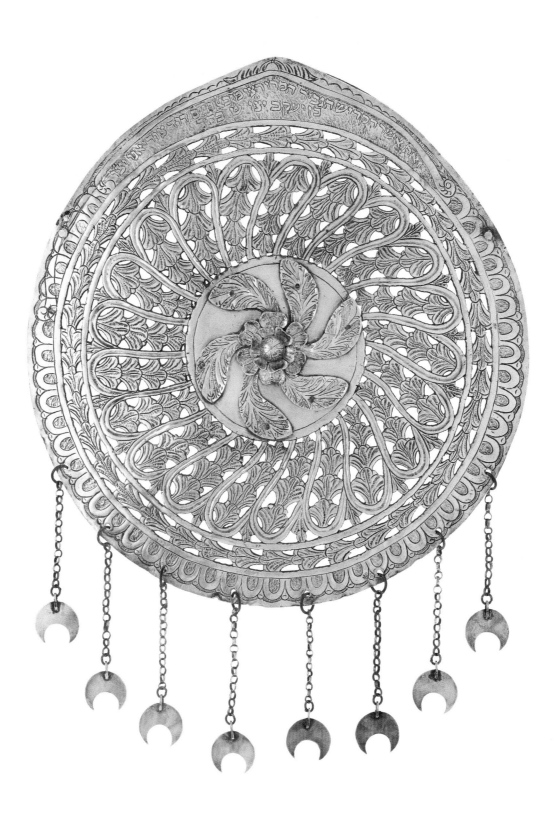

FIG. 13. Torah Shield,
Rhodes, 1859/60, Museum
purchase by the docents
of The Jewish Museum
and the Nash Aussenberg
Memorial Fund, 1991–124
(No. 245)

in the supposed form of this priestly appurtenance. The Jewish Museum has are several western European examples of this type (e.g. No. 229), some adapted from non-Jewish use.[50] The theme was taken up by the late Ludwig Wolpert, director of The Jewish Museum's Tobe Pascher Workshop, and two of his shields of this type entered the collection (Nos. 226 and 227).[51]

Another name for the Torah shield, particularly in eastern Europe, is *tzitz*, a usage rarely found on the objects themselves. The Museum possesses two shields which bear this designation, one (No. 127), dated 1839/40, is apparently from Galicia, while the other (No. 173) is a Polish shield of the early 19th century that was adapted from the backwall of a Hanukkah lamp.[52]

*c/ɔ*

# TORAH FINIALS

## *Italy*

The earliest extant Torah Finials are of tower form and originated in the Spanish domains in the late 15th century.[53] With the dispersal of Spanish Jewry, those who settled in Italy introduced the use of tower-shaped finials into that country. The Italian practice of using a pair of finials together with a cylindrical Torah Crown led to the elongation of the finial shafts and pendant chains with small bells which would clang against the inside of the crown when the Torah was carried. The earliest pair of Italian Torah Finials at The Jewish Museum (No. 388) was made in Mantua in the early 18th century; these majestic, ornate finials already display a feature which was to be come a trademark of Italian finials: long hanging chains. These finials are too heavy to have been carried atop a Torah Scroll, and they may have been intended to embellish the *bimah*, the reader's table in the synagogue — a custom originating in Spain and subsequently carried abroad to all Sephardi communities.[54] A small top finial in the form of an urn with flowers was a common feature on Italian finials, as can be seen on the Museum's No. 389, a simpler version of the classic north Italian type, in this case dedicated for use specifically on the Day of Atonement. A later version of the Italian tower form can be seen in the Museum's No. 392, made in Turin in 1816/17 and donated by a member of the well-known Ottolenghi family; here we see stories of open colonnades with objects from the Temple depicted within, a common feature on Italian Judaica. They can also be seen on an impressive pair of finials from the Piedmont, ca. 1835 (No. 393), including the Holy Ark, priestly hands, a censer, a Levitical ewer, the Fire Altar, a priestly garment, a priestly turban, the Tablets of the Law, the Temple *menorah*, the High Priest's mitre, and a flaming urn. An interesting variant of the Italian tower-form finials is No. 390, made of iron sheet and possibly once silvered; this pair is said to have come from Yugoslavia, and like other Torah ornaments from that Tyrrhenian shore is either Italian in manufacture or follows Italian fashion.[55]

An entirely different form of Italian Torah Finial in The Jewish Museum's collection is No. 399, made in Turin and dedicated in late summer, 1817. Here, too, we see several of the Temple

50. For such "breast-plates" actually made as shields, see Grossman 1995, NMAH 154765, made in London and dated 1887 (several identical shields were made); and cf. Rubenovitz 1963, ill. on pp. 25 and 26; and possibly *Historica*, No. A 31, Fig. 9.

51. omitted

52. For the same phenomenon, see Grotte 1915, p. 50, Fig. 23. For the reverse phenomenon, of Torah Shields in secondary use as Hanukkah lamp backwalls, see No. 173 and the bibliography there.

53. Cf. Cantera & Millas 1956, pp. 389–93; illustrated in Mann, Fig. 9.

54. Cf. *Gardens*, No. 194. See, e.g., *JE* V, p. 661 (Gibraltar); XI, p. 415 (Izmir); XII, p. 272 (Tunis); Pinkerfeld 1971, Pl. VII, 24 (Jerusalem); *JJA* 3/4 (1977), p. 53, Fig. 14 (Italy); Cardozo 1955, pp. 10 and 37, right (Curaçao); and many more instances.

55. Cf. *Yugoslavia*,

implements, but the basic form of the finials is a relatively short, broad cylinder with a crown attached above.

## North Africa

Similar types of Torah Finials came into use in North Africa, partly under Italian influence and possibly under direct influence from Spain.[56] The clearest example of the Italian type underlying these North African finials at the Jewish Museum is No. 396, the workmanship of which betrays its 19th-century Italian origin. The Museum's No. 408 represents the North African counterpart quite well. Its form is similar although smaller and made for a Torah Case, not for a Torah dressed in a mantle. This splendid pair of finials is most probably of Algerian workmanship. An interesting feature of its form, seen in North Africa and among Middle Eastern communities, is the little tubes at the top corners of the hexagonal body, intended to hold flowers or grain on festivals. A further or later development of this basic form can be seen in No. 407, also probably from Algeria.[57] On these finials, the sides of the tower taper, and small arched windows in each side contain bells, a feature commonly found throughout North Africa, from Tunisia to Morocco. In Morocco, where Torah Cases were not used, the finials had taller stems; later, other Moroccan types evolved.

Carved wooden finials, often gilt and painted, are another type encountered in North Africa, particularly in Tunisia. The Jewish Museum has two examples (Nos. 410 and 411). This type probably originated in northern Italy, where similar finials accompanied the gilt Torah Cases of the region. (Such Torah Cases were also used and imitated in North Africa; see below.)

## Holland and England

Another very significant offshoot of Italian finials types is found in Holland. Early in the 17th century, when the first Sephardi communities were established, Italian-made finials were most likely used, perhaps brought to Amsterdam by rabbis of Italian origin. In some instances it is difficult to distinguish between the Dutch and the Italian. The early tower type based on Italian models persisted into the 19th century. The Jewish Museum's No. 382 (long ascribed to the 17th century but clearly dated 1879/80) is a good example. In the late 17th century, however, Dutch finials took on several new features, well represented on No. 383 (early 18th century), such as the waist at the top of the stem and a small, closed crown at the pinnacle.

It is a custom in Holland, as in Italy, when the Torah Scroll is taken from the Ark and prepared for reading, to remove the large tower-form finials and replace them with smaller finials. The Jewish Museum has two fine examples of the latter (Nos. 385 and 386), both of the 18th century. These have plain stems with a very open, airy body above, made up of brackets surrounding a thin central shaft, all topped by a crown with a baluster or floral finial.

56. For a recent attempt to demonstrate the Spanish origins of several types of North African pointers, see Yaniv 1992.

57. The Hebrew date in the inscription on these finials originally read "1930," but this was spuriously modified to yield a date a century earlier. For a similar phenomenon, see Stieglitz, No. 17, finials whose 19th-century date now reads "1788."

In the latter half of the 17th century, when Dutch Jews established congregations in England, they brought with them Dutch Torah ornaments that were soon copied and then adapted to form a new style which, by the end of the 18th century, was specifically English.[58] The Jewish Museum has a pair of formal tower-shaped finials (No. 363) made in London in 1794 in an archaic style closely copying the Dutch finials of a century earlier. This archaic trend among English Sephardi silver is reflected in another pair of finials at the Museum, No. 366 made in London in 1888, a somewhat looser imitation of the early Dutch tower type.

## Germany

Dutch finials are also important for an understanding of the earliest development of German Ashkenazi finials. Prior to the early 18th century, the wooden staves of German Torah Scrolls (*atzei ḥayyim*) were often sheathed in silver. A later example is the Museum's splendid No. 254, made in Frankfurt am Main around 1735, based on an older model. These were made in the Schüler workshop, from which The Jewish Museum has several outstanding pieces of silver Judaica.[59] Extant 17th-century examples of silver Torah Staves have spherical tops (rather than a belfry as on these from Frankfurt), in imitation of the wooden handles of the Torah. The Museum has another variant form of Torah Stave Covers, made in Nuremberg in the early 18th century (No. 255). These covered only the handles, not the wooden roller disk, but like those from Frankfurt, they must have been awkward during the rolling of the Scroll. Another splendid pair (No. 256), not actually covers but permanent attachments to the upper rollers, was made in 1719–20 in the Weinolt workshop in Augsburg.[60] They seem to have been modelled, in part, after contemporaneous candlesticks and, in part, after covered chalices.

At some time in the first quarter of the 18th century, removable finials begin making their appearance in Germany. Among the earliest known are two pairs of almost identical design, made by Jeremias Zobel in Frankfurt am Main, one of which (No. 257) is now at The Jewish Museum — one of its most splendid treasures.[61] What is interesting about Zobel's finials is that they are based directly on contemporaneous Amsterdam types, having the pinched waist at the top of the stem, the hexagonal tower form, and numerous small cast elements, brackets, and finials at the angles of the several tiers. This tower form was simplified later on in 18th-century Frankfurt, and seems to have been reduced in one type there to the bare minimum of a small crown standing upon a short stem, as seen in the Museum's No. 258, made in the third quarter of the century by Conrad Hieronymus May.

At Hamburg, too, early 18th-century finials derive from the same Amsterdam types,[62] and their form is closely followed by the earliest Berlin finials of the late 18th century. Among the latter is The Jewish Museum's No. 260, crafted by August Gentzmer, who made many types of Judaica.[63] He soon modified this type and was the first to give it the specific Berlin spindle form, as can be seen in numerous examples at the Museum (such as Nos. 274 and 286, both

58. See Barnett 1974, Nos. 102-130.

59. The Museum's stave covers closely resemble a pair by Boller, now at the Israel Museum, No. 147/225. The Jewish Museum's holdings include a dozen Schüler-Boller-Schedel pieces: shields (Nos. 12 and 14–16), Torah Stave Covers (No. 254 ), hanging Sabbath lamps (F 2707; JM 37-52; F 4400), Hanukkah lamps (JM 19–64; S 563; 1883–160; F 2820), and a Burial Society beaker (F 3297).

60. And cf. Weinstein 1985, fig. 93, a later but similar pair of finials, made by Joseph Anton Seethaler.

61. The other pair of Zobel Torah Finials is in Frankfurt (Inv. No. x51:11v-w). A third pair long thought to be by Zobel, at the Skirball Museum in Los Angeles (No. 47.24), bears the master's mark of Johann Jakob Leschhorn. These finials were probably patterned after a pair by his teacher, Rötger Herfurt (cf. Christie's Amsterdam 1993, No. 654 — possibly from the Bonn synagogue; cf. *Notizblatt* 25/1929, p. 6, at the bottom of the photo).

62. Cf. Schliemann, esp. figs. 835, 836, and 838.

63. The Jewish Museum's holdings by Gentzmer include two pairs of finials (Nos. 275 and 276) and four shields (Nos. 40, 41, 67, and 68).

from around 1800, with ornamentation in Empire style typical of this period). This Berlin type was often copied at other cities during the first half of the 19th century, such as Danzig (for example, Nos. 287–290) and Breslau, where No. 293 was made ca. 1848 by Carl Korock, another prolific maker of silver Judaica.[64] This form barely changed over the years, as seen in No. 262, probably dating to the early 19th century.

An offshoot of this Berlin type, which appeared in the 19th century, modified the bulbous spindle form into a gallery with an open, columned and domed *tempietto,* but still with a large crown atop. The half dozen or so examples in The Jewish Museum's collection are well represented by No. 294, probably from about 1840, and the more complex No. 296, made in Ansbach in the mid-19th century, or the highly stylized No. 297, made in Munich in 1865 (both latter examples have matching Torah Shields).[65]

A second type of Torah Finial associated with Berlin, larger and more impressive, was also based upon Dutch tower-shaped finials; forerunners of this Berlin type can also be found at Hamburg. The Jewish Museum possesses several elegant examples, among them No. 275, apparently made by Gentzmer sometime during the 1790's. The type was copied in other cities, particularly in northern Germany, for example, No. 277, made in Danzig.[66]

In Nuremberg, an entirely different form of Torah Finials developed during the first half of the 18th century. They were more bulbous with relatively little ornamentation other than bells set into bell-shaped windows and a small crown at the top, as can be seen in The Jewish Museum's rather stark No. 263, made by Johann Conrad Weiss, or in the later No. 264, made ca. 1770 by Samuel Beckensteiner, both creators of much fine silver Judaica.[67] Later in the 18th century, this type evolved into a true tower form having a lower bulb with two or more tiers above, usually with bells hung in bell-shaped windows and a crown. The type is exemplified by the Museum's No. 301, made around 1800 by Johann Friedrich Kramer, as well as the Museum's fine finials No. 300, made in Fürth late in the 18th century. It continued well into the 19th century.

At Augsburg, too, a new tower-form finial developed at the end of the 18th century, matching the new style Torah Shields being made there. Again Gutwein was the innovator, as seen in the Museum's No. 269, made in 1803.[68] Two other impressive pairs of finials, Nos. 270 and 271, were made in the same year by Carl Bitzel, another maker of much silver Judaica.[69] This stately type of Torah Finial remained in vogue in Augsburg for several decades.

The Jewish Museum possesses an unusual single finial from Breslau (No. 267) made ca. 1760–75 by Johann Ernst Braungart. It is in the form of a tree stump which has resprouted, perhaps symbolic of the revival of some institution in Breslau (unfortunately, it is uninscribed). Another single finial from Breslau (No. 305), very elegant in style, was made in 1792/93. (It resembles later examples from Warsaw, but it is not clear where the type originated.[70]) As noted above, one common type of finial in Breslau followed the Berlin model

64. The Judaica by Korock in the Jewish Museum includes an alms box (M 27). Twelve other Jewish pieces by Korock—shields, finials, pointers, a Hanukkah lamp, a pair of tefillin cases, and a spice box—are also known, as are two pairs of candlesticks and two beakers which were definitely used by Jews.

65. For the matching shields see, respectively, No. 61 (cf. n. 36, above) and Furman, No. 5 (the latter essentially identical with the Israel Museum's 148/12, see Cohen 1978, fig. 14).

66. Cf. *Danzig 1939,* No. 81.

67. The Jewish Museum's holdings by Weiss also include a pointer (No. 517), a spice-tower (F 383), a Burial Society beaker (JM 30–51) and the silver handles to a small Torah Scroll (No. 915). Those by Beckensteiner also include a shield (No. 28), a crown (No. 450), and a pointer (No. 523).

68. The earliest known Torah Finials of this type, also made by Gutwein, in 1799, are at the Magnes Museum in Berkeley (No. 73.11). The Jewish Museum also has four shields by Gutwein (see Nos. 50–53).

69. Of the eleven known Judaica objects made by Bitzel, these two pairs of finials and a Hanukkah lamp (F 1536) are at The Jewish Museum.

70. And cf. n. 38, above, for a Warsaw example.

and is represented by No. 307, made by Otto Krutsche[71] in 1867. This pair later found its way to a synagogue in the United States, as its Yiddish dedication indicates.

As they had with German Torah Shields, silver manufacturers of the late 19th and early 20th centuries made finials in archaic styles, often marking them with false marks, as can be seen on The Jewish Museum's No. 319, probably made in Hanau.[72] The former bears an inscription dated 1917, while the latter is dated 1914. Both were dedicated by Hadji Ephraim Benguiat, the noted collector and dealer.[73]

## France

In France, a country with close ties to Sephardi North Africa and to Italy, yet adjacent to Ashkenazi lands as well, the Judaica is an admixture. Indeed, The Jewish Museum owns a rather modest pair of finials (No. 378) made in Paris around 1870 by Maurice Mayer, "Orfèvre Jouiller de l'Empereur," to accompany a splendid silver Torah case (No. 912); as well as an unusual pair of finials (No. 379) made in Paris and dedicated in 1876, presumably for an Ashkenazi Torah Scroll with thick wooden Torah Staves.

## The Austrian Empire

In Galicia Torah Finials commonly resembled the early German Torah Stave Covers, with a broad base corresponding to the roller disk and a stem with spherical termination resembling the upper handle. The Jewish Museum possesses a dozen or so Galician finials, some of them of outstanding workmanship and beauty. The earliest pair is No. 334, dedicated in 1763/64 and made in a simple style with a central knop on the stem and another atop. The outstanding example, however, is the exquisite early 19th-century No. 339, with its menagerie of lions, foxes, deer, eagles, and other birds inhabiting a wealth of openwork foliage. Another "zoo" is found on No. 336, whose motifs include a hare and a chameleon, a stag scratching its mouth, a unicorn spearing a smaller animal, grazing sheep, and a plethora of flowers. A smaller pair of finials (No. 340) made in Rzeszow in 1807 utilizes a traditional motif which goes back to ancient Near Eastern art: two birds flanking a palm tree. These finials may actually have been attached to the Torah Staves. The Hebrew dedication on another pair of Galician finials (No. 338) denotes them as "*atzei ḥayyim.*"

Another, simpler pair of Galician finials (No. 333) is topped by a large crown, a feature typical of finials in the Austro-Hungarian empire, modelled on those of Vienna. In this case, however, it may have been Galicia which inspired the capital. The Museum has a fine early example of the classic Viennese form finials, No. 322, with a typical closed crown topped by a double-headed eagle, and three arms dangling bells alongside. The typical Austro-Hungarian finials of the later 19th century, found in large numbers throughout the empire, were often made in silver-plated brass, as is the Museum's No. 328. Another common type of this same

71. Hintze 1929, No. 203 may very well be identical with this pair of finials. Otto Krutsche, who had been apprenticed to Korock (see n. 64, above), also made a pointer at The Jewish Museum (No. 565).

72. See note 98, below.

73. On Benguiat and his collection, now at The Jewish Museum, see *Treasures*, p. 10; and *JMNY* 1993, pp. 8 and 12.

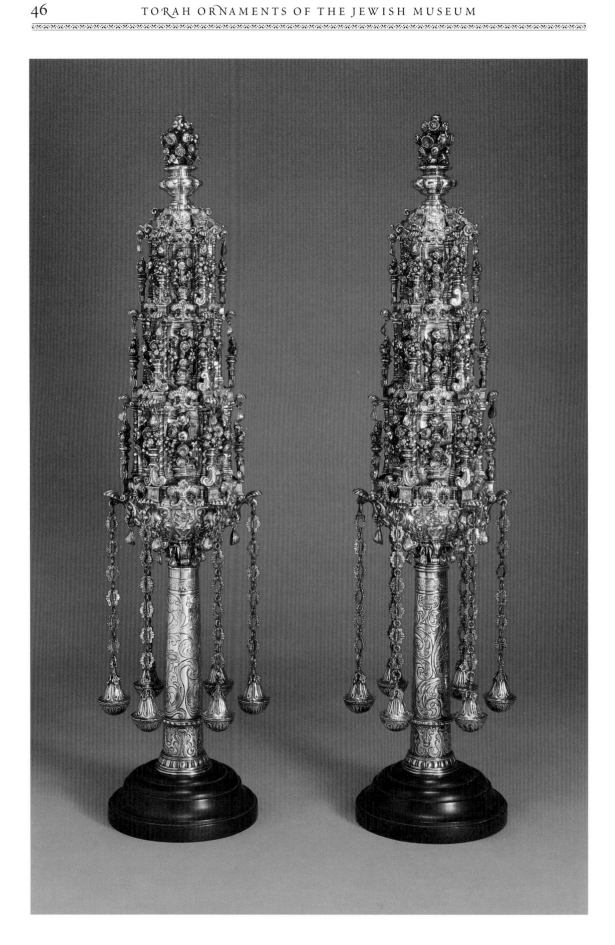

FIG. 14. Torah Finials, Mantua, early 18th century, Gift of Samuel and Lucille Lemberg, JM 20–64 a,b (No. 388)

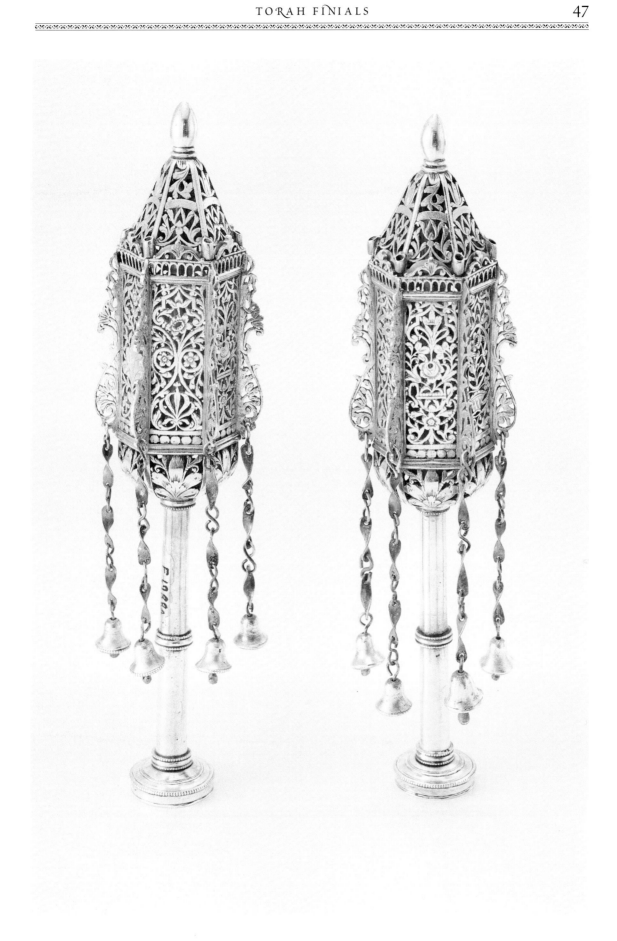

FIG. 15. Torah Finials, Algeria or Tunisia, mid-19th century, Gift of Dr. Harry G. Friedman, F 1988 a,b (No. 408)

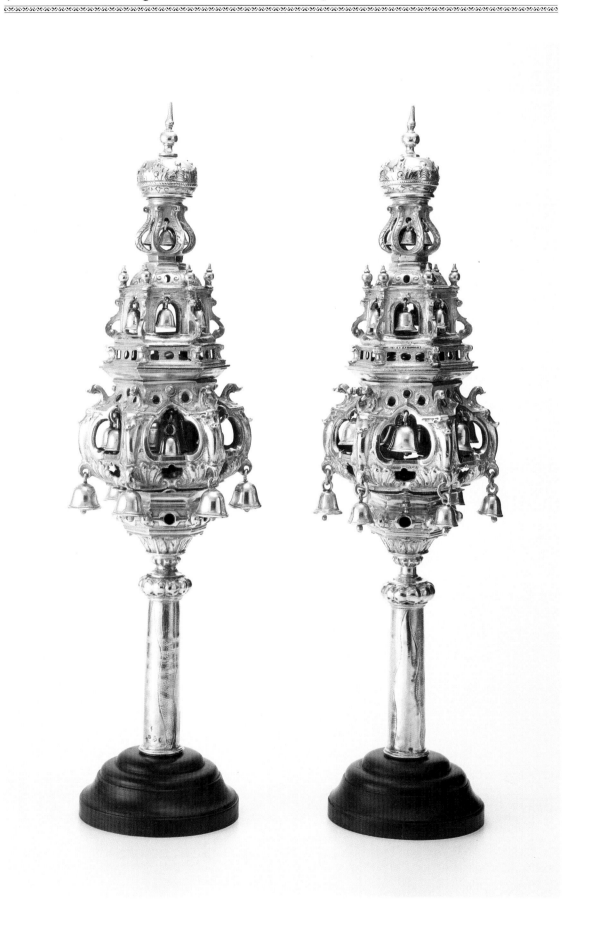

FIG. 16. Torah Finials, Amsterdam, 1705, Pieter van Hoven, active 1680–1735, Gift of Dr. Harry G. Friedman, F 2827 a,b (No. 383)

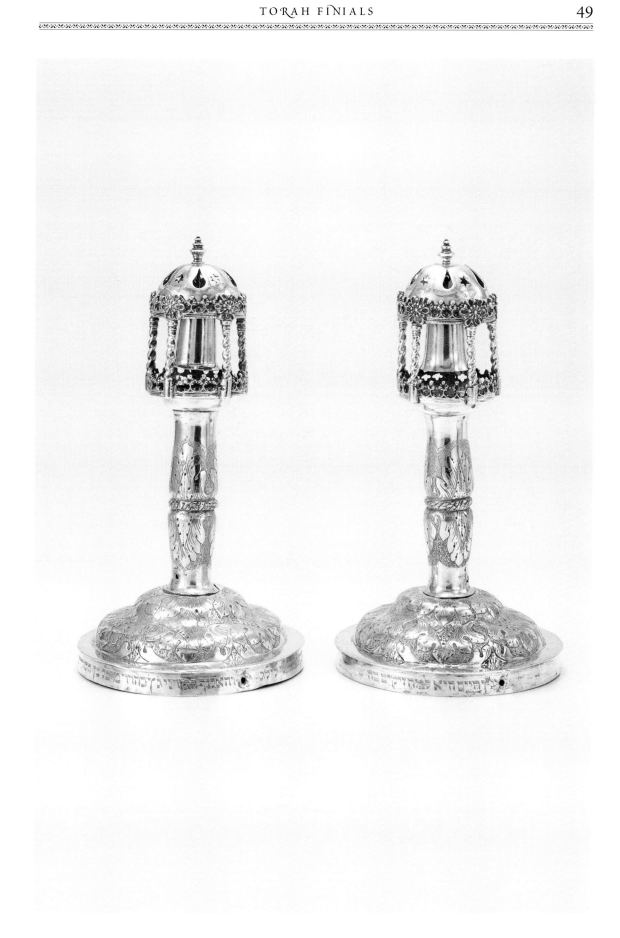

FIG. 17. Torah Finials,
Frankfurt am Main, ca.
1736–40; 1736, Georg
Wilhelm Schedel(?),
active 1722–62, Jewish
Cultural Reconstruction,
JM 42–52 a,b (No. 254)

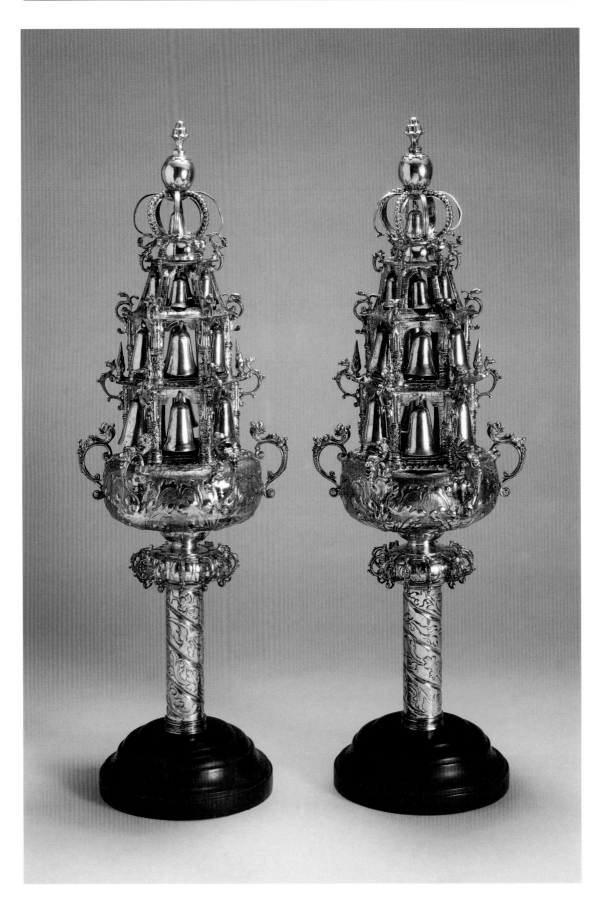

FIG. 18. Torah Finials,
Frankfurt am Main,
ca. 1720–25, Jeremias
Zobel, active 1701–41,
Gift of Dr. Harry G. Fried-
man, F 3685 a,b (No. 257)

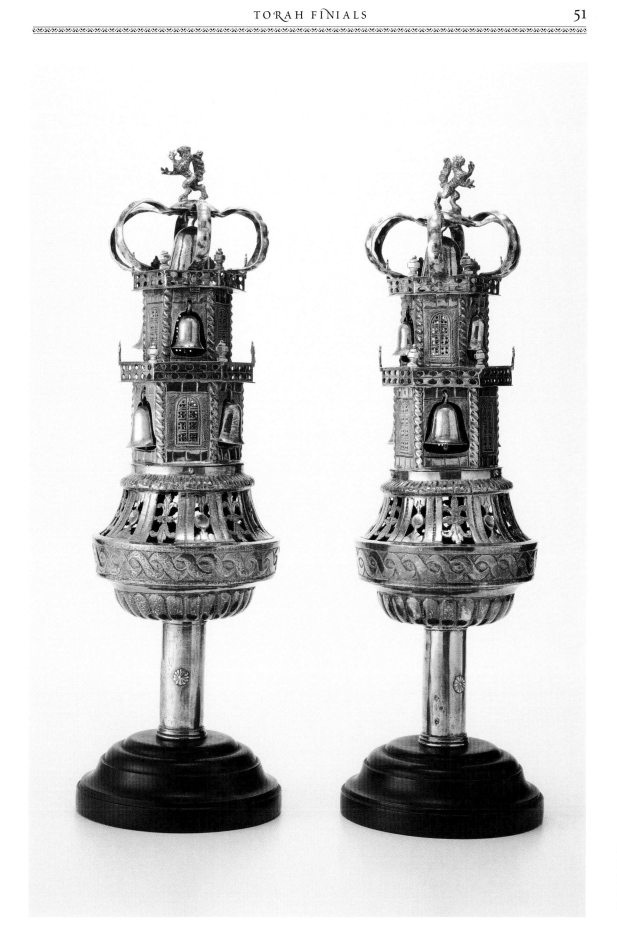

FIG. 19. Torah Finials,
Fürth, late 18th century,
Jewish Cultural Recon-
struction, JM 19–52 a,b
(No. 300)

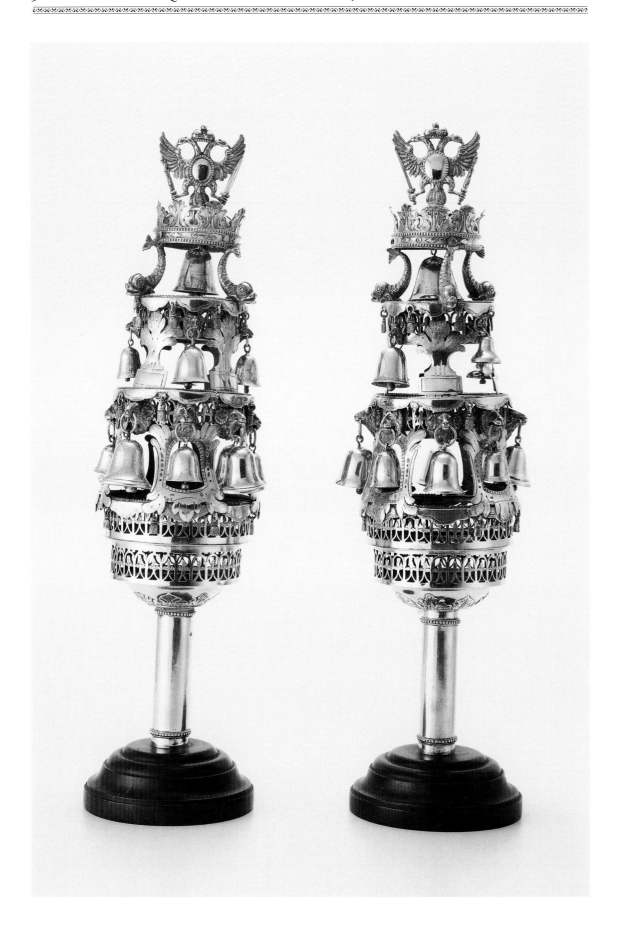

FIG. 20. Torah Finials,
Augsburg, 1803, Carl
Bitzel, active 1787–1823,
Gift of Dr. Harry G. Fried-
man, F 3920 a,b (No. 271)

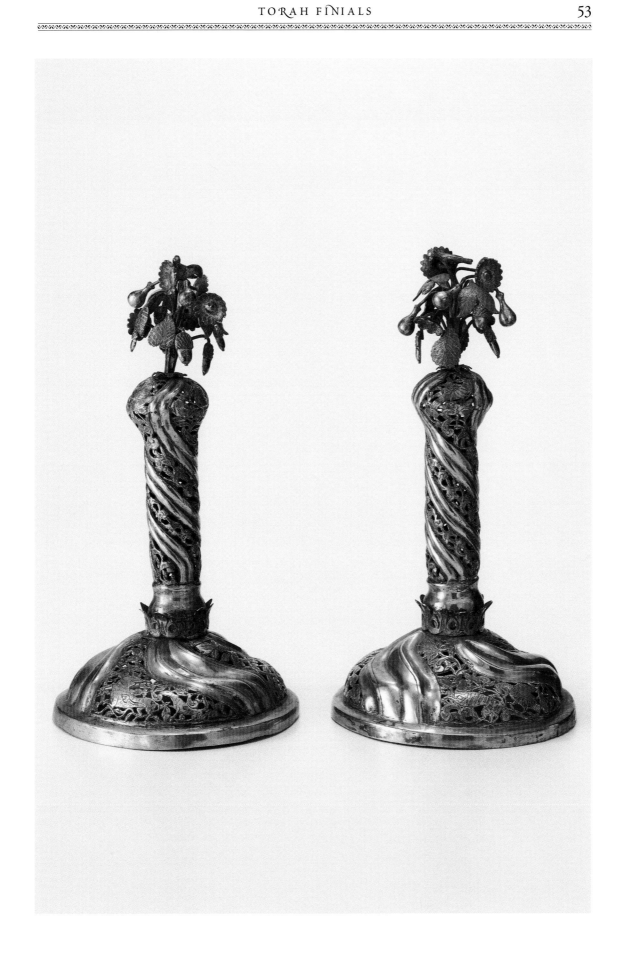

FIG. 21. Torah Finials,
Lvov(?), first quarter(?)
of 19th century, Gift of
Dr. Harry G. Friedman,
F 2544 a,b (No. 339)

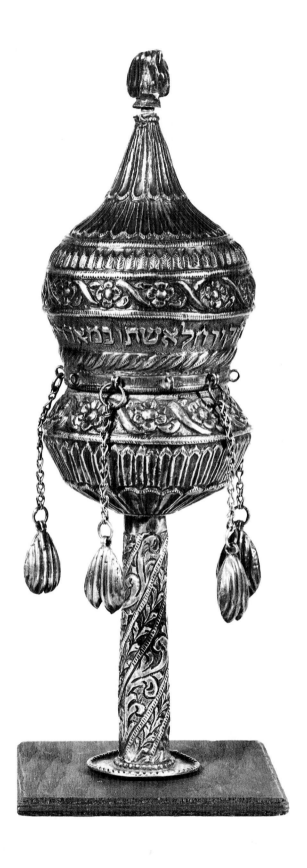

FIG. 22. Torah Finial,
Mardin 1895/6, Gift of
Dr. Harry G. Friedman,
F 4508 (No. 420)

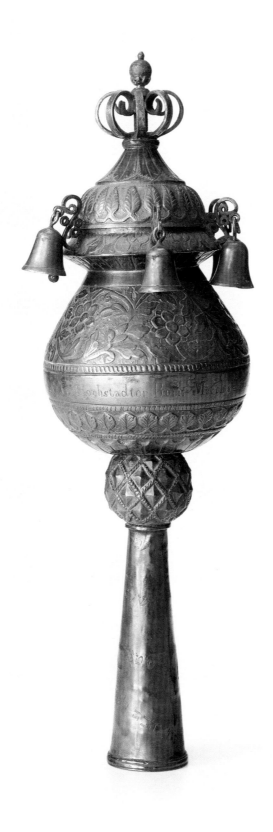

FIG. 23. Torah Finial,
Jerusalem or India, 1897/8,
Gift of Dr. Harry G. Fried-
man, F 3311 (No. 370)

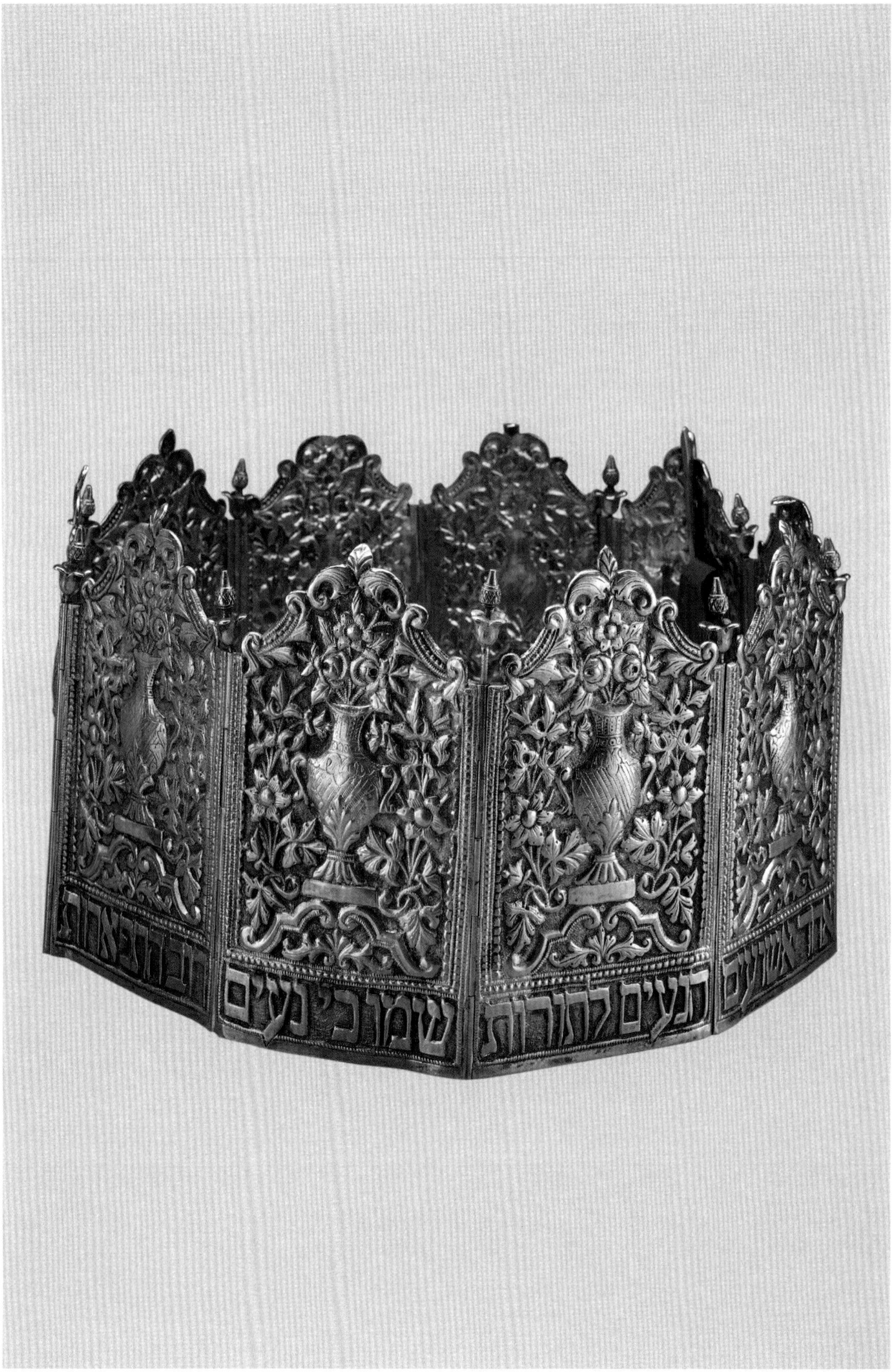

FIG. 24. Torah Crown, Algeria or Tunisia, 1898/99, Museum purchase through the Judaica Acquisitions Fund, 1990–13 (No. 499)

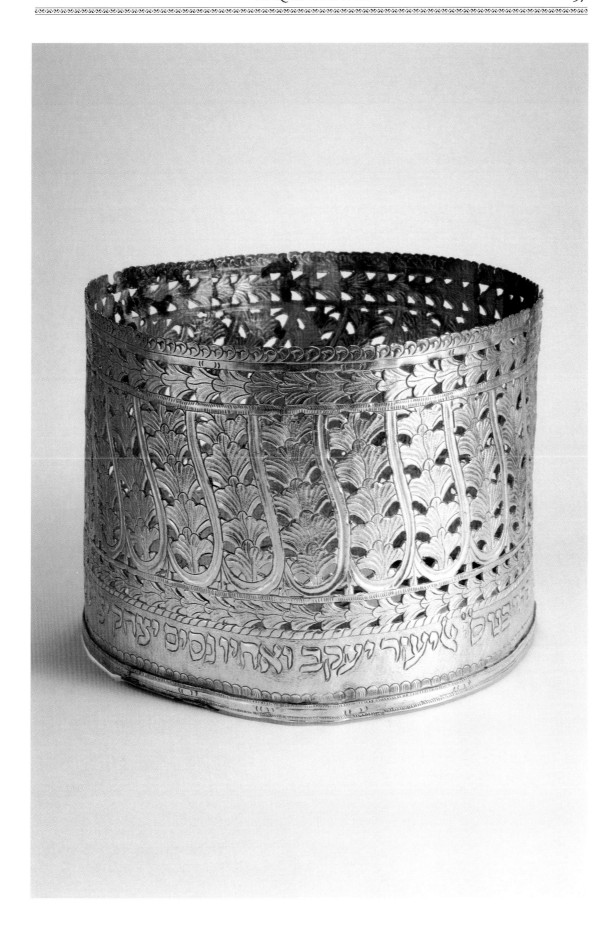

FIG. 25. Torah Crown,
Rhodes(?), 1839/40,
Museum purchase
through Kurt Thalberg in
honor of Elizabeth Cats,
1992–94 (No. 500)

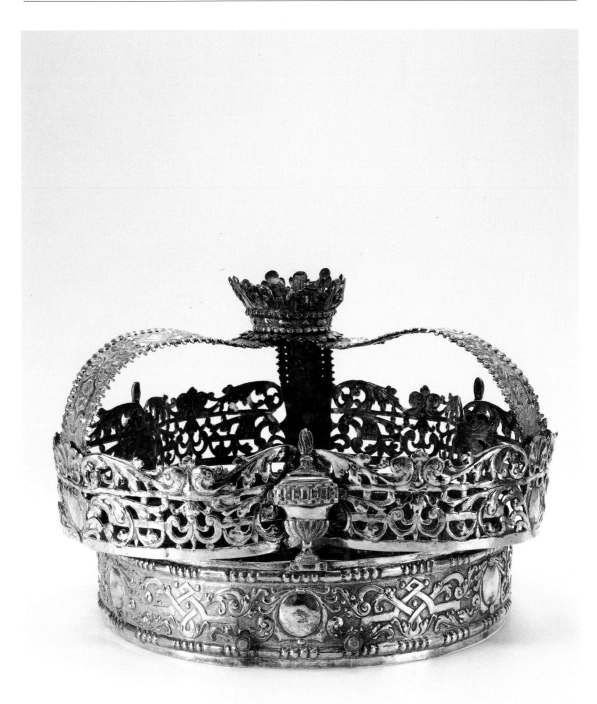

FIG. 26. Torah Crown, Nuremberg, second quarter(?) of 18th century, Jewish Cultural Reconstruction, JM 15–52 (No. 448)

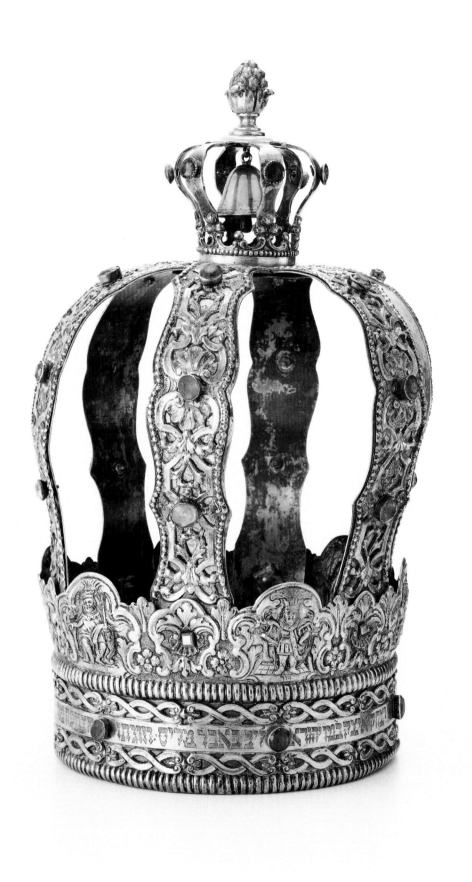

FIG. 27. Torah Crown, Breslau, 1746–58; 1782/83, George Kahlert the Younger, active 1732–73, Gift of Dr. Harry G. Friedman, F 4505 (No. 458)

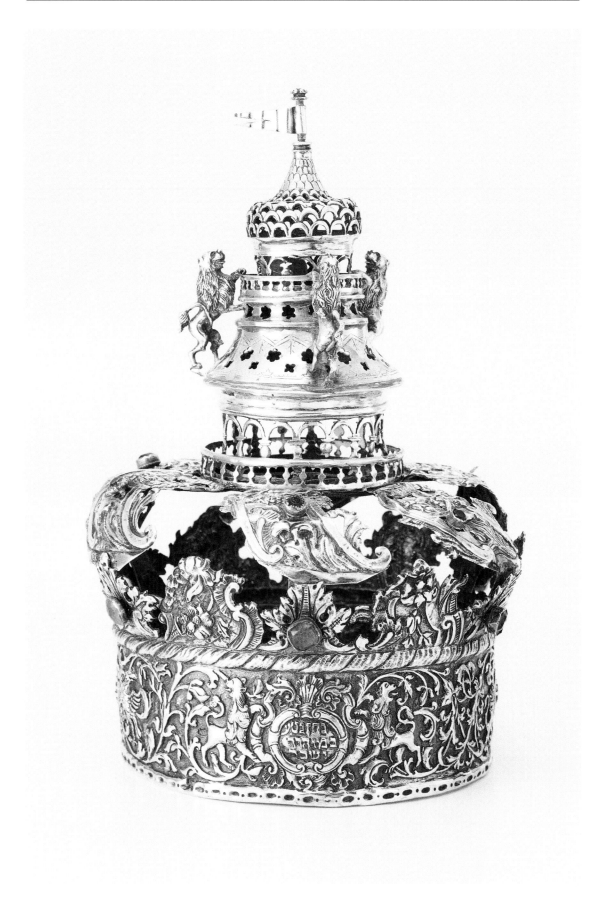

FIG. 28. Torah Crown,
Lvov, late 18th-early 19th
century, Gift of Miriam
Schloessinger, JM 17–64
(No. 468)

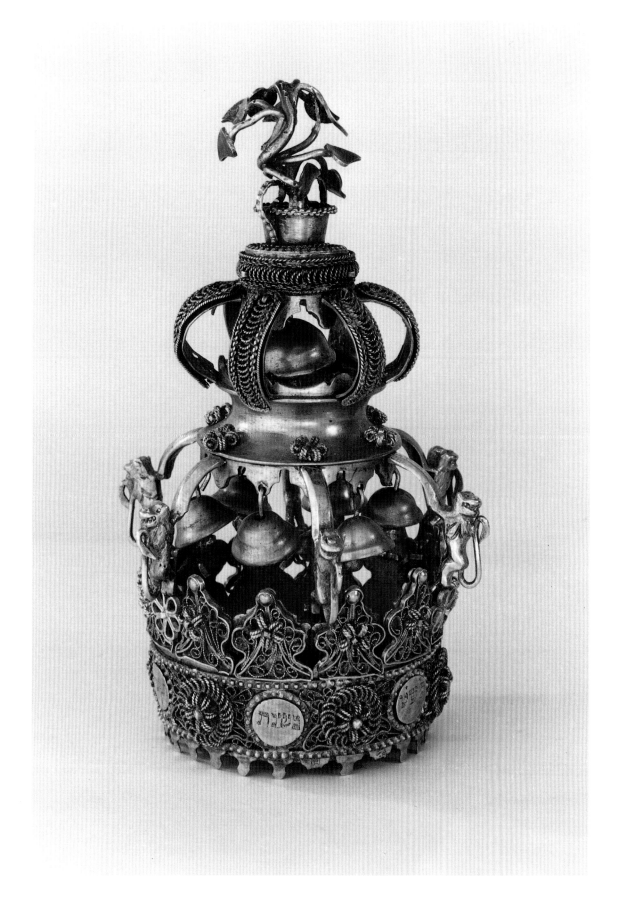

FIG. 29. Miniature Torah Crown, Northern Galicia, 1813/14, Gift of Dr. Harry G. Friedman, F 2508 (No. 467)

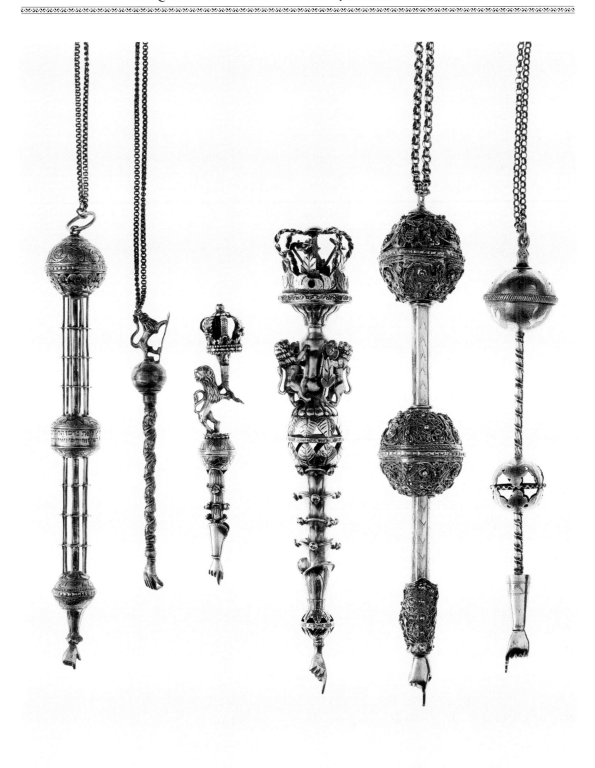

FIG. 30. Torah Pointers: Galicia, 1759/60, The Rose and Benjamin Mintz Collection, M 114 (No. 684); Lvov(?), early 19th century, The Rose and Benjamin Mintz Collection, M 116 (No. 691); Galicia(?), late 18th–early 19th century, Gift of Dr. Harry G. Friedman, F 2590 (No. 692); 20th century, Gift of Dr. Harry G. Friedman, F 5314 (No. 693); Galicia(?), early 19th century, Gift of Max M. Karp, S 1363c (No. 697); Poland, early 19th century, The Rose and Benjamin Mintz Collection, M 338 (No. 712)

period is represented by No. 327, made in Budapest. Similar types are found in Congress Poland as well, such as the fine pair No. 350 made around 1890 by Anton Riedel, one of the major producers of silver Judaica in Warsaw.

## Russia and Poland

In the Ukraine, under Russian control, the finials, like other Judaica, were often of filigree, as can be seen in the Museum's No. 352, from the second half of the 19th century. On another interesting type of finial from this region, the stem displays a hand, originally carved in bone, "holding" the upper part of the stem with the shaped finial.[74] Though The Jewish Museum has no finials of this type, it does possesses two pairs of Torah Staves of this type, No. 920 of silver-plated brass, and No. 919 made of ebony, bone, silver, and mother-of-pearl, and dated 1883.

## East European Types in Western Lands

As we have noted concerning Torah Shields in the United States late in the 19th century, Polish and Russian types of finials were copied and marked with Russian-type hallmarks, alongside the Sterling mark. Many of the Museum's examples of these finials bear Hebrew inscriptions relating to immigrants, such as No. 355 from the 1890's. One American pair (No. 353), quite different from the others and German in character, is inscribed in English: *Abraham Kantor Esq. 134 Prinz* (sic) *St. NY City*, and *Sylvester Brush*.

## The Eastern Mediterranean

In the Ottoman empire, a meeting place of East and West, we find Torah Finials generally more reminiscent of their Hebrew name, *rimmonim*. The most common types are variations of the fruit form. Typical is The Jewish Museum's No. 420, dedicated in Mardin, eastern Anatolia, in 1895/96, which closely resembles No. 421, dedicated at Ioannina in 1841/42. A variant of this basic form, No. 414, resembles a pinecone with a star-and-crescent motif atop. Another pair of finials of this type, No. 419, was dedicated to the "Portuguese congregation," but the city is unknown. Although the Museum's No. 422, a late 19th-century finial from the Benguiat Collection, is Italian in style, it probably comes from Greece. Another, grander form of Ottoman finials is represented by No. 412 of the first half of the 19th century, a tall construction of three bowl-like crowns.[75]

Many of the finials used in Eretz Israel were also of Ottoman form, but the Sephardim there developed other types as well. The Jewish Museum's No. 376 is a typical filigree form found in synagogues in Jerusalem.[76] One pair of finials and a singleton finial from Jerusalem, Nos. 368 and 369, are in a peculiar form common to a small group of Judaica made in Eretz Israel late in the 19th century, apparently for Jewish tourists and pilgrims, especially those

74. See Budapest 1987, No. 30, bearing an inscription referring to the Mishnah Society at Krivoi Rog, 250 km NW of Odessa.

75. Cf., e.g., *Sephardic Journey*, pp. 104–05 and Cat. Nos. 47a and 49.

76. Cf. *Ohel Moshe*, p. 82.

77. Cf. Fishof 1985, No. 51.

78. Cf. Bezalel 1983.

79. Cf., e.g., *Shoshanim le David*, cards 12–27.

from North Africa. They incorporate various pendants from Bedouin jewelry and may reflect a North African tradition of finial design.[77]

Another type of finials unique to Jerusalem are those made by the Bezalel workshops from 1906 to about 1930, mostly of fine filigree work.[78] Bezalel finials often reflect other traditions, as does the Museum's No. 374 in Algerian style. Some were made for use with Torah Cases (like No. 375), while others were definitely used in the Ashkenazi world (like No. 373, which bears Polish import marks from the 1920's). Bezalel work had a decided influence on craftsmanship in Eretz Israel, and filigree finials No. 372, of Yemenite form, are clear evidence of this. Older Yemenite finials, whether made in Yemen or in Eretz Israel, are usually rather austere, as is a brass pair at the Museum, No. 447, probably from late in the 19th century.

## Western Asia and India

Farther to the east, in Iraq, finials atop onion-domed Torah Cases were often simple piriforms, with small pendant bells (like No. 425, from the start of the 20th century). More complex forms evolved and are to be found wherever Iraqi ("Babylonian") communities arose,[79] as can be seen in No. 370, most probably made in India but possibly dedicated in Jerusalem in 1897/98. In India, this form came to be used with the flat-topped Torah Cases used there. The Jewish Museum's Nos. 445 and 446 both reflect this local development. The Museum's impressive gold finials No. 444 of the 19th century reflect the different tradition of the Jews of Cochin, who place either a single finial or a crown on their Torah Cases.

There are a dozen or so finials at The Jewish Museum, all apparently from Persia, or at least all made by Persian artisans, of two or three principal types: Nos. 435 and 439 are representative of two fruit forms, while No. 442 more closely resembles Sephardi tower-form finials. The Museum's No. 433 represents what is probably an older form of fruit-shaped finial, while No. 427 is of finer form and workmanship.

❧

# TORAH CROWNS

## On Torah Cases

The Torah Crown (*keter* or *'atarah*) is of two types: that associated with a Torah Case (*tiq*), generally forming an integral part of the case; and that associated with a Torah Scroll dressed in a textile mantle (*me'il*), invariably an independent element. The former is found principally in Muslim lands, while the latter type is found among the Sephardi and Ashkenazi communities.

The earliest extant example of a Torah Crown integrated with a Torah Case is the cresting on The Jewish Museum's No. 899 from mid-16th century Damascus. Later examples are found on Nos. 905 and 908). Independent, detachable crowns for Torah Cases are found in two regions, Yemen and North Africa. A fine example, made in silver of hinged panels, is No. 499, dated 1898/99. Its rhymed Hebrew wedding dedication calls it a *zer*, "wreath," and includes laudatory puns and blessings for abundant issue.

## In Sephardi Lands

The Jewish Museum's earliest crown for a dressed Torah Scroll is from Italy (No. 495), where cylindrical crowns were commonly placed atop Torah Scrolls dressed in mantles, as apparently was the custom in Spain at the time of the Expulsion in 1492. This crown was dedicated in Bolzano in 1698/99 and has dense floral ornamentation. Another crown (No. 496), apparently from Ferrara, 1764–77, shows a more typical Italian feature: a series of objects from the Holy Temple. Identical appliqués appear also on Italian Torah Finials.[80]

The Torah Crowns of Turkey and the Balkans generally follow Italian forms, although they are executed in a more provincial style.[81] The Jewish Museum possesses a pierced cylindrical crown (No. 500) dedicated in 1839/40, which is part of a set including a Torah Shield and a pair of finials (see above, p. 38). All three bear a distinctive swirled rosette design.

## Germany

Torah Crowns are more numerous in the Ashkenazi world, with a greater variety of forms. In Germany, the earliest extant examples seem to date from the first quarter of the 18th century, including The Jewish Museum's No. 448, originally from the synagogue of Friedberg in Hesse.[82] It was made in Nuremberg by an unidentified master whose mark, a rooster, is found on other fine Judaica. This crown is rather simple and quite low in construction, with only three staves and a small, open crown at the top. Another Nuremberg crown (No. 450), from the Jewish community of Schnaittach in the second half of the 18th century, follows a similar format; its maker was Johann Samuel Beckensteiner, who made other Torah ornaments now in the Museum.

In northern Germany, at Hamburg and Berlin, a taller crown evolved,[83] possibly influenced by Galician Torah Crowns (see below). The Jewish Museum's No. 449, created by Joachim Hübener of Berlin[84] in 1779 and dedicated in Danzig in 1802/03, is a colorful example of this type. Another type of crown developed at this same time in northern Germany and later became standard in Berlin. It consists of a large, closed crown resting on two stems (similar to those on finials), one of which was movable, to adjust to the handles of the Torah Scroll. The development of this form can clearly be traced through No. 454, of 1842/43, and No. 455, made by one of the early mass manufacturers of Judaica, F. A. F. Eisolt,[85] in 1854–60.

Silesia long served as a cultural gateway between Germany and the lands to the east, and this is well reflected in the Jewish ritual objects made in Breslau, such as The Jewish Museum's beautifully wrought crown No. 458, made by George Kahlert (one of Breslau's finest masters)

80. See above, p. 41.

81. Italian Judaica influenced the basic forms of that of Turkey and the Balkans. Major differences are in the details of workmanship and the motifs.

82. This crown was one of the treasures of the Hessisches Landesmuseum prior to the World War II, and came to The Jewish Museum in New York, through the Jewish Cultural Reconstruction in the early 1950's.

83. Cf. Schliemann, figs. 832–834; and Crown 53.1.8 in the Gross Family Collection, Tel Aviv.

84. For Hübener's shields, see n. 27, above.

85. Eisolt seems to have been one of the first mass-producers, making almost every type of Judaica. His silvermarks are often illegible or unrecognized, and thus his wares are often not correctly identified (cf. Gross Collection, I, p. 153, spice tower 15.1.6, where the mark is upside-down and incomplete).

in 1746–58. Panels on the circlet seem to be from an older Torah Crown, for they are dated 1730/31. Though German in workmanship, the biblical scenes around this crown and its tall form are typical of Galicia.

## Galicia

A similar Galician example is The Jewish Museum crown No. 464, from the second half of the 18th century. Here, too, are biblical depictions labelled in Hebrew, and above the staves is a canopy, topped by a crowned eagle. This splendid style culminated in one of the Museum's most important treasures, Torah Crown No. 463: Just under 20 inches tall, it bears a wealth of flora and fauna, the zodiac, and numerous inscriptions, including biblical and Mishnaic quotations and two dedications, nine years apart. There are traces of modifications, and the lower part of the crown was probably made a decade before the upper. This is the largest and most extensively ornamented Galician Torah Crown known.[86]

The Museum possesses a large group of lesser Galician crowns, variations of this same type. No. 468, from early in the 19th century, is topped by an unusual tower structure, capped by an onion dome and pennant. No. 471, dedicated in 1818 (and rededicated in 1874), has a crown above a crown, topped by an urn with a bunch of flowers. The small filigree crown No. 467, dated 1803/04, was considered sufficiently precious to have its own case. An interesting feature on this piece is the row of lions serving as staves to the main crown. These lion staves are characteristic of a large group of Galician crowns from the first decades of the 19th century,[87] several of which are in the Museum's collection (Nos. 469, dated 1809/10, and 470, dated 1810/11). In the Hebrew dedication on another Galician crown (No. 466), it is designated *zer we'atarah*, "a wreath and diadem," and the words are accompanied by minute depictions of round objects.

An entirely different form of crown co-existed in Galicia alongside the "grand" type just described. At The Jewish Museum, one fine example (No. 477), dated 1777/78, has a low circlet with four staves above, four bells and chains suspended between them, and at the top, a bird. This crown may be indicative of a Galician connection with the German crowns of the early 18th century. Another crown of this type (No. 478), probably from around 1830–40, was dedicated in memory of a son-in-law of the famous Rabbi Akiba Eger; it is ornamented in applied filigree, reminiscent of the Galician-made Hanukkah lamps of the so-called Baal Shem Tov type.

## Poland and Russia

To the north in Poland, particularly in Warsaw, a somewhat eclectic style of Torah Crown developed, showing such Galician influences as extreme height (e.g. The Jewish Museum's No. 481, made in 1882) as well as German traits (as in the globular form of No. 480, made in

86. Nothing, for instance, in Kantsedikas 1992 is comparable; cf. there, Nos. 25–27.

87. An example in Stieglitz, crown No. 7, bears an inscription dated 1725/26 — almost a century earlier than any other similar example. This inscription, however, is on a band which is not an integral part of the crown, and technically the engraving could not have been executed prior to ca. 1820. Stieglitz, crown No. 10, also bears a doubtful date, far too early for this type of crown. See also n. 57, above.

the mid-19th century). With the rise of the mass manufacture of Jewish ritual art in Warsaw toward the end of the 19th century,[88] standardized forms developed, as reflected in Nos. 483, 484 and 486, all variations on a single pattern.

In Russia during the late 19th century, traditional types were made in a rather archaic style in filigree; The Jewish Museum has two excellent examples of this work (Nos. 489, made in Moscow in 1886; and 488, made in 1885), both probably reflecting earlier Ukrainian fashion.

## East European Types in Western Lands

As with other types of Torah ornaments, crowns were made in the United States for East European immigrants at the end of the 19th century. The Jewish Museum has several such crowns, reflecting both Galician and general Polish traditions. The former is seen in No. 492, bearing spurious Russian empire marks of 1903.[89] A Warsaw style crown (No. 493) bears American marks, including the word "Sterling," alongside the Russian quality mark "84."

## Bezalel

At the Bezalel Art School in Jerusalem, founded in 1906, several types of Torah Crowns were made, often ornamented with carved ivory reliefs and semiprecious stones. They are well represented in The Jewish Museum collection by several examples, the finest of which is No. 502, made in Jerusalem and imported into Russia before World War I. Bezalel work inspired later Israeli makers, such as Smilovici in Tel Aviv, who made the Museum's crown No. 504 in the early 1950's; and Benyaminoff in Jerusalem, who made No. 505 in the 1960's.

☙

**TORAH POINTERS**

## Germany

The oldest example of a Torah Pointer at The Jewish Museum seems to be from Germany, and bears a Hebrew date equivalent to 1687/88 (No. 514).[90] In this piece we can already see the basic scheme characteristic of most Ashkenazi Torah Pointers for the next three centuries: a spherical knop at the upper end, to which a ring for a chain is attached; an upper shaft — here twisted, as on many early pointers; a central element (later generally a second spherical knop), here bearing the dedication; a lower shaft — also twisted, commonly found throughout the pointer's history; and a small hand emerging from a sleeve, with the index finger extended. In the early decades of the 18th century, the number of Torah Pointers proliferated in Germany and in other lands. We shall briefly review their development, mentioning only outstanding examples in the Museum's collection.

The inscription on another Museum pointer (No.515) shows it to be from Hildesheim, late in 1717; it displays a central knop, and its shaft is still quite thin, as is usual in early pieces. No.

88. See also p. 37.

89. See also n. 44, above.

90. Cf. Skirball Museum, Los Angeles, pointer No. 44.4 (dated 1715).

516 is another good example. A new element appears on No. 518 — long ascribed to Frankfurt around 1700, but bearing hallmarks of Lübeck of the second quarter of the 18th century. Atop the upper knop is a large figure of a rampant lion holding a shield. At some major centers of silversmithing in Germany, the same thin form with knops is preserved, as in the Nuremberg pointer No. 517 by Johann Conrad Weiss, from this same period. The spiral shaft is reminiscent of the columns appearing on contemporaneous Nuremberg Torah Shields, including several by Weiss himself.

At several other major silver centers, however, more imaginative designs began appearing late in the first quarter of the 18th century, as can be seen in the Museum's beautiful No. 519, made by Zacharias Wagner at Augsburg in 1717–18, apparently together with a Torah Shield, No. 6.[91] At Augsburg, from ca. 1738 on, we see a new turn in pointer design, a simplicity of form and decoration. The Museum's stark but elegant No. 522 by Gottfried Bartermann is the earliest example of this type.[92] This form, which became popular in many German-speaking areas, continues in the 19th century, though somewhat modified, as evidenced by No. 579 dedicated at Munich in 1818.[93]

Another imaginative form of Torah Pointer seems to have evolved around 1730 in Danzig. The Jewish Museum's No. 527 has a hefty square handle — another feature later to become quite common — with a dolphin's head emerging from a knop at the lower end, disgorging a human hand which, in turn, holds a minute Torah Pointer terminating, of course, in a pointing hand. Several pointers were subsequently made in similar form — all now at The Jewish Museum.[94] The square form of handle is also seen in No. 535, a pointer probably made in Cologne and dedicated at Deutz, just across the Rhine, in 1790/91.

By the mid-18th century, clear regional forms of Torah Pointers become evident. In northern Germany, apparently under the influence of early Dutch forms, pointers were made with the hand holding a stylus. The Museum's No. 854 was probably made in Holland, but pointer No. 575 of the same type is surely German.[95] In Berlin (and Hamburg-Altona) the typical pointer had a large spherical knop, a square handle in place of the usual upper shaft, and a twisted lower shaft. An early example is Joachim Hübener's pointer No. 530 dated 1749/50, and No. 531, from the early 1760's, which was made in Berlin by one of the Müller family. This form continued well into the 19th century.[96] The more common form with round upper shaft continued at many locales, as No. 547, from late-18th century Breslau, demonstrates.[97]

In Nuremberg and nearby Fürth, an elongated form developed with a plain upper shaft (occasionally inscribed) and a twisted, somewhat thick lower shaft. The Museum's No. 540, from the mid-1780's, is a fine example of this type made by that prolific maker of Judaica, Johann Friedrich Ehe.[98] At Augsburg at about the same time, a rather plain form emerged, in which there is a medial knop, but the upper knop is replaced by a mere domed cap, the upper

91. Cf. No. 521, from Augsburg, 1735–36, of similar form.

92. Cf. No. 523, made by Beckensteiner in Nuremberg, probably from the 1740's; and No. 525, also from Augsburg, made by Stenglin in 1765–67.

93. Cf. also No. 568, part of a set by Proll, Kassel, 1836 (see shield No. 78 and finials No. 313).

94. See Nos. 526, 528, and 529; and note Ansbacher 1985, No. 9.6 — a circumcision knife (?), ascribed to Germany, mid-19th century, the handle of which resembles those on the Danzig pointers.

95. For Dutch influence on north German Judaica, see above, pp. 43; and cf. Emden 1992, p. 16. Cf. similar pointers but without the stylus: Nos. 585 and 591, the latter with a replacement hand from a Christian digitus. Cf. No. 589 and Schaefke 1980, No. 87.

96. See also Nos. 532, 552, 555 , etc., for 19th century examples.

97. For further Breslau pointers of this form, see Brann 1918, figs. 10–11, and Sotheby's Tel Aviv 1991, No. 215.

98. Ehe made a variety of Judaica, but his mark is also found on the products of at least one Hanau workshop of the early 20th century.

and lower shafts being round or faceted, often tapering downward. At the Museum, No. 549 well represents this type and was probably made by Seethaler around 1808.[99]

Toward the end of the 19th century, the "Historismus" spirit began exerting its influence on Torah Pointers, as can be seen in numerous examples at The Jewish Museum. One of the more prolific manufacturers of Judaica in earlier styles was Emil Freund of Hanau, who supplied objects to the well-known firm of Posen in Frankfurt and Berlin. The Museum's No. 618, bearing the Posen hallmark, was cast from a copper and brass pattern now at the Museum that was used in the Freund workshop.[100] Another common design of this type is No. 618 — previously ascribed to "ca. 1700," as were other such examples in many collections.[101] The Museum also has from this period numerous pointers of a fairly uniform design, made in Germany in brass and often silver-plated, with two ribbed knops and either a large hexagonal handle or thinner, twisted shafts; No. 631 (dated 1913) exemplifies the group.

## Holland

We have already noted the early Dutch type of pointer with the hand holding a stylus. The Jewish Museum has a further example of this type, No. 855, which introduces another Dutch type characteristic of the 18th and 19th centuries: the baluster handle, which often has a hook instead of a chain, as on the Museum's No. 856. [102]

## The Austrian Empire

Turning eastward to the areas encompassed by the Austrian empire, we find earlier examples of Torah Pointers which often display an affinity with German types. No. 668 is an 18th-century example from Kashau (Kosice) in Slovakia. In the early 19th century, Vienna generally set the tone for the rest of the empire, and the Museum's No. 652, from around 1810, shows the then new technique of engine-turned ornamentation — a trademark of Viennese precious metalwork. At other major centers, elongated pointers with little ornament were made, for example, by Frederick Becker, senior and junior (Nos. 699 and 670, respectively).[103] As with other types of Judaica, influence from eastern Europe was also felt on Torah Pointers, as in No. 671 made in Brünn (Brno) early in the 19th century. In Hungary during the first part of the 19th century, German influence was dominant — as can be seen in The Jewish Museum's No. 673 from Szombathely prior to 1840, and even in No. 679 made apparently at Gyor (Raab) in 1854.[104] Later in the 19th century, the rather sweet style of Vienna pervaded and dominated the entire Austro-Hungarian empire, leaving a heavy mark even on Torah Pointers, such as the Museum's No. 656, from the end of the century.[105]

## Galicia

There was an abundance of Torah silver in this part of the Austrian empire, having a general character of its own. The Jewish Museum has a large group of Galician pointers, including

99. Cf. pointer No. 580 (Augsburg, 1825, by Muessmann); and Deneke 1988, No. 3/14 (Augsburg, 1818, by B.F. Stenglin, in a set with a shield).

100. Cf. Hanau, p. 96, fifth mark from top ("Metall- u. Silberwarenfabrik, spez. israelitische Kultgegenst."). The pattern at the Museum is (1993–1) and is from a large group of patterns presently in private hands in Tel Aviv.

101. Cf., e.g., Deneke 1988, No. 3/30 ("Meistermarke: Rose und G G." See Scheffler, *Hessens*, Hanau No. 477, mark 56 =Hanau, p. 96 bottom). This shield is the Gutgesell Brothers' model No. 1121/1, with minor variations (cf. *Pappenheim Album*. I wish to thank Rabbi Shlomo Pappenheim, Jerusalem, for access to the original album).

102. Torah Pointers with hooks but of different form are also found in Germany (cf., e.g., Moses 1931, p. 151 lower). Other baluster type pointers at The Jewish Museum include Nos. 857 and 858.

103. These two Jewish silversmiths from Pressburg produced many pieces of Torah silver; see Pataky 1994.

104. Surprisingly, the Jewish Museum of Budapest is deficient in Hungarian examples. See Budapest 1987, pp. 86–8.

105. The Berger Collection, now at the Jewish Museum of Vienna, has several examples; see Berger 1987, e.g. 1/7.6, 7.10, 7.11, 7.15, 7.16; 6/17.

several examples of one of the most interesting design types. The finest is No. 684, dedicated in 1759/60. What characterizes this type, which survived well into the 19th century, is the series of rods comprising the upper and lower shafts, numbering from as few as three to as many as six.[106] A rarer type of Galician Pointer is rather small, with a heavily twisted shaft and usually a rampant lion at the top, although variations exist; No. 691 is a handsome representative of this type.[107] A rare third type is represented by pointer No. 692, with a short, leafy lower shaft (symbolizing the Tree of Life) on which stands a rampant lion holding a cornucopia which in turn supports a crown. This pointer formerly had a loop with attached Tablets of the Law.[108] The mainstay of Galician Torah Pointers, however, was a rather standardized form having two large knops and very thin shafts, with a large ornamental cuff above the hand. The variations are innumerable, and two basic forms are represented by Nos. 697 and 712, respectively.[109] Occasionally, such pieces were formed from existing objects, such as the head of a walking stick—as in the Museum's No. 703, dedicated at Trembowla in Galicia around 1900.[110]

## Poland

Farther north in Poland and in regions to the north and east, similar types are found but generally with fewer depictions of animals and poorer workmanship. The Jewish Museum has such early examples as No. 706, from 1778/79 (with its corrupt, misspelled dedication), fancy examples like No. 734, studded with numerous glass "gems," and interesting examples such as Nos. 732 and 746 which mention in their dedications towns of essentially the same name but which are apparently lands apart.

Another group of pointers at the Museum is included under the heading of "Poland" for want of a better definition, and may well be from some other region (possibly farther to the west or southwest). These pointers, of similar shape and fine workmanship, date from the mid-18th century (for example, No. 683 and the related No. 705) through the early 19th century (No. 694). They have square or hexagonal upper shafts and tapering, spiral lower shafts, occasionally with large sleeve-cuffs.

Jewish silversmiths working in Warsaw in the second half of the 19th century and later produced numerous pointers.[111] Two at the Museum by the same smith, I. Perlman, are in entirely unrelated styles. No. 751 is Viennese in inspiration, while No. 749 resembles the Ukrainian filigree pointers. A true Ukrainian filigree pointer is the Museum's fine No. 757, dedicated by Solomon and his wife Yente in 1854/55.

## East European Types in Western Lands

As with the other Torah ornaments, pointers were also made for immigrants to the United States at the end of the 19th century. Here again are many instances of falsified Russian hall-

106. See also Nos. 686 and 687; and cf. Furman, No. 12; Stieglitz, No. 36; and PBNY 1970, No. 97.

107. This heavily twisted type seems to be typical of Lvov; cf. Kantsedikas 1992 (where several are misascribed to Germany).

108. And cf. Klagsbald 1981, No. 155 (= Klagsbald 1982, No. 49); and Rosenan 1976, No. 17 (= *Mon. Jud.*, No. E 381).

109. The basic Galician type has a rather thin shaft and large knops, giving the impression of barbells; some examples even have three knops, while a few have only the upper one.

110. The basic pointer form lends itself to adaptation from objects such as parasol handles, telescoping opera-glass handles, automatic pencils and other exotica, often in gold, ivory, and other precious materials. Few such examples are authentic and were dedicated to a synagogue.

111. For Jewish silversmiths in Warsaw, see above, n. 42.

marks, often alongside the "Sterling" mark, which served to provide potential buyers with quality marks familiar to them. Some examples merely add an "84" (for example, No. 804), but some bear impossible combinations of Russian empire marks (such as on No. 803, bearing the date 1902 in the form of a hallmark which had been superseded a decade earlier).[112] Some of these American immigrant pointers have interesting dedications—for example, No. 794 which mentions a Society for Assisting the Sick.

The Jewish Museum also possesses a number of American Torah Pointers bearing dedications from the 1860's and 1870's; one, pointer No. 790, was presented to the Hebrew Congregation of Frederick, Maryland, in October 1875, while another, No. 788, was given to Beth-Midrash Shaare Torah in New York in 1861.

## The Mediterranean

The Jewish Museum Collection includes few pointers from Mediterranean lands. Two basic types from Italy are represented — the stylus type by No. 852, late 18th-early 19th century; and the hand type, seen on one of the most splendid Torah Pointers in the Museum's collection, No. 851. This pointer has Modena hallmarks and an inscription dated 1803/04; it is fully gilt, and has a diamond bracelet on the wrist and a diamond ring on the small finger.[113]

The Jewish Museum has several pointers from Arab lands that are difficult to ascribe to specific contexts. One exception is No. 865, which bears an inscription placing it in early 20th-century Tunisia. It has a very blunt stylus tip, probably of Italian inspiration. A pointer of Moroccan workmanship and design from Eretz Israel probably dates from the beginning of this century (No. 826; its inscription ascribes it to "Jerusalem the Holy City"). There are also two pointers of Bezalel type work, probably made by graduates of that school rather than being actual Bezalel products (Nos. 827 and 828). Several Torah Pointers from the early 1950's appear to be assemblages by Smilovici of Tel Aviv (Nos. 832–828; see above, p. 67).

## Southeast Asia

Another outstanding, exotic group of Torah Pointers at The Jewish Museum includes three peculiar examples, two of which are almost identical (Nos. 869 and 870; the third is No. 868). Their tapered proportions are odd, for they thicken toward the hand. In workmanship they are Chinese and seem to have been made in one of the southeastern Asian cities where Iraqi or Persian Jews maintained synagogues.[114]

112. For the phenomenon of false Russian marks, see n. 44, above.

113. In *Gardens*, p. 292, Nos. 187 and 188 (respectively, Nos. 690 and 666) are ascribed to "Italy, eighteenth to nineteenth century" and "Italy, ca. 1830–1890"; neither, however, is Italian. (See the catalogue entries.)

114. At the Skirball Museum, Los Angeles, there are two pointers of similar proportions, one in wood and ivory and the other in silver gilt (Nos. 44.15 and 44.25). For other Judaica made by 19th- and 20th-century Chinese silversmiths in southeast Asia see Sotheby's New York 1984, No. 237 ("with Indo-Chinese marks," subsequently removed; cf. Stieglitz, No. 17). This material is unrelated to the Kai-feng Jewish community, and was made for the use of Jewish merchants in southeast Asia. See Fraser-Lu 1989, pp. 6 and 8.)

## TORAH CASES

115. I wish to thank Dr. Bracha Yaniv for discussing with me details concerning various Torah Cases. Cf., e.g., Yaniv 1982; *Shoshanim le David, passim,* and *Ohel Moshe, passim.*

116. For example, see *Treasures,* p. 154.

117. In such communities, the influx of Sephardim in the 15th–16th centuries later led to synagogues with mixed congregations; this was true in Ottoman Turkey, Syria, Eretz Israel, and Egypt, and thus Torah Cases are still found in some "Sephardi" synagogues. Note, however, that Torah Cases were in use in Spain in the 13th–14th centuries, as noted in Vivian Mann's essay, above.

118. See below, n. 131. Central elements are seen in Greece and northern Italy (cf. photo in archive, Jewish Museum), as well as France (see No. 912).

119. For photographs of Karaite and Samaritan Torah Cases in Jerusalem, cf. Pinkerfeld 1929, as well as the bibliography under No. 899.

120. Dr. Yaniv has informed me that the Synagogue Survey of the Center for Jewish Art, Jerusalem, has recorded three Samaritan Torah Cases of this type, all of the 16th century, including one almost identical with No. 899. See also Vivian Mann's essay, above.

121. For al-Rumaiḥi and the Samaritan community in Damascus, see *JE* X, p. 681a and s.v. *Samaritans;* and *EJ* 14, col. 756 and s.v. *Samaritans.*

Until recently, Torah Cases were the most neglected of all in the scholarly literature on Judaica,[115] and their context has often been confused.[116] Extant examples are limited to the Muslim lands of Western Asia and North Africa (excluding Morocco), with some examples stemming from the Balkans and Northern Italy.[117] Basically, Torah Cases are cylinders with flat, prismatic, or domed tops. Toward the end of the 18th century, an onion dome evolved on Iraqi, Persian, and Indian cases, perhaps developing out of a smaller central decorative element. The rarer conical type case is probably an offshoot of this.[118] Early in the development of the Torah Case, a crown-like circlet often appeared as an integral part of the upper edge of the case, sometimes becoming rather elaborate. Early cases may have had extensions of the staves jutting downward through the base, forming handles as seen on Karaite and Samaritan cases.[119]

The Jewish Museum possesses one of the earliest Torah Cases extant (No. 900). Originating in the Samaritan community of Damascus in 1568, it is made of brass sheet with silver inlay. This case has a low cresting above and two handles below. Like other Samaritan cases, it opens into *three* parts, and originally had three finials.[120] Its inscription mentions various persons, including Yishmael al-Rumaiḥi, a well known Samaritan commentator of 16th-century Damascus.[121]

Another Torah Case at The Jewish Museum, from India and dated 1876 (No. 899), is a rather short, plain, eight-sided prism, with two small silver finials rising from its flat top. Alongside the opening is a single, arched dedication plaque inscribed: "This Torah Scroll, and the case [*tiq*] and the finials [*rimmonim*] and the coverlet [*mappah*] and the pointer [*moreh maqom*] were dedicated by … [on] *Hoshaʻna Rabbah* 5637…." An earlier pair of such plaques, now separated from their case, is also in the Museum collection (No. 901). Similarly arched, they are ornamented in Indian fashion and, besides the typically Indian names of the donors and the date (1744/45), contain a conditional warning: "Anyone who should steal or sell or exchange or give [this *tiq* and its Scroll] in pledge shall be under all the curses in the Scriptures." The same form of dedication frame is found on cases in other lands as well.[122]

Flat-topped Torah Cases are also the norm in North Africa, although domed or pointed examples are known.[123] One clearly defined group represented at The Jewish Museum is Tunisian, deriving its form and ornamentation directly from a north Italian type of case. Some may have been made by Italian craftsmen working in Tunisia.[124] All three of The Jewish Museum's examples (Nos. 902–904), as well as two closely related examples at the Smithsonian Institution,[125] are twelve-sided prisms ornamented in high relief, with high cresting, gilt on the exterior, and shelf-like compartments in the upper part of their red interiors. One significant difference between these Tunisian examples and those from Italy is on the former of dated dedicatory inscriptions in verse, circling the case near the top and bottom. The earliest of these cases dates from 1820, while the latest is from 1837.[126] The dedication of the latest case (No. 904), which is also the best preserved, reads in part: "This is the Torah and it is pure and clear. And you shall give it . . . a crown and a diadem, within a very pleasant and beautiful case . . . with a *mappah* and *rimmonim* . . . . It was made for the repose of the soul of the noble Ḥayyah . . . of the House of Tubaya . . . of the month of Menaḥem [Av], the year 5597 of the Creation, its crafting was concluded. May her soul be with souls of righteous women, may she be bound in the bond of [eternal] life." Gilt wooden Torah Finials such as the Museum's No. 411 were used with this type of case. On another of these cases (No. 902) there are traces on the top of artificial flowers (?) made of wire and yarn. This odd feature may parallel a provision on several North African Torah Finials (including the Museum's No. 408) for affixing flowers, or possibly grain, on some festivals.[127]

This grand, gilt type of case — initially derived from Italy — was imitated in more modest forms, and these local types have many variants, spreading from Tunisia to Algeria and Libya.[128] The Jewish Museum possesses three examples, the earliest of which is 19th-century (No. 905). Within is a sticker-label inscribed in ink: "The Al-Qsar Synagogue . . ., Al-Hamma, Tunisia." Al-Ksar is one of the two villages in the Al-Hamma oasis in southern Tunisia. There are traces of Hebrew inscriptions in the upper and lower friezes and the interior is painted red, just as on the gilt examples, but the entire exterior is covered with polychrome, formal floral motifs that are presently obscured by a crude, peeling coat of reddish-brown paint. Another case at the Museum, from the Jewish Community of Malta (No. 906), appears to have originally had two Hebrew inscriptions. Its interior is painted red, and there are "shelves" above and below, each with a row of round "windows" that were originally mirrored. Just below the upper frieze are traces of studs, probably for fastening a *mappah* around the case. An interesting feature of this case is a simple, geometric inlay of mother-of-pearl on the front panel, a feature usually associated with Egypt.[129] The Museum's third case of this local type (No. 907) also has studs for a *mappah*, but its most interesting feature is its cresting in the form of round disks pierced in a "rosette" design. This form of cresting appears to be derived from a type of rosette cresting found on cases in Egypt.[130]

A somewhat similar round cresting is found on a Torah Case at the Museum, made in Ioannina, Greece, in 1927–28 (No. 908). Each disk has a large Star of David at the center. This case has a peculiar feature found apparently only in Greece: protruding from the top of the central division of the case and attached to one of the two sides is a rayed, fan-like sheet of silver, possibly a degenerate remnant of a central decorative element.[131]

The Jewish Museum collection includes three Torah Cases of Iraqi-Persian type; all three are cylindrical and have floral cresting and onion domes. The earliest one (No. 909) is from Baghdad, based on the ornamentation of the exterior silver sheeting. The frames of the

122. Dedication plaques on the sides of a Torah Case appear to have been common in most lands and remained so even after introduction of the onion dome (which obviated the need for separate plaques).

123. The few examples with pointed tops are probably variations on the onion dome, but might be survivals of an early type; cf., e.g., *EJ* 2, col. 580, illus.

124. See Yaniv 1993.

125. Grossman 1995, NMNH 217676-7, Acc. No. 207992; and Acc. No. 315221 — both apparently obtained from Ephraim Deinard, as were Nos. 902 and 903.

126. The latter has long been associated with Italy; cf. *Gardens*, No.121.

127. For a photograph of case No. 902 taken almost a century ago, see the photograph reproduced in *JE* XI, p. 133, lower left. For another pair of Tunisian-Libyan Torah Finials with holes for flowers, see the wooden example at the Magnes Museum, Berkeley, No. 79.47.7. The Museum's No. 410 may also display this feature.

128. Basing on material recorded by the Synagogue Survey, Center for Jewish Art, Jerusalem, Dr. Yaniv has concluded that for Torah cases: 12-sided=Libya, 6-sided =Tunisia; however most of the 12-sided Torah Cases at The Jewish Museum are clearly Tunisian.

129. But cf. *Broderie d'Alger*, p. 54, No. 2, an inlaid box with a similar motif.

130. Cf. Sotheby's New York 1989, No. 228, the workmanship and form of which seem clearly to be Egyptian.

131. For another example with such elements, see Sotheby's Jerusalem 1987, No. 156.

132. The onion dome seems to have come into use only toward the end of the 18th century, probably in Persia. The earliest published example of a Torah Case with an onion dome is the Israel Museum's 145/12, dated 1799; the very awkward placement of the rods for finials is indicative of its prototypic nature (cf. Katz et al. 1968, p. 167, right).

133. For other Mayer pieces, see, e.g., Klagsbald 1982, Nos. 40, 42 and 43. For the Semama family, see *EJ* 14, col. 722.

134. This method of dating was used by certain Zionist circles in Jerusalem from around the turn of the century on for several decades. It was regarded as denoting the period since the loss of Jewish independence some 1800 years before.

Hebrew dedication are identical in shape to the Indian dedication plaques described above and appear on either side of the interior of the dome. These inscriptions follow a standardized formula: "And this is the Torah which Moses put before the Israelites [Deuteronomy 4: 44]. This case, and the Torah Scroll within it, was [!] made by . . . in the year. . . ." The onion dome conceals the upper ends of the Torah Staves, and other, small rods protrude to hold finials. The dome is also topped by a fixed central finial.[132] Another Iraqi case at the Museum is very similar but is covered with leather and cloth rather than silver sheathing (No. 910). Though quite rare today, such cases were once common. When the Jews of Iraq and Kurdistan emigrated to Israel in the mid-20th century, they generally abandoned these plain cases, taking with them only the finer, silver ones.

One of the treasures of The Jewish Museum is a Torah Case with finials, made in Paris around 1870 (No. 912 and 378). The case is richly ornamented, including Jewish symbols such as the Tablets of the Law, a pair of priestly hands; a "trophy" of a *shofar*, two *lulavim* and *etrogim*; a Hanukkah lamp; and an Eternal Light. The brief Hebrew dedication mentions a woman of a well-known Sephardi family active in Tunisia, the Balkans, Italy, and Paris. The case was made by Maurice Mayer, a silversmith who also made other pieces of Judaica.[133]

Splendid Torah Cases were made by the Bezalel workshops in Jerusalem early in the 20th century. A classic example is the Museum's No. 913, made of brass inlaid in silver, with filigree and ivory embellishments depicting symbols of the Twelve Tribes and several Jewish heroes of antiquity. Its Hebrew dating is of considerable interest, for it is based on the era since the destruction of the Temple in 70 C.E. The case was dedicated to Palestinian Jewish volunteers who fought in World War I, which ended the year before this case was made.[134]

In Palestine prior to the World War I, Torah Cases were made to sell to tourists, often with bogus scrolls within. A singular example in The Jewish Museum's collection (No. 914) resembles a Karaite Torah Case with handles extending below, but its scroll is written in Samaritan script and contains only the first sixteen chapters of Genesis. In 20th-century Iran, Torah Cases were also made to be attractive to collectors. Two Torah Cases at the Museum, (Nos. F 3928 and F 3785), are both made entirely of silver in typically early 20th-century Persian workmanship. They both, however, bear Hebrew dedicatory inscriptions ascribing them to the late 18th century.

CONCLUSION

This cataloguing project of The Jewish Museum has led to a new understanding of the development and typology of Torah ornaments from Jewish communities throughout the world. Due to the composition of the collection, this development is especially detailed for Ashkenazi lands, most prominently Germany.

The following catalogue classifies the large body of material in the Museum's collection. It is hoped that this catalogue, together with further publications on other major public and private collections, will lead to a thorough and reliable typology of Torah ornaments on which future scholarship can confidently build.

# The Catalogue
## Part I · Shields

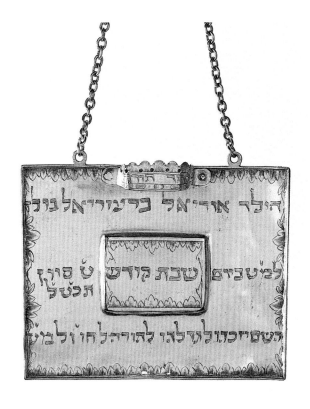

No. 1　F 2653

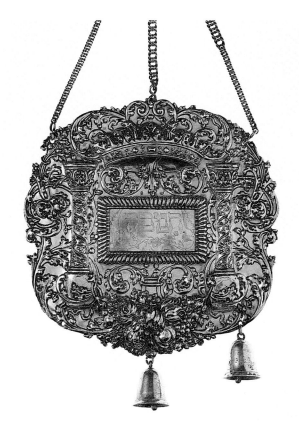

No. 2　F 248

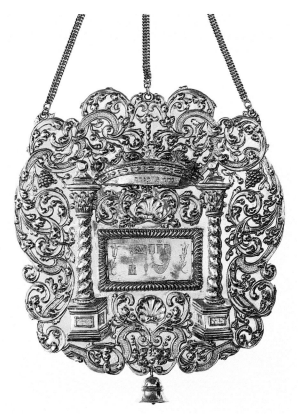

No. 3　S 34

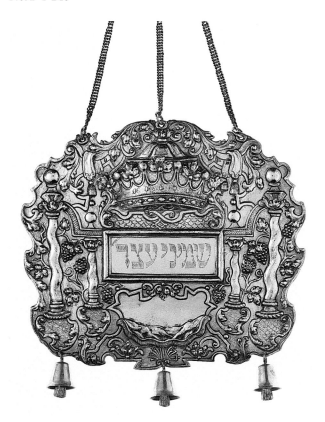

No. 4　F 3633

# Torah Shields

**1**

TORAH SHIELD F 2653 (*Illus. p. 78*)

Germany, 1669 (inscription)

Silver: chased

H 11.9 W 14.2 cm

HALLMARKS: none

INSCRIPTION: on crown: כתר תורה, "Crown of Torah"; on shield: הילד אוריאל בר עזריאל נולד/ למז"ט ביום שבת קודש ט' סיון/ תכ"ט 'ל/ השם יזכהו לגדלהו [!] לתורה לחו' ולמז"ט, "The boy Uriel son of Azriel, born unto a good fortune on the day of the Holy Sabbath, 9 Sivan [5]429 [= Saturday, 8 June 1669]. May the Lord grant him to be raised to the Torah, to the marriage canopy and to g[ood] d[eeds]."

PROVENANCE: Gustav Gumpel Collection, San Francisco

REMARKS: The words שבת קודש, "Holy Sabbath," on the raised central panel serve not only to indicate the *parashah* but also part of the date. For the relationship between this early shield and other 16th–17th century examples, see the Introduction, p. 17.

BIBLIOGRAPHY: PBNY 1950, No. 107; Kayser, No. 41

DONOR: Dr. Harry G. Friedman

**2**

TORAH SHIELD F 248 (*Illus. p. 78*)

Augsburg, 1695–1700

Domenikus Saler, active 1696–1718

Silver: repoussé, gilt

H 24.1 W 24.1 cm

HALLMARKS: *CITY:* Seling 154

        *MAKER:* Seling 1911

REMARKS: There are four *parashah* plaques, with decorative elements above the letters. The chain is original. Cf. the similar shield No. 3; and Ansbacher 1985, Nos. 7.1 and 2.5. See the Introduction, p. 24.

BIBLIOGRAPHY: Kayser, No. 43

DONOR: Dr. Harry G. Friedman

**3**

TORAH SHIELD S 34 (*Illus. p. 78*)

Augsburg, 1705

Successors of Marx Weinolt, active 1700–1747

Silver: repoussé, engraved, parcel-gilt

H 27.3 W 27.3 cm

HALLMARKS: *CITY:* Seling 163

        *MAKER:* Seling 1671

PROVENANCE: The Hadji Ephraim and Mordecai Benguiat Family Collection

REMARKS: There are four *parashah* plaques. The chain is original. This shield and Nos. 4–5 all bear the maker's mark "M over W" in a circle. The identity of the smith has long been controversial, but in 1980 the mark was identified as that of Marx Weinolt, who became a master in 1665 and died in 1700.[1] All twenty-two known pieces of Jewish silver bearing his mark (six of them at The Jewish Museum) also bear Augsburg hallmarks ranging in date from 1705 to 1733. It was thus suggested, without foundation, that the mark on the Jewish pieces was actually "MD ligature and W"— the mark of Weinolt's son, Max Daniel.[2] Reexamination of some ten of these pieces, however, shows conclusively that the mark is indeed "M over W," and that it must have been used as a workshop mark by Weinolt's two sons, Max Daniel and David (II), long after their father's death.[3]

BIBLIOGRAPHY: Kayser, No. 48; Seling II, fig. 707

DONOR: Museum purchase

1. Marx Weinolt (Seling, No. 1671) was a silversmith of outstanding capability, as the examples of his work given in Seling fully demonstrate. His mark (R³ 726) had long been identified as that of Markus Wolff (Seling, No. 1817; Master 1685, died 1716) or that of Mattheus Wolff (Seling, No. 690; died 1585), both of whose masters' marks are otherwise unknown (see, e.g., Kayser, No. 48). The latter, however, died far too early to have made the Judaica, while the former became a Master while Weinolt was still alive, and hence could not have used an identical mark.

2. See Seling, No. 1927; Master 1698, died 1731. Note that several of the Jewish Weinolt pieces bear Augsburg hallmarks from 1732-33 — that is, even after Marx Daniel's death, demonstrating that the younger son, David (II) (Seling, No. 1945; Master 1700, died 1747), continued using the mark, which they seem to have used only on Judaica. For The Jewish Museum pieces, see shields Nos. 3-5 and finials No. 256, as well as spice containers JM 35-52 (Kayser, No. 86 = Seling II, fig. 712) and F 4434.

3. An analogous phenomenon can be seen in the workshop of another branch of the Weinolt family: the mark of Marx's father, Johann Baptist I (Seling, No. 1443; Master 1628; died 1648), was "B over W" in a circle; this mark continued to be used by his widow, for sixteen years after his death, then by Johann Baptist II (Seling, No. 1660; Master 1664, died 1719), and finally by Johann Baptist III (Seling, No. 2036; Master 1710, died 1739). Thus, the same mark was in use in one workshop for 111 years!

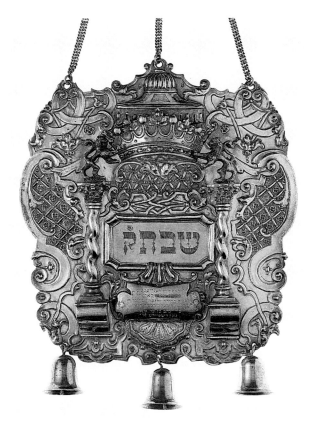

No. 5  JM 30–52

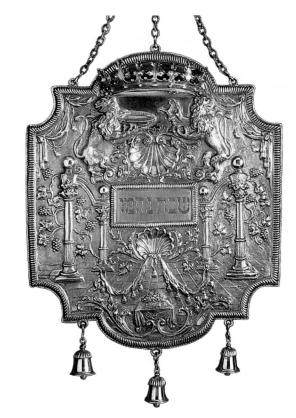

No. 6  F 70c

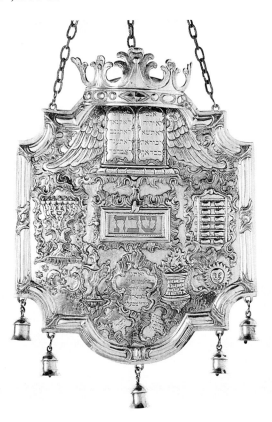

No. 7  S 996a

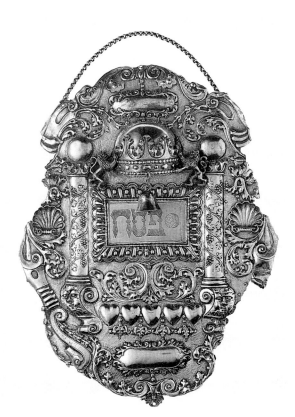

No. 8  F 5742

# 4

TORAH SHIELD F 3633  (*Illus. p. 78*)

Augsburg, 1730–32

Successors of Marx Weinolt, active 1700–1747

Silver: repoussé, cast, engraved, gilt

H 20.5  W 23.7 cm

HALLMARKS:  *CITY:* Seling 196–198

MAKER: Seling 1671

REMARKS: There is a single *parashah* plaque. See remarks, shield No. 3.

BIBLIOGRAPHY: *Jewish Museum 75*, p. [18]

DONOR: Dr. Harry G. Friedman

# 5

TORAH SHIELD  JM 30–52  (*Illus. p. 80*)

Augsburg, 1732–33

Successors of Marx Weinolt, active 1700–1747

Silver: repoussé

H 25.4  W 24.1 cm

HALLMARKS:  *CITY:* Seling 202

MAKER: Seling 1671

INSCRIPTION: on lower panel, probably a palimpsest: נדבת מרת הענריעטטע/ בת כ״ה אהרן קאהן ז״ל/ לכבוד התורה ולזכרון בהיכל ה״/ לנשמת בעלה המנוח היקר/ כה יעקב בן כ״ה מאיר/ גאלדשמידט ז״ל י, "Donation of . . . Henrietta daughter of the late . . . Aaron Kahn, in honor of the Torah and in memory, in the Temple of the Lord, of the soul of her late, dear husband, . . . Jacob son of the late . . . Me'ir Goldschmidt. Y (?)"

REMARKS: There are four *parashah* plaques, none original (added after 1954). The chain is original. See remarks, shield No. 3.

BIBLIOGRAPHY: Cohen, fig. 5

DONOR: Jewish Cultural Reconstruction

# 6

TORAH SHIELD  F 70c  (*Illus. p. 80*)

Augsburg, 1717–18

Zacharias Wagner, active 1712–33

Silver: repoussé, engraved, cast, gilt

H 42.2  W 30.3 cm

HALLMARKS:  *CITY:* Seling 178

MAKER: Seling 2054

REMARKS: There are four *parashah* plaques. The chain is probably original. Cf. pointer No. 519, made by the same maker, probably as part of a set with this shield. Cf. also Cohen, No. 11, by Johann Fassnacht, the basic scheme of which may have served as a model for the present piece.

BIBLIOGRAPHY: Kayser, No. 47; Seling 2054, ex. a), II, fig. 709; *Treasures*, pp. 94–95; *JMNY 1993*, fig. 49

DONOR: Dr. Harry G. Friedman

# 7

TORAH SHIELD  S 996a  (*Illus. p. 80*)

Augsburg (?), 1766/67 (inscription)

Silver: repoussé, engraved, gilt

H 43.2  W 30.5 cm

HALLMARKS: none

INSCRIPTION: on central cartouche: זאת ני/ הקצין פו׳מ/ כ׳ה יהושע/ שמאל [!] קלין/ מהייצפעלד, "This is the donation of Joshua Samuel Klein from Heitzfeld"; in left cartouche: וזוגתו מרת גיטל תחי׳, "and his spouse, Gittel"; in right cartouche: שנת/ תק׳כ׳ז/ לפ׳ק, "year [5]527" (= 1766/67)

REMARKS: There are six *parashah* plaques. The chain is possibly original. Kayser, No. 54, misread the date as 1742 and, since this piece came to the Museum along with a pointer bearing the hallmark of Würzburg, ca. 1740, it was also ascribed to that city and date. Cf. shield No. 6, for another tray-shaped shield. For another shield with the Temple implements, see *Menorah* 5/12 (December 1927), p. 771 right (= Moses, p. 150 right).

BIBLIOGRAPHY: Kayser, No. 54

DONOR: Dr. Harry G. Friedman

# 8

TORAH SHIELD  F 5742  (*Illus. p. 80*)

Nuremberg, ca. 1750–60

Silver: repoussé, gilt

H 36.5  W 26.7 cm

HALLMARKS:  *CITY:* "N"

MAKER: "I/CA" within inverted heart

PROVENANCE: S. Rosenberg

REMARKS: For an Augsburg shield which may have inspired this piece and shield No. 9, below, see Cohen, fig. 2 (by Bartolomäus Heuglin, 1736–37). A comment in The Jewish Museum files associates the five-hearts motif here with the Pentateuch.

DONOR: Dr. Harry G. Friedman

# 9

TORAH SHIELD  F 2416  (*Illus. p. 82*)

Oettingen, ca. 1770

Silver: repoussé, parcel-gilt; glass (not original)

H 36.8  W 31.3 cm

HALLMARKS:  *CITY:* R³ 4323

MAKER: R³ 4324

PROVENANCE: Bezalel National Museum, Jerusalem (No. 204/ 233-2-50)

REMARKS: There is one *parashah* plaque. This shield is heavily repaired. Cf. shield No. 8, apparently derived from the same Augsburg model. Almost identical pieces by the same Oettingen smith are: Israel Museum 148/75, dated 1773/74 (inscription, mentioning צעקן דארף, "Zecken-

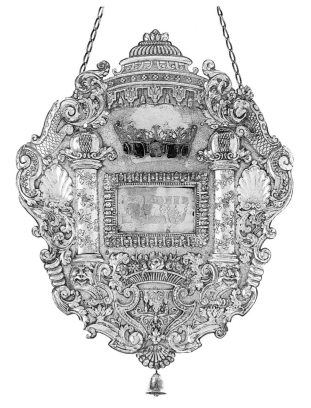

No. 9　F 2416

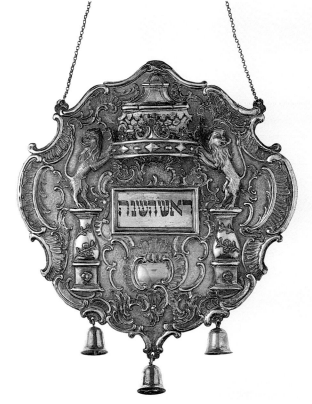

No. 10　F 3467

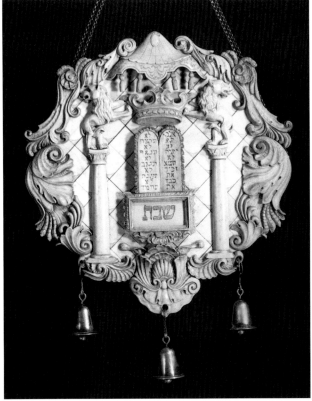

No. 11　F 4163

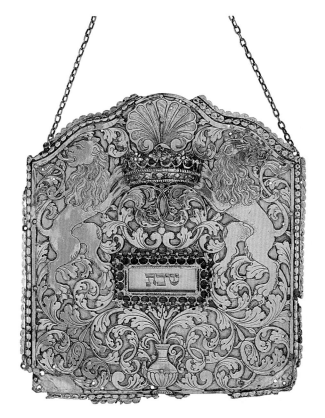

No. 12　JM 28–52

dorf"); and Ansbacher, No. 2.36. This piece was restored, apparently on the basis of the Israel Museum example, probably ca. 1952 (at which time an Austrian-type crown was replaced by the present one). It was received "as replacement of the Hanukkah Menorah given to President Truman . . . by Prime Minister Ben Gurion on the occasion of his 67th birthday" (Jewish Museum card file). [The Hanukkah lamp, numbered F 2416, had been given to the Museum by Dr. Harry G. Friedman.]

DONOR: The State of Israel (in exchange)

## 10

### TORAH SHIELD F 3467 (*Illus. p. 82*)

Tübingen, late 18th century

Silver: repoussé, parcel-gilt

H 29.8  W 28.4 cm

HALLMARKS: *CITY:* R³ 4693

*MAKER:* "GT/M" in heart

PROVENANCE: Blumka, New York

REMARKS: An inscription in Latin characters on the lower cartouche was erased. There is one *parashah* plaque. The very bottom represents an early restoration. The general style is that of Augsburg in the third quarter of the 18th century, but the workmanship is provincial.

DONOR: Dr. Harry G. Friedman

## 11

### TORAH SHIELD F 4163 (*Illus. p. 82*)

Western Europe, after 1903

Ivory (on a wooden base): carved; silver

H 25.4  W 24.1 cm

HALLMARKS: none

REMARKS: There is one *parashah* plaque (but an old photograph shows another). At one of the earliest exhibitions of Judaica held in Germany, in Düsseldorf in 1908, a silver Augsburg Torah Shield from the synagogue at Ichenhausen was displayed.[1] In 1986, a photograph was published of what is undoubtedly the same Torah Shield (now in the Jewish Museum in Augsburg), revealing an interesting fact.[2] The 1903 drawing, executed by Albert Hochreiter, distorted the proportions of the object, depicting it as much broader and rounder than it actually is.[3] The Jewish Museum's ivory Torah Shield is based on this drawing, and not on the object itself. This Torah Shield can date no earlier than 1903, the date of the drawing, another product of the broad trend of "Historismus" which thrived from 1870 to ca. 1930.[4]

BIBLIOGRAPHY: Kayser, No. 194

DONOR: Dr. Harry G. Friedman

1. Düsseldorf No. 455.
2. Ansbacher, p. 75, fig. 6.3; and see pp. 162–63.
3. *Mitt.* III-IV, p. 29, fig. 25. Nothing resembling a year letter can be discerned below the Augsburg "pineapple" in the hallmark; year let-

ters were introduced in Augsburg in 1734. See Seling 204, the mark for 1734–35; the mark here is probably one of those of the early 1730's.
4. For another Jewish Museum Torah ornament similarly inspired see shield No. 27.

## 12

### TORAH SHIELD JM 28–52 (*Illus. p. 82*)

Frankfurt am Main, 1709–25

Johann Adam Boller (?), active 1706–32

Silver: chased, pierced, engraved, parcel-gilt

H 24.4  W 23.0 cm

HALLMARKS: Scheffler, *Hessen,* 128

PROVENANCE: Synagogue of Friedberg, Germany

REMARKS: There are six *parashah* plaques (perhaps not original). The lower edge is damaged and partly missing, including the part which probably bore the maker's mark. Though the latter is missing, the workmanship and motifs point to Boller; for another openwork shield of similar form and from the same workshop, see *Wüb*, p. 164 — as noted in Mann 1986, p. 396; for another, later shield from the same workshop, of similar outline, see No. 14, below.

For a late 19th-century copy of this shield, see shield No. 13. An overwhelming majority of the Judaica objects made in Frankfurt am Main prior to 1750, some forty in number, were made in a single workshop, founded by Johann Valentin Schüler ca. 1680. Of this number, a dozen are at The Jewish Museum, and five are published in the present catalogue.[1] Schüler was joined by his younger brother, Johann Michael, in 1684, and in 1706 by Johann Adam Boller, the maker of this shield (whose sister had married the younger Schüler many years earlier). The Schüler brothers died in 1720 and 1718, respectively, leaving Boller to continue running the workshop alone. In 1726, however, apparently in an effort to assure continuity of the workshop, the childless Boller was joined by Georg Wilhelm Schedel, who had married a widowed niece of the Schüler brothers.[2] In contrast to the Schülers and Boller, who seem to have been highly innovative silversmiths, Schedel relied mainly on their (or others') designs in most of the Judaica he made.[3] By considering the objects made by these four silversmiths as the products of a single workshop, we are able to overcome many difficulties of identification and interpretation. Their stylistic unity is confirmed by examination of such minute details as repeated and continued use of identical casting patterns.[4]

BIBLIOGRAPHY: *Mitt.* III/IV, fig. 24; Düsseldorf, No. 457, pl. 30; Moses, p. 152, left; Hallo 1929, No. 5, fig. 6; Hallo 1932, No. 19; Kayser, No. 46; Mann 1982, No. 67; Mann 1986, fig. 5; *Wüb*, No. 19

DONOR: Jewish Cultural Reconstruction

1. This shield and Nos. 14–16, and finials No. 254.
2. This relationship can be deduced from the fact that Schedel's bride of 1726 was the daughter of a musician brother-in-law of the Schüler

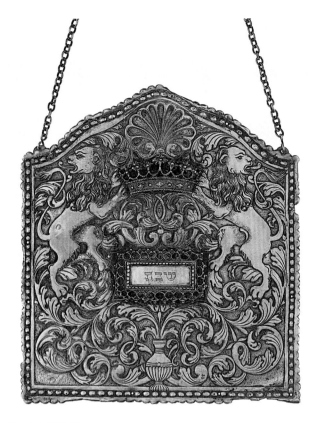

No. 13  F 3125

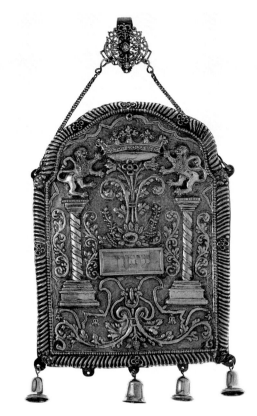

No. 14  JM 21–52

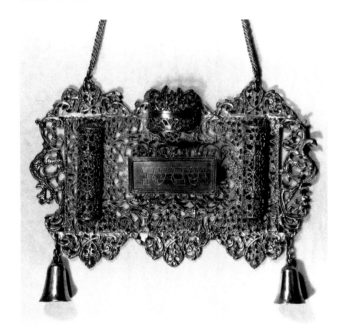

No. 15  F 740

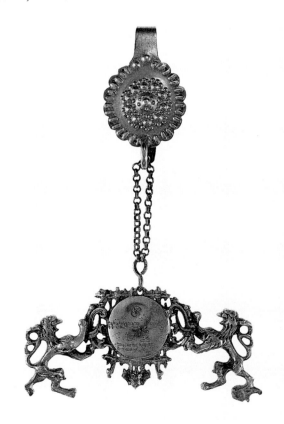

No. 16  F 4930

brothers; since none of the Schüler brothers' wives were related to the musician, he must have married their sister, and thus Schedel's bride was of Schüler blood (see Scheffler, *Hessen,* Nos. 302, 312, 356 and 388. It is notable that Boller's wife was godmother to the second issue of this marriage (in contrast to Mann 1986, p. 396).

3. Of the five known pieces of Judaica by Schedel, only an *etrog* container (cf. *Mon. Jud.,* E 630, fig. 147) might be an original design (though a similar object in a private Paris collection might have served as the prototype).

4. For a possible connection with the Leschhorn family workshop in Frankfurt, see below, remarks, shield No. 17.

## 13

TORAH SHIELD  F 3125  (*Illus. p. 84*)
Germany (?), second half of 19th century
Silver: repoussé, cast, engraved
H 25.2  W 22.9 cm
HALLMARKS: none
REMARKS: There is a single (fixed) *parashah* plaque inscribed Shabbat. This is a close copy of shield No. 12, though made in an entirely different technique, probably in the spirit of the "Historismus" movement (for which see the Introduction, p. 36).
DONOR: Dr. Harry G. Friedman

## 14

TORAH SHIELD  JM 21–52  (*Illus. p. 84*)
Frankfurt am Main, 1740's
Georg Wilhelm Schedel, active 1722–62
Silver: repoussé, engraved, parcel-gilt
H 29.3  W 21.2 cm
HALLMARKS: *CITY:* Scheffler, *Hessen,* 131 or 140
　　　　　*MAKER:* Scheffler, *Hessen,* 272
REMARKS: There are two *parashah* plaques. The chain and clasp hook are original, but part is missing. Hanukkah Lamp F 2820 and Burial Society Beaker F 3297 are by the same smith. The floral scrolling, and possibly the columns, would seem to be inspired by Augsburg designs, such as that of shield No. 2. See remarks, shield No. 12.
BIBLIOGRAPHY: *Wüb,* No. 15
DONOR: Jewish Cultural Reconstruction

## 15

TORAH SHIELD  F 740  (*Illus. p. 84*)
Frankfurt am Main, ca. 1711–12
Johann Michael Schüler, active 1684–1718
Silver: cast, engraved
H 25.4  W 24.4 cm
HALLMARKS: *CITY:* Scheffler, *Hessen,* 129
　　　　　*MAKER:* Scheffler, *Hessen,* 247
REMARKS: There are four *parashah* plaques. The breaks at the top of this shield match the broken elements at the bottom of shield fragment No. 16, which almost certainly formed the upper part of this shield (as observed already in the

1970's by then Assistant Curator Cissy Grossman). Cf. Mann 1986, pp. 393-95, for the other shields of this type by this smith. Other objects by this Schüler are "shield" No. 16 = Schoenberger, No. 10; and Klagsbald 1982, No. 27. See remarks, shield No. 12.
BIBLIOGRAPHY: Kayser, No. 44; Schoenberger, No. 4; Mann 1982, No. 65; Mann 1986, fig. 4
DONOR: Dr. Harry G. Friedman

## 16

TORAH SHIELD (Fragment)  F 4930  (*Illus. p. 84*)
Frankfurt am Main, ca. 1711–12
Johann Michael Schüler, active 1684–1718
Silver: cast, engraved, repoussé
H 5.25  W 11.3 cm
HALLMARKS: *CITY:* Scheffler, *Hessen,* 128/129
　　　　　*MAKER:* Scheffler, *Hessen,* 247
INSCRIPTION: ליב ברענלה/ קערבם, "Leib (and) Brenle . . ."
REMARKS: The clasp hook is original, bearing the maker's mark. Between the two lines of script are depictions of a Levite ewer and a rosette. See shield No. 15, of which this fragment appears to be the upper part. Cf. *Wüb,* p. 164, illus., with a similar medallion surrounded by an identical casting.
BIBLIOGRAPHY: Schoenberger, No. 2; Mann 1982, mentioned under No. 65 (mistakenly listed as F 4391)
DONOR: Dr. Harry G. Friedman

## 17

TORAH SHIELD  JM 33-52  (*Illus. p. 86*)
Frankfurt am Main, 1761 (inscription)
Rötger Herfurt, active 1748–76
Silver: repoussé
H 26.0  W 19.1 cm
HALLMARKS: *CITY:* Scheffler, *Hessen,* 147
　　　　　*MAKER:* Scheffler, *Hessen,* 287
INSCRIPTION: נתחדש ע'י הגבאים/ מקלפי של צדקה/ כהרר
ליב בעכהובין/ וכמר עזריאל לוי בק'ק רעדלהיים/ יו' ה'
כח תמוז/ תקכ'א'ל', "Restored by the *gabbaim* from the coffers of charity . . . Rabbi Leib Bechhofen and . . . Rabbi Azriel Levi, in the H[oly] C[ongregation] of Rödelheim, Thursday, 28 Tammuz, (5)521" (= 30 July 1761)
REMARKS: There are five *parashah* plaques. The clasp hook is original. The shield is lacking the ends of the scrolling on the lower right and left, which may have supported bells (as on the shield in Jacobs 1887, No. 1458). Cf. other shields by Herfurt: Israel Museum 148/35; Jacobs 1887, No. 1458 (presently said to be in a private collection, Paris); *Syn²,* No. 230; and the above noted shield, Christie's Amsterdam 1933, No. 653. Cf. also *Notizblatt* 1937, p. 19 (where two shields are noted in the synagogue of Heddernheim). See *Wüb,* under No. 24, for the persons mentioned here. See

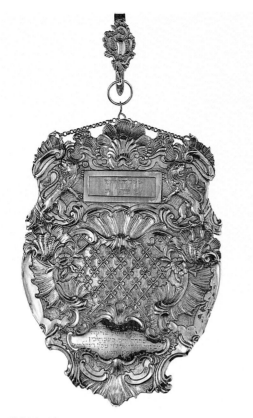

No. 17　JM 33–52

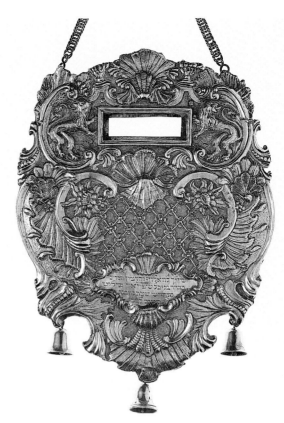

No. 18　F 4380

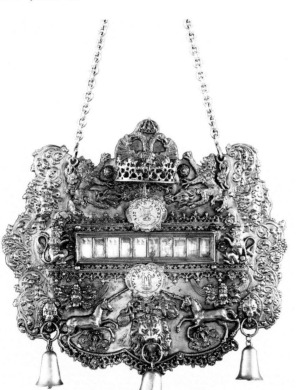

No. 19　F 3686

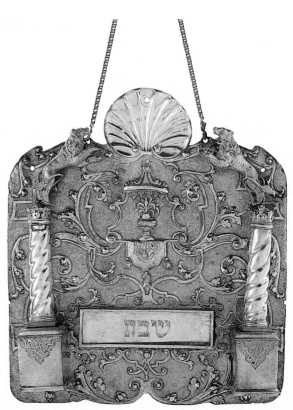

No. 20　F 2186

shield No. 18, a close copy of this shield, made exactly a century later.

Rötger Herfurt, who made this shield, became a master in 1748. A dozen years before, his sister had married another Frankfurt silversmith, Jacob Leschhorn, to whom Herfurt had been apprenticed.[1] From this and from the evidence of the objects, it is obvious that Herfurt had joined the Leschhorn family workshop, which was active for about a century.[2] Herfurt is probably best known, albeit incorrectly, as the "originator" of the typical Frankfurt Hanukkah lamp, the backwall of which depicts a menorah flanked by lions with a crown above.[3] Herfurt's true originality can be seen in his Torah Shields, a fine example of which is presented here.[4]

BIBLIOGRAPHY: Mann 1982, No. 68; Mann 1986, fig. 6; *Wüb*, No. 24

DONOR: Jewish Cultural Reconstruction

1. The Leschhorn family workshop was founded by Balthasar, active 1690-1724 (Scheffler, *Hessen,* Frankfurt No. 319 — no mark is given, but a "BLH" mark, e.g., on the Hanukkah lamp noted in n. 2, can relate only to him), continued by Jacob, active 1722-59 (*ibid.,* Frankfurt No. 386 — no Judaica by him is known); and his younger brother, Jost, active 1731-79 (*ibid.,* Frankfurt No. 405 — who made several pieces of Judaica), and finally Johann Jacob, who was apprenticed to Herfurt and was active 1769-76 (*ibid.,* Frankfurt No. 480— who made over a dozen Judaica objects). Herfurt's name is variously spelled. For the most complete published list of Judaica by him, see Mann 1986, p. 400, note 64. (There are numerous objects on the Judaica market bearing a false version of his mark, alongside a false Frankfurt hallmark.)

2. The only Leschhorn object at The Jewish Museum is a chest-type Hanukkah lamp (F 80) by Balthasar Leschhorn.

3. Originally proposed in *Notizblatt* 1937, this ascription is incorrect. A Hanukkah lamp of "Frankfurt" type at The Jewish Museum bears the mark of Georg Wilhelm Schedel and a Frankfurt city mark of the period prior to Herfurt's becoming a Master. Schedel, generally an unimaginative copyist, was probably not the first to employ the design (see remarks, shield No. 12).

4. A connection has been suggested between Herfurt's Torah Shields and the origin of the Hanukkah lamp backwalls; see Mann 1986, p. 401. But all his known shields bear city-marks later than the earliest of his Hanukkah lamps, and thus the influence was probably in the opposite direction.

# 18

## TORAH SHIELD F 4380 (*Illus. p. 86*)

Frankfurt am Main (?), 1861 (inscription)

Silver: repoussé, parcel-gilt

H 30.4 W 24.8 cm

HALLMARKS: none

INSCRIPTION: שייך להאלוף והקצין הנדיב/ כהרר מיכל שפייאר שליט/ נתחדש שנת נחמו תק טוב לפק, "Belongs to the leader …Rabbi Michel Speyer…. Renewed (in) the year (chronogram, lit.: 'Comfort, 500, good'= (5)621= 1861)."

REMARKS: This is a close copy of No. 17, and dated exactly a century later (the dating in Mann 1982 is based on a partial reading of the full date; note that the very regular, clearcut

workmanship here is decidedly typical of the 19th century). The date can be determined even more precisely if the first word of the chronogram (from Isaiah 40:1) is taken to refer to "Shabbat Naḥamu," the first Sabbath after the Ninth of Av, which in 1861 fell on July 20. There were several persons named Michel Speyer in Frankfurt in the 18th–19th century, and the identity of the one mentioned here is not clear.

BIBLIOGRAPHY: Mann 1982, mentioned under No. 68; Mann 1986, pp. 396–97

DONOR: Dr. Harry G. Friedman

# 19

## TORAH SHIELD F 3686 (*Illus. p. 86*)

Nuremberg, early 18th century (ca. 1720)

Silver: cast, engraved, parcel-gilt

H 26.6 W 30.5 cm

HALLMARKS: CITY: "N"

MAKER: "TR" (ligature) within shield

INSCRIPTION: on cartouche above *parashah* plaque box: נפתלי הירש סגל, "Naftali Hirsch Segal" (around depiction of a Levite ewer and basin); on lower cartouche: ציר*, ב(?) ה* הרר* רפאל* יצי(!), " … Zir[ele] d[aughter of ] (?) Raphael …" (around figures of Gemini).

PROVENANCE: The Monchsroth Synagogue

REMARKS: There are no plaques *per se*, but nine interchangeable, double-sided pieces bearing letters, all held by a frame which fits into the shield; the Hebrew letters are as follows: *alef/ḥet*; *alef/tav*; *ḥet/shin*; *ayin/peh*; *qof/resh*; *peh/* (Levite jug) (x 2); "/(blank) (x 3)." The extant *parashah* letters are insufficient to denote most of the readings, indicating that formerly other pieces existed (a minimum of five more double-sided pieces would be needed, and seven is likely). The depiction of the Levite ewer in the cartouche refers to the "family name" Segal, a Hebrew abbreviation for "Assistant to a Priest." The depiction of Gemini probably refers to the birth date of "Raphael." According to the Harburger Photo-Archive, this shield is from Monchsroth (as are finials No. 250). See a shield at the Skirball Museum in Los Angeles, 7.21, which is of similar form and ornamentation (Gutmann, color pl. III).

BIBLIOGRAPHY: Kayser, No. 45

DONOR: Dr. Harry G. Friedman

# 20

## TORAH SHIELD F 2186 (*Illus. p. 86*)

Nuremberg (?), ca. 1720–30

Silver: repoussé, cast, parcel-gilt

H 29.2 W 26.4 cm

HALLMARKS: none

REMARKS: There are four *parashah* plaques. The chain is probably original. Holes along the upper edge may indicate missing elements. The general scheme of decoration

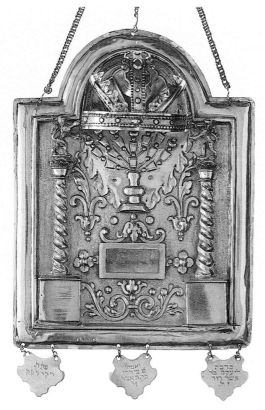

No. 21  F 3053

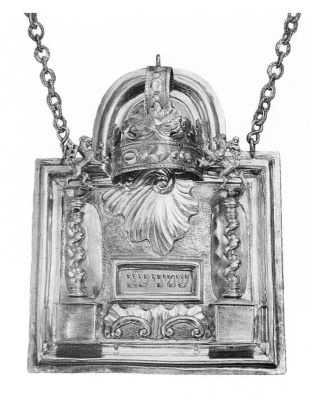

No. 22  F 876

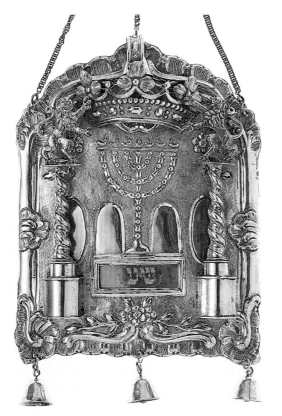

No. 23  F 1950

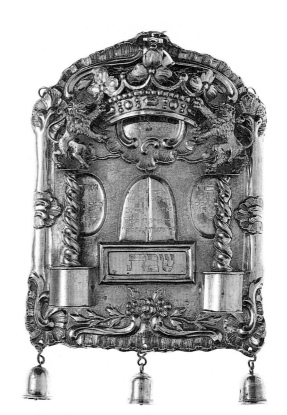

No. 24  F 4392

on this shield is reminiscent of that on several Torah Shields from Nuremberg, especially those by Johann Conrad Weiss; cf. in particular Stieglitz, No. 21 (the upper part, representing its initial form).

DONOR: Dr. Harry G. Friedman

## 21

TORAH SHIELD F 3053  (*Illus. p. 88*)
Nuremberg, 1745/46 (inscription)
Silver: repoussé, cast, engraved, parcel-gilt
H 26.0  W 20.2 cm
HALLMARKS:  *CITY:* "N"
MAKER: "GB" in oval, with medial indentations above and below
INSCRIPTION: on three pendants: אשר ב'ר'/ יעקב ר /נדבת רור (!)/ ז.ל.// ואשתו/ מ' צירלי/ בת ה' אשר זל// שנת תקו לפק, "Donation of ... Jacob son of the late ... Asher David and his wife Zirle daughter of the late . . . Asher, [in the] year (5)506" (= 1745/46)
REMARKS: The first, right-hand pendant is engraved by a different hand and may not be original. The date of the inscription is probably that of the dedication. (Kayser, No. 40, dated this piece to 1630–40 on the basis of an incorrect identification of the hallmarks.) The reference in Kayser, No. 40, to pointer F 878 (=Kayser, No. 64), appears to be erroneous. Cf. Nuremberg shields Nos. 22 and 28–31.
BIBLIOGRAPHY: Kayser, No. 40
DONOR: Dr. Harry G. Friedman

## 22

TORAH SHIELD F 876  (*Illus. p. 88*)
Nuremberg, 18th century
Silver: repoussé, cast, engraved, parcel-gilt
H 20.7  W 16.5 cm
HALLMARKS:  *CITY:* "N"
MAKER: "I/CN" (or "I/GN," or "I/GM," etc.)
REMARKS: There are four *parashah* plaques. The chain is probably original. There is red coloring in several words of the plaques.
DONOR: Dr. Harry G. Friedman

## 23

TORAH SHIELD F 1950  (*Illus. p. 88*)
Nuremberg, ca. 1783–87
Johann Friedrich Ehe, active 1773–1808
Silver: repoussé, cast
H 28.3  W 22.4 cm
HALLMARKS:  *CITY:* "N"; R³ 3777
MAKER: R³ 4304
REMARKS: There is one *parashah* plaque. The central menorah shows the biblical *kaftor vaferah* ("a knop and a flower") motif noted in Exodus 25: 33. Cf. shield No. 24, and Köln 1980, No. 39 (inscription dated 1784/85), both

similar shields; and Torah Pointer No. 540; and spice container F 861 — by the same smith, who made many other pieces of Judaica. See also No. 26, below, for a "Historismus" copy of this type of shield.

DONOR: Dr. Harry G. Friedman

## 24

TORAH SHIELD F 4392  (*Illus. p. 88*)
Nuremberg, 1783–87; 1787/88 (inscription)
Johann Friedrich Ehe, active 1773–1808
Silver: repoussé, cast, engraved, parcel-gilt
H 27.0  W 20.7 cm
HALLMARKS:  *CITY:* "N"; R³ 3777
MAKER: R³ 4304
INSCRIPTION: on upper cartouche: כ'ת', "C[rown of] T[orah]"; in sunken oval medallions, from right: קהל/ פלאץ// שנת תיק'מ'ח' לפ"ק, "Congregation [of] Plotz, [in the] year (5)548" (= 1787/88)
REMARKS: There are five *parashah* plaques (one differing from the others and probably only one original). In the date, the second letter, *qof*, seems to have been corrected from a *kaf*, but it may well have originally been a *resh* and, if so, the date would be a century later, i.e., 1887/88 (and then not contemporaneous with the shield, the "correction" to *qof* then being spurious). Cf. the similar shields Nos. 23 and 25, and the references there. An identical shield by this smith, dedicated in 1784/85, is Köln, No. 39.
DONOR: Dr. Harry G. Friedman

## 25

TORAH SHIELD JM 9–51  (*Illus. p. 90*)
Fürth, late 18th century
Silver: repoussé, engraved, parcel-gilt
H 24.0  W 19.6 cm
HALLMARKS:  *CITY:* R³ 2152, with "H"
MAKER: R³ 2157, with R³ 2154
INSCRIPTION: (probably later): on Tablets of the Law: ה מרדכי בר אלחנן, "Mordecai son of Elḥanan"
REMARKS: The *parashah* plaques, columns, and lions (?) are missing. This piece, shield No. 31, and finials No. 300, demonstrate the identical forms of Judaica used at Nuremberg and at nearby Fürth. Cf. the similar shield No. 24. For another shield from the same city, of more typical Fürth form, and for the problem of the Fürth hallmarks on Judaica, see shield No. 31.
DONOR: Jewish Cultural Reconstruction

## 26

TORAH SHIELD F 5485  (*Illus. p. 90*)
Hanau (?), early 20th century
Gutgesell Brothers (?), active after 1903
Silver: repoussé, cast, engraved

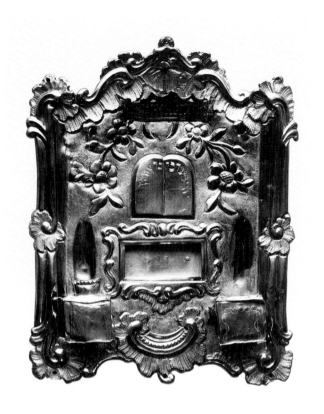

No. 25   JM 9–51

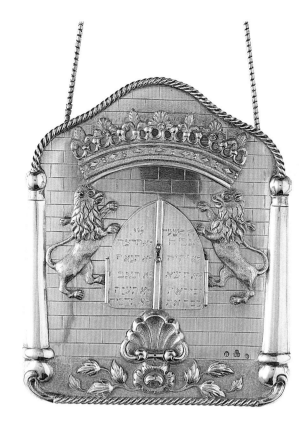

No. 26   F 5485

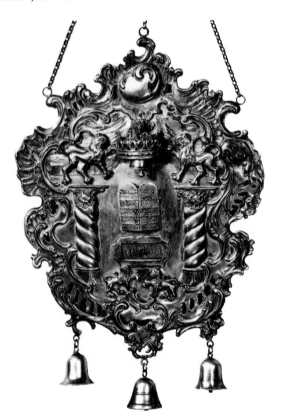

No. 27   F 2926

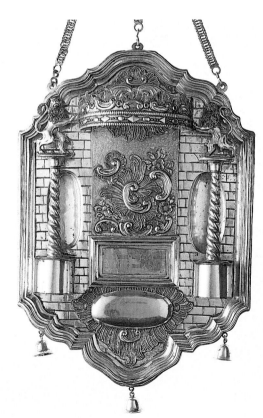

No. 28   F 3042

H 18.7 W 16.0 cm

HALLMARKS: *CITY:* "N"; R³ 3781 (both false)

      *MAKER:* R³ 4304 (Johann Friedrich Ehe—false)

REMARKS: The style and form of this shield are incongruous with shields of Johann Friedrich Ehe's time. This pattern of shield appears in the *Pappenheim Album*, under: Gebrüder Gutgesell, a firm active in the early 20th century, *Thoragarnitur* No. 1121."[1] Identical shields Nos. 26 and 27 are part and parcel of the "Historismus" trend. They are tainted by the presence of false hallmarks which would ascribe each to a different 18th-century Nuremberg silversmith—both well-known makers of Judaica. The silver marks on this piece are even more recent: it was initially accessioned in 1942 as F 988; subsequently, under unknown circumstances, it left the collection, only to return in 1964 as F 5485. Though photographs of "F 988" show no hallmarks, the object now bears those noted above. The revival of long-past styles, and the more specific imitation of particular objects, are practices well-rooted in antiquity. In the realm of Judaica, where archaism is often the rule, such nostalgic tendencies are rife. The "centenary" shields Nos. 13 and 18 are exemplars of this phenomenon. So is ivory shield No. 11, while shields Nos. 45–47 and 88–90 are typical, more recent (and partly mass-produced) manifestations.

DONOR: Dr. Harry G. Friedman

1. Torah Shield F 952, made in the early 20th century, probably in Hanau, is of the same pattern. It bears the Nuremberg "N" in an oval, a "13" and a fleur-de-lis in an oval frame—Scheffler, *Hessen,* cf. mark 505 (Neresheimer, one of the largest concerns in Hanau). (Data on this missing piece is from the Museum's records.) At the Israel Museum there is an identical casting, with the same marks (shield 148/45). A kiddush cup, Köln, No. 143, also bears the latter marks, and an almost identical piece appears in the *Pappenheim Album* among items made by Lorenz Streb of Gross-Auheim, a suburb of Hanau (pattern No. 1334). For a shield of the same pattern as Nos. 23–24, but bearing the mark of the Gutgesell Brothers, Hanau (Scheffler, *Hessen,* mark 568), see Deneke, No. 3/30. A spice container bearing Ehe's mark, PBNY 1970, No. 123, is identical with Gutgesell Brothers', pattern No. 960 in the *Pappenheim Album,* and with Christie's Amsterdam 1991, No. 123, "by Gebrüder Gutgesell."

## 27

TORAH SHIELD F 2926 (*Illus. p. 90*)

Hanau (?), early 20th century

Silver: cast, chased, parcel-gilt

H 30.6 W 22.9 cm

HALLMARKS: *CITY:* "N"; R³ 3772 (false — in casting)

     *MAKER:* R³ 4293 (B.N. Bierfreund—in casting)

PROVENANCE: Faust, Munich (8/29/51)

REMARKS: There is one *parashah* plaque. A line of soldering runs down the middle of this shield where two parts were joined together, a common practice in early 20th century castings of Torah Shields. See the remarks to shield No. 26.

DONOR: Dr. Harry G. Friedman

## 28

TORAH SHIELD F 3042 (*Illus. p. 90*)

Nuremberg, ca. 1769–73

Johann Samuel Beckensteiner, active 1743–81

Silver: repoussé, cast, gilt

H 39.8 W 28.0 cm

HALLMARKS: *CITY:* "N"; R³ 3773; "722" (in individual numbers)

     *MAKER:* R³ 4295

REMARKS: There are three *parashah* plaques. On the back of the plaque box cover, in paint: *No. 1. 3 Stuck* ("No. 1. 3 pieces," possibly referring to the number of plaques). Cf. Torah Finials No. 264; crown No. 450; pointer No. 523; and Israel Museum Torah Shield 148/70 (Feuchtwanger, No. 348), all by the same smith.

DONOR: Dr. Harry G. Friedman

## 29

TORAH SHIELD F 4885 (*Illus. p. 92*)

Nuremberg, ca. 1783–87

Wolfgang Schubert, active 1774–1803 or later

Silver: repoussé, cast, engraved, parcel-gilt

H 23.4 W 20.1 cm

HALLMARKS: *CITY:* "N"; R³ 3777

     *MAKER:* R³ 4305

REMARKS: There are three oval *parashah* plaques (not original). Cf. shields Nos. 30–31, by the same smith; other shields by Schubert are: with oval *parashah* plaques and a central menorah motif, Germanisches Nationalmuseum, Nuremberg JA 22 (*Synagoga*[1], No. C 61 = *Synagoga*[2], No. 232 = *Mon. Jud.*, No. E 373); with oval *parashah* plaques, bearing the date 1791/92 (Ansbacher, No. 2.7); with a central menorah motif, ca. 1794–97, Israel Museum, No. 148/163, Cohen, No. 20.

DONOR: Dr. Harry G. Friedman

## 30

TORAH SHIELD F 1982 (*Illus. p. 92*)

Nuremberg, ca. 1794–97; 1796/97 (inscription)

Wolfgang Schubert, active 1774–1803 or later

Silver: repoussé, cast, engraved; glass

H 19.5 W 16.7 cm

HALLMARKS: *CITY:* "N"; R³ 3780

     *MAKER:* R³ 4305

INSCRIPTION: on plinths: ליפמן ואלף ב'ה/ ואלף כ'ה/ ה'ק ה'תי, "The leader … Wolf son of Lipmann … and his spouse … Miriam daughter of … Solomon Katz"; on oval medallion: תקנז ל, "(5)557" (= 1796/97)

REMARKS: There are two *parashah* plaques. A bell is missing within the crown, as well as one at the bottom. The letters הב "H.B.," following the name of the man's father may refer

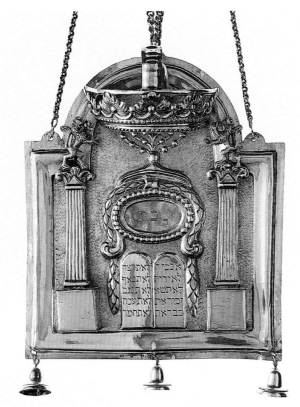

No. 29  F 4885

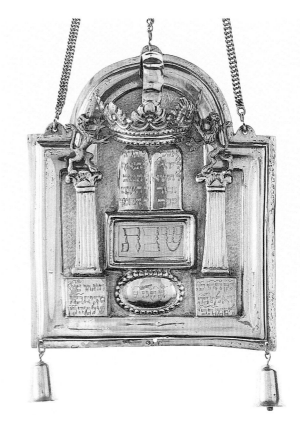

No. 30  F 1982

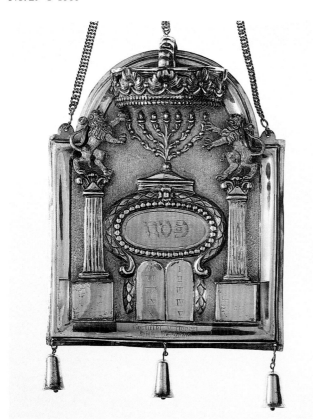

No. 31  D 136

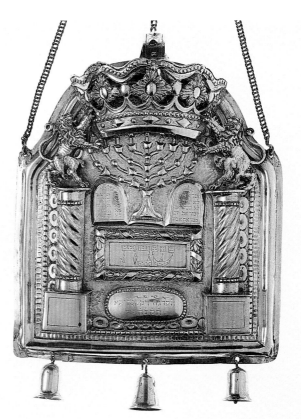

No. 32  JM 25–52

to a family or place name (e.g., Hamburg). Cf. shields Nos. 29 (with references) and 31, by the same smith as this piece.

DONOR: Dr. Harry G. Friedman

# 31

## TORAH SHIELD D 136  (*Illus. p. 92*)

Nuremberg, ca. 1800–1804

Wolfgang Schubert, active 1774–1803 or later

Silver: repoussé, cast, engraved, parcel-gilt

H 26.1  W 20.6 cm

HALLMARKS:  *CITY:* "N"; R³ 3782

        *MAKER:* R³ 4305

INSCRIPTION: on lower border: *Gestiftet v Herrn Erich Berghold*, "Donated b[y] Mr. Erich Berghold"

REMARKS: There are four oval *parashah* plaques (not original). The chain is probably original. Cf. shields Nos. 29 (with references) and 30. "The Berghold family were prominent mortgage bankers in Danzig," *Danzig 1939*, p. 87.

BIBLIOGRAPHY: *Danzig 1939/1982*, No. 59

DONOR: The Jewish Community of Danzig

# 32

## TORAH SHIELD JM 25–52  (*Illus. p. 92*)

Fürth, 1797/98 (?)

Silver: repoussé, cast, engraved

H 25.9  W 21.5 cm

HALLMARKS:  *CITY:* R³ 2152; "13" with R³ 2154 above; "G"

        (year letter= 1798 ?)

        *MAKER:* R³ 2157, with R³ 2154 above

INSCRIPTION: חק״דגח דק״ק גה יע״א ת׳ק׳נ׳ח, "H[oly] B[enevolent] S[ociety] for of the holy community of G[unzen]h[ausen] (?) …, (5)558" (= 1797/98)

REMARKS: There are four *parashah* plaques. In the inscription, גה, "G.H.," is probably Gunzenhausen (only 45 km southwest of Fürth). In the date, the letter *nun* is written over a *tzade*, apparently a correction. Kiddush cup JM 22–52 in The Jewish Museum bears the same marks (except the year letter).

The silver Judaica made in Fürth, adjacent to Nuremberg, in the 18th century and very early 19th century are unique in that all the marked pieces bear identical hallmarks, including the maker's mark "IR."[1] There is no authentic Fürth Judaica without the "IR" mark,[2] and there are no instances of non-Jewish pieces *with* it. Seemingly, one silversmith made all the Fürth Judaica — and nothing else. In an attempt to give "IR" an identity, Rosenberg (in R³) ascribed the mark to "possibly J. Rimonim." His three examples of work by "IR" are a Torah Shield and Pointer in the Stuttgart synagogue, and a Torah Shield in private Karlsruhe hands.[3] Besides these, we know today of Torah Shields, Finials and Pointers,[4] a spice container,[5] Hanukkah lamps,[6] and kiddush cups.[7]

Recently, an attempt was made to equate the Fürth "IR" with a "*JR*" (in ligature) at Nuremberg who also made Judaica, claiming that he worked in both places.[8] Since the two marks are entirely different, this seems implausible. Another suggestion is that this was the (undocumented) mark of one of the founders in 1767 of the goldsmiths guild in Fürth, one Johann Jakob Runneke;[9] but such an identification in no way answers the question of the exclusive use of this mark on Judaica.[10]

A possible solution is that the "IR" mark may have been a special guild punch reserved for marking Jewish objects made by any Fürth silversmith — the guild not allowing its members to use their own marks on such pieces. The "IR" would thus denote some such phrase as *Jüdisches Rituel*. This might find corroboration from the fact that hexagonal goblets of a type so often associated with kiddush for the Sabbath and festivals are among the objects bearing the "IR" mark.[11]

BIBLIOGRAPHY: Kayser, No. 56

DONOR: Jewish Cultural Reconstruction

1. R³ 2152 (crescent with "F"); R³ 2157 ("IR"), often with R³ 2154 ("four-square") above; and occasionally a "13" mark—as well as, in most examples, an incuse date letter, the known instances ranging from "C" to "T."

2. See note 11, below.

3. Under R³ 2157, four additional pieces by "IR" are merely mentioned. A late 1970's query from R. Cohen, then of the Israel Museum, to the Fürth Municipal Archives revealed that there was no information concerning "J. Rimonim" in the archives (cited in Deneke, under No. 2/18); cf. a corroborating postcard sent from the Fürth Archives in the early 1950's, presently bound into The Jewish Museum's copy of R³.

4. *Torah shields:* Harburger Photo-Archive, No. 326 (mentioned under Hohenems, No. 31); Mainz 1983, p. 13 (= Deneke, No. 2/18 = Moses, p. 152b); Prague 1970, No. 97 [and others]; Sotheby's NY 1983, No. 178 (now in a private collection, New York); Hohenems, No. 31 (Gross Family Collection, Tel Aviv, 51.01.45); Weinstein, figs. 77–78; Israel Museum, 148/1; 148/33; 148/40 (= *Mon. Jud.*, No. E 356); 148/44; and 148/102; and shields Nos. 25 and 32. *Torah Finials:* Deneke, Nos. 3/17 and 3/18; four pairs at the Israel Museum, 147/42, 147/58, 147/71, and 147/228; and finials No. 300. *Torah Pointers:* pointers No. 544 and 545.

5. *Stieglitz*, No. 72, and Jüdisches Museum, Frankfurt, JMF 87–117 (noted in Hohenems, No. 31, note 2).

6. The Museum's F 3483, and the almost identical Barnett, No. 244 — mistakenly ascribed to "Linsburg, late 18th century."

7. See Kayser, No. 101; *Stieglitz*, No. 108; Namenyi, No. 41 (Kugel Collection, Paris); and PBNY 1969, No. 185. See also note 10, below.

8. See Hohenems, Nos. 31 and 34.

9. See Deneke, under Nos. 2/18 and 6/22; under the latter item, the possibility of an illicit (*Schwarzarbeit*) Jewish silversmith using the "IR" mark is rejected.

10. One of the reasons for a lack of data in the Fürth Municipal Archives seems to be revealed in R³, vol. II, p. 106 top, at the beginning of the section on Fürth. There, Rosenberg mentions *der Goldschmiedeordnung von 1769, welche sich etwa 1900 bei Jacques Rosenthal in München befand* ("the Goldsmiths Ordinance of 1769, which around 1900 was to be found with Jacques Rosenthal in Munich").

11. Such goblets were in general fashion during the second quarter of the 18th century, but soon after they seem to have retained their pop

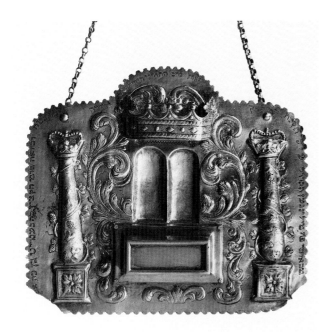

No. 33  JM 23–57

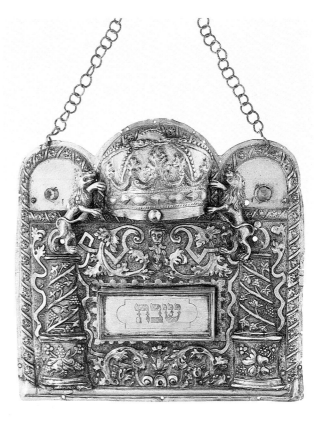

No. 34  F 2548

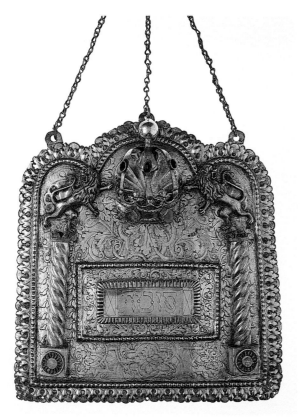

No. 35  M 283

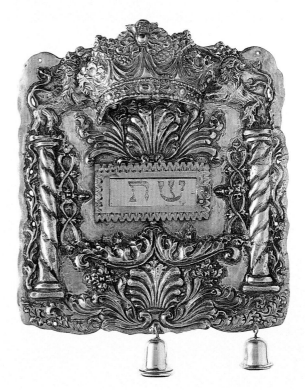

No. 36  F 4886

ularity only among the Jews. There is a spice container bearing Fürth hallmarks which do not include "IR"; its Jewishness is quite obviously of recent origin. (See Kaniel, p. 25.)

## 33

TORAH SHIELD JM 23–57 (*Illus. p. 94*)

Halberstadt, 1807 (inscription)

Silver: repoussé

H 19.6 W 23.4 cm

HALLMARKS: *CITY:* R³ 2259(var), with year letter "Y"

MAKER: R³ 2269

INSCRIPTION: on top arch: זאת נדב התורני המפורסם, continuing on left side, reading down: בתורה בחכמה וביראה, פ׳ו׳מ׳ הקצין כה בעענדיט בן כה אב . . . continuing on right side, reading up: מב(?)ארבי פה מילינגען הגדול ע׳ י׳ כ׳ (. . ?), תקסח לפק, "This was donated by the famous scholar . . . [and] . . . leader . . . Rabbi Bendit son of . . . Rabbi . . ., here, Gross Millingen, Y[om] K[ippur] e[ve], (5)568" (=11 October 1807).

REMARKS: The place mentioned in the inscription may be Mellingen, adjacent to Weimar (about 100 km from Halberstadt). Under R³ 2269 it is noted that the master's mark "Fi/M" appears on the (replacement) cover of a drinking vessel by a Halberstadt smith (but with a handle made by a Berlin silversmith) and that the vessel belonged to the Jewish Community of Halberstadt. Though the general form and style of this shield initially appear to be early, specific motifs (such as the columns), the date in the inscription and the year letter in the hallmarks, are all compatible. Cf. *AaunZ* 22 (11 June 1925), p. 173, for a much earlier German shield of very similar shape and proportions, once at the Jewish Museum in Worms.

DONOR: Dr. Ludwig Bendix

## 34

TORAH SHIELD F 2548 (*Illus. p. 94*)

Lissa (?), 18th century

Silver: repoussé, cast, parcel-gilt; glass

H 25.4 W 26.6 cm

HALLMARKS: none

REMARKS: The floral and strapwork motifs are also found on late 17th-early 18th century German shields; cf. shield No. 35, as well as Zagayski 1963, No. 19 (illus.=PBNY 1968, No. 292), and Kantsedikas, No. 58.

DONOR: Dr. Harry G. Friedman

## 35

TORAH SHIELD M 283 (*Illus. p. 94*)

Lissa (?), 18th century

Silver: cast, filigree, engraved, parcel-gilt; glass

H 28.8 W 27.8 cm

HALLMARKS: none

INSCRIPTION: on left plinth, grafitto: "A R" in script

PROVENANCE: The Rose and Benjamin Mintz Collection

REMARKS: Cf. shield No. 34 and references there.

DONOR: Museum purchase

## 36

TORAH SHIELD F 4886 (*Illus. p. 94*)

Germany or Poland (?), late 18th–early 19th century

Silver: repoussé

H 23.8 W 21.2 cm

HALLMARKS: none

REMARKS: The front cover of the *parashah* plaque box appears not to be original. The entire shield has been extensively repaired.

DONOR: Dr. Harry G. Friedman

## 37

TORAH SHIELD M 11 (*Illus. p. 96*)

Berlin, ca. 1763–72

Joachim Hübener (II), active ca. 1737–80

Silver: repoussé, cast, gilt

H 34.0 W 26.8 cm

HALLMARKS: *CITY:* Scheffler, *Berlin*, 7

MAKER: Scheffler, *Berlin*, 110

PROVENANCE: The Rose and Benjamin Mintz Collection

REMARKS: There are four *parashah* plaques. An almost identical shield by the same smith bearing the same year mark is in the Stern Collection, New York, MS/T 162; another, ca. 1760, was in the Zagayski Collection (cf. PBNY 1955, No. 156 = Hintze 1929, No. 214). Two additional shields by Hübener, Nos. 38 and 39, are of a different design. For further discussion, see the Introduction, p. 34.

DONOR: Museum purchase

## 38

TORAH SHIELD D 146 (*Illus. p. 96*)

Berlin, ca. 1770–76

Joachim Hübener (II), active ca. 1737–80

Silver: repoussé, cast, engraved, gilt

H 38.0 W 25.6 cm

HALLMARKS: *CITY:* Scheffler, *Berlin*, 8b

MAKER: Scheffler, *Berlin*, 110

PROVENANCE: The Great Synagogue, Danzig

REMARKS: There are four *parashah* plaques. This shield design seems to be of Hübener's invention. Cf. the very similar shields Nos. 39 (by Hübener) and 40–41 (by Gentzmer); Brooklyn Museum 49.228.2 and Christie's NY 1993, No. 455 (formerly Jewish Museum, F 3915) (both by Hübener); Berger 1984, No. 10 (by Gentzmer). At The Jewish Museum, by this smith, see shield No. 37, crown No. 449, and pointer No. 530.

BIBLIOGRAPHY: Danzig 1933, No. 139a (mislabeled "138a" in pl. 10); *Danzig 1939/1982*, No. 63.

DONOR: The Jewish Community of Danzig

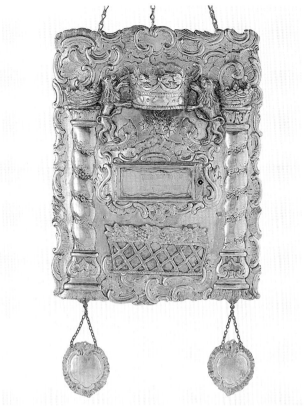

No. 37  M 11

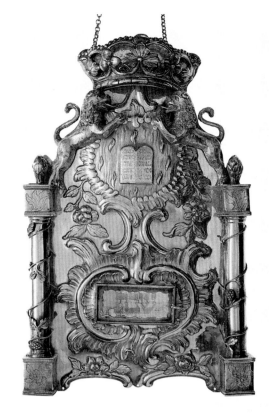

No. 38  D 146

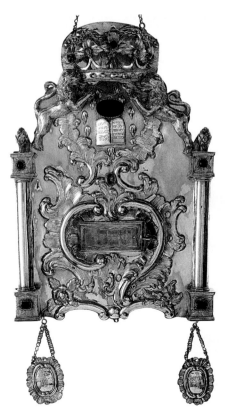

No. 39  D 150

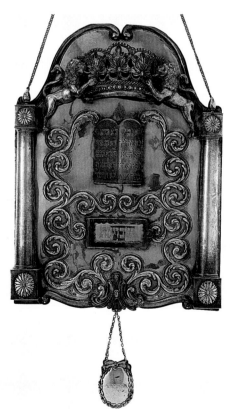

No. 40  D 139

## 39
TORAH SHIELD D 150  (*Illus. p. 96*)
Berlin, ca. 1770–80
Joachim Hübener, active 1737–80
Silver: repoussé, cast, parcel-gilt; glass
H 39.4  W 27.3 cm
HALLMARKS:  *CITY:* Scheffler, *Berlin*, 7–10 (unclear)
              *MAKER:* Scheffler, *Berlin*, 110
INSCRIPTION: (on two pendants below, at present not in orig-
   inal order; the original middle pendant is missing): עי
   הג"ב/ נעשה/ בריצוי החׂ"ק/ יצ"ו// [. . . ר שימעון] . . .// ור/
   שמואל/ פח, "M[ade] by the *gab[a'im]*, made at the desire
   of the H[oly] (Burial) S[ociety], [the *gabba'im* Simon] and
   Samuel the engraver (or 'treasurers of the month')"; see the
   remarks below.
PROVENANCE: The Schottland Synagogue, Danzig
REMARKS: There are four *parashah* plaques. Crown No. 449
   was dedicated by the same individuals. The inscription on
   the middle pendant is partially restored on the basis of
   Danzig 1933 and crown No. 449. The author interprets the
   abbreviation פח as פתח חותמות, "engraver." The editor
   suggests, based on written sources, that it stands for פרנס
   חודש, "treasurer of the month." See comparisons, shield
   No. 38.
BIBLIOGRAPHY: Danzig 1933, No. 147a; *Danzig 1939/1982*, No. 62
DONOR: The Jewish Community of Danzig

## 40
TORAH SHIELD D 139  (*Illus. p. 96*)
Berlin, 1804–08
August Ferdinand Gentzmer, active 1789–1808
Silver: repoussé, cast, engraved, parcel-gilt
H 40.3  W 29.7 cm
HALLMARKS:  *CITY:* Scheffler, *Berlin*, 12 and 30b
              *MAKER:* Scheffler, *Berlin*, 219
INSCRIPTION: on pendant: זאת נדבת, "This is the donation
   of"
PROVENANCE: The Great Synagogue, Danzig
REMARKS: There are three *parashah* plaques. The single pen-
   dant originally belonged to shield No. 69 (cf. Danzig 1933,
   No. 138b). Cf. the identical shield No. 41, by the same smith;
   and Nos. 38–39 for similar, earlier shields by Hübener. Cf.
   also Schliemann, fig. 846, an almost identical shield made
   in Hamburg in the 1820's. For other shields by Gentzmer,
   see Nos. 65 and 67.
BIBLIOGRAPHY: Danzig 1933, No. 142a; *Danzig 1939/1982*, No. 64
DONOR: The Jewish Community of Danzig

## 41
TORAH SHIELD D 141  (*Illus. p. 98*)
Berlin, 1788–1802
August Ferdinand Gentzmer, active 1789–1808

Silver: repoussé, cast, parcel-gilt
H 36.5  W 29.5 cm
HALLMARKS:  *CITY:* Scheffler, *Berlin*, 11 and 30c
              *MAKER:* Scheffler, *Berlin*, 219
PROVENANCE: The Great Synagogue, Danzig
REMARKS: There are four *parashah* plaques. On the back of
   the plaque box is engraved: "XI." For similar numbers on
   other shields — certainly synagogue inventory numbers
   — see shields Nos. 68 ("18"), 71 ("14"), and 107 ("17").
   Holes at the sides of the shield indicate the loss of a pair of
   flanking columns, as on the identical shield No. 40 (see references there).
BIBLIOGRAPHY: Danzig 1933, No. 141a; *Danzig 1939*, No. 198
DONOR: The Jewish Community of Danzig

## 42
TORAH SHIELD M 391  (*Illus. p. 98*)
Breslau, 1731–37
Johann Christophe Müller, active 1721–58
Silver: repoussé, cast, engraved, parcel-gilt
H 36.6  W 33.7 cm
HALLMARKS:  *CITY:* Hintze 1906, 17 and 32
              *MAKER:* Hintze 1906, 138
PROVENANCE: The Rose and Benjamin Mintz Collection
REMARKS: There are five *parashah* plaques; the lid of the
   *parashah* plaque box is inscribed: שבת, "Sabbath." Cf.
   Zagayski 1963, No. 17 (=PBNY 1964, No. 294), and a shield
   now in the Stern Collection, New York, MS/T 19 by the
   same smith, from 1737–45.
DONOR: Museum purchase

## 43
TORAH SHIELD F 4649  (*Illus. p. 98*)
Breslau, late 18th century
Johann Gottlob Böttiger (?), active ?–1795
Silver: repoussé, engraved
H 25.0  W 25.6 cm
HALLMARKS:  *CITY:* Hintze 1906, 23 (?)
              *MAKER:* "IG/B" in leaf
REMARKS: There is one *parashah* plaque. The lower edge of
   the shield is not original and shows a major repair. In the
   illustration in Kayser, a *parashah* plaque for Rosh Hasha-
   nah is visible. Kayser mentions more than one plaque and
   notes that all of them are later. Cf. the other "Moses and
   Aaron" shields at The Jewish Museum, Nos. 44–48. See also
   the Introduction, p. 26.[1]
BIBLIOGRAPHY: Kayser, No. 196
DONOR: Dr. Harry G. Friedman

1. Other Torah Shields bearing this theme include: a shield by Johann
   Ernst Braungart, Breslau, dated 1776/77, offered to Dr. Friedman by a
   dealer in Germany in 1959 (Jewish Museum archives); Hintze 1929,
   No. 221, another shield by Braungart, dated 1786; Sotheby's NY, 1984,
   No. 246, a shield by Johann David Klose, active in Breslau, 1816–48;

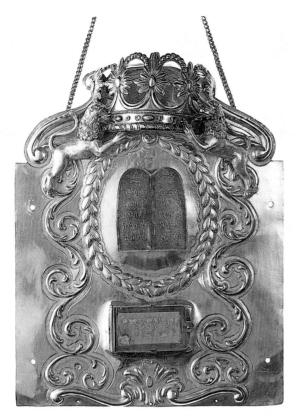

No. 41  D 141

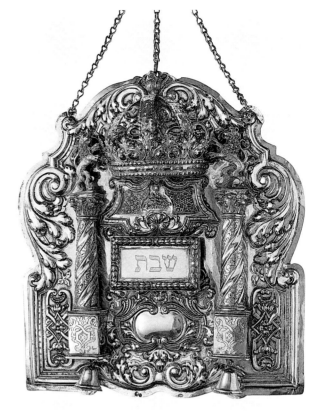

No. 42  M 391

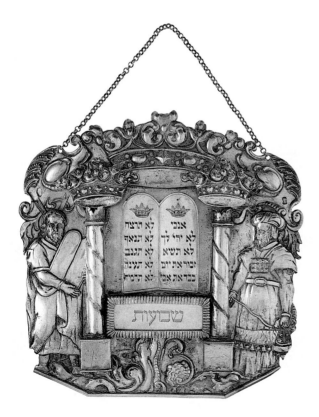

No. 43  F 4649

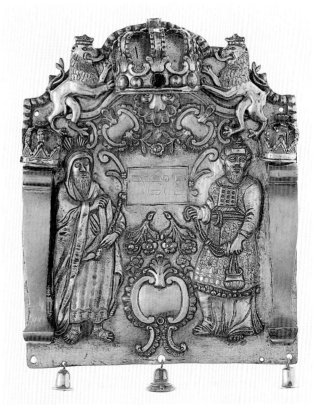

No. 44  F 3460

Steinhardt No. 68, a shield probably by Johann Christian Zwiener, Breslau, ca. 1830-40 (ex-Ehrenthal Collection); a shield seen in trade (Ha'atikos, No. 19 — Breslau, "1823," but probably later; and Perry's Tel Aviv, No. 195 — apparently from Debreczin prior to 1808).

# 44

## TORAH SHIELD  F 3460  (*Illus. p. 98*)

Germany, late 18th century

Silver: repoussé, parcel-gilt; stones

H 27.4  W 22.6 cm

HALLMARKS: none

REMARKS: There is one *parashah* plaque. None of the bells are original; numerous repairs are evident. Note that Aaron is depicted barefoot and wears a fringed garment; Moses is shod in sandles which have heart-shaped buckles. (Cf. Gerlach, e.g., pl. 98, Nos. 20 and 22, Silesia). There is an old label on the back: "R.G. 109."

DONOR: Dr. Harry G. Friedman

# 45

## TORAH SHIELD  M 293  (*Illus. p. 100*)

Probably Germany, 20th century

Silver: repoussé, engraved

H 30.3  W 24.1 cm

HALLMARKS: none

INSCRIPTION: in lower cartouche: קודש לה׳/ זאת נדבו בנימין בר גרשון/ זצ״ל וזוגתו הצנועה מרת שיינה/ רייזעל בר׳ אברהם צבי/ זצ״ל, "Dedicated to the Lord, This was donated by Benjamin son of the late Gershon and his . . . spouse . . . Sheine Reizl daughter of the late Abraham Zvi"; on Aaron's headgear: קודש ליי, Exodus 38:36, 39:30

PROVENANCE: The Rose and Benjamin Mintz Collection

REMARKS: There are no holes along the bottom for bells or pendants. Kayser dated this piece 1720 based on a very similar piece formerly in the Salomon Collection, which is actually dated 1744/45 (*Hebraica*, pl. VII = PBNY 1949, No. 221). Cf. the almost identical shields Nos. 46–47; as well as PBNY 1977, Nos. 103–104.

BIBLIOGRAPHY: Kayser, No. 51

DONOR: Museum purchase

# 46

## TORAH SHIELD  F 3474  (*Illus. p. 100*)

Probably Germany, 20th century

Silver: repoussé, gilt

H 23.8  W 19.4 cm

HALLMARKS: none

REMARKS: There are no holes along the bottom for bells or pendants. Cf. the almost identical shields Nos. 45 and 47; and PBNY 1977, Nos. 103–104.

DONOR: Dr. Harry G. Friedman

# 47

## TORAH SHIELD  JM 24–55  (*Illus. p. 100*)

Germany, 20th century

Silver: repoussé, gilt; semiprecious stones

H 43.0  W 35.5 cm

HALLMARKS: *CITY:* R³ 5; "835"
         *MAKER:* Illegible

REMARKS: There are no holes along the bottom for bells or pendants. Cf. the almost identical shields Nos. 45–46; and PBNY 1977, Nos. 103–104.

BIBLIOGRAPHY: *Biblical Images*, front cover.

DONOR: Samuel and Lucille Lemberg

# 48

## TORAH SHIELD  D 143  (*Illus. p. 100*)

Danzig, late 18th century

Johann Gottlieb Stegmann, active 1772–1804

Silver: repoussé, parcel-gilt; brass

H 29.5  W 25.0 cm

HALLMARKS: *CITY:* Czihak 507(?)
         *MAKER:* Czihak 9 and 501

INSCRIPTION: within bow motif: ארון (!)/ רבקה, "Aaron, Rebecca"

PROVENANCE: The Great Synagogue, Danzig

REMARKS: There are two *parashah* plaques. *Danzig 1939*, No. 143 records three pendants on this shield.

BIBLIOGRAPHY: Danzig 1933, No. 143a, pl. 6; *Danzig 1939/1982*, No. 68

DONOR: The Jewish Community of Danzig

# 49

## TORAH SHIELD  F 3473 (with *parashah* plaque F 1059)

(*Illus. p. 101*)

Augsburg, 1793–95

Johann Matthias Lang, active 1782–ca. 1806

Silver: repoussé

H 27.3  W 35.6 cm

HALLMARKS: *CITY:* Seling 278
         *MAKER:* Seling 2591

REMARKS: The crown at the top is missing, as apparently is some element on the lower edge, the plaque box, the original *parashah* plaques, the bells (or pendants), and the bottom border. The one extant *parashah* plaque has an interesting feature: the first and last letters were truncated, enabling the engraver to enlarge the other letters. Two spice containers by the same smith are: The Jewish Museum's F 2117 (1801); and the almost identical one at Heichal Shlomo (Bialer, p. 183, upper middle). For the significance of this shield as the forerunner of the early 19th-century Augsburg shield type, see Introduction, pp. 34–35.

BIBLIOGRAPHY: Seling, No. 2591, example a, vol. II, fig. 708

DONOR: Dr. Harry G. Friedman

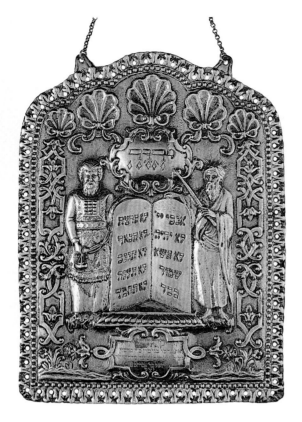

No. 45  M 293

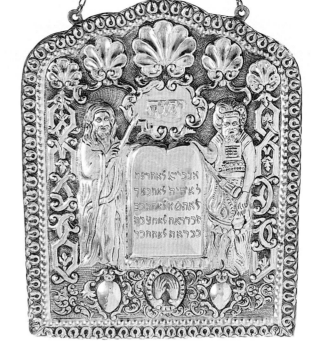

No. 46  F 3474

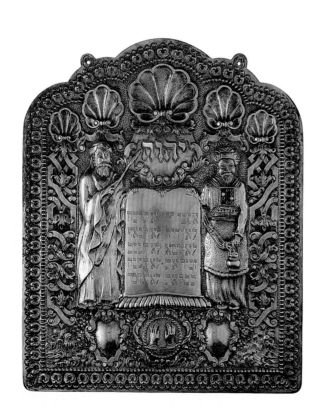

No. 47  JM 24–55

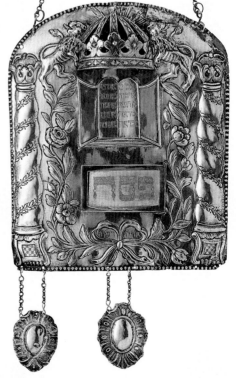

No. 48  D 143

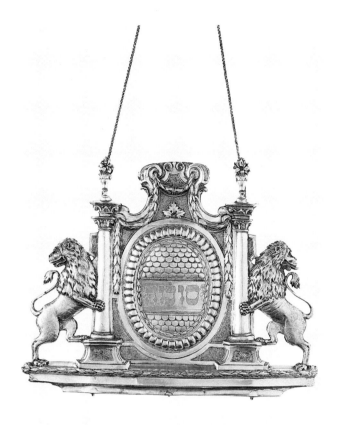

No. 49  F 3473

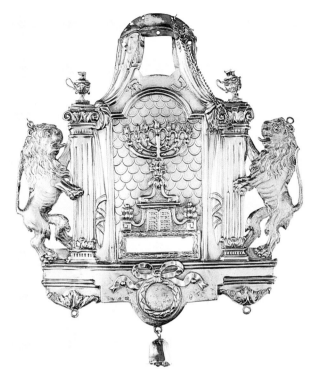

No. 50  X 1952  4

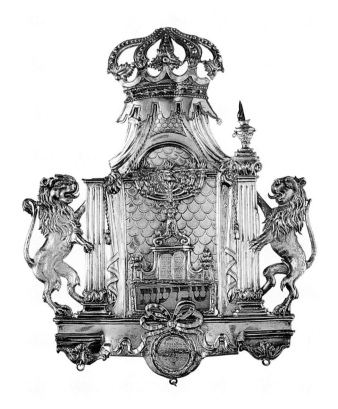

No. 51  X 1983–18

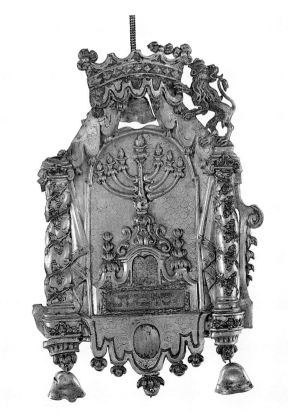

No. 52  X 1983–27

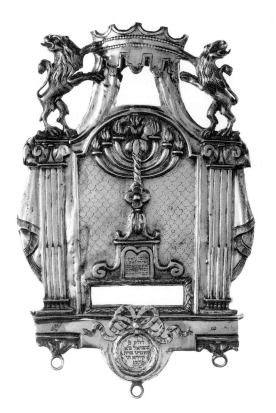

No. 53  X 1952–6

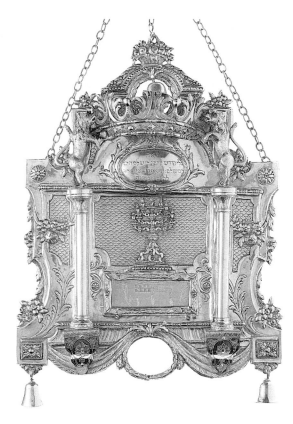

No. 54  JM 50–61

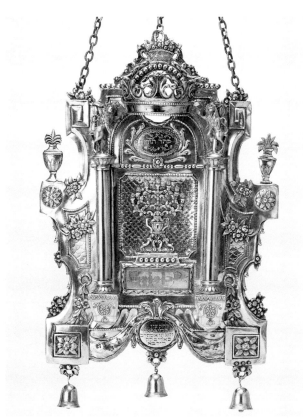

No. 55  F 60b

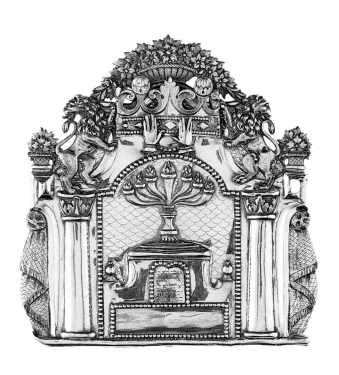

No. 56  X 1952–9

## 50

TORAH SHIELD X 1952-4  (*Illus. p. 101*)
Augsburg, 1797–99
Franz Anton Gutwein, active 1759–1805
Silver: repoussé, engraved, gilt, painted
H 36.9  W 34.9 cm
HALLMARKS:  *CITY:* Seling 281
　　　　　　　*MAKER:* Seling 2455(c or g)
INSCRIPTION: above arched frame: כ ת, "C[rown of] T[orah]"
REMARKS: The crown, the *parashah* plaques and the cover of
　　the plaque box are all missing. Only one bell survives. An
　　interesting feature is the painting of the tongues of the
　　lions with red pigment. Cf. the essentially identical shield
　　No. 51, and shields Nos. 52–53, also by Gutwein.
DONOR: Jewish Cultural Reconstruction

## 51

TORAH SHIELD X 1983-18  (*Illus. p. 101*)
Augsburg, 1797–99
Franz Anton Gutwein, active 1759–1805
Silver: repoussé, engraved, gilt
H 48.1  W 40.9 cm
HALLMARKS:  *CITY:* Seling 281
　　　　　　　*MAKER:* Seling 2455c
INSCRIPTION: שייך/ לה"ק כ' נפתלי/ בר שמואל י"צ"ו/ וזוג' מ'
תי' טעבלי/ כ' בת בערילי/, "Belongs to Naphtali son of
　　Samuel and his spouse, Berele daughter of Tevele"
REMARKS: There are four *parashah* plaques. Various parts are
　　torn or missing. See remarks, shields Nos. 52–53, which are
　　in similar condition.
DONOR: Jewish Cultural Reconstruction

## 52

TORAH SHIELD X 1983-27  (*Illus. p. 101*)
Augsburg, 1800
Franz Anton Gutwein, active 1759–1805
Silver: repoussé, gilt
H 35.0  W 23.0 cm
HALLMARKS:  *CITY:* Seling 284c (or b)
　　　　　　　*MAKER:* Seling 2455
REMARKS: There are two *parashah* plaques. The left edge is
　　torn and the lion and scrollwork there are missing, as is
　　one bell at the bottom. All the surviving bells are flattened.
　　The present chain is not original and has attached to it a
　　small fragment of a crown from another shield. Cf.
　　remarks, shield No. 50, above; and cf. shields Nos. 50–51, 53,
　　and 56.
DONOR: Jewish Cultural Reconstruction

## 53

TORAH SHIELD X 1952-6  (*Illus. p. 102*)
Augsburg, 1801; 1802/03 (inscription)
Franz Anton Gutwein, active 1759–1805

Silver: repoussé, cast, gilt
H 34.5  W 22.9 cm
HALLMARKS:  *CITY:* Seling 285
　　　　　　　*MAKER:* Seling 2455c
INSCRIPTION: לה"ק כ'/ שמואל ב"א/ וזוגתו מרת/ קילא תי'/
תרסג/ לפק, "[Belonging] to the l[eader] … Samuel son of
　　A […] and his spouse … Keila …, (5)663" (= 1902/03)
REMARKS: This shield is badly flattened; the cover of the
　　plaque box and bells are missing. See remarks, No. 50 and
　　cf. shields Nos. 51–52 and 56.
DONOR: Jewish Cultural Reconstruction

## 54

TORAH SHIELD JM 50-61  (*Illus. p. 102*)
Augsburg, 1805
Jakob Hermann Daniel Lüders, active 1776–1809
Silver: repoussé, cast, engraved, gilt
H 37.0  W 29.4 cm
HALLMARKS:  *CITY:* Seling 290
　　　　　　　*MAKER:* Seling 2550 (var.)
INSCRIPTION: זאת/ כלי קודש נדבו ר' שלמה בן/ ר' משולם:
המצוה לקיים אמרה היא גם והיא, "This is a holy vessel
　　given by Solomon son of Meshullam 'And she, she also
　　said' (Genesis 20: 5), to uphold the commandment."
REMARKS: There are three *parashah* plaques. The crown may
　　possibly not be in its original position; there are other
　　minor losses. The biblical quotation in the inscription
　　refers to Sarah and is probably an oblique reference to the
　　donor's wife, indicating she was a joint donor. A pair of
　　finials by Lüders, Stieglitz, No. 14 (the master's mark was
　　misread as "DI"), is apparently from 1818.
DONOR: Samuel and Lucille Lemberg

## 55

TORAH SHIELD F 60b  (*Illus. p. 102*)
Augsburg, 1808
Joseph Anton Seethaler, active 1766–1811
Silver: repoussé, cast, appliqué, engraved, parcel-gilt
H 34.5  W 25.5 cm
HALLMARKS:  *CITY:* Seling 294
　　　　　　　*MAKER:* Seling 2512
INSCRIPTION: on lower medallion: להקצין/ כ' ברון ב' ה'
הילבא בק"ק/ אלי כ' ב'/ אסתר וזוגתו/ ז"ל/ א', "[Belongs]
　　to the leader … Baron son of the late A[…] and his spouse
　　Esther daughter of … Eli, in the h[oly] c[ommunity of]
　　Heilbau[?]"
REMARKS: There is one *parashah* plaque. Cf. Rosenan, No. 20,
　　for another shield made by the same smith, also in 1808.
　　For finials by Seethaler, see No. 272; for an associated
　　pointer, bearing no marks, see No. 549. The latter two
　　pieces seem to form a set with this shield.
DONOR: Dr. Harry G. Friedman

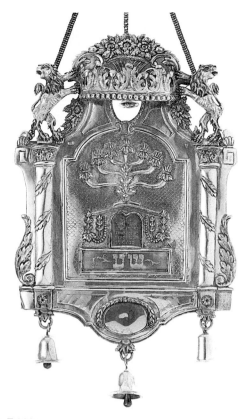

No. 57  F 239a

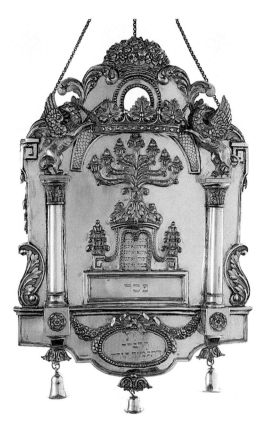

No. 58  F 3914

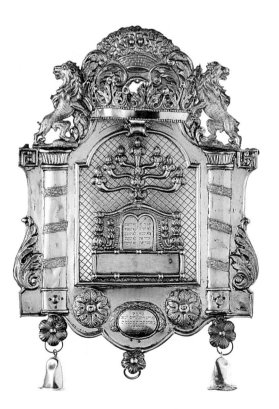

No. 59  X 1952–2

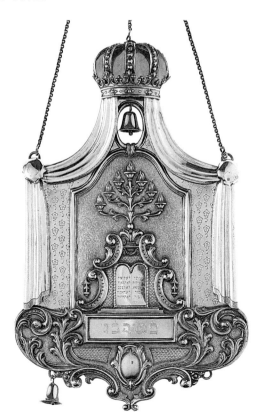

No. 60  F 1804

## 56

TORAH SHIELD X 1952–9  (*Illus. p. 102*)

Augsburg (?), early 19th century

Silver: repoussé, cast, engraved, parcel-gilt

H 21.8  W 20.4 cm

HALLMARKS: none

REMARKS: The crown is flattened, and the plaques and some elements along the bottom edge are missing. Cf. shields Nos. 50–55, of the same general form.

DONOR: Jewish Cultural Reconstruction

## 57

TORAH SHIELD F 239a  (*Illus. p. 104*)

Augsburg, 1825

Joseph Mussmann, active 1822–after 1865

Silver: repoussé, engraved, gilt

H 38.3  W 26.7 cm

HALLMARKS: *CITY:* Seling 313
　　　　　　 *MAKER:* Seling 2713a

REMARKS: There are three *parashah* plaques. For another shield by this smith, see Weinstein, fig. 6 (1824); for a pointer see No. 580, probably made as part of a set with the present piece.

BIBLIOGRAPHY: Seling 2713, ex. e.

DONOR: Dr. Harry G. Friedman

## 58

TORAH SHIELD F 3914  (*Illus. p. 104*)

Augsburg, 1838

Franz Carl Schmedding (I), active 1834–72

Silver: repoussé, cast, engraved, gilt

H 42.5  W 29.7 cm

HALLMARKS: *CITY:* Seling 326
　　　　　　 *MAKER:* Seling 2738

INSCRIPTION: in lower medallion: ז' נ'/ החברה דתלמוד תורה, "T[his was] d[onated by] the Talmud Torah Society."

REMARKS: There are four *parashah* plaques. Griffins support the crown on this piece, rather than the more common lions. For finials by the same smith, see Sotheby's NY, 1984a, No. 408 (=Christie's NY, 1980, No. 191) (1839).

BIBLIOGRAPHY: Isaacson 1979, p. 94

DONOR: Dr. Harry G. Friedman

## 59

TORAH SHIELD X 1952–2  (*Illus. p. 104*)

Augsburg (?), 1862/63 (inscription)

Silver: repoussé, die-stamped, engraved, gilt

H 37.3  W 28.5 cm

HALLMARKS: "Rindfloyd" (or "Kindfloyd"), in script; "13"

INSCRIPTION: נדבה/ מן חברת נשים י"ע"א/ לחנוכת בית

הכנסת/ ה ת'ר'כ'ג'/ קריילסהיים, "Donation from the Women's Society . . ., for the dedication of the synagogue, 5623 (=1862/63), Crailsheim"

REMARKS: This shield has been extensively repaired. The form of the Hebrew letter *heh*, both in the inscription and on the Tablets of the Law, is peculiar. Crailsheim is 100 km NW of Augsburg.

DONOR: Jewish Cultural Reconstruction

## 60

TORAH SHIELD F 1804  (*Illus. p. 104*)

Augsburg, 1865

Magnus Unsinn, active 1847–89

Silver: repoussé, parcel-gilt

H 39.9  W 26.0 cm

HALLMARKS: *CITY:* Seling 353
　　　　　　 *MAKER:* Seling 2753

REMARKS: There are six *parashah* plaques; duplications among the *parashiyot* indicate that some are not original. Cf. a shield by the same smith, Sotheby's Tel Aviv, 1991, No. 239 (dated 1873/73); for a finial by him, see No. 274 (1866).

DONOR: Dr. Harry G. Friedman

## 61

TORAH SHIELD F 4037  (*Illus. p. 106*)

Ansbach, mid-19th century

I. Rupp

Silver: repoussé, cast, engraved, parcel-gilt

H 34.3  W 22.5 cm

HALLMARKS: *CITY:* "ANSBACH"; "13"
　　　　　　 *MAKER:* "I. RUPP"

REMARKS: There are four *parashah* plaques, inscribed by a hand unfamiliar with Hebrew script. Torah Finials No. 296 are by the same smith and probably formed a set together with this piece.

DONOR: Dr. Harry G. Friedman

## 62

TORAH SHIELD F 255  (*Illus. p. 106*)

Offenbach, 1863/64 (inscription)

E. Adler

Silver: die-stamped, repoussé, engraved, gilt

H 27.6  W 21.2 cm

HALLMARKS: "13" (in oval, twice); "E. ADLER" (in rectangle)

INSCRIPTION: Flanking crown: חברת הנשים/ אפענבאך, "Women's Society, Offenbach"; below plaque-box: תרכד "(5)524" (=1863/64); below the crown, a list of members (the underlined letters are smaller):

טערץ אר' יצחק:/

רייצכה אר' יהודה: פיגלא א הח"ר אליעזר:/

פראדכה אר' אליעזר: בלומכה אר' יהודה:/

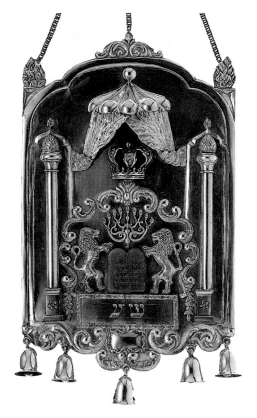

No. 61  F 4037

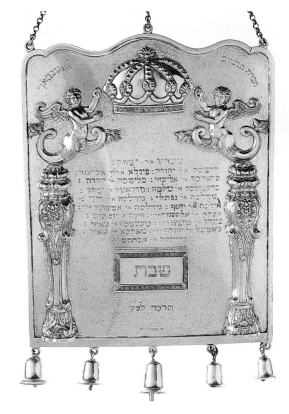

No. 62  F 255

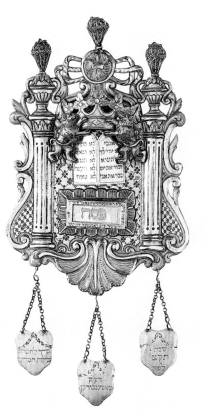

No. 63  D 130

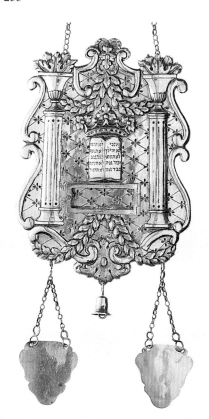

No. 64  F 1859

ברענדלכה אר׳ שלמה: גודראטה אר׳ יצחק:/

גידלכה אר׳ נפתלי: גילדכה אר׳ דוד:/

אילכה אר׳ יוסף: גידלכה אר׳ אביגדור הלוי:/

אסתר אר׳ משה הלוי: טעלצכה אר׳ מאיר:/

מאמעל אר׳ יהודה הלוי: מאלכא אר׳ מאיר:/

ברײנלה אר׳ אברהם

"Tertz wife of Isaac; Raichke wife of Judah; Feigele wife of the w[ise] Eliezer; Fredke wife of Eliezer; Blumke wife of Judah; Brendelke wife of Solomon; Gutrote wife of Isaac; Gittelke wife of Naphtali; Gittelke wife of David; Ilke wife of Joseph; Gittelke wife of Avigdor Halevi; Esther wife of Moses Halevi; Teltchke wife of Me'ir; Mamel[e ?] wife of Judah Halevi; Malka wife of Me'ir; Breinle wife of Abraham"

REMARKS: There are three *parashah* plaques. The winged mermen supporting the crown, though stock die-stampings, are an unusual motif on Torah ornaments.

DONOR: Dr. Harry G. Friedman

# 63

TORAH SHIELD D 130  (*Illus. p. 106*)
Berlin, 1788–1802; 1829/30 (inscription)
Sons of Martin Friedrich Müller
Silver: repoussé, cast, filigree, engraved, parcel-gilt
H 29.3  W 20.2 cm
HALLMARKS:  *CITY:* Scheffler, *Berlin*, 11
              *MAKER:* Scheffler, *Berlin*, 130
INSCRIPTION: on cover of plaque box: נעשה ע״י הגבאים ר׳ איצק ב/ר׳ משה גאלדשטייין/ ור׳ משה ליב דאנצגער שנת תקצ, "Made by the *gabba'im* . . . Itzik son of . . . Moses Goldstein and . . . Moses Leib Danziger, [in the] year (5)590" (=1829/30); on three pendants (they are in wrong order):

| שנת | ד׳ק׳ק׳ | שייך לחברה |
|---|---|---|
| תקצ | מאטעענבודען | גמילות חסדים |
| ל׳פ׳ק׳ | | |

"Belongs to the Benevolent Society of the h[oly] c[ommunity] of Mattenbuden, [in the] year (5)590" (=1829/30)
PROVENANCE:  The Mattenbuden Synagogue, Danzig; the Gieldzinski Collection, Danzig
REMARKS: There are two *parashah* plaques. The filigree on the urns atop the capitals and on the knot is not typical of Berlin shields and seems to be a later addition. Other shields by the Müllers include Nos. 64 and 72, as well as Sotheby's NY, 1988, No. 270 ("ca. 1805"), and *Temple Israel*, p. 12.
BIBLIOGRAPHY: Danzig 1904, No. 27; Danzig 1933, No. 130; *Danzig 1939*, No. 197
DONOR: The Jewish Community of Danzig

# 64

TORAH SHIELD F 1859  (*Illus. p. 106*)
Berlin, 1788–1802
Sons of Martin Friedrich Müller
Silver: repoussé, parcel-gilt
H 20.2  W 14.9 cm
HALLMARKS:  *CITY:* Scheffler, *Berlin*, 11
              *MAKER:* Scheffler, *Berlin*, 133
REMARKS: The bell is a replacement for a missing pendant. A *parashah* plaque appears in old Jewish Museum photographs of this piece. Shields Nos. 63 and 72 are also by the Müller family.
DONOR: Dr. Harry G. Friedman

# 65

TORAH SHIELD M 235  (*Illus. p. 108*)
Berlin, 1788–1802
August Ferdinand Gentzmer, active 1758–1808
Silver: repoussé, engraved
H 28.0  W 20.9 cm
HALLMARKS:  *CITY:* Scheffler, *Berlin*, 11
              *MAKER:* Scheffler, *Berlin*, 219
PROVENANCE: The Rose and Benjamin Mintz Collection
REMARKS: There is one *parashah* plaque. Shields Nos. 40–41 and 67 are also by this smith.
DONOR: Museum purchase

# 66

TORAH SHIELD F 5075  (*Illus. p. 108*)
Berlin, 1788–1802; 1799/1800 (inscription)
Jeremie Humbert, active ca. 1760–1802
Silver: repoussé, cast, engraved, parcel-gilt
H 39.7  W 30.1 cm
HALLMARKS:  *CITY:* Scheffler, *Berlin*, 11 and 30A/1
              *MAKER:* Scheffler, *Berlin*, 179
INSCRIPTION: below plaque box: זאת נדר הרר מרדכי בר/י ואשתו מ׳ גליקל כ״ה מיכאל ז׳/ לפרט ישרים לפק (under-lined word in larger letters), "This was vowed by . . . Mordecai son of Y[. . .] and his wife . . . Glückel daughter of the late . . . Michael, [in the] year 'upright men'" (chronogram = [5]560 = 1799/1800).
PROVENANCE: F. Gorevic & Son, New York
DONOR: Dr. Harry G. Friedman

# 67

TORAH SHIELD F 2562  (*Illus. p. 108*)
Berlin, 1788–1802
August Ferdinand Gentzmer, active 1789–1808
Silver: repoussé, cast, engraved, parcel-gilt
H 24.8  W 20.8 cm
HALLMARKS:  *CITY:* Scheffler, *Berlin*, 11
              *MAKER:* Scheffler, *Berlin*, 219

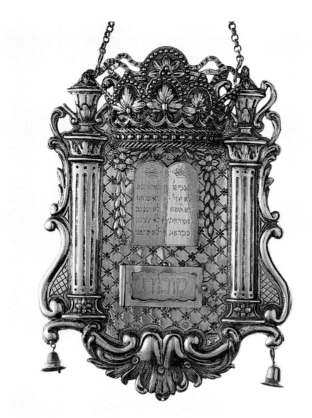

No. 65  M 235

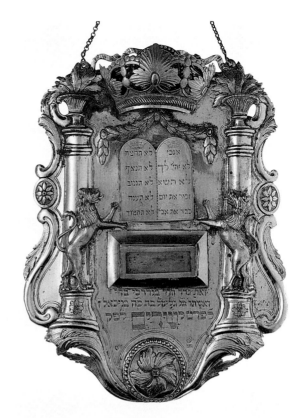

No. 66  F 5075

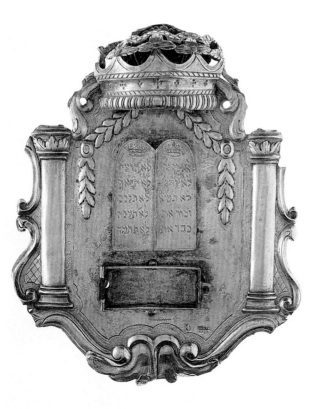

No. 67  F 2562

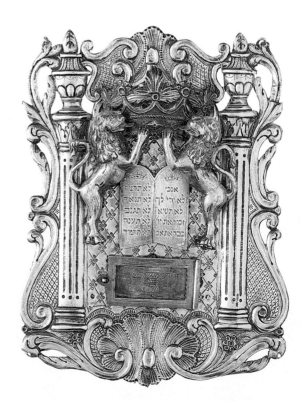

No. 68  D 138

REMARKS: The upper part of this shield is damaged; there are no loops above or below. Shields Nos. 40–41 and 65 are also by Gentzmer.

BIBLIOGRAPHY: Noted in *Danzig 1939*, No. 64

DONOR: Dr. Harry G. Friedman

## 68

TORAH SHIELD D 138  (*Illus. p. 108*)

Berlin, 1804–15

Johann Carl Franz August Sonnabendt, active ca. 1810–after 1842

Silver: repoussé, cast, engraved, parcel-gilt

H 29.6  W 22.6 cm

HALLMARKS:  CITY: Scheffler, *Berlin*, 12
MAKER: Scheffler, *Berlin*, 300

PROVENANCE: The Great Synagogue, Danzig

REMARKS: On the back of the left column is the engraved numeral "18." For other shields bearing similar numbers, see remarks, shield No. 41. According to Danzig 1933, there had been three pendants on this shield; one, inscribed: זאת נדבת, "This was donated by" (presently on shield No. 40); a second, inscribed: חברה קדישה, "Holy (Burial) Society" (presently on shield No. 73); the third (missing) was inscribed: [לפק] חבר אני לכל אשר יראוך (Psalms 119:63) forming a chronogram for (5)566 = 1806.

BIBLIOGRAPHY: Danzig 1933, No. 138a, p. 6; *Danzig 1939*, No. 199

DONOR: The Jewish Community of Danzig

## 69

TORAH SHIELD (?) D 126  (*Illus. p. 110*)

Danzig, 1805 and 1828/29 (inscriptions)

Silver: repoussé, engraved

H 27.9  W 20.5 cm

HALLMARKS: none

INSCRIPTION: above: נר תמיד, "Eternal Light"; to the right of the Tablets of the Law: נעשה/ מצדקה/ נ'ת/ ע'י/ הגבאי/ מ'ה/ יוסף/ במ יואל/ כהנא, "Made from charity (of the) Eternal Light by the *gabbai* Joseph son of Joel Kahana"; to the left of the Tablets of the Law: יום א'/ ד'/ ד'חה'ם/ של/ סוכות/ מדאנ/ ציג, "Sunday, the fourth day of the intermediate days of Sukkot from Danzig" (the last two words being a continuation of the inscription on the right); on the Tablets of the Law, below the Commandments (which are out of order): לפרט, ו'ער'י'כת נ'ר'// ל'בן' ישי'/ לפק, "Year 'And the establishing of a light for the son of Jesse' (chronogram = [5]566; entire date = 13 October 1805)"; on lower, later panel: זאת נעשה ע'י הגבאי ר' איצק ב'ר משה גאלדשטיין תקפט, "This was made by the *gabbai* Itzig Goldstein, (5)589" (= 1828/29).

PROVENANCE: The Mattenbuden Synagogue, Danzig

REMARKS: The minutes book of the same Eternal Light Soci-

ety, *Danzig 1939*/1982, No. 131, was also dedicated by Itzig Goldstein in 1832/33. Note also pointer No. 552, dedicated by Joseph Kahana on the eve of Yom Kippur, ten days before the dedication of this shield.

BIBLIOGRAPHY: *Danzig 1939*/1982, No. 69

DONOR: The Jewish Community of Danzig

## 70

TORAH SHIELD D 144  (*Illus. p. 110*)

Danzig, 1804–05 (?); 1887/88 (inscription)

Silver: repoussé, cast, engraved, parcel-gilt

H 26.3  W 20.3 cm

HALLMARKS:  CITY: Czihak 9/10 (?) with 511 (var.)
MAKER: "JK" (?) in script, in oval

INSCRIPTION: on later pendant: *Zum/ Andenken/ an/ seinen Vater/ geschenkt von/ Marcus Goldstein/* תרמ"ח, "In memory of his father, given by Marcus Goldstein, (5)648" (=1887/88)

PROVENANCE: The Mattenbuden Synagogue, Danzig

REMARKS: The cover of the plaque box, the *parashah* plaques and one flanking urn are missing. As noted in *Danzig 1939*, No. 206, on the reverse is a circular frame, within which "TB" and פסח, "Passover," were inscribed. Pointer No. 595 was also dedicated in the same year by Marcus Goldstein in memory of his father.

BIBLIOGRAPHY: *Danzig 1939*, No. 206

DONOR: The Jewish Community of Danzig

## 71

TORAH SHIELD D 133  (*Illus. p. 110*)

Danzig, 1821 or 1828; 1833/34 (inscription)

August Nathanael Lehnhard (?), active 1799–1841

Silver: repoussé, die-stamped, cast, engraved, parcel-gilt

H 35.1  W 27.5 cm

HALLMARKS:  CITY: Czihak 10 (var.); No. XXXIV (?)
MAKER: Czihak 519 (var., not in script)

INSCRIPTION: on two pendants: שייך לחברה/ תלמוד תורה/ ד'ק'ק/ מוטענבודען// תקצד לפ'ק', "Belonging to the Talmud Torah Society of the H[oly] C[ongregation of] Mattenbuden, (5)594" (=1833/34)

PROVENANCE: The Mattenbuden Synagogue, Danzig

REMARKS: There are three *parashah* plaques. The pendants appear on No. 252 in Danzig 1933, pl. 5. Danzig 1933, No. 146a, p. 6, mentions a third, middle pendant, apparently inscribed with the name "Josef Mendel Bramson." The number "14" is inscribed on the lower reverse of the shield. For other shields bearing similar numbers, see remarks, shield No. 41. Torah Finials No. 290 bear the same master's mark. This shield appears to have been modeled after shields Nos. 75 and 84, made by the Berlin silversmith Kessner.

BIBLIOGRAPHY: Danzig 1933, No. 146a, pl. 6 (mislabeled 122); *Danzig 1939*/1982, No. 67.

DONOR: The Jewish Community of Danzig

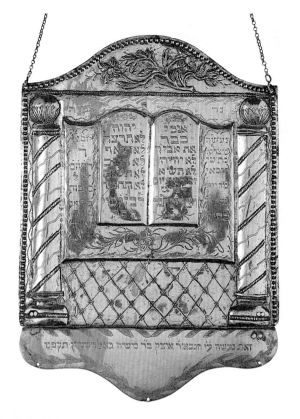

No. 69  D 126

No. 70  D 144

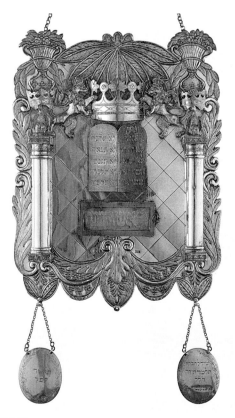

No. 71  D 133

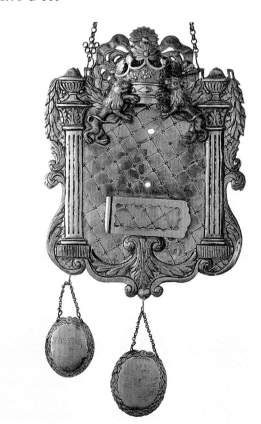

No. 72  F 1312

## 72

TORAH SHIELD F 1312 (*Illus. p. 110*)
Berlin, 1824 (inscription)
Sons of Martin Friedrich Müller
Silver: repoussé, cast, engraved
H 28.6 W 21.6 cm
HALLMARKS: *CITY:* Scheffler, *Berlin,* 12
(?, cf. 14)
*MAKER:* Scheffler, *Berlin,* 130
(one of the Müller family)
INSCRIPTION: on two pendants:ע״א מרת/ טובה// קארנאווע/
תקפד /פסח/ חה, "with his wife ... Tovah, Kornau (?), the
intermediate days of Passover (5)584" (= 1824)
REMARKS: The Tablets of the Law, visible in old photographs,
are now missing, as are other minor elements. The missing
pendant probably read: "Belonging to (or 'donation of') A
son of B." The engraving on the last pendant is peculiar,
and it may have been a practice piece; even so, its date
might provide a *terminus ad quem.* Kornau is 50 km NNE
of Osnabruck. Shield No. 63 is similar to this piece.
DONOR: Dr. Harry G. Friedman

## 73

TORAH SHIELD D 148 (*Illus. p. 112*)
Berlin, 1821–41 (?)
Johann August Gebhardt, active 1817–60
Silver: repoussé, punched, cast, die-stamped, engraved, par-
cel-gilt
H 31.3 W 25.3 cm
HALLMARKS: *CITY:* Scheffler, *Berlin,* 14; 18 (?)
*MAKER:* Scheffler, *Berlin,* 336
INSCRIPTION: on finial of crown: גא; on the single pendant:
החברה קדישא , "The Holy (Burial) Society"
REMARKS: There are four *parashah* plaques. The significance
of the inscription on the crown is unknown. According to
the photograph in Danzig 1933, No. 138b, pl. 6, the single
pendant here actually belongs to shield No. 68. See
Christie's New York 1993, No. 454 (formerly Jewish Muse-
um F 254), for a smaller shield by the same smith.
BIBLIOGRAPHY: *Danzig 1939/1982,* No. 65
DONOR: The Jewish Community of Danzig

## 74

TORAH SHIELD F 3241 (*Illus. p. 112*)
Berlin, ca. 1828–42
Gustav Heinrich Adolf Reich, active after 1828
Silver: repoussé
H 22.6 W 16.9 cm
HALLMARKS: *CITY:* Scheffler, *Berlin,* 14 and 18
*MAKER:* Scheffler, *Berlin,* 394
DONOR: Dr. Harry G. Friedman

## 75

TORAH SHIELD D 135 (*Illus. p. 112*)
Berlin, 1819–28(?)
Johann Christian Samuel Kessner, active 1804–54
Silver: repoussé, cast, engraved, parcel-gilt
H 30.5 W 24.2 cm
HALLMARKS: *CITY:* Scheffler, *Berlin,* 14
*MAKER:* Scheffler, *Berlin,* 264
REMARKS: There are four *parashah* plaques. The "indetermi-
nate third mark" noted in *Danzig 1939,* No. 200, is a double
strike of the city mark. Shield No. 84 is also by Kessner
whose shields appear to have served as models for Danzig-
made shield No. 71.
BIBLIOGRAPHY: *Danzig 1939,* No. 200
DONOR: The Jewish Community of Danzig

## 76

TORAH SHIELD D 145 (*Illus. p. 112*)
Berlin, 1854–60
Silver: repoussé, cast, engraved, parcel-gilt
H 35.4 W 28.1 cm
HALLMARKS: *CITY:* Scheffler, *Berlin,* 15 and 21
*MAKER:* "M"
PROVENANCE: The Great Synagogue, Danzig
REMARKS: There is one *parashah* plaque. According to
Danzig 1933, No. 145a, there were formerly three pendants
on this shield, inscribed: "Elḥanan son of Me'ir Halevi and
his wife Esther, [in the] year 1858." As noted in *Danzig 1939,*
No. 201, this shield is inscribed "E L," initials also found on
Torah Pointer No. 556. This shield is very similar to shield
No. 98, a late copy with early pendants.
BIBLIOGRAPHY: Danzig 1933, No. 145a; *Danzig 1939,* No. 201.
DONOR: The Jewish Community of Danzig

## 77

TORAH SHIELD X 1952–8 (*Illus. p. 113*)
Germany, 1804 (inscription)
Silver: repoussé, chased, parcel-gilt
H 22.0 W 21.6 cm
HALLMARKS: none
INSCRIPTION: in lower central cartouche:י״ט יששכר/בר יעקב
סג״ל וזוג/ מ׳ פרומט ת״י נתן/ רב״ה ב״נ ר״ה תקס״ה/ לפ״ק
ערנשבאך פה, "Yom-Tov (?) Issachar son of Jacob Segal
and his spouse ... Frumet ... [daughter of] Nathan [our]
h[oly] rabbi in N., Rosh Hashanah, (5)565 (= 6 September
1804), here, Ernsbach."
REMARKS: The crown at top is flattened, as are the columns;
there are also traces of fire damage on the shield. Ernsbach
is a very small village about 30 km NE of Heilbrunn.
DONOR: Jewish Cultural Reconstruction

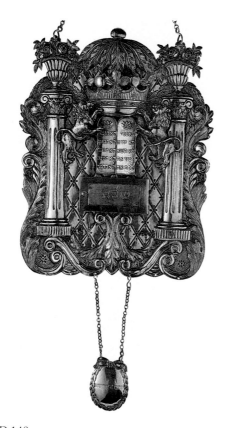

No. 73  D 148

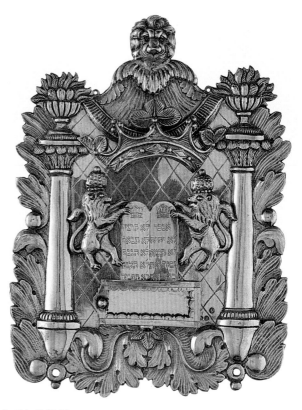

No. 74  F 3241

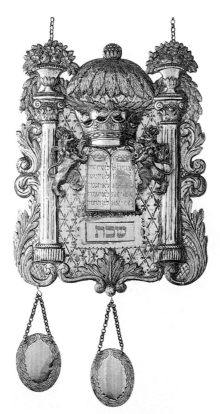

No. 75  D 135

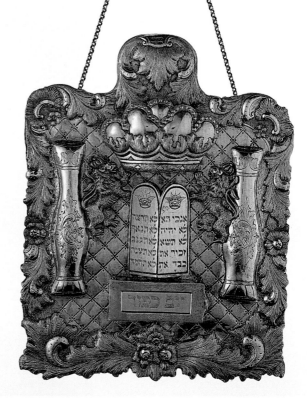

No. 76  D145

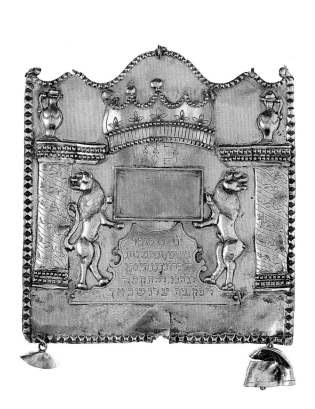

No. 77  X 1952–8

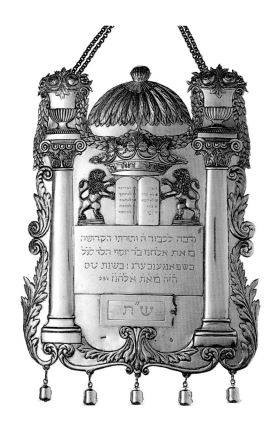

No. 78  F 3011a

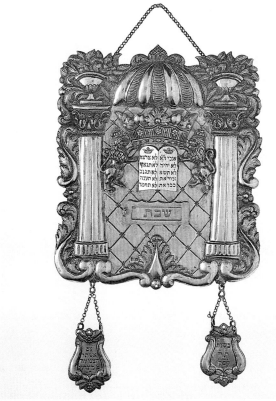

No. 79  D 132

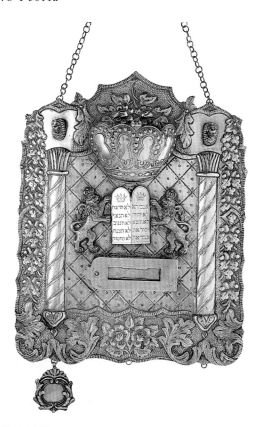

No. 80  M 461

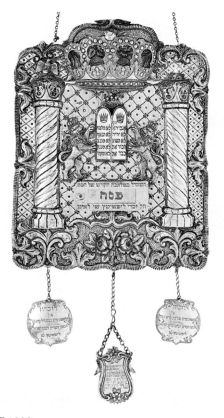

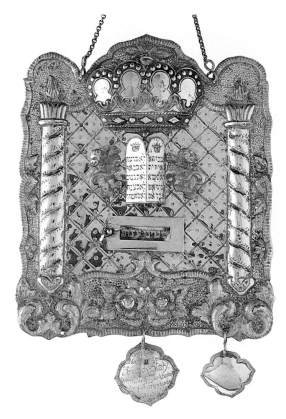

No. 81  F 1998

No. 82  F 1997

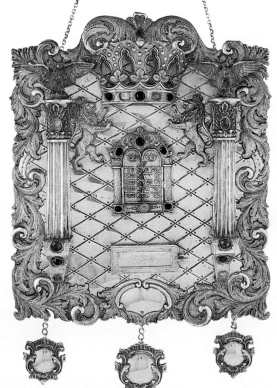

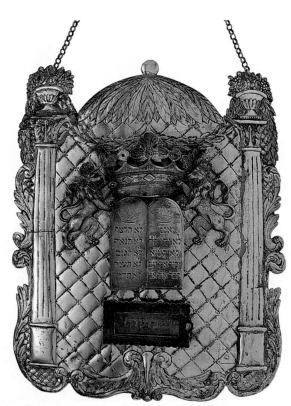

No. 83  D 134

No. 84  D 142

# 78

TORAH SHIELD F 3011a  (*Illus. p. 113*)
Kassel, 1836; 1836/37 (inscription)
Friedrich Proll, active 1824–64
Silver: repoussé, cast, engraved, parcel-gilt
H 36.5  W 28.8 cm
HALLMARKS: *CITY:* Scheffler, *Hessen,* 610
　　　　　　　 *MAKER:* Scheffler, *Hessen,* 692/93
INSCRIPTION: on central panel: נדבה לכבוד ה' ותורתו
הקדושה/ מאת אלחנן ב"ר יוסף הלוי ס'ג'ל/ בשפאנגעננבערג:
בשנת טס/ ה'ז'ה' מ'א'ת' א'ל'ח'נ'ן' לפ'ק', "Donation in
honor of the Lord and His holy Torah, by Elḥanan son of
Joseph Halevi Segal in Spangenberg. In the year 'This
Torah Shield from Elḥanan' (chronogram for [5]597 =
1836/37)"
PROVENANCE: The Spangenthal Family, Kassel; Gorevic, New
York
REMARKS: There are four *parashah* plaques. Finials No. 313
(bearing the same marks as this shield) and pointer No.
568 were acquired together with this shield. Spangenberg
is a small town 20 km SSE of Kassel.
DONOR: Dr. Harry G. Friedman

# 79

TORAH SHIELD D 132  (*Illus. p. 113*)
Danzig, 1839/40 (inscription)
Silver: repoussé, cast, engraved, parcel-gilt
H 22.8  W 19.5 cm
HALLMARKS: *CITY:* Czihak 10 (var.); No. XXXIX
　　　　　　　 *OTHER:* unclear "13," the two numerals
　　　　　　　　　　　 appearing to be crossed)
INSCRIPTION: on two pendants: עם אשתו/ הצנועה מ'/
בשנת ת'ר'/ מינדעל תי', "with his wife, . . . . Mindel . . .";
לפ"ק, "in the year (5)600" (=1839/40)
REMARKS: The two surviving pendants (of three) are hung in
the wrong order.
BIBLIOGRAPHY: Danzig 1933, No. 132; *Danzig 1939,* No. 205
DONOR: The Jewish Community of Danzig

# 80

TORAH SHIELD M 461  (*Illus. p. 113*)
Germany, mid-19th century
Silver: repoussé, die-stamped, engraved, gilt
H 30.3  W 25.5 cm
HALLMARKS:  Quadruped standing to right; "E" in script
PROVENANCE: The Rose and Benjamin Mintz Collection
REMARKS: The marks resemble the city mark of Berlin and
that of the silversmith Eisolt; cf. shield No. 81, with similar
marks.
DONOR: Museum purchase

# 81

TORAH SHIELD F 1998  (*Illus. p. 114*)
Danzig (?), mid-19th century
Silver: repoussé, engraved, parcel-gilt
H 27.8  W 21.9 cm
HALLMARKS: Bear standing to left; "E" in script
INSCRIPTION: on frame of plaque box: השתדל במלאכת
הקודש של הס"ת/ הק' זכרי' ליפשיטץ שי' לאי"ט, "He un-
dertook the sacred work of the Torah Scroll . . . Zechariah
Lipschütz..."; on the two outer pendants: האשה /לזכרון
מרת מלכה קרא בת/ הגאון הצדיק רבינו ברוך יצחק
ליפשיטץ נ"ע, "In memory of the woman … Malkah Kara
daughter of the late Gaon . . . Rabbi Barukh Isaac Lipschütz"; לזכרון האשה מרת גנענדיל קרא בת/ הגאון
הצדיק רבינו ישראל/ ליפשיטץ נ"ע, "In memory of the
woman … Gnendl Kara daughter of the late Gaon … Rabbi
Israel Lipschütz"; the middle pendant (different and larger): יעקב צבי/ בן ישראל/ גינענדל/ בת יצחק, "Jacob Zvi
son of Israel [and] Gnendl daughter of Isaac"
REMARKS: There are three *parashah* plaques. The very top of
the shield is missing. The hallmark resembles that of
Berlin as found also on the almost identical shield No. 80.
Rabbi Israel Lipschütz, mentioned in the inscription,
served several Danzig congregations from 1837 to 1860,
and was author of a commentary on the Mishnah (see
*Danzig 1939,* p. 27).
DONOR: Dr. Harry G. Friedman

# 82

TORAH SHIELD F 1997  (*Illus. p. 114*)
Germany, 1930's
Silver: cast, repoussé, engraved, gilt
H 18.3  W 16.7 cm
HALLMARKS: none
INSCRIPTION: on one pendant: *Jhren/ vorsitzenden/ Heinrich
Stahl/ Verehrung u. Dankbarkeit/die jüd. Gemeinde/ Berlin,*
"To its president Heinrich Stahl, [in] admiration and grat-
itude, [from] the Jewish Community, Berlin." Another
pendant is blank, and the third is missing.
REMARKS: Museum records indicate the former presence of a
*parashah* plaque, as well as all three pendants. Heinrich
Stahl was president of the Jewish Community of Berlin in
1933–40 and perished at Theresienstadt in 1942 (*EJ* 15, col.
326).
DONOR: Dr. Harry G. Friedman

# 83

TORAH SHIELD D 134  (*Illus. p. 114*)
Germany, late 19th-early 20th century
Silver: repoussé, cast, die-stamped, engraved, parcel-gilt; glass
H 34.5  W 29.0 cm

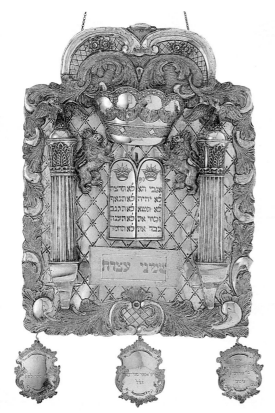

No. 85  D 122

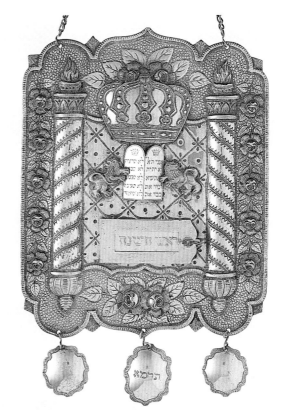

No. 86  D 147

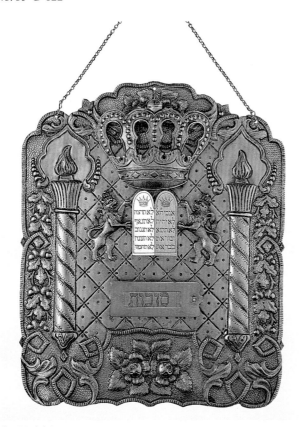

No. 87  M 9

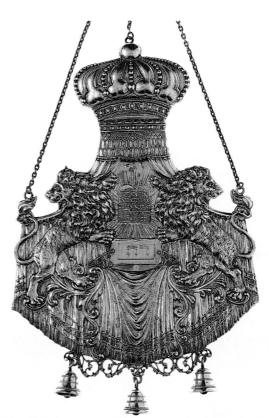

No. 89  S 33

HALLMARKS: "750"

INSCRIPTION: on miniature Torah Scroll within the Torah Ark: קדש/ ל"א, Exodus 28:36.

PROVENANCE: The Weinberg Synagogue, Danzig

REMARKS: There is one *parashah* plaque. An engraved "W" on the reverse of the shield marks it as property of the Weinberg Synagogue. Shield No. 85 is a similar but earlier example; shield No. 88, with similar elements, is from the Freund workshop, Hanau.

BIBLIOGRAPHY: *Danzig 1939*/1982, No. 61

DONOR: The Jewish Community of Danzig

# 84

## TORAH SHIELD  D 142  (*Illus. p. 114*)

Berlin, 1804–28(?)

Johann Christian Samuel Kessner, active 1804–54

Silver: repoussé, cast, engraved, parcel-gilt

H 31.7  W 26.3 cm

HALLMARKS:  *CITY:* Scheffler, *Berlin*, 12-14 (letter illegible)

MAKER: Scheffler, *Berlin*, 264

PROVENANCE: The Great Synagogue, Danzig

REMARKS: There are four *parashah* plaques. This shield is heavily repaired, and bells or pendants are missing along the bottom. If this piece is identical with Danzig 1933, No. 144a, there had originally been three pendants. A shield published in PBNY 1967, No. 402, is similar in form.

BIBLIOGRAPHY: Danzig 1933, No. 144a (?); *Danzig 1939*/1982, No. 66

DONOR: The Jewish Community of Danzig

# 85

## TORAH SHIELD  D 122  (*Illus. p. 116*)

Berlin, 1854–60; 1859/60 (inscription)

Silver: repoussé

H 39.7  W 30.7 cm

HALLMARKS:  *CITY:* Scheffler, *Berlin*, 15 and 21

MAKER: "M"

INSCRIPTION: on three pendants: שייך/ לר' ישראל משה/ ב"ר מרדכי ז"ל/ גרטה/// ע"ז/ מרת אסתר בת"ר יעקב/ ז'צ"ל// שנת כתר לפ"ק, "Belonging to Israel Moses son of the late Mordecai Gerthe (?), with his spouse Esther daughter of the late Jacob, [in the] year (5)620" (=1859/60)

PROVENANCE: The Gieldzinski Collection, Danzig

REMARKS: The name גרטה', "Gerthe," mentioned in the inscription, is problematic, though there is a town named Gerthe adjacent to Bochum. But it has an abbreviation mark at the end, which would point to a name such as Gerthheim. In the date, the letters representing the year are given in an order which forms the word כתר, "crown." *Danzig 1939*, under No. 60, mentions "no. 68 [correct to 'no. 61' = D 134 = shield No. 83], which closely resembles

F 244 [= shield No. 88] . . . . Both of these shields may be dated after 1858."

BIBLIOGRAPHY: Danzig 1904, No. 19; Danzig 1933, No. 122, pl. 7; *Danzig 1939*/1982, No. 60

DONOR: The Jewish Community of Danzig

# 86

## TORAH SHIELD  D 147  (*Illus. p. 116*)

Germany, 1880/81 (inscription)

Brass: engraved, silver-plated, parcel-gilt

H 21.9  W 17.9 cm

HALLMARKS: none

INSCRIPTION: on central pendant of three at bottom: תרמא, "(5)641" (= 1880/81)

PROVENANCE: The Weinberg Synagogue, Danzig

REMARKS: There are four *parashah* plaques. The letter "W" inscribed on the reverse of the central pendant marks this shield as property of the Weinberg Synagogue. In *Danzig 1939*, No. 203, the date is mistakenly translated as "1841." Similar, blank pendants are seen on Köln, No. 42; in both cases, the workmanship of the pendants differs radically from that of the shields, and they may not be original. Torah Shield No. 87 is almost identical.

BIBLIOGRAPHY: *Danzig 1939*, No. 203

DONOR: The Jewish Community of Danzig

# 87

## TORAH SHIELD  M 9  (*Illus. p. 116*)

Germany (?), late 19th–20th century

Silver: repoussé, cast, engraved

H 30.3  W 26.7 cm

HALLMARKS: none

PROVENANCE: The Rose and Benjamin Mintz Collection

REMARKS: There is one *parashah* plaque. There are no holes along the bottom for pendants or bells. Torah Shield No. 86 is almost identical.

DONOR: Museum purchase

# 88

## TORAH SHIELD  F 244

Germany, late 19th–early 20th century

Emil Freund (?), Hanau, active late 19th–early 20th century

Silver: repoussé, cast, gilt

H 32.7  W 27.2 cm

HALLMARKS: "750"

REMARKS: There are four *parashah* plaques. The *parashah* plaques, Tablets of the Law, and crowned lions are identical with patterns from the Emil Freund workshop in Hanau. Shield No. 83 has similar elements.

DONOR: Dr. Harry G. Friedman

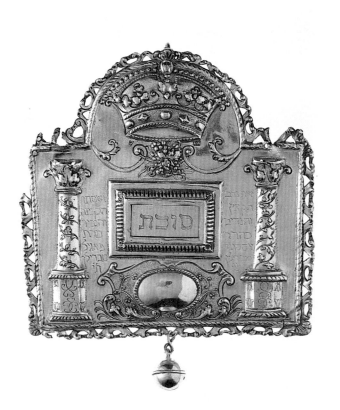

No. 90  S 1325

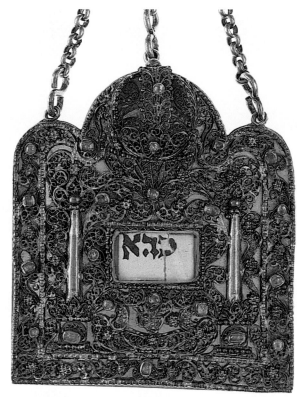

No. 91  JM 55–52

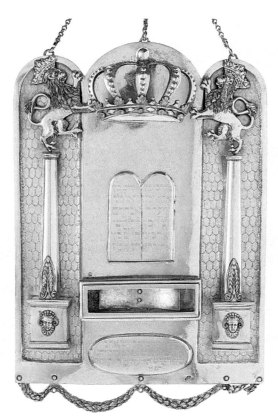

No. 92  U 8547

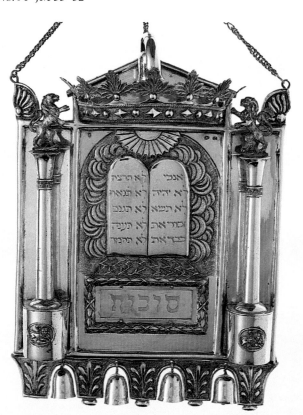

No. 93  F 1473

## 89

TORAH SHIELD S 33  (*Illus. p. 116*)

Hanau, late 19th–early 20th century

Silver: cast, chased, parcel-gilt

H 39.2  W 29.1 cm

HALLMARKS: "N"; "13"; unclear mark (all false marks)

PROVENANCE: The Hadji Ephraim and Mordecai Benguiat Family Collection

REMARKS: There are four *parashah* plaques. There are numerous examples of this shield design (either unmarked or bearing false marks). It is identical with casting patterns from the Emil Freund workshop in Hanau.

DONOR: Museum purchase

## 90

TORAH SHIELD S 1325  (*Illus. p. 118*)

Hanau, 1720's – early 1730's (?)

Daniel Marchand (I), active 1719–after 1747

Silver: repoussé, cast, engraved, traces of gilt

H 18.3  W 18.8 cm

HALLMARKS:  CITY: Scheffler, *Hessen*, 387

MAKER: Scheffler, *Hessen*, 410

INSCRIPTION: זאת נדב הקצין והנדיב כהרר זיסקינד מברילן
ש״י/, ואשתו הקצינה והגביר' מרת פאגיל מברילן תי',
"This was donated by … Süsskind from Brilon … and his wife Fogel of Brilon …."

PROVENANCE: Synagogue, Frankenberg in Westphalia (?)

REMARKS: Elements atop the capitals are missing, possibly lions or vases. For another German shield of similar shape and proportions, see the archaising shield No. 33 (Halberstadt, 1807). The provenance is based on information provided by the donor. Brilon is 60 km W of Kassel.

DONOR: Mr. Joseph Willon

## 91

MINIATURE TORAH SHIELD JM 55–52

(*Illus. p. 118*)

Nuremberg, late 18th–early 19th century

Silver: filigree, parcel-gilt; paper: ink; rubies

H 8.8  W 7.6 cm

HALLMARKS:  CITY: "N"

MAKER: "B[or E]A/WK/(star)," in oval

REMARKS: Some of the stones seem to be replacements.

DONOR: Samuel and Lucille Lemberg

## 92

TORAH SHIELD U 8547  (*Illus. p. 118*)

Nuremberg, 1815 (inscription)

Silver: repoussé, punched, engraved, cast; glass

H 39.2  W 27.7 cm

HALLMARKS:  CITY: "N"; "13" in script

MAKER (?): R³ 4315

INSCRIPTION: in oval cartouche: נדבה החברה קדישא/ הני/
של ת״ת בחג השבועות בשנת/ נש[!]חדש ש״ ת׳ק׳ע׳ה׳
פ׳ד׳ת לפק, "Donation of the T[almud] T[orah] Holy Society … on the Shavuot festival, in the year (5)575 (= 14-15 June, 1815); Renewed year (5)680" (= 1919/20); inscribed on Tablets of the Law: מרדכי כ״ץ/ אברהם כ״ץ/ מ״ה זעקל
כ״ץ/ משה כ״ץ/ יואב ב״ש/ ארי ב׳ ה׳ א'/ ליב כ״ץ/ יואל
ב״מ/ אברהם ב״מ/ ה׳ הירש סגל/ חיים כ״ץ/ ליב ב׳מ׳ז׳
כ״ץ, "Mordecai Katz; Abraham Katz; … Rabbi Zekel Katz; Moses Katz; Joab s[on of] Sh[…] Ari son of Rabbi A.…; Leib Katz; Joel son of … Abraham son of … Rabbi Hirsch Segal; Ḥayyim Katz; Leib son of Z[…] Katz."

REMARKS: Marks identical to those on this piece are found on two very similar shields: Köln, No. 44; and Deneke, No. 5/62 (dated 1820), with the lion mark (R³ 4315)and a year letter (R³ 3773, "possibly 1769-1773"). The marks on a fourth shield, PBNY 1954, No. 112, are unknown but the date given there points to R³ 3776 ("possibly 1780–1783"). The medusa heads on the column bases and the laurel wreath show the influence of neo-classicism.

## 93

TORAH SHIELD F 1473  (*Illus. p. 118*)

Nuremberg, ca. 1840

Silver: repoussé, cast, parcel-gilt

H 33.6  W 23.5 cm

HALLMARKS:  CITY: "N"; "13"

MAKER: "SC" or "CS" (ligature) in script

REMARKS: There are three *parashah* plaques and a chain is probably original, though the column on the right appears to be a replacement. The oval medallions with crouching lions are signed "ST." This shield and Nos. 94–97 all have an arcade enclosing bells along the bottom, as well as other common iconographic features. They represent a variant form of a more common Nuremberg type with a plain bottom. A close parallel with a wavy lower edge[1] forms an intermediate type (see the Introduction, p.35). Four similar shields are known besides the above.[2] The unusual clasp mechanism of the plaque boxes on Nos. 96 and 97 is identical, although the two shields are from different places. This seems to indicate some connection between them beyond their basic form. Finials No. 303 bear the same marks, as does Gross Collection, 52.1.6.

BIBLIOGRAPHY: *Oppenheim*, p. [4a]

DONOR: Dr. Harry G. Friedman

1. Köln, No. 44.

2. Idelson, p. 87 (present location unknown); PBNY 1968, No. 202 = *Ashkenaz*, p. 236, middle, dated 1845/46 (Moldovan Family Collection, New York); Grossman 1989, No. 9a (United States [?], dated 1852/53; and a shield from Nuremberg, 1842 (The Judaica Museum of the Hebrew Home for the Aged at Riverdale, B841).

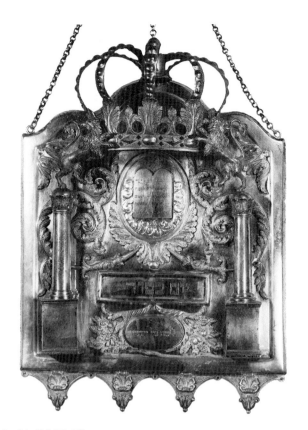

No. 94  JM 13–53

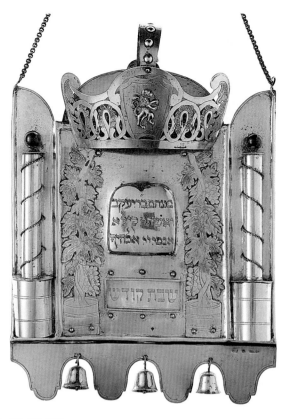

No. 95  F 1897

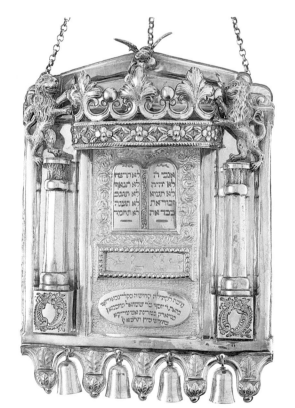

No. 96  JM 10–57

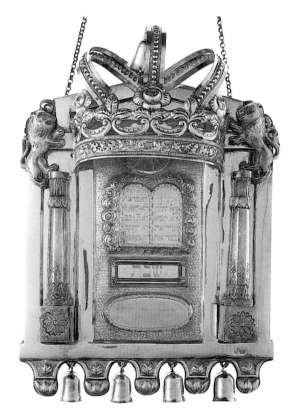

No. 97  F 5745a

## 94

TORAH SHIELD JM 13–53  (*Illus. p. 120*)
Germany, ca. 1840
Silver: repoussé, cast, engraved
H 39.2 W 28.6 cm
HALLMARKS: none
INSCRIPTION: on oval medallion: שלמה בר ישעיהו, "Solomon son of Isaiah"
REMARKS: There are four *parashah* plaques. All the bells are missing.

## 95

TORAH SHIELD F 1897  (*Illus. p. 120*)
Nuremberg, mid-19th century
Silver: chased, cast, engraved, gilt
H 34.6 W 25.1 cm
HALLMARKS: *CITY:* "NURNBERG"; "13"
          *MAKER:* "RIEDEL"
INSCRIPTION: on Tablets of the Law: מנחם ב"ר יעקוב/ ואשתו קילא/ אנוכי ה' אלקיך, "Menaḥem son of Jacob and his wife Keila"; Exodus 20:2, 5 = Deuteronomy 5:6, 9
REMARKS: There are five *parashah* plaques. For an almost identical shield, see Sotheby's NY 1983, No. 40.
DONOR: Dr. Harry G. Friedman

## 96

TORAH SHIELD JM 10–57  (*Illus. p. 120*)
Bamberg (?), 1861 (inscription)
Silver: repoussé, cast, engraved
H 33.3 W 23.7 cm
HALLMARKS: "13" (twice); "H. REES"
INSCRIPTION: on oval medallion: נדבה לקהילה קדושה בקלייננבארדא[ר]ף/ מאת ר' יוסף ב"ר שמואל טוכמאן/ בניוארק במדינת אמעריקא/ בחודש סיון תר"כא לפק, "Donation to the Holy Congregation in Kleinbardo[r]f from . . . Joseph son of . . . Samuel Tuchman in Newark in the country of America in the month of Sivan (5)621" (=1861)
PROVENANCE: "Castelbolognesi Collection, Rome" (i.e., Dr. S. Yoveli, New York)
REMARKS: There are two *parashah* plaques. The clasp on the back of the plaque box is identical in form with that on No. 97, below.
BIBLIOGRAPHY: PBNY 1957, No. 146
DONOR: Samuel and Lucille Lemberg

## 97

TORAH SHIELD F 5745a  (*Illus. p. 120*)
Altona, 1861 (?)
Silver: repoussé, engraved, parcel-gilt
H 34.2 W 24.9 cm
HALLMARKS: *CITY:* R³ 75 (var.— 1861 ?)

*MAKER:* "SC" or "SG"
PROVENANCE: Jacob Posen, New York
REMARKS: There are traces of an erased Hebrew inscription on the oval cartouche. Pointer No. 607 bears the same marks and was apparently made as a set with this piece. The clasp on the back of the plaque box is identical in form with that on shield No. 96.
DONOR: Dr. Harry G. Friedman

## 98

TORAH SHIELD D 140  (*Illus. p. 122*)
Germany, early 20th century
Silver: repoussé, cast, parcel-gilt
H 26.9 W 22.0 cm
HALLMARKS: "750"
INSCRIPTION: at bottom, on one of two oval pendants: שייך/ להמרומים[!]/ מ"ה איצק בר"ם/ גאלדשטיין, "Belonging to the exalted [in plural !] . . . Itzig son of M[oses] Goldstein"
PROVENANCE: The Great Synagogue, Danzig
REMARKS: The two pendants do not belong to this shield; in Danzig 1933, pl. 5, they are seen on "No. 129," but they may not belong there either, for they are not mentioned in its description.
BIBLIOGRAPHY: Danzig 1933, No. 140 (?); *Danzig 1939*, No. 202
DONOR: The Jewish Community of Danzig

## 99

TORAH SHIELD (Fragment) F 2971  (*Illus. p. 122*)
Germany (?), early 20th century (?)
Silver: cast, repoussé
H 14.3 W 9.9 cm
HALLMARKS: none
REMARKS: This piece, previously catalogued as an amulet, is the central piece of a Torah Shield similar to those on shields Nos. 96–97.
DONOR: Dr. Harry G. Friedman

## 100

TORAH SHIELD F 1748  (*Illus. p. 122*)
Saxony (?), mid-19th century
Silver: repoussé, engraved, parcel-gilt
H 31.3 W 24.8 cm
HALLMARKS: *CITY:* similar to R³ 65
          *MAKER:* "AB/B" in shield
INSCRIPTION: in oval cartouche: נ"י הקצין כ"ה יוסף בן/ כ"ה קאפל היימאן כ"ץ ז"ל/ בק"ק זולצבאך, "Donation of Joseph son of the late Koppel Heiman Katz, in the H[oly] C[ommunity of] Sulzbach"
REMARKS: The Sulzbach mentioned in the inscription could be one of several towns, none of which is in Saxony. A similar but not identical city hallmark appears on shield No. 101.
DONOR: Dr. Harry G. Friedman

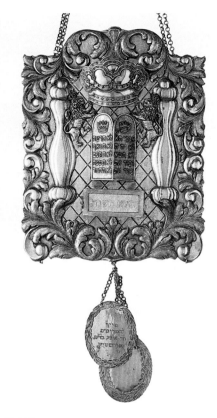

No. 98   D 140

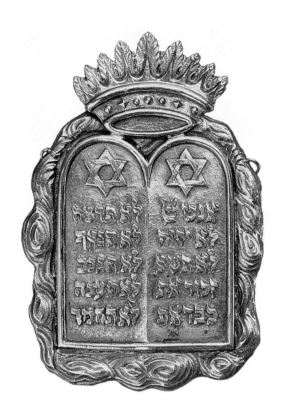

No. 99   F 2971

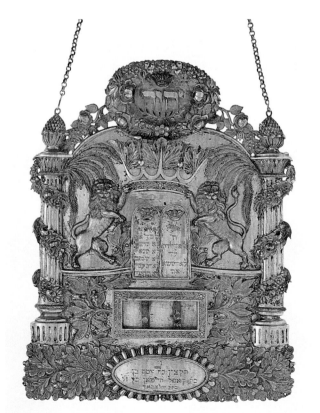

No. 100   F 1748

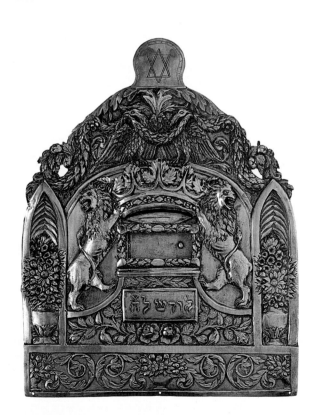

No. 101   F 3136

## 101

**TORAH SHIELD** F 3136 (*Illus. p. 122*)

Saxony (?), mid-19th century

Silver: repoussé

H 30.3 W 24.1 cm

HALLMARKS: *CITY:* R³ 9598

        *MAKER:* R³ 9599

INSCRIPTION: below plaque box: קודש ל"ה, "Dedicated to the Lord"

REMARKS: The round element at the top, bearing a star of David, is a later addition. A similar but not identical city mark is found on shield No. 100. Identical marks are found on a Hanukkah lamp in Warsaw (Martyna, No. 266).

DONOR: Dr. Harry G. Friedman

## 102

**TORAH SHIELD** JM 29-52 (*Illus. p. 124*)

Augsburg (?), late 17th century; 1712/13 (inscription)

Silver: repoussé, engraved, parcel-gilt; glass

H 16.0 W 11.9 cm

HALLMARKS: none

INSCRIPTION: on Tablets of the Law: שני'/ לחוי'ת'// ה'ב'רית/ לפ"ק, "The two Tablets of the Covenant" (Deuteronomy 9:15; chronogram: [5]473 = 1712/13); on crown: כתר תורה, "Crown of Torah"

REMARKS: There is one *parashah* plaque. Occasionally, non-Jewish objects have been adapted for Jewish ritual use, as is the case with this shield and No. 103, made from a wall calendar and a wall sconce, respectively.

Silver wall calendars were popular in late 17th- and 18th-century Germany. They are usually highly decorated plaques of irregular oval form. Three windows pierce these plaques — a large central one for the name of the month (often accompanied by an appropriate scene) and smaller ones above and below, for the year and the day of the month.[1] On the reverse were slots for holding changeable paper cards. In modifying them for use as Torah Shields, the smaller windows were usually blocked or covered, while the larger, central window was used for the *parashah* plaques.[2] Shield No. 102 is a wall calendar of the late 17th century which has been turned upside down; the former upper window showed the *parashah* plaques. On the reverse are clear traces of the large window and of the small frame for the "day" cards; behind the crown are traces of a window for the "year" cards.

BIBLIOGRAPHY: *Wüb*, No. 20

DONOR: Jewish Cultural Reconstruction

1. See Museum für Kunst und Gewerbe, Hamburg, inv. no. 1900.93 (Augsburg, ca. 1700), reproduced in Cohen, fig. 8.

2. Other calendars converted into Torah Shields: Israel Museum, 148/10 (Cohen, No. 7); Skirball, Los Angeles, 7.22 (also from Jewish Cultural Reconstruction); Klagsbald 1982, No. 33 (Consistoire de Paris); Klagsbald 1982, No. 26 (Cluny 22889 — originally made in Regensburg); two examples in Belinfante 1978, pp. 34 and 37; and a former loan to The Jewish Museum (L 10–52; now in the collection of Elmer Offenbacher, New York).

## 103

**TORAH SHIELD** D 123 (*Illus. p. 124*)

Germany (?), late 18th–early 19th century

Brass: repoussé, cast, die-stamped, engraved; glass

H 39.6 W 31.3 cm

HALLMARKS: none

INSCRIPTION: grafitto at bottom in inner oval: "Gieldzinski"

PROVENANCE: The Gieldzinski Collection, Danzig

REMARKS: A characteristic of wall sconces is their central boss — a flat or convex area left plain and highly polished to reflect candlelight.[1] It was this boss which facilitated adaptation of wall sconces for use as Torah Shields. The plain surface was often reworked or replaced, enabling the display of the *parashah* plaques and other Jewish motifs.[2] On this shield the boss has been entirely reworked in repoussé, yielding a typical combination of Torah Shield motifs. The original place of attachment of the candlestick arm has been concealed behind the setting of a large red "gemstone." Blank pendants were added below and a chain attached above.

BIBLIOGRAPHY: Danzig 1904, No. 20; Danzig 1933, No. 123; *Danzig 1939*, No. 204

DONOR: The Jewish Community of Danzig

1. See Bonn, No. 131, fig. 192 (18th century).

2. For another sconce converted into a Torah Shield, cf. Christie's NY 1982, No. 154 (ex-Castelbolognesi [=Yoveli] Collection).

## 104

**TORAH SHIELD** F 62 (*Illus. p. 124*)

Germany, 1764/65 (inscription)

Silver: repoussé, engraved, parcel-gilt

H 23.5 W 22.9 cm

HALLMARKS: none

INSCRIPTION: between priestly hands: כ ,ת, "C[rown of] T[orah]"; around disc, from right top: זה כלי קודש שייך להאלוף הקצין פו"מ כ"ה משולם בר שלמה כ"ץ ז"ל, "This holy vessel belongs to the leader ... Rabbi Meshullam son of the late Solomon Katz"; ואשתו הקצינה מ' מרים בת נפתלי נעשה מלאכי' ה'ק'ודש לפק, "And his wife ... Miriam daughter of Naphtali, the holy work was done (chronogram: [5]525)" (=1764/65); below the *parashah* "plaque" window: ממערגיטל, "from Mergital"

REMARKS: The place name at the end of the inscription may be interpreted as Mergenthal (better known as Mergentheim), 95 km due E of Mannheim. On the reverse are floral appliqué and engraved motifs.

DONOR: Dr. Harry G. Friedman

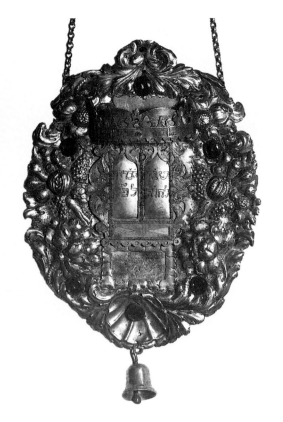

No. 102   JM 29–52

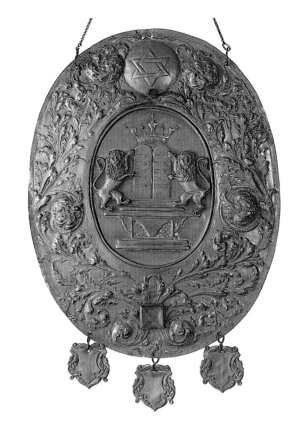

No. 103   D 123

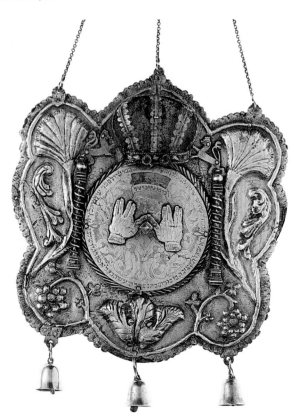

No. 104   F 62

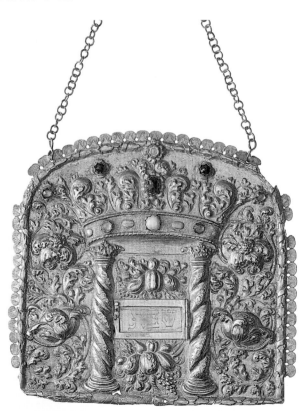

No. 105   M 8

## 105

TORAH SHIELD  M 8  (*Illus. p. 124*)

Germany (?), early (?) 18th century

Silver: repoussé, parcel-gilt; glass; semiprecious stones

H 27.2  W 29.3 cm

HALLMARKS: none

PROVENANCE: The Rose and Benjamin Mintz Collection

REMARKS: There are two *parashah* plaques. Kayser, No. 42, described this shield "Probably Augsburg, end of 17th century." The motifs are of Augsburg type, but the overall composition is not.

BIBLIOGRAPHY: Kayser, No. 42

DONOR: Museum purchase

## 106

TORAH SHIELD  JM 81–64  (*Illus. p. 126*)

Germany, 1804/05 (inscription)

Silver: repoussé, engraved

H 21.9  W 20.1 cm

HALLMARKS: none

INSCRIPTION: in lower, small medallion: תקס״ה ל, "(5)565" (=1804/05); in upper, small medallion: שמעון בר ליפמן, "Simon son of Lipmann"

REMARKS: Many repairs are evident and the shield may have been made from a preexisting object.

DONOR: Mrs. Else Seligman

## 107

TORAH SHIELD  D 137  (*Illus. p. 126*)

Germany, before 1809

Silver: repoussé, parcel-gilt, engrved, cast; glass

H 32.0  W 27.4 cm

HALLMARKS: Scheffler, *Berlin*, 30b; "10"; "MONIK"

INSCRIPTION: in lower cartouche: ח׳ק׳/ ד׳ק׳ק׳ שאטלאנד, "Holy (Burial) Society of the h[oly] c[ongregation of] Schottland"; on three pendant plaques: זנה/ יאקב/ עים (!) בנו ה/ שמעי/ עא ה/ אברם, "This was donated by … Jakob, together with his son … Shimmi, with his brother (?) Abram"; ז״נ/ הרר ליב עי/ אשתו מרת/ פריידל עבא/ הבחור שמו/ ע׳ א׳/ מרדכי, "This was donated by … Rabbi Leib, with his wife … Freidl, with his nephew (?) … Samu[el], with his brother (?) Mordecai"; ז׳נ׳א׳/ יענטה/ עב שואל/ עב ליזר, "This was donated by [the] woman Yente, together with her son Saul (?) [and] with her (?) son Lazar."

PROVENANCE: The Schottland Synagogue, Danzig; the Great Synagogue, Danzig

REMARKS: The pendants, though long attached to the shield, are surely not original; an identifying number "17," is engraved on the back of all (*Danzig 1939,* p. 93). For other shields bearing similar numbers, see shields No. 41, 68, 71.

BIBLIOGRAPHY: Danzig 1933, No. 137a; *Danzig 1939,* No. 70

DONOR: The Jewish Community of Danzig

## 108

TORAH SHIELD  F 3380  (*Illus. p. 126*)

Holland or Germany, 1836/37 (inscription)

Silver: repoussé, engraved

H 18.5  W 14.5 cm

HALLMARKS: unclear (similar to R³ 3594 [Munster]); "GS" (?); (on plaques) Voet, p. 47, No. 4; p. 48, No. 1

INSCRIPTION: in lower cartouche: נדבת/ צדיק בן אהרן כהן בעלינפאנטע/ ת׳ק׳צ׳ז׳ לפ׳ק׳, "Donation of Tzadiq son of Aaron Cohen Belinfante, (5)597"(=1836/37); in upper cartouche: נוה ישע "Neve Yesha'"

REMARKS: There are six *parashah* plaques. A tag on the reverse reads: "PERFRA//B3/R 433A." A shield of almost identical design is in the Jewish Museum, London (Barnett, No. 140: "German, *c.*1700, unmarked," with two inscriptions, dated "1702" and "1889").

DONOR: Dr. Harry G. Friedman

## 109

TORAH SHIELD  F 5423  (*Illus. p. 126*)

Vienna, 1872–1922

Silver: repoussé, engraved, appliqué, gilt

H 34.6  W 31.6 cm

HALLMARKS:  *CITY:* Rohrwasser, p. 19, second row, third from left
 *MAKER:* "N.A.G."

INSCRIPTION: in lower medallion: קופמאן/ גיי ריינגער, "*Kaufmann* Guy Ringer."

REMARKS: There is one *parashah* plaque. This shield is nearly identical with shield No. 110.

DONOR: Dr. Harry G. Friedman

## 110

TORAH SHIELD  X 1952–41  (*Illus. p. 128*)

Vienna, 1867–72

Berl Graeber (?)

Silver: repoussé, engraved, gilt

H 36.9  W 32.1 cm

HALLMARKS:  *CITY:* Neuwirth, pl. 6, 2–3
 *MAKER:* Neuwirth I/215, 315 (?)

REMARKS: There are three *parashah* plaques. This shield is nearly identical with shield No. 109.

DONOR: Jewish Cultural Reconstruction

## 111

TORAH SHIELD  F 3045  (*Illus. p. 128*)

Vienna, ca. 1820

Wenzl Massabost, active 1792–1824

Silver: repoussé, engraved, gilt

H 47.7  W 38.2 cm

HALLMARKS:  *CITY:* similar to Rohrwasser, p. 13, third row
 *MAKER:* Reitzner, 1002

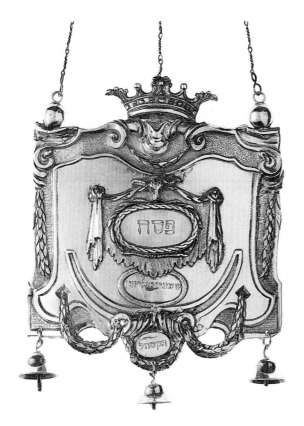

No. 106  JM 81–64

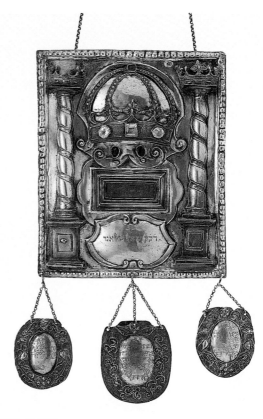

No. 107  D 137a

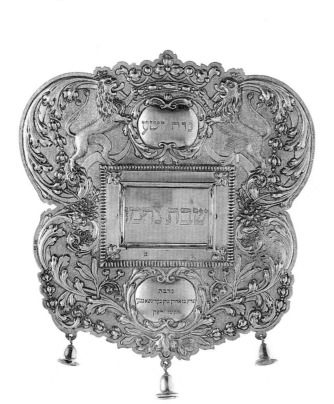

No. 108  F 3380

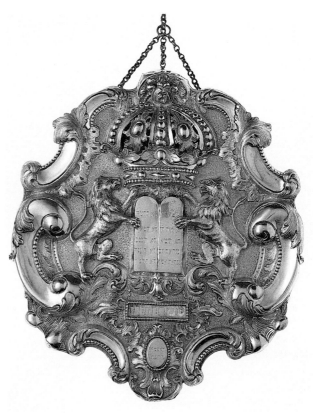

No. 109  F 5423

PROVENANCE: Gorevic, New York

REMARKS: There is one *parashah* plaque. The crown at the top is of a form often found on Hungarian Judaica; cf., Berger 1987, No. 1/5.4 (Torah Ark Curtain); and *Du* XIX/1 (1966), p. 183 (Torah Shield, ascribed to Ukraine but clearly bearing the coat of arms of Hungary).

DONOR: Dr. Harry G. Friedman

## 112

TORAH SHIELD   JM 65-59   (*Illus. p. 128*)

Vienna-Neustadt (?), 1840–63

Franz Schubert, active 1840–63

Silver: repoussé, cast

H 19.4  W 17.2 cm

HALLMARKS:   *CITY:* R³ 7961

*MAKER:* Reitzner 1364

INSCRIPTION: on lower part of Tablets of the Law: ז'נ' ה'ק' כ"ה משה ליב פעלנר/ לח"ק דק"ק פאלאנקע, "This was donated by . . . Moses Leib Felner/ to the H[oly] (Burial) S[ociety] of the h[oly] c[ommunity of] Polonka."

REMARKS: The upper part of the crown is missing. Polonka is in Byelorussia, 120 km NNW of Pinsk.

DONOR: Jewish Cultural Reconstruction

## 113

TORAH SHIELD   F 246   (*Illus. p. 128*)

Vienna, 1872–1922

Silver: repoussé

H 31.6  W 23.0 cm

HALLMARKS:   *CITY:* Neuwirth, pl. 7: 2–3; pl. 6: 12

*MAKER:* "SV" or "AS" (?)

REMARKS: There are four *parashah* plaques. This shield is very similar to shield No. 114. Another similar shield is in Prague (see Altshuler, No. 48).

DONOR: Dr. Harry G. Friedman

## 114

TORAH SHIELD   F 245   (*Illus. p. 129*)

Vienna, 1878–1908

Johann Ziehrer, active 1878–1908

Silver: repoussé, parcel-gilt

H 29.3  W 27.3 cm

HALLMARKS:   *CITY:* Neuwirth, pl. 7: 2–3; pl. 6: 12

*MAKER:* Neuwirth, II/292, No. 1452

REMARKS: There is one *parashah* plaque. Cf. the similar shield No. 113, and comparisons there. Shields Nos. 117–18 and pointers Nos. 655–56 and 664 are by the same smith.

DONOR: Dr. Harry G. Friedman

## 115

TORAH SHIELD   X 1952-3   (*Illus. p. 129*)

Vienna, 1872–1903

Firm of Josef Lechner, active 1871–1903

Silver

H 48.1  W 38.0 cm

HALLMARKS:   *CITY:* Rohrwasser, p. 19, second row, third from left

*MAKER:* Neuwirth, II/21, No. 1223

INSCRIPTION: in lower cartouche: שייך למענדל הערמאן נ"י// בן/ מ' אסתר/ ע/ה// ע/ז' מ' בלימלא תי בת מ' אסתר פראדל ע"ה "Belongs to Mendel Hermann . . . son of . . . the late Esther . . . , with his wife Blimela . . . daughter of the late . . . Esther Freidl . . ."

REMARKS: The back cover of the plaque box is missing and the shield is damaged.

DONOR: Jewish Cultural Reconstruction

## 116

TORAH SHIELD   F 3182   (*Illus. p. 129*)

Vienna, 1872–1922

Theodor Dorr (?)

Silver: repoussé, engraved, gilt

H 39.4  W 34.5 cm

HALLMARKS:   *CITY:* Rohrwasser, p. 19, second row, third from right; p. 15, upper left

*MAKER:* Neuwirth, I/154, No. 2178 (?)

REMARKS: The back cover of the *parashah* plaque box is missing.

DONOR: Dr. Harry G. Friedman

## 117

TORAH SHIELD   F 252   (*Illus. p. 129*)

Vienna, 1878–1908

Johann Ziehrer, active 1878–1908

Silver: cast (?), repoussé, engraved, parcel-gilt

H 39.3  W 27.3 cm

HALLMARKS:   *CITY:* Neuwirth, p. 19, second row, third from right

*MAKER:* Neuwirth, II/292; No. 1452

REMARKS: There are two *parashah* plaques. See shield No. 114 for other Judaica by Ziehrer at The Jewish Museum.

DONOR: Dr. Harry G. Friedman

## 118

TORAH SHIELD   F 955   (*Illus. p. 130*)

Vienna, 1878–1908

Johann Ziehrer, active 1878–1908

Silver: repoussé, engraved

H 37.9  W 25.7 cm

HALLMARKS:   *CITY:* Rohrwasser, p. 19, second row, third from left

*MAKER:* Neuwirth, II/292; No. 1452

REMARKS: See shield No. 114 for other Judaica by Ziehrer at The Jewish Museum.

DONOR: Dr. Harry G. Friedman

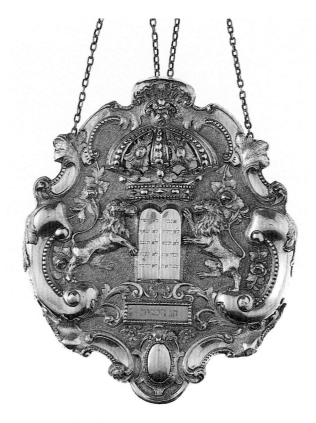

No. 110  x 1952–41

No. 111  F 3045

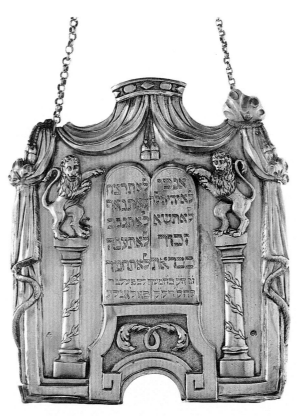

No. 112  JM 65–59

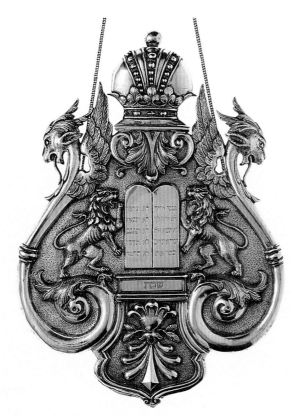

No. 113  F 246

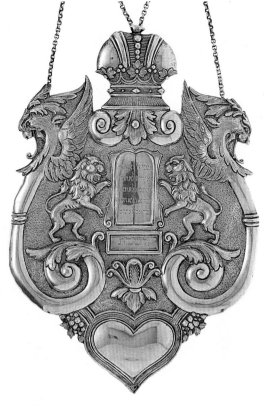

No. 114  F 245

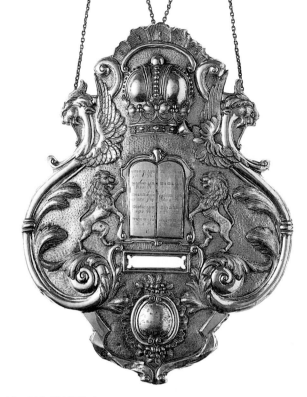

No. 115  X 1952–3

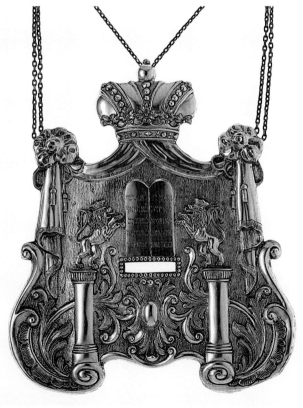

No. 116  F 3182

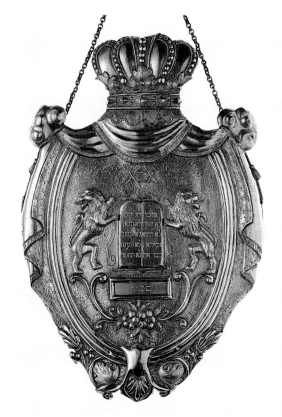

No. 117  F 252

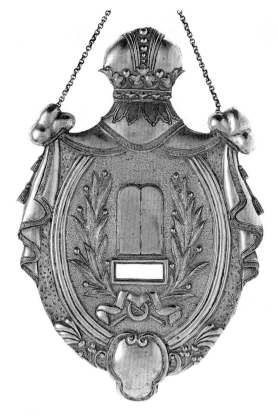

No. 118  F 955

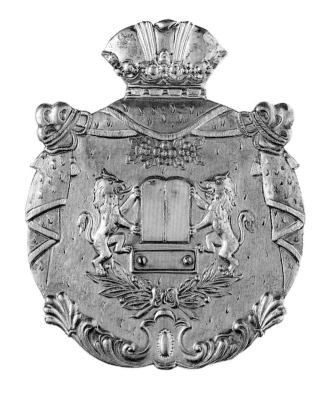

No. 119  F 1231

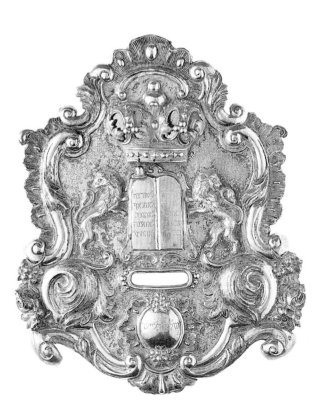

No. 120  X 1952–1

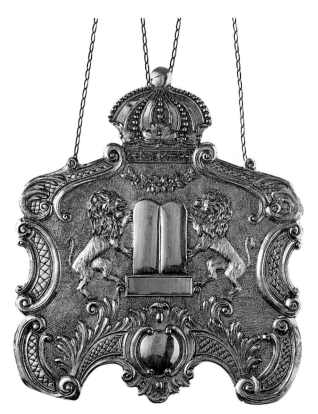

No. 121  X 1952–5

## 118A

TORAH SHIELD M 96
Austria or Poland, 2nd half of 19th century
Silver: repoussé, gilt
H 27.6 W 23.7 cm
HALLMARKS: none
PROVENANCE: The Rose and Benjamin Mintz Collection
REMARKS: The plaque box cover is missing. Though the style
of this shield is Viennese, it might be a Polish copy.
DONOR: Museum purchase

## 119

TORAH SHIELD F 1231 (*Illus. p. 130*)
Vienna (?), 19th century
Brass: silver-plated, gilt
H 30.5 W 25.1 cm
HALLMARKS: none
DONOR: Dr. Harry G. Friedman

## 120

TORAH SHIELD X 1952–1 (*Illus. p. 130*)
Vienna, 1872–1903
Georg Stumpner (?), active ca. 1886–1903
Silver: repoussé, gilt
H 43.5 W 36.5 cm
HALLMARKS: *CITY:* Rohrwasser, p. 19, 2nd row, 800 large
*MAKER:* Neuwirth, II/238, No. 855 (?)
INSCRIPTION: in lower cartouche: שלום בלייער, "Shalom
Bleier."
REMARKS: The back cover of the plaque box is missing, as are
several bells on the crown. The inscription probably refers
to the name of the donor.
DONOR: Jewish Cultural Reconstruction

## 121

TORAH SHIELD X 1952–5 (*Illus. p. 130*)
Vienna, 1880(?)–1922
Salomon Wertheimer, Simon Witz, or Sigmund Maudler
Silver: repoussé
H 46.2 W 40.2 cm
HALLMARKS: *CITY:* Neuwirth, pl. 7/2, 10
*MAKER:* "SW" or "SM" in rectangle
DONOR: Jewish Cultural Reconstruction

## 122

TORAH SHIELD F 5145 (*Illus. p. 132*)
Austria (?), late 19th century
Brass: die-stamped, engraved, silver-plated
H 34.5 W 25.0 cm
HALLMARKS: none
INSCRIPTION: on the groundline: פ' ק' נייסאנדעטצער ע' ב' פ'
א' ב' פ' א', "P … s[on of] A. Neusandetzer …"

REMARKS: There is one *parashah* plaque. For an almost identical shield see PBNY 1977, No. 102).
DONOR: Dr. Harry G. Friedman

## 123

TORAH SHIELD F 240 (*Illus. p. 132*)
Austria (?), late 19th–early 20th century
Brass: die-stamped, chased, silver-plated
H 31.8 W 22.5 cm
HALLMARKS: none
REMARKS: The back cover of the *parashah* plaque box is miss-
ing, as are the plaques.
DONOR: Dr. Harry G. Friedman

## 124

TORAH SHIELD F 3861 (*Illus. p. 132*)
Austria (?), 1935 (inscription) (?)
Silver: repoussé, engraved
H 32.8 W 24.1 cm
HALLMARKS: none
INSCRIPTION: above, flanking: נ' לק' ר' אהרן יצחק// ב'ר צבי,
הלוי "D[onated] to the c[ongregation] [by] Aaron Isaac
son of Zvi ha-Levi"; on lower panel: נפטר יח' כסלו תרצו,
"Died 18 Kislev (5)696" (= 25 November 1935)
REMARKS: The entire lower panel bears traces of an erased
three(?)- line Hebrew inscription (originally from column
base to column base). The front of the plaque box is miss-
ing.
DONOR: Dr. Harry G. Friedman

## 125

TORAH SHIELD JM 12–57 (*Illus. p. 132*)
Nágyszeben (Hermannstadt), 1776–78
Michael Gross (?), active 1767–78
Silver: repoussé, cast, parcel-gilt
H 32.3 W 22.5 cm
HALLMARKS: *CITY:* Kőseghy 1275 (var.); "13"
*MAKER:* Kőseghy 1472
PROVENANCE: The ancestors of B.W. Huebsch
REMARKS: There is one *parashah* plaque. Beneath the plaque
box, on the backwall, the word שבת, "Sabbath," is
engraved, but the work is unfinished. Various elements are
missing: a motif above the plaque box, stones on the lintel,
Aaron's censer. The positions of the Ark of the Covenant
and of the eagle may originally have been different. In the
Museum files, there is a reference to pointer No. 724 in
association with this shield. See finials No. 321, with identical marks. Cf. Perry's Tel Aviv, 1986, No. 195, a shield from
Debrezen, ca. 1800.
BIBLIOGRAPHY: Kayser, No. 195
DONOR: B.W. Huebsch

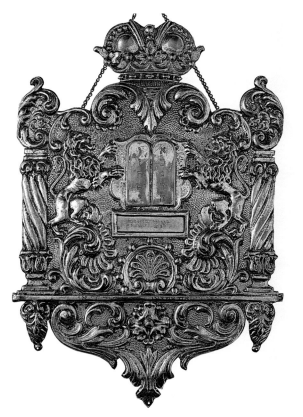

No. 122　F 5145

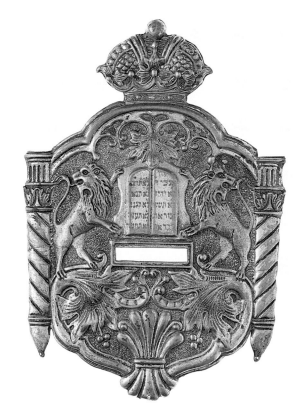

No. 123　F 240

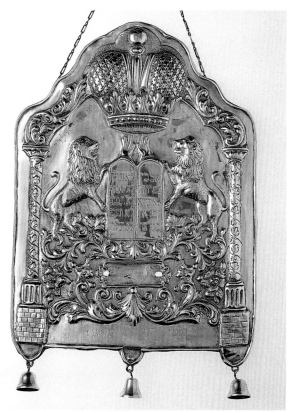

No. 124　F 3861

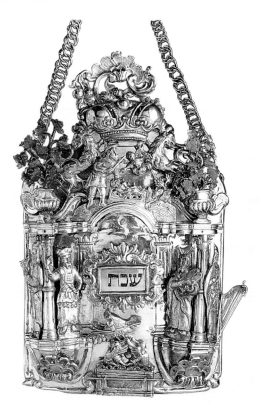

No. 125　JM 12–57

## 126

TORAH SHIELD JM 55–59 (*Illus. p. 134*)
Bohemia (?), 1802/03 (inscription)
Silver: repoussé, engraved
H 17.7 W 15.4 cm
HALLMARKS: none
INSCRIPTION: in lower cartouche: תקס״ג /לפרט, "(5)563" (=1802/03)
DONOR: Mrs. Arthur J. Sussel

## 127

TORAH SHIELD F 1945 (*Illus. p. 134*)
Galicia, 1839/40 (inscription)
Silver
H 15.5 W 12.4 cm
HALLMARKS: "TK" in rectangle
INSCRIPTION: on column bases: תר׳ //שנת, [In the] year (5)600" (=1839/40); in central, arched panel: זה הציץ שייך להאשה/ איידל צפרה/ בת ר׳ אהרן/ חייקעס, "This is the Torah Shield (*tzitz*) belonging to the woman Eidel Tzipporah daughter of Aaron Chaikes"; on both sides: זה נדר להחבורה/ קדושה// פאר מגבעות עים(!) צבאות/ ישראל, "This was pledged to the Holy Society of Decorated Turbans with the Hosts of Israel."
REMARKS: The date appears to be engraved over an erasure. The term *tzitz*, literally a blossom, is occasionally applied to a Torah Shield for, like the term *ḥoshen*, it was a name for the High Priest's breastplate; the term *pe'er migba'at*, "decorated turban," from Exodus 39:28, also refers to part of the High Priest's costume. The significance of the name of the society, and its nature, are unclear.
DONOR: Dr. Harry G. Friedman

## 128

TORAH SHIELD F 3428 (*Illus. p. 134*)
Bohemia (?), 1858/59
Silver: repoussé, engraved
H 18.5 W 14.5 cm
HALLMARKS: none
INSCRIPTION: on lower panel: ר׳ יואל/ בן מאיר/ פ(?) תריט, "Joel son of Me'ir …, (5)619" (=1858/59)
REMARKS: Within the Ark of the Law is a Torah Scroll (possibly later). There are traces of several missing elements in the upper portion of the shield.
DONOR: Dr. Harry G. Friedman

## 129

TORAH SHIELD JM 49–61 (*Illus. p. 134*)
Bohemia or Poland (?), late 18th century (?)
Silver: repoussé, engraved
H 23.8 W 18.6 cm
HALLMARKS: none
INSCRIPTION: on lower front: "S.S." (repeated in grafitto on reverse)
DONOR: Samuel and Lucille Lemberg

## 130

TORAH SHIELD X 1952–42
Pressburg, 1810
Adam Renner, active 1803–37
Silver: repoussé, engraved, parcel-gilt
H 33.8 W 25.7 cm
HALLMARKS: *CITY:* cf. Kőseghy 1816
       *MAKER:* Kőseghy 1857
INSCRIPTION: on central panel: חברה קדישא ג״ח, "Holy B[enevolent] Society"
REMARKS: The central panel is a sheet of silver soldered over the *parashah* plaque window, and thus the inscription is later.
DONOR: Jewish Cultural Reconstruction

## 131

TORAH SHIELD JM 24–59 (*Illus. p. 135*)
Pressburg, 1812
Adam Renner, active 1803–37
Silver: repoussé
H 45.7 W 28.7 cm
HALLMARKS: *CITY:* cf. Kőseghy 1817
       *MAKER:* Kőseghy 1858
INSCRIPTION: on lower reverse: ח ק׳, "H[oly] (Burial) S[ociety]"
REMARKS: The window of the plaque box has been covered over with a sheet of silver. See shield No. 130, by the same smith, for further remarks.
DONOR: Jewish Cultural Reconstruction

## 132

TORAH SHIELD X 1983–15 (*Illus. p. 135*)
Hirschberg (?), 19th century
Silver: repoussé, engraved
H 28.0 W 18.8 cm
HALLMARKS: *CITY:* R³ 2570 (var.); "12"

## 133

TORAH SHIELD M 14 (*Illus. p. 135*)
Hirschberg (?), 19th century
Silver: repoussé
H 23.7 W 19.7 cm
HALLMARKS: Stag running to right, in rectangle; "12"
PROVENANCE: The Rose and Benjamin Mintz Collection
REMARKS: There is one *parashah* plaque.
DONOR: Museum purchase

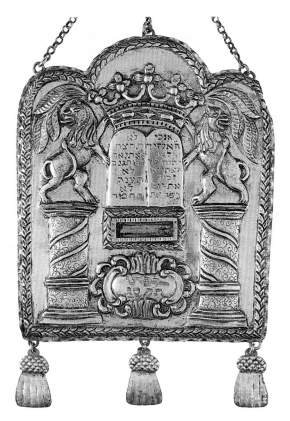

No. 126   JM 55–59

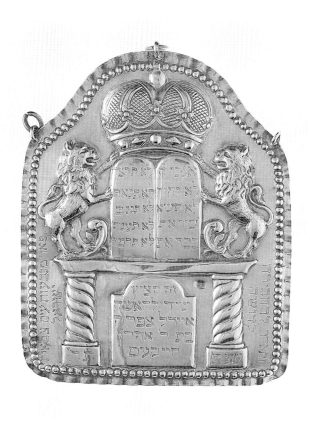

No. 127   F 1945

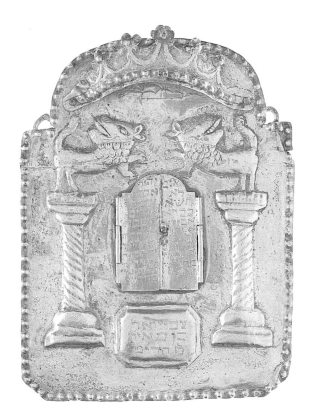

No. 128   F 3428

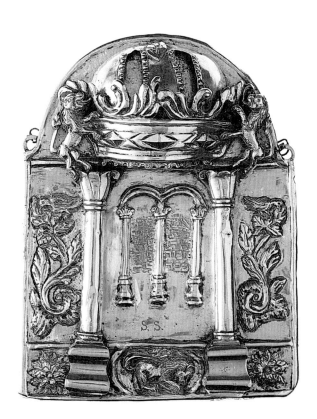

No. 129   JM 49–61

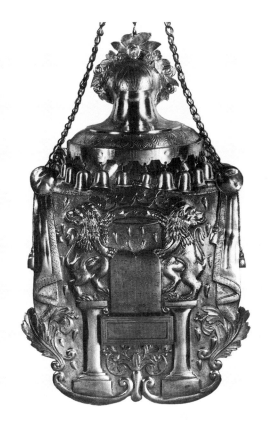

No. 131  JM 24–59

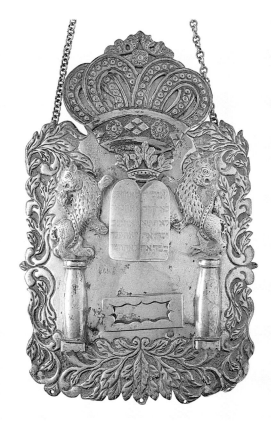

No. 132  X 1983–15

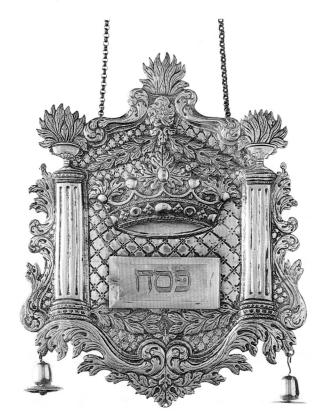

No. 133  M 14

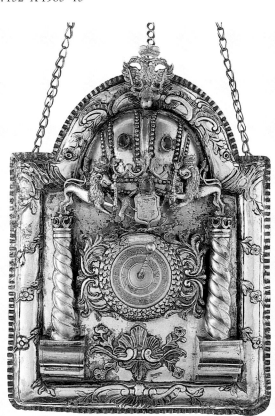

No. 134  F 3459

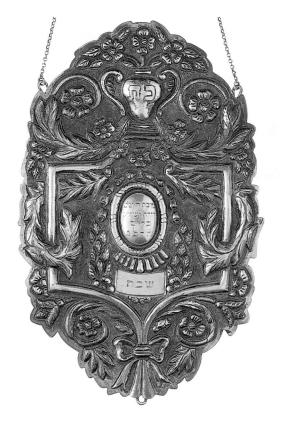

No. 135  F 5540

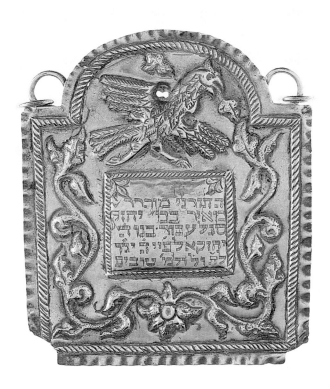

No. 136  F 3456

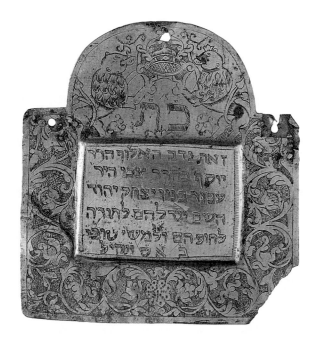

No. 137  JM 32–55

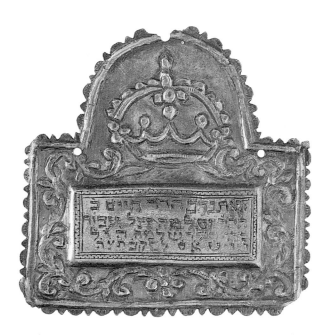

No. 138  JM 34–55

## 134

TORAH SHIELD  F 3459  (*Illus. p. 135*)

Hungary (?), late 18th–early 19th century; 1920/21 (inscription)

Silver: repoussé, cast, engraved, parcel-gilt; glass

H 31.8  W 23.6 cm

HALLMARKS: none

INSCRIPTION: on small shield: קודש/ לה׳, "Holy unto the Lord"; on disk: יעקב אריה זילבערמאנן ני׳ וזוגתו מ׳ פעסל/ בפעסט ת׳ר׳פ׳א, "Jacob Arye Silbermann . . . and his spouse . . . Pesl . . ., in Pest, (5)681" (=1920/21)

REMARKS: There is a rotating disk inscribed with seven *parashah* names. The right lion is restored; the double-headed eagle at the top may be a later addition.

DONOR: Dr. Harry G. Friedman

## 135

TORAH SHIELD  F 5540  (*Illus. p. 136*)

Hungary (?), 1862/63 (inscription)(?)

Silver: repoussé, engraved

H 27.7  W 18.4 cm

HALLMARKS: none

INSCRIPTION: in central cartouche: נדבת ה׳ ש״ם/ דורה ועיזיק/ בלום/ ת׳ר׳כ׳ג׳, "Donation of . . . Dora and Eizik Blum, (5)623" (=1862/63); on upper urn: כ ת, "C[rown of] T[orah]"

REMARKS: The Museum card file reflects a different reading of the inscription: . . . , נדבת ח׳ ש״ס, "Donation of the T[almud] S[ociety] . . . ."

DONOR: Dr. Harry G. Friedman

## 136

TORAH SHIELD  F 3456  (*Illus. p. 136*)

Galicia, early 19th century

Silver: repoussé

H 13.2  W 11.4 cm

HALLMARKS: none

INSCRIPTION: in central panel: ז׳נ׳/ התורני מהורר׳ מאיר במו״׳ יחזק׳/ סגל עבור בנו ה׳/ יחזקאל פ׳יי ה״י יג׳׳ד/ לת׳ ו׳ל ולמ׳ טובים, T[his was] d[onated by] the learned R[abbi] Me'ir [son of] Ezeki[el] Segal, on behalf of his son, the b[oy] Ezekiel ? . . , [May] the Lord ra[ise] him to the T[orah] and to [the marriage canopy] and to g[ood] d[eeds]"; on reverse, in Latin characters: "Kamienez/ Litowsk/ 1916"

REMARKS: The lower corners are broken off; several stone-settings appear to be missing.

DONOR: Dr. Harry G. Friedman

## 137

TORAH SHIELD  JM 32–55  (*Illus. p. 136*)

Galicia, 1749/50 (inscription)

Silver: chased, engraved

H 11.7  W 11.2 cm

HALLMARKS: none

INSCRIPTION: on central panel: זאת נדב האלוף כרר/ יוסף בהרר צבי היו׳/ עבור בניו יצחק (ו)יהוד(ה)/ השם יגדלהם (!) לתורה/ לחופהם (!) ולמשי (!) טוביי (!) א׳ ס׳ ת׳ק׳י׳ל׳, "This was donated by the leader . . . R[abbi] Joseph s[on of] . . . R[abbi] Zvi . . . for his sons Isaac [and] Judah, May the Lord raise them to the Torah, to their marriage canopy, and to goo[d] de[eds] . . . A[men] s[elah]. (5)510" (=1749/50); below crown: כ ת, "C[rown of] T[orah]"

DONOR: Mrs. Bernard Kahn

## 138

TORAH SHIELD  JM 34–55  (*Illus. p. 136*)

Galicia, 1754/55 (?) (inscription)

Silver: chased

H 9.7  W 10.0 cm

HALLMARKS: none

INSCRIPTION: on raised panel: זאת נדב הרר חיים ב׳/ ה׳ר׳ר׳ שלמה זצל עבור/ בנו הילד שלמה ה׳ י׳ ל׳/ ו ל ט׳א׳ס׳ לפק כ׳ת׳צ׳ה׳, "This was donated by R[abbi] Ḥayyim, s[on of] the late R[abbi] Solomon, on behalf of his son the boy Solomon. May the Lord r[aise him] to [the Torah] and to [the marriage canopy] and to g[ood deeds]. (5)495 (or [5]515)" (=1736/37 or 1754/55)

DONOR: Mrs. Bernard Kahn

## 139

TORAH SHIELD  M 206  (*Illus. p. 138*)

Galicia (?), 1779/80 (inscription)

Silver: repoussé, parcel-gilt (?)

H 15.1  W 12.4 cm

HALLMARKS: none

INSCRIPTION: on lower raised panel: כתר תורה/ זה הטס שייך להאלוף/ המרומם הרר מאיר/ בהרר דוד יצו/בשנת ת׳ק׳מ׳ לפ׳ק׳, "Crown of Torah, This Torah Shield belongs to the exalted leader R[abbi] Me'ir s[on of] R[abbi] David, in the year (5)540" (=1779/80); on the reverse: זה הטס שייך/ לח״ק ל׳מ׳ דק״ק פיסק, "This Torah Shield belongs to the H[oly] S[ociety] for [the study of] M[ishnayot] . . . of the h[oly] c[ommunity of] Pisek."

PROVENANCE: The Rose and Benjamin Mintz Collection

REMARKS: The abbreviation ל׳מ׳ in the inscription probably means "for the study of Mishnah." Shields Nos. 155 and 160 belonged to the same society.

BIBLIOGRAPHY: Kayser, No. 49

DONOR: Museum purchase

## 140

TORAH SHIELD  F 3714  (*Illus. p. 138*)

Galicia, prior to 1809

Silver: repoussé

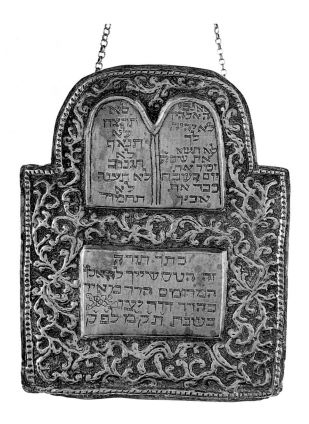

No. 139  M 206

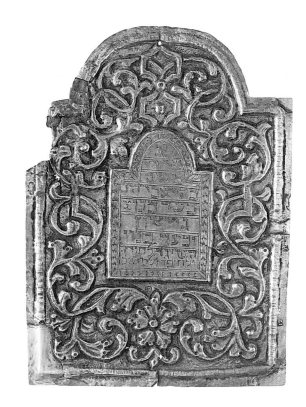

No. 140  F 3714

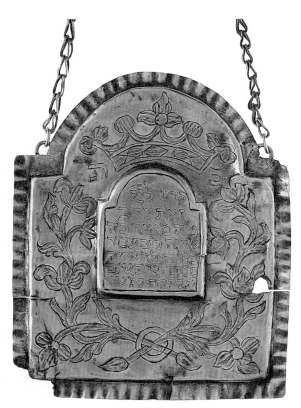

No. 141  M 203

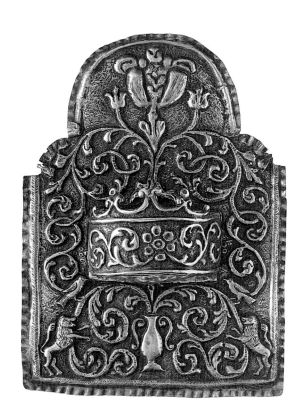

No. 142  M 428

H 15.5 W 7.3 cm

HALLMARKS: "12"; "K" in script; R³ 7884 (Austro-Hungarian re-marking)

INSCRIPTION: on the arched panel: כהר /משה /הרר /ז׳נ׳
אברהם, /בעד בנו /גרשון /ובעד בנוון(!)/ הש יגד לתתורה/
ולחופה ולמ טוב, "T[his was] d[onated by] R[abbi] Moses s[on of] Abraham, on behalf of his son Gershon, and behalf of his [other] sons (?), May the L[ord] rai[se him] to the Torah and to the marriage canopy and to goo[d] d[eeds.]"

DONOR: Dr. Harry G. Friedman

## 141

TORAH SHIELD M 203 (*Illus. p. 138*)

Galicia, early 19th century

Silver: repoussé, engraved

H 14.5 W 12.8 cm

HALLMARKS: none

INSCRIPTION: flanking crown: כ ת, "C[rown of] T[orah]"; in arched panel: קדש לה׳/ זאת נדב/ מ׳ה מאיר ב״ה/ אריה
ליב עבור/ בנו הילד אריה/ מנחם וב׳ז השם/ יג ל׳ת ל׳ח ל׳מ
ט׳ו, "Holy to the Lord, This was donated by . . . Me'ir son of . . . Arye Leib, on behalf of his son, the boy Arye Menaḥem, and by merit of this [donation] may the Lord ra[ise him] to the T[orah], to the m[arriage canopy and] to go[od] d[eeds.]"

PROVENANCE: The Rose and Benjamin Mintz Collection

REMARKS: The lower left corner of the shield is missing. In the inscription, the abbreviated phrase . . . וב׳ז השם יג may also be interpreted: "and through the beneficence of the Lord, may he be raised . . . ."

BIBLIOGRAPHY: Kayser, No. 49

DONOR: Museum purchase

## 142

TORAH SHIELD M 428 (*Illus. p. 138*)

Poland, 19th century

Silver: repoussé

H 18.1 W 13.6 cm

HALLMARKS: none

PROVENANCE: The Rose and Benjamin Mintz Collection

REMARKS: The "crown" seems originally to have been attached lower on the shield between the lions (where there are empty slots). A *parashah* plaque box may have been attached at the present position of the crown. The upper, outer corners were probably modified after damage.

DONOR: Museum purchase

## 143

TORAH SHIELD F 4890 (*Illus. p. 140*)

Galicia, 1814/15 (inscription)

Silver: repoussé, engraved

H 12.9 W 10.8 cm

HALLMARKS: none

INSCRIPTION: around central medallion: ז׳נ׳ מ׳ משה בה׳
אליעזר בנו הילד ידיד׳/ הׄשׄי יג לת׳ וח׳ ומ״ט ת׳ק׳ע׳ה׳,
"T[his was] d[onated by] Moses s[on of] Eliezer, [on behalf of] his son, the infant Jeded[iah ?], May the B[lessed] L[ord] rai[se him] to the T[orah] and to the m[arriage canopy] and to g[ood] d[eeds]. [In the year] (5)575" (=1814/15).

REMARKS: In the inscription, the word "son of " has been corrected, a *mem* having been changed to *bet*.

DONOR: Dr. Harry G. Friedman

## 144

TORAH SHIELD F 3991 (*Illus. p. 140*)

Lvov (?), prior to 1809

Silver (?): repoussé, engraved

H 20.9 W 17.3 cm

HALLMARKS: R³7989; R³7876 (var. with "D"—possibly spurious)

INSCRIPTION: on arched panel: התורני כמהורר/ האלוף/ ז׳נ׳
שלמה זלמן/ בהרר יוסף/ כץ זצל, "T[his was] d[onated] by the leader, the learned Rabbi Solomon Zalman son of the late Rabbi Joseph Katz."

REMARKS: The upper right and lower left corners of this shield are missing. The depiction of the priestly hands in the central panel symbolizes the donor's name, Katz, the Hebrew abbreviation for "Priest of Righteousness."

DONOR: Dr. Harry G. Friedman

## 145

TORAH SHIELD JM 33–55 (*Illus. p. 140*)

Galicia, early 19th century

Silver: repoussé

H 10.8 W 8.8 cm

HALLMARKS: none

INSCRIPTION: in central panel: כ ת, "C[rown of] T[orah]"

REMARKS: There are traces of an erased inscription on the central panel, beneath the present engraving. The upper corners are damaged and patched.

DONOR: Mrs. Bernard Kahn

## 146

TORAH SHIELD M 95 (*Illus. p. 140*)

Galicia, 1762/63 (inscription)

Silver: repoussé

H 13.5 W 11.9 cm

HALLMARKS: none

INSCRIPTION: in upper panel: כ ת, "C[rown of] T[orah]"; in central panel: האלוף הרר א בהר מ׳ זצל עבור בתו ז׳נ׳ ה׳ה׳
זלאטקע השׄי יג׳ לחׄו ולמט א׳ס׳ ל׳ תק׳כד לפק, "T[his was] d[onated by] the leader . . . Rabbi A. son of the late Rabbi M., on behalf of his daughter Zlotke, May the

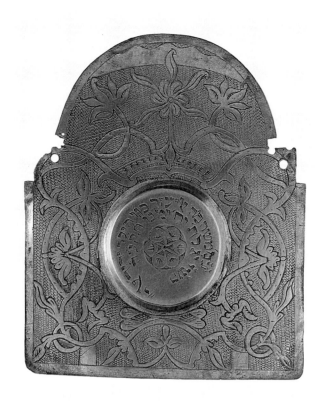

No. 143   F 4890

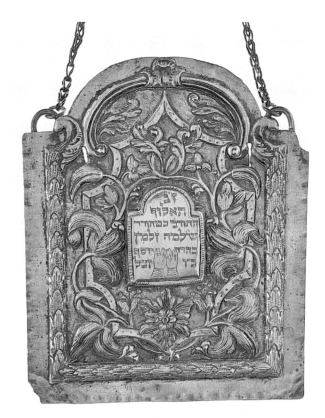

No. 144   F 3991

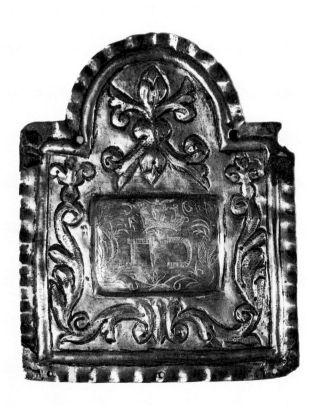

No. 145   JM 33–55

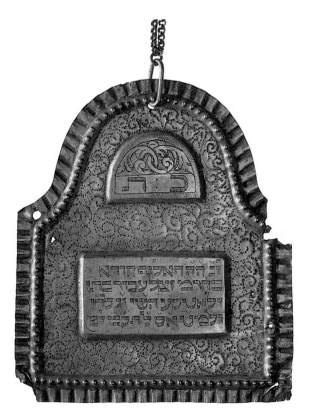

No. 146   M 95

B[lessed] Lor[d] rai[se her] to the m[arriage canopy] and to g[ood] d[eeds]. A[men], s[elah]. (5)523" (=1762/63)
PROVENANCE: The Rose and Benjamin Mintz Collection
DONOR: Museum purchase

## 147

TORAH SHIELD  M 205  (*Illus. p. 142*)
Galicia, 1848/49 (inscription) or earlier
Silver: repoussé
H 11.3  W 9.6 cm
HALLMARKS: none
INSCRIPTION: in central panel and arched panel above: /ת כ
זאת נדב/ ה' יעקב ב"ה משה/ לח"ק חייטים/ בשנת תרט,
"C[rown of] T[orah], This was donated by Jacob ... son of
... Moses to the Holy Society of Tailors, in the year (5)609"
(=1848/49).
PROVENANCE: The Rose and Benjamin Mintz Collection
REMARKS: The inscription may be a palimpsest. Shield No.
148 belonged to the same society.
DONOR: Museum purchase

## 148

TORAH SHIELD  M 204  (*Illus. p. 142*)
Galicia, 1848/49 (inscription)
Silver (?): repoussé
H 13.5  W 11.6 cm
HALLMARKS: none
INSCRIPTION: in crown: ת כ, "C[rown of] T[orah]"; in panel:
זאת נדב הרר אברהם בהרר צבי לח"ק חייטים בשנת
תרט לפק, "This was donated by R[abbi] Abraham s[on
of] R[abbi] Zvi to the H[oly] S[ociety of] Tailors, in the
year (5)609" (=1848/49).
PROVENANCE: The Rose and Benjamin Mintz Collection
REMARKS: The inscription is a palimpsest. Shield No. 147
belonged to the same society.
DONOR: Museum purchase

## 149

TORAH SHIELD  F 4557  (*Illus. p. 142*)
Galicia, 18th–19th century
Silver: engraved, traces of gilt
H 13.0  W 11.6 cm
HALLMARKS: none
INSCRIPTION: on Tablets of the Law: קודש לה', "Holy to the
Lord"
DONOR: Dr. Harry G. Friedman

## 150

TORAH SHIELD  M 13  (*Illus. p. 142*)
Poland, late 18th-early 19th century
Silver: chased, parcel-gilt
H 9.9  W 8.4 cm

HALLMARKS: obliterated
INSCRIPTION: on plaque box: שבת, "Sabbath"
PROVENANCE: The Rose and Benjamin Mintz Collection
DONOR: Museum purchase

## 151

TORAH SHIELD  F 3505  (*Illus. p. 143*)
Galicia, early 19th century
Silver: repoussé, parcel-gilt
H 17.2  W 17.9 cm
HALLMARKS: none
DONOR: Dr. Harry G. Friedman

## 152

TORAH SHIELD  M 233  (*Illus. p. 143*)
Galicia, 1809/10 (inscription)
Silver: repoussé
H 19.7  W 16.3 cm
HALLMARKS: none
INSCRIPTION: on crown: כתר תורה, "Crown of Torah"; in car-
touche: ז'נ הרר אליקום בהרר/ זאב עבור בנו הילד צבי/
הירש ה שית יגדל ה' לת/ לח'/ ומ'ט בשנת ת'קע', "T[his
was] d[onated by] ... Eliakum son of ... Zev, on behalf of
his son, the boy Zvi Hirsch, [May the] L[ord], bl[essed be
His name], raise h[im] to the T[orah], to the m[arriage
canopy] and to g[ood] d[eeds], in the year (5)570"
(=1809/10).
PROVENANCE: The Rose and Benjamin Mintz Collection
DONOR: Museum purchase

## 153

TORAH SHIELD  JM 37–54  (*Illus. p. 143*)
Russia (?), second half of 19th century
Silver: engraved
H 17.4 W 14.4 cm
HALLMARKS: rampant lion to right; "84"; "A.K(?)/18.9"
INSCRIPTION: above crown: ת כ, "C[rown of] T[orah]"; on
upper edge: זאת נדב הרב ני הגביר נחום ציחאנסקע, "This
was donated by the rabbi, the wealthy Naḥum Tziḥonska."
DONOR: Colonel Melvin L. Kralewitch

## 154

TORAH SHIELD  F 3712  (*Illus. p. 143*)
Galicia, 18th–19th century
Copper: chased
H 10.0  W 9.7 cm
HALLMARKS: none
INSCRIPTION: on central medallion: קודש לה', "Holy to the
Lord"
DONOR: Dr. Harry G. Friedman

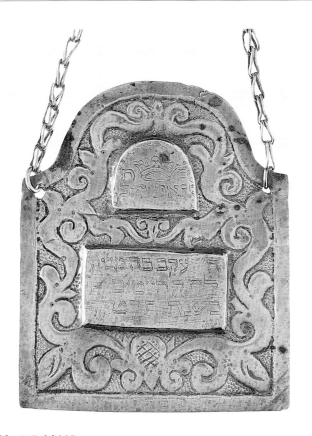

No. 147  M 205

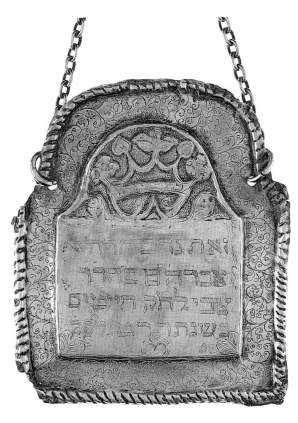

No. 148  M 204

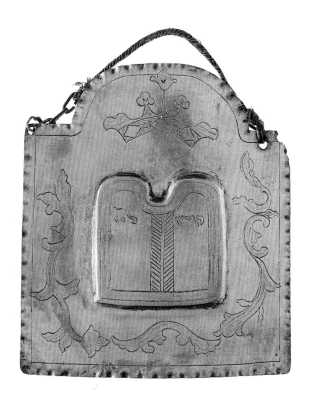

No. 149  F 4557

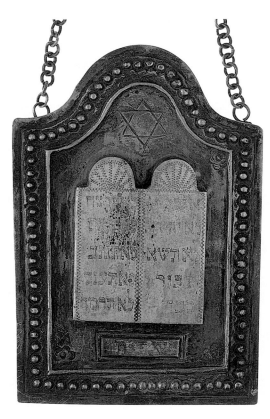

No. 150  M 13

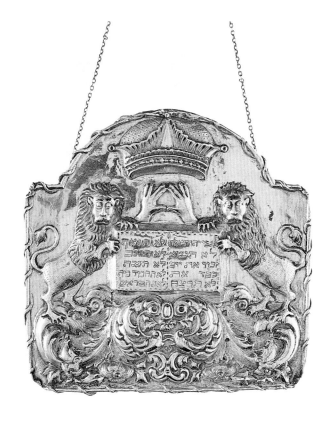

No. 151  F 3505

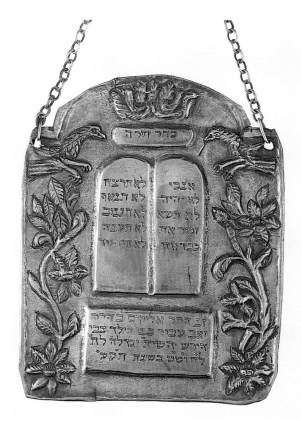

No. 152  M 233

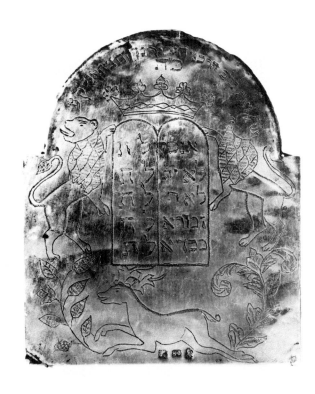

No. 153  JM 37–54

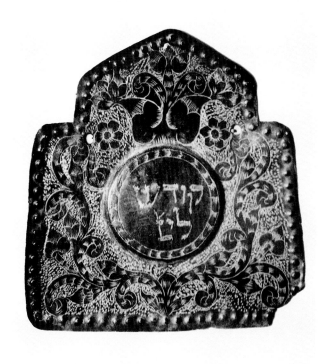

No. 154  F 3712

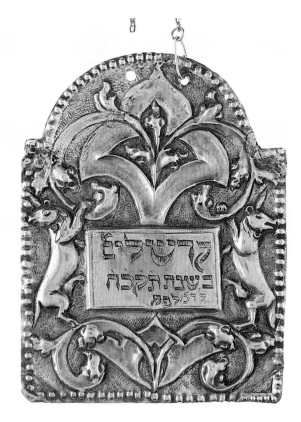

No. 155  M 210

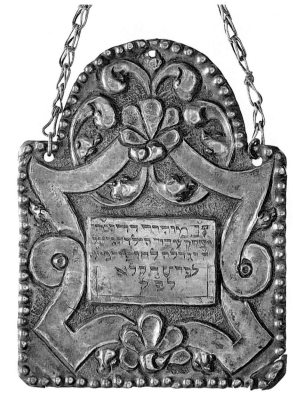

No. 156  M 207

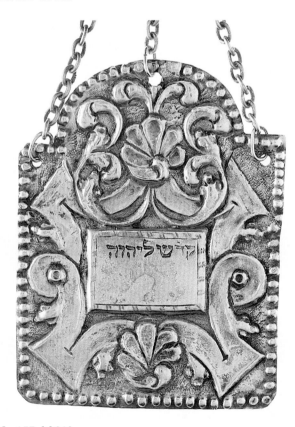

No. 157  M 212

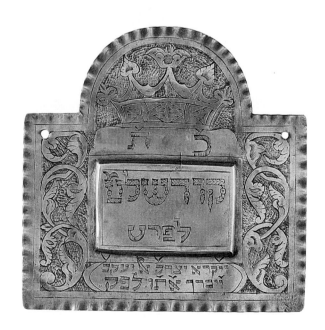

No. 158  F 2417

## 155

TORAH SHIELD M 210  (*Illus. p. 144*)

Galicia (?), 1767/68

Silver: repoussé, engraved

H 14.0  W 11.0 cm

HALLMARKS: none

INSCRIPTION: in central panel: קדש לה'/ בשנת תקכח/ לפק, "Holy to the Lord, in the year (5)528" (=1767/68)(in different script:) ,"לח"מ", "to the S[ociety for the Study of the] M[ishnah]. . ."; on reverse: שייך לח"ק ל"מ דק"ק פיסק, "Belongs to the Holy Society for [the study of] M[ishnayot] . . . of the holy community of Pisek."

PROVENANCE: The Rose and Benjamin Mintz Collection

REMARKS: See remarks, shields Nos. 139 and 160, for the society mentioned in the inscription.

DONOR: Museum purchase

## 156

TORAH SHIELD M 207  (*Illus. p. 144*)

Galicia, 1770/71 (inscription)

Silver: repoussé, engraved

H 13.3  W 10.5 cm

HALLMARKS: none

INSCRIPTION: in central panel: ז"נ מוהרר דוד במ"הר/ יצחק/ עבור הילדה גיטל/ ה' יגדלה לחופ' ולמע"ט/ לפרט תקלא/ לפ'ק, "T[his was] d[onated by] . . . R[abbi] David son of . . . R[abbi] Isaac, on behalf of the girl Gittel, May the Lord raise her to the marriag[e] canopy and to g[ood] de[eds]. (5)531" (=1770/71).

PROVENANCE: The Rose and Benjamin Mintz Collection

REMARKS: Shield No. 157 is of identical design.

DONOR: Museum purchase

## 157

TORAH SHIELD M 212  (*Illus. p. 144*)

Galicia, 19th century

Silver: repoussé

H 12.6  W 10.0 cm

HALLMARKS: none

INSCRIPTION: in central plaque: קדש ליקוק, "Holy to the Lord"

PROVENANCE: The Rose and Benjamin Mintz Collection

REMARKS: Shield No. 156 is of identical design.

DONOR: Museum purchase

## 158

TORAH SHIELD F 2417  (*Illus. p. 144*)

Galicia, 1758/59 (inscription)

Silver: chased, engraved

H 11.3  W 11.6 cm

HALLMARKS: none

INSCRIPTION: under crown: כ ת , "C[rown of] T[orah]"; in central panel: קודש לה'/ לפרט, "Holy to the Lord"; in lower panel: ויקרא יצחק' אל יעקב'/ ויברך א'תי' לפק, Genesis 28:1 (chronogram, [5]519=1758/59)

DONOR: Dr. Harry G. Friedman

## 159

TORAH SHIELD F 3713  (*Illus. p. 146*)

Galicia, 1785/86 (inscription)

Silver: repoussé

H 8.6  W 7.3 cm

HALLMARKS: none

INSCRIPTION: in central panel: זאת נדב' כה' יעקב/ מ' משה/ עבור בנו/ ראובן השם/ יגדל לת' ולח'/ ולמ"ט ב' ת'ק'מ'ו', "This is the dona[tion of] Jacob (son of ?) Moses on behalf of his son Reuben, May the Lord raise [him] to the T[orah] and to the m[arriage canopy] and to g[ood] d[eeds], in [the year] (5)546" (=1785/86).

DONOR: Dr. Harry G. Friedman

## 160

TORAH SHIELD M 211  (*Illus. p. 146*)

Galicia (?), 1782/83 (inscription)

Silver: repoussé

H 16.6  W 15.2 cm

HALLMARKS: none

INSCRIPTION: in central panel: ז"נ מהורר ארי ליב/ בהרר/ ברוך עבור/ בנו הילד יוסף השם/ יגדול (!) לת' ולח' ולמעשי'/ טובים בשנת ת'ק'מ'ג'/ לפק, "T[his was] d[onated by] R[abbi] Ari Leib s[on of] R[abbi] Barukh on behalf of his son the boy Joseph, May the Lord raise [him] to the T[orah], to the m[arriage canopy] and to g[ood] d[eeds], in the year" (=1782/83); in cartouche above: כ' ת', "C[rown of] T[orah]"; on reverse: זה הטס/ שייך לח"ק ל"מ דק"ק פיסק, "This is the Torah Shield belonging to the H[oly] S[ociety] for [the study of] M[ishnayot]. . . of the h[oly] c[ommunity] of Pisek."

PROVENANCE: The Rose and Benjamin Mintz Collection

REMARKS: The lower corners have been restored. For this society, see shields Nos. 139 and 155.

DONOR: Museum purchase

## 161

TORAH SHIELD F 4880  (*Illus. p. 146*)

Galicia, 18th–19th century

Silver: repoussé, engraved; stones

H 25.4  W 21.6 cm

HALLMARKS: none

INSCRIPTION: on crown: כתר תורה, "Crown of Torah"

REMARKS: Pairs of holes around the edge of this shield may indicate that it had been fastened to a textile, possibly a Torah Ark Curtain. This feature appears on a similar shield at the Skirball Museum, Los Angeles, 7.7.

DONOR: Dr. Harry G. Friedman

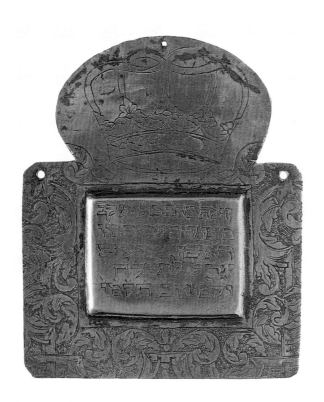

No. 159  F 3713

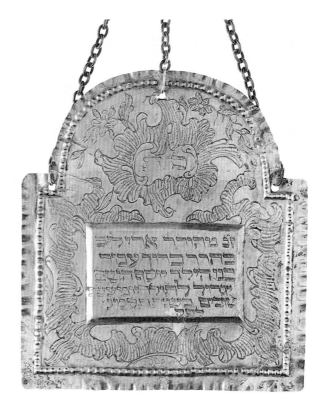

No. 160  M 211

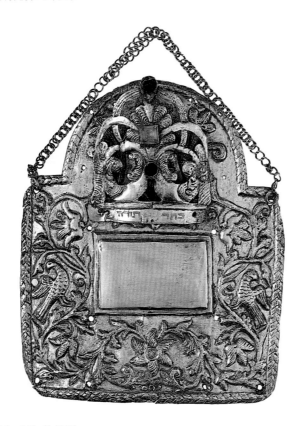

No. 161  F 4880

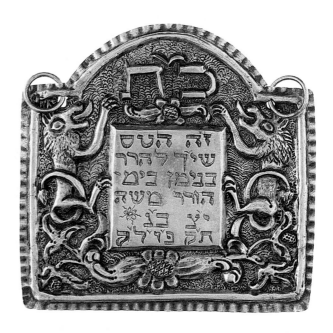

No. 162  F 4039

## 162

TORAH SHIELD  F 4039  (*Illus. p. 146*)
Galicia, 1825/26 (inscription)
Silver: repoussé
H 13.6  W 14.3 cm
HALLMARKS: none
INSCRIPTION: in central panel: זה הטס/ שייך לה'/ בנימין
ב'/ מ/ הורר משה/ י"צ ב"נ [כ"נ ?]/ ת"ק פ"ו ל"ק, "This Torah
Shield, belongs to . . . Benjamin s[on of] . . . R[abbi] Moses
. . ., (5)586" (=1825/26); above: כ"ת, "C[rown of] T[orah]."
DONOR: Dr. Harry G. Friedman

## 163

TORAH SHIELD  S 1363b  (*Illus. p. 148*)
Poland (?), 1816/17 (inscription)
Silver: engraved, parcel-gilt; stones
H 25.5  W 18.2 cm
HALLMARKS: none
INSCRIPTION: on crown: נאום אליהו במוהרר ישראל זצל,
"Word of Elijah s[on of] . . . the late R[abbi] Israel"; at bot-
tom of Tablets of the Law: תק עז לפכ, "(5)577" (=1816/17);
around outer frame of Tablets: the priestly blessing;
around inner frame: וי'יר'צ' א'ח'א'ב' ל'קראת', modified
from 1 Kings 18: 46 (chronogram for [5]577 = 1816/17);
קדש לה', "Holy to the Lord," Exodus 28: 36.
REMARKS: There is a rotating disk inscribed with six *para-
shah* names. Behind the crown is a pair of priestly hands.
Some of the stones are missing.
BIBLIOGRAPHY: Kayser, No. 18b
DONOR: Max M. Karp, New York, in memory of his father,
Micha L. Karp

## 164

TORAH SHIELD  M 167  (*Illus. p. 148*)
Poland (?), 19th century
Copper: repoussé, silvered
H 22.2  W 17.8 cm
HALLMARKS: none
INSCRIPTION: on crown: כתר תורה, "Crown of Torah"
PROVENANCE: The Rose and Benjamin Mintz Collection
REMARKS: There is a rotating disk with six *parashah* names.
DONOR: Museum purchase

## 165

TORAH SHIELD  F 2550  (*Illus. p. 148*)
Galicia, early 19th century
Copper: repoussé, silvered
H 15.1  W 12.8 cm
HALLMARKS: none
INSCRIPTION: in central panel: שבת, "Sabbath"; in lower car-
touche: ז, נ/ הרר יהוד[ה]/ ב'ה שרגא, "T[his was] d[onated
by] Juda[h] s[on of] Shraga."

PROVENANCE: S. M. Salomon Collection, London
REMARKS: The Museum card file indicates that a crown
attached to this shield, not considered original, was removed and placed on shield F 254 (deaccessioned 1993).
Various minor elements are missing, and the shield has
been extensively repaired and restored. The provenance is
based on information at The Jewish Museum.
DONOR: Dr. Harry G. Friedman

## 166

TORAH SHIELD  F 2806  (*Illus. p. 148*)
Galicia (?), early 19th century
Silver: repoussé
H 18.7  W 16.2 cm
HALLMARKS: "12"; "Szulcz" in script, in rectangle
INSCRIPTION: on crown: כתר תורה, "Crown of Torah"; on
plaque box cover: שבת, "Sabbath"
REMARKS: The plaque box cover is a replacement, and the
crown may not be original.
DONOR: Dr. Harry G. Friedman

## 167

TORAH SHIELD  F 3444  (*Illus. p. 149*)
Kamienez (?), 1768/69 (inscription)
Silver: repoussé
H 13.5  W 11.9 cm
HALLMARKS: none
INSCRIPTION: on central boss: ז'נ'/ ה'ה' הרר יהוד[ה]/ ב"ה יוס',
עב' בנו/ ב יני' מרד(כ)י ה' י' ל'/ ל ל ט, "T[his was] d[onated
by] . . . Juda[h] s[on of] Jose[ph] on be[half of] his son . . .
Mord[ecai], [May the] Lord raise him to [the Torah], to
[the marriage canopy and] to [good deeds]"; in lower car-
touche: תקכט, "(5)529" (=1768/69)
REMARKS: In the inscription, the abbreviation בי יני' may
mean "an only son, the infant."
DONOR: Dr. Harry G. Friedman

## 168

TORAH SHIELD  D 131  (*Illus. p. 149*)
Galicia, late 18th–early 19th century
Silver: repoussé, parcel-gilt
H 19.1  W 15.5 cm
HALLMARKS: none
INSCRIPTION: on central panel: נעשה עי הגבאי/ ר' איצק ב'ר'
משה/ גאלדשטיין, "Made by the *gabbai* Itzik s[on of]
Moses Goldstein"
PROVENANCE: The Mattenbuden Synagogue, Danzig
EXHIBITIONS: NYJM 1981; Braunschweig 1982
BIBLIOGRAPHY: Danzig 1904, No. 28; Danzig 1933, No. 131, pl.
7; *Danzig 1939*/1982, No. 71
DONOR: The Jewish Community of Danzig

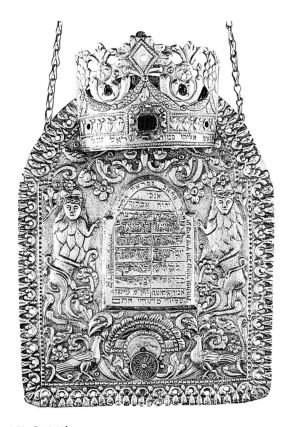

No. 163  S 1363b

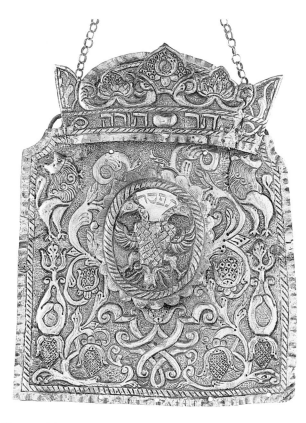

No. 164  M 167

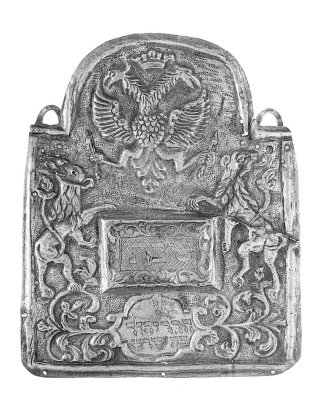

No. 165  F 2550

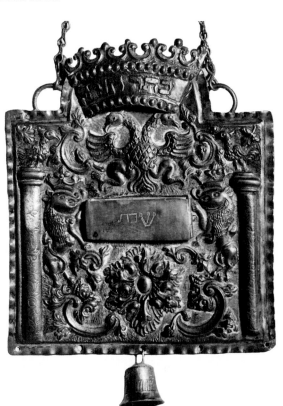

No. 166  F 2806

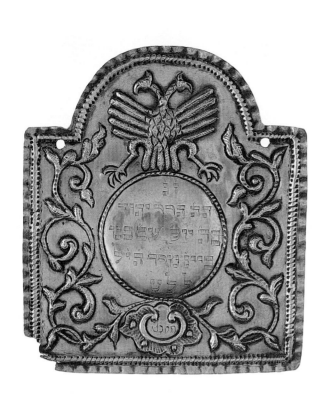

No. 167  F 3444

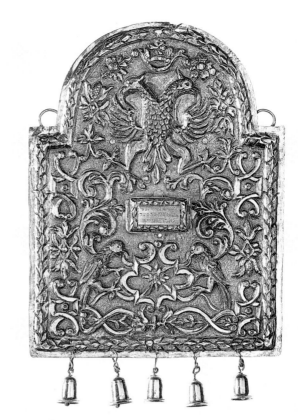

No. 168  D 131

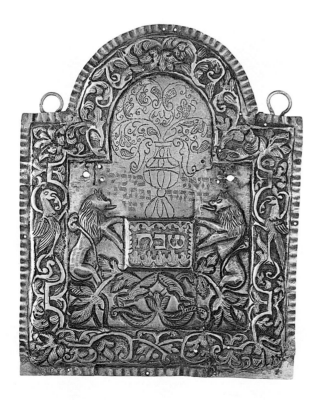

No. 169  F 2744

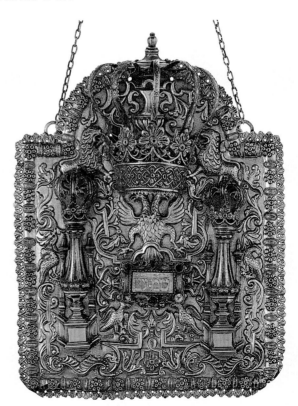

No. 170  F 2547

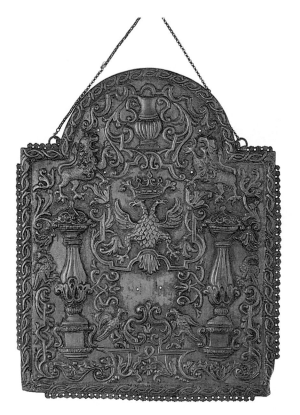

No. 171  M 286

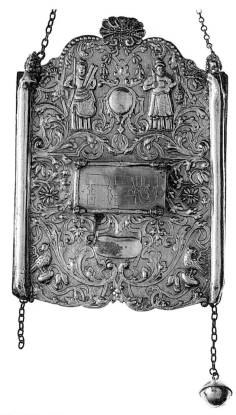

No. 172  1993–146

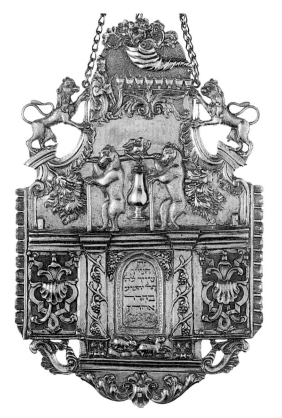

No. 173  F 2595

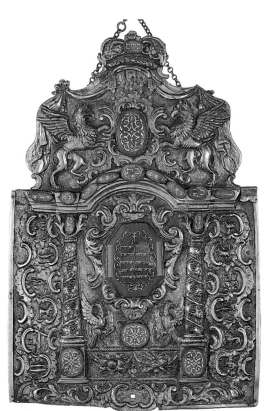

No. 174  F 2280

## 169

TORAH SHIELD  F 2744  (*Illus. p. 149*)
Galicia, 18th–19th century
Silver: repoussé
H 21.3  W 17.4 cm
HALLMARKS: none
INSCRIPTION: on central panel: שבת, "Sabbath"; flanking
vase: יחיאל מיכיל (!)/ בן כהרר נפתלי/ יצו, "Yeḥiel Michel
son of . . . R[abbi] Naphtali . . ."
DONOR: Dr. Harry G. Friedman

## 170

TORAH SHIELD  F 2547  (*Illus. p. 149*)
Galicia, early 19th century
Silver: repoussé, cast, gilt
H 21.0  W 24.8 cm
HALLMARKS: "BK" in rectangle; "12" in rectangle
REMARKS: There is one *parashah* plaque. Shield No. 171 is of
similar design.
DONOR: Dr. Harry G. Friedman

## 171

TORAH SHIELD  M 286  (*Illus. p. 150*)
Galicia, early 19th century
Brass: repoussé
H 29.2  W 24.0 cm
HALLMARKS: none
PROVENANCE: The Rose and Benjamin Mintz Collection
REMARKS: See shield No. 170, of similar design. The *parashah*
plaque box and crown are missing, as are parts of the outer
border.
DONOR: Museum purchase

## 172

TORAH SHIELD  1993–146  (*Illus. p. 150*)
Galicia (?), early 18th century
Silver: repoussé, cast
H 25.2  W 18.6 cm
HALLMARKS:  Eagle (?) in squarish oval
    MAKER: "CM" in rectangular linear frame
REMARKS: Finials No. 331 were acquired together with this
shield.
DONOR: Else Samson, in memory of Rabbi Wilhelm Buch-
heim of Dortmund

## 173

TORAH SHIELD  F 2595  (*Illus. p. 150*)
Brody (?), 18th century
Silver: repoussé, cast, engraved; velvet
H 32.9  W 21.8 cm
HALLMARKS: none

INSCRIPTION: in lower niche: זה/ הציץ/ שייך לה'/ הר יהושע/
ברזר/ אהרן, "This shield (*tzitz*) belongs to . . . Joshua s[on
of] . . . Aaron"
PROVENANCE: Matthias-Bersohn-Museum, Warsaw
REMARKS: In the inscription, the *vav* of the name Joshua is a
correction. This shield later served as a Hanukkah lamp
backwall. The uppermost piece, not original, depicts the
lighting of the Hanukkah lights, and two sockets for a row
of burners remain above the ends of the medial architrave.
The piece with two bears carrying a jar is a later addition,
probably replacing a *parashah* plaque box. The rabbits,
too, seem to be later, as does the uppermost piece, which
occupies the position of the original crown. In Lewin, this
piece is described as "Polnisch, 1730/40."
BIBLIOGRAPHY: Lewin, p. 373, upper left
DONOR: Dr. Harry G. Friedman

## 174

TORAH SHIELD  F 2280  (*Illus. p. 150*)
Lvov (?), 1800/01 (inscription)
Silver: repoussé, parcel-gilt; semiprecious stones, inlaid in
gold
H 31.4  W 21.4 cm
HALLMARKS:  CITY: defaced; Rohrwasser, p. 12, bottom row,
    right; p. 11, upper row, left ("D"=Lemberg)
    MAKER: unclear "L/LS"(?), "L/LC"(?), "L/LG"
    (?) in irregular square
INSCRIPTION: in upper cartouches: כ״ש/ט/ כ׳כ/ כ״ת/ כ׳מ,
"C[rown of a] G[ood] N[ame]; C[rown of] P[riesthood];
C[rown of] T[orah]; C[rown of] R[oyalty]"; flanking lin-
tel: שנת/ תקסא, "the year [(5)561" (=1800/01)
PROVENANCE: Miss F. Bloch, New York; Jacob Posen, New
York
REMARKS: The symbols of the zodiac follow the order of the
Hebrew year. The shield had been severely damaged and
displays heavy repairs. It was conserved in 1976. Since
then, the small piece inscribed with the date has disap-
peared. Kayser, No. 55, assumes that repairs were made in
1801 and that that date was then inscribed on a restored
piece. In the Museum card file, the maker's mark is read as
"BT/T." Similar gold inlay can be seen on shield No. 181 and
on the Museum's ring M 247 (Cracow, ca. 1800). This
shield is said to have been sent to Miss F. Bloch from Rumania for purposes of sale.
BIBLIOGRAPHY: Kayser, No. 55
DONOR: Dr. Harry G. Friedman

## 175

TORAH SHIELD  F 2546  (*Illus. p. 152*)
Pietrokov (?), 1765/66 (inscription)
Silver: repoussé, cast, parcel-gilt
H 22.7  W 15.3 cm
HALLMARKS: none

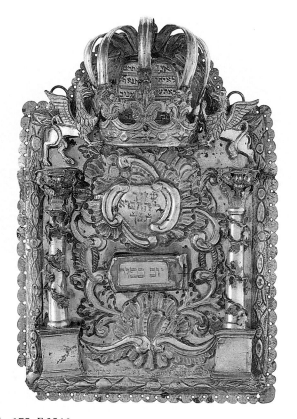

No. 175  F 2546

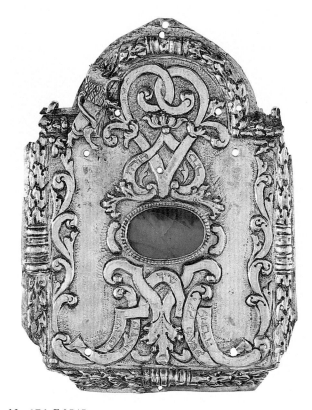

No. 176  F 2545

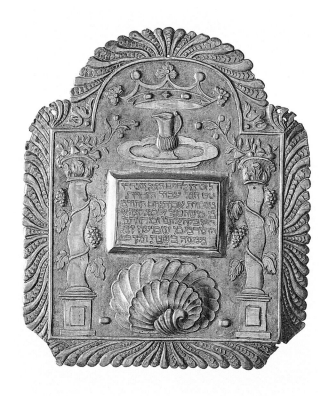

No. 177  F 5291

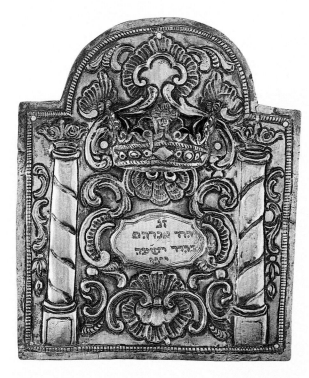

No. 178  F 838

INSCRIPTION: in central cartouche: שייך/ להחברא/ ת׳נ׳ך׳, "Belonging to the Bible (Study) Society"; between plinths: זה מעשה ידי להתפאר זאב ב׳ר׳א צורף מפיעטרוקוב/ שנת תקכו לפק, "This is my handiwork, in which I glory [Isaiah 60: 21], Zev s[on of] A(braham ?), goldsmith, from Pietrokov, [in the] year (5)526" (=1765/66)

PROVENANCE: S. M. Salomon Collection, London

REMARKS: The single *parashah* plaque has been soft-soldered over the plaque box; a gem is missing on the crown; there are various repairs evident. The Hebrew word *Ẓoref*, "goldsmith," was occasionally used as a family name.

BIBLIOGRAPHY: PBNY 1949, No. 136; Kayser, No. 53

DONOR: Dr. Harry G. Friedman

## 176

TORAH SHIELD  F 2545  (*Illus. p. 152*)

Poland, early 19th century

Silver: repoussé; glass: gilt; carnelian

H 21.7  W 16.8 cm

HALLMARKS: none

INSCRIPTION: on upper strapwork: כתר/ תורה, "Crown of Torah"; on lower strapwork: שייך/ לחברה/ דשבעה/ קרואים/ דק״ק לאסק, "Belonging to the *Shiv'ah Qeru'im* ('Seven Who Are Called') Society, of the h[oly] c[ommunity of] Lask"

REMARKS: A now-missing *parashah* plaque box has been replaced by an oval gem setting. Two flanking columns and one lion, as well as other minor elements, are missing, and considerable repairs are evident. Lask is 30 km SW of Lodz. The Lask society mentioned in the inscription was surely modeled after the society of the same name founded in Cracow in 1722; cf. a beaker of that society (bearing the names of the original "seven"), Christie's Amsterdam, 1991, No. 178, and references there; and Christie's Amsterdam, 1988, No. 536, a shield dedicated to a *Shiv'ah Qeru'im* Society in Dobra (50 km. NW of Lodz).

DONOR: Dr. Harry G. Friedman

## 177

TORAH SHIELD  F 5291  (*Illus. p. 152*)

Galicia (?), 1789/90

Silver: repoussé

H 24.6  W 21.5 cm

HALLMARKS: none

INSCRIPTION: in central panel: לזכרון לחיים הזוג שנדרו/ טס הנ״ל עבור הזכרת/ נשמות אבותיהם התורני/ מ׳ משה סג״ל ז״ל מגלוגה ש״הי/ דיין בקהילתנו ומחותנו/ התורני מ׳ שמעון זצ״ל/ נעשה בשנת ת״קן לפ״ק, "For a living memorial, the pair who pledged [this] Torah Shield for the remembrance [of the] souls of their fathers, the late scholar Moses Segal, from Glogau, who wa[s] rabbinical judge

in our congregation, and his in-law, the late scholar Simon. Made in the year (5)550" (=1789/90)

REMARKS: The pitcher and laver depicted in the upper part of the shield refer to the Levite status of Moses Segal, whose surname is a Hebrew abbreviation signifying "Assistant to a Priest."

DONOR: Dr. Harry G. Friedman

## 178

TORAH SHIELD  F 838  (*Illus. p. 152*)

Galicia or Poland, late 18th–early 19th century

Silver: repoussé, gilt; wood; brass

H 22.2  W 18.5 cm

HALLMARKS: none

INSCRIPTION: in central cartouche: ז׳נ׳/ הרר אברהם/ בהרר ישעיה/ יצו, "T[his was] d[onated by] R[abbi] Abraham [son of] R[abbi] Isaiah."

REMARKS: The shield is presently mounted on a wooden backing so the reverse could not be examined.

DONOR: Dr. Harry G. Friedman

## 179

TORAH SHIELD  F 1200  (*Illus. p. 154*)

Galicia, late 18th–early 19th century

Silver: repoussé, cast

H 28.2  W 23.0 cm

HALLMARKS: none

REMARKS: For a similar shield with dolphin columns, see Helbing 1932a, pl. I, No. 41. This Torah Shield was converted into the backwall of a Hanukkah lamp (note the slots pierced along the present lower edge); the *parashah* plaque box was removed and replaced by the pair of stags (probably taken from a shield of the type represented by No. 179). Other examples of shields converted into Hanukkah lamp backwalls include Helbing 1932a, Nos. 69 and 70 (the latter = Feuchtwanger, No. 364). For Hanukkah lamp backwall made from parts of Torah Finials, see Stern Collection, New York (H50). For secular objects converted into Torah Shields, see remarks, shield No. 102.

DONOR: Dr. Harry G. Friedman

## 180

TORAH SHIELD  M 491  (*Illus. p. 154*)

Galicia, early 19th century

Silver: repoussé; brass: cast, gilt

H 19.6  W 16.4 cm

HALLMARKS: none

PROVENANCE: The Rose and Benjamin Mintz Collection

REMARKS: There is a single *parashah* plaque. The crown, one lion and other minor elements are missing.

DONOR: Museum purchase

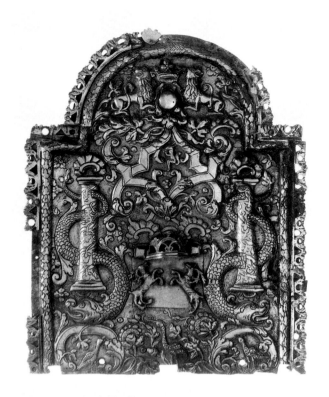

No. 179  F 1200

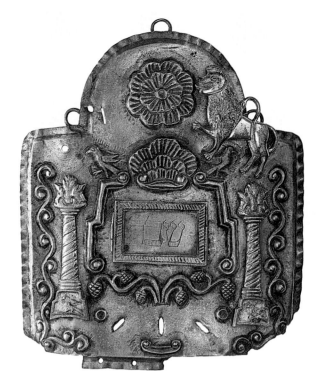

No. 180  M 491

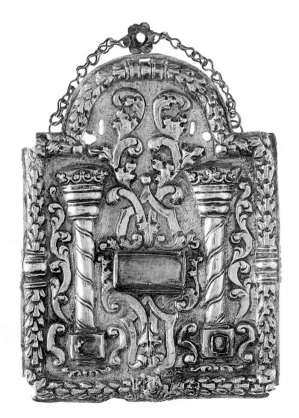

No. 181  F 2743

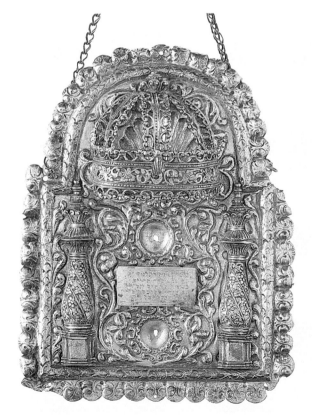

No. 182  F 5290

## 181

TORAH SHIELD F 2743 (*Illus. p. 154*)

Galicia or Ukraine, late 18th–early 19th century

Silver: repoussé

H 16.1 W 12.7 cm

HALLMARKS: none

REMARKS: At present a candleholder at the center of this shield converts it into a sconce (memorial lamp?). Various elements of the shield are missing, as shown by empty screw holes.

DONOR: Dr. Harry G. Friedman

## 182

TORAH SHIELD F 5290 (*Illus. p. 154*)

Poland, 1815/16 (inscription)

Silver: cast, chased; stones

H 26.6 W 20.9 cm

HALLMARKS: none

INSCRIPTION: in central panel: עת /לזכר נשמת ר' קלמן ז"ל/ על שפתי החיים/ נשמת המתים יזכרו/ גם אותו בתוכם יזכירו/ שנת תקע"ו לפ"ק, "In remembrance of the soul of the late Kalman, now on the edge of life; the souls of the dead shall be remembered, he too shall be remembered amongst them. [In the] year (5)576" (=1815/16)

REMARKS: The cast columns overlay chased columns; they may represent a design change requested by the patron. Several stones are missing.

DONOR: Dr. Harry G. Friedman

## 183

TORAH SHIELD F 265 (*Illus. p. 156*)

Poland or Galicia, late 18th–early 19th century

Silver: repoussé, engraved, parcel-gilt; semiprecious stones, inlaid in gold; glass; mother-of-pearl

H 17.6 W 14.2 cm

HALLMARKS: none

REMARKS: Behind the crown is an engraved festoon with fruit. Repairs are evident.

DONOR: Dr. Harry G. Friedman

## 184

TORAH SHIELD F 3517 (*Illus. p. 156*)

Galicia, ca. 1800

Silver: filigree, repoussé, die-stamped, parcel-gilt; cloisonné enamel

H 18.8 W 15.8 cm

HALLMARKS: R³ 7989 (Lemberg re-marking)

REMARKS: There are Tablets of the Law within the central Ark. The appliqués on the Ark doors are later additions. The cloisonné enamel inlay within the filigree is in blue and green. Cf. Kantzedikas, No. 67, a similar shield.

DONOR: Dr. Harry G. Friedman

## 185

TORAH SHIELD X 1963–11 (*Illus. p. 156*)

Poland, 1841/42

Silver: filigree, cast, engraved, silvered

H 18.2 W 11.8 cm

HALLMARKS: none

INSCRIPTION: on lower part of Ark doors: Numbers 10: 35; in lower panel: לפרט שנת/ בא אליהו המבשר/ לפק, "[In the] year 'Elijah the herald has come' (chronogram: [5]602)" (=1841/42); on columns: Psalms 19: 8

REMARKS: Within the Ark of the Law are two Torah Scrolls dressed in mantles. The left door of the Ark is a replacement.

## 186

TORAH SHIELD F 4038 (*Illus. p. 156*)

Poland (?), 18th–19th century

Silver: cast, repoussé, gilt

H 17.8 W 14.0 cm

HALLMARKS: *CITY:* false Danzig mark
*MAKER:* "RF"

INSCRIPTION: on central panel: שבת, "Sabbath."

PROVENANCE: Mr. Frederick Wolff

REMARKS: Within the Ark of the Law is a Torah Scroll dressed with a mantle and shield. Old repairs are in evidence. The Museum card file notes: "from the Seligsberger Collection." There is a similar shield in the Gross Family Collection, Tel Aviv.

DONOR: Dr. Harry G. Friedman

## 187

TORAH SHIELD F 839 (*Illus. p. 157*)

Cracow (?), early 19th century

Silver: repoussé

H 18.7 W 16.5 cm

HALLMARKS: R³ 7978

REMARKS: There are empty holes for attaching a now-missing crown. The lower left corner is missing.

DONOR: Dr. Harry G. Friedman

## 188

TORAH SHIELD F 241 (*Illus. p. 157*)

Galicia, 19th century

Silver: filigree, parcel-gilt; brass

H 30.2 W 23.5 cm

HALLMARKS: "12"; unclear shield

INSCRIPTION: in lower cartouche: אליהו שלמה ב"ר העשיל שטיינהארדט, "Elijah Solomon s[on of] Heschel Steinhardt"

REMARKS: One of the Ark doors is missing; the other has a perched eagle. The crown is lacking the dome-and-eagle finial found on analogous Hanukkah lamps. For a very

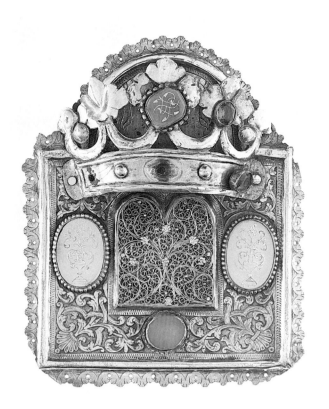

No. 183  F 265

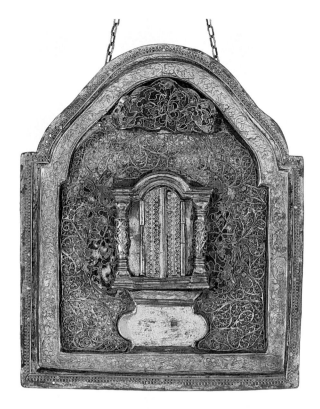

No. 184  F 3517

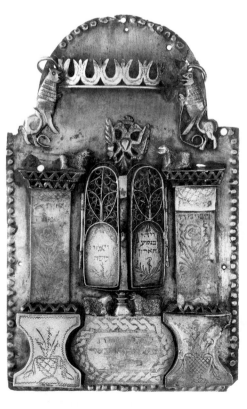

No. 185  X 1963–11

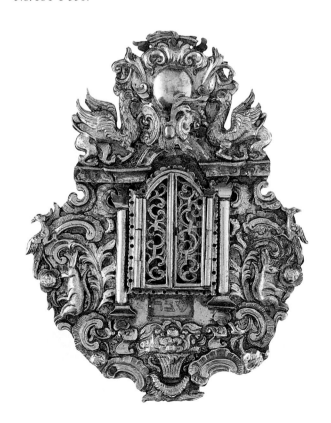

No. 186  F 4038

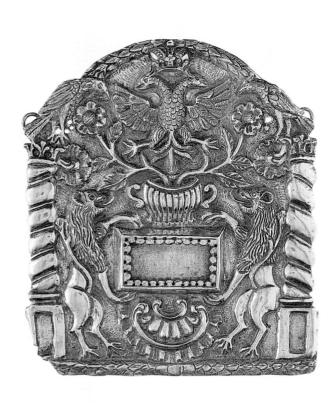

No. 187  F 839

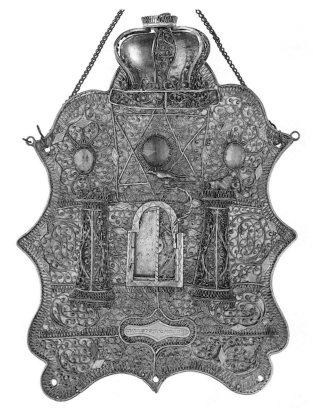

No. 188  F 241

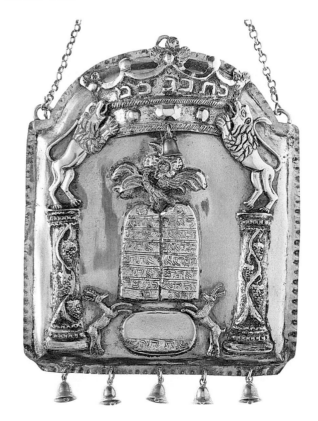

No. 189  D 128

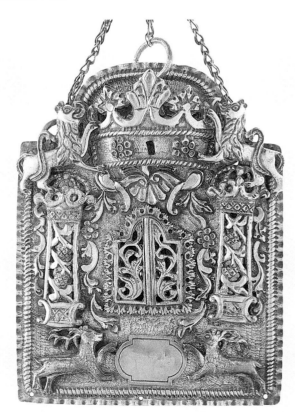

No. 190  F 1903

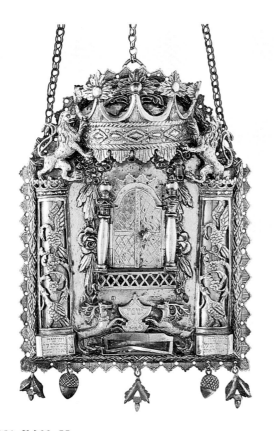

No. 191  JM 23–55

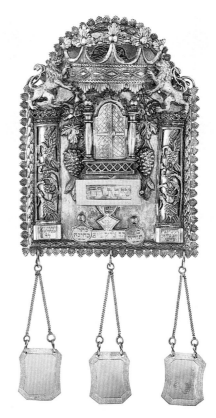

No. 192  D 125

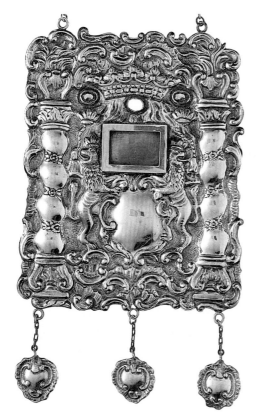

No. 193  F 3475

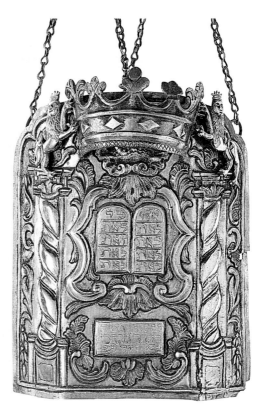

No. 194  F 1230

similar filigree shield, see Sotheby's New York, 1982, No. 364 (with finial).

DONOR: Dr. Harry G. Friedman

## 189

TORAH SHIELD  D 128  (*Illus. p. 157*)

Poland, 1806/07 (inscription)

Silver: repoussé, cast, gilt

H 18.3  W 15.2 cm

HALLMARKS: none

INSCRIPTION: on crown: כת כך כמ, "C[rown of] T[orah]; C[rown of] P[riesthood]; C[rown of Royalty]"; on Tablets of Law, below Decalogue: abbreviated Psalm 118: 20; in oval cartouche: שנת תקסז, "[In the] year (5)567" (=1806/07)

PROVENANCE: The Gieldzinski Collection, Danzig

REMARKS: This Torah shield does not appear in *Danzig 1939*.

BIBLIOGRAPHY: Danzig 1904, No. 25; Danzig 1933, No. 128, pl. 7

DONOR: The Jewish Community of Danzig

## 190

TORAH SHIELD  F 1903  (*Illus. p. 157*)

Lublin, ca. 1820

Silver: repoussé, cast, parcel-gilt

H 14.3  W 11.6 cm

HALLMARKS: none

REMARKS: Within the central Ark of the Law is a Torah Scroll. On the lower cartouche, a Hebrew inscription has been erased and a stone is missing from the crown. This shield was acquired together with crown No. 473 and pointer No. 706, the latter dated 1779, i.e., some forty years earlier than the shield. Other examples of the Lublin-type Torah Shield are: Nos. 191 and 192 (with further comparisons); Stieglitz, No. 28 (1820); Loukomski 1947, p. 174, upper left (formerly Jewish Museum, M 326; presently Ellis Island Museum, New York); and Klagsbald 1981, No. 149.

BIBLIOGRAPHY: Kayser, No. 57a

DONOR: Dr. Harry G. Friedman

## 191

TORAH SHIELD  JM 23–55  (*Illus. p. 158*)

Lublin, 1832/33 (inscription)

Silver: cast, engraved, parcel-gilt

H 19.7  W 15.2 cm

HALLMARKS: "12"; "B" in script in rectangle

INSCRIPTION: on the column plinths: Exodus 28: 10; at bottom, on shaped panel: שנת תקצג, "[In the] year (5)593" (=1832/33)

PROVENANCE: F. Gorevic, New York

REMARKS: The date on the shaped panel is presently hidden behind the plaque box. See the remarks under shield No. 192 for references.

DONOR: Samuel and Lucille Lemberg

## 192

TORAH SHIELD  D 125  (*Illus. p. 158*)

Lublin, 1838/39 (inscription)

Silver: repoussé, cast, engraved, parcel-gilt

H 20.5  W 15.9 cm

HALLMARKS: "12"; indistinct maker's name (".B./—evit—") in script within rectangle

INSCRIPTION: on lower medallions: כתר תורה/ כתר כהונה. "Crown of Torah; Crown of Priesthood"; on plinths: adapted from Exodus 28: 36, modifying the first word to read: "And I made ..."; on lower central element: שנת/ תק צדי טית, "[In the] year (5)599" (=1838/39)

PROVENANCE: The Gieldzinski Collection, Danzig

REMARKS: There is one *parashah* plaque. The hallmarks are hidden beneath the plaque box; the maker's mark is identical to that on No. 191. An almost identical shield (Martyna, No. 44) is dated 1847/48 and has the same biblical quotation, as well as the notation: שייך להחברה שומרים דקק לובלין, "Belongs to the Society of Watchmen of the h[oly] c[ommunity] of Lublin." Martyna, No. 46, with identical columns, bears a hallmark of 1866. A similar shield (in an old photograph in The Jewish Museum's Photographic Archives, shown alongside Martyna, No. 46), has identical columns and appears to be dated 1802/03 and signed "Chaim" as the maker's mark. All these shields may represent the work of several successive generations in a single Lublin workshop (cf. Martyna, No. 44). See shield No. 190 for comparisons.

BIBLIOGRAPHY: Danzig 1904, No. 22; Danzig 1933, No. 125; *Danzig 1939*, No. 207

DONOR: The Jewish Community of Danzig

## 193

TORAH SHIELD  F 3475  (*Illus. p. 158*)

Poland, 19th century (?)

Silver: repoussé; stones

H 16.6  W 13.4 cm

HALLMARKS: none

REMARKS: Some of the stones are missing.

DONOR: Dr. Harry G. Friedman

## 194

TORAH SHIELD  F 1230  (*Illus. p. 158*)

Poland, 18th–19th century

Silver: repoussé, engraved, cast, parcel-gilt

H 21.9  W 16.8 cm

HALLMARKS: none

INSCRIPTION: on rectangular panel: ז'נ' הרר משה/ בהרר מרדכי/ זצל, "T[his was] d[onated by] R[abbi] Moses s[on of the] late R[abbi] Mordecai."

REMARKS: This shield is presently bowed; if flat, it would measure 19.5 cm wide.

DONOR: Dr. Harry G. Friedman

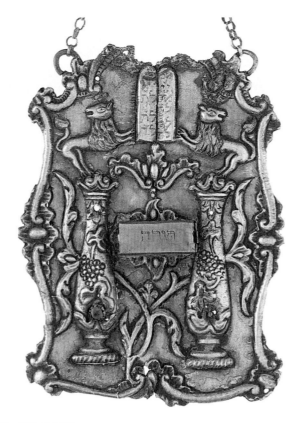

No. 195  F 2683

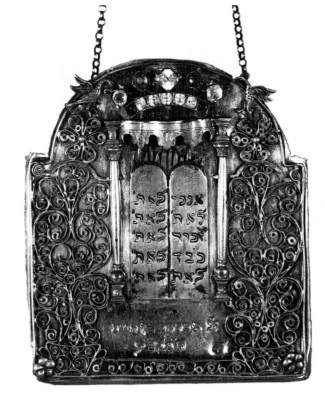

No. 196  JM 67–48

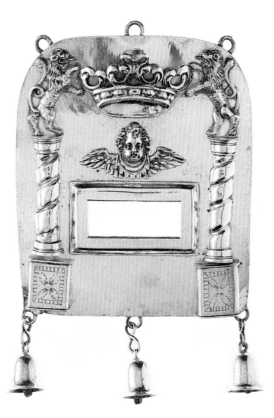

No. 197  F 249

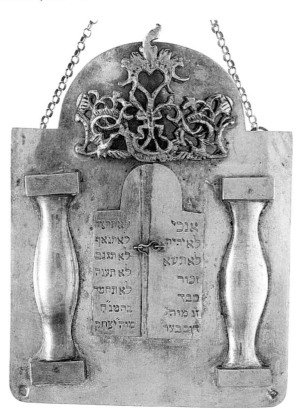

No. 198  M 342

## 195

TORAH SHIELD  F 2683  (*Illus. p. 160*)
Poland, 19th century
Silver: repoussé, engraved; stone
H 17.3  W 13.3 cm
HALLMARKS: none
INSCRIPTION: on *parashah* plaque box (later): תורה, "Torah"
REMARKS: This shield was in a fire which melted about two
cm from the top center; several stones are also missing.
The plaque box is not original and has no window.
DONOR: Dr. Harry G. Friedman

## 196

TORAH SHIELD  JM 67–48  (*Illus. p. 160*)
Galicia, 19th century
Silver: filigree, cast, chased, parcel-gilt; glass
H 10.0  W 8.9 cm
HALLMARKS: unclear, with "13"
INSCRIPTION: in lower panel: ז"נ אברהם בן חיים ת"נ לפ"ק,
"T[his was] d[onated by] Abraham son of Ḥayyim,
(5)450" (=1689/90)
PROVENANCE: Hessisches Landesmuseum, Kassel
REMARKS: The inscription is a later, spurious addition. In
Hallo 1933, this shield is associated with pointer No. 756.
BIBLIOGRAPHY: Hallo 1933, No. 24, pl. 9
DONOR: Louis Rabinowitz

## 197

TORAH SHIELD  F 249  (*Illus. p. 160*)
Poland (?), first half of 19th century
Silver: cast, chased, parcel-gilt
H 19.6  W 15.5 cm
HALLMARKS: none
REMARKS: There is one *parashah* plaque.
DONOR: Dr. Harry G. Friedman

## 198

TORAH SHIELD  M 342  (*Illus. p. 160*)
Poland, 19th century
Silver: cast, chased, gilt
H 17.5  W 12.8 cm
HALLMARKS: "12" in rectangle (twice)
INSCRIPTION: at bottom of Tablets of the Law: ז"נ מוה'/ דוב
בער/ בהמנ"ח מוה' יצחק, "T[his was] d[onated by] . . .
R[abbi] Dov Ber s[on of] the late . . . R[abbi] Isaac."
PROVENANCE: The Rose and Benjamin Mintz Collection
REMARKS: The Ark of the Law is empty.
DONOR: Museum purchase

## 199

TORAH SHIELD  JM 1–47  (*Illus. p. 162*)
Poland, 1841
Silver: chased, engraved
H 13.8  W 10.6 cm
HALLMARKS: "84"; "1841" (both crude)
INSCRIPTION: on crown: כתר תורה, "Crown of Torah"
DONOR: Mr. and Mrs. Benjamin Levy

## 200

TORAH SHIELD  F 2314  (*Illus. p. 162*)
Poland, ca. 1870
Silver: filigree, cast, engraved
H 30.7  W 23.4 cm
HALLMARKS: "12"; "A M Silber" in script, in rectangle
INSCRIPTION: on lower cartouche: ק"ק שערי בינה, "h[oly]
c[ongregation] *Sha'arei Binah* ('Gates of Wisdom')"
REMARKS: The signs of the zodiac are arranged in Hebrew
order. The three disk pendants are probably not original.
The congregation of the inscription was probably Sha'arei
Bino at 225 E. Broadway in New York City, founded in 1868
(*NY Register* 1917, p. 233). Pointer No. 749 was apparently
dedicated to the same congregation. Cf. a very similar
shield by the same smith, PBNY 1949, No. 28 (dated 1858);
and see pointer No. 700, also by A.M. Silber.
DONOR: Dr. Harry G. Friedman

## 201

TORAH SHIELD  F 5400a  (*Illus. p. 162*)
Galicia, early 19th century
Silver: filigree, gilt; glass
H 14.7  W 12.2 cm
HALLMARKS: none
INSCRIPTION: on plinths: קודש/ ליקוק, "Holy to the Lord"
PROVENANCE: Jacob Posen, New York
REMARKS: Repaired. See pointer No. 734, acquired at the same
time.
DONOR: Dr. Harry G. Friedman

## 202

TORAH SHIELD  M 6
Poland, mid-19th century
Silver: repoussé, cast, filigree, parcel-gilt
H 32.5  W 23.2 cm
HALLMARKS: "12"; "HZ" in rectangle
PROVENANCE: The Rose and Benjamin Mintz Collection
REMARKS: At The Jewish Museum there are six examples of
this type of Warsaw Torah Shield, popular in the second
half of the 19th century (shields Nos. 202–207), and many
others in various collections, e.g., *Stieglitz*, No. 3 (dated
there too early, with spurious hallmarks).
DONOR: Museum purchase

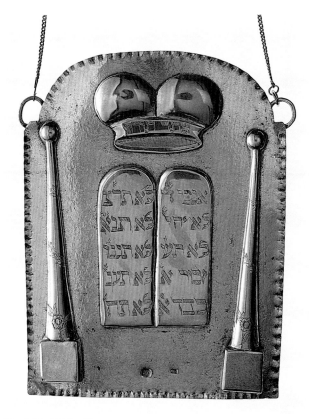

No. 199  JM 1–47

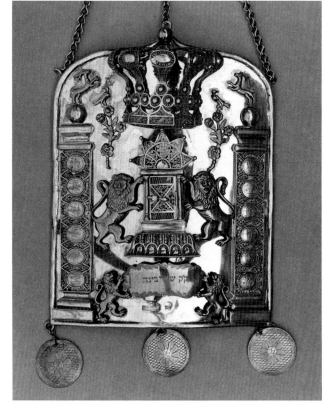

No. 200  F 2314

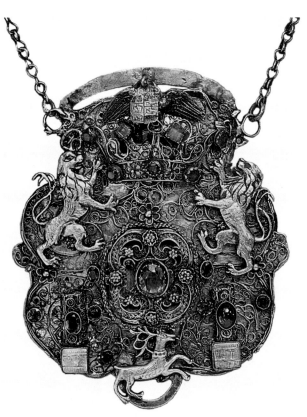

No. 201  F 5400a

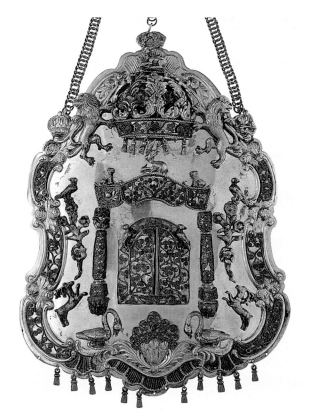

No. 203  M 456

## 203

TORAH SHIELD  M 456  (*Illus. p. 162*)
Poland, mid-19th century
Silver: cast, filigree, parcel-gilt; glass; turquoise
H 31.4  W 24.1 cm
HALLMARKS: none
PROVENANCE: The Rose and Benjamin Mintz Collection
REMARKS: See remarks, shield No. 202.
DONOR: Museum purchase

## 204

TORAH SHIELD  F 2575  (*Illus. p. 164*)
Warsaw, 1888
Anton Riedel, active 1878–1910
Silver: repoussé (or cast ?)
H 30.8  W 25.7 cm
HALLMARKS: *CITY:* Lileyko 89 (1888); 90 (right)
      *MAKER:* Lileyko 5 (both)
REMARKS: See remarks, shield No. 202. Shield No. 206 was
  made by the same smith, as were finials No. 350.
DONOR: Dr. Harry G. Friedman

## 205

TORAH SHIELD  F 250  (*Illus. p. 164*)
Warsaw, 1892/93 (inscription)
Szmul Szkarlat, active ca. 1850–1900
Silver: repoussé, cast, parcel-gilt
H 30.2  W 27.3 cm
HALLMARKS: *CITY:* Lileyko 89 (1892)
      *MAKER:* Lileyko 63 (var.)
INSCRIPTION: on right: ז', ז"ר נח הכהן ר' נ' ישעיהו ב"ר נח הכהן, "T[his
  was] d[onated by] Isaiah s[on of] N[o]ah ha-Kohen"; on
  left: על ה' מטה לוי בשנת ת'ר'נ'ג', "... the Staff of Levi, in
  the year (5)653" (=1892/93)
REMARKS: There are three *parashah* plaques. Within the Ark
  is a Torah Mantle bearing a Star of David. The expression
  "Staff of Levi" is found four times in the Book of Numbers
  (e.g., 1:49); its significance here is unclear. See shield No.
  202 for comparisons. Shield No. 207 was also made by
  Szkarlat.
DONOR: Dr. Harry G. Friedman

## 206

TORAH SHIELD  D 149  (*Illus. p. 164*)
Warsaw, ca. 1900
Anton Riedel, active ca. 1878–1910
Silver: repoussé, cast, engraved, parcel-gilt
H 30.7  W 26.0 cm
HALLMARKS: *CITY:* Lileyko 90
      *MAKER:* Lileyko 5 (both)
INSCRIPTION: in central cartouche: לזכרון אבינו/ יצחק בן

"In
remembrance of our father Isaac son of the late David
ha-Levi Speyer, (5)624–28 Sivan (5)684" (=1863/64–30
June 1924), דוד/ הלוי שפייער ז"ל/ תרכ"ד – כ"ח סיון תרפ"ד
REMARKS: See Nos. 204 and 350, by the same smith.
BIBLIOGRAPHY: *Danzig 1939/1982,* No. 72; Kantsedikas 1992,
  p. 12
DONOR: The Jewish Community of Danzig

## 207

TORAH SHIELD  S 798  (*Illus. p. 164*)
Warsaw, after 1908
Szmul Szkarlat, active ca. 1850–1900
Silver: repoussé, cast, engraved
H 38.7  W 25.7 cm
HALLMARKS: *CITY:* Postnikova 1941 (with "L"); 1939, with "L";
      1938
      *MAKER:* cf. Lileyko 63
REMARKS: There is a dressed Torah Scroll within the Ark. See
  remarks, shield No. 202. Shield No. 205 was also made by
  Szkarlat.
DONOR: Dr. Harry G. Friedman

## 208

TORAH SHIELD  JM 29–57  (*Illus. p. 165*)
Warsaw, 1852–60
Michel Swinarski, active ca. 1850–90
Silver: gilt
H 35.8  W 28.4 cm
HALLMARKS: *CITY:* Lileyko 84
      *MAKER:* Lileyko 62b, e
INSCRIPTION: on pendant: שייך למהורר שמעון/ ישעי' במהר', "Belongs to ... R[abbi]
  Simon Isaia[h] s[on of] ... R[abbi] Alexander ... [of the] אלכסנדר נ"י/ משפחת רויזען,
  Roizen Family"
REMARKS: There is one *parashah* plaque. Within the Ark are
  Tablets of the Law, inscribed "I"–"X." This shield, or one
  identical to it, appears in an old photograph in The Jewish
  Museum's Photographic Archive (marked with a collec-
  tion or catalogue number: "1947"). The pendant there,
  however, is different.
DONOR: Dr. Harry G. Friedman from Robert I. Wishnik

## 208A

TORAH SHIELD  F 3024
Vilna, 1895/96 (inscription)
Ḥayyim Katz, active 1859–97[1]
Silver: repoussé
H 13.6  W 15.8 cm
HALLMARKS: *CITY:* Postnikova 108; "84"; "A.K./1896"
      *MAKER:* "X. KATZ/VILNA" (Cyrillic), in
      rectangle

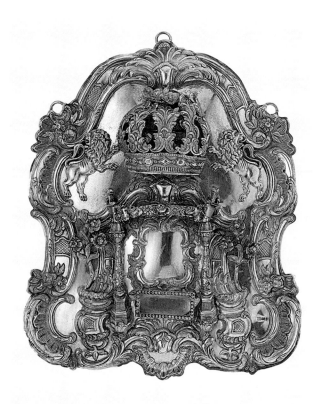

No. 204  F 2575

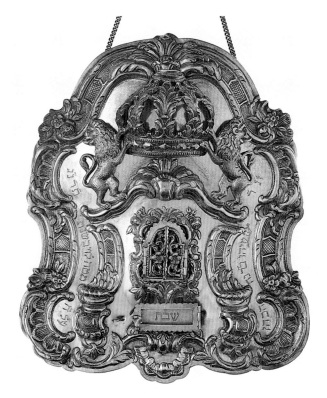

No. 205  F 250

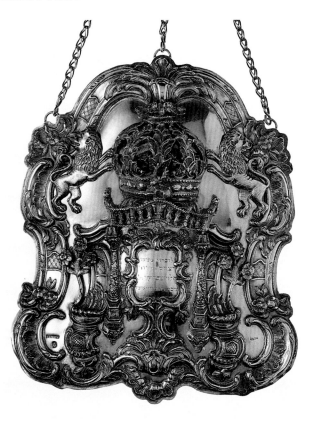

No. 206  D 149

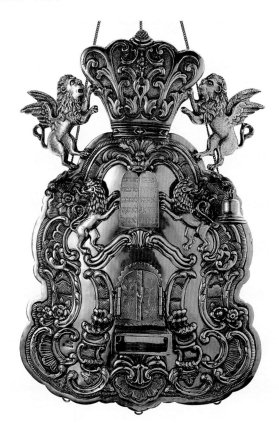

No. 207  S 798

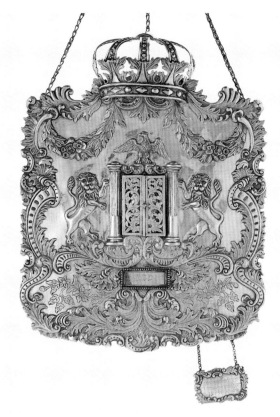

No. 208  JM 29–57

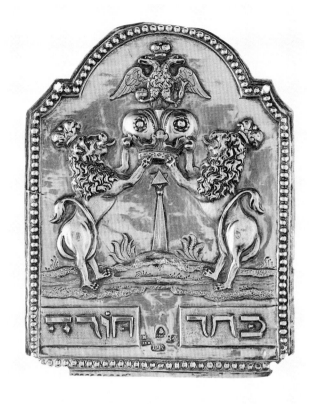

No. 209  F 963

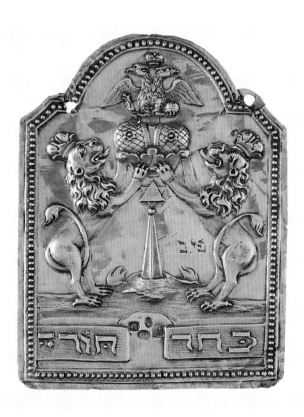

No. 210  F 964

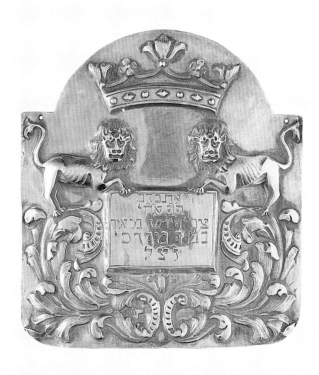

No. 211  F 2344

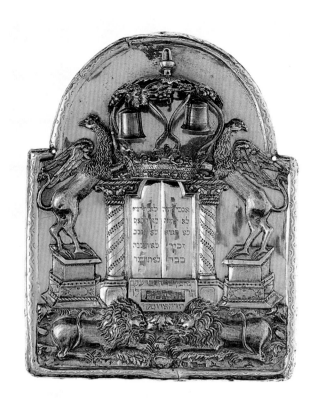

No. 212  F 242

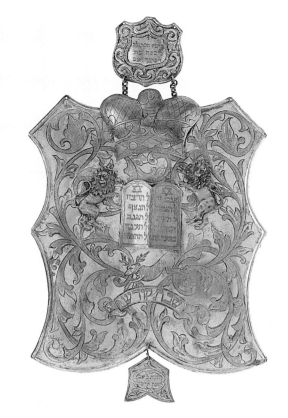

No. 213  F 247

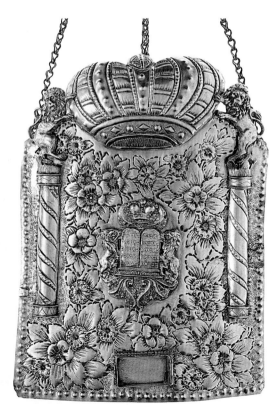

No. 214  X 1983–19

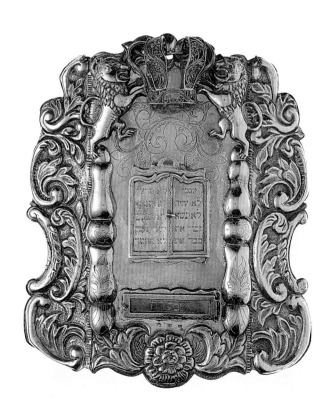

No. 215  F 1525

INSCRIPTION: above: ‏זה הציץ שייך ל"ר דוד/ יעקב ב"ר‏ ‏אברהם/ נעפט‏, "This is the Torah Shield (*tzitz*) [which] belongs to ... David Jacob son of ... Abraham Neft"; below: ‏בקלויז של חייטים ש' ת'ר'נ'ו'‏, "In the *kloiz* of [the] Tailors, y[ear] (5)656" (=1895/96)

REMARKS: There are two holes at the lower middle, for the attachment of a missing element, probably a crown. The Yiddish word *kloiz* signifies a house of study, frequently named for an occupational group.

DONOR: Jewish Cultural Reconstruction

1. Letter dated 14 December 1994, from Rūta Vitkauskiene, Vilna (who is preparing a work on Vilna silversmiths).

## 209

### TORAH SHIELD  F 963  (*Illus. p. 165*)

Moscow, 1841

Bernhard Johann Kochendorfer (?), active ca. 1831–65

Silver: repoussé

H 13.0  W 10.5 cm

HALLMARKS:  *CITY:* Postnikova 523 (but with "1841") and 616; "84" in rectangle
*MAKER:* Postnikova 1379 (?)

INSCRIPTION: in lower panels: ‏כתר/ תורה‏, "Crown of Torah"

REMARKS: Shield No. 210 is almost identical.

DONOR: Dr. Harry G. Friedman

## 210

### TORAH SHIELD  F 964  (*Illus. p. 165*)

Moscow, 1842

Silver: repoussé

H 13.0  W 10.3 cm

HALLMARKS:  *CITY:* Postnikova 520 (var.) and 618 (with "1842"); "84" in rectangle
*MAKER:* Similar to Postnikova 832

INSCRIPTION: on lower panels: ‏כתר/ תורה‏, "Crown of Torah"; in field: ‏פיכ‏

REMARKS: Cf. the almost identical, but less crude shield No. 209. The meaning of the inscription in the field is unknown.

DONOR: Dr. Harry G. Friedman

## 211

### TORAH SHIELD  F 2344  (*Illus. p. 165*)

Moscow, 1843

Silver: repoussé

H 14.4  W 13.5 cm

HALLMARKS:  *CITY:* Postnikova 523 (1843); 617; "84"
*MAKER:* Postnikova 663

INSCRIPTION: on central panel: ‏זאת נדב/ ה"ה אח'/ צבי הירש‏ ‏מאיר/ במ"ה מרדכי/ זצ"ל‏, "This was donated by ... Zvi Hirsch Me'ir s[on of the] late ... R[abbi] Mordecai."

REMARKS: The general style of this shield is Galician; cf., e.g., shield No. 151.

DONOR: Dr. Harry G. Friedman

## 212

### TORAH SHIELD  F 242  (*Illus. p. 166*)

Odessa, 1857

Silver: repoussé, parcel-gilt

H 24.4  W 19.7 cm

HALLMARKS:  *CITY:* Postnikova 1152; 1156; "84"; (on reverse:) Postnikova 528 (var.); 621 (Moscow, "1874"); "84"
*MAKER:* "RL" (?)

INSCRIPTION: around *parashah* plaque box: ‏ר' נחמן ב"ר‏ ‏דוב יעקב/ יודקאווסקי/ ת'ר/ ל'ד‏, "Naḥman s[on of] Dov Jacob Yudkowski, (5)634" (=1873/74)

REMARKS: There are three *parashah* plaques. The presence of two sets of Moscow hallmarks on this shield (one of which corresponds to the date in the inscription) is perplexing.

DONOR: Dr. Harry G. Friedman

## 213

### TORAH SHIELD  F 247  (*Illus. p. 166*)

Ukraine (?), 1906 (inscription)

Silver: chased, cast, engraved; brass

H 26.7  W 23.0 cm

HALLMARKS:  *CITY:* unidentified: "?/84"; "G.N. (Cyrillic)/ 1865"; double-headed eagle

INSCRIPTION: on the central ribbon: ‏שבת קודש‏, "Holy Sabbath"; in upper cartouche: ‏נדבה הבתולה/ ליבסה‏ ‏בת/ ר' ברוך זאב‏, "T[his] was donated by the maiden Liebse (?) daughter of Barukh Zev"; on lower pendant: ‏שבת כ" אב/ שנת ת'ר'ס'ו' (ת'ר'כ'ו'?)‏, "Sabbath, 20 Av, [in the] year (5)666 (=1906)

REMARKS: In the inscription, the third letter of the date has been tampered with; what was most probably a *samekh* seems to have been remade into a *kaf.* Cf. shield No. 188, a similarly shaped filigree shield made in Galicia but possibly used in the Ukraine.

DONOR: Dr. Harry G. Friedman

## 214

### TORAH SHIELD  X 1983–19  (*Illus. p. 166*)

United States, late 19th century

Silver: repoussé, cast, engraved, parcel-gilt

H 27.6  W 21.2 cm

HALLMARKS: engraved: "STERLING"

REMARKS: The design of this shield is reminiscent of 19th-century European shields.

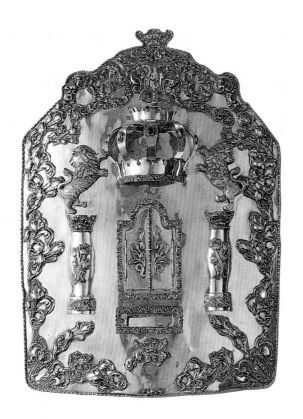

No. 216  F 1530

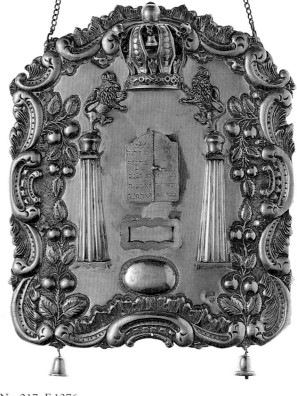

No. 217  F 1376

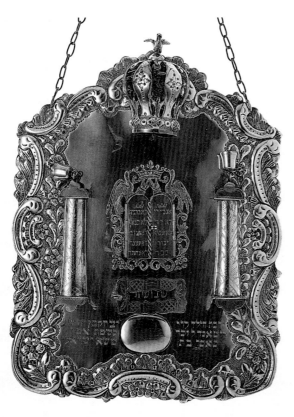

No. 218  F 3860

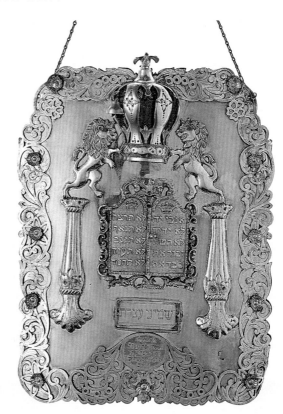

No. 219  F 1529

## 215

TORAH SHIELD  F 1525  (*Illus. p. 166*)
United States (?), 1880–90
Silver: repoussé, filigree, engraved, parcel-gilt
H 29.8  W 25.3 cm
HALLMARKS: shield with crown above illegible symbol; "84" in rectangle
MAKER: "HL" in rectangle
REMARKS: There are three *parashah* plaques. For the hallmarks, see crown No. 492; see remarks, shield No. 222.
DONOR: Dr. Harry G. Friedman

## 216

TORAH SHIELD  F 1530  (*Illus. p. 168*)
United States (?), late 19th–early 20th century
Silver: die-stamped, cast, engraved, parcel-gilt; glass
H 42.1  W 31.8 cm
HALLMARKS: none
REMARKS: There are four *parashah* plaques; one is in a different script and is a duplicate.
DONOR: Dr. Harry G. Friedman

## 217

TORAH SHIELD  F 1376  (*Illus. p. 168*)
United States (?), early 20th century
Silver: repoussé
H 32.2  W 27.5 cm
HALLMARKS: "STERLING"; "84" in rectangle with nick on left
DONOR: Dr. Harry G. Friedman

## 218

TORAH SHIELD  F 3860  (*Illus. p. 168*)
New York (?), late 19th–early 20th century
Silver: repoussé, cast, engraved
H 35.2  W 27.1 cm
HALLMARKS: "STERLING" (curved)/ "A.G."
INSCRIPTION: flanking medallion: נדבת הילד לוי/ יצחק בן יחושיע(!)/ דימאנד לזכר/ נשמת אמו/ סאסי בת/ משה ישראל, "Donation of the boy Levi Isaac son of Joshua Dimand, in memory of the soul of his mother, Sasi daughter of Moses Israel"
REMARKS: There is one *parashah* plaque. The spelling of the name Joshua is corrupt. The last letter in the Hebrew name for Moses, a *heh*, was corrected from an *alef*. For parallels, see shield No. 223.
DONOR: Dr. Harry G. Friedman

## 219

TORAH SHIELD  F 1529  (*Illus. p. 168*)
New York, ca. 1900
K. Paston
Silver: die-stamped, cast, engraved

H 36.1  W 26.4 cm
HALLMARKS: "K. PASTON" (convex) / "STERLING / NEW YORK" (concave)
INSCRIPTION: on medallion: לז״נ זוגתו חי׳ בתי׳ ב״ר נתן נטע, "In m[emory of the] s[oul of] his spouse, Ḥay[yah] Baty[ah] daughter of Nathan Neta"
REMARKS: There is one *parashah* plaque. The name of the donor is not given, only that of his late wife; thus, it is probable that either something is missing or this inscribed medallion is from another object. In the Museum records, there is a note giving the address of the maker: "18 Eldridge St., NY." Cf. shields Nos. 218 and 220 for the same form of Ark of the Law. For the general design, cf. shields Nos. 221 and 222, and the nearly identical shield at Temple Emanu-El, New York (Grossman 1989, No. 10B, stated to have been brought from Poland but probably purchased in the United States; the accompanying finials bear the mark "AG" as on shield No. 218). The same general design of Torah Shield appears in Mazin, p. 21, which is identical to shield No. 223. For an identical shield made by Paston, see Swann New York 1991, No. 309 (the name is misprinted as "P. Kraston").
DONOR: Dr. Harry G. Friedman

## 220

TORAH SHIELD (Fragment)  F 966
United States ca. 1900
Silver: cast, engraved
HALLMARKS: none
REMARKS: The Tablets of the Law on this Torah Shield are similar to those on shields Nos. 218 and 219.
DONOR: Dr. Harry G. Friedman

## 221

TORAH SHIELD  F 1527  (*Illus. p. 170*)
United States (?), 1892 or later
Silver: repoussé, cast, engraved, parcel-gilt
H 34.9  W 26.2 cm
HALLMARKS: "KC/1892"; "84" (false Russian marks)
REMARKS: There are three *parashah* plaques. This work is almost identical with shield No. 223; for other parallels, see shield No. 219.
DONOR: Dr. Harry G. Friedman

## 222

TORAH SHIELD  F 3240  (*Illus. p. 170*)
United States (?), 1881 (?)
Silver: chased, engraved, cast, parcel-gilt
H 30.1  W 22.6 cm
HALLMARKS: "W" in oval (twice); "84" in rectangle; "1881/KS"
REMARKS: The surviving *parashah* plaque is not original. Note that the last hallmark here is very similar to that on

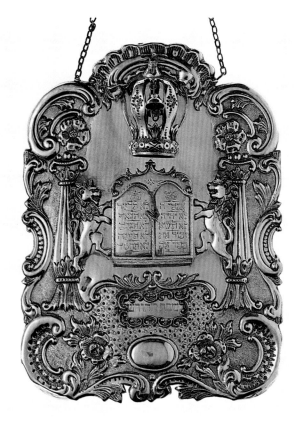

No. 221  F 1527

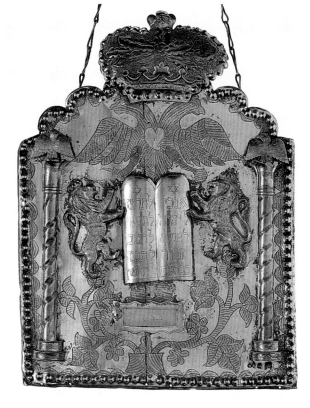

No. 222  F 3240

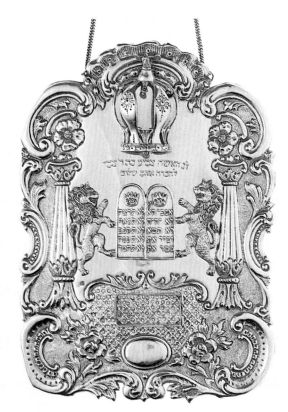

No. 223  F 1526

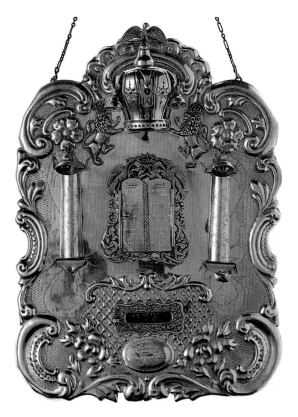

No. 224  F 1528

shield No. 221, though there the "KS" is in Cyrillic characters and above the date. Other Latin/Cyrillic initials are found on Nos. 215, 358, and 492.

DONOR: Dr. Harry G. Friedman

## 223

TORAH SHIELD  F 1526  (*Illus. p. 170*)

United States (?), early 20th century

Silver: repoussé, cast, engraved

H 35.3  W 26.3 cm

HALLMARKS: "84"; and two unclear, false St. Petersburg marks

INSCRIPTION: above Tablets of the Law: ז"נ האשה צביע בהר' צבי/ לחברה אוהב שלום, "T[his was] d[onated by] the woman Zivie d[aughter of] Zvi to the *Ohev Shalom* ('Lover of Peace') Society."

REMARKS: This shield and No. 221 are almost identical; for other parallels, see shield No. 218, and Mazin, p. 21. For the society mentioned in the inscription, see shield No. 224. Crown No. 490 was dedicated to the same society by the same person.

DONOR: Dr. Harry G. Friedman

## 224

TORAH SHIELD  F 1528  (*Illus. p. 170*)

United States (?), 1882 (?)

Silver: chased, cast, pierced, engraved, die-stamped, parcel-gilt

H 33.8  W 26.5 cm

HALLMARKS: "STERLING"; false marks

INSCRIPTION: ז"נ האשה/ דאברע ב"ר מאיר/ אשר נדבה זאת/ לחב' אוהב שלום/ תער"ב, "T[his was] d[onated by] the woman Debra d[aughter of] Me'ir who donated this to the *Ohev Shalom* Soc[iety], (5)672" (=1911/12).

REMARKS: The eagle topping the Tablets of the Law is American in form. The front of the *parashah* plaque box is missing, as are the plaques. Identical hallmarks appear on finials F 1524 (missing), which are very similar to Grossman 1989, No. 10b (marks: "AG"; "84"). The *Ohev Shalom* Society, mentioned on this shield and on shield No. 226, is also noted (according to the Museum records) on missing finials F 1524 as "דבראנזוויל", i.e., "of Brownsville" in Brooklyn. According to *NY Register* 1917, p. 276: "Oheb Sholom" was organized in 1890, and was located at 135 Thatford Avenue, Brownsville.

DONOR: Dr. Harry G. Friedman

## 225

TORAH SHIELD  F 5486  (*Illus. p. 172*)

United States (?), late 19th–early 20th century

Silver: die-stamped, engraved

H 17.8  W 12.9 cm

HALLMARKS: "84" (crude) in rectangle

INSCRIPTION: above, continuing on left: ר' שמואל טייטלבויס, "Samuel Teitelbaum…, 15 Ab, Joseph son of Nathan Dov"; below: נ"י י"צ טו' אב' ר' יוסף/ בן ר' נתן דוב below: טו כיסלו גינעדיל בת זאב וואלף, "16 Kislev, Gneidel daughter of Zev Wolf"

REMARKS: The die used for this shield would seem to have been intended for a book cover. In the inscription, the dates might refer to birthdays, for the abbreviations indicate that those named were alive at the time of dedication.

DONOR: Dr. Harry G. Friedman

## 226

TORAH SHIELD  JM 20–62  (*Illus. p. 172*)

New York and Jerusalem, completed 1960

Ludwig Yehuda Wolpert, active 1920's–1981; and Chava Wolpert Richard, active 1950's–

Silver: pierced, engraved; copper: enamelled

H 20.5  W 20.5 cm

HALLMARKS: on central element: "וולפרט" (Wolpert); "925" in oval; "ישראל" "ISRAEL"; on back of main element: Tobe Pascher Workshop mark; "WOLPERT"

INSCRIPTION: Deuteronomy 33:8.

REMARKS: This shield is essentially identical with No. 227. For Wolpert, see *Wolpert* 1982. For other Torah pieces by him at The Jewish Museum, see finials, No. 361, crown No. 510 and pointers Nos. 637, 815 and 816.

BIBLIOGRAPHY: *Wolpert* 1976, No. 18.

DONOR: Betty Wolpert and Chava Wolpert Richard

## 227

TORAH SHIELD  JM 48–64

New York, 1960

Ludwig Yehuda Wolpert, active 1924–1981; and Chava Wolpert Richard, active 1950's–

Silver: pierced, engraved; copper: enameled

H 20.5  W 19.3 cm

HALLMARKS: Tobe Pascher Workshop mark; "WOLPERT"

INSCRIPTION: As on No. 226

REMARKS: See remarks under shield No. 226.

BIBLIOGRAPHY: Kanof, p. 231; Kampf, p. 496, No. 357; Wolpert 1976

DONOR: Gift of the artists

## 227A

TORAH SHIELD  JM 2–67b

New York, 1967

Moshe Zabari, active 1958–

Silver: chased, pierced; gold; leather

H 14.9  W 17.4 cm

HALLMARKS: Tobe Pascher Workshop mark; "STERLING"; "M/ZABARI"

INSCRIPTION: מלכות, "Royalty"

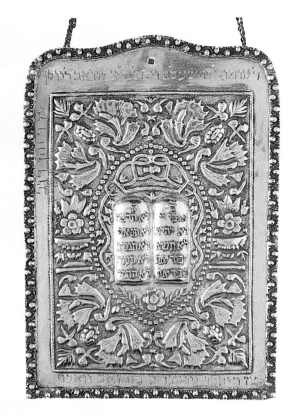

No. 225  F 5486

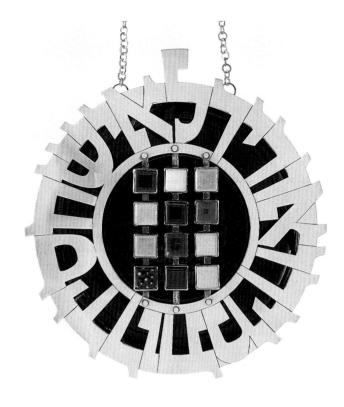

No. 226  JM 20–62

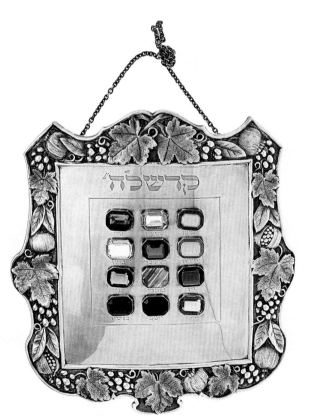

No. 229  1989–146

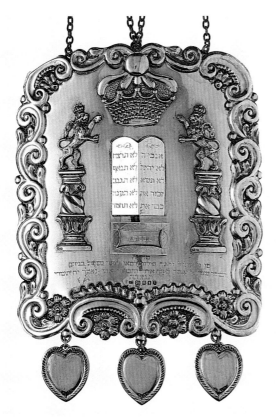

No. 230 F 4873c

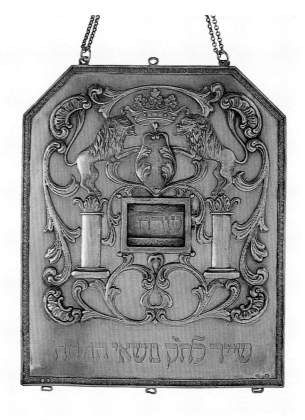

No. 231 F 5167

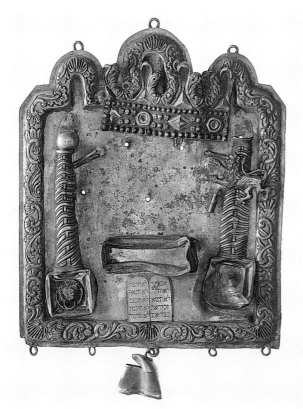

No. 232 X 1983–20

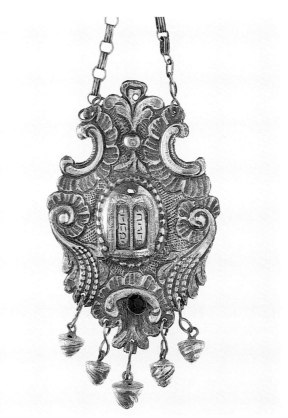

No. 233 D 127

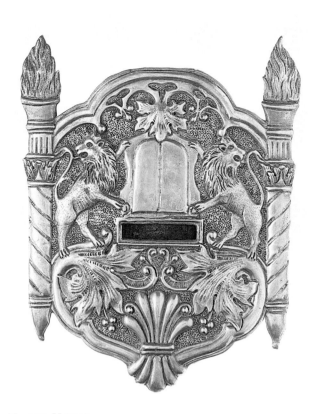

No. 234  U 9840

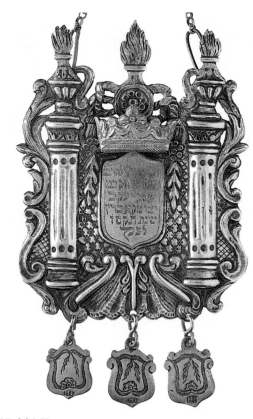

No. 235  M 265

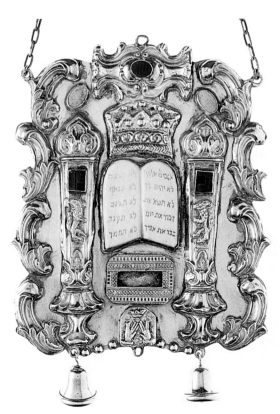

No. 236  F 4185b

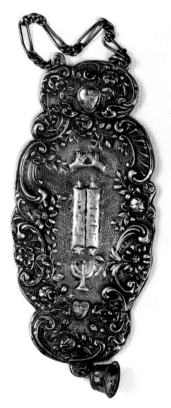

No. 237  F 5690a

REMARKS: This shield forms a set with crown No. 512 and pointer No. 816A

BIBLIOGRAPHY: Berman, No. 20

DONOR: The Abram and Frances Kanof Collection

## 228

### TORAH SHIELD 1990–20 (*Illus. p. 172*)

United States, 1961

Irving Potter (b. 1912)

Wood "intarsia"; silver

H 29.2 W 14.8 cm

HALLMARKS: "I POTTER"

REMARKS: Pointer No. 814 fits on the peg at the upper left face of this shield.

DONOR: Gift of the artist

## 229

### TORAH SHIELD 1989–146 (*Illus. p. 172*)

London, 1890–91

Joseph and Horace Savory, active late 19th century

Silver: repoussé, chased, incised; glass

H 33.7 W 34.9

HALLMARKS: *CITY:* lion; leopard's head; "P" in shield
                    *MAKER:* Pickford, p. 66, third mark

INSCRIPTION: above: קדש לה׳, "Holy to the L[ord]"

REMARKS: Several identical shields of this design were made for Alfred Marcus of the Sha'are Tefilah Synagogue in Boston; each bears a series mark. One is presently at the Smithsonian Institution (NMAH, Inv. No. 154765; see Grossman), while another was recently acquired by the Skirball Museum in Los Angeles. A fourth shield had been at Mishkan Tefilah Synagogue in Boston (successor to Sha'are Tefilah) but was recently stolen. For illustrations see Rubenovitz, pp. 25 and 26. Marcus also donated a wooden Omer Calendar from Palestine to his family's ancestral synagogue in Germany (Jewish Museum JM 23-53). The same silversmiths made finials No. 366.

DONOR: Nathan and Bluma Polmer

## 230

### TORAH SHIELD F 4873c (*Illus. p. 173*)

London, 1934

Silver: repoussé, engraved, parcel-gilt

H 27.1 W 22.7 cm

HALLMARKS: *CITY:* Jackson, p. 91, last series ("t"); Jubilee mark
                    *MAKER:* "M.S" in rectangle

INSCRIPTION: below *parashah* plaque box: מתנה/ מן ר׳ שאול
וחנה סילווערמאן לזכר נשמת בניהם/ הבחור שמואל
נפטר ב׳ ר"ח אדר והבחור צבי נפטר י"ח תשרי/ ת'נ'צ'ב'ה׳,
"Gift from Saul and Hannah Silverman in memory of the souls of their sons, the boy Samuel, died on the second day of the N[ew] M[onth] of Adar, and the boy Zvi, died on the 18th of Tishri, M[ay their] s[ouls] be b[ound up] in the [bond of eternal] l[ife]"

PROVENANCE: Joel Teitelbaum, New York

REMARKS: See Finials No. 367, made in the same year by the same smith and dedicated by the same couple. Years ago, this shield was photographed with the name plaque inverted.

DONOR: Dr. Harry G. Friedman

## 231

### TORAH SHIELD F 5167 (*Illus. p. 173*)

Verdun (?), early 19th century

Silver: repoussé, appliqué, engraved

H 28.3 W 23.0 cm

HALLMARKS: *CITY:* similar to Tardy, p. 193 (.950, provincial); gross guarantee with "53"
                    *MAKER:* "DG" above three dots, within rhomb

INSCRIPTION: at bottom: שייך לחב"ק נושאי המטה, "Belongs to the H[oly] (Burial) Society 'Bearers of the Bier'"

PROVENANCE: Jacob Posen, New York

REMARKS: The engraving of the *parashah* plaque imitates the script of the inscription. This was a society of pallbearers.

DONOR: Dr. Harry G. Friedman

## 232

### TORAH SHIELD X 1983–20 (*Illus. p. 173*)

Europe, 1781/82 (inscription)

Silver: repoussé, cast, engraved, parcel-gilt

H 28.3 W 22.3 cm

HALLMARKS: none

INSCRIPTION: on reverse: זאת/ נדבה לבה בטרם מותה
האשה גאלה בת דוד ישראל ז"ל/ לפרט יביראו׳ שלו'ם'
ינוחו ע'ל' מ'שכב'ותם ילפק, "This was donated to the synagogue, before her death, by the woman Ge'ulah daughter of the late David Israel (chronogram, Isaiah 57:2 [with variations] =(5)542)" (=1781/82)

REMARKS: Parts of this shield are damaged or missing.

DONOR: Jewish Cultural Reconstruction

## 233

### TORAH SHIELD D 127 (*Illus. p. 173*)

Europe, 19th century

Copper: repoussé, die-stamped, engraved, silvered; glass

H 13.7 W 9.2 cm

HALLMARKS: none

PROVENANCE: The Gieldzinski Collection, Danzig

BIBLIOGRAPHY: Danzig 1904, No. 24; Danzig 1933, No. 127; *Danzig 1939*, No. 209

DONOR: The Jewish Community of Danzig

## 234

### TORAH SHIELD U 9840 (*Illus. p. 174*)

Europe, late 19th–early 20th century

Brass: die-stamped, chased, traces of silver plating

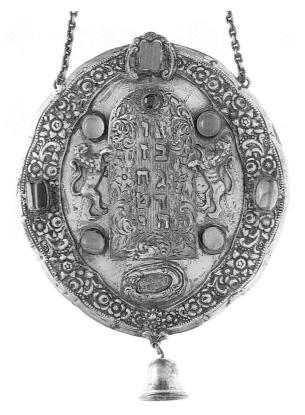

No. 238  JM 25–58

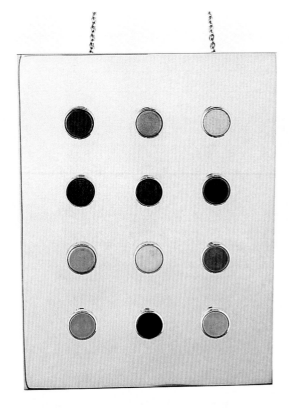

No. 239  1986–68b

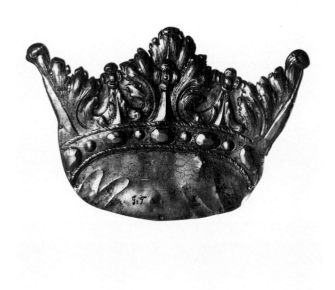

No. 240  F 5027

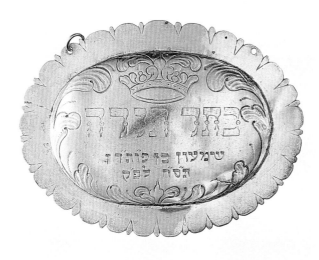

No. 241  F 4071

H 27.9 W 23.0 cm

HALLMARKS: none

REMARKS: Empty holes near the top of this shield indicate that a crown may have been attached there.

## 235

TORAH SHIELD M 265 (*Illus. p. 174*)

Europe, 19th–20th century; 1805/06 (inscription)

Silver: repoussé, cast

H 11.4 W 8.8 cm

HALLMARKS: Lion (?) to right (spurious ?); "HI" (or "HL")

INSCRIPTION: on central shield: זה שייך להיר'ר/ מוה יצחק/ במ/ יצחק יעקב/ יצו מקאברין/ שנת ת'ק'ס'ו'/ לפק, "This belongs to…R[abbi] Isaac son of [Rabbi] Isaac Jacob…of Kobryn, [in the] year (5)566" (=1805/06).

PROVENANCE: The Rose and Benjamin Mintz Collection

REMARKS: The plaque bearing the inscription is older than the rest of the shield.

DONOR: Museum purchase

## 236

TORAH SHIELD F 4185b (*Illus. p. 174*)

Tel Aviv, 1950's

Moshe Smilovici, active 1950's

Silver and white metal: die-stamped, appliqué, filigree, repoussé, parcel-gilt; ivory: carved; semiprecious stones

H 21.4 W 17.9 cm

HALLMARKS: false marks

REMARKS: This shield is a companion piece to crown No. 504. Other Smilovici pieces at The Jewish Museum are shields Nos. 237-238, crown No. 504, and pointers Nos. 832–838. He is represented in many other collections as well. On Smilovici, see Grossman 1989, under entry No. 25/26.

DONOR: Dr. Harry G. Friedman

## 237

TORAH SHIELD F 5690a (*Illus. p. 174*)

Tel Aviv, 1950's

Moshe Smilovici (?), active 1950's

Silver: die-stamped, engraved; gold: engraved; garnet

H 14.3 W 6.5 cm

HALLMARKS: "STERLING"; false Birmingham marks

INSCRIPTION: on hearts, on front and reverse: שדי, "Almighty"

REMARKS: Pointer No. 835 is apparently a matching piece. See remarks, shield No. 236 for other Smilovici pieces.

DONOR: Dr. Harry G. Friedman

## 238

TORAH SHIELD JM 25–58 (*Illus. p. 176*)

Tel Aviv, 1950's

Moshe Smilovici (?), active 1950's

Silver: cast, engraved; semiprecious stones (carnelian, chalcedony, tiger's eye, aventurine); glass

H 15.2 W 13.5

HALLMARKS: false marks

INSCRIPTION: on reverse, on crown: תורת אמת, Malachi 2:6.

PROVENANCE: Ben Ari Arts, New York

REMARKS: There are three *parashah* plaques. See remarks, shield No. 236 for other Smilovici pieces. Cf. pointer No. 838, which was acquired together with this shield.

DONOR: Samuel and Lucille Lemberg

## 239

TORAH SHIELD 1986-68b (*Illus. p. 176*)

Jerusalem, 1958

Moshe Zabari, active 1958-

Silver; enamel; leather

H 18.5 W 14.0 cm

HALLMARKS: "STERLING"; "MADE IN/ ISRAEL"; New Bezalel mark

REMARKS: This is a modern version of the High Priest's breastplate. For another modern version, see shields Nos. 226–27. The artist made this work and its matching Torah Crown (No. 506) to fulfill graduation requirements of the Bezalel School.

DONOR: Sassi and Fred Lonner

## 240

TORAH SHIELD (?) F 5027 (*Illus. p. 176*)

Italy (?), 1696 (inscription)

Silver: repoussé, gilt; glass

H 17.8 W 14.0 cm

HALLMARKS: "c/ NK (ligature)"

INSCRIPTION: on reverse, in oval: *AND: IOS: OKUN/ Ao 1696*, "Andrew (?) Joseph Okun, year 1696"

REMARKS: on the reverse, in ink: "N.G." in script

DONOR: Dr. Harry G. Friedman

## 241

TORAH SHIELD F 4071 (*Illus. p. 176*)

Italy, 1707/08 or 1847/48 (inscription)

Silver: chased, engraved

H 9.2 W 12.4 cm

HALLMARKS: none

INSCRIPTION: כתר תורה/ שמעון בן פ"וה"ר ז/ ת"ס"ח לפ"ק, "Crown of Torah. Simon son of the leader, R[abbi] Z …, (5)468" (=1707/08)

REMARKS: The letter *samekh* in the date appears to have been modified from a *resh*, and thus the actual date would be (5)608=1847/48. For similar Torah Shields in Italy, see *Mitt.* I, p. 22, fig. 14; in Turkey, see Mitrani, p. 42 (Ankara).

DONOR: Dr. Harry G. Friedman

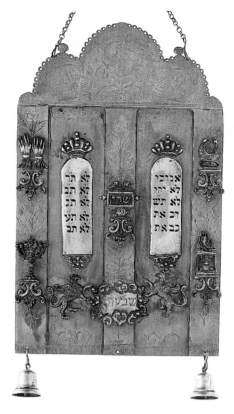

No. 242  D 124

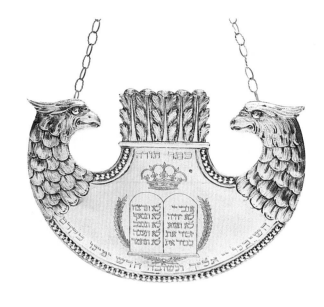

No. 243  F 3441

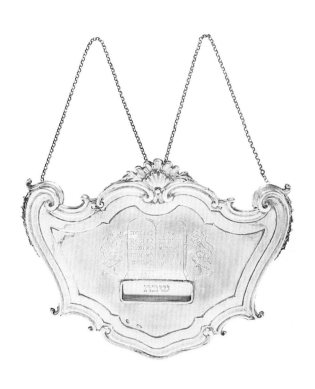

No. 244  F 5424

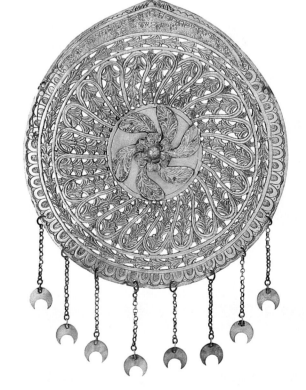

No. 245  1991–124

## 242

TORAH SHIELD D 124 (*Illus. p. 178*)

Poland, late 19th – early 20th century

Brass: chased; silver: cast, appliqué; black paint (?)

H 25.1  W 16.1 cm

HALLMARKS: none

INSCRIPTION: in central panel: שדי, "The Almighty"; in lower cartouche: שבעות, "Shavuot"

PROVENANCE: The Gieldzinski Collection, Danzig

REMARKS: The five symbols associated with the Temple are identical to those found on Italian Torah Finials, Torah Crowns (e.g., the Museum's No. 496) and amulets. The general shape and workmanship of the shield itself, however, seem to be Polish.

BIBLIOGRAPHY: Danzig 1904, No. 21; Danzig 1933, No. 124; *Danzig 1939*, No. 196

DONOR: The Jewish Community of Danzig

## 243

TORAH SHIELD F 3441 (*Illus. p. 178*)

Italy (?), 20th century

Silver: repoussé, engraved

H 18.1  W 25.3 cm

HALLMARKS: Bulgari I, 1, 168-169

INSCRIPTION: above crown: "Crown of Torah"; along lower border: Lamentations 5:21

REMARKS: There are traces of a socket on the reverse. This piece is made from the shade of an Italian oil lamp of 1815, to which 20th-century engraving has been added. See Society of Judaica Collectors, No. 617, for a complete oil lamp with the same hallmarks and an identical shade. Cf. also shield No. 244.

DONOR: Dr. Harry G. Friedman

## 244

TORAH SHIELD F 5424 (*Illus. p. 178*)

Italy (?), 20th century

Silver: repoussé, engraved

H 19.4  W 25.2 cm

HALLMARKS: *CITY:* Bulgari I, 1, No. 137

*MAKER:* Bulgari I, 1, No. 1072/73

REMARKS: The sterling silver *parashah* plaque box and the four *parashah* plaques are a 20th-century addition, as is all the engraving. This piece is made from the shade of an Italian oil lamp of 1786–90, by Mattia Venturesi (active 1760's–70's). See remarks, shield No. 243.

DONOR: Dr. Harry G. Friedman

## 245

TORAH SHIELD 1991–124 (*Illus. p. 178*)

Rhodes, 1859/60

Silver: chased, pierced

H 29.2  W 27.4 cm

HALLMARKS: none

INSCRIPTION: on upper edge: טס אשר הקדיש הגביר המר"ו רצ"ו מיכאל חיים דוד צוריאנו יצ"ו/ בן יעקב יצ"ו ש' כת"ר, "Torah shield which was dedicated by . . . R[abbi] Michael Ḥayyim David Soriano . . ., son of Jacob . . ., [in the] year (5)620" (=1859/60)

PROVENANCE: The Kahal Gadol Synagogue, Rhodes

REMARKS: This shield, crown No. 500, and a pair of finials at the Wolfson Museum, Jerusalem (Inv. No.172-04-12) formed a set, as is seen in a photograph in Levy, pl. [16b] (after Strumza). According to the Wolfson Museum records, the inscription on the finials records their dedication: ". . . Michael Ḥayyim David Soriano . . . for the life of . . . Rebecca Rizulah . . . and the lives of his son Eliezer Jacob and his brother Nissim Isa[ac] . . . ." For a marriage deed of the Soriano family in Rhodes (1830), see *JMNY* 1993, p. 29, fig. 24. For the same "chronogram," literally meaning "crown," see remarks, shield No. 85. Cf. *Sephardic Journey*, p. 204, No. 34, a similar shield from Rhodes, now in the Jewish Museum of Greece, Athens .

BIBLIOGRAPHY: Sotheby's Tel Aviv 1991, No. 221; *JMNY* 1993, p. 46, fig. 52

DONOR: Docents of the Jewish Museum through the Nash Aussenberg Memorial Fund

## 246

TORAH SHIELD 1987–67 (*Illus. p. 180*)

Ioannina, 1919 (inscription)

Silver: repoussé

H 29.4  W 22.3 cm

HALLMARKS: none

INSCRIPTION: on large dedication panel: התכשיט הזה הקדישוהו יחידי/ ק'ק'ח' יאנינא יחד עם א' ספר תורה/ של ה"מ יוסף א' מרקאדו נ"ע ופרכת/ א' עם י' הדברות ואחד זוג רמונים/ של כסף אל ק'ק'ח' נויארק יע"א/ חברה תקוה טובה תכ"בץ ביום א'/ ל"ח אלול שנת ה'תר'ע'ט' לפ"ק, "This ornament was dedicated by individuals of the H[oly] C[ongregation of] Ioannina together with one Torah Scroll of the late Joseph A. Mercado, and one Ark Curtain with the Ten Commandments, and one pair of Torah Finials of silver, to the H[oly] C[ongregation of] New York. . . . The 'Good Hope' Society . . . on the first day of the month of Elul, 5679" (=1919); on crown above: כ ת, "C[rown of] T[orah]"; at center of upper star (in cursive script): ציון, "Zion"

PROVENANCE: Congregation Sheirith Israel, Janina, the Bronx

REMARKS: For another shield with an Ottoman "sunburst" motif and Tablets of the Law, see Mitrani, p. 405 left (Istanbul, Yeniköy Synagogue).

DONOR: Congregation Sheerith Israel of Janina, through Elias Matsas

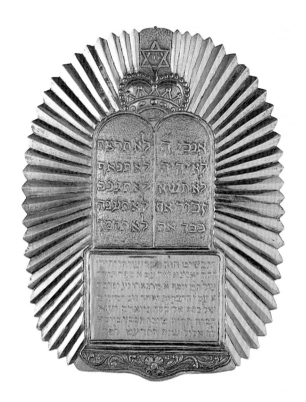

No. 246  1987–67

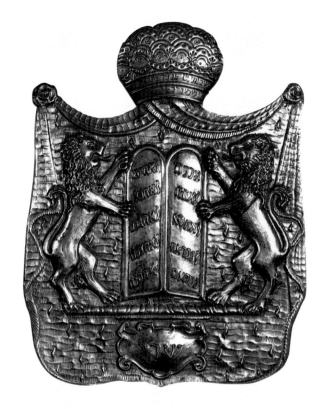

No. 247  F 2754

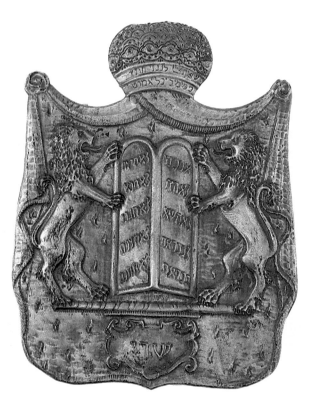

No. 248  F 2755

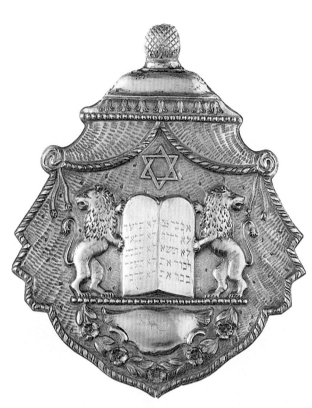

No. 249  F 2756

## 247

TORAH SHIELD  F 2754  (*Illus. p. 180*)

Italy (?), 20th century

Copper: repoussé, silver-plated

H 37.0  W 29.5 cm

HALLMARKS: none

INSCRIPTION: in lower cartouche: שדי, "The Almighty"; on crown: Psalms 16:8

REMARKS: This piece, and shields Nos. 248–250, were purchased in Rome, apparently as a group. The material and workmanship of all four objects are uniform. This piece is identical to shield No. 248.

DONOR: Dr. Harry G. Friedman

## 248

TORAH SHIELD  F 2755  (*Illus. p. 180*)

Italy (?), 20th century

Copper: repoussé, silver-plated

H 37.0  W 29.5 cm

HALLMARKS: none

INSCRIPTION: in lower cartouche: שדי, "The Almighty"; on crown: Psalms 16:8

REMARKS: See the identical shield No. 247 and the remarks there.

DONOR: Dr. Harry G. Friedman

## 249

TORAH SHIELD  F 2756  (*Illus. p. 180*)

Italy (?), 20th century

Silver (?): repoussé

H 29.2  W 23.7 cm

HALLMARKS: "S" in pointed shield; illegible mark

INSCRIPTION: in lower cartouche: שדי, "The Almighty"

REMARKS: This shield is identical to No. 250. See remarks, shield No. 247.

DONOR: Dr. Harry G. Friedman

## 250

TORAH SHIELD  F 2757  (*Illus. p. 182*)

Italy (?), 20th century

Silver (?): repoussé

H 29.2  W 23.7 cm

HALLMARKS: none

INSCRIPTION: in lower cartouche: שדי, "The Almighty"; within Star of David: ה', "The Lord"

REMARKS: This shield is similar to No. 249, though cruder in execution. See remarks, shield No. 247.

DONOR: Dr. Harry G. Friedman

## 251

TORAH SHIELD  F 2160  (*Illus. p. 182*)

20th century

Silver: repoussé

H 14.2  W 9.8 cm

HALLMARKS: none

INSCRIPTION: on lower panel: שדי, "The Almighty"

REMARKS: The workmanship on this piece is very crude.

DONOR: Dr. Harry G. Friedman

## 252

TORAH SHIELD  D 129  (*Illus. p. 182*)

Poland, late 19th–early 20th century

Silver: cast, engraved, parcel-gilt

H 16.5  W 18.1 cm

HALLMARKS:  "12" within dotted oval

    *MAKER:* Unclear name in script (see under remarks, below)

PROVENANCE: The Gieldzinski Collection, Danzig

REMARKS: In Danzig 1933, pl. 5, there are two inscribed pendants, now on shield No. 71. In the Mintz Collection, now at The Jewish Museum, there is a Hanukkah lamp (M 432), the backwall of which is almost identical to this Torah Shield; the maker's mark there, according to Museum records, reads: "Schajnler"; *Danzig 1939*, No. 208, gives the mark on the shield as "Mryngler."

BIBLIOGRAPHY: Danzig 1904, No. 26; Danzig 1933, No. 129, pl. 5; *Danzig 1939*, No. 208

DONOR: The Jewish Community of Danzig

## 253

TORAH SHIELD  (Fragment) JM 31–64  (*Illus. p. 182*)

Germany (?), 18th century (?)

Silver: chased, pierced

H 17.1  W 13.2 cm

HALLMARKS: none

PROVENANCE: Zagayski Collection, Palm Beach

REMARKS: This backsheet is made up of several panels of a 17th-century (?) casket (or book cover); there are holes and slits for the attachment of a crown, two flanking columns, and a *parashah* plaque box, all now missing.

BIBLIOGRAPHY: Zagayski 1951, No. 19; Zagayski 1963, No. 20; PBNY 1964, No. 104 (illus.).

DONOR: Purim Ball Fund Purchase

## 253A

TORAH SHIELD  F 3247  (*Illus. p. ???*)

Germany, mid-19th century

Silver: chased, cast, chased, engraved, parcel gilt; glass ("gems"); felt

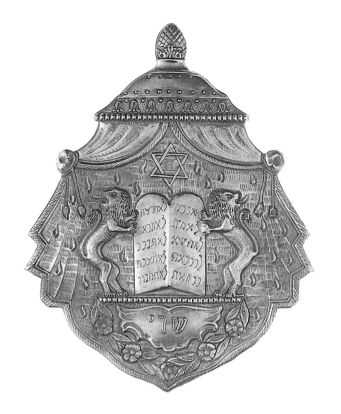

No. 250  F 2757

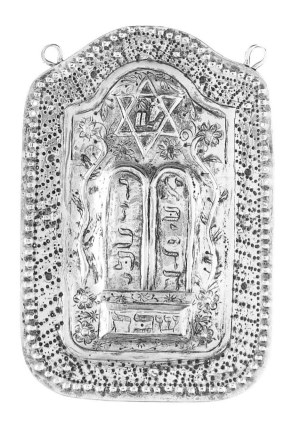

No. 251  F 2160

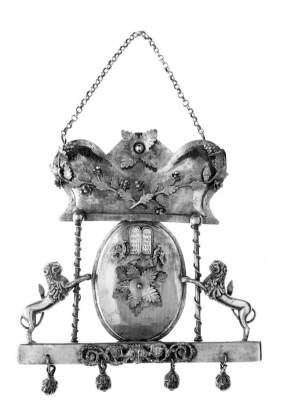

No. 252  D 129

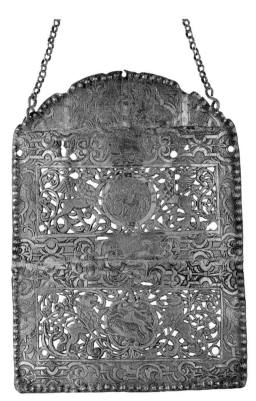

No. 253  JM 31–64

H 21.7 W 16.7 cm

HALLMARKS: *CITY:* "800 / M"; "C" in lozenge
    *MAKER:* "I. BLUM" in rectangle

INSCRIPTION: כ ת, "Crown of Torah"

REMARKS: The two *parashah* plaques appear to be replacements.

DONOR: Dr. Harry G. Friedman

## 253B

### TORAH SHIELD F 2521

Silesia (?), late 18th–early 19th century

Silver: repoussé, parcel gilt; copper (later repair)

H 18.0 W 14.5 cm

HALLMARKS: *CITY:* Scheffler, *Berlin* 30 (a?)
    *MAKER:* "I. BLUM" in rectangle

REMARKS: The *parashah* plaques are missing; the crown is possibly a replacement

DONOR: Dr. Harry G. Friedman

## 253C

### TORAH SHIELD M 278

Galicia, early 19th century

Silver: repoussé, engraved

H 14.7 W 12.8 cm

HALLMARKS: none

INSCRIPTION: (palimpsest) יוסף בן כהרר/ יעקב, "Joseph son of Rabbi Jacob"

PROVENANCE: The Rose and Benjamin Mintz Collection

REMARKS: A crown is missing, as apparently are the pair of lions and three pendants or bells.

DONOR: Museum purchase

## 253D

### TORAH SHIELD M 261

Galicia, early 19th century

Silver: repoussé, cast, engraved, parcel gilt; carnelian; coral

H 28.5 W 24.0 cm

HALLMARKS: none

INSCRIPTION: on column bases: ציזא בת ר' אהרן אשת ר' משה בר' חנוך, "Tziza daughter of Aaron, wife of Moses son of Ḥanokh"; on pendants: כ'כ'/ כ'מ', "Crown of Royalty/ Crown of Priesthood"

PROVENANCE: The Rose and Benjamin Mintz Collection

REMARKS: There is one *parashah* plaque. The central of the three pendants (probably inscribed כ'ת', "Crown of Torah") is missing.

DONOR: Museum purchase

## 253E

### TORAH SHIELD M 240

Poland (?), 1870/71 (?) (inscription)

Silver: repoussé, cast, die-stamped, engraved, gilt

H 25.9 W 20.8 cm

HALLMARKS: *CITY:* "12"
    *MAKER:* "KMF" in script, in rectangle

INSCRIPTION: Their are four *parashah* plaques. The inscriptions on the three pendants have been erased, though on the right-hand one the date can be reconstructed: בשנת/ תר[ל]א/ לפק, "In the year [5]631" (1870/71)

REMARKS: Cf. Christie's New York 1982, No. 147

PROVENANCE: The Rose and Benjamin Mintz Collection

DONOR: Museum purchase

## 253F

### TORAH SHIELD X 1976–4

Europe, late 19th–early 20th century

Silver: repoussé, cast, parcel gilt; glass ("gems")

H 18.0 W 14.5 cm

HALLMARKS: *CITY:* (on lower reverse): illegible

REMARKS: Their are two *parashah* plaques. There appears to have been some element atop the crown. This peculiar piece may not have been made as a Torah Shield.

DONOR: Charles S. Warburg

## 253G

### MINIATURE TORAH SHIELD D 151

Eastern Europe, 19th century

Silver: filigree, cast, parcel gilt

H 16.5 W 12.5 cm

HALLMARKS: none

BIBLIOGRAPHY: Danzig 1904, No. 23; Danzig 1933, No. 126; *Danzig 1939/1982*, No. 17

DONOR: The Jewish Community of Danzig

# Part II · Finials

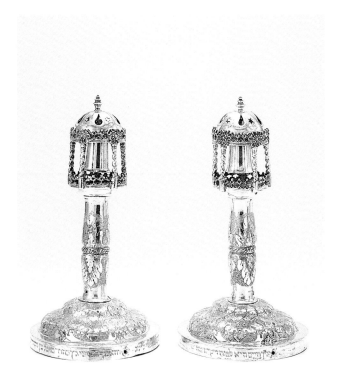

No. 254  JM 42–52a, b

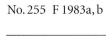

No. 255  F 1983a, b

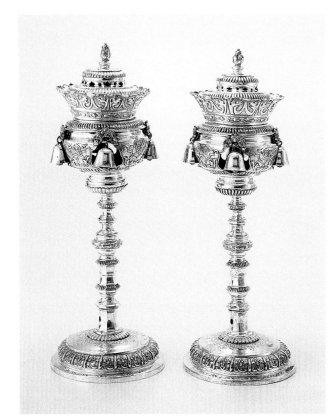

No. 256  JM 18–64a, b

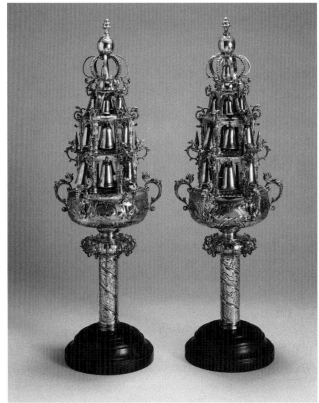

No. 257  F 3685a, b

# Torah Finials

## 254

TORAH FINIALS  JM 42–52a, b  (*Illus. p. 186*)

Frankfurt am Main, 1736

Georg Wilhelm Schedel (?), active 1722–62

Silver: chased, cast, engraved, parcel-gilt

H 25.8/26.1  DIAM 14.1 cm

HALLMARKS: Scheffler, *Hessen*, 133

INSCRIPTION: on a): נתחדש ע״י הגבאים האלוף ג׳יצ׳ כ׳ טעבלי
לילג והאלוף התורני ג׳יצ׳ כהרר מיכל בן התורני הר׳ר יוזל
שפירא זצל בחודש שבט ת׳צי׳ לפק, "Restored by the *gabba'im* … Tevele Lillig and … Rabbi Michel son of … the late Josel Spira in the month of Shevat (5)496" (=January/February 1736); on b): Proverbs 3: 18

PROVENANCE: Jewish Museum, Frankfurt am Main

REMARKS: For these two *gabba'im,* see Dietz, p. 186, No. 351 (David Lilg d. 1736[!]; and p. 290, No. 534 (Michel Joseph Spira (=Speyer). Three holes in the base of each piece, as well as a larger hole at the base of the stem, indicate that these finials had been fastened to the upper Torah Staves. They properly should be regarded as Torah Stave Covers.[1] Cf. Ellenbogen, No. 11 (Israel Museum, 147/225), a very similar pair of Torah Stave Covers bearing the semi-obliterated mark of Johann Adam Boller and a Frankfurt mark ca. 1709–25. That The Jewish Museum pair of covers is also from the Schüler workshop and by Schedel is indicated by three factors: they are patterned closely after the pair by Boller at the Israel Museum; the cast elements are identical to those employed earlier in the Schüler workshop; and most of Schedel's Judaica was copied from earlier designs of the Schüler workshop. See remarks, shield No. 12.

BIBLIOGRAPHY: *Wüb*, No. 33

DONOR: Jewish Cultural Reconstruction

---

1. For a scroll bearing stave covers with square belfries, at the Jewish Museum, Worms, see *AaunZ* 11 June 1925 (No. 22), pp. 172f. The square belfry-fragments in the Cluny Museum, by Jost Leschhorn, with the Frankfurt mark for ca. 1740-50, are very similar (Klagsbald 1981, Nos. 140-141=Klagsbald 1982, No. 25). Marks identical to those on the Cluny pieces are found on a pair of Torah Stave Covers (with later crowns) in the Gross Family Collection, Tel Aviv. The Gross staves (*sans* crowns) and the Cluny belfries may have formed a single pair of Torah Stave Covers.

The fact that the Leschhorn stave covers are so similar to the Schüler examples raises a problem requiring further study: the relationship of the Leschhorn workshop (see the introductory text to shield No. 17) to the Schüler workshop.

## 255

TORAH FINIALS  F 1983a, b  (*Illus. p. 186*)

Nuremberg, ca. 1720

Johann Jakob Fern, active 1694–1737

Silver: chased, cast, gilt

H 21.2  DIAM 6.7 cm

HALLMARKS: R³ 4273

REMARKS: The bear motifs may refer to the family name of the original owner or donor; the ewer on the shield may refer to his Levitical status. Three holes on the base of each piece were used to affix them to the wooden disks of the Torah Staves.

BIBLIOGRAPHY: Kayser, No. 25

DONOR: Dr. Harry G. Friedman

## 256

TORAH FINIALS  JM 18–64a, b  (*Illus. p. 186*)

Augsburg, 1719–20

The successors of Marx Weinolt, active 1700–ca. 1732

Silver: repoussé, cast, gilt

H 37.8  DIAM 14.3 cm

HALLMARKS:  CITY: Seling 180
MAKER: Seling 1671

PROVENANCE: Hermann Weihmann Collection, Feuchtwangen; M. Zagayski Collection, Palm Beach

REMARKS: A hole through the lower stem of each piece indicates that these finials were once affixed to Torah Staves. The form of the base and stem is reminiscent of contemporaneous baluster candlesticks, while that of the upper body recalls contemporaneous ciboria (cf. Seling II, fig. 645; and cf. Ansbacher 1985, p. 33, lower left [mislabeled 12.16;=*Mitt*. III/IV, p. 25, fig. 19=Düsseldorf, Nos. 440–441]). For the identity of the makers, and other pieces by them, see the remarks, shield No. 3. In the Harburger Photo-Archive there is also a photo of a very similar piece (formerly at Hochberg), no details of which are known.

BIBLIOGRAPHY: Munich, No. 6; Zagayski 1951, No. 5; Zagayski 1963, No. 7; PBNY 1964, No. 296

DONOR: Mrs. Henry L. Moses

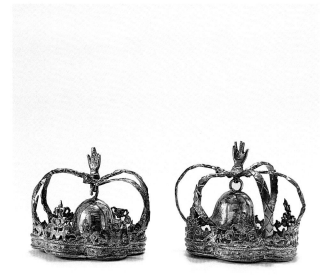

No. 258  JM 16–52a, b

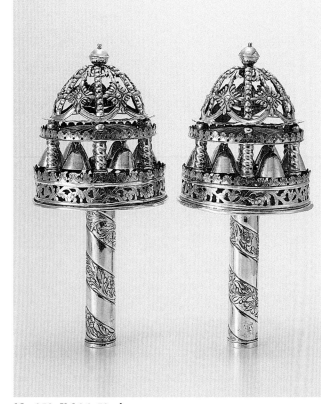

No. 259  JM 26–52a, b

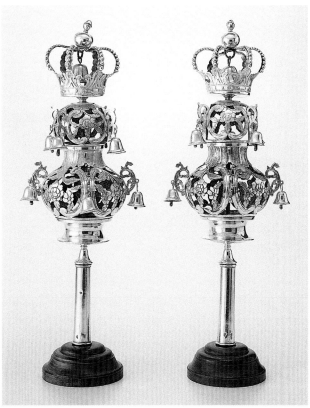

No. 260  F 1819a, b

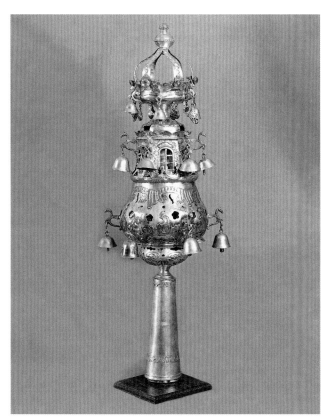

No. 261  F 71

## 257

TORAH FINIALS  F 3685a, b  (*Illus. p. 186*)
Frankfurt am Main, ca. 1720–25
Jeremias Zobel, active 1701–41
Silver: repoussé, pierced, cast, engraved, gilt
H 45.3  DIAM 16.2 cm
HALLMARKS:  *CITY:* Scheffler, *Hessen,* 128
                *MAKER:* Scheffler, *Hessen,* 256/257
PROVENANCE: The Monchsroth Synagogue
REMARKS: The form of these finials closely resembles earlier Amsterdam finials.[1] For further details, see the introduction, p. 43. A photo of these finials appears in the Harburger Photo-Archive (No. 501), where they are noted as coming from Monchsroth, 65 km SW of Nuremberg.
    Another, almost identical pair of finials by Zobel is in the Historical Museum, Frankfurt (Inv. No. x51:11v-w; *Synagoga,*[1] No. C 34=*Synagoga,*[2] No. 201=*Mon. Jud.,* No. E330).[2] A *havdalah* compendium by the same smith is at The Jewish Museum (F 3661=Kayser, No. 96).
BIBLIOGRAPHY: Kayser, No. 29; Mann 1982, No. 69; *Treasures,* pp. 84–85; Mann 1986, pp. 399–400; JMNY 1993, fig. 42
DONOR: Dr. Harry G. Friedman

1. This conclusion was arrived at independently by Dr. Annette Weber, of the Jüdisches Museum in Frankfurt.
2. A pair of finials previously attributed to Zobel (who died in 1741) is at the Skirball Museum in Los Angeles (see F. Landsberger, *Beauty,* p. 112, fig. 4). They clearly bear the mark of Johann Jakob Leschhorn, however, as well as the Frankfurt hallmark used from ca. 1750 until well into the 19th century (on Leschhorn, see the remarks, shield No. 17).

## 258

TORAH FINIALS  (Fragmentary) JM 16–52a, b
(*Illus. p. 188*)
Frankfurt am Main, ca. 1750–79
Conrad Hieronymus May, active 1746–79
Silver: chased, cast
H 8.1  DIAM 9.8 cm
HALLMARKS:  *CITY:* Scheffler, *Hessen,* 145 (var.)
                *MAKER:* Scheffler, *Hessen,* 286
PROVENANCE: The Old Synagogue, Frankfurt am Main; Museum jüdischer Altertümer, Frankfurt am Main
REMARKS: Staves are missing from both crowns, and the priestly hands atop the crowns are probably not original. By 1937, these finials were at the Jewish Museum in Frankfurt, registered as JG 027a,b. A similar pair of finials by Rötger Herfurt, at the Skirball Museum, Los Angeles, lack their original stems (47.25 = see *Ashkenaz,* p. 235, lower right).
BIBLIOGRAPHY: *Notizblatt* 1937, p. 24; *Wüb,* No. 11
DONOR: Jewish Cultural Reconstruction

## 259

TORAH FINIALS  JM 26–52a, b  (*Illus. p. 188*)
Germany, 18th century
Silver: repoussé, cast, engraved
H 27.0  DIAM 13.5 cm
HALLMARKS: "HB" in ligature, with flanking dots, in oval
PROVENANCE: Museum jüdischer Altertümer, Frankfurt am Main (?)
REMARKS: These finials show numerous repairs and are either heavily restored or are pastiches. The Museum's card file indicates that they may have been at the Jewish Museum in Frankfurt.
BIBLIOGRAPHY: *Wüb,* No. 17
DONOR: Jewish Cultural Reconstruction

## 260

TORAH FINIALS  F 1819a, b  (*Illus. p. 188*)
Berlin, ca. 1789
August Ferdinand Gentzmer, active 1789–1808
Silver: chased, cast, parcel-gilt
H 44.0  DIAM 16.1 cm
HALLMARKS:  *CITY:* Scheffler, *Berlin,* 10a
                *MAKER:* Scheffler, *Berlin,* 219
REMARKS: The scotia element beneath the body on these finials is identical to that found on similar examples from Amsterdam and Hamburg (e.g., Schliemann, fig. 839, dated 1758). Cf. the similar finials Nos. 261–262. For other finials by Gentzmer, see Nos. 275 and 276; for other objects by him at The Jewish Museum, see shields Nos. 40, 41, 65, and 67.
DONOR: Dr. Harry G. Friedman

## 261

TORAH FINIAL  F 71  (*Illus. p. 188*)
Germany (?), late 18th–early 19th century
Silver: chased, pierced, cast, parcel-gilt; glass
H 50.5  DIAM 16.6 cm
HALLMARKS:  *CITY:* fleur-de-lis, incuse
                *MAKER:* "IPL" in rectangle
REMARKS: The pendants seem to be made of various jewelry fragments. Cf. the similar finials Nos. 260 and 262.
DONOR: Dr. Harry G. Friedman

## 262

TORAH FINIALS  U 9736a, b  (*Illus. p. 190*)
Germany (?), late 18th–early 19th century
Silver: chased
H 32.0  DIAM 12.0 cm
HALLMARKS:  *CITY:* illegible; "12"
                *MAKER:* "GDS" in oval
REMARKS: Cf. the similar finials Nos. 260 and 261.

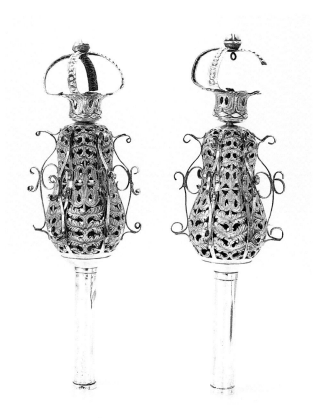

No. 262  U 9736a, b

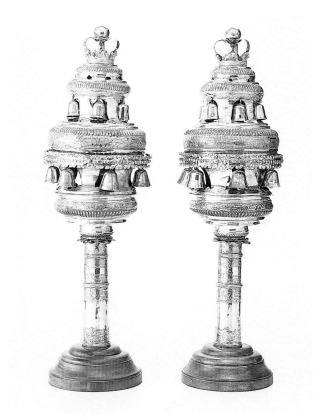

No. 263  F 70a, b

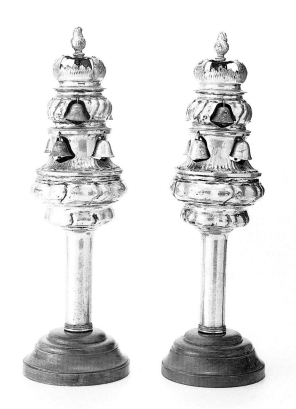

No. 264  F 3043a, b

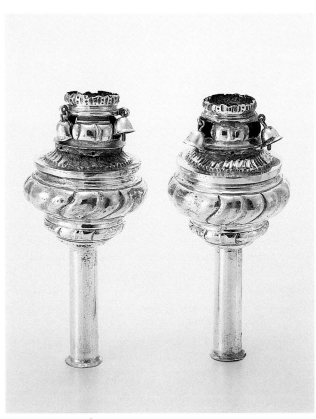

No. 265  F 877a, b

## 263

TORAH FINIALS  F 70a, b  (*Illus. p. 190*)
Nuremberg, early 18th century
Johann Conrad Weiss, active 1699–after 1751
Silver: chased, cast, gilt
H 38.0  DIAM 13.0 cm
HALLMARKS: *CITY:* R³ 3766
                    *MAKER:* R³ 4279
REMARKS: Cf. the similar finials Nos. 264 and 265. For a pair of finials by the same smith, see Rosenan, No. 7b. Other objects by Weiss at The Jewish Museum are Torah Staves No. 915, Pointer No. 517, spice container F 383, and Burial Society beaker JM 30-51.
BIBLIOGRAPHY: Kayser, No. 26
DONOR: Dr. Harry G. Friedman

## 264

TORAH FINIALS  F 3043 a, b  (*Illus. p. 190*)
Nuremberg, mid-18th century
Johann Samuel Beckensteiner, active 1743–81
Silver: repoussé, pierced, gilt
H 31.8  DIAM 10.5 cm
HALLMARKS: *CITY:* "N"
                    *MAKER:* R³ 4295
PROVENANCE: Gorevic, New York
REMARKS: In the Museum's card file, a year mark (R³ 3773=1769–73) is noted, but this was not observed on either of the finials. Other pieces by the same smith at The Jewish Museum include shield No. 28, crown No. 450, and pointer No. 523.
DONOR: Dr. Harry G. Friedman

## 265

TORAH FINIALS  F 877 a, b  (*Illus. p. 190*)
Nuremberg, second half of 18th century
Silver: repoussé, pierced, gilt
H 22.1  DIAM 10.3 cm
HALLMARKS: *CITY:* "N"
                    *MAKER:* "HC/W" or "HC/M" (the first letter could also be: E, N, B or K)
REMARKS: Around the bottom of the upper drum, there are six holes for attaching some missing elements, possibly brackets for bells. The Museum's card file identifies the maker's mark as "JC/W in trefoil," and the smith as Johann Conrad Weiss, but the identification is doubtful since this is not Weiss's mark as it appears on his known pieces.
DONOR: Dr. Harry G. Friedman

## 266

TORAH FINIAL  F 4164  (*Illus. p. 192*)
Nuremberg, ca. 1820–30
Silver: chased

H 24.5  DIAM 8.7 cm
HALLMARKS: *CITY:* "N"
                    *MAKER:* "S" in pointed shield
REMARKS: The central bell in the crown is missing.
DONOR: Dr. Harry G. Friedman

## 267

TORAH FINIAL  F 2519  (*Illus. p. 192*)
Breslau, 1761–76
Johann Ernst Braungart, active 1754–93
Silver: chased, cast
H 23.5  DIAM (base) 8.2 cm
HALLMARKS: *CITY:* Hintze 1906, 20 and 36
                    *MAKER:* Hintze 1906, 163
REMARKS: Several Torah Shields by this smith are known, including Hintze 1929, No. 221 illustrated in *JL* V, pl. clxxi, No. 6 (after col. 976), and Israel Museum 148/20.
DONOR: Dr. Harry G. Friedman

## 268

TORAH FINIALS  D 183 a, b  (*Illus. p. 192*)
Danzig (?), late 18th–early 19th century
Silver and brass: chased, pierced, cast (bells)
H 58.0  DIAM 16.5 cm
HALLMARKS: none
BIBLIOGRAPHY: Danzig 1933, No. 108, pl. 11; *Danzig 1939/1982*, No. 84
DONOR: The Jewish Community of Danzig

## 269

TORAH FINIALS  F 5105 a, b  (*Illus. p. 192*)
Augsburg, 1803
Franz Anton Gutwein, active 1759-1805
Silver: repoussé, pierced, engraved, parcel-gilt
H 33.2  DIAM 10.4 cm
HALLMARKS: *CITY:* Seling 287
                    *MAKER:* Seling 2455c
REMARKS: On the shield at the top is a coat-of-arms or a bend murrey (i.e., engraved to indicate a gold ground with a blood-red band from upper left to lower right). Other finials by Gutwein include Magnes Museum, Berkeley 73.11 (1799 — the earliest example of this type; they have broad bases added by the same smith to the original stems); Museen u. Sammlungen der Stadt Kempten, Inv. No. 4897/2–3 (1802 — see Deneke, No. 3/14); Christie's Amsterdam 1986, No. 322 (1804); Ansbacher, p. 38, No. 2.11; and R³ 1005, exs. e–f (one pair was formerly at the Stuttgart Jewish Community, while the other was in the S. Hochstetter Collection, Stuttgart). The Jewish Museum also possesses four Torah Shields by Gutwein: shields Nos. 50–53.
DONOR: Dr. Harry G. Friedman

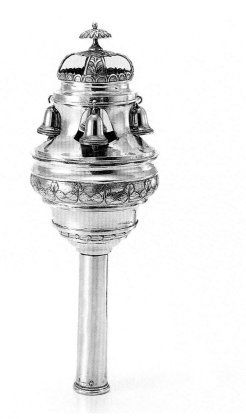

No. 266  F 4164

No. 267  F 2519

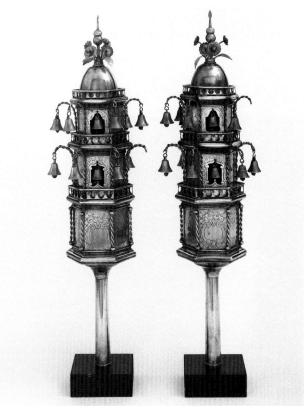

No. 268  D 183a, b

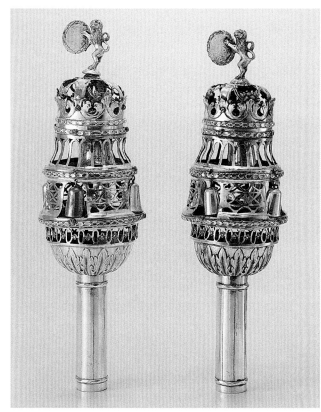

No. 269  F 5105a, b

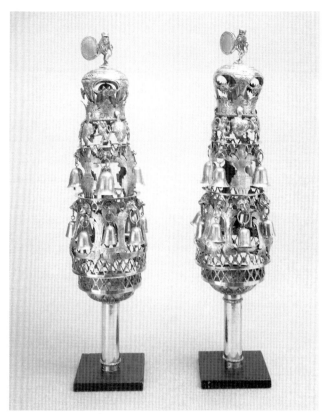

No. 270  F 3919a, b

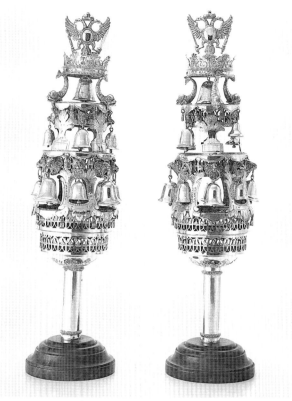

No. 271  F 3920a, b

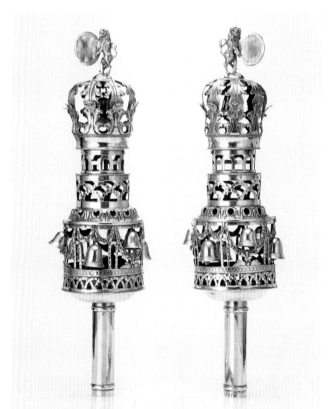

No. 272  F 60c, d

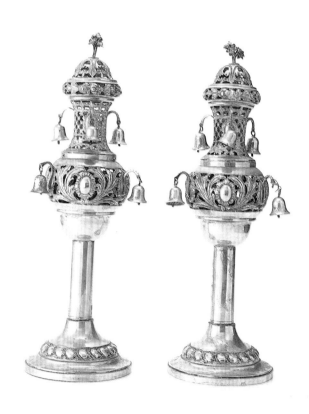

No. 273  F 1803a, b

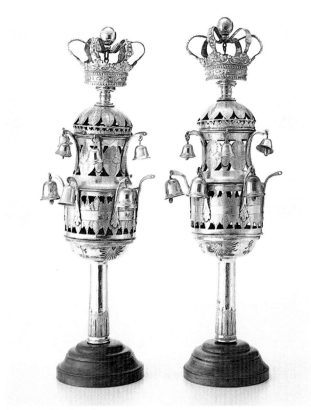

No. 274   D 187a, b

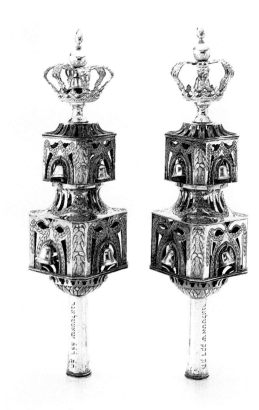

No. 275   D 184a, b

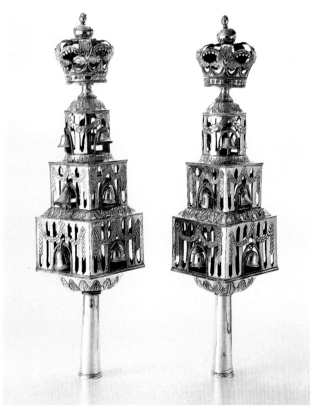

No. 276   D 173a, b

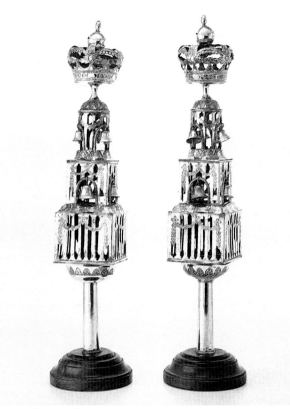

No. 277   D 174a, b

## 270

TORAH FINIALS   F 3919 a, b   (*Illus. p. 193*)

Augsburg, 1803

Carl Bitzel, active 1787–1823

Silver: chased, pierced, die-stamped, cast, gilt

H 50.0   DIAM 12.3 cm

HALLMARKS: *CITY:* Seling 287

          *MAKER:* Seling 2608

REMARKS: Cf. the Bitzel finials No. 271 (also dated 1803), and the references cited there.

BIBLIOGRAPHY: *Jewish Museum 75*, p. [20] (mistakenly ascribed)

DONOR: Dr. Harry G. Friedman

## 271

TORAH FINIALS   F 3920 a, b   (*Illus. p. 193*)

Augsburg, 1803

Carl Bitzel, active 1787–after 1823

Silver: chased, pierced, cast, engraved, gilt

H 48.0   DIAM 12.7 cm

HALLMARKS: *CITY:* Seling 287

          *MAKER:* Seling 2608

REMARKS: Cf. the Bitzel finials No. 270 (also made in 1803); for other of his finials, see PBNY 1967, No. 154=*Temple Israel*, p. 7 (1804); Sotheby's NY, 1988, No. 280 (1802); and Horowitz, No. 41 (1803). The Jewish Museum also has a Hanukkah lamp by Bitzel (F 1536; 1803). For a discussion regarding Bitzel, see under Furman, No. 6.

DONOR: Dr. Harry G. Friedman

## 272

TORAH FINIALS   F 60 c, d   (*Illus. p. 193*)

Augsburg, 1808

Joseph Antoni Seethaler, active 1766–1811

Silver: chased, pierced, cast, parcel-gilt

H 41.0   DIAM 9.5 cm

HALLMARKS: *CITY:* Seling 294

          *MAKER:* Seling 2512

PROVENANCE: The Jewish Community, Munich (?)

REMARKS: These finials are almost certainly No. 16 in the Munich exhibition of 1930. Other finials by the same smith are Weinstein, p. 88, fig. 43 (master's mark misread); Sotheby's NY 1987, No. 298 (=Sotheby's NY 1989, No. 225—1808); and PBNY 1957, No. 138 (1797 ?). At The Jewish Museum, Torah Shield No. 55 is also by Seethaler (also 1808). The unmarked pointer No. 549 may also be by him.

BIBLIOGRAPHY: Munich, No. 16

DONOR: Dr. Harry G. Friedman

## 273

TORAH FINIALS   F 1803 a, b   (*Illus. p. 193*)

Augsburg, 1866

Magnus Unsinn, active 1847–89

Silver: repoussé, traces of gilt

H 41.8   DIAM 13.0 (base 13.7) cm

HALLMARKS: *CITY:* Seling 354; R³ 3; "800"

          *MAKER:* Seling 2753; Neuwirth 1978, No. 199

REMARKS: The bases, which are not tubular but solid, are not original and bear later marks (possibly those of H. Meyen & Co., Berlin). A similar finial by the same smith is illustrated in Weinstein, fig. 95, left (misdated 1781–83). For a shield by Unsinn, see No. 60.

DONOR: Dr. Harry G. Friedman

## 274

TORAH FINIALS   D 187 a, b   (*Illus. p. 194*)

Berlin, ca. 1763–70

Joachim Hübener, active ca. 1737–80

Silver: chased, cast, engraved

H 40.5   DIAM 14.4 cm

HALLMARKS: *CITY:* Scheffler, *Berlin*, 7

          *MAKER:* Scheffler, *Berlin*, 110

REMARKS: For other pieces by Hübener at the Museum, see shields Nos. 37–39, and references there.

BIBLIOGRAPHY: *Danzig 1939*, No. 217

DONOR: The Jewish Community of Danzig

## 275

TORAH FINIALS   D 184 a, b   (*Illus. p. 194*)

Berlin, 1788–1802

August Ferdinand Gentzmer (?), active 1789–1808

Silver: chased, cast, parcel-gilt

H 47.5   DIAM 13.5 cm

HALLMARKS: *CITY:* Scheffler, *Berlin*, 11 and 30

          *MAKER:* "AG" (not in Scheffler, *Berlin*)

INSCRIPTION: on one finial: ח״ק דק״ק שאטטלאנד,"H[oly] (Burial) S[ociety] of the h[oly] c[ongregation] of Schottland"

PROVENANCE: The Schottland Synagogue, Danzig

REMARKS: Finials No. 276 are by Gentzmer; for other objects by him at the Museum, see finials No. 260.

BIBLIOGRAPHY: Danzig 1933, No. 143b (ill.); *Danzig 1939/1982*, No. 79; Emden, fig. 3; JMNY 1993, fig. 39

DONOR: The Jewish Community of Danzig

## 276

TORAH FINIALS   D 173 a, b   (*Illus. p. 194*)

Berlin, 1788–1802

August Ferdinand Gentzmer, active 1789–1808

Silver: repoussé, pierced, cast, engraved, parcel-gilt

H 52.7   W 12.0 cm

HALLMARKS: *CITY:* Scheffler, *Berlin*, 11 and 30b

          *MAKER:* Scheffler, *Berlin*, 219

INSCRIPTION: Graffiti on bottom of body: on finial A— "147E"; "147e"; on finial B— "147c" (?)

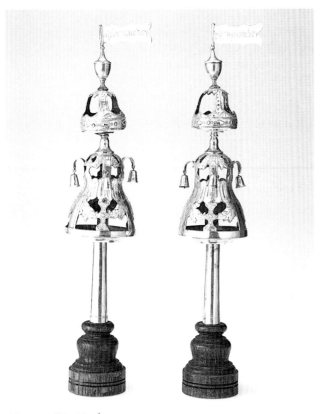

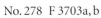

No. 278  F 3703a, b

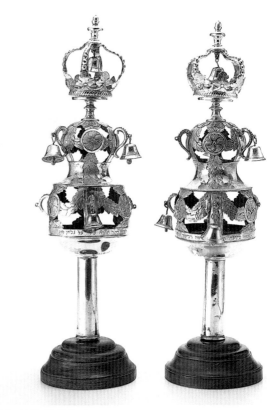

No. 279  D 179a, b

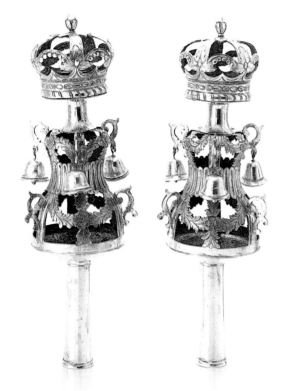

No. 280  D 180a, b

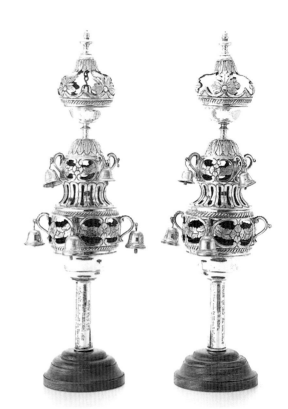

No. 281  D 178a, b

REMARKS: Finials No. 275 are also by Gentzmer; for other objects by him at the Museum, see finials No. 260.

BIBLIOGRAPHY: *Danzig 1939/1982*, No. 80; Emden, fig. 2

DONOR: The Jewish Community of Danzig

## 277

### TORAH FINIALS  D 174a, b  (*Illus. p. 194*)

Danzig, early 19th century

Johann Gottlieb Ulrich, ca. 1812–26

Silver: chased, pierced, cast, parcel-gilt

H 52.6  W 9.9 cm

HALLMARKS: *CITY:* Czihak 9; "S" incuse

*MAKER:* Cf. Czihak 526

REMARKS: As noted by V. Mann, these finials are copies of finials No. 276. For other objects by this smith at The Jewish Museum, see alms containers D 219 and D 223.

BIBLIOGRAPHY: *Danzig 1939/1982*, No. 81

DONOR: The Jewish Community of Danzig

## 278

### TORAH FINIALS  F 3703a, b  (*Illus. p. 196*)

Berlin, 1788–1802

Silver: chased, cast, pierced, gilt

H 35.5  DIAM 8.5 cm

HALLMARKS: *CITY:* Scheffler, *Berlin*, 11; "12" (also engraved "12"); French import mark "ET" (Tardy, p. 207, upper right)

*MAKER:* illegible

INSCRIPTION: on the flags: /דגל מחנה דן/ דגל מחנה אפרים
דגל מחנה ראובן/ דגל מחנה יהודה, "Banner of the Camp of Dan, Banner of the Camp of Ephraim"; "Banner of the Camp of Reuben, Banner of the Camp of Judah"

DONOR: Dr. Harry G. Friedman

## 279

### TORAH FINIALS  D 179a, b  (*Illus. p. 196*)

Berlin, 1790–1802; 1814/15 (inscription)

Casimir Ernst Burcky, active ca. 1790–1828

Silver: chased, cast, engraved, gilt

H 37.5  DIAM 12.4 cm

HALLMARKS: *CITY:* Scheffler, *Berlin*, 11

*MAKER:* Scheffler, *Berlin*, 220

INSCRIPTION: on the lower body, on both finials: נעשה מקופת
החברה קדישה דביקור חולים מק׳ק׳ וויינבערג על ידי
הגבאי ר׳ סענדר ב׳ר׳ס׳// לפרט כ׳תר ת׳ורה׳ ע׳ולה׳ ע׳ל
ג׳ב׳יהן לפק, "Made from the funds of the Holy Society for Visiting the Sick, of the h[oly] c[ongregation of] Weinberg, by the *gabbai* Sender son of S.," chronogram from Pirke Avot 4:17 (= [5]575=1814/15); on the underside of the upper crowns: "6" and, in black ink: "535"

PROVENANCE: The Weinberg Synagogue, Danzig

REMARKS: In *Danzig 1939*, the date is misread as "(5)583= 1823." See finials No. 281 by Burcky.

BIBLIOGRAPHY: Danzig 1933, No. 145b; *Danzig 1939*, No. 216

DONOR: The Jewish Community of Danzig

## 280

### TORAH FINIALS  D 180a, b  (*Illus. p. 196*)

Berlin or Danzig, early 19th century

Silver: chased, pierced, parcel-gilt

H 32.8  DIAM 10.5 cm

HALLMARKS: none

BIBLIOGRAPHY: *Danzig* 1939, No. 220

DONOR: The Jewish Community of Danzig

## 281

### TORAH FINIALS  D 178a, b  (*Illus. p. 196*)

Berlin, 1804–15; 1845 (inscription)

Casimir Ernst Burcky, active ca. 1790–1828

Silver: chased, pierced, cast, parcel-gilt

H 42.7  DIAM 15.0 cm

HALLMARKS: *CITY:* Scheffler, *Berlin*, 10a or 12, and 30a

*MAKER:* Scheffler, *Berlin*, 220

INSCRIPTIONS: on finial A: את כלי הקדש האלה נדבו
היורשים/ אשר נקבו בישמותם[!] על פחי הכסף/ לב׳ה׳כנ׳
ד׳ק״ק שאטלאנד יעא/ בשנת ת׳ר׳ה׳ לפ׳ק, "These sacred objects were donated by the heirs, who placed their names on the silver plaques for the s[ynagogue] o[f the] h[oly] c[ongregation of] Schottland . . . in the year (5)605" (= 1845); on finial B: עבור נשמת היקר כ׳ה׳ צבי הירש העררמאן
הלוי/ ואשתו היקרה מ׳ אסתר/ זכרונם לא יסוף עד דור
דורים, "On behalf of the dear soul of . . . Zvi Hirsch Herrmann ha-Levi and his dear wife Esther, their memory shall not perish for generations."

PROVENANCE: The Schottland Synagogue, Danzig

REMARKS: In *Danzig 1939* the city hallmark is given as Scheffler, *Berlin*, 11 (1788–1802). See finials No. 279 by the same smith.

BIBLIOGRAPHY: Danzig 1933, No. 142b; *Oppenheim*, p. 4a; *Danzig 1939*, No. 215

DONOR: The Jewish Community of Danzig

## 282

### TORAH FINIALS  JM 30-57a, b  (*Illus. p. 198*)

Berlin, 1804–15

Silver: chased, pierced, cast

H 30.4  DIAM 7.3 cm

HALLMARKS: *CITY:* Scheffler, *Berlin*, 12

*MAKER:* illegible

REMARKS: These finials appear in an old photo, along with other objects, in The Jewish Museum's Photographic Archive. They are marked there with the number "1942." A

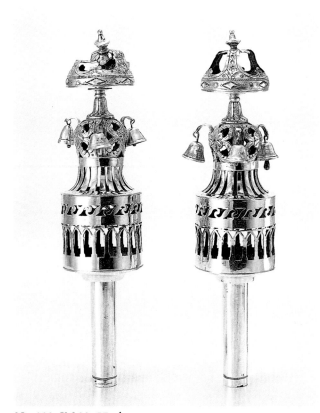

No. 282   JM 30–57a, b

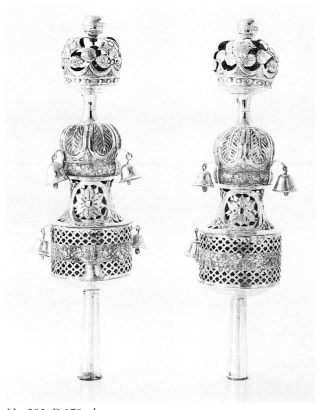

No. 283   D 170a, b

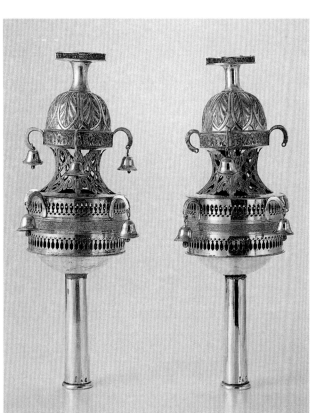

No. 284   F 2538a, b

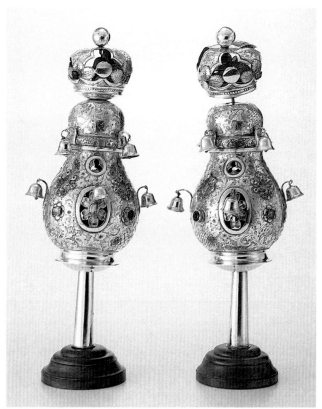

No. 285   F 1412a, b

note on the reverse reads: "Property of E. Sochat-Berkeley, 33 Rue du Clichy, Paris, 9ᵉᵐᵉ. Photo Marc Vaux, 114, Rue de Vaugiraud, Paris, VIᵉ Littré 90–01." The traces of the maker's mark may point to one of the Müller family.

DONOR: Robert I. Wishnik

## 283

TORAH FINIALS  D 170 a, b  (*Illus. p. 198*)
Berlin, 1821–39
Johann Friedrich Wilhelm Borcke, active 1816–39
Silver: chased, pierced, die-stamped, engraved, parcel-gilt
H 37.2  DIAM 9.9 cm
HALLMARKS: *CITY:* Scheffler, *Berlin*, 14
          *MAKER:* Scheffler, *Berlin*, 331
INSCRIPTION: on finial A: the German script has partly been effaced, apparently deliberately: *Danziger Wohltatig/keits-Verein; Durch den . . . / . . . A . . . / . . . / And . . . / Wohl . . .*, "Danzig Benevolent Society; Through the . . . Benev(olent Society)"; later grafitto: "142"
PROVENANCE: The Great Synagogue, Danzig (?)
REMARKS: Finials No. 284 and crown No. 453 are by the same smith.
BIBLIOGRAPHY: Danzig 1933, No. 144b; *Danzig 1939*, No. 218
DONOR: The Jewish Community of Danzig

## 284

TORAH FINIALS  F 2538a, b  (*Illus. p. 198*)
Berlin, 1821–39
Johann Friedrich Wilhelm Borcke, active 1816–39
Silver: die-stamped, cast, filigree, pierced
H 36.0  DIAM 17.0 cm
HALLMARKS: *CITY:* Scheffler, *Berlin*, 14 and 18
          *MAKER:* Scheffler, *Berlin*, 330
PROVENANCE: Salomon Collection, London; Gorevic, New York
REMARKS: The upper parts of the small crowns are missing. Finials No. 283 and crown No. 453 are by the same smith.
BIBLIOGRAPHY: PBNY 1949, No. 110
DONOR: Dr. Harry G. Friedman

## 285

TORAH FINIALS  F 1412a, b  (*Illus. p. 198*)
Berlin, 1842–47
Silver: chased, die-stamped; glass
H 42.5  DIAM 14.2 cm
HALLMARKS: *CITY:* Scheffler, *Berlin*, 14 and 19
          *MAKER:* Scheffler, *Berlin*, 404
REMARKS: A spacing element seems to be missing on either finial, between the body and the crown above. The scotia element at the bottom of the body is a late survival of a very early element on German finials; cf. the earlier finials, No. 260, with this same feature. The master's mark, in a

simplified fraktur script, is given in Scheffler, *Berlin*, as mark 404 and is ascribed to Friedrich Wilhelm August Heller, active ca. 1834–after 1869; but a note there raises the possibility that this mark, which can be read as either A H or A B, might be that of the workshop of Meyer Ascher and Jacob Ludwig Badt, established in 1844 (Scheffler, *Berlin*, No. 2193). Ascher was born in Neumark in 1807 and was apprenticed to a silversmith in Berlin 1822–26. Badt was the son of a Polish-born rabbi, became a citizen of Berlin in 1842 and was a gold and silver manufacturer and jewelry dealer there in the 1850's and 1860's.
DONOR: Dr. Harry G. Friedman

## 286

TORAH FINIALS  M 457a, b  (*Illus. p. 200*)
Berlin (?), first half of 19th century
Silver: chased, cast, pierced, parcel-gilt
H 33.8  DIAM 10.4 cm
HALLMARKS: none
PROVENANCE: The Rose and Benjamin Mintz Collection
DONOR: Museum purchase

## 287

TORAH FINIALS  D 172a, b  (*Illus. p. 200*)
Danzig, 1829–31; 1830/31 (inscription)
Silver: filigree, pierced, parcel-gilt
H 34.1  DIAM 11.0 cm
HALLMARKS: *CITY:* Czihak 9 and XXXVII
          *MAKER:* "L" in script, within square [not Czihak 470 (XIX)]
INSCRIPTIONS: on finial A: שייך להחברה קדישא דב"ח/ דק"ק מאטטענבודען, "Belongs to the Holy Society for V[isiting the] S[ick], of the h[oly] c[ongregation of] Mattenbuden"; on finial B: נעשה ע"י הגבאי/ ר' חיים אלחנן ב"ר יי פירשטענבערג/ בשנת תקצא לפ"ק, "Made by the *gabbai* Ḥayyim Elḥanan son of Y. Fürstenberg, in the year (5)591" (=1830/31); graffito on stem: "106"
PROVENANCE: The Mattenbuden Synagogue, Danzig
BIBLIOGRAPHY: Danzig 1933, No. 106; *Danzig 1939*, No. 225
DONOR: The Jewish Community of Danzig

## 288

TORAH FINIALS  D 175a, b  (*Illus. p. 200*)
Danzig, ca. 1800; 1893 (inscription)
Silver: filigree, pierced, engraved, parcel-gilt
H 47.4  DIAM 15.1 cm
HALLMARKS: *CITY:* Czihak 2-10 (blurred); "S" or "8"
          *MAKER:* "F" (?), in script; illegible mark
INSCRIPTION: on each finial, on lower, later part of stem: *Dem Andenken ihrer verstorbenen Eltern / J.H. Italiener gest. d. 2. Decbr. 1893 / Friederike Rosalie Italiener geb. Becker gest. d. 2. Octbr. 1886 / gewidmet / Danzig d. 2. December 1893*, "In

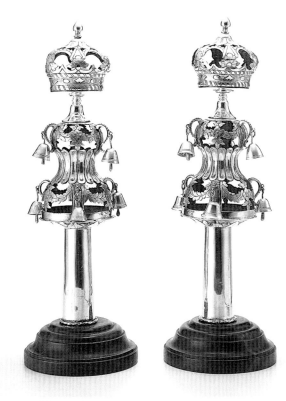

No. 286  M 457a, b

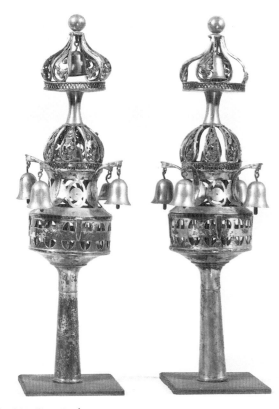

No. 287  D 172a, b

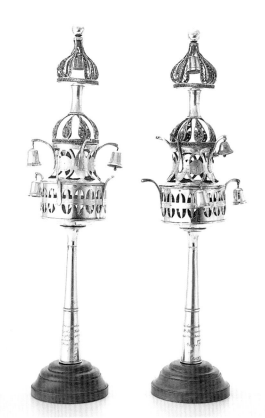

No. 288  D 175a, b

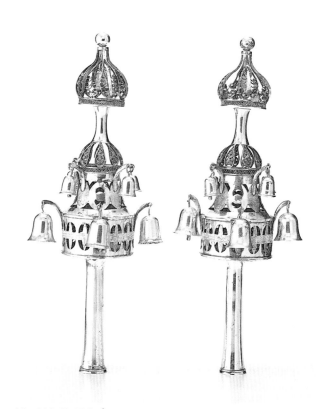

No. 289  D 176a, b

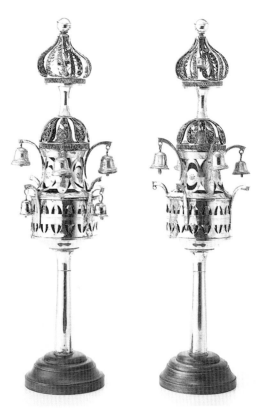

No. 290  D 181a, b

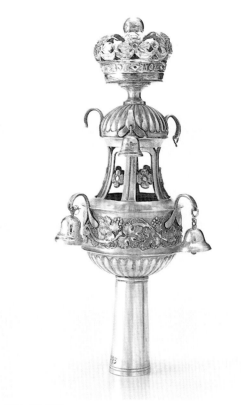

No. 291  F 1793

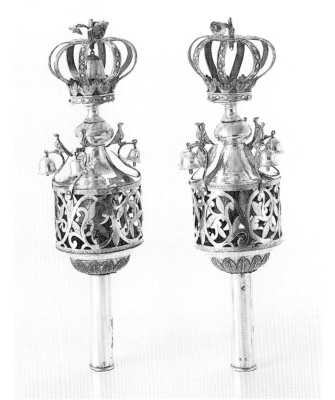

No. 292  M 129a, b

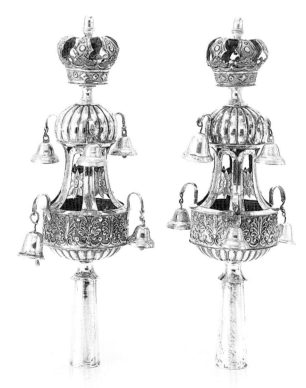

No. 293  D 177a, b

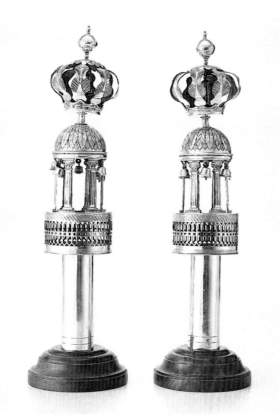

No. 294  M 454a, b

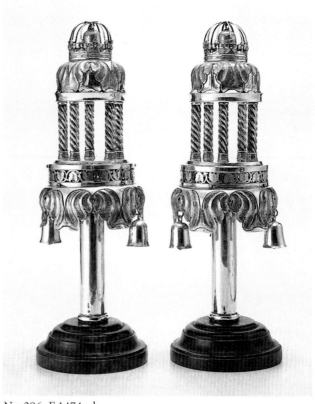

No. 296  F 1474a, b

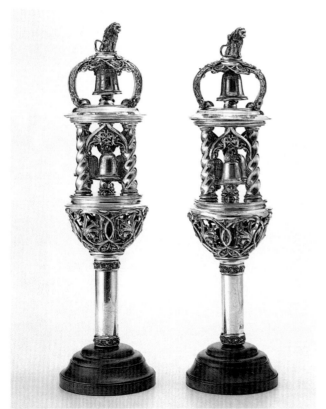

No. 297  JM 9–57a, b

No. 298  F 4752

memory of their departed parents, J.H. Italiener, died 2 December 1893 [and] Friederike Rosalie Italiener, née Becker, died 2 October 1886, dedicated Danzig, 2 December 1893"; on lower story: *Heinrich, Julius, Ludwig Italiener.*

REMARKS: The hallmarks are on the lower part of the original stem, to which an additional piece, 7.2 cm long, was added at the bottom.

BIBLIOGRAPHY: Danzig 1933, No. 147b; *Danzig 1939*, No. 224

DONOR: The Jewish Community of Danzig

## 289

TORAH FINIALS  D 176 a, b  (*Illus. p. 200*)
Danzig, early 19th century (1792–1836)
Silver: filigree, pierced, die-stamped, engraved
H 28.8  DIAM 9.4 cm
HALLMARKS: *CITY:* Czihak 2-10 (blurred)
          *MAKER:* "GFM" ("GFN"?) in script
PROVENANCE: The Gieldzinski Collection, Danzig
BIBLIOGRAPHY: Danzig 1904, No. 13; Danzig 1933, No. 105; *Danzig 1939/1982*, No. 83
DONOR: The Jewish Community of Danzig

## 290

TORAH FINIALS  D 181a, b  (*Illus. p. 201*)
Danzig, 1821–28 (?)
August Nathanael Lehnhard (?), active 1799–1841
Silver: filigree, pierced, chased, engraved, parcel-gilt
H 47.5  DIAM 15.2 cm
HALLMARKS: *CITY:* Czihak 9; "S" incuse
          *MAKER:* "ANL", probably Czihak 519 (var.) (in roman letters, not script)
REMARKS: See shield No. 71, bearing the same marks.
BIBLIOGRAPHY: Danzig 1933, No. 146b; *Danzig 1939/1982*, No. 82
DONOR: The Jewish Community of Danzig

## 291

TORAH FINIAL  F 1793  (*Illus. p. 201*)
Breslau, 1834–39
Leberecht Fournier, active 1821–49
Silver: chased, pierced, die-stamped, parcel-gilt
H 25.8  DIAM 9.3 cm
HALLMARKS: *CITY:* Hintze 1906, 26 and 46
          *MAKER:* Hintze 1906, 189
REMARKS: Cf. the similar finials No. 293; and Hintze 1929, No. 197 (illus.). The grapevine frieze is a typical feature of Breslau silver, appearing on secular objects as well as Judaica. See Sotheby's Jerusalem 1988, No. 150, a *havdalah* compendium by Breslau silversmith Gottfried Daniel Posch (Hintze 1906, 187).
DONOR: Dr. Harry G. Friedman

## 292

TORAH FINIALS  M 129 a, b  (*Illus. p. 201*)
Galicia or Silesia, first half of 19th century
Silver: chased, cast, engraved, punched
H 36.5 / 37.0  DIAM 9.7 cm
HALLMARKS: Lion to left, in rectangle; "12"
PROVENANCE: The Rose and Benjamin Mintz Collection
REMARKS: Though of Berlin type, the workmanship on this pair, and features such as the birds, point to another origin. The Museum records note a hallmark: "M.K." on these finials.
DONOR: Museum purchase

## 293

TORAH FINIALS  D 177a, b  (*Illus. p. 201*)
Breslau, 1848 or 1849
Carl Friedrich Korock, active 1835–58
Silver: chased, pierced, die-stamped, gilt
H 28.3  DIAM 7.6 cm
HALLMARKS: *CITY:* Hintze 1906, 27 (with "48" or "49");
               Hintze 1906, 47
          *MAKER:* Hintze 1906, p. 103 (= R³ 1455)
INSCRIPTION: on both finials, in script: *Lesser Gieldzinski / gewidmet der Israel: / Gemeinde zu Danzig*, "Lesser Gieldzinski, dedicated to the Jewish Community in Danzig"
PROVENANCE: The Gieldzinski Collection, Danzig; the Great Synagogue, Danzig
REMARKS: Cf. the similar finial No. 291. For other finials by the same smith, see Hintze 1929, No. 201; and Martyna, Nos. 10, 12 and 13. More than twenty Judaica objects by Korock are known, including an inscribed Burial Society alms container of 1847 at The Jewish Museum (M 29).
BIBLIOGRAPHY: *Danzig 1939/1982*, No. 85
DONOR: The Jewish Community of Danzig

## 294

TORAH FINIALS  M 454 a, b  (*Illus. p. 202*)
Germany, ca. 1820–30
Silver: die-stamped, pierced, parcel-gilt
H 42.0  DIAM 9.2 cm
HALLMARKS: none
PROVENANCE: The Rose and Benjamin Mintz Collection
REMARKS: One finial bears an earlier number, in red: "(1) 53–14a, b."
DONOR: Museum purchase

## 295

TORAH FINIALS  F 1931a, b
Frankfurt am Main, early 20th century
Successors to B. Bohrmann
Brass: chased, pierced, cast, silver-plated

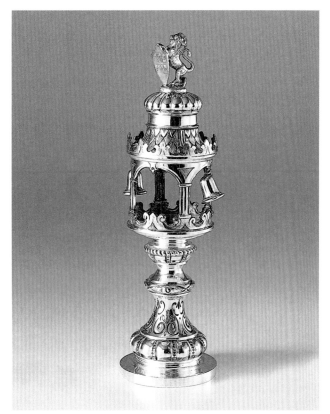

No. 299  F 3842

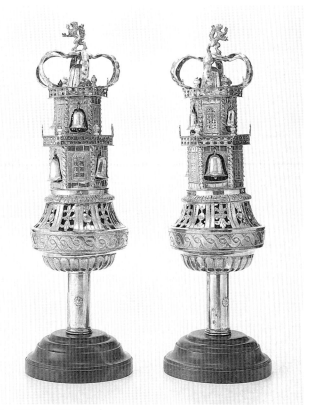

No. 300  JM 19–52a, b

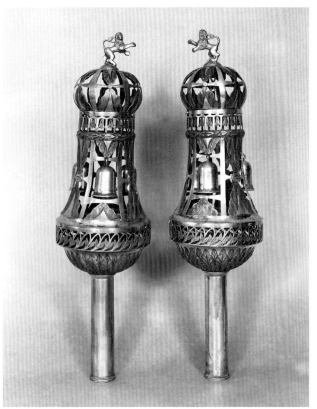

No. 301  F 1539a, b

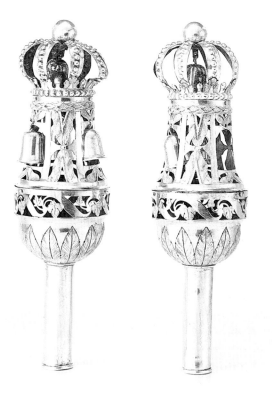

No. 302  F 1049a, b

H 38.6 DIAM 10.6 cm
HALLMARKS: *Kalender* 1951, p. 87, col. 3, No. 2
DONOR: Dr. Harry G. Friedman

## 296

TORAH FINIALS  F 1474 a, b  (*Illus. p. 202*)
Ansbach, mid-19th century
I. Rupp
Silver: chased, cast, engraved, parcel-gilt
H 35.6  DIAM 12.8 cm
HALLMARKS:  CITY: none
        MAKER: "I RUPP" in rectangle; "13"
REMARKS: Torah Shield No. 61, by the same smith and bearing the same hallmarks, has an additional mark reading "ANSBACH." It is assumed that the shield and finials formed a set.
DONOR: Dr. Harry G. Friedman

## 297

TORAH FINIALS  JM 9–57 a, b  (*Illus. p. 202*)
Munich, 1865
Kronenbitter, active ca. 1864–65
Silver: die-stamped, cast, parcel-gilt
H 37.1  DIAM 10.1 cm
HALLMARKS:  CITY: R³ 3467/68(var.), with "65"
        MAKER: "Kronenbitter" in script; "in München" in script
PROVENANCE:  Castelbolognesi Collection, Rome (= Dr. Yoveli, New York)
REMARKS: This pair and finial No. 298 (1864) represent two identical pairs of finials made by this smith. Their dates, hallmarks, workmanship, and style correspond to two Torah Shields by Kronenbitter, one in the Furman Collection, Santiago, Chile (Furman, No. 5), and the other at the Israel Museum, Jerusalem (148/12=Cohen, No. 14 — there misdated). Thus, there were two very similar sets of Torah ornaments made by Kronenbitter in 1864-65. No related pointers are known.
BIBLIOGRAPHY: PBNY 1957, No. 181; noted under Furman, No. 5
DONOR: Samuel and Lucille Lemberg (through Dr. Harry G. Friedman)

## 298

TORAH FINIAL  F 4752  (*Illus. p. 202*)
Munich, 1864
Kronenbitter, active ca. 1864–65
Silver: die-stamped, cast, parcel-gilt
H 29.2  DIAM 10.7 cm
HALLMARKS:  CITY: R³ 3467/68(var.), with "64"
        MAKER: "Kronenbitter" in script; "in München" in script

REMARKS: This finial, which had been converted into a spice container prior to its acquisition in 1958, has hallmarks identical to those on No. 297 except for the year mark (1864). It is surely the mate of a finial of identical design and marks, now in the Stern Collection, New York (T116). See remarks, finials No. 297.
DONOR: Dr. Harry G. Friedman

## 299

TORAH FINIAL  F 3842  (*Illus. p. 204*)
Germany, after 1880
Silver: cast, chased, engraved, gilt
H 25.0  DIAM 7.9 cm
HALLMARKS: R³ 3; "800"; illegible
INSCRIPTION: on small shield: כתר תורה, "Crown of Torah"
DONOR: Dr. Harry G. Friedman

## 300

TORAH FINIALS  JM 19–52 a, b  (*Illus. p. 204*)
Fürth, late 18th century
Silver: chased, pierced, cast, gilt
H 37.5  DIAM 12.0 cm
HALLMARKS:  CITY: R³ 2152; "T"; R³ 2157, with R³ 2154 above
REMARKS: For a discussion of the problem of the hallmarks, see remarks, shield No. 32, where there are references to other Fürth pieces. For similar finials, see No. 301; and PBNY 1957, No. 138 (by J. A. Seethaler, Augsburg, 1797). Other Fürth finials with R³ 2157 and R³ 2154 include Israel Museum, 147/42, 147/58 (singleton), 147/71 (inscription 1802/03; *Wüb*, No. 46 — also from Jewish Cultural Reconstruction), and 147/228; Germanisches National Museum, Inv. No. JA 36 (Deneke, No. 3/17); Private Collection, Fürth (Deneke, No. 3/18).
BIBLIOGRAPHY: Kayser, No. 27; Deneke 1988, No. 6/22
DONOR: Jewish Cultural Reconstruction

## 301

TORAH FINIALS  F 1539 a, b  (*Illus. p. 204*)
Nuremberg, late 18th–early 19th century
Johann Friedrich Kramer, active 1781–1807 or later
Silver: chased, pierced, cast, parcel-gilt
H 39.5  DIAM 11.0 cm
HALLMARKS:  CITY: "N"
        MAKER: R³ 4306, with R³ 4315
REMARKS: For this lion hallmark see shield No. 92. Cf. the similar finials, No. 300 (Fürth) and Nos. 302–304 (Nuremberg). Several Hanukkah lamps by Kramer are in private hands and in trade (Israel).
DONOR: Dr. Harry G. Friedman

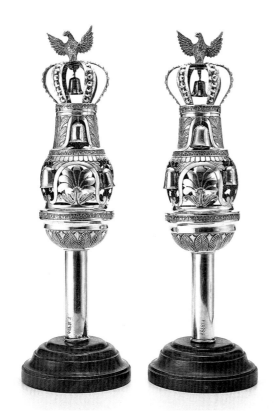

No. 303   F 1899a, b

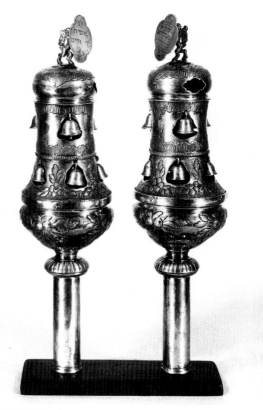

No. 304   F 4381a, b

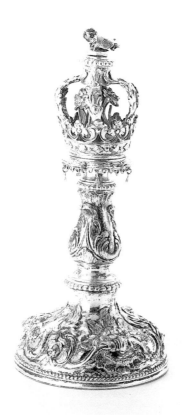

No. 305   F 2672

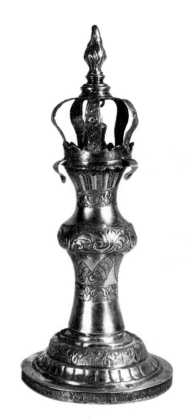

No. 306   F 3132

## 302

TORAH FINIALS  F 1049a, b  (*Illus. p. 204*)
Nuremberg, first half of 19th century
Silver: chased, traces of gilt
H 30.7  DIAM 8.8 cm
HALLMARKS: *CITY:* "N", with (date letter ?) "K" in script
        *MAKER:* illegible
REMARKS: Cf. the similar finials No. 301.
DONOR: Dr. Harry G. Friedman

## 303

TORAH FINIALS  F 1899a, b  (*Illus. p. 206*)
Nuremberg, first half of 19th century
Silver: chased, die-stamped, cast, gilt
H 38.2  DIAM 9.5 cm
HALLMARKS: *CITY:* R³ 3770; "13"
        *MAKER:* "SC" or "CS," monogram in script
REMARKS: For shields with the same marks, see No. 93 and Gross Collection, 51.1.8.
DONOR: Dr. Harry G. Friedman

## 304

TORAH FINIALS  F 4381a, b  (*Illus. p. 206*)
Nuremberg, early 19th century, 1808/09 (inscription)
Johann Jacob Rademacher (?), active 1767–91 or later
Silver: chased, cast, engraved
H 35.5  DIAM 9.4 cm
HALLMARKS: *CITY:* "N," with R³ 3800
        *MAKER:* R³ 4316
INSCRIPTION: on finial A: ז"נ/ משה/ ב'ר חיים, on finial B: קהל גלהויזן תקסט/ לפק, "This is a donation of Moses son of Ḥayyim, Gelhausen Community, (5)569" (=1808/09).
REMARKS: One lion with shield at the top is a later replacement. "Gelhausen" is probably Gelnhausen, 35 km NE of Frankfurt am Main. Pieces of rococo flatware in private hands bear the same marks as these finials, but with the year mark for 1773–76. One mark, a spoked wheel, could very well be that of J. J. Rademacher, whose name means "wheelwright" (see under R³ 4301). The dates of the Nuremberg year letter marks are very problematic.
DONOR: Dr. Harry G. Friedman

## 305

TORAH FINIAL  F 2672  (*Illus. p. 206*)
Breslau, 1792–93
Joseph Gottlieb Lederhose, active 1765–1817
Silver: repoussé, cast, parcel-gilt
H 21.7  DIAM 10.3 cm
HALLMARKS: *CITY:* Hintze 1906, 21 and 39
        *MAKER:* Hintze 1906, 167

REMARKS: For the mate of this finial, see Sotheby's Tel Aviv, 1994, No. 114, an identical finial bearing identical marks, whose only difference is the misplacement of the top element. A pair of Warsaw finials of the same design is in the Israel Museum (Stieglitz, No. 4); a "provincial" variant is finial No. 306.
DONOR: Dr. Harry G. Friedman

## 306

TORAH FINIAL  F 3132  (*Illus. p. 206*)
Poland, mid-19th century
Silver: chased, punched, cast, gilt
H 32.2  DIAM 9.5 cm
HALLMARKS: "12"
REMARKS: Cf. the similar finial No. 305, and the remarks there.
DONOR: Dr. Harry G. Friedman

## 307

TORAH FINIALS  F 261a, b  (*Illus. p. 208*)
Breslau, 1867
Carl Friedrich Otto Theodor Krutsche, active 1858-84
Silver: chased, pierced, engraved, traces of gilt
H 36.8  DIAM 11.0 cm
HALLMARKS: *CITY:* Hintze 1906, 27 (but with "67") and 49; "70"
        *MAKER:* "O.K" incuse; cf. Hintze 1906, p.107, top
INSCRIPTION: on the dome of both finials: מר אונד מיסעס שאול יוסף בראנערוויץ, "Mr. and Mrs. Saul Joseph Broner[e]witz"
PROVENANCE: Israelitisches Krankenhaus, Breslau
REMARKS: The description and date of these finials matches those of Hintze 1929, No. 203. Therefore, the inscription was almost certainly added since 1929, probably in the United States. Finials No. 308 are very similar to these. Pointer No. 565 is by the same smith. Hintze 1929, Nos. 202 and 231 are also by Krutsche and were at the same institution in Breslau.
BIBLIOGRAPHY: Hintze 1929, No. 203
DONOR: Dr. Harry G. Friedman

## 308

TORAH FINIALS  D 189a, b  (*Illus. p. 208*)
Germany (?), 19th century
Silver: chased, cast
H 41.2  DIAM 14.4 cm
HALLMARKS: "M" incuse; illegible mark, twice
INSCRIPTIONS: on finial B, in the first cartouche: כלי קדש לשרת בקדש/ לעטרת תפארת תורתינו הקדושה, "A sacred vessel to serve in sanctity, for the crowning glory of our holy Torah"; in the other cartouche: *Lewin Wollig/ Elkan Lewinsohn/ Ernestine Lewinsohn/ geb.* [i.e. *née*] *Wollig*. On finial A, in the first cartouche: קנו מהונם לכבוד צורם

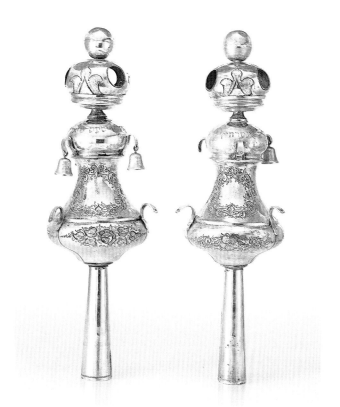

No. 307  F 261a, b

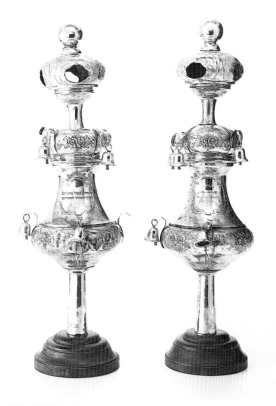

No. 308  D 189a, b

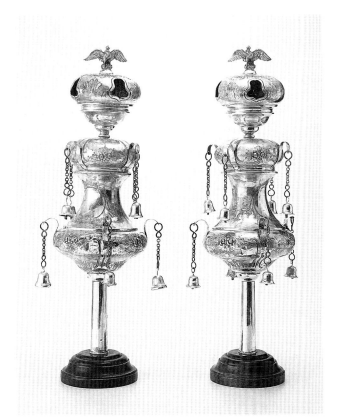

No. 310  D 188a, b

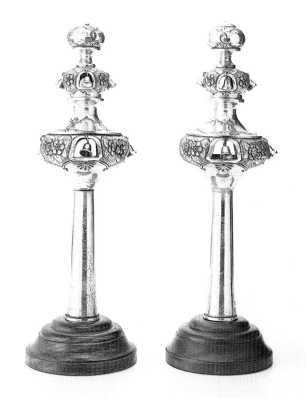

No. 311  D 185a, b

שפחתם[למ]ולנחלה ול/ לקנין ,וקונם," "They purchased [it] from their wealth in honor of their Rock and Creator, as property and estate for their family"; in the other cartouche: *Johanna Wollig/geb.* [i.e. *née*] *Franck/Elkan Lewinsohn/Ernestine Lewinsohn/geb.* [i.e. *née*] *Wollig*
BIBLIOGRAPHY: Danzig 1933, No. 141b; *Danzig 1939*, No. 242
DONOR: The Jewish Community of Danzig

## 309
TORAH FINIALS  D 171a, b
Germany, second half of 19th century
Silver: chased, parcel-gilt
H 35.5  DIAM 12.8 cm
HALLMARKS: "750"
BIBLIOGRAPHY: *Danzig 1939*, No. 219
DONOR: The Jewish Community of Danzig

## 310
TORAH FINIALS  D 188a, b  (*Illus. p. 208*)
Germany (?), 19th century
Silver: chased, cast, pierced, engraved, parcel-gilt
H 56.3  DIAM 16.5 cm
HALLMARKS: none
BIBLIOGRAPHY: Danzig 1933, No. 107; *Danzig 1939*, No. 222
DONOR: The Jewish Community of Danzig

## 311
TORAH FINIALS  D 185a, b  (*Illus. p. 208*)
Germany (?), 19th century
Silver: chased, pierced, parcel-gilt
H 30.3  DIAM 9.8 cm
HALLMARKS: none
PROVENANCE: The Weinberg Synagogue, Danzig
REMARKS: These pieces bear a "W," the identification mark of the Weinberg synagogue.
BIBLIOGRAPHY: *Danzig 1939*, No. 221
DONOR: The Jewish Community of Danzig

## 312
TORAH FINIALS  D 182a, b  (*Illus. p. 210*)
Germany (?), early 19th century
Silver: repoussé, cast, gilt; glass
H 20.6  DIAM 9.5 cm
HALLMARKS: none
REMARKS: These finials are marked with an old inventory number: "147a," which seems not to correspond with the Danzig 1933 number.
BIBLIOGRAPHY: *Danzig 1939*, No. 223
DONOR: The Jewish Community of Danzig

## 313
TORAH FINIALS  F 3011b, c  (*Illus. p. 210*)
Kassel, 1836–37
Friedrich Proll, active 1824–64
Silver: pierced
H 23.5  DIAM 7.2 cm
HALLMARKS: *CITY*: Scheffler, *Hessen*, 592
            *MAKER*: "PROLL"; Scheffler, *Hessen*, Kassel, No. 172.
REMARKS: Cf. shield No. 78 by the same smith.
DONOR: Dr. Harry G. Friedman

## 314
TORAH FINIALS  F 989a, b  (*Illus. p. 210*)
Germany (or Austria), late 19th–early 20th century
Silver (?): repoussé, pierced, parcel-gilt
H 29.6  DIAM 7.4 cm
HALLMARKS: none
DONOR: Dr. Harry G. Friedman

## 315
TORAH FINIALS  F 2584a, b  (*Illus. p. 210*)
Germany (or Holland), mid-19th century
Silver: filigree, cast
H 34.5  DIAM 11.8 cm
HALLMARKS: none
INSCRIPTIONS: on finial A: חברה גמלת חסדים ר׳ אהרון רייז ר׳ שמחה בר דוד, ". . . Benevolent Society, Aaron Reiss, Simḥah son of David"; on finial B: ר׳ יהודה ב״ר יוסף ר׳ חיים ב״ר יהודה, "Judah son of Joseph, Ḥayyim son of Judah"
DONOR: Dr. Harry G. Friedman

## 316
TORAH FINIALS  JM 20–52a, b  (*Illus. p. 211*)
Germany, second half of 19th century
Silver: chased, die-stamped, cast, parcel-gilt
H 34.8  DIAM 8.7 cm
HALLMARKS: "E.S. & Co."; "13" incuse
REMARKS: Cf. Sotheby's NY 1986, No. 329 (=Sotheby's Tel Aviv 1991, No. 247) and cf., with the same marks, Köln, No. 69.
DONOR: Jewish Cultural Reconstruction

## 317
TORAH FINIAL  F 3529  (*Illus. p. 211*)
Germany, mid-19th century
Silver: die-stamped, cast
H 33.5  DIAM 8.3 cm
HALLMARKS: none
DONOR: Dr. Harry G. Friedman

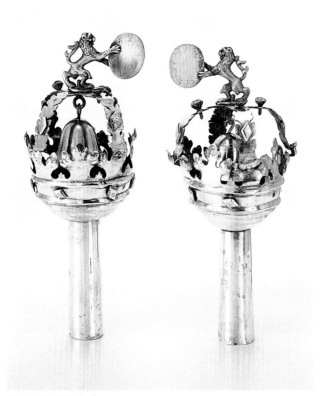

No. 312  D 182a, b

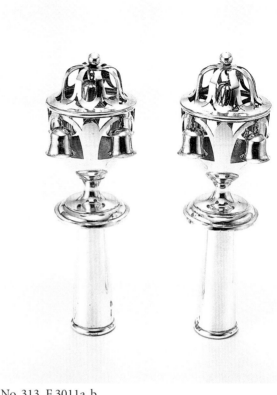

No. 313  F 3011a, b

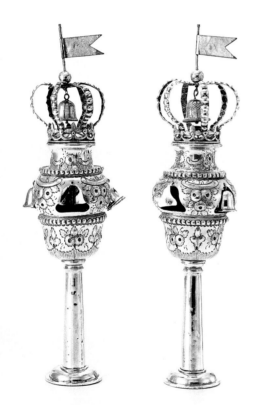

No. 314  F 989a, b

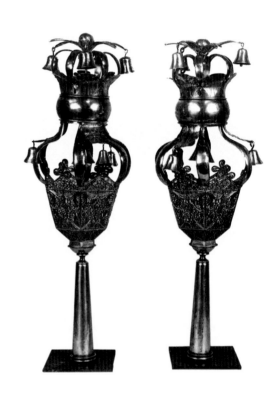

No. 315  F 2584a, b

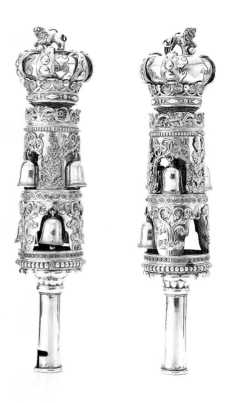

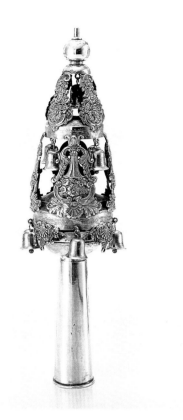

No. 316  JM 20–52a, b

No. 317  F 3529

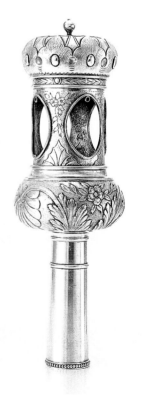

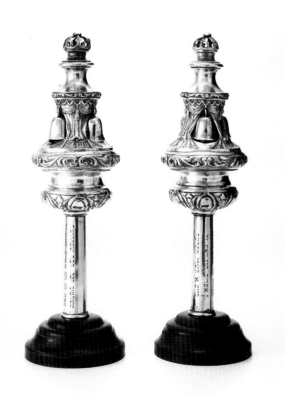

No. 318  F 4976

No. 319  U 9949a, b

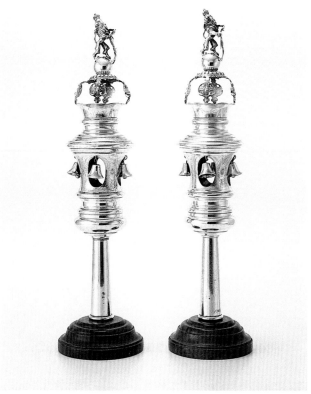

No. 320   F 263a, b

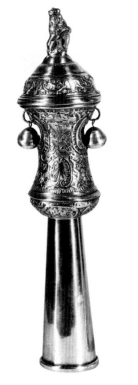

No. 320A   F 4379a, b

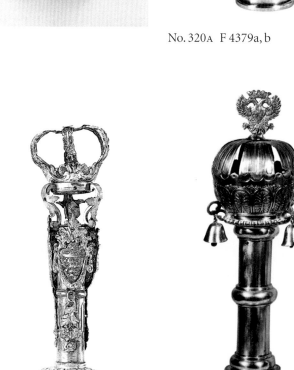

No. 321   JM 13–57a, b

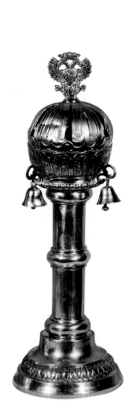

No. 322   F 3262a, b

## 318
TORAH FINIAL  F 4976  (*Illus. p. 211*)
Germany, late 19th century
Silver: chased, die-stamped
H 31.8  DIAM 10.0 cm
HALLMARKS: "BA" with star high between
REMARKS: This finial is identical in design, although larger and chased, with brass patterns for a finial used by Emil Freund in Hanau. For an example cast from these patterns, see Christie's NY 1984, No. 211.
DONOR: Dr. Harry G. Friedman

## 319
TORAH FINIALS  U 9949a, b  (*Illus. p. 211*)
Hanau (?), 1914 (inscription)
Silver: cast, engraved, gilt(?)
H 31.9  DIAM 10.1 cm
HALLMARKS: false: "N"; "13"
INSCRIPTION: on finial A: מאת /משתמש לכל דבר שבקודשה ,"ה"ג ה"מ אפרים הי"ו, "[To serve] for every thing that is sacred, from . . . Ephraim. . . ."; on finial B: המנוח מר אביו /אברהם/ ו' אפרים ה בן גיאת ז"ל/ ביום א' תשרי התר"עה "[in memory of] the deceased honorable Rabbi, his father, Abraham son of the late Ephraim Benguiat, on 1 Tishri 5675" (= 21 September 1914)
PROVENANCE: The Hadji Ephraim and Mordecai Benguiat Family Collection
REMARKS: Cf. *Historica*, fig. 5, Cat. No. A11 — an identical casting except for the top element.
DONOR: Museum purchase

## 320
TORAH FINIALS  F 263a, b  (*Illus. p. 212*)
Geislingen/Steige, late 19th–early 20th century
Württembergische Metallwarenfabrik A.G.
Brass: cast, engraved, silver-plated
H 47.0/47.5  DIAM 10.9 cm
HALLMARKS: *Kalender* 1951, p. 95, 8th row right; "1/0"
DONOR: Dr. Harry G. Friedman

## 320A
TORAH FINIALS  F 4379a, b  (*Illus. p. 212*)
Hanau or Frankfurt am Main, early 20th century
Brass or copper: cast, silver-plated
H 28.2  DIAM 6.6 cm
HALLMARKS: none
REMARKS: The lion element at the top resembles a casting pattern used in the Emil Freund workshop in Hanau.
DONOR: Dr. Harry G. Friedman

## 321
TORAH FINIALS  JM 13–57a, b  (*Illus. p. 212*)
Nágyszeben (Hermannstadt), 1776–78
Michael Gross (?), active 1767–78
Silver: repoussé, cast, parcel-gilt
H 28.8  DIAM 10.5 cm
HALLMARKS: *CITY:* Kőszegy 1275(var.); "13"
      *MAKER:* Kőszegy 1472
INSCRIPTION: in cartouches on stems of both finials: שייך לה/ שמואל/ יפ"ה/ ואשתו/ לאנה/ היפשו (?)/הבחורי' חיים/ מאיר/ שי"ח, "Belongs to . . . Samuel Jaffe and his wife Lena . . . [and their sons] the youths Ḥayyim [and] Me'ir, may they live"
REMARKS: Cf. shield No. 125, with identical marks.
DONOR: B. W. Huebsch, New York

## 322
TORAH FINIALS  F 3262a, b  (*Illus. p. 212*)
Vienna, 1803
Silver: cast, chased, parcel-gilt
H 36.0  DIAM 12.4 cm
HALLMARKS: *CITY:* Rohrwasser, p. 10, second row (1803)
      *MAKER:* "GL" in oval
DONOR: Dr. Harry G. Friedman

## 323
TORAH FINIALS  F 3421a, b  (*Illus. p. 214*)
Vienna, 1805
Franz Lorenz Turinsky, active 1789–1828
Silver: die-stamped, chased
H 15.3  DIAM 6.5 cm
HALLMARKS: *CITY:* Rohrwasser, p. 10, second row (1805)
      *MAKER:* Reitzner, No. 947
DONOR: Dr. Harry G. Friedman

## 324
TORAH FINIAL  F 3022  (*Illus. p. 214*)
Austrian Empire, 1814
Silver: cast, chased, pierced, parcel-gilt
H 27.5  DIAM (base) 8.2 cm
HALLMARKS: *CITY:* Seling 252 (false) over an Austrian Empire mark (cf. Rohrwasser, p. 12)
      *MAKER:* "AS" in shield with pointed top
REMARKS: Within the base in an old inventory or stock number: "D 733 1709 af xx." This finial may have been made from a chinoiserie object, such as an incense burner.
DONOR: Dr. Harry G. Friedman

## 325
TORAH FINIAL  F 4165  (*Illus. p. 214*)
Vienna, 1838
Silver: repoussé, gilt

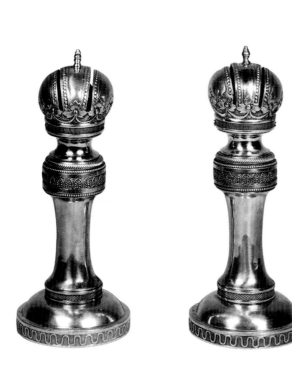

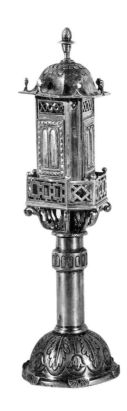

No. 323  F 3421a, b

No. 324  F 3022

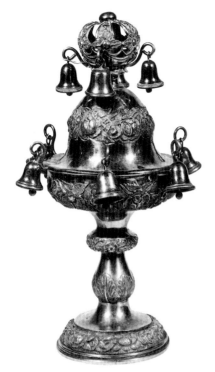

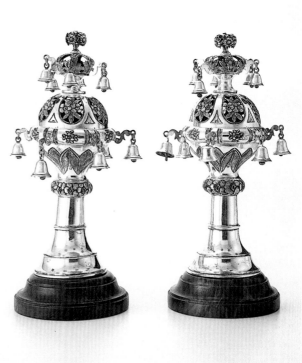

No. 325  F 4165

No. 326  F 259a, b

H 23.5 DIAM 12.5 cm

HALLMARKS: *CITY:* Rohrwasser, p. 13, third row (1838)

   *MAKER:* "OW"; illegible mark

REMARKS: An element on the stem seems to be missing, contributing to the odd proportions of this piece.

DONOR: Dr. Harry G. Friedman

## 326

### TORAH FINIALS  F 259a, b  (*Illus. p. 214*)

Vienna, 1886–1908

Johann Ziehrer, active 1878–1908

Silver: chased, pierced

H 27.6 DIAM 14.9 cm

HALLMARKS: *CITY:* Rohrwasser, p. 19, 2nd row, large 800

   *MAKER:* Neuwirth II/292, No. 1452

REMARKS: See the similar finials Nos. 328–329. For other objects at the Museum made by this smith, see shield No. 114.

DONOR: Dr. Harry G. Friedman

## 327

### TORAH FINIALS  F 1438a, b  (*Illus. p. 214*)

Budapest, 19th century

Silver: repoussé, gilt

H 32.0 DIAM 14.4 BASE DIAM 12.5 cm

HALLMARKS: *CITY:* Brestyansky 118–123

   *MAKER:* "CC" (?), in script

DONOR: Dr. Harry G. Friedman

## 328

### TORAH FINIALS  F 5377a, b  (*Illus. p. 216*)

Austrian Empire, late 19th century

Brass: die-stamped, cast, silvered

H 37.5 DIAM 11.3 cm

HALLMARKS: none

REMARKS: Cf. the similar finials Nos. 326 and 329.

DONOR: Dr. Harry G. Friedman

## 329

### TORAH FINIAL  F 3282  (*Illus. p. 216*)

Austria-Hungary, late 19th–early 20th century

Brass: cast, chased, pierced, traces of silvering

H 32.5 DIAM 14.0 cm

HALLMARKS: none

INSCRIPTION: on base: חברה בני חיים מחנה ראובן, "Sons of Life Society, Camp of Reuben"

REMARKS: Cf. the similar finial No. 328.

DONOR: Dr. Harry G. Friedman

## 330

### TORAH FINIALS  F 4640a, b

Austrian Empire, late 19th century

Brass: die-stamped, cast, traces of silvering (?)

H 34.6 DIAM 11.1 cm

HALLMARKS: none

DONOR: Dr. Harry G. Friedman

## 331

### TORAH FINIALS  1993–145a, b  (*Illus. p. 216*)

Galicia, early 18th century

Silver: chased, pierced, traces of gilt

H 23.3 DIAM 17.6 cm

HALLMARKS: none

REMARKS: No parallels are known for these finials, whose workmanship is of high quality. The gadrooning around the base is typical of the late 17th–early 18th century, but the open "crown" is quite unusual. These finials were acquired together with shield No. 172.

DONOR: Else Samson, in memory of Rabbi Wilhelm Buchheim of Dortmund

## 332

### TORAH FINIALS  F 2362a, b  (*Illus. p. 217*)

Galicia, late 18th–early 19th century

Silver: chased, filigree

H 16.7 DIAM 8.8 cm

HALLMARKS: Rohrwasser, p. 11, upper left, "mittel" (with "E"=Cracow, 1806/07)

INSCRIPTION: on circlet of crown on each: Proverbs 3: 17–18, slightly modified.

REMARKS: Cf. the similar finials No. 333.

DONOR: Dr. Harry G. Friedman

## 333

### TORAH FINIALS  F 5484a, b  (*Illus. p. 217*)

Galicia (?), late 18th–early 19th century

Silver: repoussé

H 31.0 DIAM 16.7 cm

HALLMARKS: none

REMARKS: Cf. the similar finials No. 332.

DONOR: Dr. Harry G. Friedman

## 334

### TORAH FINIALS  F 2667a, b  (*Illus. p. 217*)

Galicia, 1763/64 (inscription), with later additions

Silver: repoussé, chased, parcel-gilt

H 17.6 / 18.7 DIAM 10.6 / 10.2 cm

HALLMARKS: none

INSCRIPTION: on the base of the original finial (A): זנ׳ הה׳ האלוף הראש מרה דוד במו ניסן זצל עבור בנו כמר ארי׳ ליב ה׳ יגדלו לת׳ ולח׳ ולמ׳ טובים בשנת תקכד ל׳, "This was donated by the leader, the head, our teacher, Rabbi David son of our teacher Rabbi Nissan, of saintly memory, on behalf of his son . . . Aryeh Leib, [May the] L[ord] raise

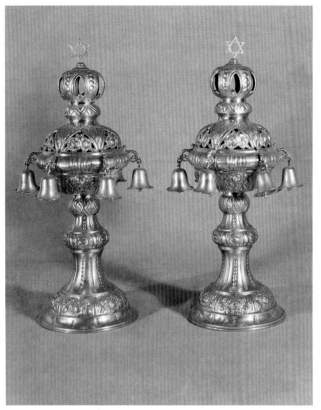

No. 327  F 1438a, b

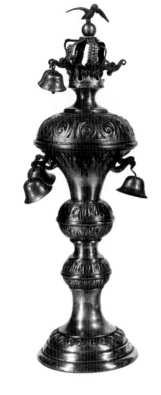

No. 328  F 5377a, b (one of pair)

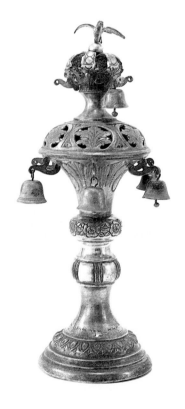

No. 329  F 3282

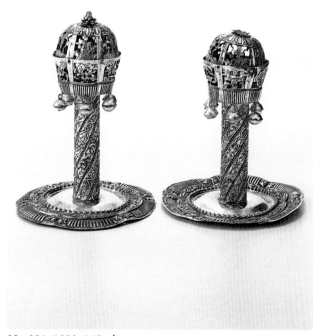

No. 331  1993–145a, b

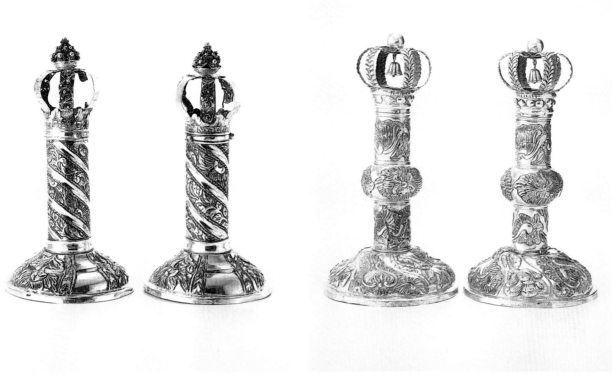

No. 332  F 2362a, b

No. 333  F 5484a, b

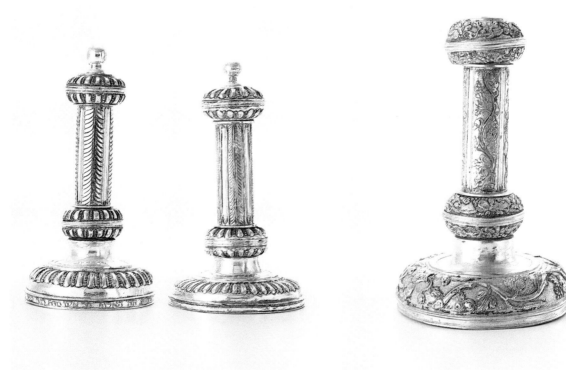

No. 334  F 2667a, b

No. 335  F 2961

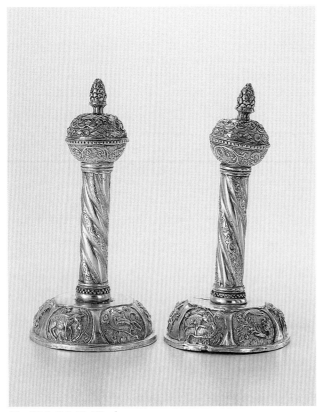

No. 336  JM 49–51a, b

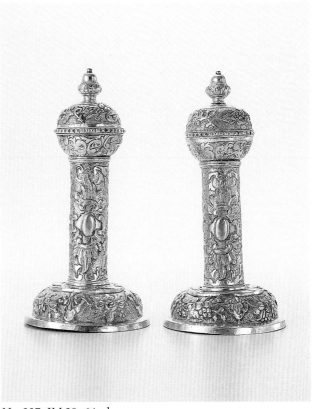

No. 337  JM 30–64a, b

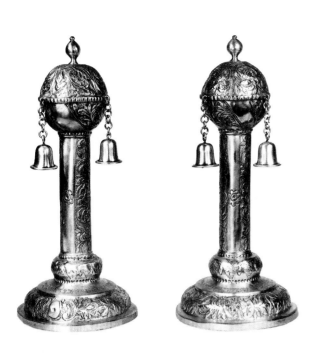

No. 338  F 3515a, b

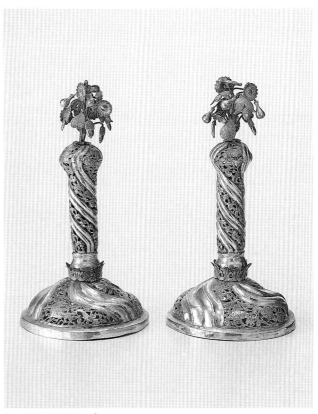

No. 339  F 2544a, b

him to the T[orah] and to [the] m[arriage canopy] and to good d[eeds]. In the year (5)524" (=1763/64)

REMARKS: One of the pair of finials is a replacement of entirely different workmanship and materials.

DONOR: Dr. Harry G. Friedman

## 335

### TORAH FINIAL  F 2961  (*Illus. p. 217*)
Galicia, late 18th–early 19th century
Silver: repoussé, pierced, parcel-gilt
H 16.9  DIAM 10.5 cm
HALLMARKS: none
REMARKS: An element is missing at the top. Cf. the similar Torah Finials No. 336.
DONOR: Dr. Harry G. Friedman

## 336

### TORAH FINIALS  JM 49–51a, b  (*Illus. p. 218*)
Galicia, late 18th-early 19th century
Silver: cast, repoussé
H 23.8  DIAM 12.9 cm
HALLMARKS: none
REMARKS: The oval medallions on the molded bases enclose flowers, a unicorn spearing a smaller quadruped, a sheep eating a leaf, a hare and a chameleon, a sunflower, and a stag scratching its mouth. Cf. the similar finials No. 335.
DONOR: Dr. Harry G. Friedman

## 337

### TORAH FINIALS  JM 30–64a, b  (*Illus. p. 218*)
Galicia, late 18th–early 19th century
Silver: chased, cast
H 18.5  DIAM 9.4 cm
HALLMARKS: CITY: Rohrwasser, p. 11, upper left (with "D"); p. 12, bottom left
PROVENANCE: Zagayski Collection, Palm Beach
REMARKS: Within the base are old inventory numbers: "J-11" (Zagayski inventory number); and "501." Cf. the similar finials No. 338.
BIBLIOGRAPHY: Zagayski 1951, No. 7; Zagayski 1963, No. 8; PB-NY 1964, No. 114
DONOR: Mr. and Mrs. Maurice Gruber

## 338

### TORAH FINIALS  F 3515a, b  (*Illus. p. 218*)
Galicia (?), 19th century; 1848/49 (inscription)
Silver: chased, die-stamped
H 27.4  DIAM 12.6 cm
HALLMARKS: none
INSCRIPTION: on base of finial B: זה העץ חיים שייך להאשה אסתר בת מו"ה יעקב זל ש' תר"טל:/ זה העץ חיים שייך לה"ה שמעון בן מו"ה אברהם צבי ז"ל ש' תר"טל, "This *etz*

*ḥayyim* ("tree-of-life," i.e., Torah Stave) belongs to the woman Esther daughter of . . . the late Rabbi Jacob, [in the] year (5)609 (=1848/49); this Torah Stave belongs to Simon son of the late Rabbi Abraham Zvi, [in the] year (5)609" (=1848/49)

DONOR: Dr. Harry G. Friedman

## 339

### TORAH FINIALS  F 2544a, b  (*Illus. p. 218*)
Lvov (?), first quarter (?) of 19th century
Silver: repoussé, chased, pierced, parcel-gilt
H 20.1 / 20.4  DIAM 11.0 cm
HALLMARKS: Rohrwasser, p. 11, "mittel," with "D"; p. 12 bottom left (both possibly false)
REMARKS: The animals inhabiting the scrollwork on these finials include birds, deer, foxes, and lions.
BIBLIOGRAPHY: Kayser, No. 23
DONOR: Dr. Harry G. Friedman

## 340

### MINIATURE TORAH FINIALS  F 3511a, b
(*Illus. p. 220*)
Rzeszow, 1807
Silver: chased, engraved, parcel-gilt
H 7.0  DIAM 4.7 cm
HALLMARKS: *CITY:* Rohrwasser, p. 12 (D6), p. 11 (Gross, D)
REMARKS: The inside of each stem is threaded for attachment to a Torah Stave.
DONOR: Dr. Harry G. Friedman

## 341

### TORAH FINIALS  F 2339a, b  (*Illus. p. 220*)
Galicia, early 19th century
Silver: repoussé, traces of gilt
H 11.2  DIAM 8.0 cm
HALLMARKS: Lileyko 83c (1851, on older objects); Tardy, p. 208 top (French import)
DONOR: Dr. Harry G. Friedman

## 342

### TORAH FINIALS  F 2340a, b  (*Illus. p. 220*)
Galicia (?), 19th century
Silver: cast, chased, gilt
H 25.5  DIAM 10.7 cm
HALLMARKS: "12"; "83" (?)
INSCRIPTION: on each base: זאת נדב ר' אברהם במהרר חיים זצל, "This was donated by R[abbi] Abraham son of our teacher, the late Rabbi Ḥayyim."
REMARKS: There are two holes around each base, possibly for attachment to the Torah Staves.
DONOR: Dr. Harry G. Friedman

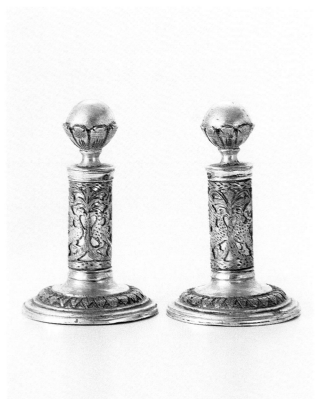

No. 340  F 3511a, b

No. 341  F 2339a, b

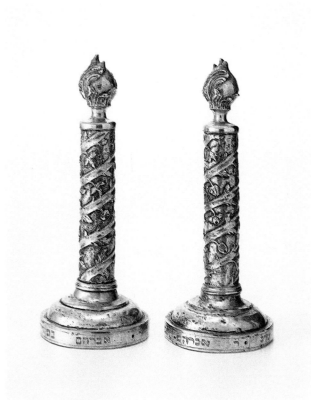

No. 342  F 2340a, b

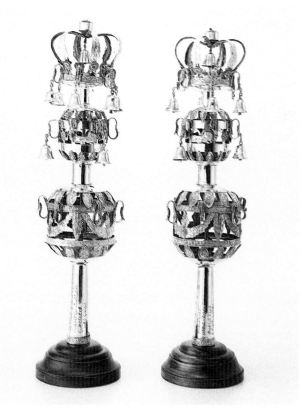

No. 343  JM 22–57a, b

## 343

TORAH FINIALS  JM 22–57a, b  (*Illus. p. 220*)
Poland, 1815 (inscription)
Silver: die-stamped, cast, engraved, parcel-gilt
H 42.2 / 43.0  DIAM 10.8 cm
HALLMARKS: "12"; "JH" (?) in script, in lozenge
INSCRIPTION: on lower stems: נדבת לב מהקטן/ יהודה ליב
גליא/ ואשתו הצנועה/ מרת גאלדה תי/ בראש השנה
שנת/ ת׳ק׳ע׳ו׳ בחודש שופר// וזאת ליהודה/ לַייא הַבַרכות/
גדולה לאלקי ישראל אתן/ גָדול אַדונינו לַו דֻומיה
הַלולו[?]/ שעזרני עד כה/ לכבוד התורה בהדור נאה
"[This is the] heartfelt donation from the humble Judah
Leib Galia (?) and his wife, the modest lady Golda …, at the
New Year, [in the] year (5)576 [=5 October 1815], in the
month of the ram's horn. And this is for Judah, Blessings to
the Lord, I shall give greatness to the God of Israel, great is
our Lord, to Him is the silence, praise Him who has helped
me thus far; in honor of the Torah, as a beautiful adorn-
ment."
REMARKS: The underlined letters in the inscription (having
superior dots in the original) form acronyms for "Leib"
and "Golda." Many bells are missing.
DONOR: Dr. Ludwig Bendix

## 344

TORAH FINIALS  F 2368a, b  (*Illus. p. 222*)
Galicia (?), early 19th century
Silver: chased, pierced, parcel-gilt
H 18.0  DIAM 7.7 cm
HALLMARKS: "12"; "ZP" in script on background of horizon-
tal lines
REMARKS: Several bells are missing.
DONOR: Dr. Harry G. Friedman

## 345

TORAH FINIALS  F 4562a, b  (*Illus. p. 222*)
Germany, second half of 19th century
Silver: chased; brass: die-stamped; glass: cut
H 26.0  DIAM 12.5 cm
HALLMARKS: "750"
REMARKS: The "crystal" finial and setting at the top seem not
to be original.
DONOR: Dr. Harry G. Friedman

## 346

TORAH FINIALS  U 7340a, b  (*Illus. p. 222*)
Hirschberg, mid-19th century
Silver: cast, chased, parcel-gilt
H 31.2 / 30.6  DIAM 10.8 cm
HALLMARKS: Stag to left; "12"
REMARKS: Most of the leaves hanging from the upper "ros-
ette" are missing. Cf. the almost identical finials No. 347.

## 347

TORAH FINIALS  F 4595a, b  (*Illus. p. 222*)
Hirschberg, mid-19th century
Silver: chased, cast, parcel-gilt
H 35.9 / 36.3  W 11.4 cm
HALLMARKS: *CITY:* R³ 2570(var.); "13"
          *MAKER:* illegible
REMARKS: Cf. the almost identical finials No. 346.
DONOR: Dr. Harry G. Friedman

## 348

TORAH FINIALS  F 4115a, b  (*Illus. p. 223*)
Poland or United States, late 19th–early 20th century
Brass: cast, chased, traces of silver-plating
H 32.2 / 32.5  DIAM 10.8 cm
HALLMARKS: none
DONOR: Dr. Harry G. Friedman

## 349

TORAH FINIALS  F 257a, b  (*Illus. p. 223*)
Germany, 19th century
Silver: cast, repoussé, engraved
H 45.5  DIAM 13.7 cm
HALLMARKS: none
REMARKS: Several bells are missing.
DONOR: Dr. Harry G. Friedman

## 350

TORAH FINIALS  D 186a, b  (*Illus. p. 223*)
Warsaw, 1890 (?)
Anton Riedel, active 1878–1910
Silver: cast, repoussé, pierced, gilt
H 39.8  DIAM 14.2 cm
HALLMARKS: *CITY:* Lileyko 90; 89
          *MAKER:* Lileyko 5
REMARKS: See shield No. 204, made by the same smith. [With-
in the base, these finials are incorrectly marked: "D 140"]
BIBLIOGRAPHY: *Danzig 1939/1982*, No. 86
DONOR: The Jewish Community of Danzig

## 351

TORAH FINIALS  F 2701a, b  (*Illus. p. 223*)
Polotsk, 1859
Silver: cast, chased, engraved
H 10.9  DIAM 5.0 cm
HALLMARKS: *CITY:* Postnikova 1713(var.); 1715 (1859); "84"
          *MAKER:* "EI" (?)
INSCRIPTION: spiralling along stems: Deuteronomy 4:44 and
Proverbs 3:18
REMARKS: The eagles at the top are possibly later additions.
The inscription on the second finial is upside down.
DONOR: Dr. Harry G. Friedman

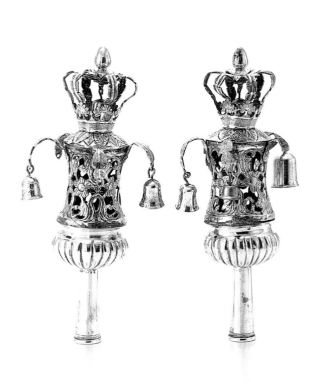

No. 344   F 2368a, b

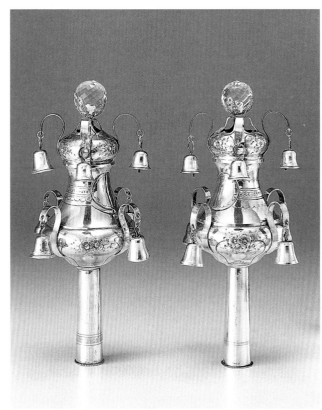

No. 345   F 4562a, b

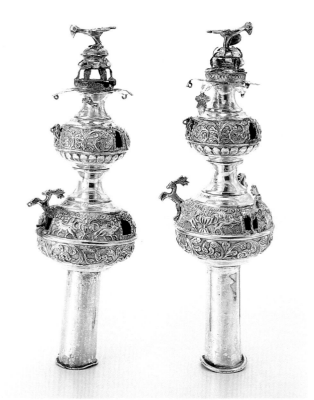

No. 346   U 7340a, b

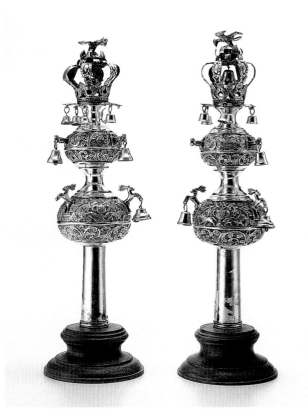

No. 347   F 4595a, b

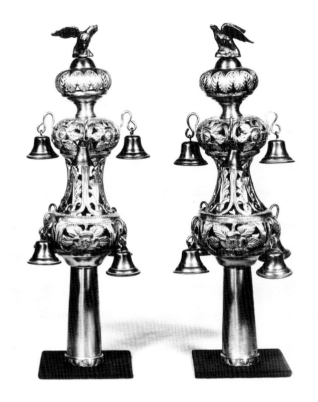

No. 348  F 4115a, b

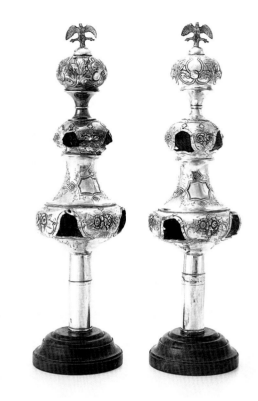

No. 349  F 257a, b

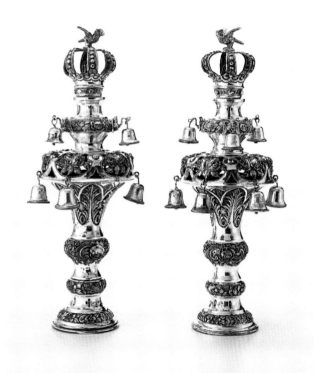

No. 350  D 186a, b

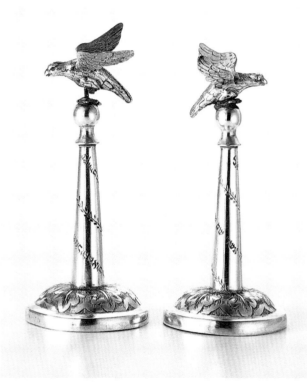

No. 351  F 2701a, b

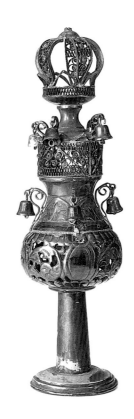

No. 352  F 1199

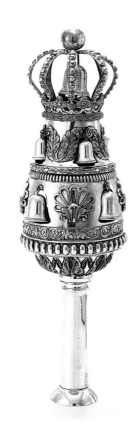

No. 353  U 7315

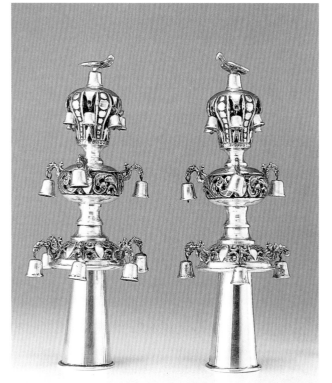

No. 354  F 1198a, b

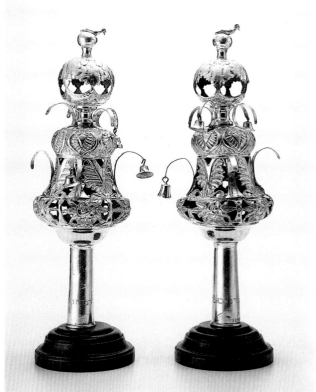

No. 355  F 5289a, b

## 352

TORAH FINIAL  F 1199  (*Illus. p. 224*)
Ukraine (?), second half of 19th century
Silver: filigree, chased
H 26.7  DIAM 7.7 cm
HALLMARKS: none
REMARKS: The top element is missing.
DONOR: Dr. Harry G. Friedman

## 353

TORAH FINIAL  U 7315  (*Illus. p. 224*)
New York, 19th century
Silver, brass: cast, chased, engraved, parcel-gilt
H 39.0  DIAM 11.5 cm
HALLMARKS: none
INSCRIPTION: on stem of finial, in script: "Sylvester Brush";
within base of stem, in dotted script: "Abraham Kantor
Esq. 134 Prinz (sic) St. NY City"
REMARKS: Prince Street is in lower Manhattan.

## 354

TORAH FINIALS  F 1198a, b  (*Illus. p. 224*)
New York, late 19th century
Silver: cast, pierced
H 28.0  DIAM 10.8 cm
HALLMARKS: "STERLING (curved)/ A.G."
REMARKS: See shield No. 218, by the same smith, for further
references.
DONOR: Dr. Harry G. Friedman

## 355

TORAH FINIALS  F 5289a, b  (*Illus. p. 224*)
United States, 1890's
Silver: chased, pierced, engraved
H 39.5 / 39.9  DIAM 19.1 cm
HALLMARKS: *CITY:* Lileyko 89 (false)
*MAKER:* dotted heart with "Ka …" (?) in script
INSCRIPTION: on stem: אנשי סאכאאשאוו // חברה קדישא ...,
"… Holy (Burial) Society, People of Sochaczew"
REMARKS: The town of Sochaczew is 20 km west of Warsaw.
For the congregation, see *NY Register* 1917, p. 162; it was
founded in 1904 and located at 121 Ludlow Street, in Man-
hattan.
DONOR: Dr. Harry G. Friedman

## 356

TORAH FINIALS  F 260a, b  (*Illus. p. 226*)
United States (?), late 19th–early 20th century
Silver: cast, die-stamped, engraved
H 41.0  DIAM 12.4 cm
HALLMARKS: "STERLING"; "84"
DONOR: Dr. Harry G. Friedman

## 357

TORAH FINIALS  F 3921a, b  (*Illus. p. 226*)
United States (?), late 19th–early 20th century
Silver: chased, parcel-gilt
H 40.8 / 41.0  DIAM 10.3 cm
HALLMARKS: eagle; "GN/ 1865" (Cyrillic); "84"; "D" (Gothic)
— false Russian marks (?)
REMARKS: Similar marks appear on shield No. 213; these
finials may also be Ukrainian.
DONOR: Dr. Harry G. Friedman

## 358

TORAH FINIALS  F 1523a, b  (*Illus. p. 226*)
United States (?), ca. 1900
Silver: chased, pierced, die-stamped, engraved, parcel-gilt
H 37.5  DIAM 11 cm
HALLMARKS: *CITY:* Moscow, 1890 — false Russian marks
*MAKER:* "H L", in rectangle
REMARKS: The top element is missing. For the hallmarks, see
shield No. 215 and crown No. 492, as well as remarks, shield
No. 222. For a shield with a maker's mark "GL," an "un-
recorded" city mark and an "1890" mark, see Sotheby's Tel
Aviv 1993, No. 251 (dedicated by *Anshei Kovno*—surely in
the United States).
DONOR: Dr. Harry G. Friedman

## 359

TORAH FINIALS  F 256a, b  (*Illus. p. 226*)
United States (?), early 20th century
Brass: cast, pierced, silver-plated
H 40.0  DIAM 13.4 cm
HALLMARKS: Lion's head to left, with "84"—false Russian
marks
DONOR: Dr. Harry G. Friedman

## 360

TORAH FINIALS  F 262a, b  (*Illus. p. 227*)
United States (?), early 20th century
Silver: filigree, repoussé, engraved
H 26.3 / 27.2  DIAM 7.9 cm
HALLMARKS: none
DONOR: Dr. Harry G. Friedman

## 361, 361A

TORAH FINIALS  JM 45–64a, b / JM 78–65a, b
(*Illus. p. 227/not illustrated*)
New York, 1960's
Ludwig Wolpert, active 1920's–1981
Silver: pierced
H 25.8  DIAM 11.8 cm
HALLMARKS: "STERLING"

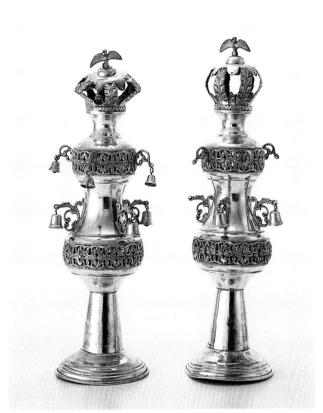

No. 356   F 260a, b

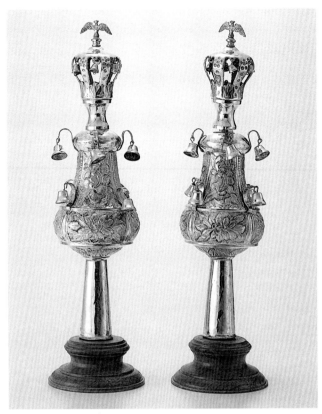

No. 357   F 3921a, b

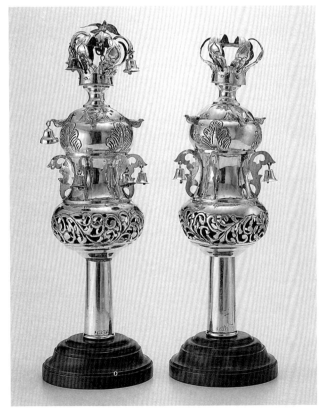

No. 358   F 1523a, b

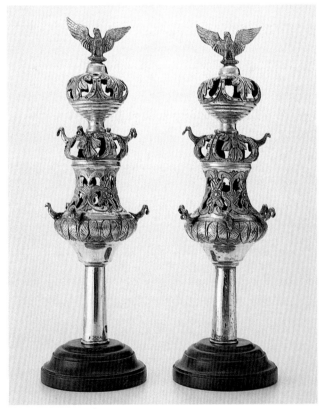

No. 359   F 256a, b

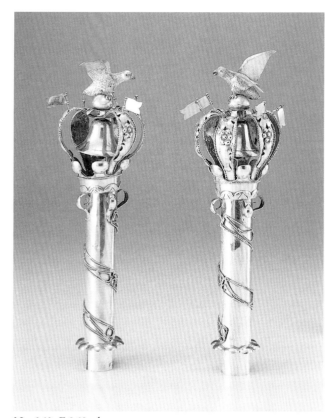

No. 360  F 262a, b

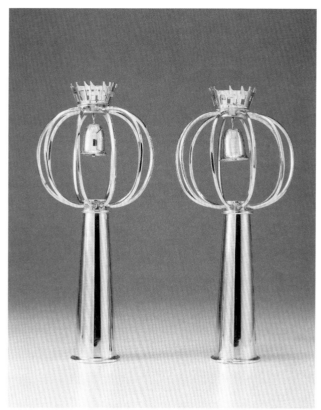

No. 361  JM 45–64a, b

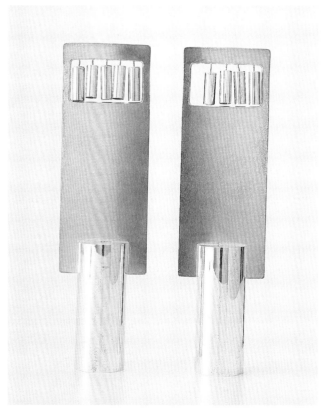

No. 362  JM 97–65a, b

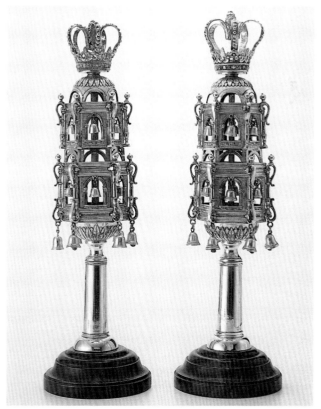

No. 363  JM 28–64a, b

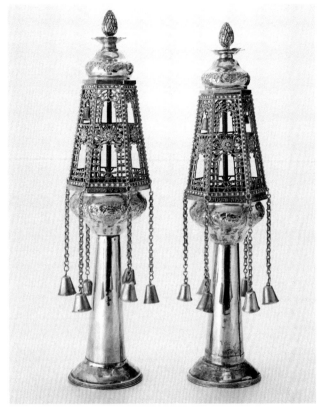

No. 364   1994–7a, b

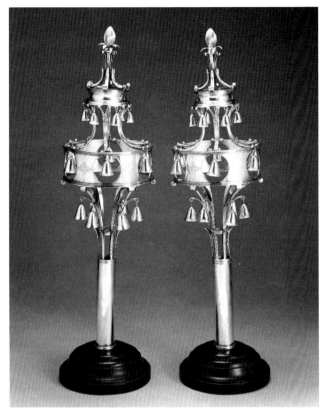

No. 365   1992–144a, b

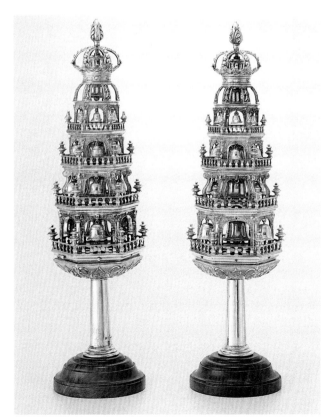

No. 366   F 4646a, b

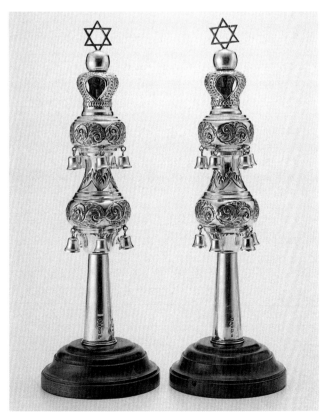

No. 367   F 4873a, b

INSCRIPTION: on crowns: Isaiah 2:3

REMARKS: These two pairs of finials are identical.

BIBLIOGRAPHY: Wolpert 1976, No.29

DONOR: Abram and Frances Kanof Collection

## 362

### TORAH FINIALS JM 97–65a, b (*Illus. p. 227*)

New York, 1964

Moshe Zabari, active 1958–

Silver: pierced, parcel-gilt

H 25.6 W 7.0 cm

HALLMARKS: inside stem: "M/ZABARI"; "STERLING"

BIBLIOGRAPHY: Berman, No. 7

DONOR: Abram and Frances Kanof Collection

## 363

### TORAH FINIALS JM 28–64a, b (*Illus. p. 227*)

London, 1794

Solomon Hougham, active late 18th–early 19th century

Silver: cast, chased, gilt

H 39.3 / 40.3 DIAM 11.3 cm

HALLMARKS: *CITY:* Lion; leopard's head; "t"; duty mark

　　　　　　*MAKER:* Pickford, p. 75, fifth mark

PROVENANCE: Zagayski Collection, Palm Beach

REMARKS: This pair of finials appears to be patterned after Barnett, No. 125, made in London in 1767. For another object by the same smith, see PBNY 1964, No. 290, a Hanukkah lamp presently in the Stern Collection, New York (H50). For a 19th–20th century American copy of this pair of finials, see Grossman 1989, No. 9b. Stone, pp. 26–27, notes the possibility that the "SH" mark might be that of "Samuel Hart, a Gold Worker, who entered his mark in June 1790. Perhaps Samuel Hart was the maker of the 1793 rimmonim [in The Jewish Museum, New York], and maybe he was a Jewish goldsmith not recorded as such by P. A. S. Phillips in his 'List of Jewish Goldsmiths.' He may also have been responsible for the pair of rimmonim dated 1796 which are in the Central Synagogue, London . . . ." Stone makes no connection, on p. 28, with two Exeter pairs of finials [one dated 1812/13] which "have the maker's mark S.H. This may be for Samuel Hart of Plymouth, father of Solomon Hart, R.A." Samuel Hart later moved to London (ca. 1820).

BIBLIOGRAPHY: "A Rare Pair of Torah Crowns," *The American Collector*, August 1941; Zagayski 1951, No. 10; Zagayski 1963, No. 10; PBNY 1964, No. 289

DONOR: Museum purchase

## 364

### TORAH FINIALS 1994–7a, b (*Illus. p. 228*)

London, 1801–02

George Smith & Thomas Hayter, active late 18th century

Silver: chased, cast, pierced, parcel-gilt

H 46.7 / 47.9 DIAM 11.8 cm

HALLMARKS: *CITY:* Pickford, p. 32 (1801–02)

　　　　　　*MAKER:* Pickford, p. 58, tenth mark

INSCRIPTION: around the lower body, on finial A: למנוחת המשכיל/ וחשוב יהודה צרפתי/ בר יצחק נע/ ולזכות אשתו/ הכלוה והצנועה/ מרים מבת, "For the repose of . . . the late Judah Sarfatti son of Isaac, and for the merit of his wife . . . Miriam . . ."; on finial B: מרים צרפתי מבת, "Miriam Sarfatti. . . ."

PROVENANCE: Etz Ḥayyim Synagogue, Gibraltar

REMARKS: Besides these finials, two other, identical pairs by the same smiths are known — one in a private collection in New York and the other in trade. A third pair by the same smiths, of 1801, is cited in Grimwade 1950, p. 105a; Grimwade 1955, p. 6. See also the similar examples in *London Temple*, No. 18, pl. V and PBNY 1986, No. 278 (probably English, 1844). The most interesting feature of these finials is their close resemblance to a common form of Moroccan finial, the earliest extant examples of which are from the second half of the 19th century (cf., Dahan, Nos. 1c, 1d and 1f). The prototype may well have been Italian (cf. Livorno 1991, p. 80).

DONOR: Purchased with funds given by Dr. Harry G. Friedman, by exchange

## 365

### TORAH FINIALS 1992–144a, b (*Illus. p. 228*)

Provincial England or English Colonies, ca. 1800

Silver: cast, chased, parcel-gilt

H 45.1 DIAM 14.3 cm

HALLMARKS: Crown; lion (pseudo-English marks); "FR" in rectangle

PROVENANCE: The Jacobo and Asea Furman Collection, Santiago, Chile

REMARKS: These finials are a variant of a known late 18th–early 19th-century English type (e.g., Christie's NY 1980, No. 192). An almost identical pair — said to be from a group of finials recently deaccessioned by a Gibraltar synagogue — bears the same maker's mark as The Jewish Museum pair, but it is flanked by a mark depicting a key (see Jackson, pp. 486 and 557–558). The second pair appeared on the Judaica market in 1993 and was later on temporary loan to the Israel Museum.

BIBLIOGRAPHY: Furman, No. 9; *Treasures*, pp. 136-137; *JMNY* 1993, No. 43

DONOR: Jacobo Furman, in memory of his wife, Asea

## 366

### TORAH FINIALS F 4646a, b (*Illus. p. 228*)

London, 1888

Joseph & Horace Savory, active late 19th century

Silver: chased, cast, gilt

H 47.0 DIAM 15.0 cm

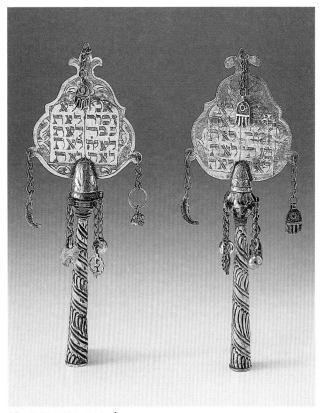

No. 368  1989–145a, b

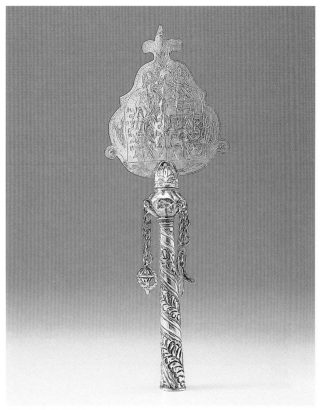

No. 369  F 2554

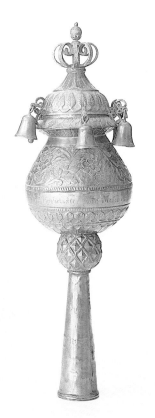

No. 370  F 3311

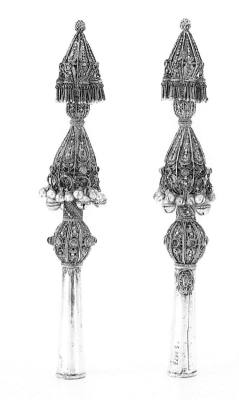

No. 371  S 1137a, b

HALLMARKS: *CITY:* Lion; leopard's head; "N"; duty mark
    *MAKER:* Pickford, p. 66, third mark

REMARKS: Cf. the very similar Dutch finials No. 380, which were made a century earlier than this pair. See shield No. 229, made by the same London silversmiths.

DONOR: Dr. Harry G. Friedman

# 367

## TORAH FINIALS   F 4873a, b   (*Illus. p. 228*)

London, 1934

Silver: chased

H 35.8   DIAM 7.4 cm

HALLMARKS: *CITY:* Lion; leopard's head; "t" (gothic); Jubilee mark
    *MAKER:* "M.S" in rectangle

INSCRIPTION: on finial B: "PRESENTED/ BY/ MR. & MRS./ S. SILVERMAN"

REMARKS: See shield No. 230, made on the same year by the same smith and dedicated by the same couple.

DONOR: Dr. Harry G. Friedman

# 368

## TORAH FINIALS   1989–145a, b   (*Illus. p. 230*)

Jerusalem, late 19th–early 20th century

Silver: chased, cast

H 22.2 / 22.8   W 8.0 cm

HALLMARKS: none

INSCRIPTION: on front side: Deuteronomy 4:44 and 33:4

REMARKS: See also finial No. 369, of the same type. Similar finials include Skirball Museum, Los Angeles, 47.3 and 47.4; and a heavier variant, at the Jewish Museum in London, integrated into the backwall of a Hanukkah lamp made in Jerusalem (Barnett, No. 228).

These finials belong to a very specific group of Judaica from Jerusalem; see, e.g., Fishof, pp. 84–85 (finials and a Hanukkah lamp made of finial plaques); Grossman (finials and other objects); and *Sephardic Journey*, Nos. 263 and 372 (Hanukkah lamps). The entire group appears to have been made by "Mughrabi" and other smiths in Jerusalem ca. 1900, particularly for the tourist trade. Examples even found their way to communities in North Africa, probably in the hands of Jewish pilgrims (Israel Museum, finials 147/120, which include pieces of Palestinian Bedouin jewelry — misascribed to "Central and Southern Morocco" in Thon, p. 92 and n. 36).

DONOR: Nathan and Bluma Polmer

# 369

## TORAH FINIAL   F 2554   (*Illus. p. 230*)

Jerusalem, late 19th–early 20th century

Silver: chased, cast, gilt

H 22.8   W 8.0 cm

HALLMARKS: none

INSCRIPTION: on front: Deuteronomy 4: 44

REMARKS: See the similar finials No. 368, and the remarks there.

DONOR: Dr. Harry G. Friedman

# 370

## TORAH FINIAL   F 3311   (*Illus. p. 230*)

Jerusalem or India, 1897/98 (inscription)

Silver: chased, engraved

H 26.5   DIAM 7.8 cm

HALLMARKS: none

INSCRIPTION: spiralling around stem: זכרון אהבה לנשמת
. . . ג׳ הוכשטאטער . . . הוריו ירושלם בחו(דש) . . . תרנח
לפק, "A loving memorial for the soul of . . . G. Hochstadter . . . his parents, Jerusalem, in the mo(nth) . . . (5)658" (=1897/98); on finial body: "In Loving memory of Sidney G. Hochstadter Born March 8th 1875 Died August 20th 1896"

REMARKS: There is a repair around the stem which has obliterated parts of the inscription. The anniversary of the death would fall on 11 Elul and the finial may have been dedicated on that day in 1899. This finial, though apparently dedicated in Jerusalem, appears to be of Indian workmanship.

DONOR: Dr. Harry G. Friedman

# 371

## TORAH FINIALS   S 1137a, b   (*Illus. p. 230*)

Israel (?), early 20th century

Silver: filigree, die-stamped, chased, gilt; glass

H 26.3   DIAM 3.9 cm

HALLMARKS: none

INSCRIPTION: at top of stem, in Arabic, in Hebrew script: רחל
בנת יחיה עמראן, "Rachel daughter of Yeḥiah Amran"

REMARKS: Cf. the similar finials No. 372; and finials No. 447, a Yemenite pair in brass, of the same basic form.

DONOR: Max Warburg

# 372

## TORAH FINIALS   F 5147a, b   (*Illus. p. 232*)

Israel, mid-20th century

Silver: filigree, die-stamped; glass

H 31.0   DIAM 3.9 cm

HALLMARKS: none

REMARKS: Cf. the similar finials No. 371; and Stieglitz, No. 18 (misdated).

DONOR: Dr. Harry G. Friedman

# 373

## TORAH FINIALS   M 259a, b   (*Illus. p. 232*)

Jerusalem, prior to mid-1914

Bezalel Workshop

Silver: filigree, die-stamped

H 36.0   DIAM 12.6 cm

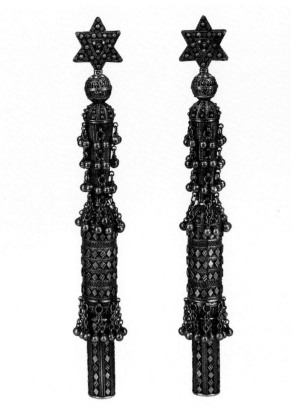

No. 372   F 5147a, b

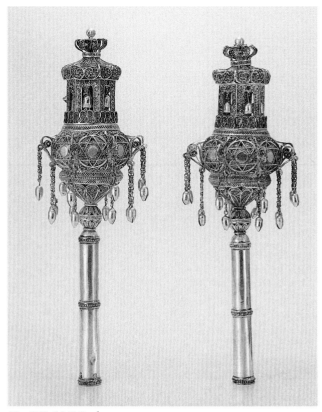

No. 373   M 259a, b

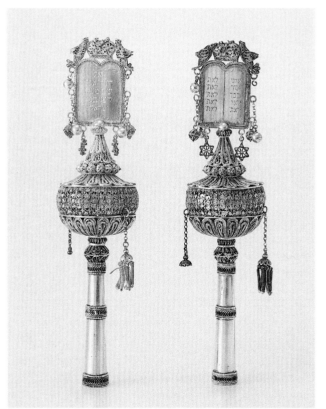

No. 374   JM 18–49a, b

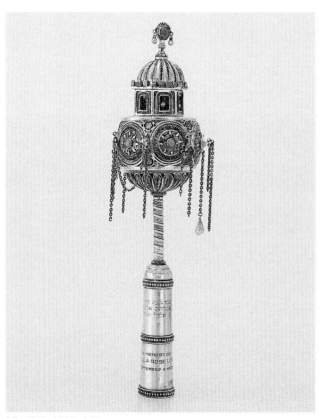

No. 375   1989–133

HALLMARKS: Postnikova 1943 (var.), with "i"=Kharkov
import, 1908-17; Lileyko 92 = Polish tax,
1920–21; engraved: "Bezalel, Jerusalem"
(Hebrew)

PROVENANCE: The Rose and Benjamin Mintz Collection

REMARKS: According to the marks, these finials were sold in
Russia. The pattern is illustrated in Bezalel 1913, p. 9, No.
70.

DONOR: Museum purchase

## 374

### TORAH FINIALS JM 18–49a, b (*Illus. p. 232*)

Jerusalem, prior to mid-1914
Bezalel Workshop
Silver: filigree, engraved
H 26.0 / 26.2 DIAM 6.2 cm
HALLMARKS: none
REMARKS: Although there is no identifying mark or inscrip-
tion, these finials are the product of one of the "Bezalel"
workshops, for the pattern appears in Bezalel 1913, p. 11, No.
66. They seem to be modeled after an Algerian finial type
(e.g., *Juifs d'Algerie*, p. 89, illus.).
DONOR: Dr. Harry Friedenwald

## 375

### TORAH FINIAL 1989–133 (*Illus. p. 232*)

Jerusalem, 1933 (inscription)
Bezalel Workshop
Silver: filigree, die-stamped; glass
H 32.5 DIAM 10.6 cm
HALLMARKS: engraved "[Bezalel] Jerusalem" (Hebrew)
INSCRIPTION: on stem: *IN MEMORY OF/ DELLA ROSE
LOUIS/ SEPTEMBER 4–1933*; לזכר דינה אשת/ אברהם
אליעזר/ י"ג אלול תרצ"ג, "In memory of Dinah, wife of
Abraham Eliezer, 13 Elul (5)693" (=4 September 1933)
REMARKS: The name "Bezalel" would have been engraved on
the other, now missing finial. This form of "signature" was
commonly used in the "Old Bezalel" workshops prior to
the school's temporary closure in 1932.
DONOR: Moshe Zabari

## 376

### TORAH FINIALS F 2057a, b (*Illus. p. 234*)

Eretz Israel, first half of 20th century
Silver: filigree
H 26.7 DIAM 7.5 cm
HALLMARKS: none
REMARKS: The form of these finials is the typical Sephardi
type found particularly in Eretz-Israel. See *Ohel Moshe* p.
82 for three similar examples.
DONOR: Dr. Harry G. Friedman

## 376A

### TORAH FINIAL 1993-237 (*Illus. p. 234*)

Israel, mid-20th century
Silver: chased, parcel-gilt
H 25.3 DIAM 8.3 cm
HALLMARKS: none
INSCRIPTION: around body: Isaiah 2:3
REMARKS: The top element, probably a Star of David, is bro-
ken off and missing.
DONOR: In memory of Ebrahim Khalil Rokhsar, by Mena
Rokhsar

## 377

### TORAH FINIAL F 1989 (*Illus. p. 234*)

France or Italy, first half of 19th century
Silver: chased, engraved
H 28.5 DIAM 10.6 cm
HALLMARKS: *CITY:* Tardy, p. 208, top (French import mark
for objects of "unknown" origin)
*MAKER:* "GP" with small fleur-de-lis above
INSCRIPTION: on stem: כתר/ תורה/ ספר, "Crown of Torah,
Scroll"; on body: ל /א /ר /ש /י, "Israel"
PROVENANCE: Berry Hill
REMARKS: The now-missing second finial was probably
inscribed on the stem, inter alia, with the word תורה,
"Torah," completing the Hebrew phrase for "Torah Scroll."
The form of this finial indicates that it was intended for a
Torah Case.
DONOR: Dr. Harry G. Friedman

## 378

### TORAH FINIALS S 1456b, c (*Illus. p. 356*)

Paris, ca. 1870
Maurice Mayer, active 1860's–70's
Silver: die-stamped, chased, parcel-gilt
H 28.7 DIAM 9.3 cm
HALLMARKS: *CITY:* Tardy, p. 204, lower left
*MAKER:* engraved: "Maurice Mayer/ Orfèvre
Jouiller de l'Empereur/ Paris"
PROVENANCE: The Hadji Ephraim and Mordecai Benguiat
Collection
REMARKS: These finials belong to Torah Case No. 912 (see the
remarks there). A single finial made by the same smith,
using the same dies but with three stories and bearing an
inscription dated 1869, was in trade in 1991.
BIBLIOGRAPHY: American Art Gallery, 1924, No. 632; *Jewish
Museum 75*, p. [13], *Treasures*, pp. 154–155
DONOR: Museum purchase

## 379

### TORAH FINIALS 1981–27a, b (*Illus. p. 234*)

Paris, 1876 (inscription)

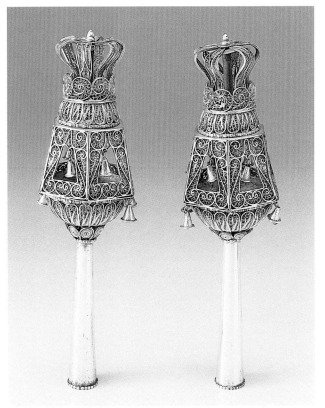

No. 376  F 2057a, b

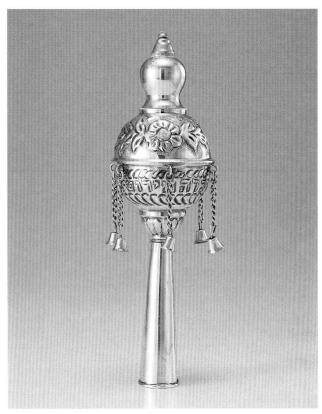

No. 376 A  1993–237

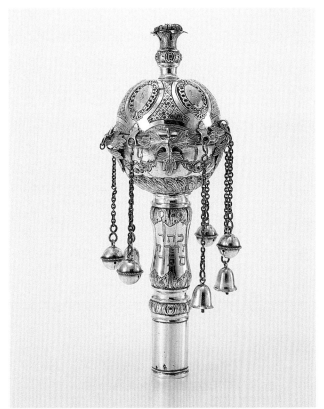

No. 377  F 1989

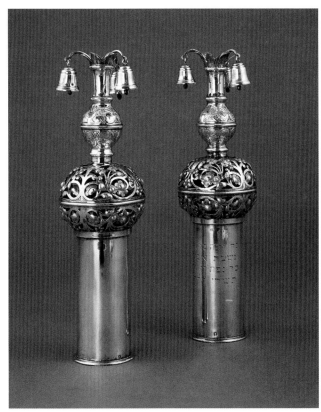

No. 379  1981–27a, b

Demarourt Brothers
Silver: repoussé, pierced, engraved
H 25.4 DIAM 7.5 cm
HALLMARKS: Tardy, p. 199, large, 800; "DEMAROU[RT]/ FRER[ES]" in lozenge
INSCRIPTION: on the stem of finial A: יונה בר יהודה נ״ל לזכר/ נשמת אביו יהודה/ בר נפתלי ז״ל ש״ה״ל/ תשרי תר״ל״ז׳ לפ״ק, "A h[eartfelt] d[onation of] Jonah son of Judah in memory of the soul of his father Judah son of the late Naphtali, Tishri (5)637" (=September/October 1876).
REMARKS: The form of these finials, with their very thick stems, is quite unusual. For a pair of finials and a pointer (dated 1878), by the same smith, see Judaica Jerusalem, Nos. 200 and 194, respectively.
BIBLIOGRAPHY: Sotheby's NY 1981, No. 259
DONOR: The Eva and Morris Feld Judaica Acquisitions Fund

## 380

TORAH FINIALS  F 3281a, b  (*Illus. p. 236*)
Holland, late 18th century (?)
Silver: cast, chased, parcel-gilt
H 42.8 DIAM 14.0 cm
HALLMARKS: none
REMARKS: Cf. the much later English finials No. 366, of similar form and type.
DONOR: Dr. Harry G. Friedman

## 381

MINIATURE TORAH FINIALS  S 23a, b
(*Illus. p. 236*)
Holland, 19th century
Silver: die-stamped, chased
H 9.0 / 9.3 W 2.9 cm
HALLMARKS: CITY: Tardy, p. 321, second row, left
MAKER: illegible
PROVENANCE: The Hadji Ephraim and Mordecai Benguiat Family Collection
DONOR: Museum purchase

## 382

TORAH FINIAL  F 4320  (*Illus. p. 236*)
Amsterdam, 1880
Silver: repoussé, pierced, engraved
H 41.3 DIAM 13.2 cm
HALLMARKS: CITY: Voet, p. 45, No. 7; p. 46, bottom, No. 2 (with "A"); p. 43 (1880)
MAKER: "Y 8 B" in rectangle
INSCRIPTION: on shaft: נדבת נשים/ אשר הביאו בית ה׳/ ביום חג תקופת שנת ארבעים שנה, "Donation of [the] women who brought [it to] the House of G[od] on the day of celebration of the fortieth anniversary."
REMARKS: The Museum card file ascribes this finial to the 17th century, and it has been so dated in various studies.
DONOR: Dr. Harry G. Friedman

## 383

TORAH FINIALS  F 2827a, b  (*Illus. p. 236*)
Amsterdam, 1705
Pieter van Hoven, active 1680–1735
Silver: cast, chased
H 45.5 DIAM 12.4 cm
HALLMARKS: CITY: Voet, p. 2, 10 (but lion-shield without crown); "T" in circle (1705); p. 48, No. 3 (tax, 1852–1927)
MAKER: Citroen 1993, p. 108b ("VHᵃ")
REMARKS: See similar finial: No. 384; Barnett, Nos. 111 (Amsterdam, 1712), 113 (London, 1724); and 115 (London, 1725); and Belinfante 1978, p. 34, an almost identical pair of finials (H 46 cm) also made by Pieter van Hoven, in 1696. For other Judaica by van Hoven, see Barnett, No. 121 (finials); J. Gutmann, *The Jewish Sanctuary*, Leiden 1983, pl. XXVIIa and b (two crowns and a pair of finials); and a pointer in the Gross Family Collection, Tel Aviv.
DONOR: Dr. Harry G. Friedman

## 384

TORAH FINIAL  F 5434  (*Illus. p. 237*)
Holland, 18th–19th century
Silver: filigree, cast, gilt
H 31.5 / 32.0 DIAM 9.7 cm
HALLMARKS: none
REMARKS: Cf. the similar finials No. 383, and the references there.
DONOR: Dr. Harry G. Friedman

## 385

TORAH FINIALS  F 5642a, b  (*Illus. p. 237*)
Amsterdam, 1739 (?)
David Robol (?), active 1729–49
Silver: cast, parcel-gilt
H 29.0 DIAM 11.1 cm
HALLMARKS: CITY: Voet, p. 13, No. 13 (?); "E"=(1739, 1764 or 1789); tax: p. 321, 1813–1905
MAKER: bird to left (Citroen 1975, No. 1027; Citroen 1993, p. 157)
PROVENANCE: Gorevic, New York
REMARKS: Cf. the similar finials No. 386 and Barnett, Nos. 121 and 122.
BIBLIOGRAPHY: *Jewish Museum 75*, p. [31]
DONOR: Dr. Harry G. Friedman

## 386

TORAH FINIALS  X 1976–3a, b
's Gravenhage, second quarter of the 18th century
Isacq S. Busard, active 1731–84
Silver: cast, chased, parcel-gilt

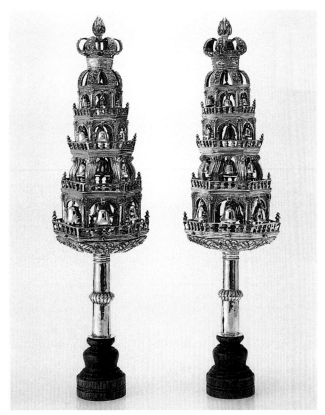

No. 380  F 3281a, b

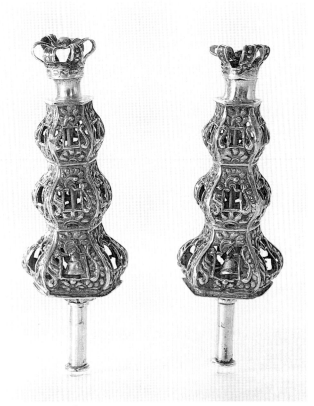

No. 381  S 23a, b

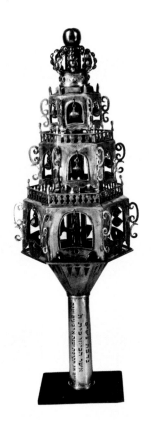

No. 382  F 4320

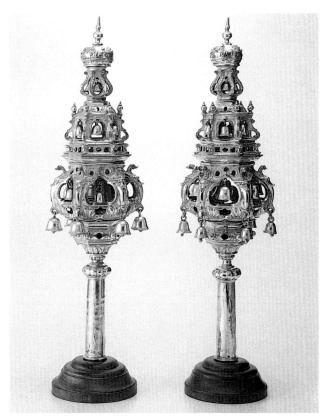

No. 383  F 2827a, b

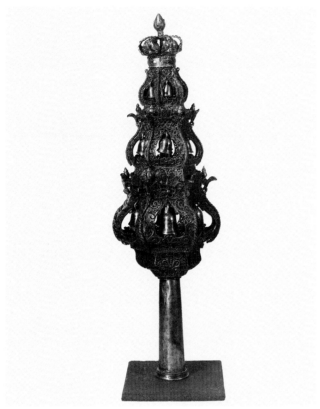

No. 384  F 5434

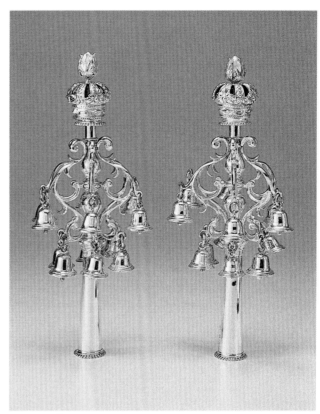

No. 385  F 5642

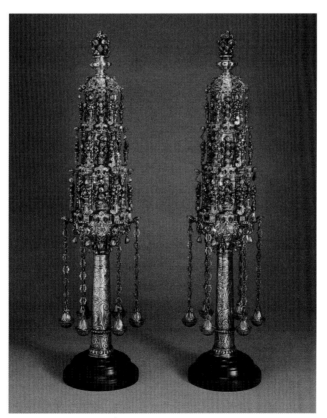

No. 388  JM 20–64a, b

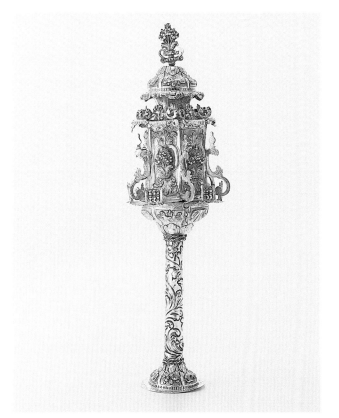

No. 389  F 3068

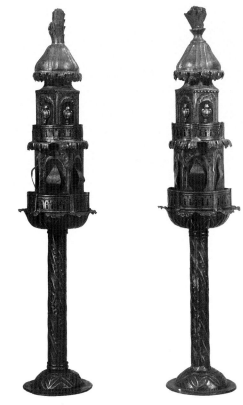

No. 390  F 5010a, b

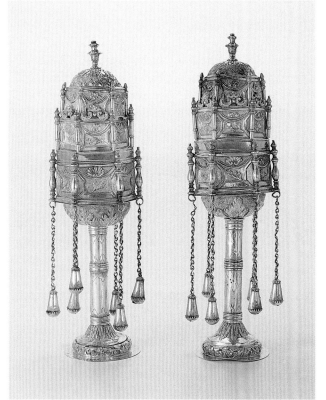

No. 391  F 264a, b

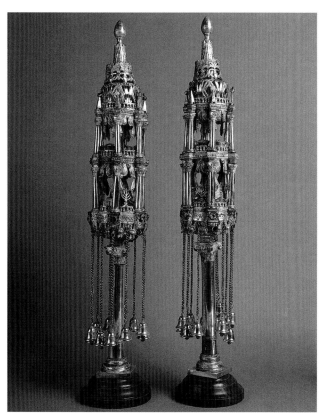

No. 392  F 2826a, b

H 19.3   DIAM 6.4 cm
HALLMARKS:   *CITY:* Voet, p. 11, No. 10
          *MAKER:* "I.B"
PROVENANCE: Mr. Charles S. Warburg, London
REMARKS: The detachable brass bases are 20th century. The
     letters "LC" are engraved on each stem. One bell is missing;
     one bell is a replacement. Cf. the similar finials No. 385, and
     the comparisons there.
BIBLIOGRAPHY: Kayser, No. 30
DONOR: Museum purchase

## 387

TORAH FINIALS   F 1932 a, b
Holland (?), first third of the 19th century
Silver: engraved, die-stamped
H 18.9 / 19.8   W 6.5 / 7.1 cm
HALLMARKS: Voet, p. 47, No. 6
PROVENANCE: Walter Schatzki, New York
DONOR: Dr. Harry G. Friedman

## 388

TORAH FINIALS   JM 20–64 a, b   (*Illus. p. 237*)
Mantua, early 18th century
Silver: cast, chased
H 61   DIAM 12.7 cm
HALLMARKS:   *CITY:* Tardy, p. 289, third row, third from right
          *MAKER:* "SIC" in circle with dot above; unclear
          mark (quartered coat of arms containing
          heraldic animals)
PROVENANCE: Zagayski Collection, Palm Beach
REMARKS: As these finials are quite heavy and large, they were
     probably used to decorate the reader's desk in a syna-
     gogue.
BIBLIOGRAPHY: Zagayski 1951, No. 1; Kayser, No. 22; Gutmann
     1964, pl. 2; Zagayski 1963, No. 3; PBNY 1964, No. 293; *Jewish
     Museum 75,* p. [37]; *Venice,* No. 9; *Treasures,* pp. 88–89; *Gar-
     dens,* No. 194
DONOR: Samuel and Lucille Lemberg

## 389

TORAH FINIAL   F 3068   (*Illus. p. 238*)
Venice, second half of 18th century
Silver: cast, repoussé, engraved
H 39.5   DIAM 12.1 cm
HALLMARKS: Pazzi 330 and 310 or 311
INSCRIPTION: on stem: קדש לה׳, "Holy to the Lord"; on
     base: מהיקרה מ״רת גיודיקה לויה ע״מ להניחו בליל כפור
     בספר כל נדרי בכל שנה ושנה, "From . . . Giudecca Levia
     i[n] o[rder] to place it on the Scroll for *Kol Nidre* on Yom
     Kippur eve, every year."
BIBLIOGRAPHY: Kayser, No. 32; *Venice,* No. 10 (where the
     name of the original donor was misread)
DONOR: Dr. Harry G. Friedman

## 390

TORAH FINIALS   F 5010 a, b   (*Illus. p. 238*)
Yugoslavia or Italy, 19th century
Sheet metal: repoussé, cut; base metal: cast; traces of
     silvering(?)
H 56.7   DIAM 11.0 cm
HALLMARKS: none
PROVENANCE: Hugo Weissmann, Boston
REMARKS: See *Dubrovnik* for similar iron finials. For the Ital-
     ian silver finial types from which No. 390 appears to de-
     rive, see finials No. 392.
BIBLIOGRAPHY: *Sephardic Journey,* No. 46
DONOR: Dr. Harry G. Friedman

## 391

TORAH FINIALS   F 264 a, b   (*Illus. p. 238*)
Turin (?), early 19th century
Silver: chased, cast
H 34.8 / 35.3   DIAM 10.6 cm
HALLMARKS:   *CITY:* Tardy, p. 291 (var.)
          *MAKER* (?): "F.L."; "FP," both incuse
DONOR: Dr. Harry G. Friedman

## 392

TORAH FINIALS   F 2826 a, b   (*Illus. p. 238*)
Turin, 1816/17 (inscription)
Silver: cast, chased, pierced, parcel-gilt; glass
H 67.4 / 68.4   DIAM 12.6 cm
HALLMARKS:   Donaver-Dabbene 21; 24=24/f.
          *OTHER:* "H . . A" in Hebrew script
INSCRIPTION: on each — on first story, on band between
     plinths: נדבת/ הקצין ר׳/ יהושע/ אוטולינגי/ שנת/
     התק״עז, "Donation of the leader . . . Joshua Ottolenghi,
     year 5577" (=1816/17)
REMARKS: These finials are quite large and were, therefore,
     probably used to ornament the reader's desk in a syna-
     gogue. The Temple symbols depicted on the first story
     include the fire altar, the Ark of the Covenant, the meno-
     rah, and the shewbread table.
BIBLIOGRAPHY: Kayser, No. 24; *Venice,* No. 6 (where the title
     of the original donor was misinterpreted); *Gardens,* No.
     199, fig. 20
DONOR: Dr. Harry G. Friedman

## 393

TORAH FINIALS   1984–74 b, c
Piedmont or Livorno, ca. 1837
Silver: cast, repoussé, pierced
H 48.1   DIAM 13.5 cm
HALLMARKS: "S Pini" in script
PROVENANCE: The Jewish Community of Malta

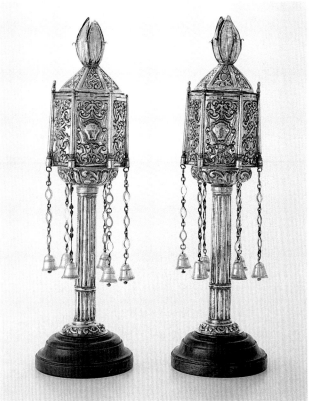

No. 394   F 1688a, b

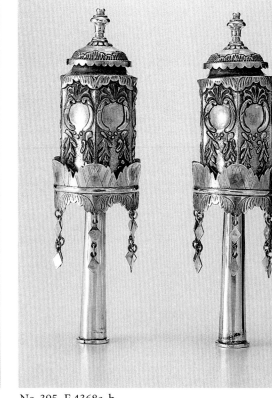

No. 395   F 4368a, b

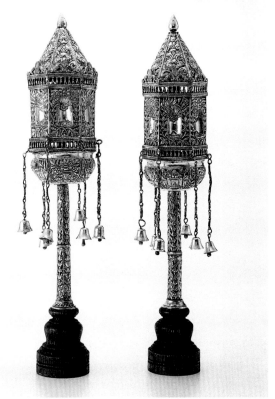

No. 396    F 2056a, b

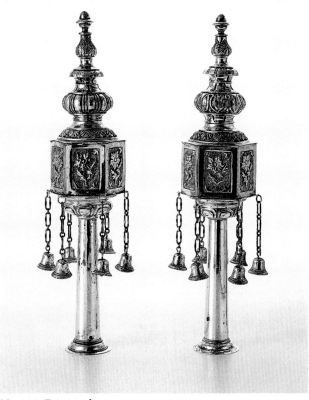

No. 397   F 5416a, b

REMARKS: The Temple symbols depicted include: the Ark of the Covenant, priestly hands, a censer, a ewer with pouring water, the fire altar, a priestly garment, the High Priest's mitre, the menorah, the Tablets of the Law. These finials came with Torah Case No. 906, which is probably Tunisian in origin. Cf. Magnes Museum, Berkeley, finials 77.333 dated 1837 and bearing the same smith's mark are very similar but have later Tunisian chains. For a third pair of finials by the same maker, dated 1845, but of different design, see Livorno, p. 81.

BIBLIOGRAPHY: *JMNY* 1993, fig. 50b

DONOR: Museum purchase

## 394

TORAH FINIALS F 1688a, b (*Illus. p. 240*)

Italy, late 18th–early 19th century

Silver: cast, repoussé, engraved

H 41.7 DIAM 11.3 cm

HALLMARKS: none

INSCRIPTION: in cartouches on sides — on finial A: Bab. Talmud Berakhot 28b; on finial B: לכבוד/ אלקינו/ נדבת/ כמ״ר/ משה/ בן/ ה׳ קצין מנחם/ אוטו״, "In honor of our Lord, donation of . . . R[abbi] Moses son of . . . [the] leader Menaḥem Otto[lenghi ?]."

REMARKS: The Museum card file records: "Place of Origin: Salenica [sic] Ca. 1710"; "Top half of two finials newly constructed . . . . Repaired . . . 1976."

DONOR: Dr. Harry G. Friedman

## 395

TORAH FINIALS F 4368a, b (*Illus. p. 240*)

Ferrara (?), 20th century

Silver: repoussé, engraved, cast

H 31.3 W 6.3 cm

HALLMARKS: none

PROVENANCE: Dr. S.Z. Yovely ("Tullio Castelbolognesi"), New York

REMARKS: According to the sale catalogue listed below, these finials were a "copy of seventeenth-century brass *rimmonim* in the Synagogue of Ferrara." The Museum card file adds that the originals were "in possession of Dr. Yovelli [sic], N.Y." in 1957.

BIBLIOGRAPHY: PBNY 1957, No. 151

DONOR: Dr. Harry G. Friedman

## 396

TORAH FINIALS F 2056a, b (*Illus. p. 240*)

Balkans or Italy, 19th century

Silver: cast, chased

H 36.4 DIAM 8.5 cm

HALLMARKS: none

REMARKS: The motifs include a flower basket, war trophies, and an elaborate gabled building. These finials are fash-

ioned in the Italian style, but the workmanship may indicate a more eastern origin.

DONOR: Dr. Harry G. Friedman

## 397

TORAH FINIALS F 5416a, b (*Illus. p. 240*)

Trieste, 1864

Silver: cast, chased

H 37.0 DIAM 9.0 cm

HALLMARKS: *CITY:* Rohrwasser, p. 13, third row (with L); Tardy, p. 52, top (Alexandria, 600; date, [early 1950's Egyptian import marks]) *MAKER:* illegible

REMARKS: The Egyptian import marks indicate that these finials were used in that country. An identical pair of finials is shown in *Juifs d'Egypte*, on a flat-topped Torah Case.

DONOR: Dr. Harry G. Friedman

## 398

TORAH FINIALS F 3470a, b (*Illus. p. 242*)

Italy or Yugoslavia (?), 20th century

Sheet metal: tinned, embossed

H 28.6 DIAM 10.4 cm

HALLMARKS: none

REMARKS: For other sheet metal finials, see No. 390.

DONOR: Dr. Harry G. Friedman

## 399

TORAH FINIALS F 5638a, b (*Illus. p. 242*)

Turin, 1817 (inscription)

Silver: repoussé, pierced, cast, parcel-gilt

H 29.9 / 31 DIAM 18.7 / 19.1 cm

HALLMARKS: Donaver-Dabbene 21 and 24/d

INSCRIPTION: on the lower band of each finial: לכבוד התורה אלול שנת נתי״ן עי״ז לפי״ק, "In honor of the Torah, Elul, year (chronogram: Psalms 68:36=5577=1817)"

PROVENANCE: Zagayski Collection, Palm Beach

REMARKS: Inside the bottom is the Zagayski Collection inventory number in red: "J-11A." For similar finials, see Frazier, p. 217 (1811); and Torino, p. 148, No. 10 (1824).

BIBLIOGRAPHY: Zagayski 1951, No. 9; Zagayski 1963, No. 13; PBNY 1964, No. 298; *Gardens*, No. 200, fig. 116

DONOR: Dr. Harry G. Friedman

## 400

TORAH FINIALS F 2343a, b (*Illus. p. 242*)

Europe, 19th century

Copper: cast, pierced, (silver-?)plated

H 32.5 DIAM 9.7 cm

HALLMARKS: none

DONOR: Dr. Harry G. Friedman

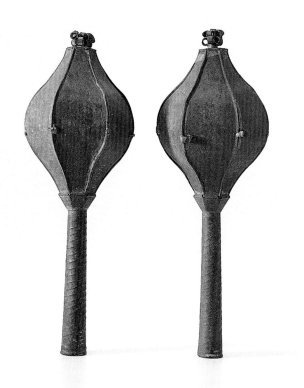

No. 398  F 3470a, b

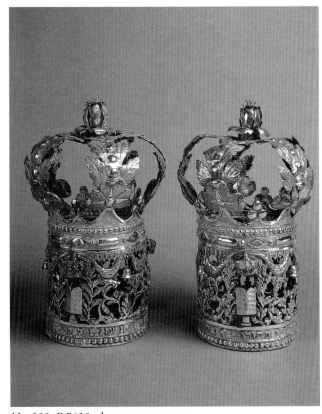

No. 399  F 5638a, b

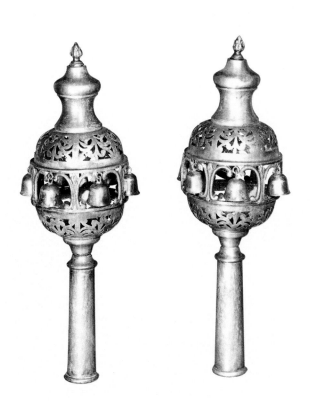

No. 400  F 2343a, b

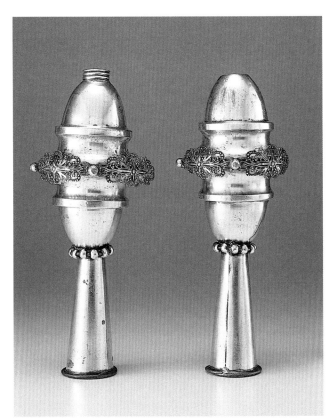

No. 401  F 2418a, b

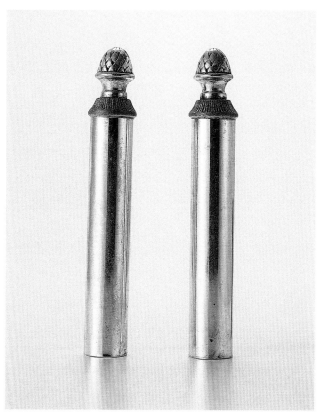

No. 402  F 4816a, b

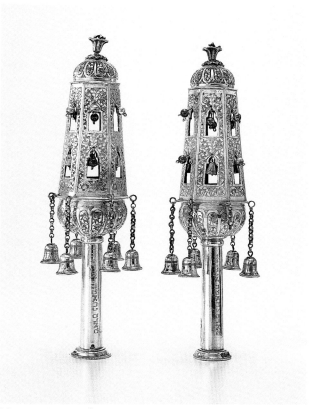

No. 403  F 5435a, b

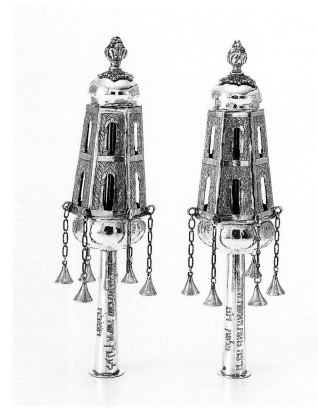

No. 404  1993–227a, b

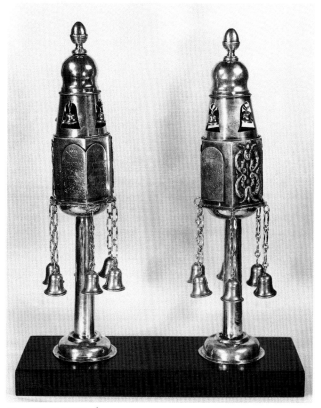

No. 405  F 5417a, b

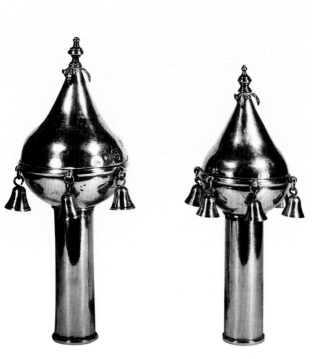

No. 406  F 5209a and b

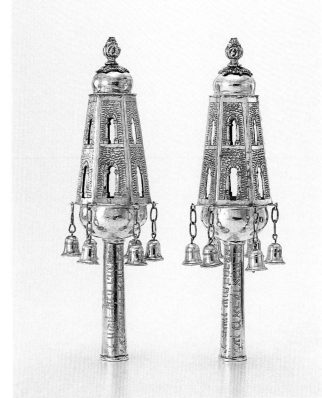

No. 407  F 5671a, b

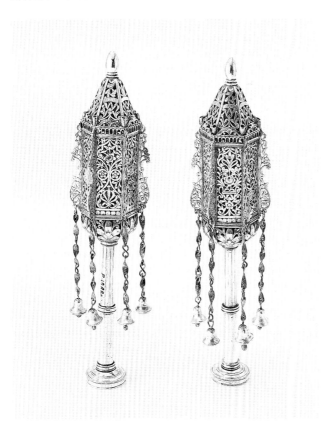

No. 408  F 1988a, b

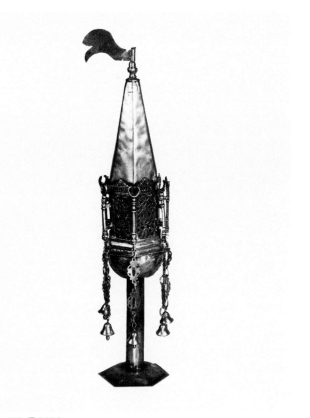

No. 409  F 2903

## 401
TORAH FINIALS  F 2418 a, b  (*Illus. p. 242*)
Europe, 19th–20th century
Brass (?): die-stamped, silver-plated
H 29.0 / 28.5  DIAM 11.0 cm
HALLMARKS: none
REMARKS: Various parts are missing on both finials.
DONOR: Dr. Harry G. Friedman

## 402
TORAH FINIALS  F 4816 a, b  (*Illus. p. 243*)
Eastern Europe (?), 19th–20th century
Silver (?); pewter: cast, silver-plated
H 21.3  DIAM 3.5 cm
HALLMARKS: none
DONOR: Dr. Harry G. Friedman

## 403
TORAH FINIALS  F 5435 a, b  (*Illus. p. 243*)
Alexandria, 1950
Silver: chased, pierced, cast
H 32.0  DIAM 9.2 cm
HALLMARKS: Tardy, p. 53, top (60); date letter (1950)
INSCRIPTION: on shaft of finial A: מאדם נחאמה אגיון היו,
  "Madame Neḥamah Agion …"
PROVENANCE: Gorevic & Son, New York
REMARKS: See the identical finials No. 404, as well as Sotheby's NY, 1981, No. 221; and *Juifs d'Egypte*, p. 151, showing two similar pairs on Torah Cases during the Simḥat Torah procession at the Eliahu Hannavi Synagogue, Alexandria, in October 1959.
DONOR: Dr. Harry G. Friedman

## 404
TORAH FINIALS  1993–227 a, b  (*Illus. p. 243*)
Alexandria, 1950
Silver: chased, pierced, cast
H 27.3  DIAM 8.0 cm
HALLMARKS: Tardy, p. 53, top (60); Arabic date letter (1950)
INSCRIPTION: on the stem of finial B: נדבה מאת האשה ורדה כלפון, "A donation from the woman Varda Kalfon …"; on the stem of finial A: לענ׳ר׳ן אישה שבתאי כלפון ת׳׳נ׳׳צ׳׳ב׳׳ה, "For the elevation of the soul of Issa Shabbetai Kalfon …"
REMARKS: Cf. the identical finials No. 403, and the references there.
DONOR: In memory of Ebrahim Khalil Rokhsar, by Mena Rokhsar

## 405
TORAH FINIALS  F 5417 a, b  (*Illus. p. 243*)
North Africa (?), 19th century
Silver: cast, engraved

H 31.2  DIAM 7.2 cm
HALLMARKS: none
REMARKS: The replacement bells are identical to those on finials No. 407.
DONOR: Dr. Harry G. Friedman

## 406
TORAH FINIALS  F 5209 a and b  (*Illus. p. 244*)
Southern Tunisia (?), late 19th–20th century
Silver: cast, parcel-gilt
H 18.6 / 20.6  DIAM 7.3 / 8.5 cm
HALLMARKS: none
REMARKS: The two finials, though similar, do not form a pair. They closely resemble wooden Torah Finials in an old photograph in The Jewish Museum's Photographic Archives inscribed: *116 — Vieilles Tapouhim en bois provenant de Djerba et Gabès (sud Tunisien).*
DONOR: Dr. Harry G. Friedman

## 407
TORAH FINIALS  F 5671 a, b  (*Illus. p. 244*)
North Africa (?), 1930 (inscription)
Silver: cast, chased, engraved
H 31.2  DIAM 8.8 cm
HALLMARKS: none
INSCRIPTION: on base body of finial A: לע׳׳ן מארקו אמון נ׳׳ע/ י׳׳ג חשון שנת התקצא, "For the e[levation of] the s[oul of] Marco Amun …, 13 Ḥeshvan year 5591" (=1830); on finial B: קודש לה׳, "Holy to the L[ord]"
REMARKS: The date has been modified by adding a vertical stroke to the *resh*, making it into a *qof*, thus adding a century to the age of the finials. The original date of death was on 4 November 1930. The bells are identical with those on finials No. 405.
DONOR: Dr. Harry G. Friedman

## 408
TORAH FINIALS  F 1988 a, b  (*Illus. p. 244*)
Algeria or Tunisia, mid-19th century
Silver: pierced, chased, parcel-gilt
H 23.8  DIAM 5.7 cm
HALLMARKS: none
PROVENANCE: Berry Hill
REMARKS: The six sockets around the upper body are most likely for holding flowers or grain, additional ornamention for the Torah Scroll on festivals (see *Beauty*, p. 96, quoting Abraham Hayarḥi "of Lunel": "… they weave and sew and pluck grass with aroma, in order to place it upon [the Torah] …"; *EJ* 14, s.v. Shavuot, col. 1322). A similar feature is found on finials No. 410, as well as on a single Tunisian/Libyan wooden finial at the Magnes Museum, Berkeley, 79.47.7. Note also the Torah Finials with flowers,

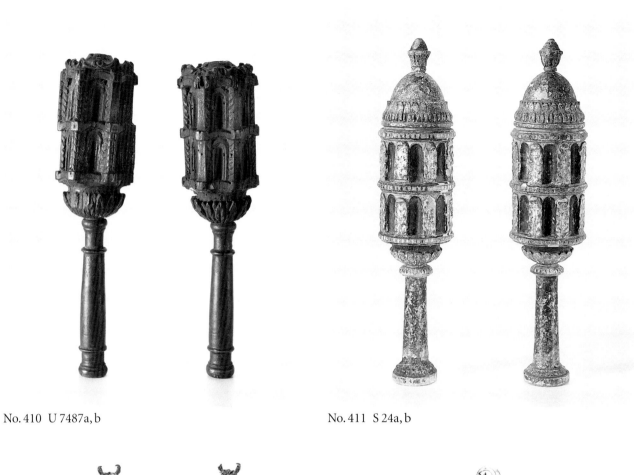

No. 410　U 7487 a, b

No. 411　S 24 a, b

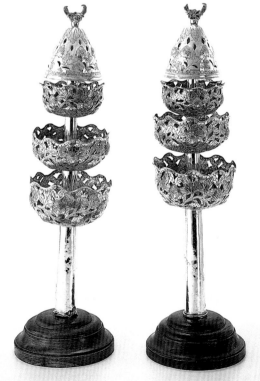

No. 412　F 3141 a, b

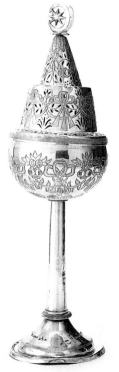

No. 413　F 1957

depicted on a Torah Case on the title page of *Ebrei in Libia*. For flowers on Afghani finials, see a photograph reproduced in Kashani, p. 15.

DONOR: Dr. Harry G. Friedman

## 409

TORAH FINIAL F 2903 (*Illus. p. 244*)
Algeria or Tunisia, late 19th–early 20th century
Silver: cast, pierced, parcel-gilt
H 25.2 DIAM 7.6
HALLMARKS: None
REMARKS: Cf. Torah Finials No. 408, which are of a form similar to that of this finial prior to its conversion into a spice container.
DONOR: Dr. Harry G. Friedman

## 410

TORAH FINIALS U 7487a, b (*Illus. p. 246*)
Tunisia, 19th century
Wood: carved, gessoed, painted, traces of gilt or bronzing
H 35.2 DIAM 8.9 cm
HALLMARKS: none
REMARKS: There are three small sockets on the top of each of these finials, apparently for flowers or grain. For this feature, see finials No. 408, and the references there. Cf. similar finials No. 411; Barnett, Nos. 101–101a; and *Sephardic Journey*, No. 327, fig. 4 (Gross Family Collection, Tel Aviv). Such finials were used in conjunction with Torah Cases of the type represented by Nos. 902–903.

## 411

TORAH FINIALS S 24a, b (*Illus. p. 246*)
Tunisia, 19th–20th century
Wood: carved, gessoed, gilt, painted
H 42.9 DIAM 9.7 cm
HALLMARKS: none
PROVENANCE: The Hadji Ephraim and Mordecai Benguiat Family Collection
REMARKS: See the similar finials No. 410, and the comparisons there. The photograph mentioned under finials No. 406 also shows a finial of this type.
BIBLIOGRAPHY: Kayser, No. 28
DONOR: Museum purchase

## 412

TORAH FINIALS F 3141a, b (*Illus. p. 246*)
Ottoman Empire, 1826/27 (inscription)
Silver: repoussé, engraved, cast
H 37.5 DIAM 10.3 cm
HALLMARKS: *Tuğra* of Maḥmūd II (1808–39)
INSCRIPTION: on finial A, spiralled around shaft, from bottom: של הארוס(?) ה/ הכ'י ה"כ יצחק ב' ברוך הכהן י"ץ ש

פ"ז, "Of the bridegroom . . . Isaac s[on of] Barukh haKohen . . ., (55)87" (= 1826/27)
REMARKS: The final letters of the inscription represent a date minus the letters representing the thousands or the hundreds. This dating agrees with the identification of the *Tuğra* hallmark as given in Mann 1982 ("of Maḥmūd II [1808–39]"—although the object itself was misdated there). A similar pair of finials is in the Israel Museum (147/214); see *Juhasz*, p. 55, fig. 30 = *Sephardic Journey*, No. 47A, fig. 47. And cf. Curiel & Cooperman, p. 160, No. 296 (illus. mid-bottom).
BIBLIOGRAPHY: Mann 1982, No. 205; Magnes 1989, p. 12; *Sephardic Journey*, No. 49
DONOR: Dr. Harry G. Friedman

## 413

TORAH FINIAL F 1957 (*Illus. p. 246*)
Ottoman Empire, 1882/83 (inscription)
Silver: cast, chased, pierced, engine-turned
H 38.0 DIAM 11.0 cm
HALLMARKS: *Tuğra* of 'Abd al-Ḥamīd II (1876–1909); *sah*
INSCRIPTION: around outer base: המשתדלים של קופה הקדושה מש[נת] ה'תר'מ'ג', "The treasurers of the Holy Fund, of the y[ear] 5653" (=1882/83); on upper base: הלא המה ה'ר דוד ציב'יליייה וה'ר משה אלבוחאירי וה'ר ברוך זאלקה ה'י, "Indeed, they are R[abbi] David Sevilla and R[abbi] Moses Albuḥairi and R[abbi] Barukh Zilka . . ."
REMARKS: The three rabbis listed here appear on finial No. 414, as well.
DONOR: Dr. Harry G. Friedman

## 414

TORAH FINIAL F 3175 (*Illus. p. 248*)
Ottoman Empire, late 19th century
Silver: chased, pierced, engraved
H 32.3 DIAM 9.4 cm
HALLMARKS: *Tuğra* of 'Abd al-Ḥamīd II (1876–1909); *sah*
INSCRIPTION: on shaft and base: קאבאר באשי ה'ר/ דוד ציבילייא הי"ו וה'ר/ משה אלבוחאיירי הי/ והר ברוך זאלכה היו והר/ שמואל ירושלמי היו/ המשתדלים של קופה קדושה יעא ש, "Kavar-bashi (?), R[abbi] David Sevilla . . . and R[abbi] Moses Albuḥairi . . . and R[abbi] Barukh Zilka . . . and R[abbi] Samuel Yerushalmi . . ., the Treasurers of the Holy Fund . . . ."
REMARKS: The names of the first three rabbis also appear on finial No. 413, dated 1882/83. Based on their names, the four rabbis may have been of Sephardi, Bukharan, Baghdadi, and Jerusalemite families, respectively. "Kavar-bashi" is either the name of a congregation, or a Turkish title (such as gâvur-başi, "Chief of Non-Muslims").
BIBLIOGRAPHY: *Sephardic Journey*, No. 47B
DONOR: Dr. Harry G. Friedman

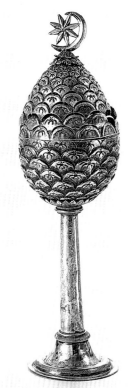

No. 414  F 3175

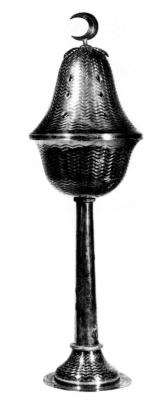

No. 415  F 1956

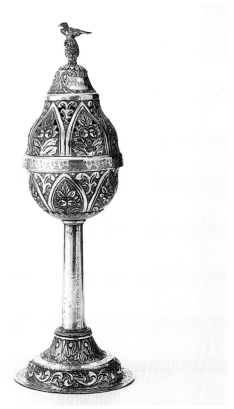

No. 416  F 3142

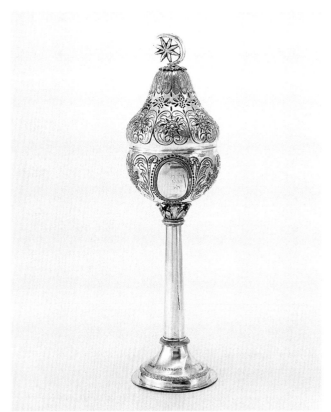

No. 417  F 3174

## 415

TORAH FINIAL  F 1956  (*Illus. p. 248*)
Ottoman Empire, 19th century
Silver: engine-turned, cast, pierced
H 39.0  DIAM 11.5
HALLMARKS: *Tuğra* (illegible)
BIBLIOGRAPHY: Mann 1982, No. 204; *Sephardic Journey*, No. 50
DONOR: Dr. Harry G. Friedman

## 416

TORAH FINIAL  F 3142  (*Illus. p. 248*)
Ottoman Empire, 1893/94 (inscription)
Silver: cast, chased, pierced, engraved, parcel-gilt
H 36.9  DIAM 12.9 cm
HALLMARKS: *Tuğra* of 'Abd al-Ḥamīd II (1876–1909); *sah*
INSCRIPTION: on stem and base: המשתדלים לחברה קדושה/
ה"ר יצחק סו אם ה"יו וה"ר יעקב נחום ה"יו וה"ר נסים יקר
5654 הי"ו שנת, "The Treasurers of the Holy (Burial) Society, R[abbi] Isaac . . . ., and R[abbi] Jacob Naḥum, and R[abbi] Nissim Yakar . . ., year 5654" (=1893/94)
DONOR: Dr. Harry G. Friedman

## 417

TORAH FINIAL  F 3174  (*Illus. p. 248*)
Ottoman Empire, 1876–1909
Silver: chased, cast
H 39.0  DIAM 10.8 cm
HALLMARKS: *Tuğra* of 'Abd al-Ḥamīd II (1876–1909); *sah*
INSCRIPTION: on base and in medallions: המשתדלים בחברה
קדושה יע"א// ה"ר דוד/ הכהן/ ה"יו// הר אהרן/ הלוי/
ה"יו ה"ה/ אבן ארי ב// ובר יעקב הי"ו, "The treasurers of the Holy (Burial) Society . . ., R[abbi] David haKohen . . ., R[abbi] Aaron haLevi . . ., and R[abbi] Jacob Ibn-Ari s[on of] H . . ."
BIBLIOGRAPHY: As noted in Mann 1982, No. 203, the *Tuğra* mark is of Abdul Hamīd II (1876–1909)
DONOR: Dr. Harry G. Friedman

## 418

TORAH FINIAL  F 5557  (*Illus. p. 250*)
Istanbul, 1792/93 (inscription)
Silver: cast, engraved
H 33.0  DIAM 10.9 cm
HALLMARKS: *Tuğra* of Selim III; *sah*
INSCRIPTION: on stem: חברת" אהבת אלים אורטה קייוא'
יע"א/ שנת התקנ"ג הגבאים ה"ה יצחק איסטאמאטי/ ה"י
הי"ו טאראגאנו נסים, "The Ahavat Elim ("Love of God") Society, Ortaköy, [in the] year 5553 (=1792/93), the *gabbaim* . . . Isaac Istamati . . . [and] Nissim Tarragano . . ."
REMARKS: In the inscription, the date has been made to read a century earlier by adding a vertical stroke to the *resh*, giving it the form of a *qof*.
DONOR: Dr. Harry G. Friedman

## 419

TORAH FINIAL  F 3389  (*Illus. p. 250*)
Ottoman Empire or Israel, late 19th–early 20th century
Silver: chased, engraved, cast
H 31.2  DIAM 9.2 cm
HALLMARKS: none
INSCRIPTION: on upper band: הקדש מקק פורטוגאל ישץ
על ידי המשתדלים בקודש מעלת::, "Dedication from the H[oly] C[ongregation of] Portugal . . ., by the Treasurers of holiness"; lower band: הגזברים סי רפאל טו קמחי היו וסי
דוד אברהם אלבילדה היו::, "The treasurers Se[ñor] Raphael . . . Kimḥi . . . and Se[ñor] David Abraham Albileda (?) . . ."
DONOR: Dr. Harry G. Friedman

## 420

TORAH FINIAL  F 4508  (*Illus. p. 250*)
Mardin, 1895/96 (inscription)
Silver: chased
H 24.0  DIAM 7.1 cm
HALLMARKS: none
INSCRIPTION: on medial band: הקדישו אותם אברהם בן
יציק ורחל אשתו במרדין ש' תר"נו, "Abraham son of Itzik and Rachel his wife, dedicated them in Mardin, y[ear] (5)656" (=1895/96)
REMARKS: Cf. the similar finials No. 421. Mardin is in southeastern Turkey, close to the border with eastern Syria.
DONOR: Dr. Harry G. Friedman

## 421

TORAH FINIALS  1987–60a, b  (*Illus. p. 250*)
Ioannina, 1841/42 (?)(inscription)
Silver: chased
H 41.0  DIAM 10.0 cm
HALLMARKS: none
INSCRIPTION: on finial A: ב'ה/ קהל קודש חדש/ יכב"ץ יאנינא
יע"א/ מ'ר/ פקיד משה ישראל/ מתתיה היו, "The synagogue of the Ne[w] Holy Congregation . . . Ioannina . . .; from . . . the officer Moses Israel Mattathiah . . ."; on lower cone: שנת תר"ב, "Year (5)602" (= 1841/42); on base: הרמונים/ האלה/ נעשו/ מהקדש/ קהל ק"/ יע"א, "These Torah Finials were made from the endowment of the H[oly] Congregation . . . ."; on finial B, the inscription is partly missing and partly the same as on finial A; on the base: הרמונים/ האלה/ נעשו/ מהקדש/ ק"ק חדש יעא, "These Torah Finials were made from the endowment of the New H[oly] C[ongregation] . . ."
REMARKS: See the similar finial No. 420. There were two synagogues in Ioannina, the "Old" and the "New," both adhering to the Romaniot rite. Torah Case No. 908 is also from Ioannina, but apparently made for the expatriate community in New York.
DONOR: Congregation Sheerith Israel of Janina, New York

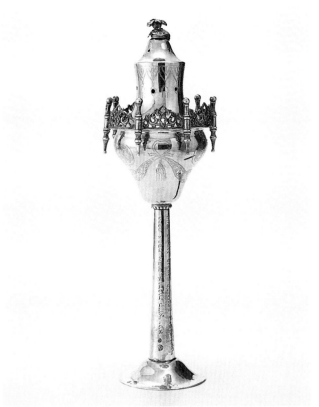

No. 418  F 5557

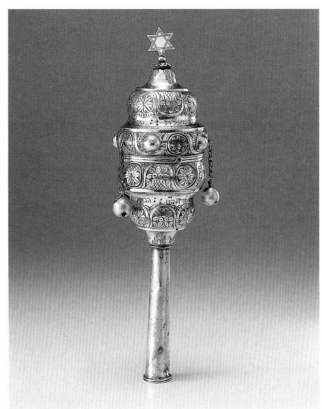

No. 419  F 3389

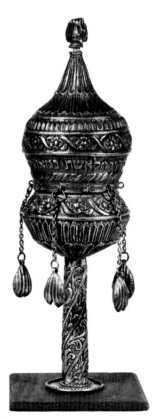

No. 420  F 4508

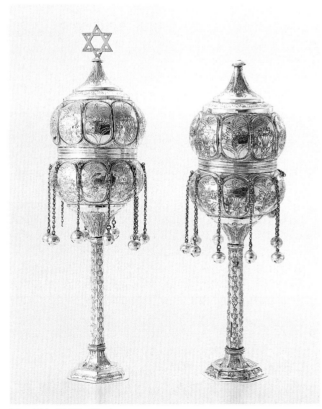

No. 421  1987–60a, b

## 422

TORAH FINIALS S 11a, b  (*Illus. p. 252*)
Western Ottoman Empire, 19th century
Silver: filigree
H 20.8  DIAM 5.5 cm
HALLMARKS: none
INSCRIPTION: on shaft of both finials: יוסף בן אפרים ו׳ גיאת
היי״ו, "Joseph son of Ephraim Benguiat …"
PROVENANCE: The Hadji Ephraim and Mordecai Benguiat
Family Collection
DONOR: Museum purchase

## 423

TORAH FINIAL X 1976-9
Western Ottoman Empire, 19th–20th century
Silver: repoussé, cast
H 26.6  DIAM 9.3 cm
HALLMARKS: none
INSCRIPTION: on the lower body is an illegible inscription in
cursive script; there is also what appears to be a date: "1174"
PROVENANCE: Charles S. Warburg, London
REMARKS: If the inscribed date is according to the Hijra, then
it is equal to ca. 1760.
DONOR: Museum purchase

## 424

TORAH FINIALS JM 2-54a, b  (*Illus. p. 252*)
Georgia, 1908–17; 1910 (inscription)
Silver: chased, cast
H 34.4  DIAM 10.8 cm
HALLMARKS: Postnikova 1941, with "o"; "M Sh" in Cyrillic
INSCRIPTION: on each finial, on each of the six sides, the first
two lines are from Exodus 28:34, referring to the finial itself
(*rimmon*); the remaining lines are as follows, on the respective sides: I — Deuteronomy 4:44; II — Deuteronomy
33:4; III — Psalms 19:8 (with abbreviations); IV — Psalms
19:9; V — Psalms 29:11; VI — Psalms 29:11, and: ל״ק שם
אליהו ו׳ ש׳/ משיח ואשתו/ ננא בת ש׳ רבי/ שנת תק״ע, "For
the … so[ul] (lit. name) of Elijah s[on of] S. Mashiaḥ and
his wife Nana daughter of S. Rabi, year (5)570" (=1809/10)
REMARKS: The Hebrew date has been modified, a vertical
stroke having been added to a *resh* to form a *qof*, thus
adding a century to the dating of the finials. Cf. *Israel Museum News* 13, 1978, p. 93, a similar pair of finials dedicated
in Jerusalem in 1925.

## 425

TORAH FINIALS S 22a, b
Iraq (?) or Turkey, first half of 20th century
Silver: chased, die-stamped, cast; wood (?); textile
H 26.7 / 27.4  DIAM 7.0 cm
HALLMARKS: none

PROVENANCE: The Hadji Ephraim and Mordecai Benguiat
Family Collection
REMARKS: The upper, cloth-covered part of the body appears
to have a wooden core. These finials have been extensively
repaired.
DONOR: Museum purchase

## 426

TORAH FINIALS F 3283a, b  (*Illus. p. 252*)
Iraq, late 19th–early 20th century
Silver
H 19.2  DIAM 5.0 cm
HALLMARKS: none
REMARKS: The oblique bottom edges on the stems indicate
that these finials were made for a domed Torah Case.
DONOR: Dr. Harry G. Friedman

## 427

TORAH FINIALS F 3726a, b  (*Illus. p. 253*)
Iran, 1851/52 (inscription)
Silver: chased, die-stamped
H 28.5  DIAM 8.0 cm
HALLMARKS: none
INSCRIPTION: on each, in cartouches: Deuteronomy 33:4;
"Year (5)612" (=1851/52)
REMARKS: Cf. the similar finials No. 428 and 429 and Skirball
Museum, Los Angeles, 47.29.
BIBLIOGRAPHY: *Jewish Museum 75*, p. [12]; *JMNY* 1993, fig. 45
DONOR: Dr. Harry G. Friedman

## 428

TORAH FINIALS F 3342a, b  (*Illus. p. 253*)
Persia, 1861/62 (inscription)
Silver: chased
H 30.0  DIAM 10.0 cm
HALLMARKS: none
INSCRIPTION: in medallions, on both finials: קודש לה / לבהכ
חכם.// אליהו/ בן יהודה// ניסן שנת/ לפ״ק תרכב, "Holy to
the Lord, to the Syna[gogue] of Ḥakham Elijah son of
Judah, Nissan year (5)522" (=1861/62); on medial band:
Deuteronomy 4: 44
REMARKS: See the similar finials No. 427 for comparisons.
DONOR: Dr. Harry G. Friedman

## 429

TORAH FINIALS F 5432a, b  (*Illus. p. 253*)
Iran, 20th century
Silver: chased, pierced, die-stamped
H 27.0  DIAM 8.7 cm
HALLMARKS: none
REMARKS: These two finials are not a true pair. On the stem of
each is a ring with several links of the chain which proba-

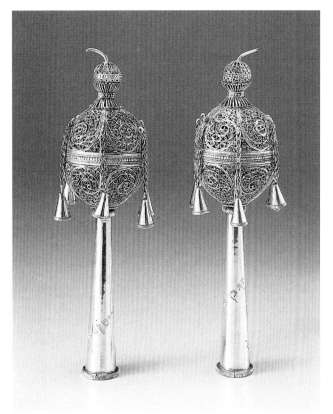

No. 422  S 11a, b

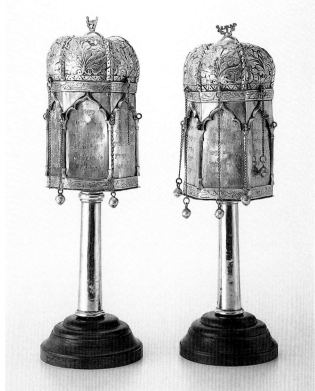

No. 424  JM 2–54a, b

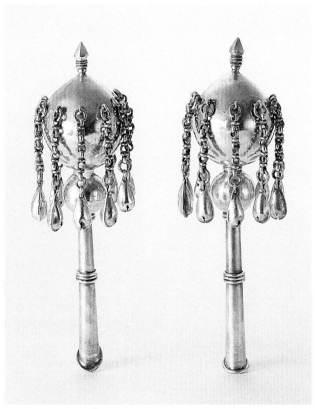

No. 426  F 3283a, b

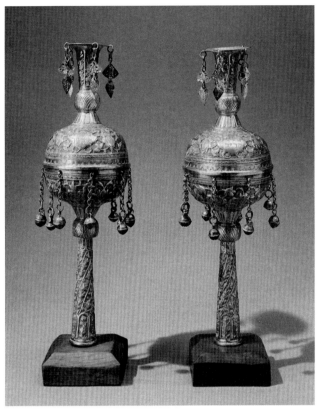

No. 427  F 3726a, b

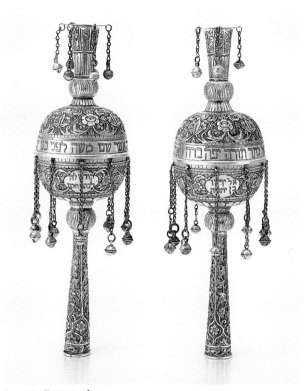

No. 428  F 3342a, b

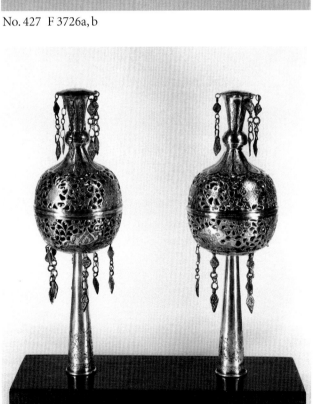

No. 429  F 5432a, b

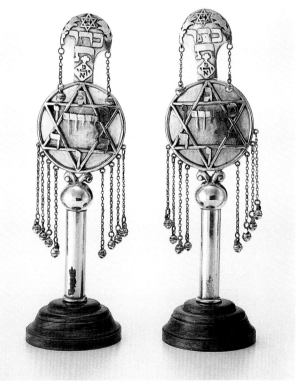

No. 431  F 3325a, b

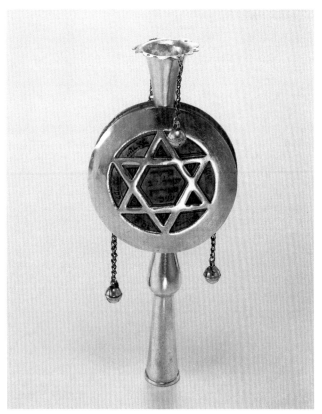

No. 432　1993–238

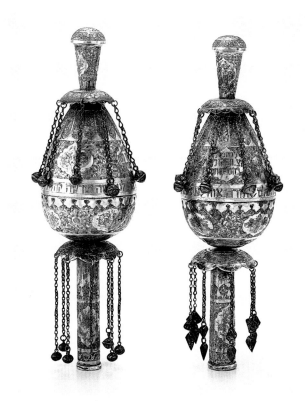

No. 433　F 3694a, b

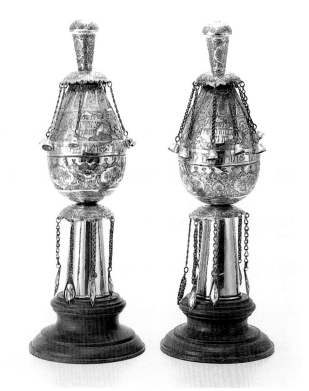

No. 434　F 4463a, b

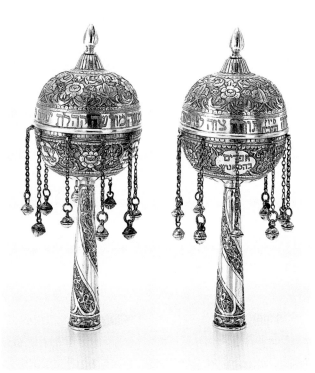

No. 435　F 3328a, b

bly had connected the two pieces. This feature appears, however, not to be original. See the similar finials No. 427 for comparisons.

DONOR: Dr. Harry G. Friedman

## 430

TORAH FINIALS  F 3261a, b

Iran, 20th century

Silver: pierced, die-stamped

H 34.5 / 36.6  W 10.4 / 10.6 cm

HALLMARKS: none

INSCRIPTION: on upper element, in Star of David: צ, "Z[ion]"; below: כתר / ת , "Crown of T[orah]"; below: on body, within Star of David, at center: ציון, "Zion"; in points: מגן דוד, "Star of David"

REMARKS: The lower inscription on the upper finial includes a large letter *dalet*, suggesting an amuletic significance. Cf. the similar finials Nos. 431–432; and Sotheby's Jerusalem 1987, No. 210.

DONOR: Dr. Harry G. Friedman

## 431

TORAH FINIALS  F 3325a, b  (*Illus. p. 253*)

Iran, first half of 20th century

Silver: pierced

H 33.5 / 33.8  W 11.1 / 11.5 cm

HALLMARKS: none

INSCRIPTION: on upper element, in Star of David: צ, "Z[ion]"; below: כתר / ת , "Crown of T[orah]"; below: on body, within Star of David, at center: ציון, "Zion"; in points: מגן דוד, "Star of David"

REMARKS: Cf. the similar finials Nos. 430 and 432.

DONOR: Dr. Harry G. Friedman

## 432

TORAH FINIAL  1993–238  (*Illus. p. 254*)

Iran, 1946/47 (inscription)

Silver: pierced, engraved ; paper: gouache

H 25.8  DIAM 10.8 cm

HALLMARKS: none

INSCRIPTION: around one side of body: קודש ל"ה נמצד ה"כ א" בנימין בן ה"ם א" עזיזאלה בן לוי שנת התשד, "Holy to [the] L[ord] …A. Benjamin son of Se[ñor] Azizolah son of Levi, year 5707" (=1946/47); on each side, on the paper insert, in the middle of Star of David: כתר / תורה י"ב/ מאירת/ עינים, "Crown of Torah, light of the eyes"; in points of star: מ/ו/ד/ו/ג/ד, "Star of David"; around: Deuteronomy 4:44

REMARKS: Cf. the similar finials Nos. 430 and 431. The donor has noted that this finial is from the Kourosh Synagogue in Teheran.

DONOR: In memory of Ebrahim Khalil Rokhsar, by Mena Rokhsar

## 433

TORAH FINIALS  F 3694a, b  (*Illus. p. 254*)

Persia, 19th–20th century

Silver: chased

H 31.0  DIAM 9.0 cm

HALLMARKS: none

INSCRIPTION: around body of finial A: Deuteronomy 33:4 and Isaiah 2:3; on medallion, on both finials: לנשמת/ הצ. והזקן נסים/ ב'ה'מ' ישועה, "For the soul of … Nissim s[on of] R[abbi] … Yeshu'ah"

REMARKS: The person mentioned in the inscription may also be mentioned on finials Nos. 437 and 443. Cf. the similar finials No. 434.

DONOR: Dr. Harry G. Friedman

## 434

TORAH FINIALS  F 4463a, b  (*Illus. p. 254*)

Persia, early 20th century

Silver: chased, pierced, die-stamped

H 29.6  DIAM 9.9 cm

HALLMARKS: Lileyko 90; "I. PERLMAN" in rectangle (both on replacement piece)

INSCRIPTION: on finial A, in upper medallions: לנשמת/ הצ" יוסף ב'ה'מי' שמואל/ לנשמת/ הצ" יוסף ב'ה'מי' שמואל "For the soul of … Joseph s[on of] R[abbi] … Samuel" (repeated twice); on main band: Deuteronomy 4:44 and Deuteronomy 33:4 (abbreviated); on finial B, in upper medallions: לנשמת/ הכבודה נורשיר(?) בת ניסן// לנשמת/ הכבודה נורשיר/ בת ניסן, "For the soul of … Nursir (?) daughter of Nissan" (repeated twice); on main band: Deuteronomy 33:4 and from the morning prayers, based on Exodus 15: 18

REMARKS: The stems on both finials have been replaced with parts from Polish finials. For two Torah Pointers by the same Warsaw smith, see Nos. 749 and 751. Cf. the similar finials No. 433.

DONOR: Dr. Harry G. Friedman

## 435

TORAH FINIALS  F 3328a, b  (*Illus. p. 254*)

Persia, early 20th century

Silver: chased

H 24.0  DIAM 9.0 cm

HALLMARKS: none

INSCRIPTION: on each finial, in medallions: כתר תורה/ יפה ברה// קודש לה/ לנהכ הרב// אפרים/ בהכ אנוש, "Crown of Torah, beautiful, radiant, Holy to the Lord, For the s[oul of] Rabbi Ephraim s[on of] Enosh"; around band: כתר תורה יפה ברה תורה צוה לנו משה מורשה קהלת יעקב סיון התריח "Crown of Torah, beautiful, radiant"; Deuteronomy 33:4; "Sivan 5618" (= May/June 1858)

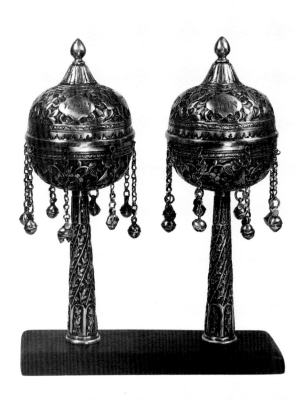

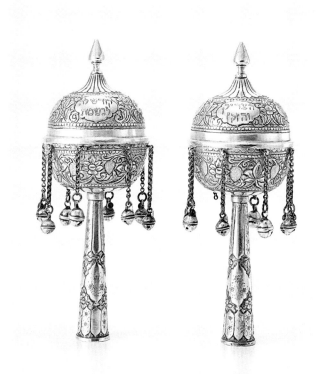

No. 436   F 3725a, b

No. 437   F 3225a, b

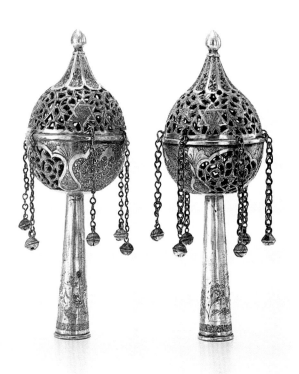

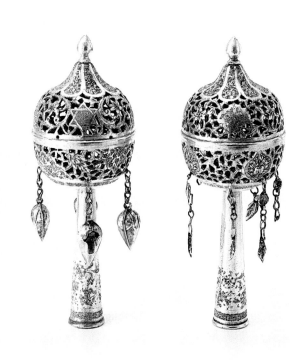

No. 438   F 4370a, b

No. 439   F 4403a, b

REMARKS: Cf. the similar finials Nos. 436–441.
DONOR: Dr. Harry G. Friedman

## 436
TORAH FINIALS  F 3725 a, b  (*Illus. p. 256*)
Iran, 20th century
Silver: chased
H 22.2  DIAM 8.5 cm
HALLMARKS: none
INSCRIPTION: on each finial, in medallions: ושמו/ אחד/ ידוד/
אחד, Zechariah 14:9
REMARKS: In the inscription, the tetragrammaton has the let-
ter *dalet* substituted for the letter *heh*. Cf. the similar finials
Nos. 435 and 437–441.
DONOR: Dr. Harry G. Friedman

## 437
TORAH FINIALS  F 3225 a, b  (*Illus. p. 256*)
Persia (?) or India (?), 19th–20th century
Silver: chased
H 23.3  DIAM 8.4 cm
HALLMARKS: none
INSCRIPTION: in cartouches: קודש/ יפה ברה/ כתר תורה/
Crown of", לה'/ לנשמת/ הצדיק/ והזקן/ ניסן בהמ/ יהושע
Torah, beautiful, radiant, Holy to the L[ord], for the soul of
the righteous . . . Nissan s[on of] R[abbi] . . . Joshua"
REMARKS: The person mentioned is also noted on finials No.
443 (and possibly also on No. 433). Cf. the similar finials
Nos. 435, 436 and 438–441.
DONOR: Dr. Harry G. Friedman

## 438
TORAH FINIALS  F 4370 a, b  (*Illus. p. 256*)
Persia, late 19th–early 20th century
Brass: chased, pierced, silvered
H 21.2  DIAM 7.5 cm
HALLMARKS: none
REMARKS: Cf. the similar finials Nos. 435–437 and 439–441.
BIBLIOGRAPHY: PBNY 1957, No. 185
DONOR: Dr. Harry G. Friedman

## 439
TORAH FINIALS  F 4403 a, b  (*Illus. p. 256*)
Iran, 20th century
Silver: chased, pierced
H 21.1 / 20.9 DIAM 7.5 cm
HALLMARKS: none
REMARKS: Cf. the similar finials Nos. 435–438 and 440–441.
DONOR: Dr. Harry G. Friedman

## 440
TORAH FINIALS  F 4881 a, b  (*Illus. p. 258*)
Iran, 20th century
Copper (?): chased, pierced, silvered
H 24.6  DIAM 8.6 cm
HALLMARKS: none
REMARKS: See the similar finials Nos. 435–439 and 441.
DONOR: Dr. Harry G. Friedman

## 441
TORAH FINIALS  F 5229 a, b  (*Illus. p. 258*)
Persia, 19th–20th century
Silver: chased, pierced, die-stamped
H 24.5  DIAM 8.6 cm
HALLMARKS: none
PROVENANCE: Ebrahim Rokhsar, New York
REMARKS: See the similar finials Nos. 435–440.
DONOR: Dr. Harry G. Friedman

## 442
TORAH FINIALS  F 4299 a, b  (*Illus. p. 258*)
Iran, 20th century
Silver: pierced, chased
H 15.4  DIAM 8.7 cm
HALLMARKS: none
REMARKS: See the similar finials No. 443. For similar work-
manship, see finials Nos. 438–441. The form of these finials
would seem to be inspired by North African examples; see
Thon, fig. 2, outer pair.
DONOR: Dr. Harry G. Friedman

## 443
TORAH FINIALS  F 4369 a, b  (*Illus. p. 258*)
Iran, 20th century
Silver: pierced, chased
H 26.5 / 27.0  DIAM 7.0 cm
HALLMARKS: none
INSCRIPTION: on stem of finial A: ל' נשמה ניסן ב'ה' ישוע ה',
"For . . . [the] soul of Nissan s[on of] Yeshua…."
REMARKS: The person mentioned in the inscription is also
noted on finials No. 437 (and possibly also on No. 433). See
the remarks under the similar finials No. 442.
DONOR: Dr. Harry G. Friedman

## 444
TWO TORAH FINIALS  1982–184 a and b
(*Illus. p. 260*)
India, 18th(?)–19th century
Gold: chased, pierced, engraved; sheet-metal (backing)
A: H 21.0  DIAM 8.5 cm  B: H 19.3  DIAM 8.8 cm
HALLMARKS: none

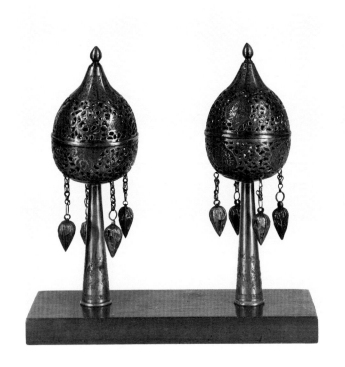

No. 440  F 4881a, b

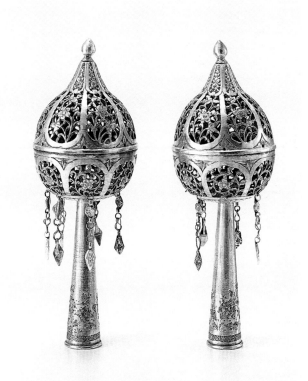

No. 441  F 5229a, b

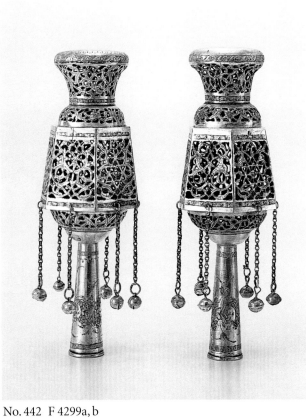

No. 442  F 4299a, b

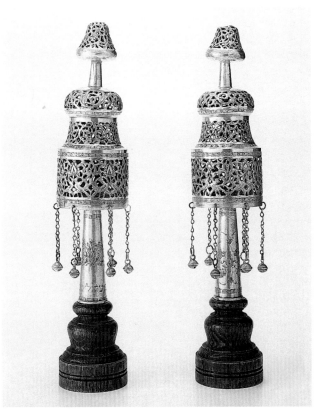

No. 443  F 4369a, b

INSCRIPTION: on the stem of finial B: שׁל מר חלגואה נ״ע ,"Of Mr. Hallegua, May he rest in peace"

REMARKS: These two similar finials were placed singly atop Torah Cases; for their context, see *Treasures*, p. 48. Two similar finials are in the Gross Family Collection, Tel Aviv.

BIBLIOGRAPHY: Christie's NY 1982, No. 160; *Treasures*, pp. 48–49

DONOR: The Michael and Luz Zak Purchase Fund

## 445

TORAH FINIALS   1987–145 b, c   (*Illus. p. 356*)

India, 1876 (?)

Silver: cast, chased

H 16.3   DIAM 7.5 cm

HALLMARKS: "15" (a synagogue mark?)

PROVENANCE: D. Cohen, Jerusalem

REMARKS: These finials belong to Torah Case No. 900. There is a grafitto on the stem "30." See the similar finial No. 446.

DONOR: The Michael and Luz Zak Purchase Fund

## 446

TORAH FINIAL   F 2509   (*Illus. p. 260*)

India, 1918/19 (inscription)

Silver: chased, cast

H 22.3   DIAM 6.9 cm

HALLMARKS: none

INSCRIPTION: on stem: לען אהרן רבקה מזרחי תנצ״בה/ נלבע ש׳ תר״עט, "For [the] [elevation of the] s[oul of] Aaron, Rebecca Mizraḥi, M[ay] h[is soul] be b[ound] in the b[onds of] l[ife], died the year (5)679" (= 1918/19)

REMARKS: Cf. the similar finials No. 445.

DONOR: Dr. Harry G. Friedman

## 447

TORAH FINIALS   F 4316 a, b   (*Illus. p. 260*)

Yemen, 19th–20th century

Brass: cast

H 29.4   DIAM 5.0 cm

HALLMARKS: none

REMARKS: Cf. finials Nos. 371 and 372, which are derived from this basic form. There are numerous parallels in public and private collections.

DONOR: Dr. Harry G. Friedman

## 447A

TORAH FINIALS   U 9737 a, b   (*Illus. p. 260*)

Uncertain origin, 19th–20th century

Silver: engraved, die-stamped

H 18.9/19.8   DIAM 6.5/7.1 cm

HALLMARKS: on lower stem: Tardy, p. 322, upper row, middle (Dutch import mark)

DONOR: Dr. Harry G. Friedman

## 447B

TORAH FINIALS   F 258 a, b

United States, early 20th century

Silver: filigree, cast, parcel gilt

H 37.6   DIAM 14.0

HALLMARKS: "STERLING"

REMARKS: On finial b, several arms for bells are missing. Some of the surviving bells are not original; one was made from a silver sheet from some other Jewish object, for there are traces of Hebrew engraving within (including אנכי, probably the beginning of the First Commandment, "I am …").

DONOR: Dr. Harry G. Friedman

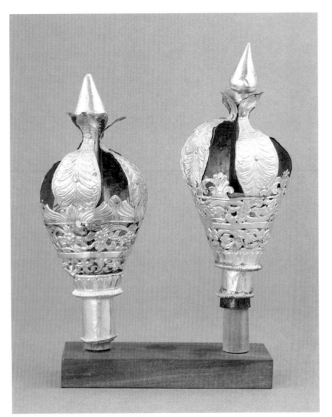

No. 444　1982–184a and b

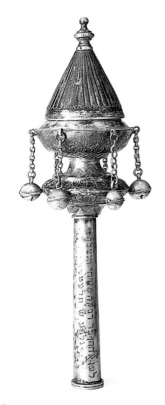

No. 446　F 2509

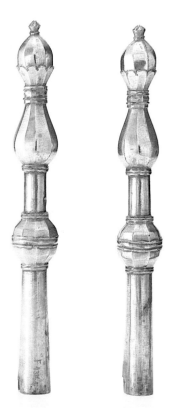

No. 447　F 4316a, b

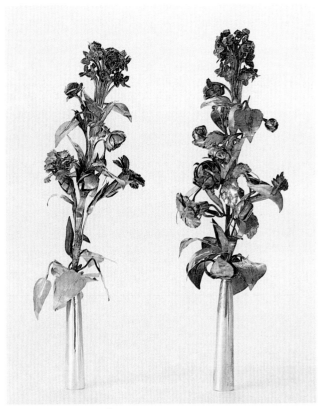

No. 447a　U 9737a, b

# Part III · Crowns

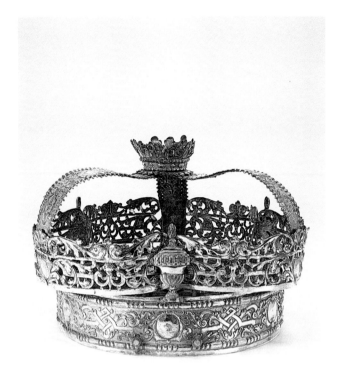

No. 448  JM 15–52

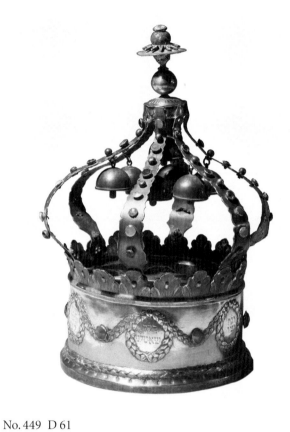

No. 449  D 61

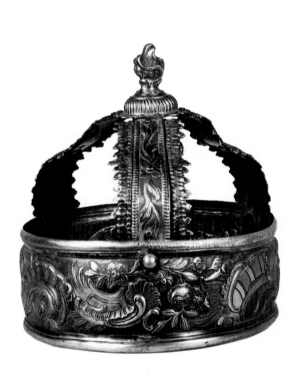

No. 450  JM 9–52

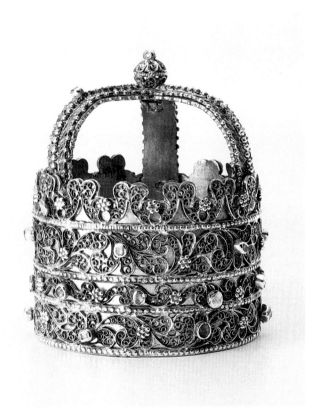

No. 451  JM 56–52

# Torah Crowns

## 448

TORAH CROWN  JM 15–52  (*Illus. p. 262*)
Nuremberg, second quarter (?) of 18th century
Silver: repoussé, cast, pierced, parcel-gilt
H 19.5  DIAM 28.0; (base) 24.4 cm
HALLMARKS: *CITY:* "N"
MAKER: Cock standing to left, in vertical oval
PROVENANCE: Friedberg Synagogue
REMARKS: This piece was badly damaged during World War II and was restored at The Jewish Museum in 1952.
BIBLIOGRAPHY: Hallo 1929, No. 23, p. 1; Moses 1931, p. 154; Hallo 1933, No. 16; Kayser, No. 38; *Wüb*, No. 10
DONOR: Jewish Cultural Reconstruction

## 449

TORAH CROWN  D 61  (*Illus. p. 262*)
Berlin, 1779; 1802/03 (inscription)
Joachim Hübener (II), active ca. 1737–80
Silver; glass; white sapphires; agates; amber
H 38.4  DIAM 28.1 cm
HALLMARKS: *CITY:* Scheffler, *Berlin*, 10b
MAKER: Scheffler, *Berlin*, 110 (var.)
INSCRIPTION: on circlet, in medallions: כתר/ תורה// שייך/
לאלופי// חברה/ קדישא// וג"ח/ יצ"ו// דק"ק/ שאטלנד//
שנת תקסג/ לפ"ק, "Crown of Torah. Belongs to the leaders of the Holy (Burial) and B[enevolence] Society of the H[oly] C[ongregation] of Schottland, (5)563" (=1802/03); on lower rim: נעשה ע"י הגבאים ר' שמעון ור' שמואל פ"ח, "Made by the *gabba'im* Simon and Samuel, o[fficers of the] m[onth] …"
PROVENANCE: The Schottland Synagogue, Danzig
REMARKS: Many of the gems seem to be replacements; the top finial has been modified, and a stone added. Two small holes on each stave suggest that there had been swags or garlands between the staves, a frequent feature on Torah Crowns. For the two *gaba'im* mentioned in the inscription, see shield No. 39, which they dedicated to the same Society. The Hebrew abbreviation פח at the end of the inscription probably stands for פרנס חודש, "treasurer of the month" (or possibly פתח חותמות, "engraver"). Hübener made shields Nos. 38 and 39 as well as pointer No. 530.
BIBLIOGRAPHY: Danzig 1933, No. 138c; *Danzig 1939/1982*, No. 74; *Treasures*, pp. 134–135; *JMNY* 1993, fig. 48
DONOR: The Jewish Community of Danzig

## 450

TORAH CROWN  JM 9–52  (*Illus. p. 262*)
Nuremberg, second half of 18th century
Johann Samuel Beckensteiner, active 1743–81
Silver: repoussé, parcel-gilt
H 22.0  DIAM 22.0 cm
HALLMARKS: *CITY:* "N"
MAKER: R³ 4295; within staves: "GA/B" in heart
INSCRIPTION: on upper band: נ"י של המונה(!) ה"ק פ"ו הר"ה
זעליגמן ז"ל בן ליב ז"ל מק"ק שנאטוך, "Donation of the deceased … R[abbi] Seligman son of the late Leib of the H[oly] C[ongregation] of Schnaittach"
PROVENANCE: The Schnaittach Synagogue
REMARKS: Another crown by the same smith (Deneke, No. 3/20) is in a private collection in Fürth. Other works by Beckensteiner at The Jewish Museum are shield No. 28, finials No. 264, and pointer No. 523. Beckensteiner also made *havdalah* compendia (e.g., Klagsbald 1982, No. 79) and Hanukkah lamps (e.g., Deneke, No. 3/123).
BIBLIOGRAPHY: Deneke, No. 3/21
DONOR: Jewish Cultural Reconstruction

## 451

MINIATURE TORAH CROWN  JM 56–52
(*Illus. p. 262*)
Nuremberg (?), 18th century
Silver: filigree; rubies; glass
H 7.3  DIAM 6.0 cm
HALLMARKS: none
REMARKS: The attribution to Nuremberg is based on the similarity of the form of this crown to others from that city (e.g., No. 450). For another miniature filigree crown, from Galicia, see No. 467.
DONOR: Jewish Cultural Reconstruction

## 452

TORAH CROWN  (Fragment) D 53  (*Illus. p. 264*)
Danzig (?), first third of 19th century
Silver: chased, cast, parcel-gilt; glass
H 21.3  DIAM 16.6 cm
HALLMARKS: Czihak 2 (?)
REMARKS: Beneath the lower band are slots for attaching this fragment to another piece, probably a circlet, as on No. 459.

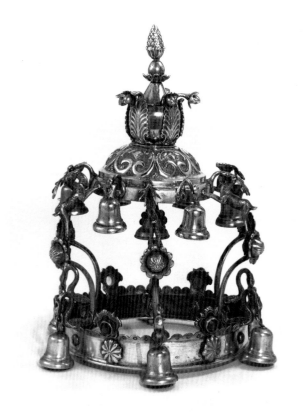

No. 452  D 53

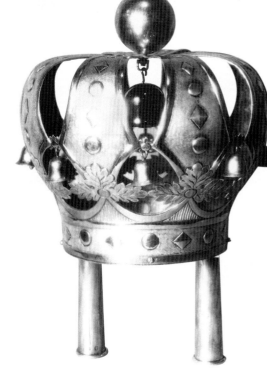

No. 453  F 1649

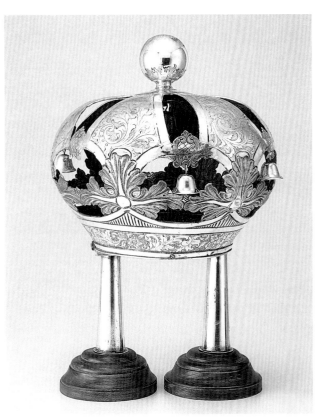

No. 454  S 987

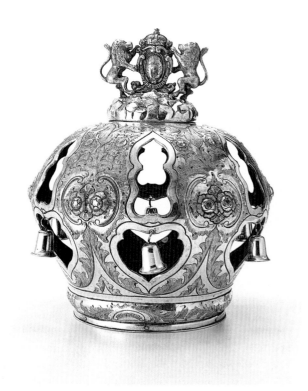

No. 455  F 3856

BIBLIOGRAPHY: Danzig 1904, No. 15; Danzig 1933, No. 53; Kayser 1950–51, p. 495; NYHS 1971, No. 149, illus. on p. 18; *Danzig 1939/1982*, No.76

DONOR: The Jewish Community of Danzig

## 453

TORAH CROWN   F 1649   (*Illus. p. 264*)
Berlin, 1821–39
Johann Friedrich Wilhelm Borcke, active ca. 1821–39
Silver: chased, parcel-gilt
H 32.1   DIAM 22.7 cm
HALLMARKS: *CITY:* Scheffler, *Berlin*, 14 and 18
  *MAKER:* Scheffler, *Berlin*, 331
REMARKS: Another crown by the same smith is in the Mark and Peachy Levy Collection, Los Angeles. Other Judaica by Borcke include finials (Nos. 283–84) and an alms container (D 226), all in The Jewish Museum's Collection, a shield and a Hanukkah lamp at the Israel Museum (148/121 and 118/704), and a spice container at the Skirball Museum (53.100). For similar Berlin crowns, see Nos. 454–455.
BIBLIOGRAPHY: Mann 1982, No. 70
DONOR: Dr. Harry G. Friedman

## 454

TORAH CROWN   S 987   (*Illus. p. 164*)
Berlin, 1842–43
Silver: chased, pierced, engraved, parcel-gilt
H 37.0   DIAM 25.6 cm
HALLMARKS: Scheffler, *Berlin*, 14 and 19
REMARKS: This crown, initially lent to the Museum in 1936, was later donated by Dr. Harry G. Friedman in 1959. For similar Berlin crowns, see Nos. 453 and 455.
DONOR: Dr. Harry G. Friedman

## 455

TORAH CROWN   F 3856   (*Illus. p. 164*)
Berlin, 1854–60
Friedrich August Ferdinand Eisolt, active ca. 1833–58
Silver: repoussé, cast
H 32.0   DIAM 27.5 cm
HALLMARKS: *CITY:* Scheffler, *Berlin*, 15 and 21
  *MAKER:* Scheffler, *Berlin*, 414 (var.)
REMARKS: Note that the original (cruciform ?) finial of the small crown at the top has been partly removed. The arms below the small crown are those of Bavaria quartered with a rampant lion. There is an empty hole for a half-crown with large Tablets of the Law, visible in an older photograph. For other Berlin crowns of this general type, see Nos. 453–454.
BIBLIOGRAPHY: *Jewish Museum 75*, p. [5]
DONOR: Dr. Harry G. Friedman

## 456

TORAH CROWN   D 57   (*Illus. p. 166*)
Germany (Danzig ?), late 19th century
Brass: repoussé, engraved; silver: engraved; glass
H 37.5   DIAM 16.6 cm
HALLMARKS: none
INSCRIPTION: on two bosses: כתר תורה, "Crown of Torah"; חברה קדישא, "Holy (Burial) Society"
BIBLIOGRAPHY: Danzig 1933, No. 57; *Danzig 1939*, No. 213
DONOR: Jewish Cultural Reconstruction

## 456A

TORAH CROWN   D 60   (*Illus. p. 166*)
Danzig (?), late 19th–early 20th century
Brass: chased, engraved, parcel-gilt
H 18.5   DIAM ca.20.0 cm
HALLMARKS: none
INSCRIPTION: on circlet: כתר / תורה, "Crown of Torah"
PROVENANCE: The Great Synagogue, Danzig
REMARKS: This crown is apparently made up of pre-existing elements. Museum records indicate that various studs were replaced in the early 1950's.
BIBLIOGRAPHY: Danzig 1933, No. 60; *Danzig 1939*, No. 212
DONOR: The Jewish Community of Danzig

## 457

TORAH CROWN (Fragment)   F 1894   (*Illus. p. 166*)
Germany (?), late 19th–early 20th century
Silver: repoussé, pierced, parcel-gilt
H 9.6   DIAM 10.4 cm
HALLMARKS: none
REMARKS: This is probably a fragment of a larger crown, since the lower opening is only 5.4 cm in diameter.
DONOR: Dr. Harry G. Friedman

## 458

TORAH CROWN   F 4505   (*Illus. p. 166*)
Breslau, 1746–58; 1782/83 (inscription)
George Kahlert the Younger, active 1732–73
Silver: chased, pierced, cast, parcel-gilt; glass; sheet metal
H 40.3   DIAM 23.8 cm
HALLMARKS: *CITY:* Hintze 1906, Nos. 19 and 34
  *MAKER:* Hintze 1906, No.148
INSCRIPTION: on circlet: ז'נ האלו' התו' מו' יצחק איצק ב'
מו יהודא ליב ב' אבר' מליס. וזוגתו הצנועה מר' מינדיל
בת הרב מו' שלמה א'ב'ד' מראטרדם ש' קד"שי'ם י"ביו"(!)
ל'א'ל'ה'ם, "T[his is the] d[onation of] R[abbi] Isaac Itzik son of Judah Leib son of Abr[aham] from Liss[a], and his spouse Mindel daughter of R[abbi] Solomon, H[ead of the] R[abbinical] C[ourt], of Rotterdam, [in the] year

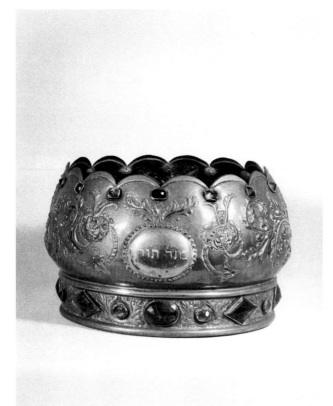

No. 456  D 57

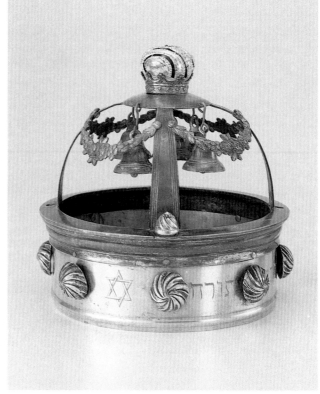

No. 456A  D 60

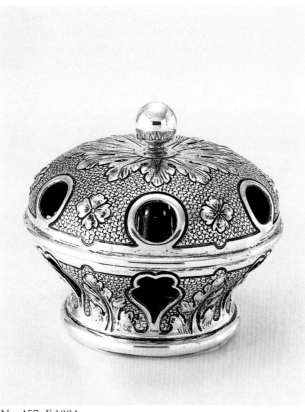

No. 457  F 1894

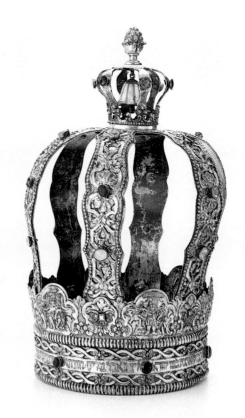

No. 458  F 4505

'Holy ones will come to the Lord' (chronogram for [5]543= 1782/83)."

PROVENANCE: P. W. Rosenfeld Collection, Berlin (?); The Antique Porcelain Collector, Inc., New York

REMARKS: Six scenes around the upper part of the circlet bear Hebrew tituli naming biblical subjects ("Abraham and the Offering of Isaac"; "Jacob"; "Moses"; "Aaron"; "David"; "Solomon"). There are tubes to fit over the Torah Staves, one fixed and the other sliding; these were probably added in the early 19th century. The Museum records note that, "on the second tier, the semiprecious stones are missing and (are) replaced by square silver knobs." Although made at Breslau, in Silesia, the form of this crown resembles that of the Galician Torah Crowns.

R. Isaak Itzig b. R. Judah Leib is cited in Louis Lewin's *Geschichte der Juden in Lissa* (p. 259). He died in 1814. The woman in the inscription is most likely the daughter of Rabbi Solomon Ezekiel who was Chief Rabbi in Rotterdam (1725–35) (letter from Nahum M. Sarna, 1957, in The Jewish Museum archives. See also *EJ* IX, p. 229d). The provenance is based on a note on the back of a photograph in the Museum's Photographic Archives. For a Torah Shield by the same smith, see Hintze 1929, No. 212.

DONOR: Dr. Harry G. Friedman

## 459

TORAH CROWN F 4588 *(Illus. p. 268)*
Central Europe (?), 19th century
Silver: cast, die-stamped, traces of gilt
H 32.3 DIAM 11.8 cm
HALLMARKS: none
DONOR: Dr. Harry G. Friedman

## 460

TORAH CROWN D 59 *(Illus. p. 268)*
Central Europe, 19th–20th century
Brass and silver: cast, chased, parcel-gilt; glass
H 23.9 DIAM 15.8 cm
HALLMARKS: none
REMARKS: The base of this Torah Crown appears to be a Madonna crown to which the staves and finial were added. Some of the stone settings and several bells are missing. *Danzig 1939*, No. 78, cites "a similar crown from Brno, dated 1813."
BIBLIOGRAPHY: Danzig 1933, No. 59; *Danzig 1939/1982*, No. 78
DONOR: The Jewish Community of Danzig

## 461

TORAH CROWN F 3492 *(Illus. p. 268)*
Austrian Empire, second half of 19th century
Silver: repoussé, cast, traces of gilt
H 46.8 DIAM 26.2 cm

HALLMARKS: none
DONOR: Dr. Harry G. Friedman

## 462

TORAH CROWN F 5797 *(Illus. p. 268)*
Hungary, 20th century
Silver: die-stamped, cast, chased
H 34.5 DIAM 29.8 cm
HALLMARKS: "MADE IN / HUNGARY"; "925"; "STERLING" (erased); "Silver" (erased)
DONOR: Dr. Harry G. Friedman

## 463

TORAH CROWN F 2585 *(Illus. p. 269)*
Galicia, 1764/65; 1773 (inscriptions)
Silver: repoussé, cast, pierced, engraved, parcel-gilt; glass
H 50.0 DIAM 29.0 cm
HALLMARKS: R³ 7884, R³ 7989 (on both circlets, staves, and griffins, but not on dome or eagle)
INSCRIPTION: on lower circlet, middle register (each panel separately):

ז"נ/ ה'ה האלוף/ המרוממ התורני הר/ הנגיד המפורסם מ'ו
משה ב'ה/ יצחק מענקס זל איש צבי ואש תו(!)/ החשובה
והגבירה מרת/ רחל בת מ שמעון זל/ עבור בניהם שיזכו
לג'ד/ לתורה ול'ח ול'מט'ו א'ס. לסדר ולפרט והיה
כ'אש'ר' (!)/ משה' יזו וגבר ישראל/ לפק

"T[his was] d[onated by] Rabbi ... Moses son of the late R[abbi] Isaac Menkes, man of glory, and his wife ... Rachel daughter of the late Simon, on behalf of their sons, may they be worthy to r[aise them] to the Torah, to the m[arriage canopy] and to g[ood] d[eeds]. A[men], s[elah]. In the year (chronogram from Exodus 17:11=[5]525= 1764/65)."

ואת אמי מו'ר/ החשובה והצ'נ/ החסידה מ' זיסל/ בת
מהו' ישראל/ איסר זצל
"And my mother ... Zissel daughter of the late Rabbi Israel Isser."

<u>יזכור</u>/ אלקים את נשמת/ אדוני אבי מורי ה'ה/ האלוף
המרוממ מ'/ שמעון ב'מ אברהם/ ז'ל בעבור שאני נודר/
זאת בעד הזכרית (!)/ נשמתה (!) ות'נ צב'ה/ א'ס
"May the Lord remember the soul of ... my father ... the late Simon son of the late Abraham, for I vow this on behalf of the remembrance of his (lit. her) soul and M[ay his] s[oul] be b[ound up] in the b[onds of] life. A[men], s[elah]."

כתר תורה/ וכתר כהונה/ וכתר מלכות
"Crown of Torah, and Crown of Priesthood, and Crown of Royalty."

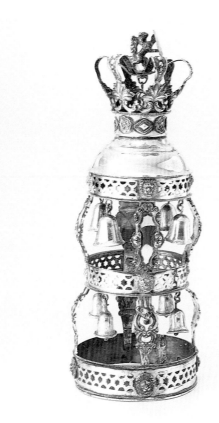

No. 459  F 4588

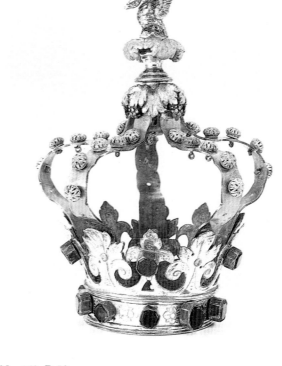

No. 460  D 59

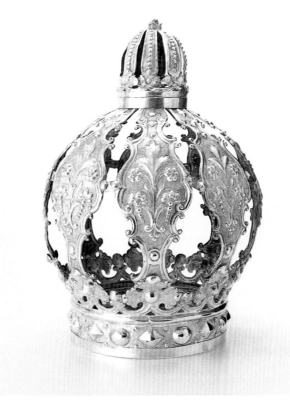

No. 461  F 3492

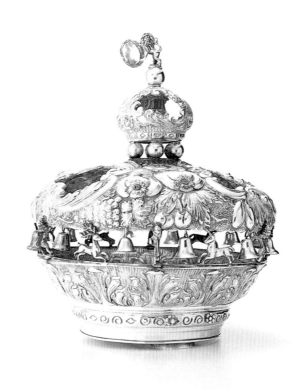

No. 462  F 5797

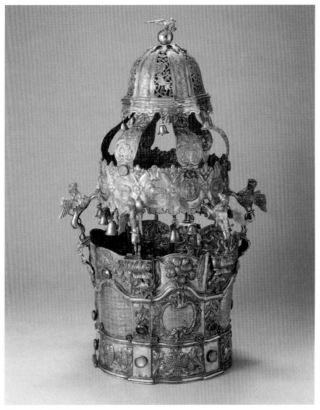

No. 463  F 2585

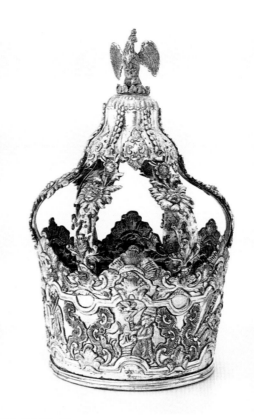

No. 464  JM 30–55

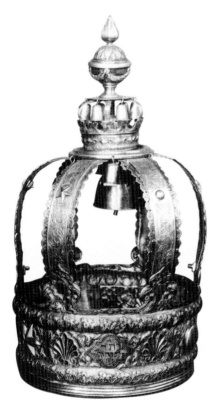

No. 465  S 560

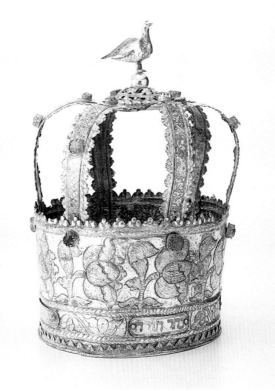

No. 466  F 5636

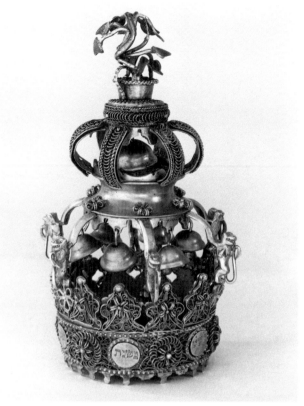

No. 467  F 2508

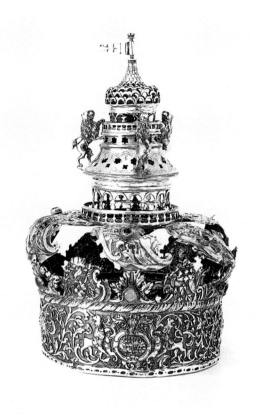

No. 468  JM 17–64

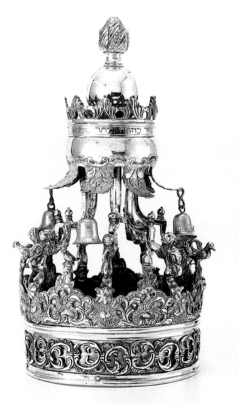

No. 469  D 52

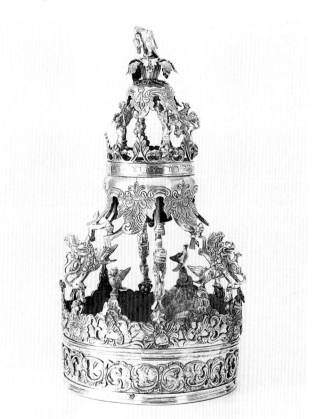

No. 470  M 319

ויזכור/ אלקים את נשמת/ אמי הצנועה והחסודה (!)/
ה׳ח מ׳ ייטה בת הרבני מ׳/ צבי הירש זל בעבור/ שאני נודר
בעד הזכרת/ נשמתה ות׳נצ ב׳ה/ אס

"May the Lord remember the soul of my mother . . . Yetta daughter of the late Rabbi Tzvi Hirsch, for I vow on behalf of the remembrance of her soul, and May her soul be bound up in the bonds of eternal life. A[men], s[elah]."

וכתר/ שם טוב עול׳/ על גביהן

"And the Crown of a Good Name exceeds them all" (Ethics of the Fathers 4: 17).

On upper circlet:

מזל/ ניסן/ נגמר ב׳ע׳ר׳ה׳ ת׳ק׳ל׳ד׳

"Aries. Completed on the e[ve] o[f] R[osh] H[ashanah], (5)534" (=17 September 1773).

This is followed by the eleven remaining months with their corresponding zodiac signs.

REMARKS: For pierced work similar to that on the upper cupola, see finials No. 339. For less elaborate crowns of this type see, e.g., Kantzedikas, Nos. 3, 12, and 25–27. A wooden, blind-tooled leather case, apparently late 18th-century, came with this crown: H ca. 60.5; DIAM 34.5 cm.

BIBLIOGRAPHY: Kayser, No. 35; Kayser 1950–51; Roth, p. 121, fig. 114; *Treasures*, pp. 102–03; *JMNY* 1993, fig. 46

DONOR: Dr. Harry G. Friedman

# 464

## TORAH CROWN  JM 30–55  (*Illus. p. 269*)

Galicia, late 18th–early 19th century

Silver: repoussé, cast, parcel-gilt

H 27.5  DIAM 17.0 cm

HALLMARKS: none

INSCRIPTION: אברהם/ ויצחק, "Abraham and Isaac"; משה, "Moses"; אהרין(!), "Aaron"; שלימה(!), "Solomon"; דוד, "David"; יעקב, "Jacob"

REMARKS: The tituli for David and Solomon have been interchanged. The orthography of the tituli may reflect local pronunciation. For a similar canopy, see Kantsedikas, No. 3.

BIBLIOGRAPHY: Kayser, No. 191

DONOR: Mrs. Bernard Kahn, New York, in memory of her husband

# 465

## TORAH CROWN  S 560  (*Illus. p. 269*)

Galicia, late 18th–early 19th century

Silver: repoussé, die-stamped, cast, parcel-gilt, nielloed

H 38.0  DIAM 21.2 cm

HALLMARKS: none

INSCRIPTION: on circlet, in three medallions: כתר/ תורה//, כתר/ מלכות// וכתר/ כהונה/ וכתר/ ש״טוב, "Crown of Torah, Crown of Royalty, and Crown of Priesthood, and

Crown of a Good N[ame]"; on boss: שבת, "Shabbat."

PROVENANCE: Hugo Helbing, Munich; Felix M. Warburg Collection, New York

REMARKS: Within are two tubes attached to the sides; within one, in black ink, is: "560/JTSA." The word יכתר is in smaller script. The occurrence of the word "Shabbat" on this crown would seem to negate the oft-assumed Polish tradition of using Torah Finials on the Sabbath and Torah Crowns on festivals. The 1932 Helbing catalogue notes the presence of a hallmark, apparently no longer visible.

BIBLIOGRAPHY: Helbing 1932a, No. 37 and pl.I; Kayser, No. 18a

DONOR: Mr. and Mrs. Felix M. Warburg

# 466

## TORAH CROWN  F 5636  (*Illus. p. 269*)

Galicia, late 18th-early 19th century

Silver: chased, cast, parcel-gilt, nielloed; semiprecious stones

H 32.9  DIAM 22.3 cm

HALLMARKS: none

INSCRIPTION: on plaques around the circlet: כתר תורה// נזר/ ועטרה/ ולתפארה, "Crown of Torah, diadem and coronet, and for splendor"

PROVENANCE: Michael Zagayski Collection, Palm Beach; G. Gumbel Collection, San Francisco

REMARKS: There is an old number written within, in red: "J-1C"— the Zagayski Collection number. Note that the inscription reflects the biblical imagery of עטרת תפארת, "a glorious diadem" (Proverbs 4: 9). All three words, כתר, נזר, and עטרה, are biblical terms for noble or priestly headgear.

BIBLIOGRAPHY: PBNY 1950, No. 128; Zagayski 1951, No. 15; Zagayski 1963, No. 2; PBNY 1964, No. 291

DONOR: Dr. Harry G. Friedman

# 467

## MINIATURE TORAH CROWN  F 2508

(*Illus. p. 270*)

Northern Galicia, 1813/14 (inscription)

Silver: filigree, cast, engraved, parcel-gilt

H 11.6  DIAM 7.4 cm

HALLMARKS: CITY: "L:[12]" (Cyrillic); partial mark — upper part of pair of scales
MAKER: "A(J)" (ligature in script)

INSCRIPTION: on medallions: כ׳ת׳// כ׳כה׳ר׳// כ׳מ׳// כתשט// בשבת/ תקעד, "C[rown of] T[orah], C[rown of] P[riesthood], C[rown of] R[oyalty], "C[rown of a] G[ood] N[ame], on the Sabbath in the year (5)574" (=1813/14)

PROVENANCE: H. Rosenau, New York

REMARKS: The bottom is closed with a sheet of silver having two rectangular openings for the Torah Staves. The Hebrew for "Crown of Royalty" is in smaller script and,

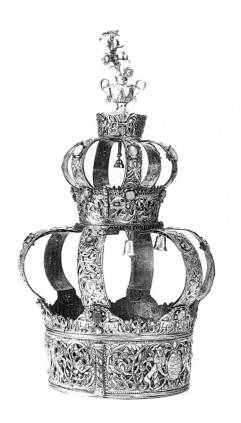

No. 471   S 1363a

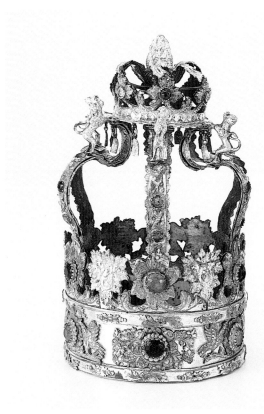

No. 472   F 4040

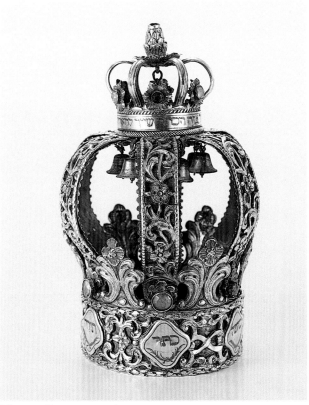

No. 473   F 1904

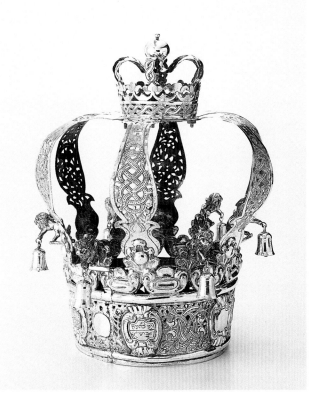

No. 474   F 3601

therefore, probably a restoration. All three hallmarks appear on a silver lamp at the Israel Museum (Stieglitz, No. 143), formerly in the Oppenheimer Collection, London, and said to have come from a synagogue in Sweden (*Beauty*, p. 299, fig. 11). On the basis of style and workmanship, both this crown and the lamp should be ascribed to early-19th-century Polish Galicia. The crown has a contemporaneous, fitted green leather case.

DONOR: Dr. Harry G. Friedman

## 468

TORAH CROWN   JM 17–64   (*Illus. p. 270*)

Lvov, late 18th–early 19th century

Silver: chased, pierced, cast, parcel-gilt; glass

H 26.8   DIAM 18.3 cm

HALLMARKS: *CITY:* Rohrwasser, p. 11, single-letter group, "D"; p. 12, bottom, left

INSCRIPTION: on circlet, in cartouches: כתר/ מלכות/ נתן נטע/ במוהר"ר' ישכר (!)/ כתר תורה/ טויב' בת/ מוהר' ז/אב/ ואלף, "Crown of Royalty, Nathan Neta son of Rabbi Issacher, Crown of Torah, Toiv[a] (or "Taub[e]") daughter of Rabbi Zev Wolf"

PROVENANCE: Michael Zagayski Collection, Palm Beach

REMARKS: Within, old mark in red: "J–1B" (the Zagayski Collection number). For similar ornamentation of the circlet, see crown No. 471. Lions decoratively arranged around the upper section appear on several crowns in the Museum of Historical Treasures, Kiev (e.g., Kantsedikas, Nos. 1 and 27, the latter, a related crown dated 1785, formerly in Lvov). A pair of Torah Finials of similar style is in the Stern Collection, New York (T 14, bearing a Lvov re-mark of 1807; see Zagayski 1963, No. 9=PBNY 1964, No. 105). The Zagayski 1963 catalogue ascribed this crown to the 17th century, while the 1951 exhibition catalogue ascribed the lower part to "ca. 1760" and the upper part to "17th ct." The parallels noted support the present dating.

BIBLIOGRAPHY: Zagayski 1951, No. 14; Zagayski 1963, No. 1

DONOR: Miriam Schloessinger

## 469

TORAH CROWN   D 52   (*Illus. p. 270*)

Galicia, 1809/10 (inscription)

Silver: chased, cast, gilt

H 24.7   DIAM 13.5 cm

HALLMARKS: "12"; "BM" (?), (ligature in script)

INSCRIPTION: on upper band: Ethics of the Fathers 4:17; לפרט ת"ק"ע' "(5)570" (=1809/10)

REMARKS: In the more elaborate examples of Torah Crowns of the lion-stave type, there is an upper tier of smaller staves. Many of these crowns are inscribed with dates and indicate a period of production spanning the first three decades of the 19th century. Both this crown and No. 470

are classic examples of the smaller, more modest version.[1] The type may have evolved from another Galician type of crown, with floral staves.[2] The transitional form has lions standing on floral staves.[3] Some of the group are very elaborate: two-tiered, with stags or griffins in the upper tier[4] and a bird or eagle atop the finial.[5]

BIBLIOGRAPHY: Danzig 1904, No. 14; Danzig 1933, No. 52; Kanof 1960, fig. 15; *Danzig 1939/1982*, No. 77

DONOR: The Jewish Community of Danzig

1. A fine example, with colored stones is Kayser, No. 39 (formerly F 268=Christie's New York 1993, No. 456).
2. See, e.g., Stieglitz, No. 10, ascribed there to Germany (and bearing a spurious 1740 date).
3. See Kantsedikas, No. 6.
4. For stags, see a crown formerly in the Feinberg Collection, PBNY 1967, No. 460. For griffins, see Stieglitz, No. 7, dated (spuriously) 1726.
5. For a bird, see PBNY 1949, No. 115, dated 1811; and a 1929 photo in The Jewish Museum's Photographic Archive, showing a crown in the Lublin Synagogue, dated 1826. For an eagle, see *Central Synagogue Calendar*, opp. week of September 13–18, a crown dated 1816.

## 470

TORAH CROWN   M 319   (*Illus. p. 270*)

Galicia, 1810/11 (inscription)

Silver: cast, chased, parcel-gilt

H 27.9   DIAM 15.6 cm

HALLMARKS: none

INSCRIPTION: Ethics of the Fathers 4:17; תקעא "(5)571" (=1810/11)

PROVENANCE: The Rose and Benjamin Mintz Collection

REMARKS: See crown No. 469, of the same type.

DONOR: Museum purchase

## 471

TORAH CROWN   S 1363a   (*Illus. p. 272*)

Galicia, 1817/18; 1874 (inscriptions)

Silver: chased, pierced, parcel-gilt; semiprecious stones; glass

H 52.0   DIAM 29.8 cm

HALLMARKS: none

INSCRIPTION: on circlet, in three medallions: כלל/ כסף קודש/ מהנגיד ר' שמעון/ ב"ר יהודא ז"ל/ ו"ז ש"ר"ה ב"ת דוב/ ול"ב"נ"י"ה ם" לפק, "Completed with sanctified silver from . . . Rabbi Simon s[on of the] late Judah, and h[is spouse] Sarah daughter of Dov, and for their sons" (=chronogram for (5)634=1873/74); סלסלה/: ותרוממך/ שי'ל"ר"ם/ וליא: כתר: לראשיך, adapted from Proverbs 4: 8; ר'ב'/ לאוהבי/ 'תורתיד/ ל'פ'ק', Psalms 119: 165 (=chronogram for [5]578=1817/18)

PROVENANCE: Michael Karp, New York

REMARKS: The word וליא in the second chronogram is to be read לויה.

For very similar ornamentation on the circlet, see crown No. 468. The top was restored in 1950 by Posen, New York.

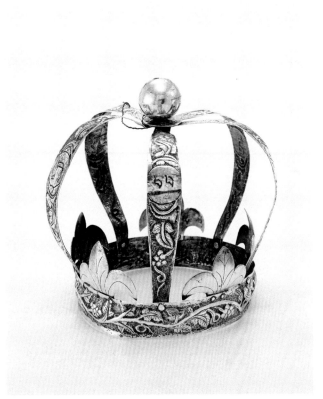

No. 475  F 3528

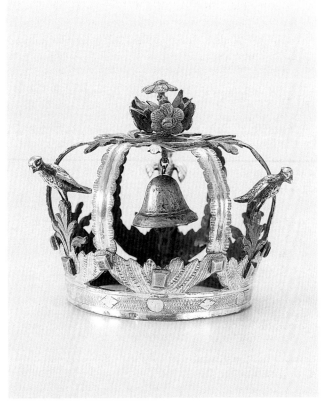

No. 476  F 2349

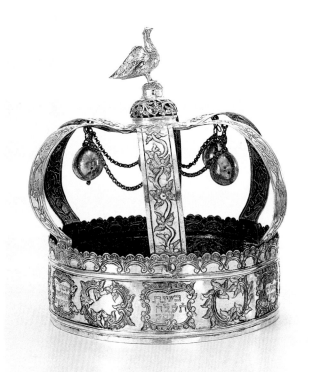

No. 477  M 15

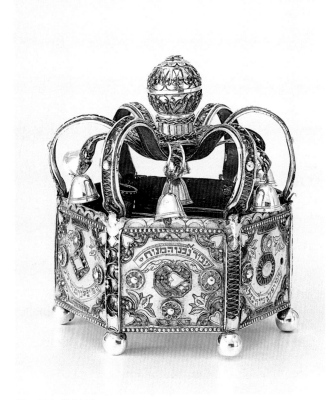

No. 478  F 3131

A letter from the donor, dated February 24, 1947, notes that his father had purchased the crown in 1910 from a family in Rumania, in whose possession it had been since the Kishinev pogrom.

DONOR: Max M. Karp, in memory of his father, Michael Karp

## 472
### TORAH CROWN  F 4040  (*Illus. p. 272*)
Galicia, late 18th–early 19th century
Silver: cast, chased, engraved, gilt; glass
H 24.0  DIAM 16.5 cm
HALLMARKS: none
REMARKS: Old number within, in ink: "7011⁵". The 1932 Helbing sale catalogue (see below) already notes that one of the lions is missing.
BIBLIOGRAPHY: Helbing 1932b, No. 92 (illus.).
DONOR: Dr. Harry G. Friedman

## 473
### TORAH CROWN  F 1904  (*Illus. p. 272*)
Galicia (?), ca. 1780 (?)
Silver: cast, chased, engraved, gilt, nielloed; stones; glass
H 18.1  DIAM 12.0 cm
HALLMARKS: none
INSCRIPTION: on circlet, in six medallions: Ethics of the Fathers 4:17; on upper band: זה הכתר שייך להאלו' המרומ' הרר דוד בהר' ירוחם זל, "This crown belongs to . . . Rabbi David son of the late Rabbi Yeruḥam."
PROVENANCE: Leo Seifter
REMARKS: In Kayser, No. 57b, this crown is dated "1779," based on the date of Torah Pointer No. 706, which was dedicated by the same person in 1778/79. Cf. also shield No. 190, which was acquired by the Museum at the same time.
BIBLIOGRAPHY: Kayser, No. 57b
DONOR: Dr. Harry G. Friedman

## 474
### TORAH CROWN  F 3601  (*Illus. p. 272*)
Galicia, early 19th century
Silver: chased, pierced, cast, parcel-gilt
H 31.6  DIAM 26.8 cm
HALLMARKS: none
INSCRIPTION: The first inscription is engraved in five cartouches on the circlet, arranged in two superimposed lines, the top reading: Ethics of the Fathers 4:17; the second line reads: נאום אברהם אבוש יַח'רר יצחק, "Signed (?) by Abraham Avush son of (?) Isaac." Another inscription appears beneath cartouches: מלאחת (!)/ הקדש עש'/ כ' חיים במ'/ צבי (ה)ירש/ ז(ל)/ אשתו/ בראנדל/ (ב)ת כה/ שמואל (ל)'ז, "Sacred work made by . . . Ḥayyim son of the late . . . Zvi Hirsch; [and] his wife Braindel daughter of the late Samuel."

REMARKS: A sixth cartouche is blank. The spellings and the order of the inscription are corrupt.
DONOR: Dr. Harry G. Friedman

## 475
### TORAH CROWN  F 3528  (*Illus. p. 274*)
Galicia, 19th century
Silver: chased, cast
H 14.8  DIAM 16.0 cm
HALLMARKS: none
INSCRIPTION: ת,/ נ /א/ ה/ ו', "May God rest his soul."
REMARKS: The significance of the inscription is unknown.
DONOR: Dr. Harry G. Friedman

## 476
### TORAH CROWN  (Fragment)  F 2349  (*Illus. p. 274*)
Galicia, late 18th–early 19th century
Silver and bronze: chased, cast, engraved, parcel-gilt
H 10.8  DIAM 13.8 cm
HALLMARKS: Rohrwasser, p. 12, bottom, left; p. 11, top row, left, mid (with "D"); a false Augsburg mark
INSCRIPTION: on lower part of circlet: זנ אברהם בן חיים, ת"נ לפ"ק "T[his was] d[onated by] Abraham son of Ḥayyim, (5)450" (=1689/90)
PROVENANCE: Hessisches Landesmuseum, Kassel
REMARKS: See Torah Shield No. 196, which bears the same false inscription (and is of the same provenance). For a Torah Crown having the same small upper crown, see a photograph in the Photographic Archive of The Jewish Museum, taken in "Kazimierz on the Vistula" (near Lublin). The photograph bears the mark of the Jewish Exploration Society, Warsaw Branch.
BIBLIOGRAPHY: *Notizblatt* 1929, p. 3, fig. 2 ; Hallo 1932, No. 17
DONOR: Dr. Harry G. Friedman

## 477
### TORAH CROWN  M 15  (*Illus. p. 274*)
Lithuania (?), 1777/78
Silver: chased, pierced, cast
H 28.3  DIAM 27.0 cm
HALLMARKS: none
INSCRIPTION: on circlet, in cartouches: שמות/ האלופם (!)/ (!) הגבאים/ מהור'/ יהוד'/ בהרר גרש'/ זצ'ל/ מהו' נתן/ נטע במהור'/ יצחק סגל// מהורר/ אליעזר בהר/ מהור' יחזקיאל// אבד'/ כמו הורר/ יצחק סגל// בשנת/ ת' ק' ל' ח' לפק, "Names of the leaders, the *gabba'im* Rabbi Juda[h] son of the late Rabbi Gersh[on]; Rabbi Nathan Neta son of Rabbi Isaac Segal; Rabbi Eliezer son of Rabbi Ezekiel; Chief of the Rabbinical Court, Rabbi Isaac Segal. In the year (5)538" (=1777/78)
PROVENANCE: The Rose and Benjamin Mintz Collection
BIBLIOGRAPHY: Loukomski, p. 171 (illus.)=Gilbert, fig. 16
DONOR: Museum purchase

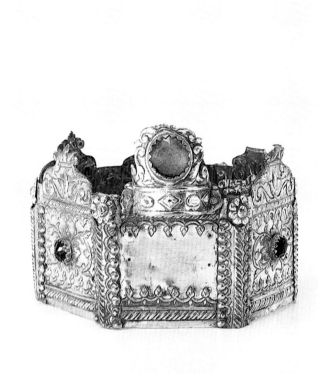

No. 479  F 2563

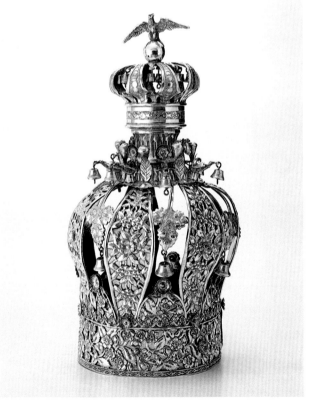

No. 481  S 797

No. 480  JM 22–59

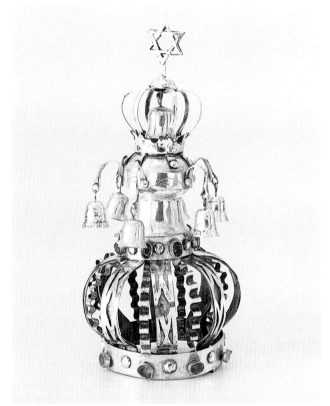

No. 482  M 16

## 478

TORAH CROWN  F 3131  (*Illus. p. 274*)

Lithuania or Belorussia, prior to 1837

Silver: filigree, die-stamped, cast, engraved, gilt; brass

H 19.5  DIAM 16.5 cm

HALLMARKS: none

INSCRIPTION: on circlet, in ribbons: זה הכ׳ת נדב הגביר/ המופלג מו׳ה בצלאל/ עבור נ׳ בנו המנוח המופלג ומהולל/ מ׳ יעקב נ׳ע׳ חתן של/ ה׳:ג:מ׳: עקיבא: איגר נ׳י ,"This is the C[rown of] T[orah], donated by Bezalel on behalf of the s[oul of] his son, the late . . . Jacob, son-in-law of the Gaon Akiva Eger." On remnant in beak of bird-finial: ה נ (?)

REMARKS: Within are two sliding shafts for the Torah Scroll staves. In 1952, three filigree rosettes were restored by Jacob Posen, New York.

Rabbi Akiba Eger's name is followed here by the Hebrew abbreviation meaning "May his light shine"—used only for the living. Therefore, the crown must precede 1837, the year of Eger's death. For crowns of similar, angled form, see crown No. 479 and several photographs of crowns in the Photographic Archive at The Jewish Museum, taken between the two World Wars, one of them from Zabludow (20 km SE of Bialystok).

BIBLIOGRAPHY: Kayser, No.37

DONOR: Dr. Harry G. Friedman

## 479

TORAH CROWN  F 2563  (*Illus. p. 276*)

Lithuania (?), early 19th century

Silver: repoussé, parcel-gilt; glass

H 11.7  DIAM 17.5 cm

HALLMARKS: none

REMARKS: Only the stub of one stave remains. The entire upper part of this crown is missing. On one side there are traces of a former dedication plaque. Crown No. 478 is of similar form.

DONOR: Dr. Harry G. Friedman

## 480

TORAH CROWN  JM 22–59  (*Illus. p. 276*)

Warsaw (?), late 19th century

Brass: cast, chased, die-stamped, engraved, silver-plated

H 25.9  DIAM 23.9 cm

HALLMARKS: "A.BAUMINGER" in rectangle

IINSCRIPTION: in two panels on the lower band: ז״נ שיינדיל בת אסתר מרים/ שלמה שמואל בן חבר ר׳ אליעזר הלוי, "T[his was] d[onated by] Sheindel daughter of Esther Miriam [and] Solomon Samuel son of . . . Eliezer ha-Levi"; Ethics of the Fathers 4:17

REMARKS: Three of the original six stag-heads are missing. Older Museum photographs of this crown show a spheri-

cal finial topped by a flying eagle — elements now missing. Within are two tubes for the Torah Staves. A similar crown is in the collection of the Comunità Israelitica di Roma; for others, see PBNY 1949, Nos. 101 and 118.

DONOR: Breziner Sick and Benevolent Society

## 481

TORAH CROWN  S 797  (*Illus. p. 276*)

Warsaw, 1882

Silver: die-stamped, chased, cast

H 42.3  DIAM 22.0 cm

HALLMARKS: *CITY*: similar to Postnikova, No. 529 but with an eagle and "1882"

REMARKS: Several leaves and bells are missing.

DONOR: Dr. Harry G. Friedman

## 482

TORAH CROWN  M 16  (*Illus. p. 276*)

Poland (?), 19th–20th century

Silver and alpacca (?): pierced, gilt; glass

H 21.8  DIAM 10.1 cm

HALLMARKS: none

PROVENANCE: The Rose and Benjamin Mintz Collection

REMARKS: This crown was obviously made for a small Torah Scroll.

DONOR: Museum purchase

## 483

TORAH CROWN  F 843  (*Illus. p. 278*)

Poland (?), late 19th–early 20th century

Brass: die-stamped, cast, silver-plated

H 43.3  DIAM 21.5 cm

REMARKS: Cf. the similar crowns Nos. 484 and 486; and Mazin, p. 20, top.

DONOR: Dr. Harry G. Friedman

## 484

TORAH CROWN  F 4485  (*Illus. p. 278*)

Poland (?), late 19th–early 20th century

Brass: die-stamped, cast, silver-plated

H 32.2  DIAM 32.0 cm

PROVENANCE: Samuel Narefsky, New York

REMARKS: The top finial is missing, as are most of the bells. See crown No. 483 for comparisons.

DONOR: Dr. Harry G. Friedman

## 485

TORAH CROWN  F 4667  (*Illus. p. 278*)

Poland (?), 19th–20th century

Silver: chased, cast, engraved, parcel-gilt; glass

H 20.0  DIAM 12.6 cm

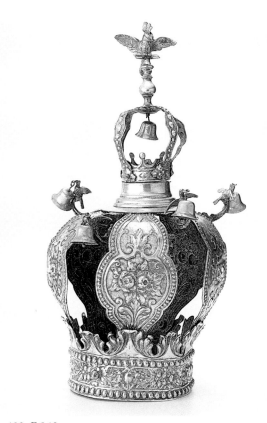

No. 483  F 843

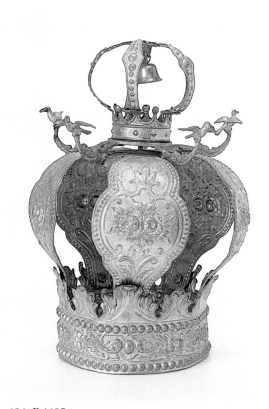

No. 484  F 4485

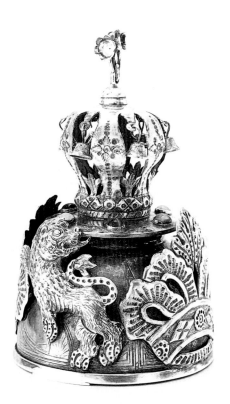

No. 485  F 4667

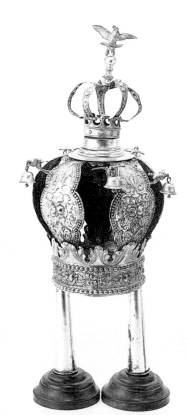

No. 486  F 1451

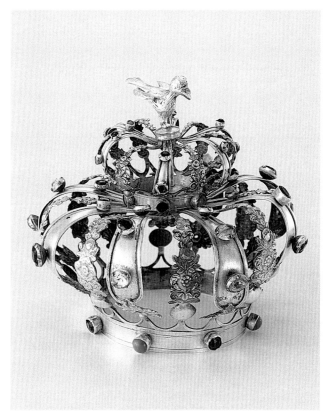

No. 487  F 3711

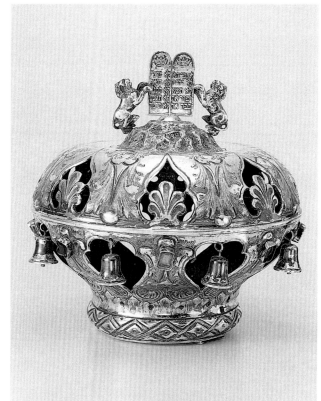

No. 488  D 62

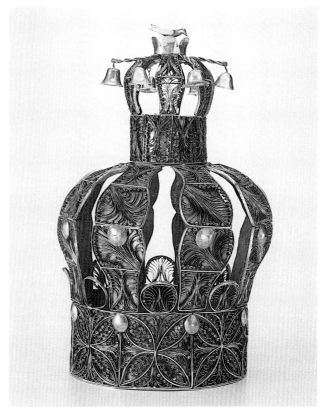

No. 489  F 269

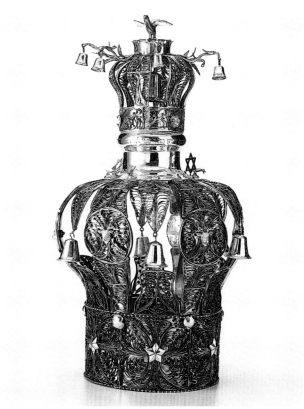

No. 490  F 1522

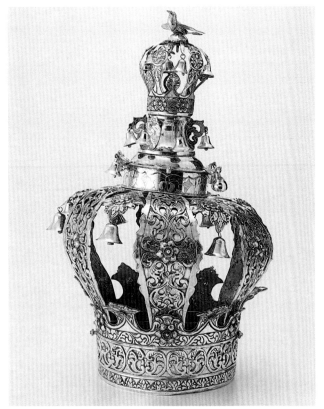

No. 492  F 1521

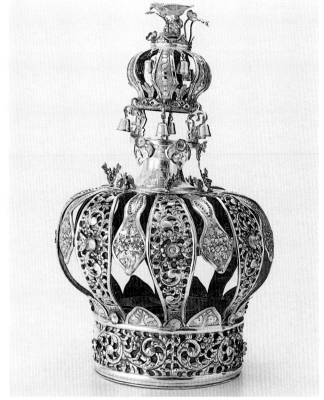

No. 493  F 1694

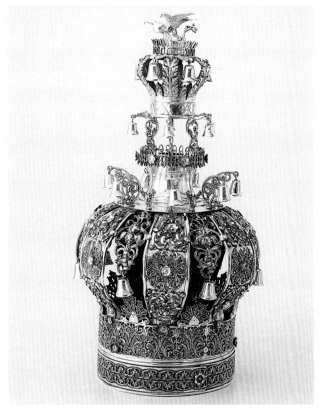

No. 494  F 1475

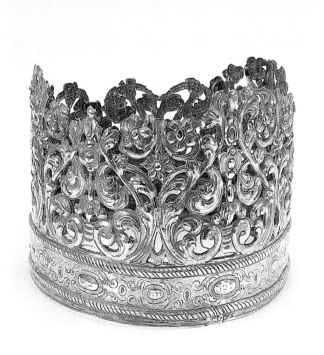

No. 495  D 58

HALLMARKS: none

REMARKS: This crown is apparently based on an inverted bowl, to which various decorative elements were added.

DONOR: Dr. Harry G. Friedman

## 486

TORAH CROWN  F 1451  (*Illus. p. 278*)

Poland or Germany, late 19th–early 20th century

Brass: die-stamped, cast, partly silver-plated

H 58.8  DIAM 24.0 cm

REMARKS: Cf. crowns Nos. 483–484; and Mazin, p. 20, top.

DONOR: Dr. Harry G. Friedman

## 487

TORAH CROWN  (Fragment) F 3711  (*Illus. p. 279*)

Poland, 19th century

Silver: cast, die-stamped; glass

H 10.1  DIAM 11.5 cm

HALLMARKS: none

DONOR: Dr. Harry G. Friedman

## 488

TORAH CROWN  D 62  (*Illus. p. 279*)

Russia, 19th century

Silver: cast, chased; glass

H ca. 25.5  DIAM 26.0 cm

HALLMARKS: none

PROVENANCE: The Weinberg Synagogue, Danzig

REMARKS: On back of Tablets of the Law, grafitto: "138" (or "38"). A "W" engraved on the underside indicates that this crown belonged to the Weinberg Congregation.

BIBLIOGRAPHY: *Danzig 1939/1982*, No. 75

DONOR: The Jewish Community of Danzig

## 489

TORAH CROWN  F 269  (*Illus. p. 279*)

Ukraine (?), 1885

Silver: filigree, cast, engraved, parcel-gilt; brass

H 42.8  DIAM 25.7 cm

HALLMARKS: none

REMARKS: Extensively repaired in 1976. Crown No. 490 is similar.

DONOR: Dr. Harry G. Friedman

## 490

TORAH CROWN  F 1522  (*Illus. p. 279*)

United States (?), late 19th–early 20th century

Silver: filigree, cast, parcel-gilt

H 48.2  DIAM 25.3 cm

HALLMARKS: Eagle; "84"; "D.P/18 . ." (Cyrillic) (false Russian marks)

INSCRIPTION: ז״נ האשה צביע בת ר׳ צבי לחברה אוהב שלום, "T[his was] d[onated by] the woman Zivie daughter of Zvi to the Lover of Peace Society."

REMARKS: Several minor elements are missing. No. 489 is a similar crown. Shield No. 223 was dedicated to the same society by the same person.

DONOR: Dr. Harry G. Friedman

## 491

TORAH CROWN  U 7338

United States (?), late 19th–early 20th century

Brass: die-stamped, cast; glass

H 18.0  DIAM 15.7 cm

HALLMARKS: none

## 492

TORAH CROWN  F 1521  (*Illus. p. 280*)

United States (?), ca. 1903

Silver: cast, repoussé, pierced, parcel-gilt

H 50.4  DIAM 29.5 cm

HALLMARKS: *CITY:* crown over ?, in shield; "B.C./1903"; "84"
*MAKER:* "GL" (Cyrillic) in rectangle

INSCRIPTION: in cartouche on lower band: תורה /כתר, "Crown of Torah"

REMARKS: Within the crown there are two short sockets for the Torah Staves. Numerous bells are missing. The hallmarks are false Russian marks, almost identical with those appearing on shield No. 215 (maker: "HL") and similar to those on finials No. 358 (maker: "HL"). Note that Cyrillic "GL" may represent "HL"—"H" in Cyrillic being represented by "G." Thus, the maker's mark here may indeed represent the actual name of the maker of all three of these objects. The "assayer's mark," which includes the year, is of a type that went out of use in the 1890's. This crown is patterned after a Polish model, as is the similar crown No. 493. For another shield marked "GL," with "unrecorded" city-mark and an "1890" date mark, see Sotheby's Tel Aviv 1993, No. 251 (dedicated by "Anshei Kovno," surely in the United States).

DONOR: Dr. Harry G. Friedman

## 493

TORAH CROWN  F 1694  (*Illus. p. 280*)

United States (?), 20th century

Silver: cast, repoussé, parcel-gilt

H 45.8  DIAM 28.3 cm

HALLMARKS: "STERLING" in rectangle; "84" in rectangle; "AG" in oval

REMARKS: Like crowns Nos. 492 and 494, this crown is patterned after Polish examples. For a similar maker's mark, see shield No. 218. The "84" mark is crudely rendered.

DONOR: Dr. Harry G. Friedman

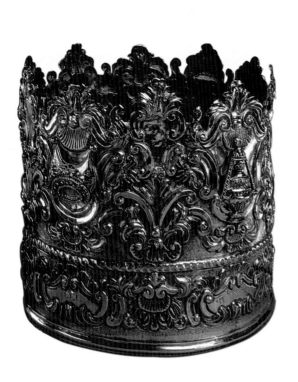

No. 496  F 3688

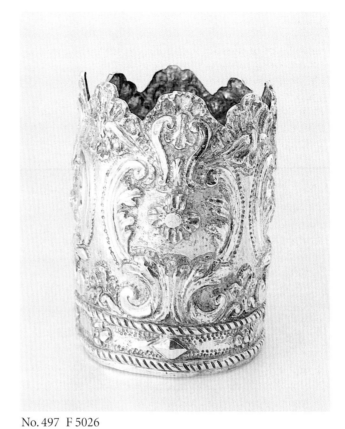

No. 497  F 5026

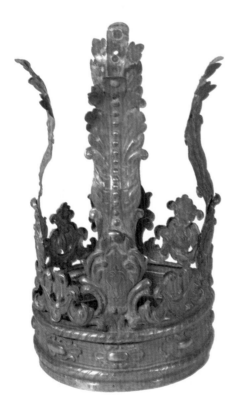

No. 498  F 2331

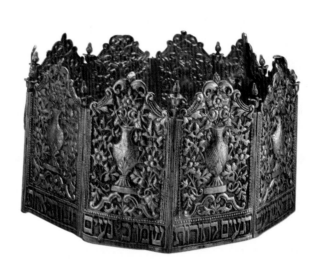

No. 499  1990–13

## 494

TORAH CROWN  F 1475  (*Illus. p. 280*)

Uncertain origin, late 19th century

Silver: cast, die-stamped, chased, punched

H 52.0  DIAM 27.3 cm

HALLMARKS: none

INSCRIPTION: in circlet, on plaque: ר׳ זאת נדבו האחים אליהו ור׳ שמשון העלמאן עבור נשמות צבי הירש בר׳ שמשון חיים יוסף בר׳ אברהם חוה בת ר׳ אליהו "This was donated by the brothers Elijah and Samson Helman on behalf of the souls of Zvi Hirsch son of Samson, Ḥayyim Joseph son of Abraham, Eve daughter of Elijah."

REMARKS: See the almost identical crown No. 493.

DONOR: Dr. Harry G. Friedman

## 495

TORAH CROWN  D 58  (*Illus. p. 280*)

Bolzano, 1698/99 (inscription)

Copper: repoussé

H 15.5  DIAM 18.7 cm

HALLMARKS: none

INSCRIPTION: on circlet: נדבת/ יורשי/ כמר/ זלמן/ ב״ש/ ז״ל/ ב/ב/ל/ ידיו (יריד ?)/ בולזאן/ שנת/ תנ/ט/ לפ׳ק "Donation of the heirs of the late Zalman son of S., [my] s[ons are] b[lessed] to [God] (the fair of?) . . . Bolzano, year (5)459" (=1698/99)

REMARKS: For a similar north Italian copper crown, see Skirball Museum, Los Angeles, 58.4, dated 1797.

BIBLIOGRAPHY: Danzig 1933, No. 58; *Danzig 1939/1982*, No. 73; *Venice*, No. 7

DONOR: The Jewish Community of Danzig

## 496

TORAH CROWN  F 3688  (*Illus. p. 282*)

Ferrara, 1764–77

Giovanni Maria Ronchi (active 1764–1801)

Silver: repoussé, engraved, cast, parcel-gilt, punched

H 18.3  DIAM 19.5–20.0 cm

HALLMARKS: Bulgari, IV, 2658, 2717

INSCRIPTION: in cartouches: עזריאל חי//| ב״כ״ר ידידיד חי הלוי//| יליד צינטו//| (. . .) "Azriel Ḥai son of Yedidi[ah] Ḥai ha-Levi, native of Cento . . ."

BIBLIOGRAPHY: Kayser, No. 36; *Jewish Patrons*, No. 8; *Gardens and Ghettos*, No. 206

DONOR: Dr. Harry G. Friedman

## 497

TORAH CROWN  F 5026  (*Illus. p. 282*)

Italy, 18th–19th century

Silver: repoussé

H 15.0  DIAM 11.9 cm

HALLMARKS: none

REMARKS: Museum records note a hallmark, "Rome, 1650–1700"; however, the "mark" is merely the result of hammering.

DONOR: Dr. Harry G. Friedman

## 498

TORAH CROWN  F 4578  (*Illus. p. 282*)

Italy (?), early 19th century

Silver: repoussé, parcel-gilt

H 11.0  DIAM 15.0 cm

HALLMARKS: none

INSCRIPTION: on lower circlet: *OFFERTA DA* ואסתר סורי, "Donation of [. . .] and Esther Suri"

REMARKS: The staves were originally bent to form the arc of the crown. A portion of the inscription seems to be missing.

DONOR: Dr. Harry G. Friedman

## 498A

TORAH CROWN  F 2331

Belgium, 1831–68

Silver: die-stamped

H 12.6  DIAM 17.8 cm

HALLMARKS: *CITY:* Tardy, p. 85, lower left, 800
*MAKER:* illegible

PROVENANCE: Frank Wallach, New York

REMARKS: This crown, which resembles a Madonna crown, may have been used as a crown for a small Torah. An old inventory number, "21," is engraved on the lower edge. This form of crown was commonly used in Italy in the first half of the 19th century.

DONOR: Dr. Harry G. Friedman

## 499

TORAH CROWN  1990–13  (*Illus. p. 282*)

Algeria or Tunisia, 1898/99 (inscription)

Silver: repoussé

H 15.0  DIAM 26.0 cm

HALLMARKS: none

INSCRIPTION: around lower circlet:

זר נעים/ בציצים חרות
אחד אשועים¹/ הנעים לתורות
שמו כי נעים/ רוב התפארות
אברהם נעים/ ואשתו רות
יראו זרעים/ ופרי פירות

"A pleasant wreath, engraved with blossoms,
One of the wealthy, who adorn the Torah,
For his name is pleasant, abounding in glory:
Abraham Naʻim, and his wife Ruth,
May they behold seeds and fruit of fruits."

REMARKS: This crown, intended for use with a Torah Case, was surely dedicated on the occasion of a wedding, as the

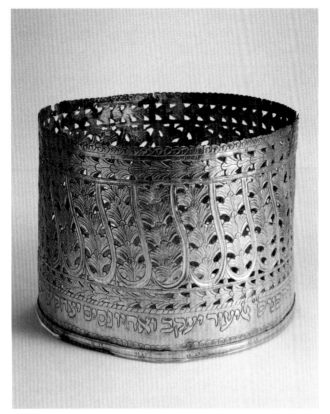

No. 500  1992–94

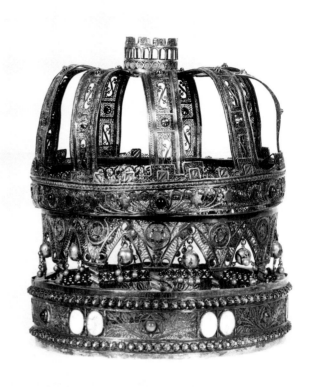

No. 501  S 650

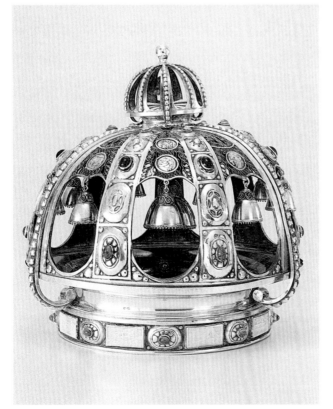

No. 502  M 260

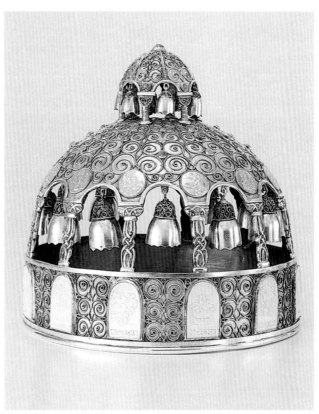

No. 503  JM 28–57

poetic inscription would indicate. The inscription contains repeated puns on the bridegroom's family name, which means "pleasant."

BIBLIOGRAPHY: Sotheby's Tel Aviv 1990, No. 265; *JMNY 1993*, fig. 47

DONOR: Judaica Acquisitions Fund

---

1. Note the orthographic "error," *alef* for *heh* not uncommon in North Africa and based on regional pronunciation.

## 500

### TORAH CROWN  1992–94  (*Illus. p. 284*)

Rhodes (?), 1839/40 (inscription)

Silver: chased, pierced

H 16.3  DIAM 22.1 cm

HALLMARKS: none

INSCRIPTION: ‏[כתר] אשר נדב לב הגביר רצ״ו ס״י מיכאל חיים‎
‏דוד צוריאנו ולחיי בנו ס״י אליעזר יעקב ואחיו נסים יצחק‎
‏יצ״ו ש׳ כ״תר‎: "[Crown] that which is the heartfelt donation of Se[ñor] Michael Ḥayyim David Soriano, and for the life of his son Se[ñor] Eliezer Jacob and his brother Nissim Isaac . . . , y[ear] (5)620" (=1839/40)

PROVENANCE: The Kahal Gadol Synagogue, Rhodes

REMARKS: For the attribution, and that of the matching finials, see the companion Torah Shield No. 245.

BIBLIOGRAPHY: See Torah Shield No. 245

DONOR: Museum purchase through Kurt Thalberg in honor of E. Cats

## 501

### TORAH CROWN  S 650  (*Illus. p. 284*)

Jerusalem, 1910–14

Bezalel Workshops

Silver: filigree, engraved, parcel-gilt; ivory: carved; chrysophrase

H 25.2  DIAM 22.7 cm

HALLMARKS: none

INSCRIPTIONS: on upper band of lower circlet: *DECEMBER 22, 1824. in memoriam LAZARUS KOHNS DECEMBER 3, 1910*; on ivory plaques (with symbols): the Hebrew names of eight of the twelve Israelite tribes; on upper circlet: Proverbs 3: 18; within small crown finial, grafitto: "‏גIII‎" (probably an assembly mark)

REMARKS: Although not signed or marked, the workmanship is very typical of early Bezalel pieces. For other Bezalel crowns, see Nos. 502–503.

DONOR: The Library of The Jewish Theological Seminary of America

## 502

### TORAH CROWN  M 260  (*Illus. p. 284*)

Jerusalem, before 1917

Bezalel Workshops

Silver: repoussé, die-stamped, filigree; semiprecious stones; ivory: carved

H 22.9  DIAM 23.8 cm

HALLMARKS: Lileyko, 92 (1920–21); Postnikova, 1943 (var.) (Russian import mark)

PROVENANCE: The Rose and Benjamin Mintz Collection

REMARKS: One rectangular ivory plaque is missing; the others bear depictions of David's Tower, the Dome of the Rock, Absalom's Tomb, Rachel's Tomb, Zachariah's Tomb, the Bnei Ḥezir Tomb, Mount Sinai (?), and Safed (?). The ivory medallions are carved with symbols of the zodiac, in Hebrew order. Within the bottom is a bar with two oval holes for the Torah Staves. Other Bezalel crowns at The Jewish Museum are Nos. 501 and 503.

DONOR: Museum purchase

## 503

### TORAH CROWN  JM 28–57  (*Illus. p. 284*)

Jerusalem, 1920's

Bezalel Workshops

Silver: filigree, die-stamped; ivory: carved; turquoise

H 18.0  DIAM 17.7 cm

HALLMARKS: "Bezalel" (Hebrew)

INSCRIPTION: on ivory plaques: the Hebrew names of the twelve Israelite tribes

REMARKS: Other Bezalel crowns at The Jewish Museum are Nos. 501 and 502.

DONOR: Henry Gamson

## 504

### TORAH CROWN  F 4185a  (*Illus. p. 286*)

Tel Aviv, early 1950's

Moshe Smilovici, active 1950's

Silver: die-stamped, cast, chased, parcel-gilt; bone (?); carnelian; malachite; turquoise; agate

H 22.0  DIAM 28.4 cm

HALLMARKS: none

INSCRIPTIONS: on upper surface of main crown: the blessings recited before each reading of the Torah

REMARKS: This crown is a companion piece to shield No. 236. On Smilovici, and for other pastiches by him, see shield No. 236.

DONOR: Dr. Harry G. Friedman

## 505

### TORAH CROWN  U 7333  (*Illus. p. 286*)

Jerusalem, early 1960's

Nissan Benyaminoff, active ca. 1932–90

Silver and brass: cast, chased, pierced, die-stamped, gilt; amethyst; banded agate; moss agate; aventurine; tiger's eye

H 23.0  DIAM 22.5 cm

HALLMARKS: "MADE IN/ ISRAEL"; "HAND MADE"; "BENYAMINOFF"

REMARKS: The maker, born in Urmia, Iranian Kurdistan, in 1912, was a silversmith and antiques dealer in Jerusalem.

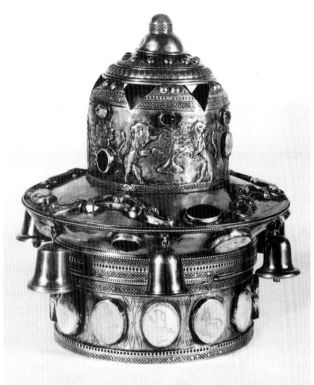
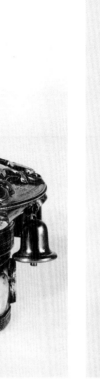

No. 504  F 4185a

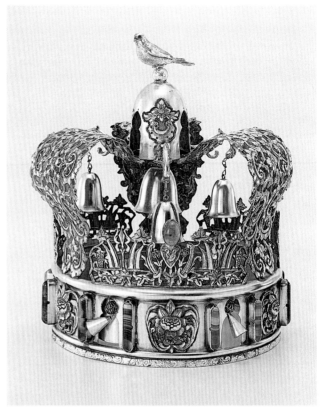

No. 505  U 7333

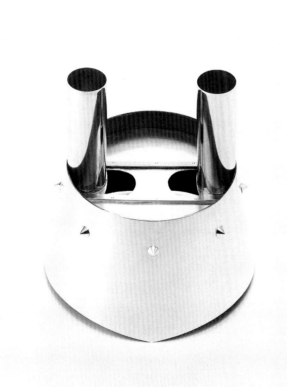

No. 506  1986–68a

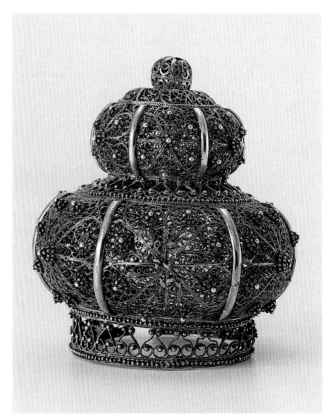

No. 507  D 54

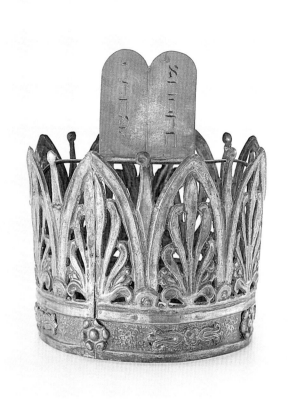

No. 508  D 56

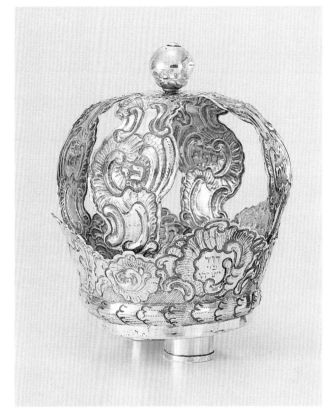

No. 509  F 5541

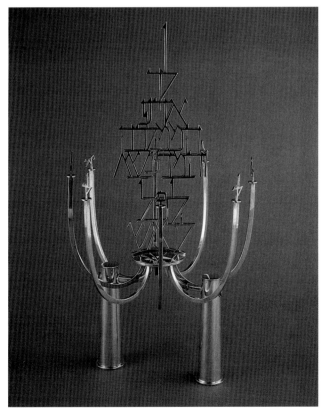

No. 510  1982–30

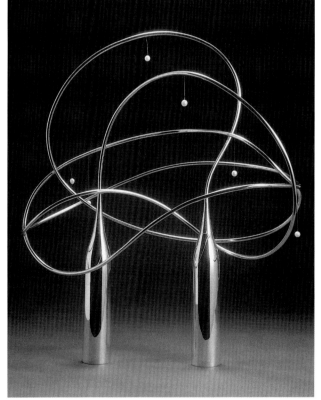

No. 511  JM 85–69

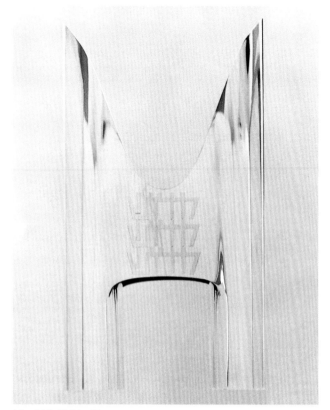

No. 512  JM 2–67c

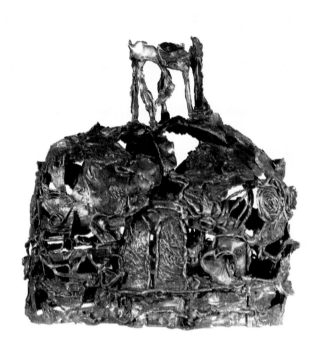

No. 513  JM 1–67

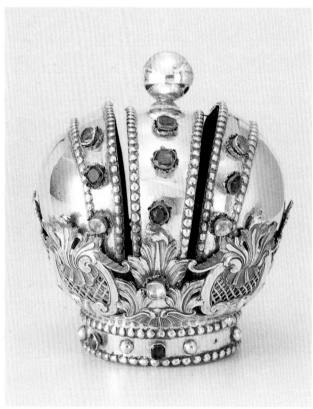

No. 513a  F 1749

## 506

TORAH CROWN 1986–68a (*Illus. p. 286*)
Jerusalem, 1958
Moshe Zabari, active 1958–
Silver
H 22.5 DIAM 22.3 cm
HALLMARKS: New Bezalel mark; "ISRAEL"; "925" in oval
REMARKS: This crown forms a set with shield No. 239.
DONOR: Fred and Sassi Lonner

## 507

MINIATURE TORAH CROWN D 54 (*Illus. p. 286*)
Europe, 19th century
Silver: filigree
H 10.0 DIAM 9.3 cm
HALLMARKS: none
REMARKS: This crown is part of a set with shield F 253G and
pointer No. 765.
BIBLIOGRAPHY: Danzig 1904, No. 18; Danzig 1933, No. 54;
*Danzig 1939/1982*, No. 18
DONOR: The Jewish Community of Danzig

## 508

TORAH CROWN D 56 (*Illus. p. 287*)
Europe, late 19th–early 20th century
Brass: die-stamped, pierced, chased, engraved, traces of silver
plating
H 16.2 DIAM 14.3 cm
HALLMARKS: none
BIBLIOGRAPHY: Danzig 1933, No. 56; *Danzig 1939*, No. 211
DONOR: The Jewish Community of Danzig

## 509

TORAH CROWN F 5541 (*Illus. p. 287*)
Europe, late 19th–20th century (?)
Silver: repoussé
H 19.0 DIAM 14.7 cm
HALLMARKS: none
INSCRIPTIONS: on upper cartouches: Psalms 36: 10; on lower
band: ז״נ// דוד/ ב״ר/ ישיהו[!] // מנדז/ ת׳ק׳מ׳, "T[his was]
d[onated by] David son of Isaiah [?] Mendez …"
PROVENANCE: Gorevic, New York
REMARKS: In the lower inscription, the final letters appear to
indicate a date equal to 1779/80, but the first letter seems to
have been modified or added; thus this is probably not a
date at all. In fact, the entire inscription is problematic and
possibly spurious. For a crown of similar form but with
taller staves, cf. Sotheby's Tel Aviv 1994, No. 125 (mistakenly
ascribed to the Balkans).
DONOR: Dr. Harry G. Friedman

## 510

TORAH CROWN 1982–30 (*Illus. p. 287*)
New York, 1953
Ludwig Wolpert, active 1920's–1981
Silver
H 48.2 DIAM 27.3 cm
HALLMARKS: "WOLPERT"; "STERLING"; mark of Tobe
Pascher Workshop, The Jewish Museum
INSCRIPTION: at center: 1 Chronicles 29:11; on arms: לך, "Unto
you"
REMARKS: For other Wolpert pieces, see Nos. 226, 227, 361, 815,
and 816.
BIBLIOGRAPHY: Wolpert 1982, p. [8], illus.
DONOR: Betty Wolpert and Chava Wolpert Richard

## 511

TORAH CROWN JM 85–69 (*Illus. p. 287*)
New York, 1959
Moshe Zabari, active 1958–
Silver; pearls
H 39.0 W 34.3 cm
HALLMARKS: none
REMARKS: This crown was made at the Tobe Pascher Work-
shop of The Jewish Museum.
BIBLIOGRAPHY: Berman, No. 25 (the photograph published is
actually of The Jewish Museum piece, although the Quit-
man Collection crown cited there is identical); *Treasures*,
pp. 194–95.
DONOR: Albert A. List Family

## 512

TORAH CROWN JM 2–67a (*Illus. p. 288*)
New York, 1966
Moshe Zabari, active 1958–
Silver and gold; leather (lining)
H 17.6 L 26.7 W 27.9 cm
HALLMARKS: Tobe Pascher Workshop mark; "M/ZABARI";
"STERLING"
INSCRIPTION: קדש קדש קדש, Isaiah 6:3
BIBLIOGRAPHY: Berman, No. 20, illus. p. 22
DONOR: The Abram and Frances Kanof Collection

## 513

TORAH CROWN JM 1–67 (*Illus. p. 288*)
New York, 1966
Hana Geber, active ca. 1935–90
Silver: cast, patinated
H 17.6 L 26.7 W 27.9 cm
HALLMARKS: "HG" (ligature); חנה גבר
INSCRIPTION: on small upper crown: קדוש, "Holy"
DONOR: Albert A. List Family

## 513A

TORAH CROWN (?)   F 1749   (*Illus. p. 288*)

Munich, second quarter of 18th century

Silver: repoussé, pierced, parcel-gilt; glass

H 17.7   DIAM 17.5 cm

HALLMARKS: *CITY:* R³ 3452; (?—with truncated corners)

            *MAKER:* R³ 3532

REMARKS: There are traces of a now-missing element at the top of the upper knop. The small size of this crown, particularly the diameter at the base (ca. 10 cm), might indicate that it was intended for a *Haftorot* Scroll.

DONOR: Dr. Harry G. Friedman

# Part IV · Pointers

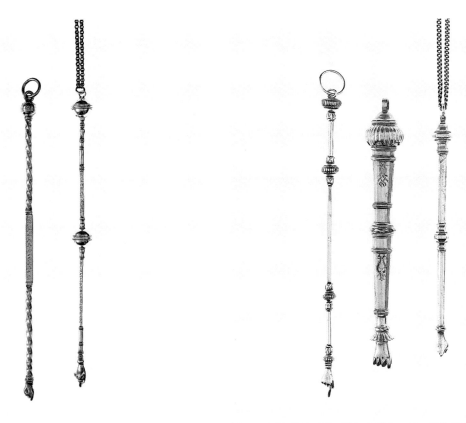

No. 514  JM 48–52;  No. 515  F 3634        No. 516  F 4321;  No. 520  S 996в;  No. 521  JM 59–59

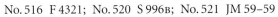

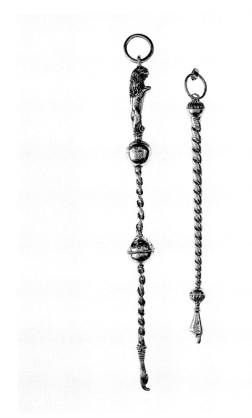

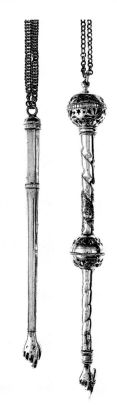

No. 518  JM 47–52;  No. 517  F 4041а        No. 522  JM 50–52;  No. 575  1976–24

# Torah Pointers

## 514

TORAH POINTER  JM 48–52  (*Illus. p. 292*)

Germany, 1687/88 (inscription)

Silver: cast, chased, engraved

L 27.5  DIAM 1.4 cm

HALLMARKS: none

INSCRIPTION: on central shaft: וואלף בן הרר זלמן/ שץ זצל/ ריי־כלי/ בת יצחק אשת וואלף ש' ת'מ'ח' ל', "Wolf son of the late Zalman Schatz, (and) Rei-khle/ daughter of Isaac wife of Wolf, [in the] year (5)448" (=1687/88); on upper knop: אשת מערל ליב/ מלאקס היים/ תקפא, "Merl wife of (?) Leib/ from Lochsheim, (5)581" (=1820/21)

PROVENANCE: Formerly at Museum Jüdischer Altertümer, Frankfurt am Main

REMARKS: The first two words of the second inscription are out of order. Museum records indicate the place name as "Rochsheim." Kayser, No. 67, suggested that this pointer was "perhaps originally from the Old Synagogue of Frankfurt." Skirball Museum, Los Angeles, 44.4 (dated 1714/15) is a similar pointer.

BIBLIOGRAPHY: Kayser, No. 67; *Wüb*, No. 37

DONOR: Jewish Cultural Reconstruction

## 515

TORAH POINTER  F 3634  (*Illus. p. 292*)

Germany (?), 1717 (inscription)

Silver: cast, chased; brass (chain)

L 26.3  DIAM 2.1 cm

HALLMARKS: none

INSCRIPTION: on shaft: הירץ ב'פ'ו' כ"ה שמעון/ שליט הילדיסים מרחשון ת'ע'ח' ל'פ'ק'// וגיטכי בת ה"ר"ר איצק/ שליט הילדיסים מרחשון תעחל, "Hertz son of the . . . leader Rabbi Simon Hildesheim, Marḥeshvan (5)478 (=October/early November 1717), and Gitke daughter of Rabbi Itzik . . . Hildesheim, Marḥeshvan (5)478" (=October/early November 1717).

DONOR: Dr. Harry G. Friedman

## 516

TORAH POINTER  F 4321  (*Illus. p. 292*)

Germany, 18th century

Silver: cast, chased

L 24.7  DIAM 1.6 cm

HALLMARKS: Dutch tax mark (Voet, p. 47, lower, No. 4)

MAKER: "SW" in rectangle (see remarks below)

REMARKS: The maker's mark, identical with R³ 754, is identified in R³ as that of Simon Wickhart, and thus this piece had previously been attributed to "Augsburg, 1680." Seling has recently ascribed other "SW" marks to Wickhart, excluding this mark from Augsburg altogether.

DONOR: Dr. Harry G. Friedman

## 517

TORAH POINTER  F 4041a  (*Illus. p. 292*)

Nuremberg, first half of 18th century

Johann Conrad Weiss, active 1699–after 1751

Silver: cast, engraved

L 21.0  DIAM 1.7 cm

HALLMARKS: CITY: "N" in circle

MAKER: R³ 4279

REMARKS: The spiralled shaft is remarkably similar to that of the columns on Torah shields (e.g. Christies' Amsterdam 1985, No. 422) and a Hanukkah lamp (cf. *Ashkenaz*, p. xix) by the same smith. Other objects by Weiss at The Jewish Museum are: finials No. 263, Torah Staves No. 915, spice container F 383; and Burial Society beaker JM 30–51 (Kayser, No. 175).

DONOR: Dr. Harry G. Friedman

## 518

TORAH POINTER  JM 47–52  (*Illus. p. 292*)

Lübeck (?), second quarter of 18th century (?)

Johann Wichmann (?), ca. 1712–58

Silver: cast, chased

L 28.2  DIAM 2.4 cm

HALLMARKS: CITY: R³ 3150 (?)

MAKER: R³ 3217 (var.) (?); cf. Warncke, p. 343

INSCRIPTION: on upper and medial knops: חיים בנימין/ מאסלר// סערכי מנחם מאסלר, "Ḥayyim Benjamin of Uslar; Sarke (daughter of) Menaḥem of Uslar"

PROVENANCE: Museum Jüdischer Altertümer, Frankfurt am Main

REMARKS: Uslar, mentioned in the inscription, lies 38 km N of Kassel. This pointer was previously attributed to Frankfurt am Main, on the basis of the hallmarks; however, the neck of the eagle in the mark is compatible only with a *Doppeladler*, precluding Frankfurt as the place of origin, and

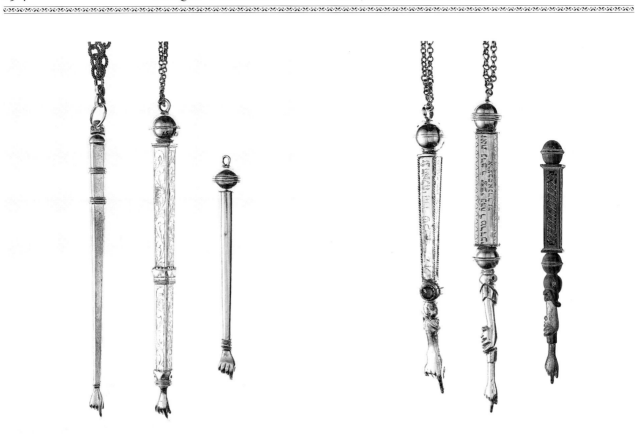

No. 523  F 878;  No. 524  JM 27–57;  No. 525  F 4803      No. 526  D 33;  No. 528  D 31;  No. 529  D 43

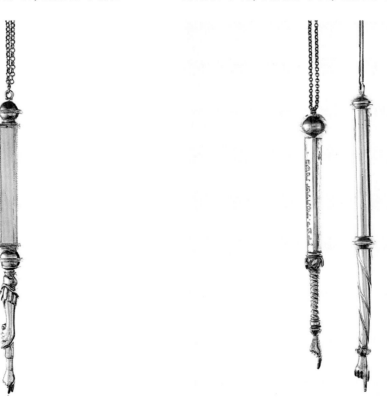

No. 527  D 37      No. 530  D 23;  No. 540  F 1045

hence also the ascription to Johannes Willems III.
BIBLIOGRAPHY: Kayser, No. 66; Mann 1982, No. 72
DONOR: Jewish Cultural Reconstruction

## 519

TORAH POINTER  F 70d
Augsburg, 1717–18 (?)
Zacharias Wagner, active 1712–33
Silver: cast, chased, gilt
L 21.4  DIAM 3.0 cm
HALLMARKS: *CITY:* Seling 177 (?)
              *MAKER:* cf. Seling 2054
REMARKS: The master's mark here, and on shield No. 6, is
    otherwise unrecorded.
BIBLIOGRAPHY: Kayser, No. 63; Seling 2054, ex. a)
DONOR: Dr. Harry G. Friedman

## 520

TORAH POINTER  S 996b  (*Illus. p. 292*)
Würzburg (?), second quarter of 18th century
Silver: cast, engraved, gilt
L 21.9  DIAM 3.2 cm
HALLMARKS: *CITY:* similar to R³ 4941
REMARKS: The date is based on that of shield No. 7 with which
    this pointer forms a set.
BIBLIOGRAPHY: cf. Kayser, No. 54
DONOR: Dr. Harry G. Friedman

## 521

TORAH POINTER  JM 59–59  (*Illus. p. 292*)
Augsburg, 1735–36
Johann II Pepfenhauser (?), active 1697–1754
Silver: cast
L 19.2  DIAM 1.8 cm
HALLMARKS: *CITY:* Seling 205
              *MAKER:* "IP" in indented oval; cf. Seling 1919h
              and 2418
REMARKS: A Seder egg-cup at the Skirball Museum (50.2)
    bears the same maker's mark; see *Mitt.* III/IV, p. 83, fig. 112.
DONOR: Jewish Cultural Reconstruction

## 522

TORAH POINTER  JM 129–52  (*Illus. p. 292*)
Augsburg, 1737–39
Gottfried Bartermann, active 1733–69
Silver: cast, gilt
L 22.1  DIAM 1.7 cm
HALLMARKS: *CITY:* Seling 212
              *MAKER:* Seling 2248
DONOR: Jewish Cultural Reconstruction

## 523

TORAH POINTER  F 878  (*Illus. p. 294*)
Nuremberg, 18th century
Johann Samuel Beckensteiner, active 1743–81
Silver: cast, gilt
L 22.0  DIAM 1.1 cm
HALLMARKS: *CITY:* "N" in circle
              *MAKER:* R³ 4295
REMARKS: The chain is original. The Museum's shield No. 28,
    finials No. 264 and crown No. 450, were made by the same
    smith.
BIBLIOGRAPHY: Kayser, No. 64; Deneke, No. 3/38
DONOR: Dr. Harry G. Friedman

## 524

TORAH POINTER  JM 27–57  (*Illus. p. 294*)
Germany, 18th century
Silver: cast, engraved, parcel-gilt
L 24.0  DIAM 2.4 cm
HALLMARKS: none
REMARKS: In the Museum's files, this pointer was attributed to
    "Halberstadt, ca. 1700"; no supportive evidence for this
    has been found.
DONOR: Dr. Ludwig Bendix

## 525

TORAH POINTER  F 4803  (*Illus. p. 294*)
Augsburg, 1751–53 (or 1765–67)
Johann Christoph Stenglin, active 1737–1776
Silver: cast
L 16.6  DIAM 2.3 cm
HALLMARKS: *CITY:* Seling 321 (or 248–50)
              *MAKER:* Seling 2293i
DONOR: Dr. Harry G. Friedman

## 526

TORAH POINTER  D 33  (*Illus. p. 294*)
Danzig, East Prussia, 1739 (inscription)
Silver: cast, chased; glass (or garnet)
L 25.4  DIAM 3.0 cm
HALLMARKS: none
INSCRIPTION: on upper shaft: ז"נ האלוף הרר שכנא ב'נ' מ
זל/ עבור בנו מאיר ש"י נולד במזט/ ביום ו' עש"ק חי תמוז
ת"צט ל"פ/ הש' יגדל לתורה ולחופה ולמעט אמן ,"This was
    donated by Shakhna son of the late ..., on behalf of his son
    Me'ir, born in go[od] for[tune] on Friday, E[ve of the]
    h[oly] S[abbath] ..., 18 Tammuz, (5)499 (=July 24, 1739),
    May the Lord raise [him] to the Torah and to the marriage
    canopy and to go[od] de[eds]. Amen."
BIBLIOGRAPHY: *Danzig 1939/1982,* No. 93
DONOR: The Jewish Community of Danzig

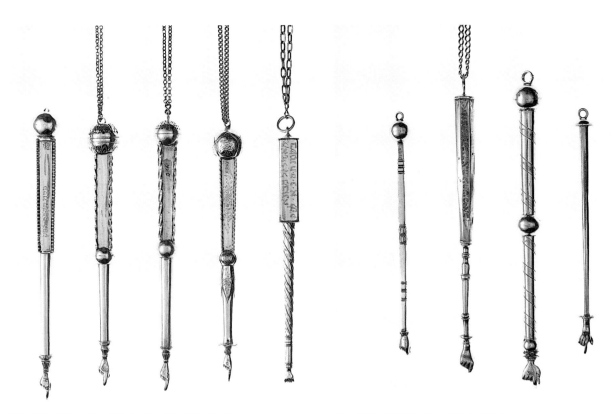

No. 531  F 74;  No. 532  D 21;  No. 533  D 36;
No. 534  F 3234;  No. 535  F 3433

No. 538  F 1822;  No. 536  F 3756;
No. 537  F 2403;  No. 539  F 4377

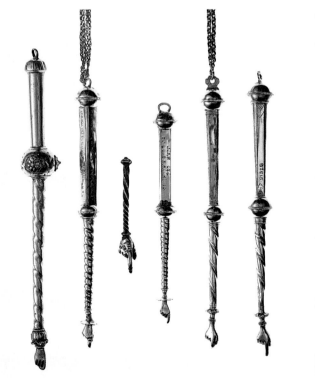

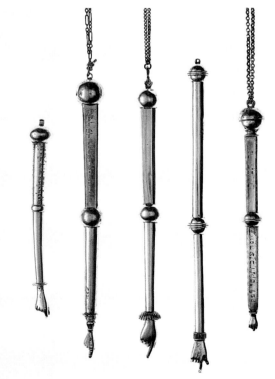

No. 541  F 311;  No. 542  D 24;  No. 543  D 19;
No. 544  F 1751;  No. 545  S 1326;  No. 546  F 3868

No. 547  F 3636;  No. 548  F 301;  No. 550  F 2303;
No. 551  F 3425;  No. 552  D 25

## 527

**TORAH POINTER** D 37 (*Illus. p. 294*)

Danzig, 1748–66

Silver: cast, engraved

L 29.8 DIAM 2.6 cm

HALLMARKS: Czihak XII ("Nebenzeichen")

REMARKS: This appears to be the earliest of the three pointers of this type from Danzig. The more precise dating given in *Danzig 1939/1982* is based on interpretation of the one mark on the piece as "Czihak 448", and on the possible absence of the assayer's mark, a feature that appeared after 1730. Cf. pointers Nos. 528 and 529.

BIBLIOGRAPHY: *Danzig 1939/1982*, No. 92

DONOR: The Jewish Community of Danzig

## 528

**TORAH POINTER** D 31 (*Illus. p. 294*)

Danzig, 1780's; 1868 (inscription)

Silver: cast, chased

L 28.2 DIAM 2.9 cm

HALLMARKS: *CITY:* Czihak 9 and xxviii

*MAKER:* illegible

INSCRIPTION: on shaft: זאת נדב ר' צבי ב/ה/ח' ר' מרדכי אלעכסאנדר ז"ל// ניפטר יד' אייר ת/ר/כ/ח'// ע/א' מ' קאשה ט/ו/ בת ה/ר/ר/ יעקב// לחברה קדישא ו/ג/ח' ד/ק/ק' שאטטלאנד, "This was donated by Tsvi son of . . . the late Rabbi Mordecai Alexander, who died on 14 Iyyar, (5)628 [=May 6, 1868], with his wife, Kasha Tovah (?) daughter of Jacob, to the Holy [Burial] Society and [Society for] Visiting the Sick of the Holy Congregation of Schottland"

PROVENANCE: The Schottland Synagogue, Danzig

REMARKS: Beneath the later inscription is a lightly scratched "draft" of the text, which probably served to guide the smith.

BIBLIOGRAPHY: Danzig 1933, No. 147c; *Danzig 1939/1982*, No. 91

DONOR: The Jewish Community of Danzig

## 529

**TORAH POINTER** D 43 (*Illus. p. 294*)

Danzig, 19th century

Wood: carved, painted

L 21.5 W 2.7 cm

HALLMARKS: none

PROVENANCE: The Gieldzinski Collection, Danzig

REMARKS: Formerly painted all over. See the similar pointer No. 527. For a modern copy of this piece in silver, see Steinhardt, No. 82.

BIBLIOGRAPHY: Danzig 1904, No. 30; Danzig 1933, No. 30; *JL* V, pl. clxxiii, 3rd from bottom; *Danzig 1939/1982*, No. 94

DONOR: The Jewish Community of Danzig

## 530

**TORAH POINTER** D 23 (*Illus. p. 294*)

Berlin, 1749/50 (inscription)

Joachim Hübener (II), active ca. 1737–1780

Silver: cast, chased

L 23.0 DIAM 2.6 cm

HALLMARKS: Scheffler, *Berlin*, 110 (var.)

INSCRIPTION: on upper shaft: שייך להח' כה שלמה ברה זל/ ואשתו מ" פריידה בת כה" זלמן זל/ בשנת ירו/נ/ת/י/י' תמ/ת/י לפק, "Belonging to . . . Solomon son of the late . . . H . . ., and his wife . . . Freyda daughter of the late . . . Zalman, in the year (Song of Songs 5: 2 and 6:9, a chronogram for [5]510 [=1749/50])"

BIBLIOGRAPHY: *Danzig 1939/1982*, No. 87

DONOR: The Jewish Community of Danzig

## 531

**TORAH POINTER** F 74 (*Illus. p. 296*)

Berlin, 1788–1802, and/or the 1760's

Müller Family

Silver: cast, chased

L 29.9 DIAM 3.1cm

HALLMARKS: *CITY:* Scheffler, *Berlin*, 11 or 7

*MAKER:* Scheffler, *Berlin*, 130

INSCRIPTION: on upper shaft: שייך להו/ה' כ' הענך בכ' משה ליב ז/ל/ מנשב(?) ואשתו הצנועה/ מ' לאה בת כ' יוסף בש ז/ל' מהש ובנו ה/ו/ה' כ' משה ליב שי/ ואשתו הצנועה מ' רחל בת כ' בער פנטי כ/ץ' ז/ל//פסח ת/ק/כ/ב' ל/פ/ק', "Belonging to . . . Henokh son of . . . the late Moses Leib, of . . .(?), and his . . .wife Leah daughter of . . . the late Joseph Basch, of Halberstadt, and his son . . . Moses Leib . . . and his . . .wife Rachel daughter of the late Baer . . . Katz, Pesaḥ [5]522" (=1762); on later lower shaft: ובנו התה' כ' הענך בן כה' משה ליב ז/ל/ ואשתו הצנועה מ' גיטל נפתלה זל', "And his son...Henokh son of...the late Moses Leib, and his ...wife Gittel daughter of...the late Naphtali"

REMARKS: The spelling of the name Naphtali is corrupt.

DONOR: Dr. Harry G. Friedman

## 532

**TORAH POINTER** D 21 (*Illus. p. 296*)

Germany, before 1809

Silver: cast, chased, pierced

L 27.4 DIAM 3.4 cm

HALLMARKS: *CITY:* Scheffler, *Berlin*, 30A 1

PROVENANCE: The Weinberg Synagogue, Danzig

REMARKS: There is an engraved "W" on the lower shaft, indicating that this piece belonged to the Weinberg congregation in Danzig.

BIBLIOGRAPHY: *Danzig 1939/1982*, No. 229

DONOR: The Jewish Community of Danzig

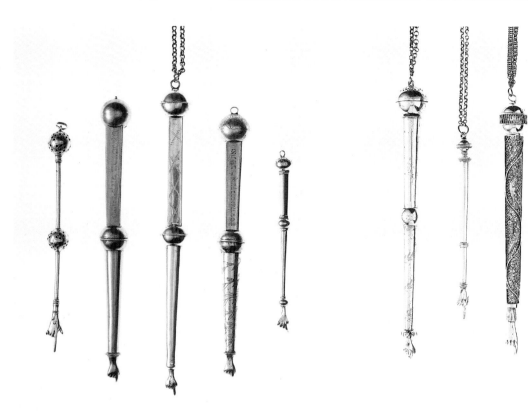

No. 553  F 1949;  No. 554  D 26;  No. 555  D 34;
No. 558  D 30; No. 559  F 3758

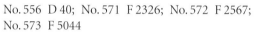

No. 556  D 40;  No. 571  F 2326;  No. 572  F 2567;
No. 573  F 5044

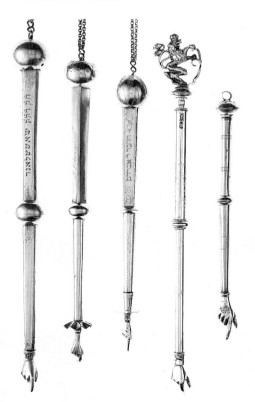

No. 560  D 35;  No. 561  D 20;  No. 562  M 177;
No. 563  F 3301; No. 564  F 4075

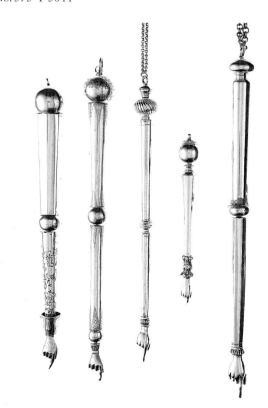

No. 565  F 280;  No. 566  F 2441;  No. 567  F 5554;
No. 569  D 51; No. 570  F 4239

## 533
TORAH POINTER D 36 *(Illus. p. 296)*
Berlin, 1821–50
Silver: cast, pierced
L 28.9 DIAM 3.0 cm
HALLMARKS: *CITY:* Scheffler, *Berlin*, 14
         *MAKER:* illegible
BIBLIOGRAPHY: *Danzig 1939/1982*, No. 228
DONOR: The Jewish Community of Danzig

## 534
TORAH POINTER F 3243 *(Illus. p. 296)*
Berlin, mid-19th century
Friedrich August Ferdinand Eisolt (?), active ca. 1833–58
Silver: cast, chased
L 26.9 DIAM 3.45 cm
HALLMARKS: *CITY:* Scheffler, *Berlin*, 4b (var.)
         *MAKER:* Scheffler, *Berlin*, 415 (var.)
REMARKS: Cf. the marks on pointer No. 562, also possibly by Eisolt.
DONOR: Dr. Harry G. Friedman

## 535
TORAH POINTER F 3433 *(Illus. p. 296)*
Deutz, 1790/91 (inscription)
Silver: cast, chased
L 26.4 DIAM 2.8 cm
HALLMARKS: none
INSCRIPTION: on upper shaft: שייך (ל)פום כ״ה מאיר/ בן/ מהורר משה אברם// זל מהאקינברוך/ בק״ק דייץ// וזוגתו א״ה מ״ רידלכא/ בת כה״רר מאיר// קאסיל ז״ל מבונא/ בשנת ת׳ק׳נ׳א׳ לפ״ק, "Belonging (to) the treasurer and teacher Rabbi Me'ir son of . . . the late Rabbi Moses Abram of Hackenbroch, in the holy congregation of Deutz, and his wife . . . Ridlke (?) daughter of the late . . . Rabbi Me'ir Cassel, of Bonn, in the year (5)551" (=1790/91)
REMARKS: This pointer was probably made in Cologne, a noted silversmithing center across the Rhine from Deutz.
DONOR: Dr. Harry G. Friedman

## 536
TORAH POINTER F 3756 *(Illus. p. 296)*
Berlin (?), 1887/88 (inscription)
Ernst Philipp Gasser (?), active 1760's–1770's
Silver: cast, chased, gilt
L 24.3 DIAM 1.7 cm
HALLMARKS: *CITY:* obliterated
         *MAKER:* Scheffler, *Berlin*, 180 (?)
INSCRIPTION: on upper shaft: זאת נדבה/ האשה היקרה/ מרת חנה בילא הערשמאנן/ שנת הגדול תרמ״ח, "This was donated by Ḥannah Beila Herschmann in the great (?) year (5)648" (=1887/88)
DONOR: Dr. Harry G. Friedman

## 537
TORAH POINTER F 2403 *(Illus. p. 296)*
Germany (?), early 19th century
Silver: cast, engraved, traces of gilt
L 25.8 DIAM 2.3 cm
HALLMARKS: "13"; "HS" or "SH"
INSCRIPTION: on back of hand: א״פ.
REMARKS: The significance of the Hebrew abbreviation is unknown.
DONOR: Dr. Harry G. Friedman

## 538
TORAH POINTER F 1822 *(Illus. p. 296)*
Stuttgart (?), 18th/19th century
Silver: cast, chased
L 19.8 DIAM 1.7 cm
HALLMARKS: *CITY:* similar to R³ 4626, but with "O"
         *MAKER:* "FC/M" or "FL/M" in trefoil
REMARKS: Cf. the similar German pointer No. 570 and the Dutch pointer No. 854. F 1822 was previously numbered as F 5956.
DONOR: Dr. Harry G. Friedman

## 539
TORAH POINTER F 4377 *(Illus. p. 296)*
Germany (?), 1st half of 19th century
Silver: cast, gilt
L 19.9 DIAM 1.7 cm
HALLMARKS: none
DONOR: Dr. Harry G. Friedman

## 540
TORAH POINTER F 1045 *(Illus. p. 294)*
Nuremberg, ca. 1783–87
Johann Friedrich Ehe, active 1773–1808
Silver: cast, chased
L 27.1 DIAM 2.3 cm
HALLMARKS: *CITY:* "N" in circle, with R³ 3777
         *MAKER:* R³ 4304
INSCRIPTION: on upper arm: ה מ ה
REMARKS: The significance of the Hebrew abbreviation is unknown.
DONOR: Dr. Harry G. Friedman

## 541
TORAH POINTER F 311 *(Illus. p. 296)*
Germany (?), late 18th–early 19th century
Silver: cast, pierced, applique
L 31.6 DIAM 4.0 cm
HALLMARKS: none
DONOR: Dr. Harry G. Friedman

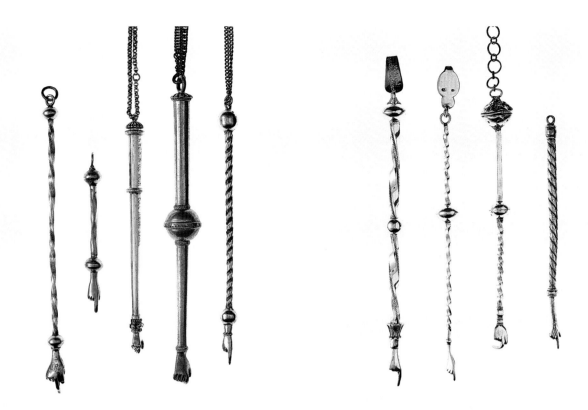

No. 577 JM 81–52; No. 578 F 5489; No. 579 JM 13–52;
No. 580 F 239b; No. 581 F 5944

No. 588 F 4269; No. 589 F 2426; No. 590 F 295;
No. 898a U 9181

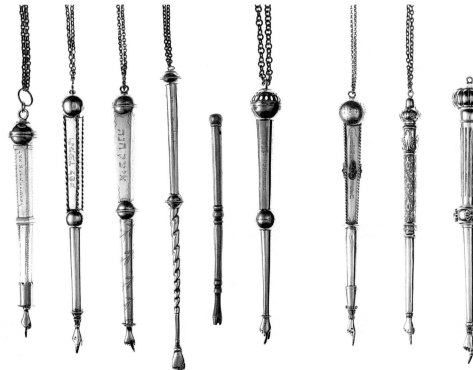

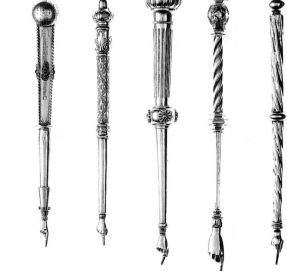

No. 593 F 1343; No. 594 F 1046; No. 595 D 22;
No. 596 D 41; No. 597 D 29; No. 598 F 2963

No. 599 F 279; No. 600 F 1598; No. 601 F 3918;
No. 602 F 3455; No. 605 F 918

## 542

TORAH POINTER  D 24  (*Illus. p. 296*)
Danzig (?), 1814 (inscription)
Silver: cast, engraved
L 26.6  DIAM 2.7 cm
HALLMARKS: none
INSCRIPTION: on upper shaft: שייך לאלופי חברה גמילת חסדים/ ונעשה מן נדבת אנשי אלופי חברה ג"ח/ ע"י הגבאים ר' איצק בר"מ גאלדשטיין, ור' הירש בר"ע ערב ר"ה שנת תקעה לפק, "Belonging to the officers of the Benevolent Society, and made from the donation of members [and] officers of the Benevolent Society, by the *gaba'im* Itzik son of M[ordecai] Goldstein and Hirsch son of . . ., the eve of Rosh Hashanah, year (5)575" (=September 14, 1814); on the upper knop, in German script: "Emigdirekt Danzig 25.9.27"
PROVENANCE: The Mattenbuden Synagogue, Danzig
REMARKS: Cf. the similar pointer No. 543. The German inscription refers to the "Aid Association for Jewish Emigrants in Danzig" (see *Danzig 1939*/1982, No. 29, as well as the introductory essay there by G. Bacon).
BIBLIOGRAPHY: *Danzig 1939*/1982, No. 88
DONOR: The Jewish Community of Danzig

## 543

TORAH POINTER  D 19  (*Illus. p. 296*)
Danzig, 1830/31 (inscription)
Silver: cast, chased
L 21.5  DIAM 2.4 cm
HALLMARKS: *CITY:* Czihak 5–6 var.; Czihak, No. XXXVII (var.) (?)
       *MAKER:* "(?) F" in script (not in Czihak)
INSCRIPTION: on upper shaft: זאת נדר ר' איצק גאלדשטיין לחברה ת"[ת]/ דק'ק' מאטענבודען// עבור נשמות אביו ר' משה ב'ר' מרדכי// ונשמות אשתו הצנועה מרת חנה// בת ר' חיים צוטרויען ז"ל/ תקצא לפ'ק', "This was vowed by Itzik Goldstein to the Talmud Torah Society of the Holy Congregation of Mattenbuden for the souls (*sic*) of his father Moses son of Mordecai, and the souls of his wife Hannah daughter of the late Ḥayyim Zutreuen (?), [5]591" (=1830/31)
PROVENANCE: The Mattenbuden Synagogue, Danzig
REMARKS: Cf. similar pointer No. 542. On the maker's mark, see under *Danzig 1939*/1982, No. 89.
BIBLIOGRAPHY: Danzig 1933, No. 143c; *Danzig 1939*/1982, No. 89
DONOR: The Jewish Community of Danzig

## 544

TORAH POINTER  F 1751  (*Illus. p. 296*)
Fürth, late 18th century
Silver: cast, engraved
L 26.6  DIAM 2.6 cm
HALLMARKS: R³ 2152; R³ 2157 with R³ 2154
REMARKS: Pointer No. 545 bears almost identical marks.
DONOR: Dr. Harry G. Friedman

## 545

TORAH POINTER  S 1326  (*Illus. p. 296*)
Fürth, late 18th century
Silver: cast, chased, parti-gilt
L 27.9  DIAM 2.9 cm
HALLMARKS: R³ 2152; "13"; "O"; R³ 2157, with R³ 2154
REMARKS: Pointer No. 544 bears almost identical marks.
DONOR: Joseph Willon

## 546

TORAH POINTER  (fragment)  F 3868  (*Illus. p. 296*)
Germany (?), 18th–19th century
Silver: cast, engraved
L 11.4  W 2.0 cm
HALLMARKS: none
REMARKS: Only the lower shaft and hand are preserved.
DONOR: Dr. Harry G. Friedman

## 547

TORAH POINTER  F 3636  (*Illus. p. 296*)
Breslau, late 18th century
Carl Gottfried Haase (?), active 1756–96
Silver: cast, chased
L 20.3  DIAM 2.6 cm
HALLMARKS:  *CITY:* similar to Hintze 1906, 23
       *MAKER:* similar to Hintze 1906, 164
INSCRIPTION: on upper shaft: ז"נ כ"ה דוד במ"ו ליזר/ גאלדשטיקר נרו/ מברעסלא/ ואשתו מ' מייטל בת/ כ"ה אביגדר זצל, "This was donated by David son of Leizer Goldsticker from Breslau and his wife Meitl daughter of the late Avigdor"
DONOR: Dr. Harry G. Friedman

## 548

TORAH POINTER  F 301  (*Illus. p. 296*)
Berlin, 1788–1802; 1811/12 (inscription)
Gottlob Ludwig Howaldt (?), active ca. 1799–1838
Silver: cast, engraved
L 29.1  DIAM 3.0 cm
HALLMARKS:  *CITY:* Scheffler, *Berlin*, 11 (or 12)
       *MAKER:* Scheffler, *Berlin*, 326–27 (?)
INSCRIPTION: on upper shaft: שייך ל'ר נפתלי הירש עם/ אשתו מרת רחל תי' מפייזער/ בשנת תקעב לפק, "Belonging to Naphtali Hirsch with his wife Rachel, of Peiser[n], in the year (5)572" (=1811/12)
REMARKS: Peisern (Pyzdry) lies 55 km SE of Posen. Torah Pointer No. 718 also mentions Peisern.
DONOR: Dr. Harry G. Friedman

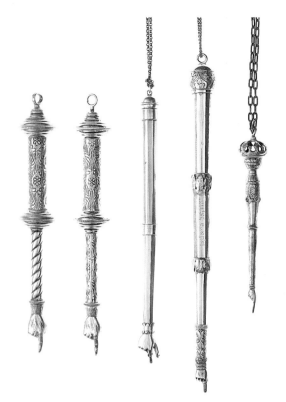

No. 603  F 5384;  No. 604  F 293;  No. 606  F 2348;
No. 607  F 5745b; No. 610  F 77

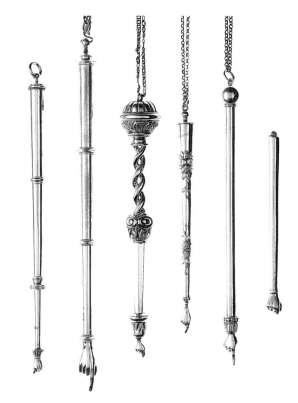

No. 608  F 308;  No. 609  F 309;  No. 611  F 2048;
No. 612  F 4705; No. 613  F 306;  No. 614  F2570

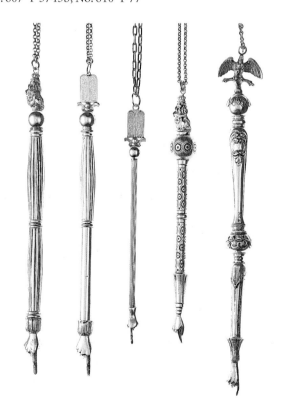

No. 615  F 3917;  No. 616  F 3916;  No. 617  F 827;
No. 619  F 5016; No. 620  F 276

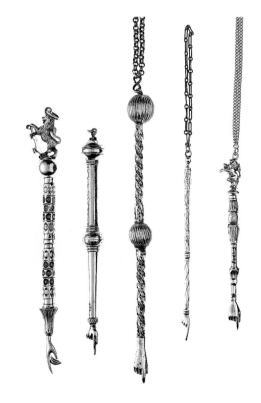

No. 618  S 28;  No. 791  F 1383;  No. 796  F 2390;
No. 798  F 2215; No. 809  F 4798

# 549

TORAH POINTER  F 60a

Augsburg (?), ca. 1800

Joseph Antoni Seethaler (?), active 1766–1811

Silver: cast

L 27.7  DIAM 2.8 cm

HALLMARKS: none

REMARKS: For the attribution, see shield No. 55, dated 1808, with which this pointer forms a set.

DONOR: Dr. Harry G. Friedman

# 550

TORAH POINTER  F 2303  (*Illus. p. 296*)

Nuremberg, ca. 1800

Silver: cast, parcel-gilt

L 28.3  DIAM 2.5 cm

HALLMARKS: *CITY:* "N"; illegible year letter

*MAKER:* illegible

DONOR: Dr. Harry G. Friedman

# 551

TORAH POINTER  F 3425  (*Illus. p. 296*)

Germany (?), first half of 19th century

Silver: cast, engraved

L 32.0  DIAM 2.2cm

HALLMARKS: "13" in square with protrusion above; "JP" in rectangle

DONOR: Dr. Harry G. Friedman

# 552

TORAH POINTER  D 25  (*Illus. p. 296*)

Danzig, 1805 (inscription)

Johann Christoph Wonecker II (?), active 1763–1813

Silver: cast, engraved

L 23.6  DIAM 2.6 cm

HALLMARKS: *CITY:* Czihak 9–10 var.; Czihak XXI (?)

*MAKER:* Czihak 495 (?)

INSCRIPTION: on upper shaft: נעשה מצדקה נ״ת/ עי הגבאי מה יוסף במה/ יואל כהנא מדאנציג/ נר תמיד, "Made from the Eternal Light charity by the *gabbai* Joseph son of . . . Joel Kahana of Danzig, Eternal Light [Society]"; on lower shaft: יום ד עיכ ת׳ק׳ס׳י׳ לפק, "Wednesday, Yom Kippur eve, (5)566" (=October 2, 1805)

REMARKS: On the Eternal Light Society see Torah Shield No. 69 and *Danzig 1939*/1982, p. 118.

BIBLIOGRAPHY: *Danzig 1939*/1982, No. 90

DONOR: The Jewish Community of Danzig

# 553

TORAH POINTER  F 1949  (*Illus. p. 298*)

Germany (?), early 19th century

Silver: cast, pierced; garnet(?)

L 21.9  DIAM 2.3 cm

HALLMARKS: *CITY (?):* Fleur-de-lis in circle

*MAKER:* unclear, partial

DONOR: Dr. Harry G. Friedman

# 554

TORAH POINTER  D 26  (*Illus. p. 298*)

Danzig, early 19th century

Base metal: cast; white metal wash

L 28.3  DIAM 3.1 cm

HALLMARKS: none

INSCRIPTION: on upper shaft: שייך לקהל ברייטגאס, "Belongs to the Breitgasse Congregation"

PROVENANCE: The Breitgasse Synagogue, Danzig

BIBLIOGRAPHY: *Danzig 1939*/1982, No. 243

DONOR: The Jewish Community of Danzig

# 555

TORAH POINTER  D 34  (*Illus. p. 298*)

Berlin, 1817–20, 1820/21 (inscription)

Johann August Gebhardt, active 1817–1860

Silver: chased, cast

L 30.6  DIAM 3.3 cm

HALLMARKS: *CITY:* Scheffler, *Berlin*, 13; "g" in circle

*MAKER:* Scheffler, *Berlin*, 336

INSCRIPTION: on upper shaft: שייך לח״ק/ נעשה ע״י ר׳ שלמה יס׳ט׳ ור׳ יוזפא ב׳ר׳מ׳/ בשנת תק״פא לפק, "Belongs to the H[oly] (Burial) S[ociety]; made by Solomon . . . and Juspa son of M . . ., in the year (5)581" (=1820/21)

REMARKS: In the inscription, the abbreviation following the name Solomon could represent the family name יסטרוב, Jastrow, or may represent a blessing: "May his fate be good" (an unusual feature in Ashkenazi inscriptions). For another pointer by the same smith, see Scheffler, *Berlin*, No. 1714, ex. e, Märkisches Museum, Berlin, Inv. No. S. 2399. Another object by Gebhardt at the Jewish Museum is shield No. 73.

BIBLIOGRAPHY: Danzig 1933, No. 146c; *Danzig 1939*/1982, No. 227

DONOR: The Jewish Community of Danzig

# 556

TORAH POINTER  D 40  (*Illus. p. 298*)

Danzig, 1814–19

Silver: cast, chased

L 27.9  DIAM 3.2 cm

HALLMARKS: *CITY:* Czihak 5–6; Czihak XXXVI

*MAKER:* "S"(?)

INSCRIPTION: "E.L.", in script

BIBLIOGRAPHY: *Danzig 1939*/1982, No. 234

DONOR: The Jewish Community of Danzig

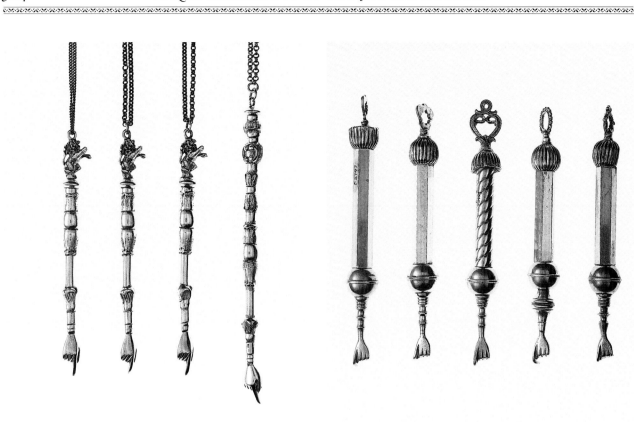

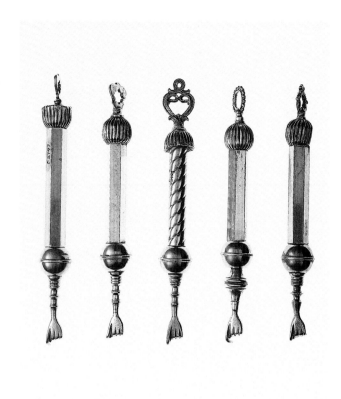

No. 621   F 2018;   No. 622   F 2809;   No. 623   F 310;
No. 624   F 3523

No. 625   F 2797;   No. 626   F 5959;   No. 627   F 2443;
No. 628   1987–63;   No. 629   U 9178

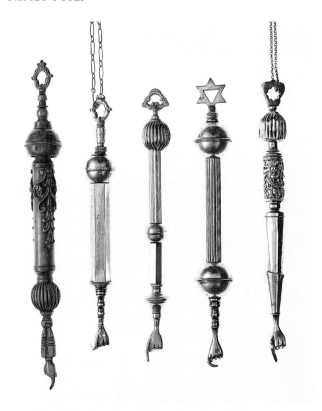

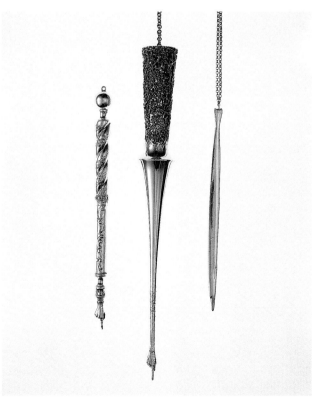

No. 630   S 827;   No. 631   F 3795;   No. 632   F 271;
No. 633   F 2047;   No. 634   F 2317

No. 635   F 270;   No. 636   JM 17–66;   No. 637   JM 49–52

## 557

TORAH POINTER JM 101–47 (*Illus. p. 326*)
Germany (?), 1815 (inscription)
Wood: carved, punched
L 29.5 W 2.0 cm
INSCRIPTION: on lower shaft: נעשה ע״י כה אפרים/ אלטין
בוסיק ביום/ ג ד״ח אלול ת׳ק׳ע׳ה׳ ל", "Made by Ephraim
Alten-Buseck on the 3rd day of the month of Elul, (5)575"
(=September 8, 1815)
REMARKS: Museum records indicate that this pointer is from
Alten Buseck, which is 55 km N of Frankfurt.
DONOR: Dr. Harry Friedenwald

## 558

TORAH POINTER D 30 (*Illus. p. 298*)
Probably Thorn, 1825/26 (inscription)
Silver: cast, engraved
L 26.5 DIAM 3.3 cm
HALLMARKS: *ASSAY MASTER:* "S," Czihak IV (116)
INSCRIPTION: on upper shaft: זאת נדב ר׳ איצק ב׳ר׳ם
גאלדשטיין/ להחברה קדישא וב״ח מאטענבודען/ עבור
נשמת אשתו הצנועה/ מ׳ חנה ז״ל תקפו לי'פ'ק, "This was
donated by Itzik son of M(oses) Goldstein to the Matten-
buden Holy [Burial] Society and [Society for] Visiting the
Sick, on behalf of the soul of his . . . wife, the late Hannah,
(5)586" (=1825/26)
PROVENANCE: The Mattenbuden Synagogue, Danzig
REMARKS: The mark belonged to Joseph Staniezewski (d.
1826) *Altermann* from 1821–26.Cf. the inscription on
pointer No. 595, another donation of Itzik Goldstein.
BIBLIOGRAPHY: *Danzig 1939/1982*, No. 235
DONOR: The Jewish Community of Danzig

## 559

TORAH POINTER F 3758 (*Illus. p. 298*)
Germany, 19th century
Silver: cast
L 17.9 DIAM 1.8 cm
HALLMARKS: none
DONOR: Dr. Harry G. Friedman

## 560

TORAH POINTER D 35 (*Illus. p. 298*)
Thorn, before 1811
Daniel Clausen I ?
Silver: cast, engraved
L 33.5 DIAM 3.4 cm
HALLMARKS: "10"; Czihak IV (113)
INSCRIPTION: on upper shaft: שאטאלאנד ד״ק״ק" ח״ק",

"H[oly] (Burial) S[ociety] of the H[oly] C[ongregation
of] Schottland"
PROVENANCE: The Schottland Synagogue, Danzig
BIBLIOGRAPHY: Danzig 1933, No. 140c; *Danzig 1939*, No. 232
DONOR: The Jewish Community of Danzig

## 561

TORAH POINTER D 20 (*Illus. p. 298*)
Germany (?), 19th century
Silver: cast, engraved, gilt(?)
L 20.4 DIAM 3.1 cm
HALLMARKS: none
INSCRIPTION: on upper shaft, in Latin script: "J. Leburg"
BIBLIOGRAPHY: *Danzig 1939/1982*, No. 251
DONOR: The Jewish Community of Danzig

## 562

TORAH POINTER M 177 (*Illus. p. 298*)
Berlin (?), second quarter of 19th century
Friedrich August Ferdinand Eisolt, active ca. 1833–58
Silver: cast, engraved
L 26.5 DIAM 3.2 cm
HALLMARKS: *CITY:* cf. Scheffler, *Berlin*, 14–17
*MAKER:* "E" in script, Scheffler, *Berlin*, 415 (?)
INSCRIPTION: on upper shaft: החבר ר׳ אברהם/ בן החבר /ז״נ
ר׳ מיכאל/ ב״ר״פ בראש, "This was donated by the member
Abraham son of the member Michael son of P. Barasch"
PROVENANCE: The Rose and Benjamin Mintz Collection
DONOR: Museum purchase

## 563

TORAH POINTER F 3301 (*Illus. p. 298*)
Germany, 19th century
Silver: cast, chased, engraved, gilt
L 34.0 W 5.0 cm
HALLMARKS: "T T" or "1 1", synagogue mark?
INSCRIPTION: on shield: משה בר דוד, "Moses son of David"
DONOR: Dr. Harry G. Friedman

## 564

TORAH POINTER F 4075 (*Illus. p. 298*)
Germany (?), mid-19th century
Silver: cast, chased, engraved
L 23.2 DIAM 2.2 cm
HALLMARKS: none
INSCRIPTION: on back of hand: מ׳ ק/׳ פ (or מ״ץ ק״ל/ פ)
REMARKS: The meaning of the abbreviated inscription is
unclear.
DONOR: Dr. Harry G. Friedman

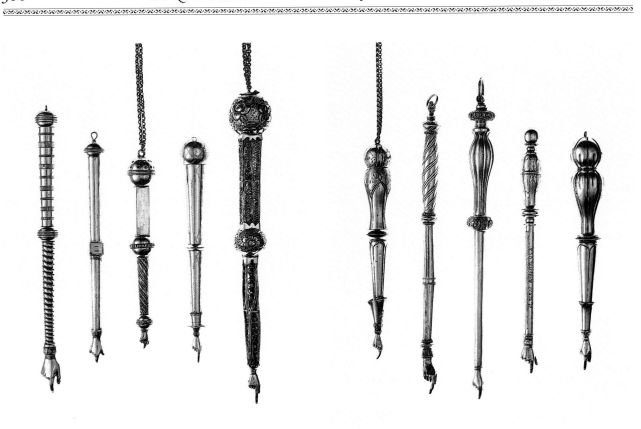

No. 638  F 3721;  No. 639  F 2504;  No. 640  F 291;
No. 641  D 18;  No. 642  F 5657

No. 643  D 27;  No. 644  F 3519;  No. 645  F 2442;
No. 646  F 2450;  No. 647  F 273

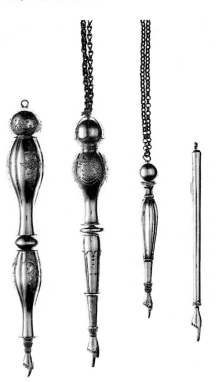

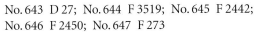

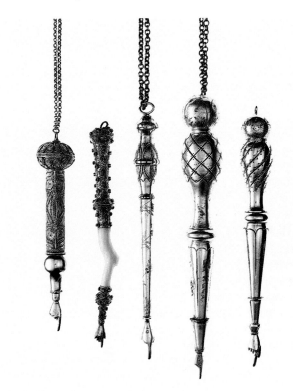

No. 648  D 38;  No. 649  JM 60–55;  No. 650  JM 34–56;
No. 651  F 3426

No. 653  F 1044;  No. 654  F 934;  No. 655  F 289;
No. 657  F 884;  No. 658  F 2313

## 565

TORAH POINTER  F 280  (*Illus. p. 298*)
Breslau, 1870 (?)
Carl Krutsche, active 1858–1884
Silver: cast, chased, engraved, nielloed
L 27.8  DIAM 3.3 cm
HALLMARKS: *CITY:* Hintze 1906, Type XX (?)(year illegible)
　　　　　　*MAKER:* Hintze 1906, p. 107 top
REMARKS: See finials No. 307, by the same smith. Cf. Brann,
　　figs. 10 and 11, and Martyna, No. 53, for identical pointers
　　by Korock to whom Krutsche had been apprenticed.
DONOR: Dr. Harry G. Friedman

## 566

TORAH POINTER  F 2441  (*Illus. p. 298*)
Germany (?), 1878/79 (inscription)
Silver: cast, engraved, chased
L 29.4  DIAM 3.0 cm
HALLMARKS: none
INSCRIPTION: on upper knop: יד של כסף/ נדב ר חנוך רייכמאן
עם אש/ תו. כלה בת ק. נטע וי: בערין בשנת/ תרלט,
　　"Pointer of silver donated by Ḥenoch Reichman with his
　　wife Kalle daughter of . . . Neta . . . Berin(?), in the year
　　(5)639" (=1878/79)
DONOR: Dr. Harry G. Friedman

## 567

TORAH POINTER  F 5554  (*Illus. p. 298*)
Nuremberg, late 18th–early 19th century
Silver: cast, gilt
L 26.9  DIAM 2.3 cm
HALLMARKS: *CITY:* "N" in circle
　　　　　　*MAKER:* Shield with branch (?)
DONOR: Dr. Harry G. Friedman

## 568

TORAH POINTER  F 3011d
Kassel (?), ca. 1836 (?)
Silver: cast, parcel-gilt
L 24.2  DIAM 2.7 cm
HALLMARKS: none
REMARKS: This pointer apparently formed a set with Torah
　　shield No. 78 and finials No. 313.
DONOR: Dr. Harry G. Friedman

## 569

TORAH POINTER  D 51  (*Illus. p. 298*)
Danzig, after 1838

Georg Friedrich May, active 1838–?
Silver: cast, parcel-gilt
L 16.1  DIAM 2.3 cm
HALLMARKS: *CITY:* Czihak 5–6(?); illegible mark
　　　　　　*MAKER:* Czihak 555
PROVENANCE: Gieldzinski Collection, Danzig
BIBLIOGRAPHY: Danzig 1904, No. 37; Danzig 1933, No.49;
　　*Danzig 1939/1982*, No. 233
DONOR: The Jewish Community of Danzig

## 570

TORAH POINTER  F 4239  (*Illus. p. 298*)
Germany (?), late 19th–early 20th century
Silver: cast, chased
L 32.9  DIAM 3.0 cm
HALLMARKS: none
INSCRIPTION: on lower shaft: מאיר שוטץ, "Me'ir Schutz"
DONOR: Dr. Harry G. Friedman

## 571

TORAH POINTER  F 2326  (*Illus. p. 298*)
Germany (?), 19th century
Silver: cast
L 18.9  DIAM 1.8 cm
HALLMARKS: none
DONOR: Dr. Harry G. Friedman

## 572

TORAH POINTER  F 2567  (*Illus. p. 298*)
Berlin, Prussia, 1817–19
Silver: filigree, cast
L 26.1  DIAM 2.9 cm
HALLMARKS: *CITY:* Scheffler, *Berlin*, 13
　　　　　　*MAKER:* "L" (? Scheffler, *Berlin*, 1379)
DONOR: Dr. Harry G. Friedman

## 573

TORAH POINTER  F 5044  (*Illus. p. 298*)
Germany (?), 19th century
Silver: cast, chased, engraved
L 34.0  DIAM 3.1 cm
HALLMARKS: "FM" in rectangle
INSCRIPTION: on shaft: כ' יעקב בן כ' יהודה כ"ץ/ קילה בת כ'
שמעון מווע זל/ אליעזר בן כ' יהודה כ"ץ/ פראדכה בת כ'
דוד סיג'ל' מדדורף, "Jacob son of Judah Katz; Keila daugh-
　　ter of the late Simon Mowe(?); Eliezer son of Judah Katz;
　　Fradke daughter of David Segal of Dadorf (?)."
REMARKS: The continuation of the inscription may have been

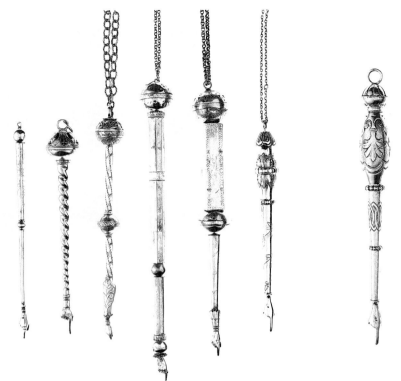

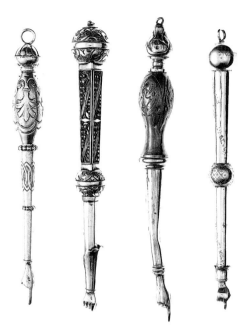

No. 667  F 5488;  No. 668  F 296;  No. 671  F 5946;
No. 674  F 300;  No. 679  U 9179;  No. 656  F 2302

No. 659  F 2449;  No. 660  F 2464;  No. 661  F 5961;
No. 662  F 2505

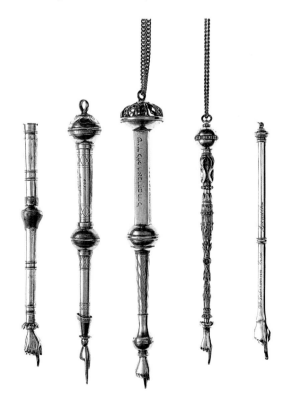

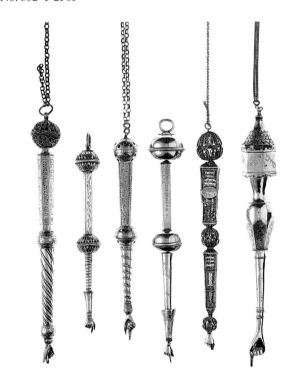

No. 676  U 9180;  No. 677  F 4509;  No. 678  U 9175;
No. 680  F 4494;  No. 681  F 3244

No. 683  F 75;  No. 694  F 2017;  No. 705  F 304;
No. 746  JM 31–57;  No. 757  F 284;  No. 764  F 2553

erased. The place name at the end of the inscription may represent Dodendorf, south of Magdeburg.

DONOR: Dr. Harry G. Friedman

## 574
### TORAH POINTER  F 4849

Germany (?), 19th century
Silver: cast, engraved
L 18.2  DIAM 1.3 cm
HALLMARKS: none
DONOR: Dr. Harry G. Friedman

## 575
### TORAH POINTER  1976–24  (*Illus. p. 292*)
Northern Germany, late 18th–early 19th century
Silver: cast, pierced, chased
L 27.0  DIAM 2.5 cm
HALLMARKS: none

## 576
### TORAH POINTER  F 4270
Wehrheim, late 18th–early 19th century
Silver: cast, engraved
L 18.7  DIAM 1.9 cm  (hook: H 2.0  W 4.5 cm)
HALLMARKS: none
INSCRIPTION: on hook: קהל/ וויר/ היים, "Congregation of Wehrheim"
REMARKS: Wehrheim is 32 km NNW of Frankfurt am Main.
DONOR: Dr. Harry G. Friedman

## 577
### TORAH POINTER  JM 81–52  (*Illus. p. 300*)
Germany (?), first half of 19th century
Silver: cast
L 26.5  W 2.1 cm
HALLMARKS: none
INSCRIPTION: on back of hand: ה ש (or ה ס), "H. Sh." (or "H. S.")
REMARKS: The significance of the Hebrew abbreviation is unknown.

## 578
### TORAH POINTER  F 5489  (*Illus. p. 300*)
Germany (?), 19th century
Silver: cast
L 14.2  DIAM 1.7 cm
HALLMARKS: none
REMARKS: This piece, somewhat crudely made, may have been cut down from a longer pointer.
DONOR: Dr. Harry G. Friedman

## 579
### TORAH POINTER  JM 13–52  (*Illus. p. 300*)
Munich, 1818
Silver: cast, engraved
L 21.2  DIAM 1.8 cm
HALLMARKS: none
INSCRIPTION: on shaft: ני מהיישיש הרה אלחנן/ בהרר זעליגמן שנאטיך// מינכען ר׳ח א״ש/ תקע״ח לפק, "Donation from the elder Elḥanan son of Seligman Schnaittach, Munich, 1 (*Rosh Ḥodesh*) Adar II, (5)578" (=March 9, 1818)
DONOR: Jewish Cultural Reconstruction

## 580
### TORAH POINTER  F 239B  (*Illus. p. 300*)
Augsburg, 1825 or 1850
Joseph Heinrich Mussmann, active 1822–after 1865
Silver: cast, die-stamped, gilt
L 27.0  DIAM 3.4 cm
HALLMARKS: *CITY:* Seling 313 or 338
             *MAKER:* Seling 2713
REMARKS: The earlier dating is preferable since that is the date of shield No. 57 by the same smith. The two pieces probably formed a set.
DONOR: Dr. Harry G. Friedman

## 581
### TORAH POINTER  F 5944  (*Illus. p. 300*)
Germany (?), mid-19th century
Silver: cast
L 23.3  DIAM 1.9 cm
HALLMARKS: illegible
REMARKS: The hallmarks appear to be in the casting, indicating that this piece was copied directly from another pointer.
DONOR: Dr. Harry G. Friedman

## 582
### TORAH POINTER  F 2137
Germany (?), 19th century
Silver: cast
L 20.5  DIAM 1.6 cm
HALLMARKS: "800" (?); star(?) above "I"
REMARKS: Museum records indicate that this pointer formed a set with Torah Staves No. 918. The set "originally belonged to the Berthold Auerbach family and late[r to the] Steffin [?] family of N.Y."
DONOR: Dr. Harry G. Friedman

## 582A
### TORAH POINTER  U 9177
Germany, 18th– early 19th century
Silver: cast, engraved

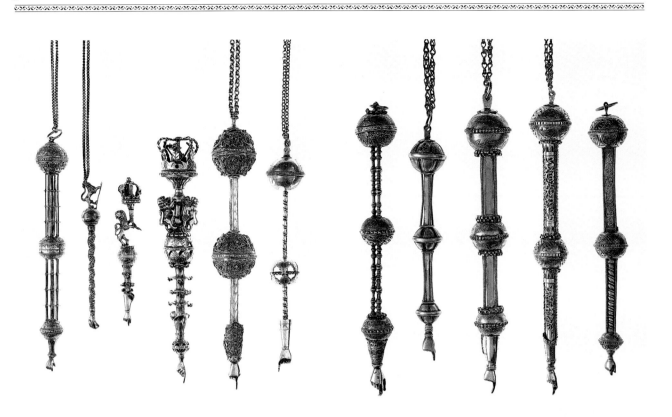

No. 684  M 114;  No. 691  M 116;  No. 692  F 2590;
No. 693  F 5314;  No. 697  S 1363c;  No. 712  M 338

No. 685  JM 32–64;  No. 686  M 279;  No. 687  D 42;
No. 688  M 19;  No. 689  D 16

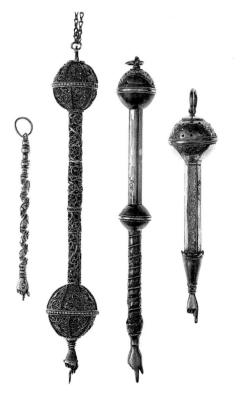

No. 690  F 4078;  No. 698  F 5335;  No. 695  F 305;
No. 696  F 4076

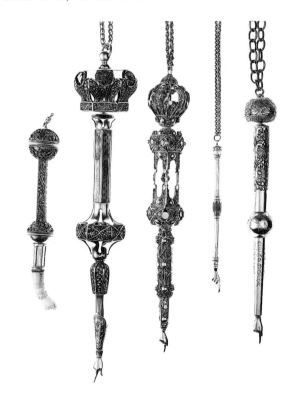

No. 699  D 46;  No. 700  F 2319;  No. 701  F 4602;
No. 702  JM 57–52;  No. 703  F 1545

L 19.9  DIAM 1.7 cm

HALLMARKS: none

INSCRIPTION: on hook: יד, "[Torah] Pointer" (or initials "Y.D.")

DONOR: Jewish Cultural Reconstruction

# 583

## TORAH POINTER  X 1976–2a, b

Germany, early 19th century

Silver: cast, engraved

L 24.5  DIAM 2.1 cm

HALLMARKS: none

INSCRIPTION: on upper knop: שרה אשת אברהם ווארבורג, "Sarah wife of Abraham Warburg"

PROVENANCE: Charles S. Warburg, London

DONOR: Museum purchase

# 584

## TORAH POINTER  JM 82–52

German (?), late 18th/early 19th century

Silver: cast, engraved

L 34.1  DIAM 1.9 cm

HALLMARKS: unclear; "WN"

INSCRIPTION: on back of hand: ז״ח (or ד״ח, ז״ה, ד״ה)

REMARKS: The significance of the Hebrew abbreviation is unknown.

DONOR: Jewish Cultural Reconstruction

# 585

## TORAH POINTER  F 4271

Germany (?), early 19th century

Silver: cast

L 20.3  W 1.8 cm

HALLMARKS: none

DONOR: Dr. Harry G. Friedman

# 586

## TORAH POINTER  F 4478

Germany (?), early 19th century

Silver: cast, chased, gilt

L 16.8  W 1.3 cm

HALLMARKS: none

DONOR: Dr. Harry G. Friedman

# 587

## TORAH POINTER  JM 82–64

Germany (?), early 19th century

Silver: cast

L 26.1  DIAM 2.1 cm

HALLMARKS: none

REMARKS: According to the donor this piece originally belonged to the Levy family, of Trier, who donated it to a syn-agogue in Beilstein, on the Mosel, along with other objects. Upon moving to Gerolstein in 1900, the family took the pointer with them as they had a synagogue in their home. In 1938, the donor's brother brought the pointer to the United States.

DONOR: Else Seligman

# 588

## TORAH POINTER  F 4269  (*Illus. p. 300*)

Germany (?), first half of 19th century

Silver: cast

L 26.3  DIAM 2.5  (clasp: L 4.2  W 1.7 cm)

HALLMARKS: "13"; "G.C.H." in rectangle (both on clasp)

INSCRIPTION: on clasp: ליב בן משה שוואב/ ת׳ר׳ט׳ז׳ לפ״ק, "Leib son of Moses Schwab, (5)516" (=1855/56)

REMARKS: The clasp is made from a spoon handle, and is probably a later addition to the pointer.

DONOR: Dr. Harry G. Friedman

# 589

## TORAH POINTER  F 2426  (*Illus. p. 300*)

Germany (?), early 19th century

Silver: cast

L 24.4  DIAM 2.2 cm  (clasp: L 2.2 W 5.0 cm)

HALLMARKS: "(?)D/C" in script; "13"

REMARKS: The clasp is apparently made from a spoon. In Museum files, this pointer is ascribed to "Hamburg, 1790–1800."

DONOR: Dr. Harry G. Friedman

# 590

## TORAH POINTER  F 295  (*Illus. p. 300*)

Germany (?), first half of 19th century

Silver: cast, pierced

L 23.5  DIAM 3.0 cm

HALLMARKS: none

DONOR: Dr. Harry G. Friedman

# 591

## TORAH POINTER  F 5945

Germany, early 19th century

Silver: cast

L 30.0  DIAM 1.8 cm

HALLMARKS: none

REMARKS: Repairs are evident. The right hand has two fingers extended, and is probably a replacement taken from (or intended for) a Christian digitus. Cf. F 2626, an actual digitus made in Germany in the mid-19th century. This Christian scepter, used to bless the congregation in church, was received by the Museum as a pointer. For another digitus in a public Judaica collection, see Harvard, No. 88. For a digitus in a German collection, see Schäfke.

DONOR: Dr. Harry G. Friedman

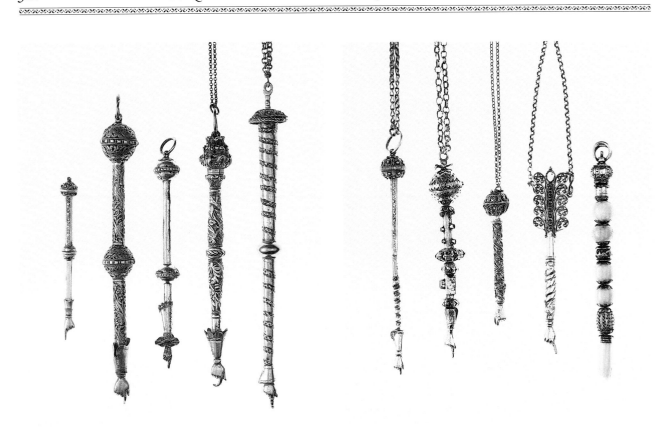

No. 704  F 2592;  No. 707  F 3637;  No. 708  F 3724;
No. 709  D 17;  No. 710  M 18

No. 706  F 1905;  No. 734  F 5400b;  No. 761  JM 71–48;
No. 765  D 50;  No. 756A  D 44

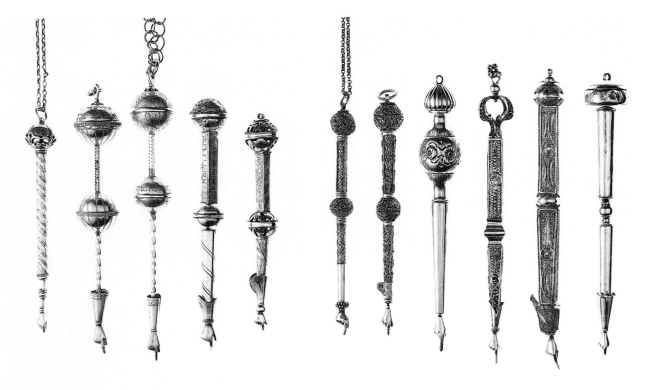

No. 711  F 1805b;  No. 714  JM 59–55;  No. 715  F 3118;
No. 716  F 4074;  No. 717  JM 93–67

No. 713  M 17;  No. 735  F 2568;  No. 736  F 2139;
No. 737  F 287;  No. 738  F 272b;  No. 739  F 307

## 592 (*no entry*)

## 593
### TORAH POINTER F 1343 (*Illus. p. 300*)
Germany (?), 1824/25 (inscription)
Silver: cast, chased, engraved
L 33.0  DIAM 2.5 cm
HALLMARKS: none
INSCRIPTION: on upper arm: אברהם ברוקמאן, "Abraham Bruckman"; palimpsest over an older text that reads, in part: [ת] ק פ ה (?=[5]585=1824/25 ?)
DONOR: Dr. Harry G. Friedman

## 594
### TORAH POINTER F 1046 (*Illus. p. 300*)
Germany, first half of 19th century
Brass: cast
L 22.2  DIAM 1.5 cm
HALLMARKS: none
DONOR: Dr. Harry G. Friedman

## 594A
### TORAH POINTER JM 63-64
Speyer (inscription), 1866 (inscription)
Silver: engraved
L 17.4  DIAM 3.1 cm
HALLMARKS: none
INSCRIPTION: on flat upper element, on upper side: כת/ מתנת יד/ הח' [?הלזי] שייך/ לה"ק כ"ש כ'/ משה טובי'/ יצו/ מק"ק פיורדא/ ואשתו/ המהוללת/ אשת חייל/ מ' רבקה/ ת"י/ מעברבאך, "C[rown of] T[orah]. Donation . . . This belongs to the l[eader] . . . Moses Tobi[as] . . . of the h[oly] c[ommunity of] Fürth, and his . . . wife, a woman of valor, . . . Rebecca . . . , from Eberbach"; on lower side: מתנה/ מרבי' טובי' הר'/ נפתלי/ יוסף/ טרייפוס/ ואשתו/ מרת/ צערלא/ בת מרדכי/ ביום יב' לחודש/ אייר ת'ר'כ'ו' לפק'/ שפייער "Gift from . . . Tobi[as son of] . . . Naphtali Joseph Dreyfus (?), and his wife . . . Zerla daughter of . . . . Mordecai, on the 12th day of the month of Iyar [5]626 (= 27 April, 1866), Speyer"; on shaft, grafitto: מ.ק., "M.K."
REMARKS: The two main inscriptions are of entirely different engraving. Eberbach is 20 km NE of Heidelberg.
DONOR: Nathan Cummings

## 595
### TORAH POINTER D 22 (*Illus. p. 300*)
Germany (?), 1824/25 (inscription)
Silver: cast, engraved
L 28.2  DIAM 3.0 cm
HALLMARKS: illegible
INSCRIPTION: on upper shaft: איצק חנה/ תקפה, "Itzik, Hannah, (5)585" (=1824/25); Zum Andenken an seinen Vater geschenkt von: Marcus Goldstein, "In memory of his father, donated by Marcus Goldstein"
BIBLIOGRAPHY: *Danzig 1939/1982*, No. 226
DONOR: The Jewish Community of Danzig

## 596
### TORAH POINTER D 41 (*Illus. p. 300*)
Germany, 1814/15 (inscription)
Silver: cast, pierced, engraved
L 28.2  DIAM 3.6 cm
HALLMARKS: Scheffler, *Berlin*, 30; "12" (or "13"); an illegible mark
INSCRIPTION: on upper shaft: ז' נ' ר' אהרון ב'ר'מ' מוויינבערג/ בשנת תקעה לפ'ק'/ לחברה גמילת הריעים/ ד'ק'ק' דאנציג "This was donated by Aaron son of M. of Weinberg, in the year (5)575 [=1814/15], to the Friends Benevolent Society of the Holy Community of Danzig"
REMARKS: An old tag attached to this object bears the number "138," referring to the Danzig 1933 number.
BIBLIOGRAPHY: Danzig 1933, No. 138d; *Danzig 1939/1982*, No. 230
DONOR: The Jewish Community of Danzig

## 597
### TORAH POINTER D 29 (*Illus. p. 300*)
Northern Germany, 1816/17 (inscription)
Silver: cast, chased
L 27.7  DIAM 2.8 cm
HALLMARKS: defaced
INSCRIPTION: on upper shaft: זאת נדבו/ אלופי חברה קדישה/ פה דנציק/ ת'ק'ע'ז' לפ"ק, "This was donated by the officers of the Holy (Burial) Society, here [in] Danzig, (5)577" (=1816/17); engraved near upper loop: "XII"
BIBLIOGRAPHY: *Danzig 1939/1982*, No. 231
DONOR: The Jewish Community of Danzig

## 598
### TORAH POINTER F 2963 (*Illus. p. 300*)
Germany, 1862/63 (inscription)
Silver: cast, chased, engraved
L 24.1  DIAM 3.2 CM
HALLMARKS: none
INSCRIPTION: on upper shaft, on two sides: ישראל בן ר' מרדכה שנת תרכז// לאה אשת ר' ישראל, "Israel son of Mordke, Leah wife of Israel, year (5)523" (=1862/63)
REMARKS: The last two letters of the date are hidden by the medial band.
DONOR: Dr. Harry G. Friedman

## 599
### TORAH POINTER F 279 (*Illus. p. 300*)
Germany (?), late 19th–early 20th century; 1879 (inscription)
Silver: cast, engraved; glass

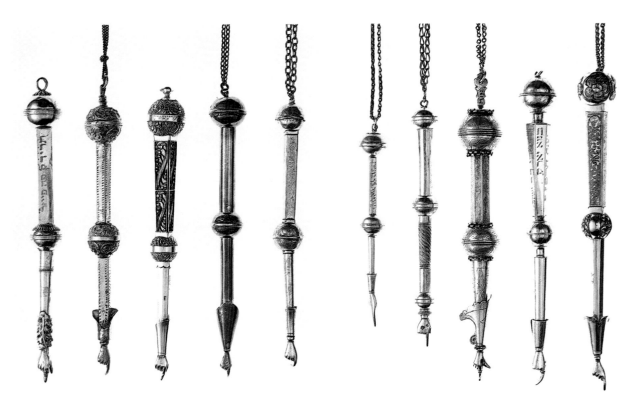

No. 718 F 303; No. 719 M 371; No. 720 F 285;
No. 721 F 2228; No. 722 M 238

No. 723 D 49; No. 724 JM 15–57; No. 725 M 192;
No. 726 F 2523; No. 727 F 1541

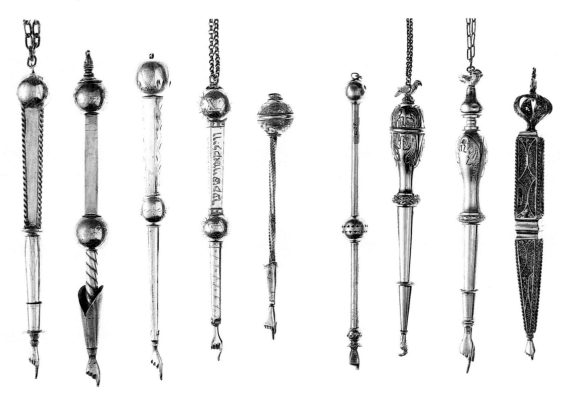

No. 728 F 274; No. 729 F 3723; No. 730 F 1823;
No. 732 F 299; No. 733 F 2347

No. 740 U 9182; No. 741 F 2288; No. 742 F 275;
No. 743 S 847; No. 744 M 426

L 26.3 DIAM 3.2 cm
HALLMARKS: unclear mark
INSCRIPTION: on shaft: חנוכה // ת'ר'ם', "Hanukkah (5)640"
 (=10–17 December, 1879)
REMARKS: This pointer was made in a late 18th-century north
 German style.
DONOR: Dr. Harry G. Friedman

## 600

TORAH POINTER  F 1598  (*Illus. p. 300*)
Germany, late 19th–early 20th century
Silver: cast, chased
L 25.9 DIAM 2.3 cm
HALLMARKS: R³ 3; "800"
DONOR: Dr. Harry G. Friedman

## 601

TORAH POINTER  F 3918  (*Illus. p. 300*)
Germany, 1899/1900 (inscription)
Silver: cast, chased, engraved
L 29.2 DIAM 2.7 cm
HALLMARKS: R³ 3; "800"
  *MAKER:* illegible
INSCRIPTION: on lower shaft: לכבוד ספר תורה/ שהניח זקני
 מורי כמר יהודה ז"צ"ל/ נדבתי יד הזאת אנכי נכדו/ מ'ר'ד'כ'י'
 בן' מ'נ'חם' ק'ו'ל'פ'א ז"ל/ לפ"ק, "In honor of the Torah
 Scroll which was left by my grandfather and teacher, the
 late R. Judah, I donated this pointer, I, his grandson,
 Mordecai son of the late Menaḥem Kulpa (chronogram
 =[5]660)" (=1899/1900)
DONOR: Dr. Harry G. Friedman

## 602

TORAH POINTER  F 3455  (*Illus. p. 300*)
Germany, ca. 1900
Silver: die-stamped, cast, engraved
L 33.2 DIAM 2.4 cm
HALLMARKS: R³ 5; "800"
INSCRIPTION: on lower arm, in Latin script: "Geschenk von
 David Anschel," "Donation from David Anschel"
DONOR: Dr. Harry G. Friedman

## 603

TORAH POINTER  F 5384  (*Illus. p. 302*)
Germany (?), late 19th century
Brass: cast, plated
L 25.9 DIAM 3.6 cm
HALLMARKS: none
REMARKS: cf. the similar pointer No. 604.
DONOR: Dr. Harry G. Friedman

## 604

TORAH POINTER  F 293  (*Illus. p. 302*)
Germany (?), late 19th century
Brass: cast, partly silvered
L 25.5 DIAM 3.6 cm
HALLMARKS: none
REMARKS: Cf. the similar pointer No. 603.
DONOR: Dr. Harry G. Friedman

## 605

TORAH POINTER  F 918  (*Illus. p. 300*)
Germany (?), late 19th century
Silver: cast
L 28.3 DIAM 2.0 cm
HALLMARKS: none
REMARKS: The chain and the shield-shaped loop are not orig-
 inal elements.
DONOR: Dr. Harry G. Friedman

## 606

TORAH POINTER  F 2348  (*Illus. p. 302*)
Germany (?), late 19th century
Silver: cast, stamped
L 27.7 W 2.4 cm
HALLMARKS: Tardy, p. 208, top
DONOR: Dr. Harry G. Friedman

## 607

TORAH POINTER  F 5745b  (*Illus. p. 302*)
Altona, ca. 1861 (? or earlier)
Silver: cast, chased, engraved, traces of gilt
L 34.0 DIAM 2.6 cm
HALLMARKS: *CITY:* cf. R³ 75
  *MAKER:* "SC" or "SG"
INSCRIPTION: on opposing facets of the middle shaft (in
 Hebrew and Latin characters): יחזקאל הייאמאן, "Ezekiel
 Heyman"
REMARKS: The city mark, although resembling that of 1761, is
 probably a century later. See shield No. 97 bearing identical
 marks; parallels clearly place the shield in the mid-19th
 century. It was made as a set with this pointer.
DONOR: Dr. Harry G. Friedman

## 608

TORAH POINTER  F 308  (*Illus. p. 302*)
Germany, 19th–20th century
Brass: cast, silver-plated
L 30.0 DIAM 1.9 cm
HALLMARKS: none
REMARKS: The hand is a left hand, an unusual feature on
 pointers. Cf. the similar pointer No. 609.
DONOR: Dr. Harry G. Friedman

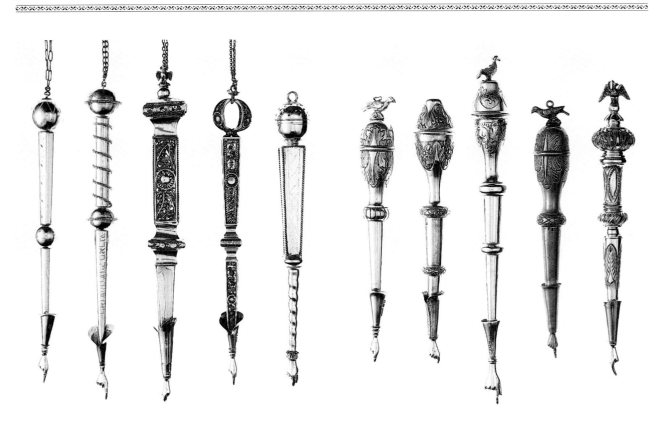

No. 745  F 1531;  No. 747  F 1860;  No. 748  F 288;
No. 749  F 2306;  No. 750  D 28

No. 751  F 2439;  No. 752  F 283;  No. 753  F 2524;
No. 754  F 3295;  No. 755  F 4077

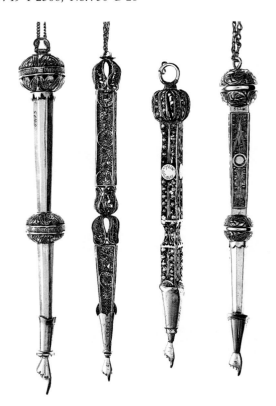

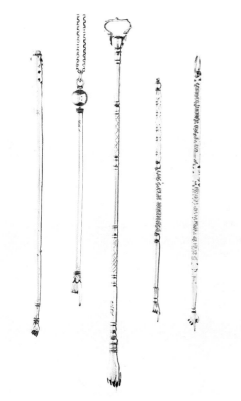

No. 756  U 9173;  No. 758  F 2465;  No. 759  F 2815;
No. 760  S 526

No. 767  F 1047;  No. 768  F 3106;  No. 862  F 3910;
No. 863  F 5376;  No. 864  F 5403

## 609

TORAH POINTER  F 309  (*Illus. p. 302*)
Germany, 19th century
Silver: cast
L 35.2  DIAM 2.7 cm
HALLMARKS: none
REMARKS: Cf. pointer No. 608, with a similar hand.
DONOR: Dr. Harry G. Friedman

## 610

TORAH POINTER  F 77  (*Illus. p. 302*)
Germany or Austria, late 19th–early 20th century
Silver: cast, gilt
L 18.3  DIAM 2.9 cm
HALLMARKS: none
DONOR: Dr. Harry G. Friedman

## 611

TORAH POINTER  F 2048  (*Illus. p. 302*)
Germany (?), early 20th century
Lazarus Posen Wwe.(?), active 1869–1930's
Silver: cast, chased
L 26.3 DIAM 4.4 cm
HALLMARKS: two marks, obliterated
DONOR: Dr. Harry G. Friedman

## 612

TORAH POINTER  F 4705  (*Illus. p. 302*)
Frankfurt am Main, late 19th–early 20th century
Lazarus Posen Wwe., active 1869–1930's
Silver: cast, repoussé, gilt
L 23.0 DIAM 2.0 cm
HALLMARKS: R³ 3; "800"
         MAKER: "POSEN"
DONOR: Dr. Harry G. Friedman

## 613

TORAH POINTER  F 306  (*Illus. p. 302*)
Germany, late 19th–early 20th century
Bronze: cast, silver-plated
L 28.6  DIAM 2.2 cm
HALLMARKS: none
DONOR: Dr. Harry G. Friedman

## 614

TORAH POINTER  F 2570  (*Illus. p. 302*)
Central Europe, late 19th–early 20th century
Silver: cast
L 18.6  W 1.7 cm
HALLMARKS: none
DONOR: Dr. Harry G. Friedman

## 615

TORAH POINTER  F 3917  (*Illus. p. 302*)
Hanau, early 20th century
Emil Freund, active early 20th century
Brass: cast, silver-plated
L 30.7  DIAM 2.1 cm
HALLMARKS: *MAKER: Hanau*, p. 96, 5th down
REMARKS: Cf. the similar pointer No. 616, also made by
    Freund.
DONOR: Dr. Harry G. Friedman

## 616

TORAH POINTER  F 3916  (*Illus. p. 302*)
Hanau, early 20th century
Emil Freund, active early 20th century
Silver: cast, chased, gilt
L 30.7  W 2.4 cm
HALLMARKS: R³ 3; "800"
         *MAKER: Hanau*, p. 96, 5th mark down.
REMARKS: Cf. the similar pointer No. 615 made by the same
    smith.
DONOR: Dr. Harry G. Friedman

## 617

TORAH POINTER  F 827  (*Illus. p. 302*)
Hanau, early 20th century
Emil Freund (?), active early 20th century
Silver: cast
L 24.0  W 2.3 cm
HALLMARKS: none
REMARKS: The hand is a left hand. Basing on identical cast-
    ings on pointer No. 616, this piece can be attributed to Emil
    Freund.
DONOR: Dr. Harry G. Friedman

## 618

TORAH POINTER  S 28  (*Illus. p. 302*)
Hanau, late 19th–early 20th century
Silver: cast, engraved, parcel-gilt
L 23.7  W 3.3 cm
HALLMARKS: none
PROVENANCE: The Hadji Ephraim and Mordecai Benguiat
    Family Collection
REMARKS: On the basis of the *Pappenheim Album* model No.
    664c, the maker was either Emil Freund or Gebruder Gut-
    gesell; cf. *Hanau*, p. 96. Cf. the similar pointer No. 619; and
    pointer No. 620, with an identical casting of the hand and
    cuff. For copies of this pointer design, made in the United
    States, see pointers Nos. 810–811. Numerous similar exam-
    ples have been published, e.g., *Mon. Jud.*, No. E 385, as-
    cribed to the 17th century.
DONOR: Museum purchase

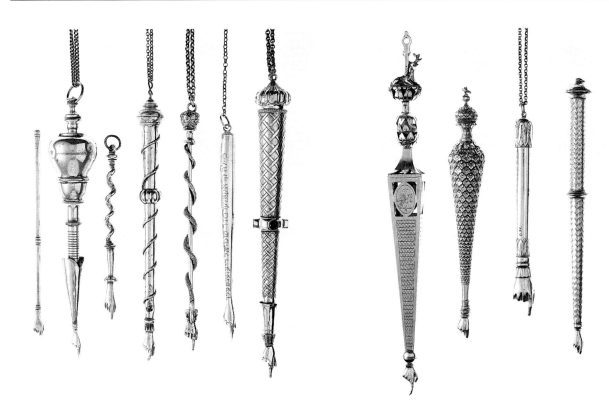

No. 771  F 3722;  No. 772  F 3096;  No. 773  D 45;  No. 774
D 47;  No. 777  F 2076;  No. 778  S 856;  No. 779  D 39

No. 780  F 5678;  No. 781  F 2742;  No. 782  D 32;
No. 783  F 5953

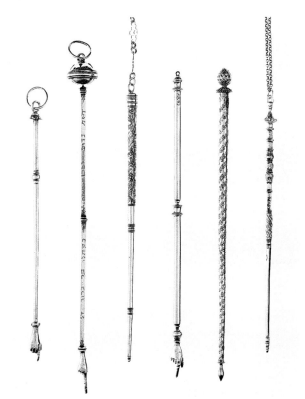

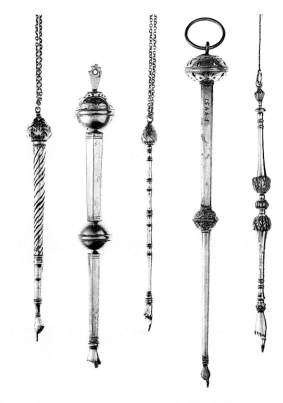

No. 784  F 4272;  No. 786  F 1597;  No. 852  F 5479;
No. 871  F 1542;  No. 881  S 26;  No. 878A  F 5476

No. 785  F 1920;  No. 787  F 3315;  No. 853  F 3710;
No. 877  F 4451;  No. 880  S 25

## 619

TORAH POINTER  F 5016  (*Illus. p. 302*)
Hanau (?), late 19th–early 20th century
Silver: cast
L 25.7  DIAM 2.6 cm
HALLMARKS: "800"
REMARKS: cf. the similar pointer No. 618, and the remarks there.
DONOR: Dr. Harry G. Friedman

## 620

TORAH POINTER  F 276  (*Illus. p. 302*)
Hanau (?), late 19th century
Silver: cast, gilt
L 35.0  DIAM 4.7 cm
HALLMARKS: none
REMARKS: Cf. pointer No. 618, with same hand-and-cuff casting.
DONOR: Dr. Harry G. Friedman

## 621

TORAH POINTER  F 2018  (*Illus. p. 304*)
Germany, late 19th–early 20th century
Silver: cast, gilt
L 16.6  W 2.1 cm
HALLMARKS: R³ 3; "800"; "W" (or "M")
REMARKS: This piece is relatively heavy and crudely made. Cf. the identical pointers Nos. 622, 623, and the similar pointer No. 624.
DONOR: Dr. Harry G. Friedman

## 622

TORAH POINTER  F 2809  (*Illus. p. 304*)
Germany, late 19th–early 20th century
Silver: cast, gilt
L 16.5  W 2.1 cm
HALLMARKS: "800"
REMARKS: Cf. the identical pointers Nos. 621, 623, and the similar pointer No. 624.
DONOR: Dr. Harry G. Friedman

## 623

TORAH POINTER  F 310  (*Illus. p. 304*)
Germany, 20th century
Silver: cast, chased
L 16.5  W 2.2 cm
HALLMARKS: none
REMARKS: Cf. the identical pointers Nos. 621–622, and the similar pointer No. 624.
DONOR: Dr. Harry G. Friedman

## 624

TORAH POINTER  F 3523  (*Illus. p. 304*)
Germany, late 19th–early 20th century
Silver: cast, chased, gilt
L 20.8  DIAM 1.5 cm
HALLMARKS: R³ 3; "800"
REMARKS: This poorly cast piece is relatively heavy. The hand may be a replacement. Cf. the similar pointers Nos. 621–623.
DONOR: Dr. Harry G. Friedman

## 625

TORAH POINTER  F 2797  (*Illus. p. 304*)
Germany, late 19th–early 20th century
Brass: cast, die-stamped, turned, plated
L 27.7  DIAM 3.5 cm
HALLMARKS: none
REMARKS: Pointers Nos. 625–634 seem to have been made in a single workshop. The traditional ascription to Germany is problematic, in the light of another group of pointers (Nos. 790–796), which is here attributed to the United States. The latter group includes inscriptions which indicate their American use. It is possible that both groups are actually from a common source, either in Europe or in the United States.
DONOR: Dr. Harry G. Friedman

## 626

TORAH POINTER  F 5959  (*Illus. p. 304*)
Germany, late 19th–early 20th century
Brass: cast, die-stamped, silver-plated
L 25.9  DIAM 3.6 cm
HALLMARKS: none
DONOR: Dr. Harry G. Friedman

## 627

TORAH POINTER  F 2443  (*Illus. p. 304*)
Germany, 19th century
Brass: cast, die-stamped, turned, plated
L 27.2  DIAM 3.5 cm
HALLMARKS: none
DONOR: Dr. Harry G. Friedman

## 628

TORAH POINTER  1987–63  (*Illus. p. 304*)
Germany, 19th century
Brass: cast, traces of silver-plating
L 26.7  DIAM 3.5 cm
HALLMARKS: none
INSCRIPTION: on shaft: יצחק בן אוריאל, "Isaac son of Uriel."
REMARKS: The hand is a left hand, an unusual feature on Torah pointers.

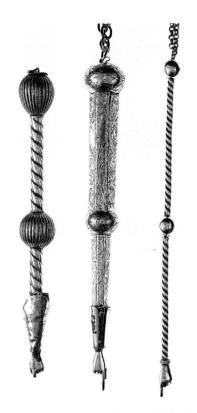
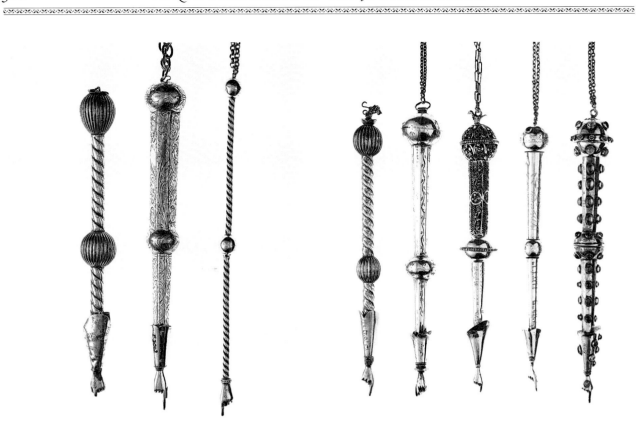

No. 794  F 290;  No. 804  F 3062;  No. 790  U 8542

No. 797  F 1967;  No. 799  JM 54–59;  No. 800  F 916;
No. 805  F 1342;  No. 806  F 5491

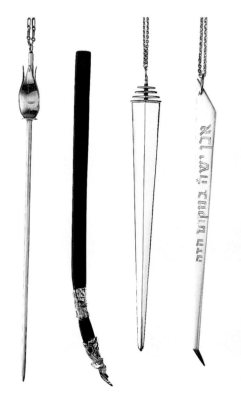
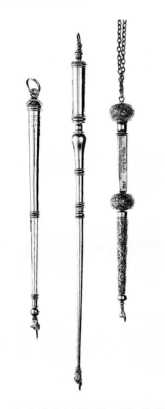

No. 813  JM 26–61;  No. 816B  1984–16;
No. 816  1992–162;  No. 815  1992–133

No. 817  F 5478;  No. 818  F 4668;  No. 819  F 4874

DONOR: Congregation Sheerith Israel of Janina, through Elias Matsas

## 629
TORAH POINTER  U 9178  (*Illus. p. 304*)
Germany, 19th century
Brass: cast, plated
L 26.1  DIAM 3.6 cm
HALLMARKS: none

## 630
TORAH POINTER  S 827  (*Illus. p. 304*)
Germany, late 19th–early 20th century
Brass: cast
L 33.5  DIAM 4.1 cm
HALLMARKS: none
DONOR: Mr. and Mrs. Al Schiff

## 631
TORAH POINTER  F 3795  (*Illus. p. 304*)
Germany, 1913 (inscription)
Silver: cast, engraved, silver-plated
L 26.5  DIAM 3.6 cm
HALLMARKS: none
INSCRIPTION: /ז״ן אתי טוראק בעד הילד זלמן רודאלף
ב׳ חשון ת׳ר׳ע׳ד׳, "This is the donation of Ettie Tourak on behalf of the boy Zalman Rudolph, 2 Heshvan (5)674" (=[Sunday,] November 2, 1913)
REMARKS: The hand of the pointer is a left hand, an unusual feature.
DONOR: Dr. Harry G. Friedman

## 632
TORAH POINTER  F 271  (*Illus. p. 304*)
Germany (?), 19th century
Brass: cast, plated
L 27.6  DIAM 3.0 cm
HALLMARKS: none
REMARKS: The hand of the pointer is a left hand, an unusual feature.
DONOR: Dr. Harry G. Friedman

## 633
TORAH POINTER  F 2047  (*Illus. p. 304*)
Europe, late 19th–early 20th century
Brass: cast, "gilt"
L 29.5  DIAM 4.0 cm
HALLMARKS: none
DONOR: Dr. Harry G. Friedman

## 634
TORAH POINTER  F 2317  (*Illus. p. 304*)
Germany, late 19th–early 20th century
Brass: cast, die-stamped, silver-plated
L 29.8  DIAM 2.7 cm
HALLMARKS: none
DONOR: Dr. Harry G. Friedman

## 635
TORAH POINTER  F 270  (*Illus. p. 304*)
Germany, early 20th century
Silver: cast
L 27.0  DIAM 2.0 cm
HALLMARKS: $R^3$ 3 or 5
DONOR: Dr. Harry G. Friedman

## 636
TORAH POINTER  JM 17–66  (*Illus. p. 304*)
Berlin, 1960
Michael Langner
Silver: cast, parcel-gilt
L 36.8  DIAM 4.2 cm
HALLMARKS: "900"
          *MAKER:* "ML"
DONOR: Mrs Albert A. List

## 637
TORAH POINTER  JM 49–52  (*Illus. p. 304*)
Germany, ca. 1930
Ludwig Wolpert, active 1920's–1981
Silver: cast (?), chased
L 22.6  DIAM 1.3 cm
HALLMARKS: "800"; "WOLPERT" (engraved)
REMARKS: This is the only piece by Wolpert at The Jewish Museum which was made by him while he was still in Germany.
DONOR: Jewish Cultural Reconstruction

## 638
TORAH POINTER  F 3721  (*Illus. p. 306*)
Austrian Empire, early 19th century
Silver: cast, die-stamped
L 30.6  DIAM 2.5 cm
HALLMARKS: *CITY:* indistinct Austrian Empire mark
          *MAKER:* illegible
DONOR: Dr. Harry G. Friedman

## 639
TORAH POINTER  F 2504  (*Illus. p. 306*)
Austro-Hungarian Empire, mid-19th century
Silver: chased, engraved, traces of gilt

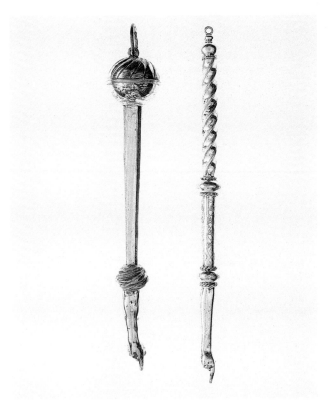

No. 820  F 5952;  No. 821  F 3635

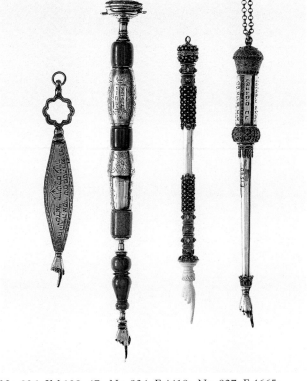

No. 826  JM 108–47;  No. 834  F 4419;  No. 827  F 4665;
No. 828  F 1540

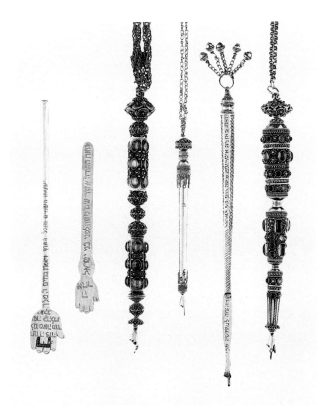

No. 841  F 3231;  No. 845  F 3235;  No. 898b  F 2219;
No. 847  1987–61;  No. 848  F 2220;  No. 849  1989–149

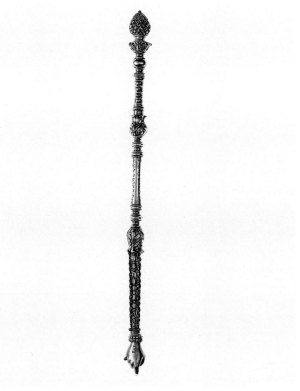

No. 851  JM 86–48

L 24.7  DIAM 2.4 cm

HALLMARKS: *CITY:* indistinct Austro-Hungarian mark, mid-19th century, with "13" at center, surrounded by date

INSCRIPTION: on medial knop: ם / ת, (?)

REMARKS: The significance of the inscription is unknown.

DONOR: Dr. Harry G. Friedman

## 640

TORAH POINTER  F 291  (*Illus. p. 306*)

Scheibbs, late 19th century

Silver: cast, chased

L 21.2  DIAM 3.0 cm

HALLMARKS: *CITY:* Rohrwasser, p. 19, 2nd row (750 large, with "A4")

INSCRIPTION: Erased.

DONOR: Dr. Harry G. Friedman

## 641

TORAH POINTER  D 18  (*Illus. p. 306*)

Austro-Hungarian Empire, late 19th century

Silver: cast, engraved

L 23.8  DIAM 3.1 cm

HALLMARKS: none

INSCRIPTION: on upper cuff: "W."

PROVENANCE: The Weinberg Synagogue, Danzig

REMARKS: The letter inscribed on the cuff indicates this pointer belonged to the Weinberg Congregation of Danzig.

BIBLIOGRAPHY: *Danzig 1939/1982*, No. 250

DONOR: The Jewish Community of Danzig

## 642

TORAH POINTER  F 5657  (*Illus. p. 306*)

Austro-Hungarian Empire (?), late 19th–20th century

Silver: filigree, cast, chased, pierced

L 33.3  DIAM 4.7 cm

HALLMARKS: none

DONOR: Dr. Harry G. Friedman

## 643

TORAH POINTER  D 27  (*Illus. p. 306*)

Austro-Hungarian Empire, second half of 19th century

Silver: cast, chased

L 23.1  DIAM 3.0 cm

HALLMARKS: none

BIBLIOGRAPHY: *Danzig 1939/1982*, No. 244

DONOR: The Jewish Community of Danzig

## 644

TORAH POINTER  F 3519  (*Illus. p. 306*)

Austro-Hungarian Empire, 1862–1922

Silver: cast, chased, engraved, gilt

L 30.9  DIAM 2.1 cm

HALLMARKS: *CITY:* Rohrwasser, p. 19, second row (800 small) (?) — indistinct

*MAKER:* "SI" or "IS"

DONOR: Dr. Harry G. Friedman

## 645

TORAH POINTER  F 2442  (*Illus. p. 306*)

Austria (?), late 19th century

Silver: cast

L 32.4  DIAM 2.9 cm

HALLMARKS: none

DONOR: Dr. Harry G. Friedman

## 646

TORAH POINTER  F 2450  (*Illus. p. 306*)

Austria (?), 1929/30 (inscription)

Silver: cast, engraved

L 26.2  DIAM 2.4 cm

HALLMARKS: none

INSCRIPTION: ז'נ' בן ציון שלעזינגער ת'ר'צ', "This was donated by Ben-Zion Schlesinger, (5)690" (=1929/30)

DONOR: Dr. Harry G. Friedman

## 647

TORAH POINTER  F 273  (*Illus. p. 306*)

Austro-Hungarian Empire, late 19th–early 20th century

Silver (?): cast, chased, gilt

L 25.3  DIAM 3.7 cm

HALLMARKS: none

REMARKS: Cf. pointers Nos. 648–650. This type is probably derived from the Viennese type represented, e.g., by pointer No. 658.

DONOR: Dr. Harry G. Friedman

## 648

TORAH POINTER  D 38  (*Illus. p. 306*)

Austro-Hungarian Empire (?), late 19th–early 20th century

Silver: cast, chased

L 29.5  DIAM 4.3 cm

HALLMARKS: none

REMARKS: Cf. pointers Nos. 647 and 649–650.

BIBLIOGRAPHY: *Danzig 1939/1982*, No. 246

DONOR: The Jewish Community of Danzig

## 649

TORAH POINTER  JM 60–55  (*Illus. p. 306*)

Austro-Hungarian Empire (?), early 20th century

Silver: cast, chased

L 26.8  DIAM 4.0 cm

HALLMARKS: none

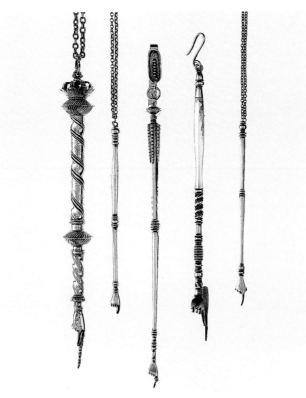

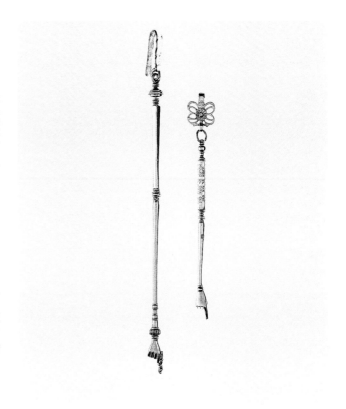

No. 854   F 3518;   No. 857   F 3050;   No. 858   JM 6–53;           No. 855   F 3648;   No. 856   F 3665
No. 859   F 5629;   No. 860   F 917

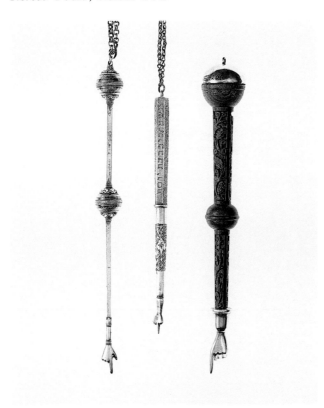

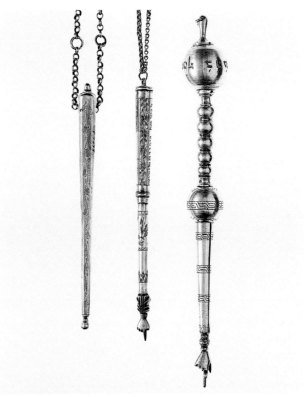

No. 861   F 281;   No. 866   F 4459;   No. 867   F 4206         No. 865   F 4479;   No. 878   F 4458;   No. 865a   1993–244

REMARKS: Cf. pointers Nos. 647–648 and 650, which are similar.

DONOR: Mrs. Bernard Kahn

# 650

TORAH POINTER   JM 34–56   (*Illus. p. 306*)
Austria, early 20th century
Silver: die-stamped, cast
L 17.3   DIAM 2.4 cm
HALLMARKS: none
REMARKS: Cf. pointers Nos. 647–649.
DONOR: Mark Schweid

# 651

TORAH POINTER   F 3426   (*Illus. p. 306*)
Austro-Hungarian Empire, 1872–1922
Silver: cast
L 21.2   DIAM 2.4 cm
HALLMARKS: *CITY:* Rohrwasser, p. 19, second row, right (800; city letter illegible)
          *MAKER:* "WM" in rectangle
DONOR: Dr. Harry G. Friedman

# 652

TORAH POINTER   F 2404
Vienna, 1807–14
Silver: cast, chased, engine-turned
L 25.3   DIAM 2.1 cm
HALLMARKS: *CITY:* Rohrwasser, p. 13, second row, left
          *MAKER:* Illegible
DONOR: Dr. Harry G. Friedman

# 653

TORAH POINTER   F 1044   (*Illus. p. 306*)
Vienna, 1820's or later
Silver: filigree, cast
L 19.3   DIAM 3.7 cm
HALLMARKS: *CITY:* Rohrwasser, p. 13, upper (?)
          *MAKER:* "BC" in script, in oval
DONOR: Dr. Harry G. Friedman

# 654

TORAH POINTER   F 934   (*Illus. p. 306*)
Vienna, 1872–1922
Silver: chased, gilt; coral; semiprecious stones
L 22.4   DIAM 2.6 cm
HALLMARKS: Rohrwasser, p. 19, second row, right (750)
BIBLIOGRAPHY: Kayser, No. 61
DONOR: Dr. Harry G. Friedman

# 655

TORAH POINTER   F 289   (*Illus. p. 306*)
Vienna, 1872–1922
Johann Ziehrer, active 1878–1908
Silver: cast, chased
L 25.3   DIAM 2.7 cm
HALLMARKS: *CITY:* Rohrwasser, p. 19, second row (800, large)
          *MAKER:* "JZ" in oval
REMARKS: See the identical pointer No. 656 and pointer fragment No. 664, as well as shields Nos. 117–118 and finials No. 326, by the same smith.
DONOR: Dr. Harry G. Friedman

# 656

TORAH POINTER   F 2302   (*Illus. p. 308*)
Vienna, 1872–1922
Johann Ziehrer, active 1878–1908
Silver: cast, chased
L 24.1   DIAM 2.8 cm
HALLMARKS: *CITY:* Rohrwasser, p. 19, 800, small
          *MAKER:* "JZ" in oval
REMARKS: See pointer No. 655 for parallels.
DONOR: Dr. Harry G. Friedman

# 657

TORAH POINTER   F 884   (*Illus. p. 306*)
Vienna (?), late 19th century
Silver: cast, chased; brass (hand)
L 18.3   DIAM 4.1 cm
HALLMARKS: none
INSCRIPTION: on upper shaft: אליעזר, "Eliezer"; on lower shaft: בר ארי'/ הלוי: עז'חמ', "Son of Aryeh Halevi, with his spouse H ... M ...(?)."
REMARKS: See the similar pointers Nos. 655–656 and 658–661.
DONOR: Dr. Harry G. Friedman

# 658

TORAH POINTER   F 2313   (*Illus. p. 306*)
Vienna (?), late 19th–early 20th century
Brass: chased, silver-plated
L 25.6   DIAM 3.4 cm
HALLMARKS: none
REMARKS: See the similar pointers Nos. 654–657 and 659–661.
DONOR: Dr. Harry G. Friedman

# 659

TORAH POINTER   F 2449   (*Illus. p. 308*)
Vienna, 1872–1922
Silver: cast, chased
L 25.6   DIAM 2.8 cm
HALLMARKS: *CITY:* Rohrwasser, p. 19, second row (800 small)
          *MAKER:* "M.S" in truncated rectangle

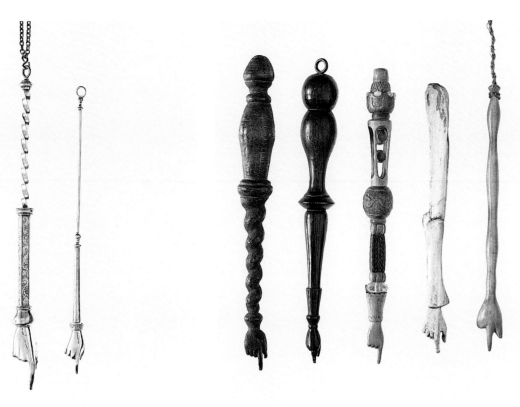

No. 868  F 2265;  No. 870  F 2527

No. 894  F 5950;  No. 896  F 5949;  No. 764A  M 296;
No. 898  F 2569;  No. 891A  D 48

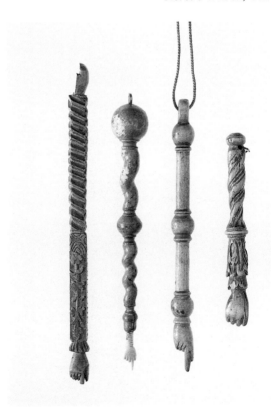

No. 557  JM 101–47;  No. 889  M 373;  No. 893  F 4848;
No. 895  JM 14–52

REMARKS: Cf. the similar pointers Nos. 655–658 and 660–661.
DONOR: Dr. Harry G. Friedman

## 660

TORAH POINTER  F 2464  (*Illus. p. 308*)
Vienna, 1872–1922
H. Sudfeld & Co., active late 19th–early 20th century
Silver: chased, cast, traces of gilt
L 28.3  DIAM 4.5 cm
HALLMARKS:  CITY: Rohrwasser, p. 19, second row (800 small)
MAKER: Neuwirth 1976, No. 240
REMARKS: A small shield (חצי כתר) from the Dubrovnik syn-
agogue bears the same hallmarks; cf. *Dubrovnik*. Cf. the
similar pointers Nos. 655–659 and 661.
DONOR: Dr. Harry G. Friedman

## 661

TORAH POINTER  F 5961  (*Illus. p. 308*)
Vienna (?), late 19th–early 20th century
Brass and copper: cast, chased, traces of silver-plating
L 28.3  DIAM 3.2 cm
HALLMARKS: none
REMARKS: Cf. the similar pointers Nos. 655–660.
DONOR: Dr. Harry G. Friedman

## 662

TORAH POINTER  F 2505  (*Illus. p. 308*)
Vienna (?), 1872–1922
Silver: cast, chased, engraved
L 26.3  DIAM 3.0 cm
HALLMARKS:  CITY: Rohrwasser, p. 15, top left (?)
MAKER: "J.V" in rectangle
INSCRIPTION: on upper knop: עשהו אברהם נתן ראזע בערג,
"It was made by Abraham Nathan Rose(n ?)berg"; on
upper shaft: נדבה מאת כ"ה ארי בן יהודה צבי ס'ג'ל/
ס' בעשעניא, "Gift from ... Rabbi Ari son of Judah Zvi Segal
...(?)"
REMARKS: The Editor has suggested interpreting the final
word of the inscription as "in Essegney," south of Nancy on
the Moselle. Cf. the similar pointer No. 663.
DONOR: Dr. Harry G. Friedman

## 663

TORAH POINTER  F 5404
Vienna, after 1872
Silver: cast
L 27.7  DIAM 2.5 cm
HALLMARKS: "G K" in oval (cf. Neuwirth 1976, Nos. 827–28)
REMARKS: cf. the similar pointer No. 662.
DONOR: Dr. Harry G. Friedman

## 664

TORAH POINTER (fragment)  F 312
Vienna, 1872–1922
Johann Ziehrer, active 1878–1908
Silver: cast, chased, engraved
L 15.0  DIAM 2.0 cm
HALLMARKS:  CITY: Rohrwasser, p. 19 (800, large)
MAKER: "JZ" in oval
REMARKS: Cf. pointers Nos. 655 and 656, by the same smith.
DONOR: Dr. Harry G. Friedman

## 665

TORAH POINTER (fragment)  U 8726
Vienna, 1872–1922
Silver: cast, gilt
L 9.7  W 1.6 cm
HALLMARKS:  CITY: Rohrwasser, p. 19, second row, middle (800)
MAKER: "CS" or "GS" in oval (?)
REMARKS: Broken off at the lower knop.

## 666

TORAH POINTER  F 2389
Vienna, 1922–1938
Julius Thurin, active 1st half of 20th century
Silver: cast, chased
L 12.5  DIAM 1.2 cm
HALLMARKS:  CITY: Rohrwasser, p. 33 (Silber 800); "800"
MAKER: Neuwirth, No. 1394
REMARKS: In *Gardens*, No. 188, this pointer was regarded as
Italian, in accord with Museum records ("Italy, 17th–18th
century, silver-plated brass").
BIBLIOGRAPHY: *Gardens*, No. 188
DONOR: Dr. Harry G. Friedman

## 667

TORAH POINTER  F 5488  (*Illus. p. 308*)
Czernowitz, 1789
Silver: cast, engraved, traces of gilt
L 24.3  DIAM 1.8 cm
HALLMARKS: Rohrwasser, p. 55.
INSCRIPTION: on upper shaft: זּינ' ה'נ' האשה מרת גיטל תה"י/
ע"ב יוסף נ"י ווּיסבער/ עבור ערשטע ניישטעטער החברה,
"This was donated by ... the woman ...Gittel ..., with her
husband Joseph Weisber(g ?), for the First Neustadter
Society"; on lower shaft: possible traces of script
REMARKS: See *NY Register* 1917, p. 200b, for the First Neu-
stadter Congregation.
DONOR: Dr. Harry G. Friedman

## 668

### TORAH POINTER   F 296   (*Illus. p. 308*)
Kaschau (?), 18th century
Silver: cast, pierced, chased
L 24.2   DIAM 4.1 cm
HALLMARKS: *CITY:* cf. Kőszeghy 808–820
            *MAKER:* "C/BL"
REMARKS: This pointer has been repaired. A later disk, soldered to the end of the upper knop, was made from a silver coin of the Austrian empire (now ca. 1.8 cm in diam), inscribed: "...E CAROL*D:G ... AUSTRIA IM...."
DONOR: Dr. Harry G. Friedman

## 669

### TORAH POINTER   F 5947
Pressburg (Bratislava), 1816 (?)
Fridericus Becker, Sr., active ca. 1800–27
Silver: cast, engraved
L 28.2   DIAM 2.3 cm
HALLMARKS: *CITY:* cf. Kőszeghy 1823
            *MAKER:* Kőszeghy 1853/1855(?)
REMARKS: See pointer No. 670, by Fridericus Becker, Jr. A Jewish Cultural Reconstruction identification tag is attached to this piece.
DONOR: Jewish Cultural Reconstruction

## 670

### TORAH POINTER   U 9183
Pressburg, 1837 (?)
Fridericus Becker, Jr., active 1830's–ca. 1848
Silver: cast, engraved
L 26.0   DIAM 2.4 cm
HALLMARKS: *CITY:* similar to Kőszeghy 1831
            *MAKER:* Kőszeghy 1864/65
REMARKS: Cf. pointer No. 669, by the smith's father.

## 671

### TORAH POINTER   F 5946   (*Illus. p. 308*)
Brünn (Brno) (?), 1806–24, or earlier
Silver: cast, chased, pierced
L 26.1   DIAM 3.4 cm
HALLMARKS: Rohrwasser, p. 52, bottom, left ("F" — tax)
DONOR: Dr. Harry G. Friedman

## 672

### TORAH POINTER   F 2440
Steinamangen (Szombathely), early 19th century
Joseph Bruckner, active ca. 1828
Silver: cast
L 30.2   DIAM 2.1 cm

HALLMARKS: *CITY:* Kőszeghy 2078
            *MAKER:* Kőszeghy 2083
REMARKS: See pointer No. 673, possibly from the same city.
DONOR: Dr. Harry G. Friedman

## 673

### TORAH POINTER   F 298
Steinamangen (Szombathely)(?), early 19th century
Silver: cast, chased, filigree, parcel-gilt; ruby
L 25.0   DIAM 2.8 cm
HALLMARKS: *CITY:* Kőszeghy 2078 (?), or 1810–11
INSCRIPTION: On square upper shaft: ש . . . ז"ה שייך להק' ר ב
    תק/. . . לפק, "This pointer belongs to the leader ... B ... sh ... [5]5.." (=sometime before 1840)
REMARKS: The filigree piece is probably not original. Cf. pointer No. 672, possibly from the same city.
DONOR: Dr. Harry G. Friedman

## 674

### TORAH POINTER   F 300   (*Illus. p. 308*)
Austro-Hungarian Empire, 1820
Silver: cast, engraved; traces of gilt; garnet
L 33.9   DIAM 3.8 cm
HALLMARKS: Rohrwasser, p. 59 (?)
DONOR: Dr. Harry G. Friedman

## 675

### TORAH POINTER   X 1952–35
Budapest, 1834(?)
Franciscus (Ferenc) Schmidt, active 1820–ca. 1865
Silver: cast, chased
L 33.1   DIAM 2.6 cm
HALLMARKS: *CITY:* Kőszeghy 315/316, but with 1834(?)
            *MAKER:* Kőszeghy 523
REMARKS: Cf. pointer No. 676, and the references there.
DONOR: Jewish Cultural Reconstruction

## 676

### TORAH POINTER   U 9180   (*Illus. p. 308*)
Budapest, 1844
Franciscus (Ferenc) Schmidt, active 1820–ca. 1865
Silver: cast
L 22.0   DIAM 2.1 cm
HALLMARKS: *CITY:* Kőszeghy 417
            *MAKER:* Kőszeghy 523
REMARKS: An upper knop seems to be missing. See pointer No. 675, and a Levite ewer and an alms box (Budapest 1987, Nos. 56 and 63), all by the same smith.

## 677

### TORAH POINTER   F 4509   (*Illus. p. 308*)
Szekesfehervar (?), mid–19th century(?); dated 1933/34

Silver: cast, chased, engraved

L 25.6  DIAM 3.3 cm

HALLMARKS: *CITY:* Kőszeghy 1866 (var.) or 2048 (var.) (?)
MAKER: "WB", script in ligature (? — or "13"?)

INSCRIPTION: on upper shaft, in Latin characters: "Gotzl Lipot es neje/ adomanya/ 5694" ("Leopold Gotzl donated it, 1933/34")

REMARKS: One or two additional lines are erased at the end of the inscription.

DONOR: Dr. Harry G. Friedman

# 678

TORAH POINTER  U 9175  (*Illus. p. 308*)

Hungary (?), mid–19th century

Silver: cast, filigree, engraved

L 26.9  DIAM 3.9 cm

HALLMARKS: none

INSCRIPTION: on upper shaft: שייך לה״ק ר׳ אברהם תרל(?!) דקק זעקאווי/ ל׳ אן כא יבא גואל צדק בקרוב/ לז נש בצלאל ב״ר אליעזר הכהן כץ, "Belonging to the leader Avraham Tarel(?) of the holy community of Zekawi (?) . . . . May the savior of righteousness come soon; in memory of the soul of Bezalel son of Eliezer ha-Kohen Katz"

REMARKS: The last line of the inscription is a later addition. "Zekawi(?)" might be Szekely, 90 km E of Miskolcz.

DONOR: Jewish Cultural Reconstruction

# 679

TORAH POINTER  U 9179  (*Illus. p. 308*)

Raab (Gyor), 1854(?)

Bernardus Friedman, active 1852–71

Silver: cast, engraved, pierced

L 30.9  DIAM 4.1 cm

HALLMARKS: *CITY:* Rohrwasser, p. 68 (like 1851, but 1854 ?)
MAKER: Kőszeghy 767

DONOR: Jewish Cultural Reconstruction

# 680

TORAH POINTER  F 4494  (*Illus. p. 308*)

Grosswardein (Oradea), 19th century

Silver: cast, filigree, chased, parcel-gilt

L 22.1  DIAM 2.2 cm

HALLMARKS: *CITY:* Kőszeghy 1522–34, 41 (?)
MAKER: "AM" in rectangle

DONOR: Dr. Harry G. Friedman

# 681

TORAH POINTER  F 3244  (*Illus. p. 308*)

Hungary, early 20th century

Silver (?): cast

L 22.5  W 1.7 cm

HALLMARKS: none

INSCRIPTION: on shaft: *D*r *Liebermann Erno/ Ajandeka*, "Donated by Dr. Erno Liebermann"

DONOR: Dr. Harry G. Friedman

# 681A

TORAH POINTER  F 5960

Hungary, after 1937

Silver: filigree, cast

L 23.5  DIAM 1.6 cm

HALLMARKS: partially obliterated Hungarian mark, after 1937; "T" in circle; unclear mark (maker's?)

INSCRIPTION: traces on the upper shaft

DONOR: Dr. Harry G. Friedman

# 682

TORAH POINTER  F 829

19th century

Wood: carved

L 21.2  W 2.9 cm

HALLMARKS: none

DONOR: Dr. Harry G. Friedman

# 683

TORAH POINTER  F 75  (*Illus. p. 308*)

Galicia (?), 1753/54 (inscription)

Silver: filigree, cast, chased

L 27.5  DIAM 3.3 cm

HALLMARKS: none

INSCRIPTION: on upper arm: יד הלז שייך להחברא/ חייטים הקובעי׳ שיעור מידי/ שבת בשבתו אצל הרב מ׳ יואל/ דיין בר א׳ד׳ ע׳י הכשרי׳ והפרנסים/ והגבאים והנאמנים דבאי/ שתא יד׳ר׳ש׳ לטובה ליפ׳ק, "This pointer belongs to the Society of Tailors who establish a study session every Sabbath with the Rabbi, our Teacher, Joel Dayan son of A . . . Dayan(?), [commissioned] by the Worthies and Officers and Treasurers and Trustees of those who attend. Year 'May he expound for a good purpose' (chronogram, [5]514)" (=1753/54)

DONOR: Dr. Harry G. Friedman

# 684

TORAH POINTER  M 114  (*Illus. p. 310*)

Galicia, 1759/60 (inscription)

Silver: cast, chased, parcel-gilt

L 25.5  DIAM 3.7 cm

HALLMARKS: none

INSCRIPTION: זאת נדבו החבר היקר נשא(?) עשירי איש כמתנת/ ידו לפרט והיה כ׳אש׳ר יר׳ים משה ידו וגבר ישראל לפק, "This was donated by the associat[es], the honorabl[es], . . ., the wealthy, 'each with his own gift' (Deuteronomy 16:17), (chronogram, Exodus 17:11 =[5]520 (=1759/60)"

PROVENANCE: The Rose and Benjamin Mintz Collection

REMARKS: Cf. similar pointers Nos. 685–689; and Furman, No. 12; Stieglitz, No. 36; PBNY 1970, No. 97; and Köln 1980, No. 32.
DONOR: Museum purchase

## 685

TORAH POINTER   JM 32–64   (*Illus. p. 310*)
Lvov (?), late 18th–early 19th century
Silver: cast, chased, pierced, engraved, parcel-gilt; garnet
L 27.8   DIAM 3.9 cm
HALLMARKS: *CITY:* Rohrwasser, p. 11, top, left ("12 D"); p. 12, bottom, left and right; p. 13, top, left (D) — all re-marks and tax stamps; and cf. p. 62
INSCRIPTION: on upper knop: ז״נ האלוף המרומם מהורר יעקב בן מהרר יהודא ליב כ״ץ, "This is the donation of Jacob son of Judah Leib Katz"
REMARKS: The floral motif of the upper knop is inhabited by a pair of griffins supporting a Levitic laver, and a pair of lions supporting a pair of priestly hands. The similar lower knop is inhabited by a running stag, an eagle and a leopard — a reference to Pirke Avot 5: 23. The motifs on the upper knop may refer to the donor's priestly rank, expressed in the inscription by the word "Katz", an abbreviation for "Priest of Righteousness" that was often used as a family name. The garnet in the ring on the index finger is not original. Cf. the parallels cited under pointer No. 684.
DONOR: Purim Ball Fund

## 686

TORAH POINTER   M 279   (*Illus. p. 310*)
Galicia (?), early 19th century
Silver: cast, chased
L 21.9   DIAM 3.5 cm
HALLMARKS: none
PROVENANCE: The Rose and Benjamin Mintz Collection
REMARKS: The hand appears to be a replacement. Cf. the parallels cited under pointer No. 684.
DONOR: Museum purchase

## 687

TORAH POINTER   D 42   (*Illus. p. 310*)
Galicia, 19th century
Silver: cast, chased; brass
L 28.5   DIAM 4.5 cm
HALLMARKS: none
REMARKS: The index finger has been restored in brass. Cf. the parallels cited under pointer No. 684.
BIBLIOGRAPHY: *Danzig 1939*, No. 247
DONOR: The Jewish Community of Danzig

## 688

TORAH POINTER   M 19   (*Illus. p. 310*)
Galicia, 1800/01 (inscription)

Silver: cast, pierced, chased, engraved, parcel-gilt; glass
L 28.9   DIAM 4.0 cm
HALLMARKS: none
INSCRIPTIONS: on upper shaft: זה (!) היד שייך להאלו/ הרר יהודה ברץ זל עם/ אישתו יטה, "This pointer belongs to the leader, the late Judah Baratz with his wife Yetta"; on lower shaft: בשנת תקסא/ לפ״ק, "In the year (5)561" (=1800/01)
PROVENANCE: The Rose and Benjamin Mintz Collection
REMARKS: Cf. the parallels cited under pointer No. 684.
DONOR: Museum purchase

## 689

TORAH POINTER   D 16   (*Illus. p. 310*)
Galicia, 1833/34 (inscription)
Silver: cast, chased
L 25.8   DIAM 3.8 cm
HALLMARKS: none
INSCRIPTION: on upper knop: שייך לקהל ד׳ק׳ק׳ מאטעננבודען תקצד לפ׳ק׳, "Belonging to the Holy Congregation of Mattenbuden, (5)594" (=1833/34)
PROVENANCE: The Mattenbuden Synagogue, Danzig
REMARKS: See the parallels cited under pointer No. 684.
BIBLIOGRAPHY: Danzig 1933, No. 48; *Danzig 1939/1982*, No. 236
DONOR: The Jewish Community of Danzig

## 690

TORAH POINTER   F 4078   (*Illus. p. 310*)
Galicia, early 19th century
Silver: cast, chased, gilt
L 13.2   W 1.1 cm
HALLMARKS: none
REMARKS: In *Gardens*, No. 187, this pointer was published as Italian, following information in Museum records. Cf. the similar pointers No. 691; and Kantsedikas, No. 74a–c (misascribed to late 19th-century Germany).
BIBLIOGRAPHY: *Gardens*, No. 187
DONOR: Dr. Harry G. Friedman

## 691

TORAH POINTER   M 116   (*Illus. p. 310*)
Lvov (?), early 19th century
Silver: cast, chased, gilt
L 16.2   W 2.5 cm
HALLMARKS: Rohrwasser, p. 62 (D)
PROVENANCE: The Rose and Benjamin Mintz Collection
REMARKS: Cf. the parallels cited under pointer No. 690, as well as the identical pointer in *JL* V, pl. clxxiii, 6th from the top.
DONOR: Museum purchase

# 692

TORAH POINTER  F 2590  (*Illus. p. 310*)
Galicia (?), late 18th–early 19th century
Silver: cast, chased, engraved
L 16.3  DIAM 3.2 cm
HALLMARKS: none
REMARKS: Cf. Klagsbald 1982, No. 49; Rosenan, No. 17 (with a "13" mark and a master's mark reading "IHS").
BIBLIOGRAPHY: Kayser, No. 58
DONOR: Dr. Harry G. Friedman

# 693

TORAH POINTER  F 5314  (*Illus. p. 310*)
20th century
Galicia (?), Silver: cast, spun, chased, punched
L 27.0  DIAM 4.5 cm
HALLMARKS: none
REMARKS: This pointer is one of several copies of a pointer in the Musée de Cluny. See Klagsbald 1982, No. 49; Harvard, No. 81; Sotheby's NY 1988, No. 265; and see similar pointer No. 692.
DONOR: Dr. Harry G. Friedman

# 694

TORAH POINTER  F 2017  (*Illus. p. 308*)
Galicia (?), 1803/04 (inscription)
Silver
L 20.8  DIAM 2.8 cm
HALLMARKS: none
INSCRIPTION: on two sides of the upper shaft: שלמה זלמן ראזען, /לפרט שנת תקסד לפק, "Solomon Zalman Rosen, [in the] year (5)564" (=1803/04)
REMARKS: Cf. the similar pointer No. 695.
DONOR: Dr. Harry G. Friedman

# 695

TORAH POINTER  F 305  (*Illus. p. 310*)
Galicia (?), first half of the 19th century
Silver: cast, pierced, engraved
L 25.1  DIAM 3.3 cm
HALLMARKS: none
REMARKS: Cf. the similar pointer No. 694.
DONOR: Dr. Harry G. Friedman

# 696

TORAH POINTER  F 4076  (*Illus. p. 310*)
Lvov (?), early 19th century
Silver: cast, punched, chased, engraved, pierced; brass
L 16.8  DIAM 3.7 cm
HALLMARKS: Rohrwasser, p. 11, 2nd group, "D"

REMARKS: The shaft seems to have been shortened, and a medial knop is probably missing.
DONOR: Dr. Harry G. Friedman

# 697

TORAH POINTER  S 1363c  (*Illus. p. 310*)
Galicia (?), early 19th century
Silver: cast, filigree, engraved
L 29.5  DIAM 5.2 cm
HALLMARKS: none
DONOR: Max M. Karp

# 698

TORAH POINTER  F 5335  (*Illus. p. 310*)
Galicia (?), 19th century
Silver: filigree, cast
L 26.3  DIAM 4.1 cm
HALLMARKS: none
REMARKS: Cf. the similar pointer in Altshuler, No. 60, ill. on p. 122.
DONOR: Dr. Harry G. Friedman

# 699

TORAH POINTER  D 46  (*Illus. p. 310*)
Galicia (?), mid-19th century
Silver: filigree, stamped, cast, parcel-gilt; coral: carved
L 23.9  DIAM 3.9 cm
HALLMARKS: none
PROVENANCE: The Gieldzinski Collection, Danzig
REMARKS: The lower shaft and the coral hand appear to be replacements.
BIBLIOGRAPHY: Danzig 1904, No. 33; *JL* V, pl. clxxii, 6th from top; Danzig 1933, No. 46; *Danzig 1939/1982*, No. 241
DONOR: The Jewish Community of Danzig

# 700

TORAH POINTER  F 2319  (*Illus. p. 310*)
Poland, mid-19th century
A.M. Silber
Silver: filigree, cast, engraved, parcel-gilt
L 39.9  DIAM 7.5 cm
HALLMARKS: "12"/"AMZ"; "12"/"A.M. Silber" in script
PROVENANCE: M. Mirsky & Son, New York
REMARKS: The index finger has been replaced. For a Torah shield by the same smith, see No. 200. Some of the filigree elements on this pointer are similar to those on a pointer formerly at the Jewish Museum (F 2354, marked "JS" and "13," and is similar to unmarked pointer No. 701).
BIBLIOGRAPHY: Kanof, fig. 36
DONOR: Dr. Harry G. Friedman

## 701

TORAH POINTER　F 4602　(*Illus. p. 310*)
Poland, mid-19th century
Silver: cast, filigree
L 34.3　DIAM 4.8 cm
HALLMARKS: none
PROVENANCE: Ben Ari Arts, New York
REMARKS: Cf. the remarks under pointer No. 700.
DONOR: Dr. Harry G. Friedman

## 702

TORAH POINTER　JM 57–52　(*Illus. p. 310*)
Galicia (?), 19th century
Silver: cast, engraved, chased; agate
L 18.4　DIAM 1.2 cm
HALLMARKS: Rohrwasser, p. 13, top, right (tax).
REMARKS: The upper stone is a replacement, and possibly the hand is, as well.
DONOR: Lucille and Samuel Lemberg

## 703

TORAH POINTER　F 1545　(*Illus. p. 310*)
Trembowla (?), 1898 (inscription)
Silver: cast, chased, engraved
L 30.5　DIAM 4.0 cm
HALLMARKS: none
INSCRIPTION: on lower shaft: זאת נדב החתן/ להח' ע'/ טרעמבאוולא ק' א' פ' ג' חשון/ פרעזענטעט פאן/ היינריך ציפפערבלאט, "This was donated by the bridegroom to the Assistance Society(?), Trembowla . . . o[fficers], l[eaders] and t[reasurers] (?), 3 Ḥeshvan [in the year 5659]. Presented by Heinrich Zifferblat"; and in Latin script: "H Z 1898"
REMARKS: The upper knop and arm are from a walking-stick. The date would appear to be October 19, 1898. Trembowla is 135 km SW of Lvov. The inscription here, however, may indicate that this pointer was presented to an immigrant association in the United States. See *NY Register*, p. 827b for the Trembowler Young Friends Society.
DONOR: Dr. Harry G. Friedman

## 704

TORAH POINTER　F 2592　(*Illus. p. 312*)
Poland (?), 1769/70 (inscription)
Silver: cast, filigree, engraved, nielloed
L 13.0　DIAM 1.5 cm
HALLMARKS: none
INSCRIPTION: on upper shaft: הבחור שמואל בהרר מאיר סגל/ ב מ אפרים פישל ב מ יצחק זל/ כ הרר מאיר ב מ אפרים פישל ס/ בשנת תק למד לפק, "The youth Samuel son of Rabbi Me'ir Segal son of . . . Ephraim Fischel son of . . . the late Isaac. Rabbi Me'ir son of Ephraim Fischel Segal, in the

year (5)530" (=1769/70)
REMARKS: The inscription appears to have been made in two stages. First, Me'ir Fishel "Segal" was inscribed in two lines together with the date; later his son Samuel added two lines on the free facets of the upper shaft. The hand appears to be later, as does the portion below the medial knop. These elements may represent a restoration that occasioned the additional inscription.
DONOR: Dr. Harry G. Friedman

## 705

TORAH POINTER　F 304　(*Illus. p. 308*)
Poland, 1776/77 (inscription)
Silver: cast, chased, pierced
L 22.6　DIAM 2.8 cm
HALLMARKS: none
INSCRIPTION: on upper shaft: זג האלפי הכריהשכמה [?]—/ בשנת תקלז ל, "This was donated by . . . the officers . . ., in the year (5)537" (=1776/77)
REMARKS: The hand is probably not original.
DONOR: Dr. Harry G. Friedman

## 706

TORAH POINTER　F 1905　(*Illus. p. 312*)
Poland (?), 1778/79 (inscription)
Silver: cast, filigree, engraved, gilt; brass
L 15.9　DIAM 1.8 cm
HALLMARKS: none
INSCRIPTION: on upper shaft: בנאם גבאים הרר דוד בהרר ירוחם זל/ ט (?) בנו הבכור יהודא ליב לגדלו לתורה/ לחופה (!) ולמשים (!) טובים (!)/ בשנת תקלט לפק, "As witnessed [by] the *gabba'im*, Rabbi David son of the late Rabbi Yeruḥam . . . [on behalf of] his eldest son Judah Leib, that [he may] raise him to the Torah, to the wedding canopy and to good deeds, in the year (5)539" (=1778/79)
REMARKS: The Hebrew of the text is corrupt.
DONOR: Dr. Harry G. Friedman

## 707

TORAH POINTER　F 3637　(*Illus. p. 312*)
Poland, late 18th–early 19th century
Silver: pierced, engraved, parcel-gilt
L 23.0　DIAM 3.1 cm
HALLMARKS: none
DONOR: Dr. Harry G. Friedman

## 708

TORAH POINTER　F 3724　(*Illus. p. 312*)
Poland (?), late 18th–early 19th century
Silver: cast, pierced, engraved, gilt
L 17.2　DIAM 2.2 cm
HALLMARKS: none
DONOR: Dr. Harry G. Friedman

## 709

TORAH POINTER D 17 (*Illus. p. 312*)

Breslau or Warsaw, 1st half of 19th century

Silver: cast, chased, parcel-gilt

L 20.5 DIAM 2.7 cm

HALLMARKS: none

REMARKS: For a nearly identical but finer pointer, part of a set of Torah implements, see Stieglitz, No. 5, bearing questionable Warsaw hallmarks of the end of the 18th century. The same designs were used contemporaneously in Breslau, Warsaw and Berlin in the 19th century (see under finial No. 305), and the origin of the Museum's pointer is thus indefinite.

BIBLIOGRAPHY: *JL* V, pl. clxxiii, 2nd from top; Danzig 1933, No. 47 (Pl. 5); *Danzig 1939/1982*, No. 96

DONOR: The Jewish Community of Danzig

## 710

TORAH POINTER M 18 (*Illus. p. 312*)

Poland (?), early 19th century

Silver: cast, filigree, chased

L 26.0 DIAM 3.2 cm

HALLMARKS: none

PROVENANCE: The Rose and Benjamin Mintz Collection

DONOR: Museum purchase

## 711

TORAH POINTER F 1805b (*Illus. p. 312*)

Poland, late 18th–early 19th century

Silver: cast, pierced, chased

L 19.2 DIAM 2.9 cm

HALLMARKS: none

DONOR: Dr. Harry G. Friedman

## 712

TORAH POINTER M 338 (*Illus. p. 310*)

Poland, early 19th century

Silver: cast, engraved

L 25.6 DIAM 4.4 cm

HALLMARKS: none

PROVENANCE: The Rose and Benjamin Mintz Collection

REMARKS: The pointing hand is a left hand, an unusual feature on pointers.

DONOR: Museum purchase

## 713

TORAH POINTER M 17 (*Illus. p. 312*)

Poland, early 19th century

Silver: cast, filigree, parcel-gilt

L 23.3 DIAM 2.7 cm

HALLMARKS: "12" in square

*MAKER:* "ALZ" in rectangle

PROVENANCE: The Rose and Benjamin Mintz Collection

REMARKS: The lower shaft and hand may have been replaced.

DONOR: Museum purchase

## 714

TORAH POINTER JM 59–55 (*Illus. p. 312*)

Poland, 19th century

Silver: cast, chased, pierced, engraved

L 23.7 DIAM 4.4 cm

HALLMARKS: none

INSCRIPTION: on upper knop: אליעזר בן צבי אריה/ אבא בן שמואל, "Eliezer son of Zvi Aryeh; Abba son of Samuel"

DONOR: Mrs. Bernard Kahn

## 715

TORAH POINTER F 3118 (*Illus. p. 312*)

Poland (?), 1919 (inscription)

Silver: chased, engraved, pierced, traces of gilt

L 25.9 DIAM 3.8 cm

HALLMARKS: none

INSCRIPTION: on medial knop: נדבת ר' ב"צ ראטניר בעד נשמת בנו יצחק/ ובתו רחל הנהרגים עקה"ש ט"ו אדר ראשון תרע"ט, "Donation of Ben-Zion Ratner on behalf of the soul of his son Isaac/ and his daughter Rachel, who were killed for the sanctification of God, 15 Adar I, (5)679" (= February 14, 1919)

REMARKS: The formula employed in the inscription indicates that the deceased were martyred, apparently in a pogrom. On the basis of style, this pointer seems to have been made in the first half of the 19th century.

DONOR: Dr. Harry G. Friedman

## 716

TORAH POINTER F 4074 (*Illus. p. 312*)

Poland, 1827/28 (inscription)

Silver: cast, chased, pierced

L 22.2 DIAM 3.4 cm

HALLMARKS: "12"

*MAKER:* "DBM" (?) in script

INSCRIPTION: on upper shaft: זה היד שייך לה"ה/ הרבני מו"ה בנימין/ במהורר משה י"ץ/ שנת ת"קפ"ח לפ"ק, "This pointer belongs to … Rabbi Benjamin son of … Rabbi Moses …, year (5)588" (=1827/28)

DONOR: Dr. Harry G. Friedman

## 717

TORAH POINTER JM 93–67 (*Illus. p. 312*)

Poland, first half of 19th century

Silver: cast, engraved, pierced, parcel-gilt

L 19.2 DIAM 3.3 cm

HALLMARKS: "12"; "HP" in flat oval

DONOR: Mr. and Mrs. Arthur Wiesenberger

## 718

TORAH POINTER   F 303   (*Illus. p. 314*)

Peisern (Pyzdry), 1853/54 (inscription)

Silver: cast, die-stamped, chased; garnet

L 29.2   DIAM 3.7 cm

HALLMARKS: "12" in square

INSCRIPTION: on upper shaft: שייך לחברה ג"ח אשר/ נדבו/
אנשי חברה בשנת/ ת'ר'י'ד' לפ"ק פה פייזר, "Belongs to the
Society for Visiting the Sick, donated by (the) members of
(the) Society in the year (5)514 [=1853/54], here, Peiser[n]"

REMARKS: Peisern is located 55 km SE of Posen; for another
pointer used in this town, see No. 548.

DONOR: Dr. Harry G. Friedman

## 719

TORAH POINTER   M 371   (*Illus. p. 314*)

Poland (?), 19th century

Brass: cast, chased, tinned

L 27.9   DIAM 3.9 cm

HALLMARKS: none

PROVENANCE: The Rose and Benjamin Mintz Collection

REMARKS: The chain is original.

DONOR: Museum purchase

## 720

TORAH POINTER   F 285   (*Illus. p. 314*)

Poland or Ukraine, late 19th century

Silver: cast, filigree, chased, engraved

L 28.4   DIAM 3.9 cm

HALLMARKS: "84"

REMARKS: The hand may be a replacement.

DONOR: Dr. Harry G. Friedman

## 721

TORAH POINTER   F 2228   (*Illus. p. 314*)

Poland, 19th century

Brass: cast, plated (?)

L 27.4   DIAM 3.8 cm

HALLMARKS: none

DONOR: Dr. Harry G. Friedman

## 722

TORAH POINTER   M 238   (*Illus. p. 314*)

Poland (?), 19th century

Brass: silvered

L 26.0   DIAM 3.3 cm

HALLMARKS: none

PROVENANCE: The Rose and Benjamin Mintz Collection

DONOR: Museum purchase

## 723

TORAH POINTER   D 49   (*Illus. p. 314*)

Poland, 19th century

Silver: cast, engraved

L 19.3   DIAM 2.9 cm

HALLMARKS: none

INSCRIPTION: שניאור בר בן ציון/ הכהן, "Shneur son of Ben-
Zion ha-Kohen."

BIBLIOGRAPHY: *Danzig 1939*, No. 238

DONOR: The Jewish Community of Danzig

## 724

TORAH POINTER   JM 15–57   (*Illus. p. 314*)

Poland, 19th century

Silver: cast

L 23.7   DIAM 2.6 cm

HALLMARKS: "12"; mark over mark, both illegible

INSCRIPTION: on upper knop, in script: "D.L"

DONOR: B. W. Huebsch

## 725

TORAH POINTER   M 192   (*Illus. p. 314*)

Poland, 19th century

Silver: cast, engraved

L 29.8   DIAM 4.5 cm

HALLMARKS: "12"; Lileyko 98

PROVENANCE: The Rose and Benjamin Mintz Collection

BIBLIOGRAPHY: Loukomski, p. 175, upper left

DONOR: Museum purchase

## 726

TORAH POINTER   F 2523   (*Illus. p. 314*)

Poland (?), 1876/77 (inscription)

Silver: cast, engraved

L 30.3   DIAM 3.8 cm

HALLMARKS: none

INSCRIPTION: on upper shaft: שייך לכ'/ טובי ב"ר יעקב/ בנוא
 יארק/ שנת תרכז לפק/ (blank) /(blank), "Belongs to
Tuvi(ah) son of Jacob in New York, [in the] year (5)627"
(=1876/77).

DONOR: Dr. Harry G. Friedman

## 727

TORAH POINTER   F 1541   (*Illus. p. 314*)

Poland (or Russia), 1904/05 (inscription)

Silver: cast, chased, engraved, nielloed

L 31.0   DIAM 3.7 cm

HALLMARKS: "84" in rectangle (crude)

INSCRIPTION: on lower shaft: ז"נ/ נחמן בר" שמואיל (!)/
זונוויל/ עם זוגתי (!)/ פייגע בר"/ חיים דוב/ שנת ת"ר"סה

"This was donated by Naḥman son of Samuel Zanwil, with his spouse Feige daughter of Ḥayyim Dov, [in the] year (5)665" (=1904/05)

REMARKS: Some parts of this pointer appear to be later restorations.

DONOR: Dr. Harry G. Friedman

## 728
TORAH POINTER  F 274  (*Illus. p. 314*)
Poland, 1922–39
Silver: cast, engraved
L 26.0  DIAM 3.0 cm
HALLMARKS: Lileyko 94 (800); 96 (round); 98
INSCRIPTION: On upper shaft: traces of an erased Hebrew inscription
DONOR: Dr. Harry G. Friedman

## 729
TORAH POINTER  F 3723  (*Illus. p. 314*)
Poland or Germany, late 19th–early 20th century
Brass: cast
L 27.8  DIAM 3.2 cm
HALLMARKS: none
DONOR: Dr. Harry G. Friedman

## 730
TORAH POINTER  F 1823  (*Illus. p. 314*)
Poland (?), late 19th century
Silver: cast, engraved
L 27.0  DIAM 3.1 cm
HALLMARKS: none
INSCRIPTION: on upper arm: רחל בת יהודה לייב/ א. ש. פ. ס., "Rachel daughter of Judah Leib …"
REMARKS: The meaning of the abbreviation at the end of the inscription is unknown. This pointer is unusually heavy.
DONOR: Dr. Harry G. Friedman

## 731
TORAH POINTER  F 292
Eastern Europe, early 19th century
Bronze: cast, pierced, chased, engraved, silver-washed
L 26.8  W 3.5 cm
HALLMARKS: none
DONOR: Dr. Harry G. Friedman

## 732
TORAH POINTER  F 299  (*Illus. p. 314*)
Poland (?), 19th century
Silver, cast, chased, engraved
L 22.4  DIAM 3.0 cm
HALLMARKS: none

INSCRIPTION: on upper shaft: ז'נ' ר' אהרן/ בן אברהם אבא לח'בה/ ווילקאוווישקער, "This was donated by … Aaron son of Abraham Abba to the Wilkowishker Synagogue Society"
REMARKS: The hand might not be original. The Society was probably located in New York; see *NY Register*, p. 348b, the Wolkowisker Young Men's Beneficial Association.
DONOR: Dr. Harry G. Friedman

## 733
TORAH POINTER  F 2347  (*Illus. p. 314*)
Poland (?), 19th century
Silver: cast, chased
L 20.3  DIAM 3.4 cm
HALLMARKS: none
REMARKS: The medial knop is missing.
DONOR: Dr. Harry G. Friedman

## 734
TORAH POINTER  F 5400b  (*Illus. p. 312*)
Galicia (?), 19th century
Silver: cast, filigree, pierced, engraved; glass
L 14.5  DIAM 2.5 cm
HALLMARKS: none
PROVENANCE: Jacob Posen, New York
DONOR: Dr. Harry G. Friedman

## 735
TORAH POINTER  F 2568  (*Illus. p. 312*)
Poland, prior to 1851
Silver: filigree, cast, chased, parcel-gilt
L 24.3  DIAM 3.2 cm
HALLMARKS: *CITY:* Lileyko 83c
DONOR: Dr. Harry G. Friedman

## 736
TORAH POINTER  F 2139  (*Illus. p. 312*)
Poland or Ukraine, late 19th–early 20th century
Silver: cast, filigree, chased
L 26.8  DIAM 3.8 cm
HALLMARKS: "84"
  *MAKER:* "W.S"
REMARKS: Cf. the similar pointer No. 720.
DONOR: Dr. Harry G. Friedman

## 737
TORAH POINTER  F 287  (*Illus. p. 312*)
Poland or Russia, late 19th–early 20th century
Silver: filigree
L 30.1  DIAM 4.3 cm
HALLMARKS: "84" in square
REMARKS: Cf. the similar pointer No. 738.
DONOR: Dr. Harry G. Friedman

## 738

TORAH POINTER   F 272b   (*Illus. p. 312*)
Poland or Russia, late 19th–early 20th century
Silver: cast, filigree, parcel-gilt
L 30.4   DIAM 3.1 cm
HALLMARKS: none
REMARKS: Cf. pointer No. 737, of similar form.
DONOR: Dr. Harry G. Friedman

## 739

TORAH POINTER   F 307   (*Illus. p. 312*)
Poland, 19th century
Silver: chased, engraved
L 28.4   DIAM 4.7 cm
HALLMARKS: none
DONOR: Dr. Harry G. Friedman

## 740

TORAH POINTER   U 9182   (*Illus. p. 314*)
Poland (?), 19th century
Silver: cast, pierced
L 29.0   DIAM 2.5 cm
HALLMARKS: none
REMARKS: The Jewish Cultural Reconstruction tag on this
    piece indicates that it was recovered in Europe.
DONOR: Jewish Cultural Reconstruction

## 741

TORAH POINTER   F 2288   (*Illus. p. 314*)
Poland, late 19th–early 20th century
Brass: cast, chased, silver-plated
L 26.7   DIAM 3.8 cm
REMARKS: This type of Polish pointer is based on a Viennese
    model, e.g., pointer No. 658.
DONOR: Dr. Harry G. Friedman

## 742

TORAH POINTER   F 275   (*Illus. p. 314*)
Poland or United States, early 20th century
Silver: cast, chased
L 29.7   DIAM 3.6 cm
HALLMARKS: none
DONOR: Dr. Harry G. Friedman

## 743

TORAH POINTER   S 847   (*Illus. p. 314*)
Poland (?), late 19th–early 20th century
Silver: filigree, cast
L 28.9   W 3.9 cm

HALLMARKS: none
DONOR: Dr. Harry G. Friedman

## 744

TORAH POINTER   M 426   (*Illus. p. 314*)
Poland, 19th century
Wood: carved, gessoed, painted (polychrome); glass (mir-
    ror); silver (chain)
L 23.6   W 2.3 cm
PROVENANCE: The Rose and Benjamin Mintz Collection
REMARKS: There are numerous traces of green, black and red
    (?) paint on various parts of this piece. The chain is later (a
    loop bears evidence of once having had a hallmark).
    Pointer M 394, formerly at The Jewish Museum, is another
    example with the "ball in a cage" motif typical of folk carv-
    ing.
DONOR: Museum purchase

## 745

TORAH POINTER   F 1531   (*Illus. p. 316*)
Warsaw, 1882
Silver: cast, engraved
L 29.1   DIAM 3.5 cm
HALLMARKS: Cf. Tardy, p. 353, mark for 1886, but with eagle
    and "1882" (not in Lileyko)
REMARKS: Cf. similar pointers Nos. 746 and 747.
DONOR: Dr. Harry G. Friedman

## 746

TORAH POINTER   JM 31–57   (*Illus. p. 308*)
Warsaw, 1851–1915
Silver: cast, engraved, stamped
L 26.7   DIAM 4.2 cm
HALLMARKS: *CITY:* Lileyko 90
             *MAKER:* illegible
INSCRIPTION: on upper shaft: /(!) חנה דינע/ בת ר' מרדחי
    ואלקאוויטש תר, "Hannah Dina daughter of . . . Mordecai
    Wolkowitch, (5)6??"
REMARKS: The date is incomplete, but lies between 1851 and
    1938/39. Cf. the similar pointers Nos. 745 and 747.
DONOR: Robert I. Wishnik

## 747

TORAH POINTER   F 1860   (*Illus. p. 316*)
Warsaw, 1851–1915
Silver: cast, engraved
L 31.4   DIAM 4.0 cm
HALLMARKS: Lileyko 90
REMARKS: Cf. the similar pointers Nos. 745–746.
DONOR: Dr. Harry G. Friedman

## 748
TORAH POINTER  F 288  (*Illus. p. 316*)
Warsaw (?), late 19th–early 20th century
Silver: cast, filigree, chased, parcel-gilt(?)
L 34.0  W 4.3 cm
HALLMARKS: none
REMARKS: Crudely repaired. Cf. the similar pointers Nos. 749
    and 760.
DONOR: Dr. Harry G. Friedman

## 749
TORAH POINTER  F 2306  (*Illus. p. 316*)
Warsaw, late 19th–early 20th century
I. Perlman
Silver: cast, engraved, parcel-gilt
L 29.8  DIAM 4.2 cm
HALLMARKS: *CITY:* Lileyko 90
            *MAKER:* "I.P." in square (not in Lileyko)
INSCRIPTION: on cuff: שערי בינה /לה׳, "[Dedicated] to God,
    the Gates of Knowledge"
REMARKS: The name in the inscription, "Sha'arei Binah,"
    probably refers to the "Sha'arei Bino" congregation in New
    York City; see shield No. 200, also dedicated to that con-
    gregation. See pointer No. 751 by the same smith; and the
    similar pointer No. 760.
DONOR: Dr. Harry G. Friedman

## 750
TORAH POINTER  D 28  (*Illus. p. 316*)
Danzig, mid-19th century
Silver: cast, engraved, pierced
L 29.7  DIAM 3.5 cm
HALLMARKS: *CITY:* Czihak 3 or 5
            *MAKER:* two illegible marks
BIBLIOGRAPHY: *Danzig 1939/1982*, No. 237
DONOR: The Jewish Community of Danzig

## 751
TORAH POINTER  F 2439  (*Illus. p. 316*)
Warsaw, late 19th–early 20th century
I. Perlman
Brass: cast, chased, silver-plated; silver: cast
L 25.9  W 3.8 cm
HALLMARKS: *CITY:* Lileyko 90
            *MAKER:* "I. PERLMAN" in rectangle
REMARKS: This silver pointer has been restored extensively
    with brass parts. Cf. similar pointers Nos. 752–754 and 757;
    and pointer No. 749, with Perlman's abbreviated mark:
    "I.P." Persian finials No. 434 are restored with stems from a
    pair of finials made by Perlman.
DONOR: Dr. Harry G. Friedman

## 752
TORAH POINTER  F 283  (*Illus. p. 316*)
Warsaw, 1851–1915
Silver: cast, chased
L 26.1  DIAM 4.3 cm
HALLMARKS: Lileyko 90 (eagle)
REMARKS: Cf. the similar pointers Nos. 751 and 753–754.
DONOR: Dr. Harry G. Friedman

## 753
TORAH POINTER  F 2524  (*Illus. p. 316*)
Warsaw, late 19th–early 20th century
Silver: cast, chased
L 33.5  DIAM 4.0 cm
HALLMARKS: *CITY:* Lileyko 90 (eagle)
REMARKS: cf. the similar pointers Nos. 751–752 and 754.
DONOR: Dr. Harry G. Friedman

## 754
TORAH POINTER  F 3295  (*Illus. p. 316*)
Warsaw (?), late 19th–early 20th century
Brass: cast, chased, silver-plated (traces)
L 24.5  W 3.8 cm
HALLMARKS: none
REMARKS: cf. the similar pointers Nos. 751–753.
DONOR: Dr. Harry G. Friedman

## 755
TORAH POINTER  F 4077  (*Illus. p. 316*)
Warsaw, early 1920's (?)
Silver: cast, chased, parcel-gilt
L 28.5  DIAM 4.0 cm
HALLMARKS: *CITY:* Lileyko 94 (875, with "W"); 98; Tardy, p. 374,
            upper, second row, left and second row, right
            *MAKER:* "F.C." in oval
DONOR: Dr. Harry G. Friedman

## 756
TORAH POINTER  U 9173  (*Illus. p. 316*)
Moscow (?), 1898
Silver: cast, chased, stamped
L 32.2  DIAM 4.1 cm
HALLMARKS: *CITY:* similar to Postnikova 529, but with "1898"
            *MAKER:* illegible
REMARKS: The date 1898 is too late for this type of hallmark,
    and the mark may be false.
DONOR: Jewish Cultural Reconstruction

## 756A
TORAH POINTER  D 44  (*Illus. p. 312*)
Russian Empire, late 19th century
Silver: cast, engraved, parcel-gilt; coral: carved

L 17.0  DIAM 1.7 cm

HALLMARKS: none

PROVENANCE: The Gieldzinski Collection, Danzig

REMARKS: The silver elements are from various preexisting items.

BIBLIOGRAPHY: Danzig 1904, No. 31; *JL* V, pl. clxxii, fifth from top; Danzig 1933, No. 44; *Danzig 1939/1982*, No. 97

DONOR: The Jewish Community of Danzig

## 757

TORAH POINTER  F 284

Ukraine, 1854/55 (inscription)

Silver: filigree, cast, engraved

L 24.8  DIAM 2.7 cm

HALLMARKS: none

INSCRIPTION: on upper shaft: //זאת נדב// ה' שלמה// בן משה// ואשתו/ יענטה בת/ יעקב// תרטו/ לפק, "This was donated by . . . Solomon son of Moses and his wife Yente daughter of Jacob, [5]615" (=1854/55)

DONOR: Dr. Harry G. Friedman

## 758

TORAH POINTER  F 2465  (*Illus. p. 316*)

Ukraine (?), mid-19th century

Silver: filigree, cast

L 30.2  DIAM 2.6 cm

HALLMARKS: "84" in rectangle; on chain: Rohrwasser, p. 33 (800, toucan); illegible maker's mark

INSCRIPTION: . . . ז, . . . נ . . . אליהו . . . בר . . . יצחק, "This was donated by . . . Elijah . . . son of . . . Isaac . . ."

REMARKS: The chain is from Austria, 20th century. Cf. the similar pointers Nos. 757 and 759.

DONOR: Dr. Harry G. Friedman

## 759

TORAH POINTER  F 2815  (*Illus. p. 316*)

Ukraine (?), 19th century

Silver: filigree, cast, engraved; brass

L 27.6  DIAM 3.5 cm

HALLMARKS: none

INSCRIPTION: on upper shaft: ערשטער/ אנטערשטיצונג/ קראנקען/ קריסנאפאלער, "First Krisnopol [Society for the] Support for the Sick"

REMARKS: The brass ferrule is not original. "Krisnopol" is possibly Krasnopolje, 100 km NW of Kharkov, in northeastern Ukraine. For the Krassnapoler Young Men's Aid Society, see *NY Register* 1917, p. 796a. For a similar society, see pointer No. 794. The inscription may indicate that this pointer was made in the United States. Cf. the similar pointers Nos. 757 and 758.

DONOR: Dr. Harry G. Friedman

## 760

TORAH POINTER  S 526  (*Illus. p. 316*)

Ukraine or United States, late 19th–early 20th century

Silver: filigree, cast, chased, parcel-gilt

L 29.0  DIAM 3.5 cm

HALLMARKS: "84" in rectangle (twice)

PROVENANCE: William Cowen Collection (No. 83)

REMARKS: The hallmark might be an American imitation. Cf. the similar pointers Nos. 757, 748 and 749.

DONOR: Museum purchase

## 761

TORAH POINTER  JM 71–48  (*Illus. p. 312*)

Ukraine (?), 19th century

Silver: cast, filigree

L 10.1  DIAM 2.0 cm

HALLMARKS: none

PROVENANCE: Hessisches Landesmuseum, Kassel

REMARKS: The hand is a left hand. As noted by Rudolf Hallo, there is an inscription identical to that on shield No. 196, naming the original donor and giving the date: 1689/90 — obviously a later addition.

BIBLIOGRAPHY: Hallo 1932, No. 17

DONOR: Louis Rabinowitz

## 762

TORAH POINTER  F 2591

Ukraine (?), 19th century

Silver and brass: cast, filigree, parcel-gilt

L 11.3  DIAM 1.5 cm

HALLMARKS: none

DONOR: Dr. Harry G. Friedman

## 763

TORAH POINTER  F 4603

Ukraine or Galicia, 2nd half of 19th century

Bone: carved, inlaid; horn; silver: cast

L 29.3  DIAM 3.0 cm

DONOR: Dr. Harry G. Friedman

## 764

TORAH POINTER  F 2553  (*Illus. p. 308*)

Ukraine (?), 19th century

Silver: cast, chased, engraved

L 28.8  W 3.7 cm

HALLMARKS: "3" with pentagram/ "H 54" with 5-pointed star.

INSCRIPTION: on panels of upper section: שלמה/ חיים/ ב"ר/ מרדכי/ יוסף/ וויניצקע, "Solomon Ḥayyim son of Mordecai Joseph Winitzke"

REMARKS: The upper part appears to be a spice container. The family name in the inscription derives from Winnitza in the Ukraine.

DONOR: Dr. Harry G. Friedman

# 764A

## TORAH POINTER  M 296  (*Illus. p. 326*)

Russia (?), 19th–20th century
Wood: carved; unidentified; coral (beads); amber
L 25.5  DIAM 2.7 cm
PROVENANCE: The Rose and Benjamin Mintz Collection
DONOR: Museum purchase

# 764B

## TORAH POINTER  M 372

Russia (?), 19th–20th century
Horn: carved; bone: carved
L 27.2  DIAM 2.5 cm
PROVENANCE: The Rose and Benjamin Mintz Collection
DONOR: Museum purchase

# 765

## TORAH POINTER  D 50  (*Illus. p. 312*)

Europe, first half of 19th century
Silver: filigree, cast; garnets; amethyst
L 13.3  W 2.7 cm
HALLMARKS: none
REMARKS: See the comments in *Danzig 1939/1982*, No. 95. The upper filigree element is reminiscent of early 19th-century hairpins; see *JL II*, pl. LXXIII, lower right.
BIBLIOGRAPHY: *Danzig 1939/1982*, No. 95
DONOR: The Jewish Community of Danzig

# 766

## TORAH POINTER  F 317

Europe, early 20th century (?)
Wood: carved, turned
L 24.5  DIAM 1.5 cm
REMARKS: The hand is realistically rendered.
DONOR: Dr. Harry G. Friedman

# 767

## TORAH POINTER  F 1047  (*Illus. p. 316*)

Europe, 18th century
Silver: cast, chased
L 27.3  W 1.7 cm
HALLMARKS: none
REMARKS: The upper knop is missing.
DONOR: Dr. Harry G. Friedman

# 768

## TORAH POINTER  F 3106  (*Illus. p. 316*)

Western Europe, 19th century
Silver: cast, chased, gilt
L 21.6  DIAM 2.1 cm
HALLMARKS: none
DONOR: Dr. Harry G. Friedman

# 769

## TORAH POINTER  F 2055

Europe, late 19th–early 20th century
Silver: cast, engraved
L 28.4  DIAM 2.8 cm
HALLMARKS: none
REMARKS: The hand is a left hand, an unusual feature on pointers.
DONOR: Dr. Harry G. Friedman

# 770

## TORAH POINTER  F 3104

Europe, 19th century
Silver: cast, chased
L 16.2  DIAM 1.3 cm
HALLMARKS: none
DONOR: Dr. Harry G. Friedman

# 771

## TORAH POINTER  F 3722  (*Illus. p. 318*)

Europe, early 19th century(?)
Silver: cast, gilt(?)
L 21.3  W 1.2 cm
HALLMARKS:  *MAKER:* "GBS" in rectangle
INSCRIPTION: on upper shaft: ח״ג
REMARKS: For an identical inscription, see pointer No. 774.
DONOR: Dr. Harry G. Friedman

# 772

## TORAH POINTER  F 3096  (*Illus. p. 318*)

Europe, 19th century
Copper and brass: silver-plated; silver
L 27.0  DIAM 5.0 cm
DONOR: Dr. Harry G. Friedman

# 773

## TORAH POINTER  D 45  (*Illus. p. 318*)

Europe, 19th century
Brass: cast
L 17.9  DIAM 1.6 cm
BIBLIOGRAPHY: Danzig 1904, No. 32; *JL* V, pl. clxxiii, bottom; Danzig 1933, No. 45; *Danzig 1939/1982*, No. 248
DONOR: The Jewish Community of Danzig

# 774

## TORAH POINTER  D 47  (*Illus. p. 318*)

Europe, 19th century
Silver: cast, chased, engraved, gilt
L 27.3  DIAM 2.8 cm
HALLMARKS: none
INSCRIPTION: on shaft: ח״ג

REMARKS: The abbreviated inscription was interpreted in *Danzig 1939/1982*, No. 249, as "Holiday." For an identical inscription, see pointer No. 771.

BIBLIOGRAPHY: Danzig 1904, No. 35; Danzig 1933, No. 47; *Danzig 1939/1982*, No. 249

DONOR: The Jewish Community of Danzig

## 775
### TORAH POINTER   S 421a
Uncertain origin, mid-19th century
Silver: cast, die-stamped, engraved, parcel-gilt
L 28.5   DIAM 3.7 cm
HALLMARKS: none
REMARKS: Cf. pointer No. 776, which is identical but for the addition of stones and the absence of a medial crown element.

## 776
### TORAH POINTER   S 421b
Europe, mid-19th century
Silver: die-stamped, cast, engraved, parcel-gilt; stones
L 28.7   DIAM 3.7 cm
HALLMARKS: none
REMARKS: A medial knop seems to be missing. No. 775 is identical.
PROVENANCE: The Hadji Ephraim and Mordecai Benguiat Family Collection
DONOR: Museum purchase

## 777
### TORAH POINTER   F 2076   (*Illus. p. 318*)
Europe, late 19th century
Silver: cast
L 25.5 DIAM 2.0 cm
HALLMARKS: illegible
DONOR: Dr. Harry G. Friedman

## 778
### TORAH POINTER   S 856   (*Illus. p. 318*)
Europe, 19th century
Silver: cast, chased, engraved; diamond
L 22.3 DIAM 2.0 cm
HALLMARKS: indistinct mark (on ring).
INSCRIPTION: on shaft: נדבת לב כה' חנוך בן כה' מרדכי לזכרון נשמת זוגתו/ כיילה קראקאואר בת ר' שמואל ריעזענפעלד, "Heartfelt donation of Ḥanokh son of Mordecai in memory of the soul of his spouse, Keila Krakauer daughter of Samuel Riesenfeld"; near the upper end: "MC" in script

## 779
### TORAH POINTER   D 39   (*Illus. p. 318*)
Europe, 19th century

Silver: cast, chased, engraved, gilt; glass
L 31.3   DIAM 3.6 cm
HALLMARKS: none
INSCRIPTION: "W"
PROVENANCE: The Weinberg Synagogue, Danzig
REMARKS: The inscribed initial signifies that this object belonged to the Weinberg Congregation in Danzig.
BIBLIOGRAPHY: *Danzig 1939/1982*, No. 239
DONOR: The Jewish Community of Danzig

## 780
### TORAH POINTER   F 5678   (*Illus. p. 318*)
Uncertain origin, 20th century (?)
Silver, cast, chased, pierced
L 33.3   W 4.2 cm
HALLMARKS: none
INSCRIPTION: adjacent to depictions on the shaft: /צ(בי)/ נ(שר)/ א(ריה)/, "Hart, eagle, lion," a reference to the *Ethics of the Fathers* 5:23
REMARKS: Cf. *JL* V, pl. CLXXIV, 3rd from top. The two examples are almost identical and might be one and the same; any differences could be explained by modifications made after the 1931 publication.
DONOR: Dr. Harry G. Friedman

## 781
### TORAH POINTER   F 2742   (*Illus. p. 318*)
Europe, 19th century
Silver: cast, chased, pierced
L 23.5   DIAM 3.3 cm
HALLMARKS: traces of English marks on loop
REMARKS: The loop, which bears the hallmarks, is probably not original.
DONOR: Dr. Harry G. Friedman

## 782
### TORAH POINTER   D 32   (*Illus. p. 318*)
Europe, late 19th century
Silver: cast, chased
L 18.8   W 2.2 cm
HALLMARKS: none
BIBLIOGRAPHY: *Danzig 1939/1982*, No. 245
DONOR: The Jewish Community of Danzig

## 783
### TORAH POINTER   F 5953   (*Illus. p. 318*)
Europe, 19th century
Silver: cast, chased
L 25.5   DIAM 2.8 cm
HALLMARKS: none
DONOR: Dr. Harry G. Friedman

## 784
TORAH POINTER  F 4272  (*Illus. p. 318*)
Europe (?), second half of 19th century
Silver: cast, traces of gilt
L 23.7  DIAM 1.4 cm
HALLMARKS: none
DONOR: Dr. Harry G. Friedman

## 785
TORAH POINTER  F 1920  (*Illus. p. 318*)
Europe (?), late 19th century (?)
Silver: cast, die-stamped, chased
L 25.4  DIAM 2.8 cm
HALLMARKS: none
DONOR: Dr. Harry G. Friedman

## 786
TORAH POINTER  F 1597  (*Illus. p. 318*)
Europe, 19th century (?)
Silver: cast, pierced, punched
L 31.0  DIAM 3.1 cm
HALLMARKS: none
INSCRIPTION: on shaft: זאת נדיב[!] לספירן[!] תורה נפתלי בר ברוך ז״ל, "This was donated for the Torah Scroll [by] Naphtali son of Barukh"; in different script and on a different facet: ואשתו הינדל בת ה׳ק׳ דוד זל, "And his wife Hindel daughter of the martyr . . . David"
DONOR: Dr. Harry G. Friedman

## 787
TORAH POINTER  F 3315  (*Illus. p. 318*)
Europe (?), 19th century (?)
Silver: cast, chased
L 32.1  DIAM 4.8 cm
HALLMARKS: none
DONOR: Dr. Harry G. Friedman

## 788
TORAH POINTER  F 272a
United States, 1861 (inscription)
Silver, cast, engraved
L 27.0  DIAM 3.7 cm
HALLMARKS: none
INSCRIPTION: on upper shaft: נדבה/ מ׳ר׳ אליהו בר׳ יהודא ני׳י׳/ לבהמ״ד שערי תורה/ בעד הזכרת נשמת אחיו/ המנוח ר׳ אברהם בר יהודא/ תהא נשמתו צרורה בצרור החיים/ נוא יארק ר׳ח׳ ניסן ה״תרכ״א, "Donation of . . . Rabbi Elijah son of . . . Judah . . . , to *Beth Midrash* [Study Hall] *Sha'arei Torah*, for the remembrance of his late brother . . . Abraham son of . . . Judah, May his soul be bound up in the bond of [eternal] life, New York, 1 Nissan 5621" (=12 March 1861)
DONOR: Dr. Harry G. Friedman

## 789
TORAH POINTER  F 1752
United States or England, 1867 (inscription)
Silver: cast
L 26.3  DIAM 2.7 cm
HALLMARKS: none
INSCRIPTION: on lower shaft (in English): "Pres^d by Sophia Patz. 1867."
DONOR: Dr. Harry G. Friedman

## 790
TORAH POINTER  U 8542  (*Illus. p. 320*)
United States, 1875
Silver: cast, engraved
L 31.0  DIAM 1.7 cm
HALLMARKS: none
INSCRIPTION: on knops (in English): "Presented by/ Gemiluth Chesed Society of Frederick.// to/ Heb. Cong. of Frederick. Md. Oct. 30th 1875"
REMARKS: Pointers 790–796 seem to have been made in a single workshop. Some of the group bear inscriptions indicating their use in America. An origin in the United States is problematic, however, because of another, related group of pointers (Nos. 625–34), which is ascribed to Germany. It is possible that both groups are actually from a common source, either in the United States or in Europe.

## 791
TORAH POINTER  F 1383  (*Illus. p. 302*)
United States, 2nd half of 19th century
Silver: cast, chased
L 20.3  DIAM 2.3 cm
HALLMARKS: none
INSCRIPTION: זה (!) היד נדבה האשה/ רייזיל נחמה לזכרון בעלה/ הר׳ ר׳/ אריה ליב זל גאלדשמיט/ לחברת/ בני אברהם אנשי ווילנא, "This pointer was donated by the woman Reizel Neḥamah in memory of her husband Rabbi Arieh Leib Goldschmidt, to the Society of the Sons of Abraham, Men of Vilna"
DONOR: Dr. Harry G. Friedman

## 792
TORAH POINTER  F 4524
United States (?), late 19th–early 20th century
Brass: cast, silver-plated
L 28.6  DIAM 3.1 cm
INSCRIPTION: on cuff: ז״נ ה״ר/ אברהם בן צבי/ א[!]ז׳ה׳/ רבקה/ בת מאניש/ שנת ע״ת ק״ש, "This was donated by Abraham son of Zvi, with his spouse Rebecca daughter of Mannes (?), year (?)"

REMARKS: According to ordinary *gematria* (computation), the date in the inscription would read (5)870, equivalent to 2110 C.E. Cf. the identical pointer No. 793, and the similar pointers Nos. 794–796. See also pointer No. 799 for further remarks.

DONOR: Dr. Harry G. Friedman

## 793
### TORAH POINTER   F 1546
United States (?), late 19th–early 20th century

Brass: fabricated, cast, silver-plated

L 28.9   DIAM 3.1 cm

HALLMARKS: none

REMARKS: Cf. the identical pointer No. 792 and the similar pointers Nos. 794–796. See also pointer No. 799 for further remarks.

DONOR: Dr. Harry G. Friedman

## 794
### TORAH POINTER   F 290   (*Illus. p. 320*)
United States (?), late 19th century

Brass: cast, engraved, silver-plated

L 27.5   DIAM 3.1 cm

HALLMARK: illegible

INSCRIPTION: in Yiddish, on cuff: פרעזענט/ פין יצחק ראזענטאל/ צו די ערשטע מיאלענר/ קראנקין אינטערשטיצען/ פעריין, "Present from Isaac Rosenthal to the First Mialener Society for Support of the Sick"

REMARKS: The cuff is possibly of silver and, if so, not original. The society was for immigrants from Miala, ca. 50 km NW of Posen. For a similar society, see pointer No. 759. Cf. the identical pointers Nos. 795–796 and the similar pointers Nos. 792–793. See also pointer No. 799 for further remarks.

DONOR: Dr. Harry G. Friedman

## 795
### TORAH POINTER   F 3757
United States (?), late 19th century

Silver: repoussé, cast

L 28.5   DIAM 3.1 cm

HALLMARKS: on cuff: "W" in circle; "84" in square

REMARKS: The cuff is not original to this piece. Cf. the identical pointers Nos. 794 and 796, and the similar pointers Nos. 792–793. See also pointer No. 799 for further remarks.

DONOR: Dr. Harry G. Friedman

## 796
### TORAH POINTER   F 2390   (*Illus. p. 302*)
United States (?), 19th century

Silver: cast, engraved(?)

L 26.5   DIAM 2.5 cm

HALLMARKS: none

REMARKS: This piece is heavier than the others of its group. Cf. the identical pointers Nos. 794–795, and the similar pointers Nos. 792–793. See also pointer No. 799 for further remarks.

DONOR: Dr. Harry G. Friedman

## 797
### TORAH POINTER   F 1967   (*Illus. p. 320*)
United States or Poland, late 19th century

Brass: cast, die-stamped, engraved, traces of silver plating

L 29.0   DIAM 3.0 cm

INSCRIPTION: ז"נ ר' בנימין כץ, "This was donated by Benjamin Katz"

DONOR: Dr. Harry G. Friedman

## 798
### TORAH POINTER   F 2215   (*Illus. p. 302*)
United States(?), late 19th–early 20th century

Silver: cast

L 17.2   DIAM 0.9 cm

HALLMARKS: "84" and griffin (?) in double-square frame

REMARKS: Cf. pointer No. 798A, with a similar hallmark.

DONOR: Dr. Harry G. Friedman

## 798A
### TORAH POINTER   F 4607
Russian Empire, late 19th–early 20th century

Silver: cast

L 33.9   DIAM 4.2 cm

HALLMARKS: "84" and griffin (?)

REMARKS: This pointer bears the same mark as No. 798.

DONOR: Dr. Harry G. Friedman

## 799
### TORAH POINTER   JM 54-59   (*Illus. p. 320*)
United States(?), 1880's

Silver: cast, engraved

L 29.3   DIAM 4.1 cm

HALLMARKS: False St. Petersburg mark for 1882 (on cuff)

REMARKS: This pointer is apparently an American imitation of a Russian piece, as are the similar pointers Nos. 800–804.

DONOR: Mrs. Arthur J. Sussel

## 800
### TORAH POINTER   F 916   (*Illus. p. 320*)
United States, or St. Petersburg, 1888(?)

Silver: filigree, cast, engraved

L 29.1   DIAM 4.0 cm

HALLMARKS: False Russian mark; cf. Postnikova, No. 1185 — "1888" (modified from "1838")

INSCRIPTION: on lower shaft: /זײ׳נ ח״ק אנשי בני אדאבינער‏‎ ‏ב׳א׳ס׳ין׳ ת׳ק׳פ׳ז׳ נויארק‎, "This was donated by the Holy (Burial) Society of the People of . . . Adubiner, . . . (5)587 [=1926/27] New York"

REMARKS: The hallmarks are dubious. See pointer No. 799 for further remarks. See *NY Register*, p. 750a, for the Dubiner-Wohliner Aid Society.

DONOR: Dr. Harry G. Friedman

# 801

TORAH POINTER  F 1861

United States (?), late 19th–early 20th century

Silver: cast, engraved, gilt

L 28.9  DIAM 3.4 cm

HALLMARKS: Imitation Russian marks, including "84."

INSCRIPTION: ‏זײ׳ נ ה׳ נדב יצחק מאיר בן טויבע‎, "This pointer was donated by Isaac Meir son of Taube"

REMARKS: The denoting of a man as his *mother's* son is rare in Ashkenazi dedications. It is, however, quite usual among Hassidim and common among Sephardim. In the present instance, the mother may have been the actual donor, honoring her son. See pointer No. 799 for further remarks.

DONOR: Dr. Harry G. Friedman

# 802

TORAH POINTER  U 9174

United States, early 20th century (see below)

Silver (silver-plated ?): cast, engraved

L 28.5  DIAM 3.6 cm

HALLMARKS: "84"

INSCRIPTION: on medial knop: ‏זײ׳נ׳ א׳ג׳‎, "This was donated by …"

REMARKS: See pointer No. 799 for further remarks.

DONOR: Jewish Cultural Reconstruction

# 803

TORAH POINTER  F 302

United States (?), 1902 (?)

Silver: cast, engraved

L 28.0  DIAM 4.0 cm

HALLMARKS: Imitation Russian marks: "84"; "(?)/1902"

REMARKS: See pointer No. 799 for further remarks.

DONOR: Dr. Harry G. Friedman

# 804

TORAH POINTER  F 3062  (*Illus. p. 320*)

United States (?), late 19th–early 20th century

Silver: cast, etched, traces of parcel–gilding

L 30.0  DIAM 3.8 cm

HALLMARKS: "84"; "STERLING"

REMARKS: See pointer No. 799 for further remarks.

DONOR: Dr. Harry G. Friedman

# 805

TORAH POINTER  F 1342  (*Illus. p. 320*)

New York, early 20th century

Silver: cast, engraved

L 27.9  DIAM 3.1 cm

HALLMARKS: "STERLING" (curved)/ "A.G."

INSCRIPTION: on lower shaft: ‏ירוחם פישל מינץ‎, "Yeruḥam Fischel Mintz"

REMARKS: There are two pointers of similar pattern in the Eis-Levy Collection, Oakland, bearing the same marks as those on this piece. For a Torah Shield with the same marks, see No. 218. See also pointer No. 806 and crown No. 493, bearing an oval mark with the same initials, possibly from the same period and place.

DONOR: Dr. Harry G. Friedman

# 806

TORAH POINTER  F 5491  (*Illus. p. 320*)

United States (?), 1911/12 (inscription)

Silver: cast, engraved; semiprecious stones and glass

L 30.4  DIAM 4.3 cm

HALLMARKS: "84"; "AG" in oval

INSCRIPTION: on medial knop: /זײ׳נ ר׳ זכריה בר ישראל‏‎ ‏לערשטע ראארימור קאנג׳ תרעב‎, "This was donated by Zekhariah son of Israel to the First Rorimor Congregation, (5)572" (=1911/12).

REMARKS: For a Torah crown bearing the same marks, see No. 493; cf. also pointer No. 805, with a similar mark.

DONOR: Dr. Harry G. Friedman

# 807

TORAH POINTER  F 286

United States (?), late 19th–early 20th century

Silver: filigree, cast

L 27.8 DIAM 3.6 cm

HALLMARK:  "STERLING"

MAKER: illegible

DONOR: Dr. Harry G. Friedman

# 808

TORAH POINTER  F 297

United States (?), early 20th century

Silver: cast, engraved

L 28.4  DIAM 4.0 cm

HALLMARK: "STERLING", on cuff

INSCRIPTION: on lower arm: /זײ׳נ ר׳ יעקב מרדכי׳ ב״ר טודרס‏‎ ‏ריקאן׳ ע״ז מורים עטיל׳ בת ר׳ בן ציון‎, "This was donated by Jacob Mordecai son of Todros Reikan (?) w[ith his] s[pouse] Miriam Ethel daughter of Ben-Zion."

DONOR: Dr. Harry G. Friedman

## 809

TORAH POINTER  F 4798  (*Illus. p. 302*)
United States or Germany, early 20th century
Silver
L 16.1  W 2.0 cm
HALLMARK: "STERLING"
DONOR: Dr. Harry G. Friedman

## 810

TORAH POINTER  F 4710
United States (?), early 20th century
Silver: cast
L 21.9  DIAM 1.8 cm
HALLMARK: "925"
REMARKS: Cf. the identical pointer No. 811. These pointers appear to be American copies of a common Hanau design, Nos. 618–619.
DONOR: Dr. Harry G. Friedman

## 811

TORAH POINTER  F 4799
United States (?), early 20th century
Silver: cast, traces of gilt
L 21.8  DIAM 2.0 cm
HALLMARK: "925"
REMARKS: Cf. the identical pointer No. 810 for further remarks.
DONOR: Dr. Harry G. Friedman

## 812

TORAH POINTER  F 5200
United States or Israel, 20th century
Silver: chased; white metal: cast, engine-turned
L 51.5  DIAM 4.5 cm
HALLMARKS: none
INSCRIPTION: on upper shaft: לך יי הגבורה, (adapted from 1 Chronicles 29:11)
DONOR: Dr. Harry G. Friedman

## 813

TORAH POINTER  JM 26–61  (*Illus. p. 320*)
Larchmont, NY, 1960
Herman Roth
Silver: chased
L 28.7  W 2.3 cm
HALLMARKS: none
DONOR: Abram and Frances Kanof

## 814

TORAH POINTER  1990–21
United States, 20th century

Irving Potter, b. 1912
Wood: "intarsia," carved
L 27.5  W 4.3 cm
REMARKS: This pointer is part of a set with Torah Shield No. 228, and is made to hang from a peg on the shield.
DONOR: Gift of the artist

## 815

TORAH POINTER  1992–133  (*Illus. p. 320*)
New York, ca. 1948 (design)
Ludwig Wolpert, active 1920's–1981
Silver: engraved
L 24.5  W 1.8 cm
HALLMARKS: "WOLPERT"; on loop: "STERLING"; "PORTU-GAL"
INSCRIPTION: אכן יש ה' במקום הזה, Gen. 28:16
DONOR: Betty Wolpert, widow of the artist

## 816

TORAH POINTER  1992–162  (*Illus. p. 320*)
New York, 1950's (?)
Ludwig Wolpert, active 1920's–1981
Silver
L 23.4  W 2.9 cm
HALLMARKS: "WOLPERT/925"
DONOR: Betty Wolpert, widow of the artist

## 816 A

TORAH POINTER  JM 2–67c
New York, 1966
Moshe Zabari, active 1954–
Silver: appliqué
L 14.2  W 2.6 cm
HALLMARKS: Tobe Pascher Workshop mark; "M/ZABARI"; "STERLING"
INSCRIPTION: ש, "The Al[mighty" (?)
REMARKS: This pointer forms a set with shield No. 227A and crown No. 512.
BIBLIOGRAPHY: Berman,  No. 20
DONOR: The Abram and Frances Kanof Collection

## 816 B

TORAH POINTER  JM 1984–16  (*Illus. p. 320*)
New York, 1984
Shirley Kagan, active 1972–
Ebony: carved; silver: cast; amethyst
L 27.9  W 1.5 cm
HALLMARKS: "S. Kagan 84"
BIBLIOGRAPHY: JMNY 1993, fig. 59
DONOR: Museum purchase

## 817

TORAH POINTER  F 5478  (*Illus. p. 320*)

England (?), 1811/12 (inscription)

Silver: cast, engraved

L 34.0  DIAM 2.6 cm

HALLMARKS: none

INSCRIPTION: at top of shaft: בשנת/ תקע״ב/ לפ״ק, "In the year (5)572" (=1811/12)

REMARKS: Some later reworking is evident.

DONOR: Dr. Harry G. Friedman

## 818

TORAH POINTER  F 4668  (*Illus. p. 320*)

England (?), late 19th–early 20th century

Brass: cast, silver-plated

L 47.0  DIAM 2.7 cm

DONOR: Dr. Harry G. Friedman

## 819

TORAH POINTER  F 4874  (*Illus. p. 320*)

London, 1929

Silver: cast, chased

L 30.8  DIAM 3.4 cm

HALLMARKS: *CITY:* Pickford, p. 39 (1929)

　　　　　*MAKER:* "MR"

INSCRIPTION: on upper shaft: מתנה מ׳מרת ליבע רחל בת ר׳ בצלאל, "Gift from . . . Liebe Rachel daughter of Bezalel"

DONOR: Dr. Harry G. Friedman

## 820

TORAH POINTER  F 5952  (*Illus. p. 322*)

France, second half of 19th century

Silver: cast, chased

L 30.8  DIAM 5.2 cm

HALLMARKS: "K" below ewer within upright lozenge; "SCHWARTZ"

REMARKS: Cf. other pointers with realistic arms, pointer No. 821 and, Sotheby's NY 1987, No. 301 (Strasbourg, 1819–38).

DONOR: Dr. Harry G. Friedman

## 821

TORAH POINTER  F 3635  (*Illus. p. 322*)

France, late 19th century

Silver: cast, chased, engraved, parcel-gilt

L 33.5  DIAM 2.5 cm

HALLMARKS: none

REMARKS: See No. 820, and the reference there.

DONOR: Dr. Harry G. Friedman

## 822

TORAH POINTER  F 2210

Jerusalem, early 20th century

Wood: turned, carved, pierced; bone (inlay); ink: stamped

L 31.2  DIAM 4.4 cm

INSCRIPTION: on upper knop: כותל מערבי, "Western Wall"

REMARKS: See the similar pointers Nos. 823 and 824.

DONOR: Dr. Harry G. Friedman

## 823

TORAH POINTER  F 4205

Jerusalem, early 20th century

Wood: turned, carved, pierced; bone (inlay); mother-of-pearl: carved; brass and iron (repairs); cord

L 29.6  DIAM 4.2 cm

REMARKS: See the similar pointers Nos. 822 and 824.

DONOR: Dr. Harry G. Friedman

## 824

TORAH POINTER  F 4951

Jerusalem, mid–20th century

Wood: turned, carved; mother-of-pearl: carved; ink: stamped

L 29.3  DIAM 3.5 cm

INSCRIPTION: on medial knop: ירושלים, "Jerusalem"

REMARKS: Unlike similar pointers Nos. 822 and 823, the upper knop of this piece is not hollow and pierced and does not unscrew; the hand is mother-of-pearl.

DONOR: Dr. Harry G. Friedman

## 825

TORAH POINTER  F 1395

Jerusalem, early 20th century

Olive wood: carved; pen and ink

L 22.8  DIAM 4.0 cm

HALLMARKS: none

INSCRIPTION: on upper knop: ירושלם, "Jerusalem"

REMARKS: The pierced upper knop originally opened to allow the insertion of spices. The hand is missing.

DONOR: Dr. Harry G. Friedman

## 826

TORAH POINTER  JM 108–47  (*Illus. p. 322*)

Jerusalem, early 20th century

Silver: cast, engraved

L 17.4  W 2.8 cm

HALLMARKS: none

INSCRIPTION: וזאת התורה אשר שם משה לפני בני/ ישראל ירושלם עה״ק, Deuteronomy 4: 44; "Jerusalem, the Holy City"

REMARKS: This pointer is Moroccan in form (cf. *La Vie Juive*, fig. 76), but the inscription is typical of pointers from Eretz-Israel (e.g., Feuchtwanger, No. 181).

DONOR: Dr. Harry Friedenwald

## 827

TORAH POINTER  F 4665  (*Illus. p. 322*)
Jerusalem, early 20th century
Bezalel workshops (?), active 1906–32
Silver: filigree; ivory: turned, carved
L 23.7  DIAM 1.9 cm
HALLMARKS: none
DONOR: Dr. Harry G. Friedman

## 828

TORAH POINTER  F 1540  (*Illus. p. 322*)
Jerusalem, first half of 20th century
Silver: cast, filigree; enamel
L 24.3  DIAM 2.5 cm
HALLMARKS: "'AMANUTH'"/„אמנות",,
INSCRIPTION: on upper shaft: עץ החיים היא/ למחזיקים בה/
ותומכיה מאשר/ דרכיה דרכי נועם/ וכל נתיבותיה שלום/
ירושלם, Proverbs 3: 17–18; "Jerusalem"
REMARKS: On the basis of its style, quality and workmanship,
this piece may have been made in a Bezalel workshop, or
by a Bezalel graduate. The trademark "Amanuth" means
"art, craft."
DONOR: Dr. Harry G. Friedman

## 829

TORAH POINTER  F 2263
Israel (?), first half of 20th century
Silver: cast, filigree
L 28.9  DIAM 3.1 cm
HALLMARKS: none
DONOR: Dr. Harry G. Friedman

## 830

TORAH POINTER  F 2142
Israel, first half of 20th century
Silver: filigree, cast
L 22.8  DIAM 2.4 cm
HALLMARKS: none
DONOR: Dr. Harry G. Friedman

## 831

TORAH POINTER  1985–206
Jerusalem, after 1932
Silver: filigree, cast, die-stamped
L 16.1  DIAM 1.7 cm
HALLMARKS: *CITY:* "JERUSALEM/ ST. 925"
      *MAKER:* "Bezalel/Jerusalem" (on applied plaque)
REMARKS: On the basis of its design and craftsmanship, this
pointer was made after the closing of the Bezalel work-
shops in 1932. The Bezalel mark was commonly misap-
plied to later metalwork made in Israel.
DONOR: Mrs. Paula Elman

## 832

TORAH POINTER  F 3012a
Tel Aviv, 1950's
Moshe Smilovici, active 1950's
Silver: filigree, cast, engraved; gold: engraved; semiprecious
stones
L 34.2  (W 6.6) DIAM 2.7 cm
HALLMARKS: none
REMARKS: See pointers Nos. 833–838, all pastiches by Smilo-
vici. For other pointers by him, and a brief background, see
Grossman 1989, Nos. 25 and 26. Other objects by this smith
at the Museum are Torah Shields Nos. 236–238 and Torah
Crown No. 504.
DONOR: Dr. Harry G. Friedman

## 833

TORAH POINTER  F 4185c
Tel Aviv, 1950's
Moshe Smilovici, active 1950's
Silver: die-stamped, chased; ivory (?): carved; semiprecious
stones
L 26.1  W 3.3 cm
HALLMARK: "925" (on chain)
INSCRIPTION: on hand: שדי, "The Almighty"
REMARKS: Initials have been erased from the side of the upper
shaft. This Torah Pointer is associated with shield No. 236
and crown No. 504. Cf. the Smilovici pointer No. 832, and
references there.
DONOR: Dr. Harry G. Friedman

## 834

TORAH POINTER  F 4419  (*Illus. p. 322*)
Tel Aviv, 1950's
Moshe Smilovici, active 1950's
Silver: cast, engraved; ceramics; plastic
L 30.1 (?)  W 4.2 cm
HALLMARKS: *CITY:* Lileyko 94c; 96a
      *MAKER:* "KiM"
INSCRIPTION: on lower shaft: וזאת התורה/ אשר שם/ משה
לפני/ בני ישראל, Deuteronomy 4: 44
REMARKS: See No. 832 and references there.
DONOR: Dr. Harry G. Friedman

## 835

TORAH POINTER  F 5690b
Tel Aviv, 1950's
Moshe Smilovici, active 1950's
Silver: cast, die-stamped; gold: engraved
L 13.9  W 1.8 cm
HALLMARKS: none
INSCRIPTION: on upper knop: שדי, "The Almighty"; on upper
shaft: של יד, "Of a hand (or "pointer")"

REMARKS: The second inscription is a peculiar choice for a Torah pointer. It often appears on *tefillin* cases to indicate which of the two *tefillin* is to be placed on the head (e.g., JM 69–48, Kayser, No. 162). See No. 832 and references there.

DONOR: Dr. Harry G. Friedman

## 836

TORAH POINTER JM 39–74

Tel Aviv, 1950's (?)

Moshe Smilovici, active 1950's

Silver: cast, chased, gilt; diamonds; glass

L 19.7 W 1.7 cm

HALLMARKS: none

REMARKS: See No. 832 and references.

## 837

TORAH POINTER F 5039

Tel Aviv, 1950's

Moshe Smilovici, active 1950's

Silver: chased, engraved; gold: appliqué, engraved; ivory: carved; semiprecious stones; glass

L 33.2 DIAM 6.0 cm

HALLMARKS: Moscow, 1880's; illegible mark in oval; partly defaced mark

INSCRIPTION: on main shaft, spiralled: וישלח יקוק בעם את הנחשים השרפים ויעש משה נחש נחשת איש והביט אל בראשית שמות, Numbers 21: 6, 9; on lid: נחש הנחשת ויקרא במדבר דברים, "Genesis, Exodus, Leviticus, Numbers, Deuteronomy"

REMARKS: See No. 832 for references.

DONOR: Dr. Harry G. Friedman

## 838

TORAH POINTER JM 26–58

Tel Aviv, 1950's

Moshe Smilovici, active 1950's

Brass: die-stamped, cast, silver-plated; silver

L 27.8 W 3.8 cm

HALLMARKS: Lileyko 96 (left); "5"; "M.T"

INSCRIPTION: on shaft: תורת/ אמת// תורת/ אמת, Malachi 2:6

REMARKS: See No. 832 for references; and shield No. 238 which was acquired with this piece.

DONOR: Samuel and Lucille Lemberg

## 839

TORAH POINTER F 2593

Israel (?), 20th century

Silver: cast, chased, engraved, gilt, nielloed

L 16.0 DIAM 1.4 cm

HALLMARKS: none

INSCRIPTION: וזאת התורה אשר שם משה/ על פי יקוק ביד משה, Deuteronomy 4: 44

REMARKS: The inscription may be a later addition.

DONOR: Dr. Harry G. Friedman

## 840

TORAH POINTER F 3230

Israel, mid-20th century

Silver: engraved; glass

L 25.8 W 3.7 cm

HALLMARKS: none

INSCRIPTION: on shaft, reading up to upper end: שמע ישראל ה' אלהינו ה' אחד שם כבוד מלכותו לעולם ועד, Deuteronomy 6:4 and "Blessed be the name of His glorious majesty forever and ever"; on hand: תורה צוה לנו/ משה מורשה/ קהלת יעקב, Deuteronomy 33:4

REMARKS: Cf. similar pointers Nos. 841–846.

DONOR: Dr. Harry G. Friedman

## 841

TORAH POINTER F 3231 (*Illus. p. 322*)

Israel, mid-20th century

Silver: engraved; turquoise

L 25.5 W 3.7 cm

HALLMARKS: none

INSCRIPTION: on shaft: ישמחו השמים ותגל הארץ ויאמרו בגוים ה' מלך, 1 Chronicles 16:31

REMARKS: Cf. similar pointers Nos. 840 and 842–846.

DONOR: Dr. Harry G. Friedman

## 842

TORAH POINTER F 3232

Israel, mid-20th century

Silver: engraved

L 17.3 W 3.6 cm

HALLMARKS: none

INSCRIPTION: on shaft: תורה צוה לנו משה מורשה קהלת יעקב, Deuteronomy 33:4; on hand: ה/ אחד, from Deuteronomy 6:4

REMARKS: Cf. similar pointers Nos. 840–841 and 843–846.

DONOR: Dr. Harry G. Friedman

## 843

TORAH POINTER F 3233

Israel, mid-20th century

Silver: engraved

L 17.3 W 3.6 cm

HALLMARKS: none

INSCRIPTION: on shaft: תורה צוה לנו משה מורשה קהלת יעקב, Deuteronomy 33:4; on hand: ה/ אחד, from Deuteronomy 6:4

REMARKS: Cf. similar pointers Nos. 840–842 and 844–846.

DONOR: Dr. Harry G. Friedman

## 844

TORAH POINTER  F 3234

Israel, mid-20th century

Silver: engraved

L 17.2  W 2.6 cm

HALLMARKS: none

INSCRIPTION: on shaft: תורה צוה לנו משה מורשה קהלת יעקב, Deuteronomy 33:4; on hand: ה/ אחד, excerpt from Deuteronomy 6:4

REMARKS: Cf. similar pointers Nos. 840–843 and 845–846.

DONOR: Dr. Harry G. Friedman

## 845

TORAH POINTER  F 3235  (*Illus. p. 322*)

Israel, mid-20th century

Silver: engraved

L 17.3  W 2.6 cm

HALLMARKS: none

INSCRIPTION: on shaft: וזאת התורה אשר שם משה לפני בני ישראל, Deuteronomy 4:44; on hand: ה/ אחד, from Deuteronomy 6:4

REMARKS: Cf. similar pointers Nos. 840–844.

DONOR: Dr. Harry G. Friedman

## 846

TORAH POINTER  F 3236

Israel, mid-20th century

Silver: engraved

L 17.3  W 2.3 cm

HALLMARKS: none

INSCRIPTION: on shaft and hand: וזאת התורה אשר שם משה לפני בני ישראל, Deuteronomy 4:44

REMARKS: Cf. similar pointers Nos. 840–845.

DONOR: Dr. Harry G. Friedman

## 847

TORAH POINTER  1987–61  (*Illus. p. 322*)

Israel, second half of 20th century

Silver: filigree, cast

L 18.2  DIAM 1.3 cm

HALLMARKS: "MADE IN/ ISRAEL/ 925"

DONOR: Gift of Congregation Sheerith Israel of Janina, New York, through Elias Matsas

## 848

TORAH POINTER  F 2220  (*Illus. p. 322*)

Israel (?), second half of 20th century

Silver: cast, filigree; glass

L 26.5  DIAM 3.3 cm

HALLMARKS: none

DONOR: Dr. Harry G. Friedman

## 849

TORAH POINTER  1989–149  (*Illus. p. 322*)

Israel (?), 2nd half of 20th century

Silver

L 30.1  DIAM 1.6 cm

HALLMARKS: none

INSCRIPTION: on upper shaft: תורת ה' תמימה משיבת נפש ע'ה' נ'מ'פ'/ וזאת התורה אשר שם משה לפני בני ישראל, Psalms 19: 8, partly abbreviated; Deuteronomy 4: 44; on lower shaft: תורה צוה לנו משה מ'ק'י, Deuteronomy 33: 4, partly abbreviated.

REMARKS: Cf. a similar pointer at the Magnes Museum, Berkeley, No. 73.45.

DONOR: Anna Ternbach

## 850

TORAH POINTER  F 5281

Italy (?), 18th century (?)

Silver: cast

L 22.9  W 1.8 cm

HALLMARKS: none

DONOR: Dr. Harry G. Friedman

## 850A

TORAH POINTER  1993–250

Jerusalem, 1993

Yaakov Greenvurcel, active 1970's–

Aluminum: anodized; silver

L 23.5  W 3.2 cm

HALLMARKS: on the cuff: "JG" monogram; "Israel"; ישראל; on the hand: "STERLING"

DONOR: The Artist

## 851

TORAH POINTER  JM 86–48  (*Illus. p. 322*)

Modena, Italy, 1803/04

Silver: cast, engraved, gilt; diamonds

L 36.7  DIAM 2.5 cm

HALLMARKS: *CITY:* R³ 7396 (var.)
            *MAKER:* "GB" in oval

INSCRIPTION: on shaft: קדש לה' לפני(?) ההיכל יעא/ נדבת מרת אסתר תנ"צבה/ אשת כ' אפרים קמיאו יצ"ו/ שנת הת"קסד ליצירה, "Dedicated to God before the Ark [or 'to (the congregation of) *Penei Heikhal* ("Interior of the Tabernacle")'], may the Lord establish it, donation of . . . Esther, may her soul be bound up in the bond of [eternal] life, wife of Ephraim Cameo . . ., year 5564 of the Creation"

PROVENANCE: Comunità Israelitica di Roma

REMARKS: The number "673" on the hand is probably a synagogue inventory number. For other pointers with a similar arrangement of diamonds (bracelet and ring) see Klags-

bald 1981, No. 150, and Emden, p. 17 — a feature generally found only on Dutch (or Dutch inspired) pointers.
DONOR: American Joint Distribution Committee

## 852
TORAH POINTER  F 5479  (*Illus. p. 318*)
Italy (?), 18th-19th century
Silver: cast, chased
L 25.5  DIAM 1.1 cm
HALLMARKS: illegible
DONOR: Dr. Harry G. Friedman

## 853
TORAH POINTER  F 3710  (*Illus. p. 318*)
Italy (?), 19th century
Silver: cast, chased
L 23.4  DIAM 1.9 cm
HALLMARKS: "YC"(?); "ET" (Tardy, p. 207 — French import mark, after 1864)
DONOR: Dr. Harry G. Friedman

## 854
TORAH POINTER  F 3518  (*Illus. p. 324*)
Holland, or Northern Germany, late 17th–early 18th century
Silver: cast, chased, engraved
L 26.8  DIAM 3.4 cm
HALLMARKS: Tardy, p. 321, "20"; p. 322 (boar); p. 322 upper left (shield) — all Dutch tax marks
BIBLIOGRAPHY: Kayser, No. 65
REMARKS: The hand holds a stylus.
DONOR: Dr. Harry G. Friedman

## 855
TORAH POINTER  F 3648  (*Illus. p. 324*)
Amsterdam, 18th century
Silver: cast, gilt
L 28.5  DIAM 1.6 cm (clasp: L 4.8  W 1.3 cm)
HALLMARKS: CITY: Voet, p. 2, No. 18(var.); Voet, p. 48, No. 3; on clasp: Tardy, p. 317 ("O" with crown)
  MAKER: "BM" in rectangle (not in Citroen 1993)
REMARKS: A similar pointer is in the Jewish Museum, London: Barnett, No. 164.
DONOR: Dr. Harry G. Friedman

## 856
TORAH POINTER  F 3665  (*Illus. p. 324*)
Amsterdam, 1762–74
Musnier & Maurenbrecher, active 1762–74
Silver: cast, chased
L 17.0  DIAM 1.3 cm (clasp: W 2.2 cm)
HALLMARKS: CITY: Voet, p. 2, No. 18 (var.); Tardy, p. 192, middle (French import, 1809–19); Voet, p. 47, No. 6 (Dutch import, 1814–31)

MAKER: "JvC" in monogram, in oval (Citroen 1993, p. 70)
INSCRIPTION: on shaft: /זעליג בר משה/ מאיר בר הירש ווינר/ חיים העלפוט ואשתו פרומט/ חיים בר אברהם כהן/ קאשמן בר שמואל כהן/ אברהם בר משה כהן/ יוזפא בר ליב כהן/ ר' שמעון בר ר תנחום, "Selig son of Moses; Meyer son of Hirsch Wiener; Ḥayyim Helfut and his wife Frumet; Ḥayyim son of Abraham Cohen; Cosman son of Samuel Cohen; Abraham son of Moses Cohen; Juspa son of Leib Cohen; Rabbi Simon son of Rabbi Tanḥum"
REMARKS: The Amsterdam mark is of a form not found in the literature (Kayser, No. 62, cites R³ 7567).
BIBLIOGRAPHY: Kayser, No. 62
DONOR: Dr. Harry G. Friedman

## 857
TORAH POINTER  F 3050  (*Illus. p. 324*)
Holland or Germany, 18th-19th century
Silver: cast, traces of gilt
L 17.3  DIAM 1.0 cm
HALLMARKS: none
DONOR: Dr. Harry G. Friedman

## 858
TORAH POINTER  JM 6–53  (*Illus. p. 324*)
Amsterdam, 1818 (clasp 1817)
Silver: cast; diamond
L 26.0  DIAM 1.5 cm (clasp: L 1.2 w 1.3 cm)
HALLMARKS: CITY: Voet, p. 45, No. 7; p. 46, No. 2; p. 43 ("J" in script, on hand; "H" in script, on clasp)
  MAKER: "C/MD" in square
DONOR: Mr. Rupert L. Joseph

## 859
TORAH POINTER  F 5629
Holland (?), 19th century
Silver: cast, chased, engraved
L 25.0  W 1.7 cm
HALLMARKS: none
DONOR: Dr. Harry G. Friedman

## 860
TORAH POINTER  F 917  (*Illus. p. 324*)
Holland, 19th century
Silver: cast
L 16.9 w 1.2 cm
HALLMARKS: none
DONOR: Dr. Harry G. Friedman

## 861
TORAH POINTER  F 281  (*Illus. p. 324*)
Georgia, Caucasus (?), 1901 (inscription)
Silver: die-stamped, engraved, nielloed

L 26.4   DIAM 2.4 cm

HALLMARKS: none

INSCRIPTION: on upper arm: /אסתר בת צפניה/ חדש תשרי
שנת תרסב/ לפק, "Esther daughter of Zephaniah, month
of Tishri, [5]662" (=September/October 1901)

DONOR: Dr. Harry G. Friedman

## 862

### TORAH POINTER   F 3910   (*Illus. p. 316*)

Near East, late 19th–early 20th century

Silver: cast, chased

L 35.8   W 3.0 cm

HALLMARKS: none

DONOR: Dr. Harry G. Friedman

## 863

### TORAH POINTER   F 5376   (*Illus. p. 316*)

Egypt, 19th century

Silver: cast, chased

L 23.3   DIAM 0.9 cm

HALLMARKS: none

INSCRIPTION: on medial shaft: נדבה מאת האשה מ'/ רחל
לינדא אסמאעלון/ לק"ק בית יתומים יב"ץ, "Donation
from the woman ... Rachel Linda Isma'eloun to the holy
congregation of the Orphanage ..., May it be built in righteousness"

DONOR: Dr. Harry G. Friedman

## 864

### TORAH POINTER   F 5403   (*Illus. p. 316*)

Alexandria, mid-20th century

Silver: cast, chased

L 24.9   W 1.3 cm

HALLMARKS: none

INSCRIPTION: on shaft: /למנוחת נ'ר'ן' הבתולה נטלי די מנדיל
ת'נ'צ'ב'ה' יום ט' תשרי ש' תר'מ' ל'פק, "For the repose of
the soul ... of ... Natalie di Mendil, May her soul be bound
in the bond of [eternal] life, 9 Tishri, (5)640" (=September
26, 1879); on lower shaft: יד (?), "Torah pointer(?)"

REMARKS: Since this pointer is of typically mid-20th century
workmanship and form, the date in the inscription must
refer to the date of the death of the woman mentioned.

DONOR: Dr. Harry G. Friedman

## 865

### TORAH POINTER   F 4479   (*Illus. p. 324*)

Tunisia, 1905–42

Silver: cast, engraved

L 19.9   W 1.7 cm

HALLMARKS: Tardy, p. 405 upper (head)

REMARKS: The shaft is pierced near the top for attaching a
chain.

DONOR: Dr. Harry G. Friedman

## 865A

### TORAH POINTER   1993–244   (*Illus. p. 324*)

Iran, 20th century

Silver: cast, chased, engraved

L 29.7   W 3.8 cm

HALLMARKS: none

INSCRIPTION: יוסף ב' מ' שמואל, "Joseph son of ... Samuel"

DONOR: In memory of Ebrahim Khalil Rokhsar, by Mena
Rokhsar

## 866

### TORAH POINTER   F 4459   (*Illus. p. 324*)

Iraq (?), 20th century

Silver: cast, chased

L 20.4   DIAM 1.3 cm

HALLMARKS: none

INSCRIPTION: on upper handle: לנשמת כוכב בת יוסף, "For
the soul of Kokhav (or Arabic "Kaukab") daughter of
Joseph"

DONOR: Dr. Harry G. Friedman

## 867

### TORAH POINTER   F 4206   (*Illus. p. 324*)

India, 20th century

Wood: carved; brass: cast

L 26.2   DIAM 3.8 cm

REMARKS: This pointer is modelled after a European original.
Details of the carving and the combination of the hard,
reddish wood and brass, however, reveal its south Asian
origin.

DONOR: Dr. Harry G. Friedman

## 868

### TORAH POINTER   F 2265   (*Illus. p. 326*)

Southeast Asia, mid-19th century

Silver: cast, chased, parcel-gilt

L 26.0   W 2.8 cm

HALLMARKS: none

REMARKS: The workmanship here, as on Nos. 869 and 870, is
typical of Chinese silversmiths scattered throughout
southeast Asia. The form and proportions are quite foreign to other known types of Torah pointers. At the
Skirball Museum, Los Angeles, there are two pointers of
similar proportions and origin — 44.14 (wood and ivory)
and 44.25 (silver). Cf. pointer No. 869, possibly by the same
smith.

DONOR: Dr. Harry G. Friedman

## 869

### TORAH POINTER   F 2526

Southeast Asia, 19th century

Silver: cast, chased, parcel-gilt

L 26.0 W 2.8 cm

HALLMARKS: none

REMARKS: See No. 868 for comments and references.

DONOR: Dr. Harry G. Friedman

## 870

### TORAH POINTER F 2527 (*Illus. p. 326*)

Southeast Asia, 19th century

Silver: cast, chased, engraved

L 23.0 W 1.9 cm

HALLMARKS: none

REMARKS: See No. 868 for comments and references.

DONOR: Dr. Harry G. Friedman

## 871

### TORAH POINTER F 1542 (*Illus. p. 318*)

Germany, 20th century

Koch & Bergfeld, Bremen

Silver: cast, parti-gilt

L 28.0 W 1.4 cm

HALLMARKS: "800"; Neuwirth 1978, No. 286

REMARKS: Cf. No. 872, possibly by the same maker.

DONOR: Dr. Harry G. Friedman

## 872

### TORAH POINTER F 1543

Germany (?), late 19th–early 20th century

Silver: cast, gilt

L 27.4 DIAM 1.3 cm

HALLMARKS: "800"

REMARKS: Cf. pointer No. 871, possibly by the same smith.

DONOR: Dr. Harry G. Friedman

## 873

### TORAH POINTER F 1544

Uncertain origin, 20th century

Silver: die-stamped, cast

L 23.2 DIAM 1.9 cm

HALLMARKS: "13" (numbers marked separately); trace of second mark

REMARKS: The upper handle is a replacement.

DONOR: Dr. Harry G. Friedman

## 874

### TORAH POINTER F 2054

Europe, 19th century (?)

Silver: cast, parcel-gilt

L 16.7 DIAM 1.6 cm

HALLMARKS: *CITY:* illegible

　　　　　*MAKER:* "SI" or "IS"

DONOR: Dr. Harry G. Friedman

## 875

### TORAH POINTER F 2346

Uncertain origin, 19th century (?)

Silver: cast, chased

L 31.0 DIAM 3.5 cm

HALLMARKS: none

REMARKS: Repaired.

DONOR: Dr. Harry G. Friedman

## 876

### TORAH POINTER F 3337

Uncertain origin, 20th century

Silver: cast, chased

L 29.4 DIAM 4.1 cm

HALLMARKS: none

DONOR: Dr. Harry G. Friedman

## 877

### TORAH POINTER F 4451 (*Illus. p. 318*)

Uncertain origin, 1806/07 (?)(inscription)

Silver: cast, chased, pierced, parcel-gilt

L 37.3 DIAM 4.9 cm

HALLMARKS: none

　　　　　*MAKER:* "NS" or "SN" in rectangle.

INSCRIPTION: on upper shaft: מיכאל ב״ר / (erased) מינדא / בת שמואל/ שנת ת״קל״ט ל', "Michael son of . . . Minda daughter of Samuel, year (5)539" (=1778/79)

REMARKS: The date has been modified, probably from תקסז or תקס (1806/07). The script is poorly formed and inconsistent.

DONOR: Dr. Harry G. Friedman

## 878

### TORAH POINTER F 4458 (*Illus. p. 324*)

Uncertain origin, 20th century

Silver: cast, chased, engraved

L 21.1 DIAM 1.7 cm

HALLMARKS: none

INSCRIPTION: לנשמת ניסן בה מ ישועה, "For the soul of Nissan son of . . . Rabbi Joshua"

REMARKS: The lower parts of this pointer seem to be later replacements.

DONOR: Dr. Harry G. Friedman

## 878A

### TORAH POINTER F 5476 (*Illus. p. 318*)

Uncertain origin, 20th century

Silver: cast

L 23.8 DIAM 1.7 cm

HALLMARKS: none

INSCRIPTION: on medial shaft: בשנת תקל״ה, "In the year (5)535" (=1774/75) (*sic*)

DONOR: Dr. Harry G. Friedman

# 879
## TORAH POINTER   F 5490
Italy, 18th century
Silver: coral: carved; semiprecious stones
L 20.2   W 2.8 cm
HALLMARKS: none
DONOR: Dr. Harry G. Friedman

# 880
## TORAH POINTER   S 25   (*Illus. p. 318*)
Lisbon, early 19th century
Silver: cast, chased, parcel-gilt
L 29.2   DIAM 2.1 cm
HALLMARKS: *CITY:* Tardy, p. 334
           *MAKER:* "I F V.A" (?)
PROVENANCE: The Hadji Ephraim and Mordecai Benguiat
     Family Collection
Inscription: מורה באצבע לאור באור/ החיים נשמת המו"ה
     אברהם/ סיכסו נ"ע בר יחייא ה'ר', "Point with the finger
     toward the light, in the light of the life of … the
     late Rabbi Abraham Seixo, son of Yiḥya …"
REMARKS: A large metallic thread tassel (15 cm long) is at-
     tached.
DONOR: Museum purchase

# 881
## TORAH POINTER   S 26   (*Illus. p. 318*)
Italy, 19th century
Silver: cast, chased
L 28.3   DIAM 1.5 cm
HALLMARKS: none
PROVENANCE: The Hadji Ephraim and Mordecai Benguiat
     Family Collection
DONOR: Museum purchase

# 882
## TORAH POINTER   F 315
Uncertain origin, 20th century
Brass: die-stamped, turned; iron: wrought
L 21.9   DIAM 2.7 cm
DONOR: Dr. Harry G. Friedman

# 883
## TORAH POINTER   F 316
Uncertain origin, 20th century
Bone and ivory: carved and turned
L 23.7   DIAM 1.5 cm
REMARKS: The uppermost element of this object is missing.
DONOR: Dr. Harry G. Friedman

# 884
## TORAH POINTER   F 2122
Uncertain origin, 20th century
Bone and ivory: turned, carved; metal (chain)
L 25.2   W 1.5 cm
REMARKS: The shaft is possibly a replacement.
DONOR: Dr. Harry G. Friedman

# 885
## TORAH POINTER   F 3173
Uncertain origin, 20th century
Bone: carved, turned
L 20.2   DIAM 2.6 cm
HALLMARKS: none
DONOR: Dr. Harry G. Friedman

# 886
## TORAH POINTER   S 1193
Uncertain origin, 19th century (?)
Ivory: carved
L 23.2   W 1.7 cm
DONOR: M. Vaxer

# 887
## TORAH POINTER   U 9185
Uncertain origin, 20th century
Ivory: carved
L 21.2   W 1.8 cm

# 888
## TORAH POINTER   F 78
Uncertain origin, 20th century
Bone: carved; wood: turned
L 17.5   DIAM 2.0 cm
DONOR: Dr. Harry G. Friedman

# 889
## TORAH POINTER   M 373   (*Illus. p. 324*)
Poland (?), 19th century (?)
Wood: turned; bone: carved; brass
L 25.7   DIAM 3.6 cm
PROVENANCE: The Rose and Benjamin Mintz Collection
REMARKS: The handle of this pointer appears to be a later
     replacement.
DONOR: Museum purchase

# 891
## TORAH POINTER   F 5028
Uncertain origin, 19th century (?)
Horn: carved, turned, pierced; wood (?)

L 24.7 DIAM 2.2–2.5 cm
DONOR: Dr. Harry G. Friedman

## 891A
TORAH POINTER  D 48  (*Illus. p. 326*)
Central Europe, 19th century
Wood: carved
L 23.5 DIAM 2.3 cm
HALLMARKS: none
INSCRIPTION: "W"
PROVENANCE: The Great Synagogue, Danzig
REMARKS: A braided metallic-thread ribbon is attached to the
loop.
BIBLIOGRAPHY: *Danzig 1939/1982*, No. 48
DONOR: The Jewish Community of Danzig

## 892
TORAH POINTER  F 2609
Uncertain origin, 20th century
Wood: carved
L 10.9 W 3.3 cm
DONOR: Dr. Harry G. Friedman

## 893
TORAH POINTER  F 4848  (*Illus. p. 326*)
Uncertain origin, 20th century
Wood: turned, carved; cord
L 25.0 DIAM 2.3 cm
DONOR: Dr. Harry G. Friedman

## 894
TORAH POINTER  F 5950  (*Illus. p. 326*)
Uncertain origin, 20th century
Wood: turned, carved, stained
L 27.7 DIAM 3.3 cm
DONOR: Dr. Harry G. Friedman

## 895
TORAH POINTER  JM 14–52  (*Illus. p. 326*)
Schnaittach, 18th–19th century
Wood: carved
L 17.9 DIAM 2.3 cm
PROVENANCE: from the Schnaittach Synagogue; Schnaittach,
Heimatmuseum
DONOR: Jewish Cultural Reconstruction

## 896
TORAH POINTER  F 5949  (*Illus. p. 326*)
Uncertain origin, 19th–20th century
Wood: turned, carved; iron (loop)

L 26.5 DIAM 3.4 cm
DONOR: Dr. Harry G. Friedman

## 898
TORAH POINTER  F 2569  (*Illus. p. 326*)
Uncertain origin, 19th–20th century
Wood: carved
L 24.7 W 2.3 cm
DONOR: Dr. Harry G. Friedman

## 898A
TORAH POINTER  U 9181  (*Illus. p. 300*)
Europe, 19th century (?)
Brass: cast, chased, (silver-?) plated
L 21.3 W 1.3 cm
HALLMARKS: none

## 898B
TORAH POINTER  F 2219  (*Illus. p. 322*)
Israel, mid–20th century
Silver: filigree, cast; glass ("gems")
L 26.3 W 3.2 cm
REMARKS: Repaired.
DONOR: Dr. Harry G. Friedman

# Part V · Cases

᭞᭞᭞
᭞᭞
᭞

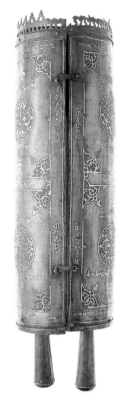

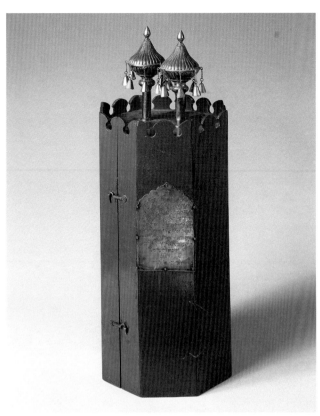

No. 899  S 21

No. 900  1987–145a, b, c

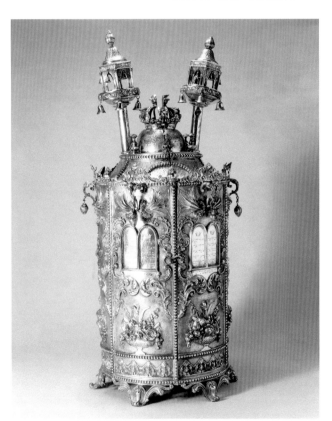

No. 912  S 1456

# Torah Cases

## 899

### SAMARITAN TORAH CASE S 21 (*Illus. p. 356*)

Damascus, 1568 (inscription)

Brass: chased, pierced, silver-inlaid, cast

H 64.1 DIAM 18.0 cm

HALLMARKS: none

INSCRIPTIONS: Samaritan script on three panels (see diagram of one panel):[1]

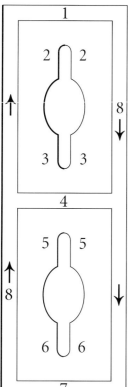

1. בשם יק׳(וק) עשה זה הארון
למ׳(כתב)/ הק׳(דוש) בד׳[2] העבד
השש[3] יוסף/ בן אב סכוה רמבני מטר[4]
5. מיd על יד הרבן אבי עזי
6. מיd בן הרבן יוסף בדמשק
7. בשנת ו וע. וט. ק. לממי׳(לכת)/
בני יש׳(מעאל)[5] יק׳(וק) יכפר לו
חטא/ [6׳] אמן וכתבו[7] ישמעאל
הרמחי[8]

2. אלוקים יראה/ יקוק אלקינו[9]/
יקוק שמו [10]

3. יקוק יראה/ יקוק אחד לבדו/
יקוק נסי [11]

4. יברכך/ יקוק/ וישמרד[12]

5. יקוק אלקיי[13]/ יקוק אל

6. יקוק גבור/ רחום וחנון[14]

8. ויהי[15] בנסע/ הארון ויאמר/ משה
קומה/ יקוק ויפוצו/ איביך וינוסו/
משנאיך מפניך[16]

"In the name of the Lo[rd], this case for the H[oly] Sc[ripture] was made, with H[eavenly assistance],[2] by the aged[3] servant Joseph son of Ab Sakhwa of the sons of Matar[4]; by means of the Rabban Abi Uzzi son of the Rabban Joseph in Damascus; in the year 976 of the Kin[gdom of] the Ishma[elites].[5] May the L[ord] let his sin be atoned. Let Amen be said.[6] And it was written[7] by Yishmael Haramḥi.[8]

| | | |
|---|---|---|
| God shall be feared. | The Lord is our God.[9] | The Lord is His name![10] |
| The Lord shall be feared. | The Lord is one alone. | The Lord is my banner.[11] |

May the Lord bless you and protect you.[12] The Lord! The Lord is my God.[13] God compassionate and gracious.[14] The Lord is God. The Lord is mighty.

When[15] the Ark was to set out, Moses would say: Advance, O Lord! May Your enemies be scattered, and may Your foes flee before You!"[16]

PROVENANCE: The Hadji Ephraim and Mordecai Benguiat Family Collection

REMARKS: The case opens as three panels, the two outer ones with handles below, to facilitate raising the case before the congregation. Originally, each of the three parts had a rod (*etz ḥayyim*) which protruded above, to hold a finial.

Several similar cases are still at Nablus (see *JE* XI, p. 133 upper right; Pinkerfeld 1929; *JL* V, col. 69; color pl. opp. cols. 71–72; *EJ* 14, col. 727, fig. 1; Stahl, p. 49). Another similar Samaritan Torah Case is in the collection of the University of Michigan (see Anderson, pp. 62–64).

BIBLIOGRAPHY: *JL* V, col. 71 (illus.); JMNY 1944, p. [15]; Kayser, No. 4.

DONOR: Museum Purchase

1. As presented here, the dedicatory passages of the inscription are followed by the laudatory texts. The lines are to be read horizontally, from panel to panel. The breaks between panels are denoted by diagonal strokes (see diagram). An exception is lines 5 and 6, where the text on the middle panel is integral with the dedication, whereas that on the two flanking panels is laudatory.

2. Probably בסעדא דשמיא or the like.

3. Possibly כשש, misspelling קשש, "aged."

4. The last two words have variously been interpreted as דמבני מטר or דמבני פטר, "of the sons of Matar" or "Petar." The reading, not to speak of the interpretation, is most problematic.

5. The previous dating of 1565 was apparently based on the incorrect reading of the *vav* as a *gimel*. The literal translation would be "in the year 6 and 70 and 9[x]100 of the Kingdom of the Ishmaelites." Such a dating is supported by the mention of a known personage; see note 8, below.

6. Possibly abbreviating יאמר.

7. The reading is difficult; presumably, the "it" would refer to the Torah Scroll within.

8. For Yishma'el al-Rumaiḥi (Hebrew Haramḥi), see *JE* X, p. 681a; *EJ* 14, col. 756; his *Molad Moshe*, written in Arabic (ed. by S.J. Miller, New York, 1949), was completed in 1537.

9. Deuteronomy 6:4.

10. Exodus 15:3.

11. Exodus 17:15.

12. Numbers 6:24.

13. Deuteronomy 4:5; 18:16.

14. Exodus 34:6.

15. Between this and the next word are three crudely inserted words, not inlaid in silver. They seem to read: עמר עי.י. עמר, and do not appear to relate to the surrounding text. This later addition requires further study.

16. Numbers 10:35.

## 900

### TORAH CASE 1987–145a  (*Illus. p. 356*)

India, 1876 (inscription)

Wood: painted; silver: chased; brass

H 44.2   DIAM 23.5 cm

HALLMARKS: none

INSCRIPTIONS: on plaques: זה/ ספר תורה והתיק/ והרמונים והמפה ומ"מ/ הקדישה אותם ס"י רחל/ הנקרא שמה לרובאי/ פיזרכרה מב'ת/ אשת" משה בנימן פיזרכר ה"יו"/ יום כ"א לחודש תשרי/ ליום הושענה רבא/ שנת ה'ת'ר'ל'ז'/ לפ"ג/ אס, "This Torah Scroll and the case and the finials and the mantle and the po[inter] (*moreh maqom*) were dedicated by … Rachel, called … Pizarkara …, wife of Moses Benjamin Pizarkar …, 21 Tishri, Hoshana Rabba, the year 5637. A[men]. S[o may it be]."

REMARKS: Torah Finials No. 445 belong to this case.

DONOR: The Michael and Luz Zak Purchase Fund

## 901

### TORAH CASE PLAQUES F 5430a,b

India (?), 1744/45 (inscription)

Brass: chased

H 13.3   W 9.2 cm (each)

HALLMARKS: none

INSCRIPTIONS: on plaque A: וזאת/ התורה שהקדישה/ כ'א' ברכרדאר יצ'ו בן כ'א'/ משה יצ'ו' לקרותה (!) בצבור/ כל מי יהיה/; on plaque B: /שיגנוב או ימכור/ או יחליף או ימשכן בכלל הקללות/ שבכ'ד' ספרים ערוכים/ והקוראים ישמחו בה/ א'מ'נ'ס' נשלם בשנת/ ה'ת'ק'ה' ליצירה, "And this is the Torah which was dedicated by … Berkerdar (?) … son of … Moses … to read it in public. Anyone who should steal or sell or exchange or pawn [it] shall be under all the curses in the Scriptures. And the readers shall rejoice in it, A[men]. E[ternity.] S[elah]. Completed in the year 5505" (= 1744/45)

REMARKS: There is an old number on a label on the reverse of plaque A: "668."

DONOR: Dr. Harry G. Friedman

## 902

### TORAH CASE S 503

Tunisia, 1820 (inscription)

Wood: carved, gessoed, painted, gilt

H 52.0   DIAM 31.5 cm

HALLMARKS: none

INSCRIPTIONS: on the upper frieze, reading from the opening: זו/ תורה התורה ב/ ותיק נאה/ סגורה במו ת./ (?)כתורה/ להרמכ/ ס והרא/ ש סבורה (?)/ נעשה/ למנוח/ ת; on the lower frieze, from the opening: או(?)א/ נ(?)בון שנ/ שער(?) בלא ב/ נים ולו פ(?)/ יר אי שמו/ ו משה /. . . ./ . . . ./ . . . . / תו מל/. כ(?)א ב/ אדרש/ תקף לפ(?)/) . ., "This is the Law. The Torah [Scroll] closed in a pleasing case crowned … to elevate you and the head. … Made for the repose of a wise m[an of] G[od] who was left without sons and … his name is Moses … (day) of Adar, y[ear] [5]580 …" (=1820).

PROVENANCE: Judge Mayer Sulzberger, 1904

REMARKS: In *JE* XI, p. 133, this Torah case is ascribed: "from Tafilet, Morocco."

In the *JE* photograph, floral elements are seen attached to the top of the case. Traces of these are extant in the form of several nails with wire, wrapped with red and green woolen threads. On the top of the case are remains of a blue and green floral printed wallpaper; there are traces of a patterned paper on the bottom as well. There is a lower "shelf" within.

BIBLIOGRAPHY: *JE* XI, p. 133, lower left; Yaniv 1993, p. 96, n. 34.

DONOR: Dr. A. Marks

## 903

### TORAH CASE S 508

Tunisia, 1832 (inscription)

Wood: carved, gessoed, gilt

H 74.0   DIAM 46.0 cm

HALLMARKS: none

INSCRIPTIONS: on the upper frieze: זאת התורה/ (ה)תורה/ בנ(?)כת ביד/ באושרה ב/ ותיק נאה יפ/ ה מראה כ/ מו תגין[1] /. . .; on the lower frieze: ה לשם יקר/ יד(?)ה)ו אנכר/ בכל מדה/ מפוארה ברום/ ריחו משומר/ ה האליתו ל/ — /— /— /— ה כהונה לו/ מתו אדה בכ/ט באב שנת/ תקצה /—, "This is the Torah. [The] Torah [Scroll] … with her wealth, in a pleasing case, beautiful in appearance, like *tagin*[1] for a precious name … splendid in every measure, at the height of his scent, his lamentation is preserved for. …, priesthood … on the 29th of [the month of] Av year (5)592" (= 25 August, 1832)

PROVENANCE: Judge Mayer Sulzberger, 1904

REMARKS: This case is in very poor condition and the inscription very faint. The entire interior surface is painted with floral motifs on a light red background; above and below, there are "shelves."

BIBLIOGRAPHY: Yaniv 1993, p. 96, n. 34 (listed mistakenly as U 8456).

DONOR: Karekin Beshir

---

1. The word *tagin*, lit. "crowns," may refer to the crown-like embellishments at the top of certain letters in a Torah Scroll.

## 904

### TORAH CASE  JM 24–49

Tunisia, 1837 (inscription)

Wood: carved, gessoed, gilt; paint; ink

H 73.0  DIAM 41.0 cm

HALLMARKS: none

INSCRIPTIONS: on upper frieze, from the opening around:

זאת ת/ורה והיא זכ/ה וברה . . ולה ת/ תן כדמות כתר ו/
עטרה..בתוך נרתי/ק מאד נאה/ ויפה צרורה.../ עם מפה ורמוני/
ים הלה היא בפ/ (?)הדורה נעשה/ למנחת נפש ה./ ת' היקרה.. חי/
ה שמה

on lower frieze:

—/ — / מים ולבית טובייא/ .א' הכי נקרא . . לח/
ודש מנחם שנת/ התק ותשעים ושבע/ ליצירת/ מלאכתו נגמרה/
תהיה נפשה עם נפ/ שות נשים צדקניו/ ת בצרור החיים/
צרורה . . ./ ת'נ'צ'ב'ה'

"This is [the] Torah and it is pure and clear.
And you shall give it an image like a crown and a diadem,
Within a very pleasing case and beautifully bound,
With these mantle [*mappah*] and finials [*rimmonim*] it . . . was ornamented. . . . It was made for the repose of the soul of the dear . . . Ḥayyah is her name. . . . and of the House of Tubaya . . . indeed [she?] was called. . . . in the month of Menaḥem [Av], year 5500 and ninety-seven of the Creation (= August 1837), its crafting was concluded. May her soul be with the souls of righteous women, in the bond of life may she be bound. M[ay] s[he be] b[ound] in [the bond of (eternal)] l[ife]."

REMARKS: The interior is painted red, with gold details. The lower "shelves" have eight circular "windows" each. Cf. the similar Torah case No. 903; and, Klagsbald 1981, No. 122.

BIBLIOGRAPHY: *Venice*, No. 16; *Gardens*, No. 121; Yaniv 1993, p. 96, n. 34

DONOR: Joseph E. Adler

## 905

### TORAH CASE  F 4568

El-Ḥamma, 19th century (?)

Wood: carved, painted; iron (nails, hinges and clasp)

H 84.0  DIAM 36.0 cm

HALLMARKS: none

INSCRIPTIONS: illegible traces in upper and lower friezes; on a paper label within: (*sic*) בהכנ"ס אלקסר זיע"א/ אלחאמרה טוניסיה, "The Al-Ksar Synagogue . . ., El-Ḥamma, Tunisia."

PROVENANCE: The Bezalel National Museum, Jerusalem

REMARKS: The Al-Ksar mentioned on the label is one of the two villages in the El-Ḥamma oasis, 30 km west of Gabes in Tunisia. Above the label, written in ink, is the Bezalel Museum inventory number: "2816-6-50."

The surface is painted in a red-brown that covers the original painted polychrome floral ornamentation. The interior is painted salmon red. There is a similar polychrome Torah Case at the Israel Museum, Jerusalem.

BIBLIOGRAPHY: Yaniv 1993, p. 91, n. 27

DONOR: Dr. Harry G. Friedman

## 906

### TORAH CASE  1984–70a

Tunisia or Libya, first half of 20th century

Wood: pierced, painted; mother-of-pearl: inlaid; glass (mirrors)

H 78.8  DIAM 37.0 cm

HALLMARKS: none

PROVENANCE: The Jewish Community of Malta

REMARKS: A Hebrew inscription may have adorned the upper frieze. On a panel to the left of the opening is a crudely carved "3," possibly intended to indicate the order of reading, like the plaques of a Torah Shield. There are traces of studs around the case, just below the upper frieze, probably for fastening a mantle.

The interior is painted red. There are top and bottom "shelves," each pierced by eight holes; the upper holes were originally backed with mirrors (fragments of which remain). Torah Finials No. 393 were acquired with this case. For a similar inlay on a wooden casket from Algeria, see *Broderie d'Alger*, p. 54, No. 2.

BIBLIOGRAPHY: *Sephardic Journey*, No. 337, color pl. 11, left; *JMNY 1993*, fig. 50a

DONOR: Museum purchase

## 907

### TORAH CASE  F 4594

Tunisia or Libya, early 20th century

Wood; textiles

H 69.6  DIAM 39.6 cm

HALLMARKS: none

PROVENANCE: Ben Ari Arts, New York

REMARKS: There are nail hooks at the top of every other panel, for suspending a mantle. The clasp is a machine-made replacement. The interior is lined with a pink fabric. On the inside at top left is a number inscribed in pencil: "378" (or "318"). See Sotheby's NY 1989, No. 228, for an Egyptian (?) Torah Case with a metal crown similar to the one on this case.

BIBLIOGRAPHY: Yaniv 1993, p. 96, n. 34 (?)

DONOR: Dr. Harry G. Friedman

## 908

### TORAH CASE  F 5146

Ioannina, 1927 (inscription)

Silver (?) and brass: fabricated, die-stamped, engraved; glass; textile

H 76.0  DIAM 36.8 cm

HALLMARKS: none

INSCRIPTIONS: on crowns: כ ת, "C[rown of] T[orah]"; on large plaques: זה התיק הקדישו היקר חיים שלמה אליה/ לק״ק שארית ישראל יאנינא לחייו ולחיי כל בני ביתו/ ובא אל הקודש בראש השנה משנת התרפ״ח, "This Torah Case was dedicated by . . . Ḥayyim Solomon Elia to the H[oly] C[ongregation] Sheerith Israel, Ioannina, for [the benefit of] his life and the lives of all the members of his household, and came to the synagogue (lit. "the Holy") on the New Year of the year 5688" (= 27 September 1927); and: ספר התורה הזה הקדישו היקר אליסף יהודה מצא/ היו לק״ק שארית ישראל יאנינא לחייו ולחיי כל בני ביתו/ ובא אל הקודש בי״ד לח׳ אדר משנת התרפ״ז, "This Torah Scroll was dedicated by . . . Eliasaf Judah Maza . . . to the H[oly] C[ongregation] Sheerith Israel, Ioannina, for [the benefit of] his life and the lives of all the members of his household, and came to the synagogue (lit. "the Holy") on the 14th of the m[onth] of Adar of the year 5687" (= 16 February 1927); on each bowl-shaped plaque: מורה תבנית התיק היקר יוסף שמואל מצא הי״ו, "The designer of the precious Torah Case [was] Joseph Samuel Matsa . . ."; on small stars of David: ציון, "Zion"

PROVENANCE: N. Sakiel & Son, New York

DONOR: Dr. Harry G. Friedman

## 909

### TORAH CASE   JM 27–56

Iraq, 1907/08

Silver: chased, die-stamped; wood; textile: printed; glass (mirror): painted

H 85.2   DIAM 28.5 cm

HALLMARKS: none

INSCRIPTIONS: inside right: וזאת/ התורה אשר/ שם משה לפני/ בני ישראל: תיק/ זה וסת שבו/ עשתה אותו שרה/ בת שאול חי/ אהרן מבת׳ על/ נש׳ בתה המ׳/ רוזה כתון בת/ המ׳ עזרא שלום, "And this is the Torah which Moses put before the Children of Israel (Deut. 4:44): This case, and the T[orah] S[croll] in it, was made by Sarah daughter of Saul Ḥai Aaron . . . (and) her daughter . . . Rosa Khatoun daughter of . . . Ezra Shalom"; on lower strip, right and left: שנת תרסח, Deuteronomy 33:4, and "year [5]668" (= 1907/08); on exterior, upper frieze, from opening: תיק זה וסת׳ שבו עשתה אותו האשה שרה בת/ האשה טובה בת זבידה נע׳ תנצבה׳, "This case and the T[orah] S[croll] within it was made by . . . . Sarah daughter of . . . Tovah daughter of the late Zabida . . ."; on exterior, lower frieze, from opening: על מנת בכל מקום שירצו בעלי הספר תורה להוציאו ולהניחו למקומות אחרים הרשות בידם ובידן], "For the sake of owners of the Torah Scroll, wherever they may wish to take it and place it in other places, permission is in their hands and in the hand of . . ."

PROVENANCE: The Bevis Marks Synagogue

REMARKS: There is an incorrect accession number in pencil: "F 4147." The brass nails used in this case are all old, while the iron ones are recent.

DONOR: The Bevis Marks Synagogue

## 910

### TORAH CASE   JM 28-56

Iraq, 1918/19 and 1919/20 (inscriptions)

Wood; textile; leather; brass; iron; glass; gouache on paper

H 87.1   DIAM 26.3 cm

HALLMARKS: none

INSCRIPTIONS: on interior of dome, on right: שדי/ ועתה כתבו לכם/ את ההתשוירירהה הזאת ולמדה את בני ישראל "The Almighty. And now write for yourselves this TORAH [within the small letters, the word: "Poem"], and it was taught to the Children of Israel" (based on Deuteronomy 31:19); on interior of dome, on left: שדי/ תיק זה וס׳ת/ שבו הקדישו ה׳ר/ משה יוסף יחזקאל/ בחייו ש׳ תרעט/ ונפטר יום ר׳ח/ טבת שנת התרף/ תנצבהא "The Almighty. This case and the Torah Scroll which is in it were dedicated by . . . Moses Joseph Ezekiel in his lifetime, year (5)679 (= 1918/19), and he died on 1 Tevet of the year 5680 (= 23 December 1919). M[ay his] s[oul be] b[ound] in [the bond of eternal] l[ife], A[men]."

REMARKS: The interior is lined with a multicolored "mattress ticking."

DONOR: The Bevis Marks Synagogue

## 911

### TORAH CASE   JM 29–56

Iraq (?), 1942/43; 1951 (inscriptions)

Wood; brass: die-stamped, chased; textile; glass; paper: painted

H 77.2   DIAM 22.2 cm

HALLMARKS: none

INSCRIPTIONS: on interior of dome, on right: וזאת/ התורה אשר/ שם משה לפני/ בני ישראל:/ תיק זה וסת/ שבו הזקנה/ עזיזה בת/ יעקב כהן מבת/ עשתה אותו; on left: ה׳ יאריך ימיה/ בטוב אכיר״/ שנת התשג׳ "This is the Torah that Moses set before the Children of Israel [Deut. 4:44]. This case and the Torah Scroll within it were made by the elder woman Aziza daughter of Jacob Cohen. . . . May the Lord increase her days with goodness, . . ., year [5]703" (= 1942/43); on upper interior rim of case, on right: יום א 19 אדר א 5711; on left: נפ הז עזיזה בת רבקה "The e[lderly woman] Aziza daughter of Rebecca di[ed] on Sunday 19 Adar I 5711" (= 25 February 1951).

REMARKS: The interior of the case is lined with striped cloth. The top metal element is missing. The date at the end of the inscription is in Arabic numerals. Beneath the last two inscriptions, there appears to have been an earlier inscription or motif.

DONOR: The Bevis Marks Synagogue

# 912

TORAH CASE S 1456a (*Illus. p. 356*)

Paris, ca. 1870

Maurice Mayer, active 1860s–1870s

Silver: die-stamped, repoussé, cast, engraved, parcel-gilt; wood; textile

H 62.0 DIAM 31.0 cm

HALLMARKS: *CITY:* Tardy, p. 204, second row, left (= export, 1840–79)

*MAKER:* engraved on upper dome, in script: *Maurice Meyer/ Orfèvre Joaillier de l'Empereur/ Paris*

INSCRIPTION: on later plaques: לבית שמאמא /החסידה חנה ז"ל, "The righteous Ḥannah, late of the house (family) Semama, of blessed memory"

REMARKS: The hallmark and the nature of the dedication plaques and inscription indicate that this Torah Case was probably used in North Africa or in the western Ottoman Empire.

The Semama family included several very wealthy members who lived in Paris, Livorno and Corfu during the time this Torah Case was manufactured; one of them could have been its patron (see *EJ* 14, col. 722). Torah finials No. 378, by the same smith, embellish this case.

BIBLIOGRAPHY: American Art Galleries, No. 632; JMNY 1944, p. [14]; *Jewish Museum 75*, p. [13]; *Treasures*, pp. 154–55

DONOR: Museum purchase

# 913

TORAH CASE F 1984

Jerusalem, 1919

Bezalel workshops, active 1906–32

Brass: chased, filigree, silver-plated; silver: inlaid, repoussé; ivory: carved

H 37.5 DIAM 18.0 cm

HALLMARKS: none; on bottom: "886."

INSCRIPTIONS: on sides:

| בעם | למתנדבים |
|---|---|
| א'תתמ"ט | ארץ ישראל |

Deuteronomy 6:4; Judges 6:12; "For volunteers from among the People, Eretz-Israel, 1849" (= 1919; see remarks for explanation); around the base of the dome: Numbers 10:35; Isaiah 2:3

REMARKS: The ivory medallions bear symbols of the Twelve Tribes; the clasp medallion shows Judea being freed (by Bar Kokhba or Judah Maccabee?). The era of the date in the inscription is based on the destruction of the Temple in 70 C.E. The dedication refers to volunteers from Palestine in the British Army during the First World War.

BIBLIOGRAPHY: Bezalel 1983, No. 828

DONOR: Dr. Harry G. Friedman

# 914

TORAH CASE JM 22–51

Israel, early 20th century

Sheet-iron: coppered; brass; ink on paper

H 52.0 DIAM 17.5 cm

HALLMARKS: none

INSCRIPTION: on final sheet of scroll (in Samaritan script): אלי מאה ועשרין י.פר שני אלפ'/ ושלשה מאות ותשע ועשרין/ לממלכת ען . . ס, "Eli (?) one hundred and twenty . . . two thousand and three hundred and twenty-nine [years] of the kingdom of [the Ishmaelites] . . ." (= 1911).

REMARKS: The scroll within the case, in Samaritan script (30 columns on 5 sheets of paper), includes Genesis 1:1 to Genesis 16:16, besides the colophon. The case is not of Samaritan form, and was probably made for the tourist trade.

# Part VI · Staves

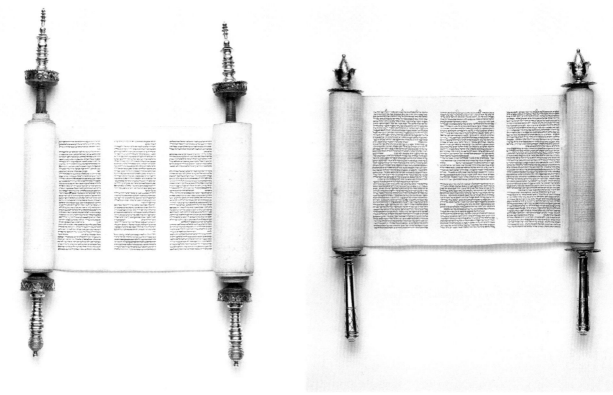

No. 915　JM 54–52a, b

No. 918　F 2154a, b

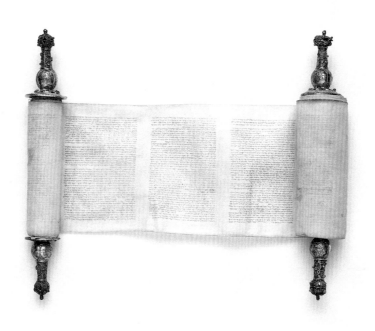

No. 916　F 1933a, b

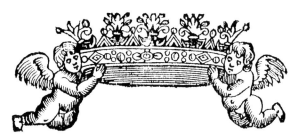

# Torah Staves

## 915

**TORAH STAVES** JM 54–52 a,b  (*Illus. p. 364*)

Nuremberg, early 18th century

Johann Conrad Weiss, active 1699–after 1751

Silver: turned, pierced, engraved; wood

H 39.0  DIAM 4.1 cm (each)

HALLMARKS: *CITY:* "N"; R³ 3790 (?)

      *MAKER:* R³ 4279

REMARKS: A pair of Torah Finials (No. 263), a Torah Pointer (No. 517), a Burial Society beaker (JM 30–51) and a spice container (F 383) at the Museum are all by the same master.

BIBLIOGRAPHY: Kayser, No. 19; Mann 1982, No. 8

DONOR: Samuel and Lucille Lemberg

## 916

**TORAH STAVES** F 1933 a,b  (*Illus. p. 364*)

Europe, 18th–19th century

Silver: filigree, chased, parcel-gilt

H 22.5  DIAM 3.5 cm (each)

HALLMARKS: none

REMARKS: The donor "was told that the scroll was found in Germany buried in the ground to hide it from the Nazis. Munich or the neighborhood was given as the location. But the story is unconfirmed." (Museum records).

DONOR: Dr. Harry G. Friedman

## 917

**TORAH STAVES** F 2952 a,b

Ukraine, second half of 19th century

Brass: cast, chased, engine-turned, silver-plated

H 26.3  DIAM 8.9 cm

HALLMARKS: none

REMARKS: The bottom ends are threaded to fit into now-missing discs. For parallels, see the Museum's wood and bone Torah Staves F 5358.

DONOR: Dr. Harry G. Friedman

## 918

**TORAH STAVES** F 2154 a,b  (*Illus. p. 364*)

Germany (?), 19th century

Silver: cast, engraved

H 32.2  DIAM 4.2 cm

HALLMARKS: *CITY:* shield with bend (cf. Tardy, p. 41, Karlsruhe, right)

      *MAKER:* "B" incuse

REMARKS: Museum records indicate that these Torah Staves formed a set with Torah Pointer No. 582. The set "originally belonged to the Berthold Auerbach family and later to the Steffin family of New York."

DONOR: Dr. Harry G. Friedman

## 919

**TORAH STAVES** JM 73–48 a,b

Central Europe, 19th–20th century

Silver: engraved, gilt; tourmaline

H 30.5  DIAM 7.9 cm

HALLMARKS: none

DONOR: Louis M. Rabinowitz, New York

## 920

**TORAH STAVE COVERS** F 4818 a,b

Europe, 1915

Silver: engraved

DIAM 10.5 cm (each)

HALLMARKS: none

INSCRIPTION: אכבד את ה׳ מהוני זה כתב ידי אשר חנני
ה׳ ואך זה כל הוני עלי אדמות וכתבתי/ אני דובער ב"ר
משה ז"ל סופר את הספר הזה מבראשית/ ועד לעיני
כל ישראל לשם קדושת ספר תורה// בעז"ה׳ ית׳ ובעזרת
עזרתי ציפה פייגה בת ר׳ זאב הכהן ז"ל החילותי בדמעה
במוצאי יו׳ ה"כ תר"סח וגמרתי ברנה יום א טז שבט הע"תר

"I will honor the L[ord] from my wealth. This is my hand-writing [with] which the L[ord] has favored me, and this is my entire wealth on earth, and I, Dober (=Dov Baer) son of the late ... Moses, scribe, wrote this [Torah] Scroll, from "In the beginning" [Gen. 1:1] to "before all Israel" [Deut. 34:10], for the sanctification of the Torah Scroll, with the help of the Lord, blessed be He, and with the help of my helper, Zippah Feige daughter of the late ... Zev ha-Kohen. I began with a tear on the evening after the Da[y of] A[tonement], [5]668 (=September 18, 1907), and I finished in joy on Sunday, 16 Shevat [5]675" (=January 31, 1915).

REMARKS: The wooden handles and discs of the staves are missing.

DONOR: Dr. Harry G. Friedman

# Hallmarks

## *Pictorial*

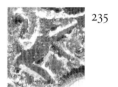 235

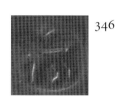 346

 496

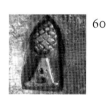 520

## *Alphabetical*

 60

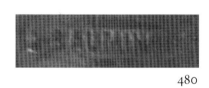 480

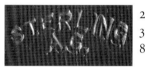 218
354
805

 467

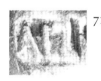 713

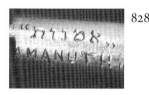 828

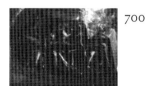 700

 700

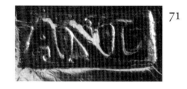 71

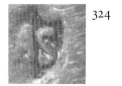 324

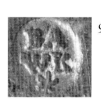 91

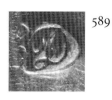 589

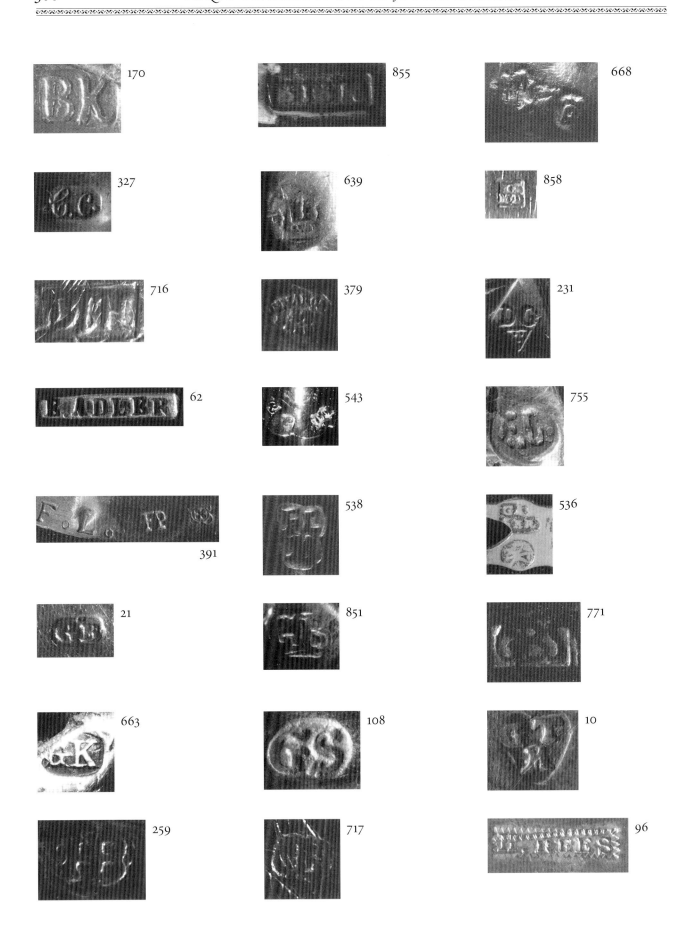

170

855

668

327

639

858

716

379

231

62

543

755

391

538

536

21

851

771

663

108

10

259

717

96

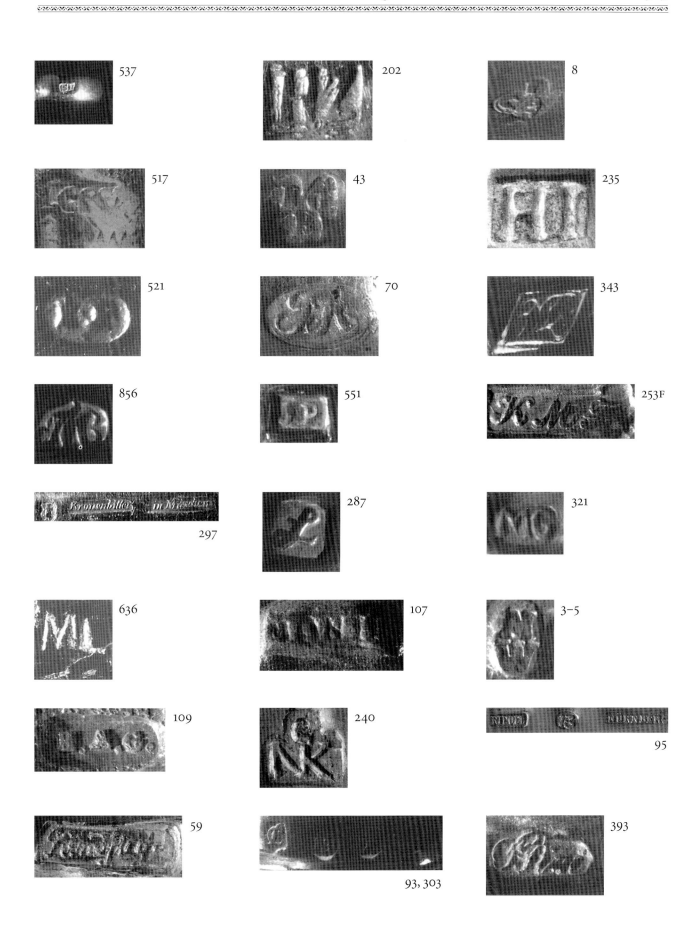

537

202

8

517

43

235

521

70

343

856

551

253F

297

287

321

636

107

3–5

109

240

95

59

93, 303

393

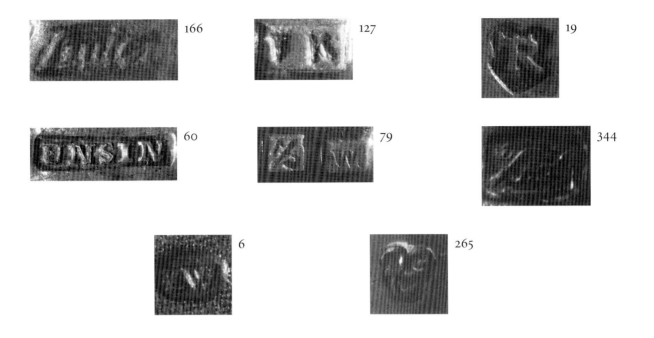

## Illegible

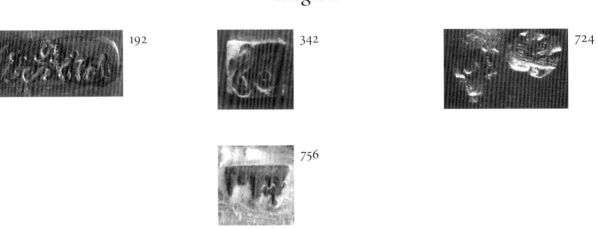

## Numerals

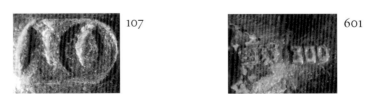

## Cyrillic

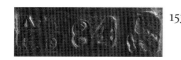 153

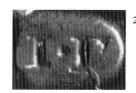 210

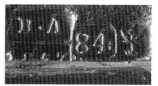 212

## Hebrew

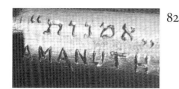 828

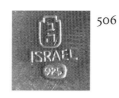 506

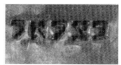 503

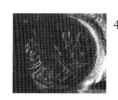 392

## Turkish

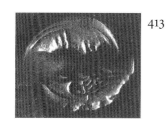 413

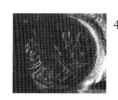 414

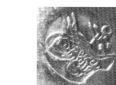 416

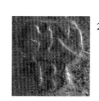 418

## False German

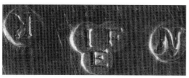 

26

 27

 80

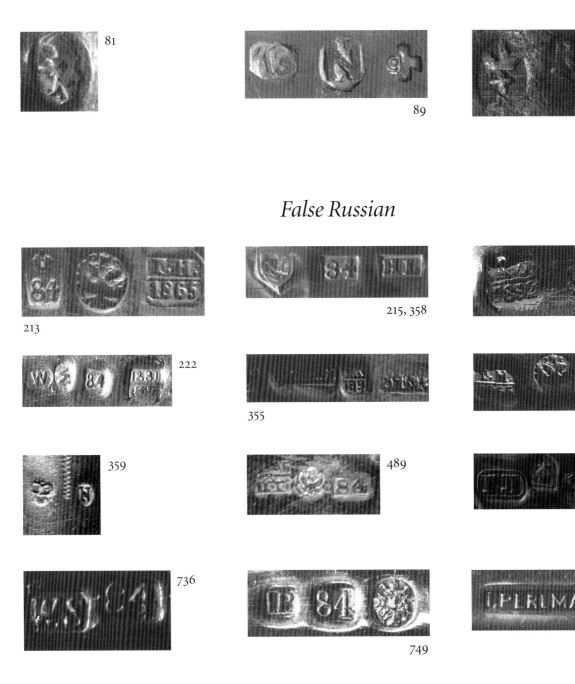

81

89

186

## False Russian

213

215, 358

221

222

355

357

359

489

492

736

749

751

799

801

# Pastiches and Dubious Objects

❦

## TORAH SHIELD  F 5605

Uncertain origin, 20th century; dated 1786
Silver: repoussé, cast, engraved
H 29  W 24.6 cm
HALLMARKS: none
INSCRIPTION: above: כתר תורה, "Crown of Torah"; at center:
נדבת הקצין האלון האלוף מוהר/ ר׳ יוסף וואהל ר׳ח׳
ניסן ת׳ק׳מ׳ו׳, "Donation of . . . Rabbi Joseph Wohl, 1 Nissan
(5)546" (= 1786)
REMARKS: This shield is a pastiche of old and new elements,
with a recent inscription.
DONOR: Dr. Harry G. Friedman

## TORAH FINIALS  F 2617a, b

Uncertain origin, 20th century
Silver(?): pierced; brass (bells)
H 32.3  DIAM 10.1 cm
HALLMARKS: "22"; pointed oval (mostly obliterated)
REMARKS: These pastiches are made from a pair of openwork
flower vases, with the glass liners removed.
DONOR: Dr. Harry G. Friedman

## TORAH FINIALS  F 3224a, b

Israel (?), 20th century
Silver: chased, engraved
H 22.4  DIAM 8.0 cm
HALLMARKS: none.
INSCRIPTION: on each, repeated twice: ה׳ הוא/ האלקים, "The
Lord is God"; in smaller script: סיון התקצו, "Sivan 5596"
(= May–June 1836).
REMARKS: The bodies of these pastiches are made from gob-
lets; the inscriptions on the tops are recent.
DONOR: Dr. Harry G. Friedman

## TORAH FINIALS  F 4727a, b

Uncertain origin, 20th century
Brass: spun, die-stamped, cast
H 36.2  DIAM 10.6 cm
HALLMARKS: none
REMARKS: These pastiches are made up from goblets, seg-
ments of bracelets and parts of lamps.
DONOR: Dr. Harry G. Friedman

## TORAH FINIALS  F 5194a, b

Uncertain origin, 20th century
Brass: die-stamped, cast, pierced
H 23.5  W 7.0 cm
HALLMARKS: none
REMARKS: These pieces, apparently from lanterns, were never
actually made into finials. Cf. the similar No. F 5222.
DONOR: Dr. Harry G. Friedman

## TORAH FINIALS  F 5222a, b

Uncertain origin, 20th century
Brass: die-stamped, cast, pierced; glass
H 29.4  DIAM 14.3 cm
HALLMARKS: none
REMARKS: These pastiches are made from parts of lanterns;
cf. the similar No. F 5194.
DONOR: Dr. Harry G. Friedman

## TORAH FINIALS  F 5675a, b

United States(?), early 20th century
Brass: cast
H 27.1 / 27.3  DIAM 13.5 cm
HALLMARKS: none
REMARKS: This pair is made from castings and other pieces of
electric lamps.
DONOR: Dr. Harry G. Friedman

## TORAH FINIALS  F 5780a, b

Uncertain origin, 20th century
Brass: cast, plated
H 23.5  DIAM 7.0 cm
HALLMARKS: none
REMARKS: These heavy pastiches are made of various pieces
welded together. Cf. No. F 5785, of similar character.
DONOR: Dr. Harry G. Friedman

## TORAH FINIALS  F 5785a, b

Uncertain origin, 20th century
Brass, copper, iron (?)
H 29.1  DIAM 9.8 cm
HALLMARKS: none
REMARKS: These heavy pastiches are made of various pieces
welded together. Cf. No. F 5780, of similar character.
DONOR: Dr. Harry G. Friedman

## TORAH FINIAL  X 1976–8

Uncertain origin, 20th century
Silver : cast, filigree, chased, pierced
H 25.0  DIAM 11.0 cm
HALLMARKS: none
PROVENANCE: Charles S. Warburg, London
REMARKS: This pastiche is made up of varied pieces.
DONOR: Museum purchase

## TORAH CROWN  D 55

Uncertain origin, 19th century
Wood: turned, gessoed, painted, embossed; brass: filigree, engraved, chased, painted, enameled (?); glass; mother-of-pearl
H 19.9  DIAM 13.5 cm
HALLMARKS: none
INSCRIPTION: on irregular plaque: כתר תורה, "Crown of Torah"; above, on plaque: the Tetragrammaton.
REMARKS: This crown, resembling a Venetian doge's head-gear, is probably from a non-Jewish figure of Aaron the High Priest.
BIBLIOGRAPHY: *Danzig 1939*, No. 214.
DONOR: The Jewish Community of Danzig

## TORAH CROWN  F 2489

Uncertain origin, 20th century
Silver (plated ?): die-stamped
H 14.3  DIAM 18.5 cm
HALLMARKS: none
REMARKS: This crown is made up of pieces, probably from a lamp; the eagle atop is American in character.
DONOR: Dr. Harry G. Friedman

## TORAH CROWN  F 3462

Uncertain origin, 20th century
Brass: repoussé, silvered; glass
H 16.1  DIAM 13.3 cm
HALLMARKS: none
REMARKS: The lower diameter of this crown precludes its use as a Torah Crown. For the general form, see Helbing 1932a, No. 64.
DONOR: Dr. Harry G. Fricdman

## TORAH CROWN  F 4385

Uncertain origin, 20th century
Silver: repoussé, cast
H 16.9  DIAM 18.7 cm
HALLMARKS: *CITY:* "G" crowned
         *MAKER:* "ICI" (?)
PROVENANCE: Dr. Hugo Weissmann, Boston
REMARKS: This pastiche, bearing hallmarks of Ghent, is made up from varied parts; the circlet and cresting may have been a bowl.
DONOR: Dr. Harry G. Friedman

## TORAH CROWN  F 4386

Uncertain origin, 19th–20th century
Silver: chased, pierced
H 20.5  DIAM 20.4 cm
HALLMARKS: none
PROVENANCE: Dr. Hugo Weissmann, Boston
REMARKS: The lower part of this pastiche is made up from a Madonna crown.
DONOR: Dr. Harry G. Friedman

## TORAH CROWN  F 5138

Uncertain origin, 19th–20th century
Brass: cast
H 19.4  DIAM 17.5 cm
HALLMARKS: none
REMARKS: Though the body of this pastiche is quite heavy, the stave tubes and bar are not.
DONOR: Dr. Harry G. Friedman

## TORAH CROWN  F 5139

Uncertain origin, 19th–20th century
Brass: cast
H 15.5  DIAM 14.0 cm
HALLMARKS: none
REMARKS: The inner bar with two "stave tubes" is a late addition to this small, heavy crown.
DONOR: Dr. Harry G. Friedman

## TORAH CROWN  F 5501

Edinburgh, 1875; 20th century
James Aitchison, active late 19th century
Silver: chased, cast, die-stamped
H 16.6  DIAM 14.5 cm
HALLMARKS: *CITY:* Thistle; "T"
         *MAKER:* "AITCHISON" within rectangle (see Jackson, p. 507)
PROVENANCE: A. Belinsky, New York
REMARKS: The stamped inscription inside the staves: "PAT'D JUNE 9, 91", in combination with the 1875 date of the hallmarks, indicate that this piece is a pastiche. The Museum card file notes: "Upper crown may not originally be pertaining to the lower crown.... Leave[s] and Flower ornament originally from a band."
DONOR: Dr. Harry G. Friedman

## TORAH CROWN  F 5701

Uncertain origin, 19th century
Silver
H 12.1  DIAM 24.0 cm
HALLMARKS: illegible
PROVENANCE: Gorevic, New York
REMARKS: The ornamental embellishments are probably later additions.
DONOR: Dr. Harry G. Friedman

## TORAH CROWN  U 7316
Uncertain origin, 19th-20th century
Brass: chased, cast
H 23.5  DIAM 24.5 cm
HALLMARKS: none
REMARKS: This crown is very heavy, and is probably not a
  Torah Crown at all.

## TORAH CROWN  U 7339
Uncertain origin, 20th century
Silver: repoussé
H 8.7  DIAM 1.7 cm
HALLMARKS: none
REMARKS: This is a typical Madonna crown.

## TORAH POINTER  F 277
Uncertain origin, 20th century
Silver: die-stamped, pierced; mother-of-pearl: carved
L 25.7  DIAM 1.8 cm
HALLMARKS: "COXOLA"; "800"
REMARKS: This pastiche is made up from an Argentinian
  *mate* tea strainer-straw (*bombilla*). See Nos. F 278, F 313
  and F 956; and *Südamerika*, Nos. 365-88.
DONOR: Dr. Harry G. Friedman

## TORAH POINTER  F 278
Uncertain origin, 20th century
Silver: chased; ivory: carved
L 26.1  DIAM 1.9 cm
HALLMARKS: "800" and "CE"; clock(?)
REMARKS: See remarks, the similar F 277.
DONOR: Dr. Harry G. Friedman

## TORAH POINTER  F 313
Uncertain origin, 20th century
Silver: cast, filigree, die-stamped
L 27.2  W 2.0 cm
HALLMARKS: "800"; "PESSINA"
REMARKS: See remarks, the similar No. F 277.
DONOR: Dr. Harry G. Friedman

## TORAH POINTER  F 314
Uncertain origin, mid-20th century
Silver: cast, chased, die-stamped
L 25.2  DIAM 1.8 cm
HALLMARKS: "1"; traces of two marks
REMARKS: This piece is a pastiche of varied preexistent ele-
  ments.
DONOR: Dr. Harry G. Friedman

## TORAH POINTER  F 318
Uncertain origin, 20th century
Wood: turned, carved; brass (loop and ring)

L 33.2  DIAM 2.8 cm
HALLMARKS: none
REMARKS: The hand of this piece has been recarved from a
  handle.
DONOR: Dr. Harry G. Friedman

## TORAH POINTER  F 319
Uncertain origin, 19th–20th century
Wood: carved, stained
L 23.5  W 3.4 cm
INSCRIPTION: near top: ת//ק//ע//ה, "(5)575" (= 1814/15); on
  shaft: יצחק בן רחל, "Isaac son of Rachel"
REMARKS: There are similar pieces in many collections. For a
  genuine "ball-in-a-cage" pointer, see No. 744.
DONOR: Dr. Harry G. Friedman

## TORAH POINTER  F 828
Uncertain origin, 20th century
Silver: cast, die-stamped, appliqué
L 20.5  DIAM 2.0 cm
HALLMARKS: none
REMARKS: This pastiche is made up from a handle.
DONOR: Dr. Harry G. Friedman

## TORAH POINTER  F 879
Uncertain origin, 20th century
Silver: cast, chased
L 23.9  DIAM 1.4 cm
HALLMARKS: two illegible marks
REMARKS: The upper part of this piece was made from a han-
  dle.
DONOR: Dr. Harry G. Friedman

## TORAH POINTER  F 944
Uncertain origin, 20th century
Silver: cast, chased, engraved, engine-turned, nielloed
L 20.9  DIAM 1.7 cm
HALLMARKS: *CITY:* Russian mark after 1896
       *MAKER:* "(?)K" in rectangle (incomplete)
INSCRIPTION: on element of shaft, in Cyrillic script:
  *KAVKAZ*, "Caucasus"
REMARKS: This pastiche includes a handle from Georgia in
  the Caucasus (cf. No. S 268).
DONOR: Dr. Harry G. Friedman

## TORAH POINTER  F 956
Uncertain origin, 20th century
Silver and gold: chased, die-stamped
L 17.8  DIAM 1.8 cm
HALLMARKS: "800"
REMARKS: See remarks, the similar F 277.
DONOR: Dr. Harry G. Friedman

## TORAH POINTER  F 1201
Uncertain origin, 20th century
Ivory: carved; brass: pierced, silver(?)-plated
L 23.3  DIAM 2.2 cm
HALLMARKS: none
REMARKS: This pastiche is made up from an umbrella handle.
DONOR: Dr. Harry G. Friedman

## TORAH POINTER  F 1502
Uncertain origin, 20th century (?)
Silver: cast, chased
L 26.3  DIAM 3.6 cm
HALLMARKS: none
REMARKS: This pastiche is made up from 19th-century walk-ing-stick handles.
DONOR: Dr. Harry G. Friedman

## TORAH POINTER  F 1750
Uncertain origin, 20th century
Silver: cast, chased, enameled; semiprecious stones
L 20.4  DIAM 2.6 cm
HALLMARKS: none
REMARKS: This piece is made from a handle of Hungarian manufacture.
DONOR: Dr. Harry G. Friedman

## TORAH POINTER  F 1752
Uncertain origin, 20th century
Silver: chased, cast; mother-of-pearl; carnelian
L 24.9  DIAM 3.3 cm
HALLMARKS: "STERLING" (twice)
REMARKS: This piece is made from a parisol handle; the hand is of the same type as on No. F 2051 and other pastiches.
DONOR: Dr. Harry G. Friedman

## TORAH POINTER  F 1782
Uncertain origin, 20th century
Silver: cast, die-stamped, parcel-gilt
L 30.8  W 4.5 cm
HALLMARKS: none
REMARKS: This pastiche is made from a scepter, with several parts removed. See the similar pointers Nos. F 1783, F 1784 and F 2698.
DONOR: Dr. Harry G. Friedman

## TORAH POINTER  F 1783
Uncertain origin, 20th century
Silver: cast, chased, gilt
L 39.2  DIAM 3.2 cm
HALLMARKS: none
REMARKS: See remarks, the similar No. F 1782.
DONOR: Dr. Harry G. Friedman

## TORAH POINTER  F 1784
Uncertain origin, 20th century
Silver: cast, chased, parcel-gilt
L 30.0  W 2.1 cm
HALLMARKS: none
REMARKS: See remarks, the similar No. F 1782.
DONOR: Dr. Harry G. Friedman

## TORAH POINTER  F 1785
Uncertain origin, 20th century
Silver: stamped, cast, engraved
L 25.2  DIAM 3.4 cm
HALLMARKS: Tardy, p. 321, bottom right (Dutch tax)
REMARKS: The upper element of this pastiche is from a han-dle, with the stylus added.
DONOR: Dr. Harry G. Friedman

## TORAH POINTER  F 1786
Uncertain origin, 20th century
Silver: die-stamped, cast; ivory (?): carved; serpentine; car-nelian
L 27.0  W 3.5 cm
HALLMARKS: sword (Dutch or Belgian import mark)
REMARKS: This pastiche has a large fist at the top, and a ser-pentine stylus. See the similar Nos. F 1959 and F 2131.
DONOR: Dr. Harry G. Friedman

## TORAH POINTER  F 1805a
Uncertain origin, 20th century
Silver
L 32.9  DIAM 2.4 cm
HALLMARKS: none
REMARKS: The realistic hand of this piece was made with its index finger bent over.
DONOR: Dr. Harry G. Friedman

## TORAH POINTER  F 1813
Uncertain origin, 20th century
Silver: cast, chased, engraved
L 30.0  DIAM 3.3 cm
HALLMARKS: none
REMARKS: This pastiche is made from a walking-stick handle. There are traces of an engraved monogram.
DONOR: Dr. Harry G. Friedman

## TORAH POINTER  F 1919
Uncertain origin, 20th century
Silver: cast, chased
L 27.2  W 4.5 cm
HALLMARKS: none
REMARKS: This pastiche is made from various pieces includ-ing a triangular stylus; the upper part of the shaft is of workmanship different from the rest. Cf. No. F 1921 for a similar shaft.
DONOR: Dr. Harry G. Friedman

## TORAH POINTER  F 1921

Uncertain origin, 20th century
Silver: cast, chased
L 28.6  DIAM 3.8 cm
HALLMARKS: none
REMARKS: This pastiche is made of varied pieces (compare F 1919), with a left hand.
DONOR: Dr. Harry G. Friedman

## TORAH POINTER  F 1927

Uncertain origin, 20th century
Ivory; silver: pierced, stamped, engraved, cast
L 27.6  W 3.0 cm
HALLMARKS: (on loop): twin-frames, one with "84" — unclear. Russian, after 1880
REMARKS: This piece is made from an ivory dagger sheath, with pierced silver overlay; there are traces of two bands around the upper part, for attaching it to a belt. The middle finger is pointing (rather than the index finger).
DONOR: Dr. Harry G. Friedman

## TORAH POINTER  F 1934

Uncertain origin, 20th century
Celluloid: carved and turned; silver: cast, chased, gilt; carnelian
L 32.0  DIAM 2.9 cm
HALLMARKS: "SILVER/ STERLING" (partly defaced)
INSCRIPTION: in cursive "Ashkenazi" script: חום סרגן (?) בעיר לסבן, "…in [the] city [of] Lisbon"
REMARKS: See remarks, No. F 1752, with some common elements.
DONOR: Dr. Harry G. Friedman

## TORAH POINTER  F 1959

Uncertain origin, 20th century
Silver: cast, chased; ivory (walrus ?); lead (filling)
L 24.5  DIAM 3.9 cm
HALLMARKS: none
REMARKS: The upper element of this pastiche is in the form of a large fist (see the similar element on No. F 1786); the main silver parts are from a candlestick.
DONOR: Dr. Harry G. Friedman

## TORAH POINTER  F 1985

Uncertain origin, 20th century
Silver: cast, chased, pierced
L 28.6  DIAM 2.7 cm
HALLMARKS: none
REMARKS: This piece is a crudely joined and finished pastiche of varied elements, some of which were preexistent.
DONOR: Dr. Harry G. Friedman

## TORAH POINTER  F 2019

Uncertain origin, 20th century
Ivory: turned, inlaid; silver: cast
L 123.0  DIAM 1.3 cm
HALLMARKS: none
REMARKS: The lower shaft of this pastiche is made from a cigarette holder; the hand is identical to those on Nos. F 2049 and F 2128.
DONOR: Dr. Harry G. Friedman

## TORAH POINTER  F 2049

Uncertain origin, 20th century
Ivory: turned; silver: cast; glass
L 27.9  DIAM 2.6 cm
REMARKS: The three elements of this pastiche are crudely glued together; the hand is identical to those on Nos. F 2019 and F 2128.
DONOR: Dr. Harry G. Friedman

## TORAH POINTER  F 2050

Uncertain origin, 20th century
Silver: cast, filigree, chased; turquoise; garnets; amethysts
L 17.9  DIAM 2.6 cm
HALLMARKS: none
REMARKS: This pastiche is made from a handle; the chain is typical of Yemenite workmanship.
DONOR: Dr. Harry G. Friedman

## TORAH POINTER  F 2051

Uncertain origin, 20th century
Bone and ivory: carved; silver: cast
L 20.5  W 1.4 cm
HALLMARKS: none
REMARKS: The upper shaft of this pastiche is made from a parisol handle, with its hand pierced for a chain; the middle shaft is made from an Indian pen-handle or needle-case. See the similar Nos. F 2124 and F 2285.
DONOR: Dr. Harry G. Friedman

## TORAH POINTER  F 2052

Uncertain origin, 20th century
Silver: cast
L 40.4  DIAM 1.9 cm
HALLMARKS: Crowned "E" (?)
REMARKS: This piece is made from several baluster handles soldered together, with a long stylus tip.
DONOR: Dr. Harry G. Friedman

## TORAH POINTER  F 2053

Europe, late 19th–20th century
Silver: die-stamped, engraved; lead (filling)
L 28.7  DIAM 2.4 cm

HALLMARKS: none

INSCRIPTION: in oval medallion on arm: ‎/משה‎ בן‎ יעקב‎ נ"ז
‎קלש, "This was donated by Jacob son of Moshe Kalish (?)"

REMARKS: The shaft of this pastiche is made from a handle.

DONOR: Dr. Harry G. Friedman

## TORAH POINTER  F 2107

Uncertain origin, 20th century

Bone: turned, carved, drilled; silver: cast, gold-plated; gold:
chased

L 20.9  DIAM 2.2 cm

HALLMARKS: none

REMARKS: The upper element of this piece is a handle; the upper and lower shaft is made from a bone pen handle. See
remarks, No. F 2285, with similar elements.

DONOR: Dr. Harry G. Friedman

## TORAH POINTER  F 2120

Uncertain origin, 20th century

Ivory: carved, turned; bone: burnt; silver

L 17.9  W 1.8 cm

HALLMARKS: none

REMARKS: This pastiche is made from a Chinese cigarette
holder. The hand is missing.

DONOR: Dr. Harry G. Friedman

## TORAH POINTER  F 2124

Uncertain origin, 20th century

Bone: carved; celluloid(?)

L 18.6  W 1.9 cm

REMARKS: The upper shaft of this piece is made of an Indian
pierced needle-case or pen handle, with a large, fist-
shaped finial pierced for a chain; the tip is a long, flat stylus. See remarks, No. F 2051.

DONOR: Dr. Harry G. Friedman

## TORAH POINTER  F 2127

Uncertain origin, 20th century

Ivory: carved, turned; silver: cast

L 27.5  DIAM 3.6 cm

HALLMARKS: none

REMARKS: This piece is made from a parisol handle; the hand
is of the same type as found on No. F 2051.

DONOR: Dr. Harry G. Friedman

## TORAH POINTER  F 2128

Uncertain origin, 20th century

Ivory: turned, carved; silver: cast

L 26.3  DIAM 2.9 cm

HALLMARKS: none

REMARKS: This pastiche is made of varied parts; the hand is
identical to those on Nos. F 2019 and F 2049.

DONOR: Dr. Harry G. Friedman

## TORAH POINTER  F 2129

Uncertain origin, 20th century

Ivory: carved; silver: cast

L 32.3  DIAM 2.5 cm

HALLMARKS: none

REMARKS: This pastiche is made from a umbrella or parasol
handle.

DONOR: Dr. Harry G. Friedman

## TORAH POINTER  F 2131

Uncertain origin, 20th century

Ivory, bone, plastic, and mother-of-pearl: turned, carved; silver: cast

L 25.9  DIAM 4.0 cm

HALLMARKS: none

REMARKS: This pastiche includes an upper element with a
large fist. See No. F 1786 for a similar fist.

DONOR: Dr. Harry G. Friedman

## TORAH POINTER  F 2133

Uncertain origin, 20th century

Ivory: carved; silver: cast, chased; rose quartz; glass

L 21.0  DIAM 2.6 cm

HALLMARKS: "STERLING" (in "finger ring")

REMARKS: This pastiche is made from a parisol handle.

DONOR: Dr. Harry G. Friedman

## TORAH POINTER  F 2136

Uncertain origin, 20th century

Silver: cast, chased

L 19.6  DIAM 2.3 cm

HALLMARKS: Lileyko 90 (both)

REMARKS: This pastiche is made up of varied pieces.

DONOR: Dr. Harry G. Friedman

## TORAH POINTER  F 2187

Uncertain origin, 20th century

Ivory: carved; silver: cast, gilt

L 32.5  W 2.3 cm

HALLMARKS: none

REMARKS: This pastiche is made from a long parisol handle;
the hand is identical with that on No. F 2051, but is gilt.

DONOR: Dr. Harry G. Friedman

## TORAH POINTER  F 2201

Uncertain origin, 20th century

Ivory and bone: turned, carved; silver: filigree, cast; glass

L 34.9  DIAM 4.9 cm

HALLMARKS: none

REMARKS: The upper element of this pastiche is in the form of
a large, closed fist; for a similar feature, see remarks, No. F
1786.

DONOR: Dr. Harry G. Friedman

## TORAH POINTER  F 2262

Uncertain origin, 20th century

Brass: die-stamped, engine-turned; silver: cast, gold-plated; plastic

L 19.7  DIAM 2.2 cm

HALLMARKS: none

REMARKS: This pastiche is made from an opera-glass handle.

DONOR: Dr. Harry G. Friedman

## TORAH POINTER  F 2264

Europe, 19th century

Silver: cast, chased, parcel-gilt

L 37.1  DIAM 2.5 cm

HALLMARKS: none

REMARKS: This pastiche is made of varied pieces; the hand is a left hand.

DONOR: Dr. Harry G. Friedman

## TORAH POINTER  F 2283

Uncertain origin, 20th century

Ivory: turned, carved, drilled

L 23.2  DIAM 1.8 cm

INSCRIPTION: יד, "[Torah] Pointer"

DONOR: Dr. Harry G. Friedman

## TORAH POINTER  F 2285

Uncertain origin, 20th century

Bone: carved; silver: cast; parchment

L 19.0  W 1.2 cm

HALLMARKS: none

REMARKS: This pastiche is made of a pierced needle case or pen handle; within is an inscribed parchment. See Nos. F 2051 and F 2107, with similar elements; and the remarks, Nos. F 2539 and F 3309, also with inserted parchments.

DONOR: Dr. Harry G. Friedman

## TORAH POINTER  F 2539

Uncertain origin, 20th century

Bone and ivory: carved, turned; silver: stamped; parchment

L 21.6  DIAM 3.0 cm

HALLMARKS: none

REMARKS: See remarks, No. F 2285, also with an enclosed parchment.

DONOR: Norman F. Goetz, through Dr. Harry G. Friedman

## TORAH POINTER  F 2594

Uncertain origin, 20th century

Bone: carved, turned; silver

L 21.3  W 1.8 cm

HALLMARKS: none

REMARKS: The disproportionately large index finger is a feature found also on No. F 2793.

DONOR: Dr. Harry G. Friedman

## TORAH POINTER  F 2627

Uncertain origin, 20th century

Bone, ivory and plastic: turned; silver: cast

L 21.2  W 2.1 cm

HALLMARKS: none

REMARKS: The lower shaft of this pastiche is made from a pen. On a tag attached to it is the note: "Ivory sphere on top is missing."

DONOR: Dr. Harry G. Friedman

## TORAH POINTER  F 2682

Uncertain origin, 20th century

Silver: wrought, cast, chased, stamped

L 19.3  W 2.5 cm

HALLMARKS: none

REMARKS: This piece appears to be made of a preexisting handle.

DONOR: Dr. Harry G. Friedman

## TORAH POINTER  F 2698

Uncertain origin, 20th century

Silver: cast, chased, parcel-gilt

L 27.4  W 1.5 cm

HALLMARKS: none

REMARKS: See remarks, the similar No. F 1782.

DONOR: Dr. Harry G. Friedman

## TORAH POINTER  F 2751

Uncertain origin, 20th century

Bone and ivory: carved; porcelain; brass: gilt; glass

L 18.0  DIAM 1.4 cm

HALLMARKS: none

INSCRIPTION: on upper shaft: נ(?)' יו ט' קמחי, "D[onation of](?) Yo[m]-T[ov] Kimḥi"

REMARKS: The left hand of this pastiche is attached with glue; the chain is made of plastic.

DONOR: Dr. Harry G. Friedman

## TORAH POINTER  F 2793

Uncertain origin, 20th century

Bone and horn: carved; bronze paint

L 15.6  W 1.7 cm

HALLMARKS: none

REMARKS: The uppermost part of this piece is missing. The left hand has a disproportionately large pointing index finger; see the similar feature on No. F 2594.

DONOR: Dr. Harry G. Friedman

## TORAH POINTER   F 2945

Uncertain origin, 20th century
Silver: cast, repoussé, turned, parcel-gilt
L 36.3   DIAM 3.6 cm
HALLMARKS: none
REMARKS: This pastiche is made from various pieces.
DONOR: Dr. Harry G. Friedman

## TORAH POINTER   F 3057

Uncertain origin, 20th century
Brass: cast, chased, engine-turned, gilt
L (extended): 26.8 (contracted): 17.5   DIAM 1.6 cm
HALLMARKS: none
INSCRIPTION: erased monogram in script, obliterated by a
    rosette chased over it.
REMARKS: This pastiche is made from the telescoping handle
    of an opera glass.
DONOR: Dr. Harry G. Friedman

## TORAH POINTER   F 3105

Uncertain origin, 20th century
Silver: cast, chased, engraved, traces of parcel-gilding
L 20.3   W 1.8 cm
HALLMARKS: none
REMARKS: This pastiche is made from a case for some
    unidentified object.
DONOR: Dr. Harry G. Friedman

## TORAH POINTER   F 3309

Uncertain origin, 20th century
Bone: turned, carved, drilled; silver: cast
L 19.2   DIAM 1.1 cm
HALLMARKS: none
REMARKS: This pastiche is made from a pen handle. Within
    the shaft is a parchment, probably from a *mezuzah*; for a
    similar feature, see Nos. F 2285 and F 2539.
DONOR: Dr. Harry G. Friedman

## TORAH POINTER   F 3454

Uncertain origin, 20th century
Copper: chased, cast, engine-turned, gilt; mother-of-pearl
L (extended) 22.0   DIAM 1.6 cm
HALLMARKS: none
REMARKS: This pastiche is made from the telescoping handle
    of an opera-glass.
DONOR: Dr. Harry G. Friedman

## TORAH POINTER   F 3590

Uncertain origin, 20th century
Wood: turned; ivory: carved; cord and tassel
L 28.7   DIAM 2.6 cm
REMARKS: This pastiche is made from a finely-turned (pari-
    sol ?) handle, with a crudely rendered hand.
DONOR: Dr. Harry G. Friedman

## TORAH POINTER   F 4000

Israel (?), 20th century
Brass: gilt(?); garnet; plastic: carved, engraved
L 28.6   W 3.1 cm
HALLMARKS: none
INSCRIPTION: on medial knop: the Tetragrammaton; on low-
    er knop: ב״ה, "W[ith] D[ivine help]"; in oval on lower
    shaft: שדי, "Almighty"
REMARKS: This pointer is made of recent elements and re-
    carved pieces of plastic.
DONOR: Dr. Harry G. Friedman

## TORAH POINTER   F 4026

Uncertain origin, 20th century
Brass: cast, silver-plated; silver: cast, die-stamped (chain)
L 23.8   DIAM 1.8 cm
HALLMARKS: none
REMARKS: The upper shaft of this pastiche is a handle; the
    lower shaft is from a button-hook; the hand is crudely at-
    tached.
DONOR: Dr. Harry G. Friedman

## TORAH POINTER   F 4085

Uncertain origin, 20th century
Ebony; silver: chased, cast, gilt, enameled; semiprecious
    stones
L 41.2   DIAM 2.7 cm
HALLMARKS: none
REMARKS: The top knop of this pastiche is from a handle of
    Hungarian workmanship; the hand is probably of the
    early 19th century.
DONOR: Dr. Harry G. Friedman

## TORAH POINTER   F 4236

Uncertain origin, 20th century
Bone and ivory: turned, carved; silver: cast
L 32.4   DIAM 1.9 cm
HALLMARKS: none
REMARKS: This pastiche is made of varied parts; the "cuff" is a
    Near Eastern bead.
DONOR: Dr. Harry G. Friedman

## TORAH POINTER   F 4238

Germany, 19th–20th century
Silver: cast, engraved, traces of gilt
L 30.4   DIAM 3.2 cm
HALLMARKS: crown/"13"
INSCRIPTION: *IOSEPH/ SEBASTIAN/ FREIHERR/ ZWEY-*
    *ER/ "DAS-RECHT-SOLL-SPRECHEN"*, "Joseph Sebastian
    Freiherr Zweyer. 'Justice shall be spoken'."
REMARKS: The hand of this pastiche is a later addition. The
    hallmark might be that of Kronstadt (similar to Kőszeghy
    135 and 139).
DONOR: Dr. Harry G. Friedman

## TORAH POINTER  F 4240

Uncertain origin, 20th century

Ivory: carved and turned; silver (chain)

L 22.0  DIAM 1.9 cm

HALLMARKS: none

INSCRIPTION: Psalms 19:8

REMARKS: This pastiche is made up from a parisol handle with additional elements, one probably Persian. The inscribed band is recarved. The hand is undersized and oddly carved.

DONOR: Dr. Harry G. Friedman

## TORAH POINTER  F 4250

Uncertain origin, 20th century

Silver: chased, engine-turned, cast, parcel-gilt

L 38.9  DIAM 4.4 cm

HALLMARKS: Dutch import (Tardy, p. 327 [835] — since 1953)

REMARKS: The shaft of this pastiche includes several baluster handles; some of the pieces may be from Torah Pointers.

DONOR: Dr. Harry G. Friedman

## TORAH POINTER  F 4263

Uncertain origin, 20th century

Ivory: carved; brass: die-stamped; gold: chased; glass

L 31.3  DIAM 2.3 cm

HALLMARKS: none

REMARKS: This pastiche is made from a long parisol handle.

DONOR: Dr. Harry G. Friedman

## TORAH POINTER  F 4528

Uncertain origin, 20th century

Ivory: carved; metal (chain)

L 19.0  W 2.9 cm

REMARKS: The upper shaft of this pastiche is made from a flat handle; the oversized hand is carved to hold a pen or stylus.

DONOR: Dr. Harry G. Friedman

## TORAH POINTER  F 4663

Uncertain origin, 20th century

Silver: cast, parcel-gilt

L 40.3  W 4.8 cm

HALLMARKS: none

INSCRIPTION: on upper shaft: ז״נ מו״ה משה יעקב/ ק״ק רומא, "T[his was] d[onated by] . . . Moses Jacob, h[oly] c[ommunity of] Rome."

REMARKS: This pastiche is made up from a baluster stylus, with an added cluster of spheres and a ball-bead chain.

DONOR: Dr. Harry G. Friedman

## TORAH POINTER  F 4666

Uncertain origin, 20th century

Brass: cast, stamped, silver(?)-plated

L 27.7  DIAM 3.1 cm

HALLMARKS: none

INSCRIPTION: on lower shaft: זואת(!) נדבת/ האישה רחל בת אברהם, "This is the donation of the woman Rachel daughter of Abraham."

REMARKS: This pastiche is made of varied pieces, including a loop-finial of the type seen on pointer No. 626. The Museum card file notes that an attached watch chain "was taken off."

DONOR: Dr. Harry G. Friedman

## TORAH POINTER  F 4704

Uncertain origin, 20th century

Silver(?): cast, die-stamped; ebony (?)

L 35.7  DIAM 2.2 cm

HALLMARKS: none

REMARKS: The upper part of this pastiche is made from a walking-stick or parisol handle.

DONOR: Dr. Harry G. Friedman

## TORAH POINTER  F 4743

Uncertain origin, 20th century

Bone and ivory: turned, carved; silver: die-stamped; enamel

L 33.5  DIAM 3.1 cm

HALLMARKS: none

REMARKS: This pastiche is made of varied pieces. Of the semiprecious stones mentioned in the Museum card file, only traces of the glue which had held them remain along the shaft.

DONOR: Dr. Harry G. Friedman

## TORAH POINTER  F 5184

Israel (?), 20th century

Ivory: carved; silver: stamped

L 25.7  W 3.1 cm

HALLMARKS: none

INSCRIPTION: on upper shaft: גבור/ כאריה, from Ethics of the Fathers 5:20; on lower shaft: Deuteronomy 33:4

REMARKS: This pastiche is made of varied parts.

DONOR: Dr. Harry G. Friedman

## TORAH POINTER  F 5199

Uncertain origin, 20th century

Silver: cast, chased, die-stamped

L 47.8  DIAM 5.0 cm

HALLMARKS: none

INSCRIPTION: from 1 Chron. 29:11, adapted

REMARKS: This pastiche is made up of varied pieces; the hand appears to be older than the rest.

DONOR: Dr. Harry G. Friedman

## TORAH POINTER  F 5322

Uncertain origin, 20th century

Silver: chased, cast, filigree, die-stamped, pierced; ivory

L 65.2  DIAM 5.5 cm

HALLMARKS: none

REMARKS: This pastiche is made from a walking-stick, probably English.

DONOR: Dr. Harry G. Friedman

## TORAH POINTER  F 5339

Uncertain origin, 20th century

Gold and silver: repoussé; agate; diamonds; emeralds

L 13.9  W 1.0 cm

HALLMARKS: none

REMARKS: This piece is made from the handle of a pen.

DONOR: Dr. Harry G. Friedman

## TORAH POINTER  F 5352

Uncertain origin, 20th century

Tortoise-shell; silver(?): oxydized, gilt (or gold ?), cast

L 36.6  DIAM 3.2 cm

HALLMARKS: none

REMARKS: The upper part of this pastiche is made of a walking-stick.

DONOR: Dr. Harry G. Friedman

## TORAH POINTER  F 5401

Malta, 1760 (inscription); 20th century

Silver: cast, chased, engraved

L 33.3  DIAM 0.8 cm

HALLMARKS: MAKER: "SC" in irregular rectangle

INSCRIPTION: בשנת תקד"ה לפ"ק, "In the year (5)525" (= 1764/65)

REMARKS: The hand of this pastiche is reengraved; one finger has been restored.

DONOR: Dr. Harry G. Friedman

## TORAH POINTER  F 5402

Uncertain origin, 20th century

Silver: cast, engraved

L 25.7  DIAM 2.0 cm

HALLMARKS: none

INSCRIPTION: on upper and lower shaft: יהודה בן ישראל/ שנת ת"ק"ל"ב, "Judah son of Israel, year (5)532" (= 1771/72)

REMARKS: The workmanship of this piece and its inscription are recent.

DONOR: Dr. Harry G. Friedman

## TORAH POINTER  F 5487

Hungary (?), 20th century

Silver: chased, cast, gilt; ivory: carved; turquoise; garnet; opal; semiprecious stones; traces of enamel

L 28.0  DIAM 2.9 cm

HALLMARKS: none

REMARKS: The varied parts of this pastiche include a piece of ivory carved with a dragon motif.

DONOR: Dr. Harry G. Friedman

## TORAH POINTER  F 5492

Uncertain origin, 20th century

Silver: cast, engraved; enamel

L 28.3  W 2.9 cm

HALLMARKS: English, French, Belgian and other marks

REMARKS: This pastiche is made up from a French enamelled handle, a Belgian cigarette holder, an English ferule and other parts.

DONOR: Dr. Harry G. Friedman

## TORAH POINTER  F 5493

Uncertain origin, 20th century

Wood: carved

L 32.4  W 2.3 cm

INSCRIPTION: נחום// הוד ה' תקצר(?), "Naḥum, the glory of the Lord …"

REMARKS: In the Museum records, the final word in the inscription is interpreted as a date ([5]590 = 1829/30). The top element is in the form of a pig. The pierced work on the hand differs from the other workmanship on this piece; the hand is recarved.

DONOR: Dr. Harry G. Friedman

## TORAH POINTER  F 5555

Uncertain origin, 20th century

Silver: cast, chased, engraved

L 28.3  W 3.2 cm

HALLMARKS: none

REMARKS: This pastiche is made of varied pieces.

DONOR: Dr. Harry G. Friedman

## TORAH POINTER  F 5954

United States, 20th century

Silver: cast, chased

L 22.1  DIAM 1.8 cm

HALLMARKS: "STERLING SILVER"; "1"

REMARKS: This pastiche is made from an opera-glass or parisol handle.

DONOR: Dr. Harry G. Friedman

## TORAH POINTER  F 5957

Uncertain origin, 20th century

Silver and brass(?): gilt; agate

L 13.8  W 1.5 cm

HALLMARKS: none

REMARKS: The agate handle of this pastiche may be from a gilder's burnisher; other of the elements are old but their combination in this form is recent.

DONOR: Dr. Harry G. Friedman

## TORAH POINTER  F 5960

Uncertain origin, 20th century
Silver: cast, filigree, engine-turned
L 23.4  DIAM 1.6 cm
HALLMARKS: partly obliterated, including a 19th-century mark and partial Dutch maker's mark
REMARKS: This piece is made from varied parts which bear traces of incongruous hallmarks.
DONOR: Dr. Harry G. Friedman

## TORAH POINTER  JM 72–48

Uncertain origin, 20th century
Silver: engraved, gilt
L (extended): 23.8; (compressed): 9.8  DIAM 1.4 cm
HALLMARKS: erased (on ring).
REMARKS: In the Museum card file, this piece is noted as belonging to Torah Scroll JM 73–48. This pastiche is made from the telescoping handle of an opera glass.
DONOR: Louis M. Rabinowitz, New York

## TORAH POINTER  JM 46–52

Uncertain origin, 20th century
Plastic: turned, carved, engraved, painted
L 19.6  DIAM 1.5 cm
HALLMARKS: none
PROVENANCE: Museum jüdischer Altertümer, Frankfurt am Main
REMARKS: See *AaunZ* No. 17, 17 July 1930, p. 132, fig. 4, lower middle: a well-carved pointer of bone, the original from which this piece was copied.
BIBLIOGRAPHY: *Wüb*, No. 36.
DONOR: Jewish Cultural Reconstruction

## TORAH POINTER  JM 21–59

Uncertain origin, 20th century
Silver: cast, stamped, engine-turned, engraved, chased; bone and ivory: carved and pierced; glass
L 36.2  DIAM 3.7 cm
HALLMARKS: none
REMARKS: This pastiche is made up from walking-stick heads and other preexisting elements.
DONOR: Samuel Moscowitz

## TORAH POINTER  S 268

Uncertain origin, late 19th-early 20th century
Silver: die-stamped, cast, chased, engraved, nielloed
L 30.0  DIAM 2.0 cm
HALLMARKS: unclear (Russian ?)
INSCRIPTION: on upper shaft, in Cyrillic script: *KAVKAZ*, "Caucasus"
PROVENANCE: The Hadji Ephraim and Mordecai Benguiat Family Collection
REMARKS: The upper knop of this pastiche is made from a

bottle-stopper; the upper shaft is from a Georgian souvenir object (cf. No. F 944).
DONOR: Museum purchase

## TORAH POINTER  U 9176

19th–20th century
Silver: die-stamped, cast, engraved
L 20.4  DIAM 2.3 cm
HALLMARKS: none
REMARKS: The upper part of this pastiche is the main piece of a baby-rattle or teething ring cum whistle. On the attached tag is the note: "JCR 25" (this is not the usual Jewish Cultural Reconstruction tag).

## TORAH POINTER  U 9186

Uncertain origin, 20th century
Silver: stamped, cast; copper: stamped; mother-of-pearl: carved; glass
L 18.1  DIAM 3.6 cm
HALLMARKS: *CITY:* Rohrwasser, p. 19, 2nd row (800, small)
          *MAKER:* "JK"(?) in square
REMARKS: This pastiche is made up of various preexisting pieces of several materials.

## TORAH POINTER  U 9187

Uncertain origin, 20th century
Bone: carved
L 8.6  DIAM 1.9 cm
HALLMARKS: none
REMARKS: The fine-quality bone of this piece has been re-carved.

## TORAH POINTER  X 1976–7

Uncertain origin, 20th century
Silver: cast, etched, die-stamped
L 35.6  DIAM 2.5 cm
HALLMARKS: "84"
PROVENANCE: Charles S. Warburg, London
REMARKS: This pastiche is made from a walking-stick or umbrella handle.
DONOR: Museum purchase

## TORAH CASE  F 3785

Iran, 20th century
Silver: chased; wood; iron; textile
H 68.6  DIAM 30.5 cm
HALLMARKS: none
REMARKS: This case, and the similar No. F 3928, are unique in form. The inscriptions here, including the dedication, are similar to those on No. F 3928.
DONOR: Dr. Harry G. Friedman

TORAH CASE  F 3928

Iran, 20th century

Silver: chased; wood; iron; textile, printed

H 66.3  DIAM 25.8 cm

HALLMARKS: none

INSCRIPTIONS: There are extensive biblical and kabbalistic texts in Hebrew; in the corner of one panel, the dedication: מתנה לבית הכנסת/ רבי חנינא שירנא שיראז חודש/ סיון התק'נ'ב' הצעיר/ אשר יעקב/ כהן, "Gift to the synagogue [of] Rabbi Ḥanina..., Shiraz, [the] month of Sivan 5552 (= May–June 1792),... Asher Jacob Kohen."

REMARKS: This case, and the similar No. F 3785, are unique in form.

DONOR: Dr. Harry G. Friedman

# Index of Places of Origin

# Index of Makers

❦❦❦❦
❦❦❦
❦❦
❦

*N.B. Figures indicate catalogue entries*

# Index of Person and Place Names in the Inscriptions[*]

ৎৎৎৎ
ৎৎৎ
ৎৎ
ৎ

*N.B. Figures indicate catalogue entries*

# Bibliography

❦❦❦❦❦
❦❦❦❦❦
❦❦❦
❦❦

*AaunZ* = *Aus alten und neuen Zeit*, biweekly of the "Israelitisches Familienblattes." Hamburg, 1898–1938.

Altschuler = Washington, D.C., Smithsonian Institution, *The Precious Legacy. Judaic Treasures from the Czechoslovak State Collections*, ed. by D. Altshuler, exhibition catalogue, 1983.

American Art Gallery = New York, American Art Gallery, *The Magnificent Benguiat Collection*, sale catalogue, April, 1924.

Anderson = R.T. Anderson, *Studies in Samaritan Manuscripts and Artifacts. The Chamberlain-Warren Collection* (American Schools of Oriental Research Monograph Series 1). Cambridge, MA, 1978.

Ansbacher = B.M. Ansbacher, *Zeugnisse jüdischer Geschichte und Kultur*. Augsburg, 1985.

*Ashkenaz* = New York, Yeshiva University Museum, *Ashkenaz, The German Jewish Heritage*, ed. by G. Hirschler, 1988.

Barnett = R.D. Barnett, ed., *Catalogue of the Permanent and Loan Collection of the Jewish Museum London*. London, 1974.

*Beauty* = J. Gutmann, ed., *Beauty in Holiness. Studies in Jewish Customs and Ceremonial Art*. New York, 1970.

Belinfante 1978 = Amsterdam, Jewish Historical Museum, *Jewish Historical Museum* (Nederlandse Musea III), by J.C.E. Belinfante, Haarlem, 1978.

———— 1991 = J.C.E. Belinfante et al., *The Esnoga, a Monument to Portuguese-Jewish Culture*. Amsterdam, 1991.

Bendt = V. Bendt, *Judaica Katalog. Abteilung Jüdisches Museum*. Berlin, 1989.

Berger 1984 = Munich, München Stadtmuseum, *Das jüdische Jahr. Kunst und Kult des Judentums*, by M. Berger et al., exhibition catalogue, 1984.

———— 1987 = Vienna, Historisches Museum der Stadt Wien, *"Heilige Gemeinde Wien." Judentum in Wien. Sammlung Max Berger*, exhibition catalogue, 1987.

Berman = New York, The Jewish Museum/Los Angeles, Skirball Museum, *Moshe Zabari: A Twenty-five Year Retrospctive*, by N.M. Berman, exhibition catalogue, 1986.

Bezalel 1913 = *Preisverzeichnis der Erzeugnisse der Kunstgewerbeschule Bezalel in Jerusalem*. [Berlin, 1913].

———— 1983 = Jerusalem, Israel Museum, *Bezalel, 1906-1929*, 2 vols., ed. by N. Shilo-Kohen, exhibition catalogue, 1983.

Bialer = Y.L. Bialer and E. Fink, *Jewish Life in Art and Tradition. From the Collection of the . . . Wolfson Museum. . . .* Jerusalem, 1980 (2nd ed.) .

*Blackbook* = Jerusalem, Yad Vashem, *Blackbook of Localities whose Jewish Population was Exterminated by the Nazis*. Jerusalem, 1965.

Bonn = Bonn, Rheinisches Landesmuseum Bonn, *Rheinische Goldschmiedekunst der Renaissance- und Barockzeit*. Köln, 1975.

Brann = M. Brann, "Der Silberschatz der Zülzer Judengemeinde", *Ost und West* 1918, XVIII, cols. 335–56.

Braunschweig = R. Hagen and R. Busch, *Jüdisches Kultgerät. Eine Auswahl aus den Sammlungen*. Braunschweig, 1984.

Budapest = I. Benoschofsky and A. Scheiber, eds., *The Jewish Museum of Budapest*. Budapest 1987.

Bulgari = C.G. Bulgari, *Stato Pontifico. Raccolta dei Bolli . . . per l'Argento e per l'Oro . . .*, Rome, 1974.

Central Synagogue = C. Grossman, *The Jewish Family's Book of Days*. New York, n.d.(1993).

Cantera and Millas = F. Cantera and J.M. Millas, *Las inscripciones hebraicas de España*. Madrid, 1956.

Christie's Amsterdam 1988 = Christie's Amsterdam, *Fine Judaica*, sale catalogue, May 11, 1988.

———— 1991 = Amsterdam, Christie's, *Judaica . . .*, sale catalogue, June 19, 1991.

———— 1993 = Christie's Amsterdam, *Dutch and Foreign Silver, Judaica . . .*, sale catalogue, 10 June, 1993.

Christie's New York 1980 = New York, Christie's, *An Important Collection of Judaica* (Kaniel Coll.), sale catalogue, October 9, 1980.

———— New York 1982 = New York, Christie's, *Fine Judaica . . .*, sale catalogue, October 26, 1982.

———— New York 1993 = New York, Christie's, *Important Silver . . . and Judaica*, sale catalogue, April 22, 1993.

Citroen 1975 = K.A. Citroen, *Amsterdam Silversmiths and their Marks* I. New York-Amsterdam, 1975.

———— 1993 = K. Citroen, *Dutch Goldsmiths' and Silversmiths' Marks and Names prior to 1812. A Descriptive and Critical Repertory*. Leiden, 1993.

Cohen = Y. (R.) Cohen, "Torah Breastplates from Augsburg in the Israel Museum", *The Israel Museum News* 14 (1978), pp. 74–85.

Croft-Murray = Edward Croft-Murray, "A Note on the Painting of Moses and Aaron", in A.G. Grimwade et al., *Treasures of a London Temple*. London, 1951.

Curiel and Cooperman = R. Curiel and B.D. Cooperman, *The Ghetto of Venice*, London 1990.

Czihak = E. v. Czihak, *Die Edelschmiedekunst früherer Zeiten in Preussen. Zweiter Teil: Westpreussen*. Leipzig 1908.

*Dahan* = Tel Aviv, Eretz Israel Museum, *From the Remotest West, Ritual Articles from Synagogues in Spanish Morocco. The Hananiah Dahan Collection*, ed. by N. Bahrouzi, exhibition catalogue, 1989.

*Danzig 1904* = *Katalog der alten jüdischen Kultusgegenstände Gieldzinski-Stiftung in der Neuen Synagoge zu Danzig*. Danzig, 1904.

———— *1933* = *Sammlung jüdischer Kunstgegenstände der Synagogen-gemeinde Danzig*. Danzig, 1933.

*Danzig 1939* = New York, The Jewish Museum, *Danzig 1939: Treasures of a Destroyed Community*, by V. B. Mann and J. Gutmann, exhibition catalogue, 1980.

*Danzig 1939/1982* = *Danzig 1939* and *Danzig 1982*.

Danzig 1982 = Braunschweig, Braunschweigisches Landesmuseum, *Danzig 1939: Schätze einer zerstörten Gemeinde*, by V. B. Mann and J. Gutmann, exhibition catalogue, 1982 (identical with *Danzig 1939* up to object No. 134; the remainder of the catalogue items, Nos. 135–288 not in the German catalogue).

Deneke = Nuremberg, Germanisches Nationalmuseum Nürnberg, *Siehe der Stein schreit aus der Mauer. Geschichte und Kultur der Juden in Bayern*, by B. Deneke, ed., exhibition catalogue, 1988.

Dietz = Alexander Dietz, *Stammbuch der Frankfurter Juden. Geschichtliche Mitteilungen über die Frankfurter jüdischen Familien von 1349–1949*. Frankfurt am Main, 1907.

Donaver-Dabbene = V.D. Donaver and R. Dabbene, *Argenti italiani dell'800*. Vol. I, *Punzoni di garanzia degli Stati Italiani*, Milan, 1987.

*Dubrovnik* = New York, Yeshiva University Museum, exhibition catalogue (forthcoming).

Dusseldorf = Düsseldorf, Kunstgewerbe-Museum, *Ausstellung von Bauten und Kultus-Gegenstanden für Synagoge und Haus*, ed. by H. Frauberger, exhibition catalogue, 1908.

*Ebrei in Libia* = M. Cohen and M.M. Moreno: *Gli Ebrei in Libia (Usi e Costumi)*. Rome, 1932.

*EJ* = *Encyclopaedia Judaica* 1–16, Jerusalem, 1972.

Ellenbogen = R. Ellenbogen, *Judaic Treasures Fashioned by Johann Jacob Leschhorn, an Eighteenth Century Frankfurt-am-Main Silversmith*. New York, 1988.

Emden = Emden, Ostfriesichen Landesmuseum, *Zeugnisse zerstorten Vergangenheit. Jüdisches Kultgerät aus Emden 1639–1806*, by W.B. Gross, R. Grafman and A. Weber, exhibition catalogue, 1992.

Fallon = John P. Fallon, *Marks of London Goldsmiths and Silversmiths 1837–1914*. London, 1992.

Feuchtwanger = Jerusalem, Israel Museum, *Jewish Tradition in Art. The Feuchtwanger Collection of Judaica*, by I. Shachar, trans. R. Grafman. Jerusalem, 1981.

Fishof = Jerusalem, Israel Museum, *From the Secular to the Sacred. Everyday Objects in Jewish Ritual Use*, by I. Fishof, exhibition catalogue, 1985.

Fraser-Lu = S. Fraser-Lu, *Silverware of South-East Asia* (Images of Asia series). Singapore, 1989.

Furman = New York, The Jewish Museum, *Personal Vision. The Furman Collection of Jewish Ceremonial Art*, by Susan L. Braunstein, exhibition catalogue, 1985.

*Gardens* = New York, The Jewish Museum, *Gardens and Ghettos. The Art of Jewish Life in Italy*, ed. by V. B. Mann, exhibition catalogue, Berkeley, 1989.

Gilbert = Martin Gilbert, *The Jews of Russia, Their History in Maps and Photographs*. London, 1976.

Grimwade 1950 = A.G. Grimwade, "The Ritual Silver of Bevis Marks Synagogue — I," *Apollo* 51 (1950), pp. 103–05; II, pp. 130–32.

Grimwade 1955 = A.G. Grimwade, *Anglo-Jewish Silver*. London, 1955 (= *Transactions of the Jewish Historical Society of England* 1955), pp. 113–25.

Gross Collection = B. Narkiss and B. Yaniv, *The Gross Family Collection*. Part One. Volume One: *Objects*. Jerusalem, 1985.

Grossman = G.C. Grossman, *The Judaica Collection at the Smithsonian . . .*, Washington, D.C. (forthcoming).

Grossman 1989 = C. Grossman, *A Temple Treasury. The Judaica Collection of Congregation Emanu-El of the City of New York*. New York, 1989.

Grotte = A. Grotte, *Deutsche, böhmische und polnische Synagogentypen vom XI. bis Anfang des XIX. Jahrhunderts*. Berlin, 1915.

Gutmann = J. Gutmann, *Jewish Ceremonial Art*. New York-London, 1964.

Ha'atikos = New York, Ha'atikos, *Important Judaica . . .*, sale catalogue, February 1, 1988.

Hallo 1929 = R. Hallo, "Jüdische Kultaltertümer aus Edelmetall in der Ausstellung Religiose Kunst aus Hessen und Nassau, Marburg a/Lahn, Sommer 1928," *Notizblatt* 23–24 (1929).

———— *1932* = R. Hallo, "Judaica," Religiose Kunst aus Hessen und Nassau. Kritischer Gesamtkatalog der Ausstellung Marburg 1928, exhibition catalogue, Marburg, 1932, pp. 207–47 (= R. Hallo, *Jüdische Kunst aus Hessen und Nassau*. Berlin, 1933).

Hanau = Hanau, Magistrat der Stadt Hanau, *450 Jahre altstädter Rathaus. Deutsches Goldschmiedehaus Hanau*. Hanau, 1988.

Harburger Photo-Archive = The Harburger Collection of Photographic Negatives, at the Archives of the Jewish People, The Hebrew University, Jerusalem.

Harvard = Cambridge, MA, Harvard University Library, *Catalogue of the . . . Tumen Collection of Jewish Ceremonial Objects . . .*, by V. Gilboa, 1993.

*Hebraica* = H. Gutmann, *Hebraica. Documents d'art juif. Orfèvrerie, Peinture*. Paris, 1930.

Heidingsfelder = B. Heidingsfelder, *Allgemeines Lexicon sämtlicher jüdischen Gemeinden Deutschlands*. Frankfurt am Main, 1884.

Helbing 1932a = Munich, Hugo Helbing, *Jüdische Kultgeräte, Silber, Waffen . . .*, sale catalogue, Feb. 12–13, 1932.

———— 1932b = Munich, Hugo Helbing, *Jüdische Kultgeräte, Silber, Gläser...*, sale catalogue, April 14, 1932.

Hintze 1906 = E. Hintze, *Die Breslauer Goldschmiede. Eine archivalische Studie*. Breslau 1906.

———— 1929 = Breslau, Schlesisches Museum für Kunstgewerbe und Altertümer, *Katalog der ... Ausstellung Das Judentum in der Geschichte Schlesiens*, ed. by E. Hintze, exhibition catalogue, 1929.

*Historica* = Berlin, Jüdischen Gemeindehaus, *Historica Hebraica. Jüdische Kunst — Kultur und Geschichte aus dem Staatlichen Jüdischen Museum Prag*, exhibition catalogue, 1965.

Hohenems = Hohenems, Jüdisches Museum, *Geschichten von Gegenständen. Judaika aus dem Beziehungsraum der Hohenemser Juden. The Gross Family Collection, Tel Aviv*, ed. by E. Grabherr, exhibition catalogue, 1994.

Horowitz = Miami, Temple Israel, *Exhibition of Jewish Ceremonial and Jewish Folk Art* (Horowitz Collection), exhibition catalogue, 1930.

Huth = H. Huth, *Die Kunstdenkmäler in Baden-Württemberg Stadtkreis Mannheim*. Munich, 1982.

Idelson = A.Z. Idelson, *The Ceremonies of Judaism*, New York, 1930.

*Ingathering* = New York, Jewish Museum, *Ingathering. Ceremony and Tradition in New York Public Collections*, by Irene Winter, exhibition catalogue, 1968.

Isaacson = B. Isaacson, *Dictionary of the Jewish Religion*. Englewood, NJ, 1979.

*Italian Silver* = London, Victoria and Albert Museum, *Italian Secular Silver* (Small Picture Book No. 57). London, 1962.

Jackson = C. J. Jackson, *English Goldsmiths and their Marks*. London, 1921 (reprinted New York, 1964).

Jacobs = London, Royal Albert Hall, *Catalogue of the Anglo-Jewish Historical Exhibition*, by J. Jacobs and L. Wolf, exhibition catalogue, 1888.

*JE* = *The Jewish Encyclopaedia* I–XII, NY and London, 1901.

*Jewish Museum 75* = New York, The Jewish Museum, *The Jewish Museum at 75*, brochure, [1979].

*JL* = *Jüdisches Lexikon* I–V, Berlin, 1931.

JMNY 1947 = New York, Jewish Museum, *The Jewish Museum. Inaugural Exhibition. The Giving of the Law and The Ten Commandments*, exhibition brochure, [1947].

JMNY 1993 = V. B. Mann with Emily D. Bilski, *The Jewish Museum New York*. London, 1993.

Judaica Jerusalem = Jerusalem, Judaica Jerusalem (Society for Documentation of the Ancient Hebrew Book), *Exhibition and Auction ... Judaica*, sale catalogue, October 4, 1994.

Juhasz = Jerusalem, The Israel Museum, *Sephardi Jews in the Ottoman Empire*, ed. by E. Juhasz, exhibition catalogue, 1990.

*Juifs d'Algerie* = J. Lalour and J.-L. Allouche, eds., *Les Juifs d'Algerie. Images et textes*. Paris, 1984.

*Juifs d'Egypte* = Editions du Scribe, *Juifs d'Egypte. Images et textes*. Paris, 1984.

Kalender = *Deutscher Goldschmiede-Kalender 1951*. Stuttgart, 1951.

Kaniel = M. Kaniel, *A Guide to Jewish Art*, New York, 1989.

Kanof = A. Kanof, *Jewish Ceremonial Art and Religious Observance*. New York, [1969].

Kantsedikas = A. Kantsedikas, Y. Volkovinskaya and T. Romanovskaya, *Silver* (Masterpieces of Jewish Art ... in the Commonwealth of Independent States, Vol. 3). Moscow, 1992.

Kashani = R. Kashani, *The Jews of Afghanistan*. Jerusalem 1975.

Katz et al. = K. Katz et al., *From the Beginning. Art and Archaeology in the Israel Museum*. Jerusalem-London, 1968.

Kayser = S.S. Kayser and G. Schoenberger, *Jewish Ceremonial Art*. Philadelphia, 1959 (2nd ed.).

Kayser 1950–51 = S.S. Kayser, "A Polish Torah Crown," *Hebrew Union College Annual* 23/2 (1950–51), pp. 493–501.

Kiefer = Isidor Kiefer, "Dan Museum der israelitischen Gemeinde Worms," *Zeitschrift für die Geschichte der Juden in Deutschland* V, 1934, pp. 182–86.

*Kings and Citizens* = New York, The Jewish Museum, *Kings and Citizens. The History of the Jews in Denmark 1622–1983* I–II, exhibition catalogue, 1983.

Klagsbald 1981 = Paris, Musée de Cluny, *Catalogue raisonné de la collection juive du Musée de Cluny*, by V. Klagsbald, exhibition catalogue, 1981.

———— 1982 = Jerusalem, Israel Museum, *Jewish Treasures from Paris...*, by V. Klagsbald, exhibition catalogue, 1982.

Köln = L. Franzheim, *Judaica. Kölnisches Stadtmuseum*. Köln, 1980.

La vie juive = Jerusalem, The Israel Museum, *La vie juive au Maroc*, exhibition catalogue, by A. Muller-Lancet and D. Champoult, 1986.

Lazar = H. Lazar, "Du nouveau dans l'art sacré juif," *L'Oeil* 288/289 (1979), pp. 62–63.

Levy = I. J. Levy, *Jewish Rhodes: A Lost Culture*. Berkeley, CA, 1989.

Lewin = D. Lewin, "Das Matthias-Bersohn-Museum in Warschau," *Aus aletr und neuer Zeit* 47 (July 1929), pp. 372–73.

Lileyko = H. Lileyko, *Srebra warszawskie w zbiorach Muzeum Historycznego m. st. Warszawy*. Warsaw 1979; the silversmiths' marks are listed on pp. 90–98, and numbered from 1 to 73; for convenience, the author has continued the numbering as follows: p. 99, 74–82e; p. 100, 83–91b; p. 101, 92–99; p. 102, 100–105 (No. 101a–d).

Livorno = *La nazione Ebrea di Livorno. Itinerari di vita*, exhibition catalogue, Livorno, 1991.

Loukomski = G. K. Loukomski, *Jewish Art in European Synagogues*. London, 1947.

Magnes = Berkeley, Judah L. Magnes Museum, *Embellished Lives, Customs and Costumes of the Jewish Communities of Turkey* exhibition catalogue, 1989.

Lewin = D. Lewin, "Das Matthias-Bersohn-Museum in Warschau," *AaunZ* 47, July 1929, pp. 372–373.

Lileyko = H. Lileyko, *Srebra warszawskie w zbiorach Muzeum Historycznego m. st. Warszawy*. Warsaw 1979; the silversmiths' marks are listed on pp. 90–98, and numbered from 1 to 73; for convenience, the author has continued the numbering as follows: p. 99, 74–82e; p. 100, 83–91b; p. 101, 92–99; p. 102, 100–105 (No. 101a–d).

Livorno = *La nazione Ebrea di Livorno. Itinerari di vita*, exhibition catalogue, Livorno, 1991.

Loukomski = G. K. Loukomski, *Jewish Art in European Synagogues*. London, 1947.

Magnes = Berkeley, Judah L. Magnes Museum, *Embellished Lives, Customs and Costumes of the Jewish Communities of Turkey* exhibition catalogue, 1989.

Mainz = Mainz, Mittelrheinischen Landesmuseum, *Ausstellung der Judaica-Sammlung in Mittelrheinischen Landesmuseum Mainz*, exhibition catalogue, 1983.

Mann 1982 = New York, The Jewish Museum, *A Tale of Two Cities. Jewish Life in Frankfurt and Istanbul 1750-1870*, by V. B. Mann, exhibition catalogue, 1982.

———— 1986 = V. B. Mann, "The Golden Age of Jewish Ceremonial Art in Frankfurt. Metalwork of the Eighteenth Century," *Leo Baeck Institute Year Book* 31 (1986), pp. 389–403.

Martyna = E. Martyna, *Judaica w zbiorach Muzeum Narodowego w Warszawie*. Warsaw, 1993.

Mazin = R. Mazin and Co. Ltd., *Catalogue No. 51. Daily and Festival Prayer Books, Bibles, Pentateuchs, Books Suitable for Presentation, Rituals for Home and Synagogue, Jewish Museum, Wall Pictures, Etc.*. London, 1916.

Mitrani = E. Mitrani and E. Alok: *Anatolian Synagogues*. Istanbul, 1992.

*Mitt.* I = H. Frauberger, *Zweck und Ziel der Gesellschaft zur Erforschung Jüdischer Kunstdenkmäler zu Frankfurt a.M.* (*Mittheilungen der Gesellschaft zur Erforschung jüdischer Kunstdenkmäler* I., October 1900), Frankfurt am Main 1900.

———— III–IV = H. Frauberger, *Über alte Kultus Gegenstände in Synagoge und Haus* (*Mittheilungen der Gesellschaft zur Erforschung jüdischer Kunstdenkmäler* III. IV.), Frankfurt am Main 1903.

*Mon. Jud.* = Köln, Kölnischen Stadtmuseum, *Monumenta Judaica. 2000 Jahre Geschichte und Kultur der Juden am Rhein. Katalog*, ed. by K. Schilling, exhibition catalogue, 1963.

Moses = E. Moses, "Jüdische Kult- und Kunstdenkmäler in den Rheinlanden", *Aus der Geschichte der Juden im Rheinland. Jüdische Kult- und Kunstdenkmäler*. Düsseldorf, 1931.

Munich = Munich, Verband Bayerischer Israelitischer Gemeinden and Der Israelitischen Kultusgemeinde, *Ausstellung jüdischer Kult-Geräte und Einrichtungen für Synagoge und Haus*, [by Th. Harburger,] exhibition catalogue, 1930.

Namenyi = Paris, Musée d'art juif, *Art religieux juif. Reflêt des styles, 13ᵉ siècle au 19ᵉ siècle*, by E. Namenyi, exhibition catalogue, 1954.

Neuwirth 1976 = W. Neuwirth, *Lexikon Wiener Gold- und Silberschmiede und ihre Punzen. 1867-1922* I–II. Vienna, 1976.

———— 1978 = W. Neuwirth, *Markenlexikon für Kunstgewerbe 1. Die Edle und unedle Metalle. 1875-1900*. Vienna, 1978.

*NY Register* 1917 = New York, Kehillah, *The Jewish Communal Register of New York City, 1917-1918*. New York, 1918.

*Notizblatt* 1929 = R. Hallo, *Jüdische Kultaltertümer aus Edelmetall in der Ausstellung Religiose Kunst aus Hessen und Nassau, Marburg a/Lahn, Sommer 1928* (Notizblatt der Gesellschaft zur Erforschung jüdischer Kunstdenkmäler Nos. 23 and 24). Frankfurt am Main, 1929.

———— 1937 = H. Gundersheimer and G. Schonberger, *Frankfurter Chanukkah-leuchter aus Silber und Zinn* (Notizblatt der Gesellschaft zur Erforschung jüdischer Kunstdenkmäler No. 34). Frankfurt am Main, 1937.

NYHS = New York, The New York Historical Society, *City of Promise*, exhibition catalogue, 1971.

Ohel Moshe = Jerusalem, Center for Jewish Art, *Ohel Moshe: The Synagogue and its Ritual Objects*. Jerusalem, 1984 (Hebrew).

*Oppenheim* = New York, The Jewish Museum, *The Paintings of Moritz Oppenheim. Jewish Life in 19th Century Germany*, by Norman L. Kleeblatt, exhibition brochure, 1981.

Pappenheim Album = Album (ca. 1930) of "order catalogue" photographs of several manufacturers of metal and porcellain Judaica in Frankfurt am Main, Hanau and other German cities, formerly in the possession of a Hamburg family (apparently that of E. Joelson; see below) and now belonging to Rabbi Shlomo Pappenheim, Jerusalem. The manufacturers include Posen (Frankfurt am Main; little material), Lorenz Streb (Gross-Auheim near Hanau), the Gutgesell Brothers (Hanau), and "Kunstgewerbestube E. Joelson, Bogenstr. 119, Hamburg 27 [formerly Parkallee Nr. 20], Tel. Nordsee 6444" — original owner of the album and who also made mixed-media Judaica.

Pataky = I. Pataky-Brestyànszky, "The Becker Family: Silversmiths of Bratislava," *Jewish Art* 19/20 (1993/94), pp. 180–93.

Pazzi = P. Pazzi, *I Punzoni dell'Argenteria e Oreficeria Veneziana*. Venice, 1990.

PBNY 1949 = New York, Parke-Bernet, *Jewish Ritual Silver*, sale catalogue, December 6, 1949.

———— 1950 = New York, Parke-Bernet Galleries, *Pre-Columbian . . . Gothic and Renaissance Art. Jewish Ritual Silver*, sale catalogue, October 18, 1950.

———— 1954 = New York, Parke-Bernet, *Rare Near Eastern Pottery . . ., Jewish Ritual Silver . . .*, sale catalogue, February 19, 1954.

———— 1957 = New York, Parke-Bernet, *Judaica . . . Collection of Tullio Castelbolognesi, Rome*, sale catalogue, February 14, 1957.

———— 1964 = New York, Parke-Bernet, *The Michael M. Zagayski Collection of Rare Judaica*, sale catalogue, June 23, 1967.

———— 1967 = New York, Parke-Bernet, *The Charles E. Feinberg Collection of Valuable Judaica*, sale catalogue, June 23, 1967.

———— 1968 = New York, Parke-Bernet, *Judaica*, sale catalogue, March 13, 1968.

———— 1969 = New York, Parke-Bernet, *Judaica*, sale catalogue, May 28, 1969.

———— 1970 = Parke-Bernet, New York, *Valuable Judaica*, sale catalogue, May 20, 1970.

———— 1977 = New York, Parke-Bernet, *Judaica and Other Works of Art*, sale catalogue, March 16, 1977.

Perry's Tel Aviv, 1986 = Tel Aviv, Perry's, *Judaica . . .*, sale catalogue, September 17, 1986.

Pickford = I. Pickford, *Pocket Edition. Jackson's Hallmarks, English, Scottish, Irish Silver and Gold Marks from 1300 to the Present Day*. Woodbridge (Suffolk), 1991.

Pinkerfeld 1929 = J. Pinkerfeld, "Alte palaestinensische Thorarollen und ihr Schmuck (Jüdische Kunstsammlungen/VII)," *Aus alter und neuer Zeit* (biweekly of the "Israelitischen familienblattes," Hamburg), No. 46, July 11, 1929, pp. 364–365.

———— 1971 = J. Pinkerfeld, *Synagogues in Eretz-Israel*, Jerusalem, 1971 (Hebrew).

Postnikova = M.M. Postnikova-Losseva, *Russian Jewellery, its Centres and Masters, XVIth-XIXth Centuries*. Moscow, 1974 (Russian) (= Slavisches Institut, *Verzeichnis der Russischen Gold- und Silbermarken*. Munich, 1971).

R³ = M. Rosenberg, *Der Goldschmiede Merkzeichen* I–IV. Frankfurt am Main, 1922 (3rd ed.).

Reitzner = V. Reitzner, *Edelmetalle und deren Punzen* (Alt-Wien-Lexikon für Österreichische und Süddeutsche Kunst und Kunstgewerbe, III). Vienna, 1952.

Rohrwasser = A. Rohrwasser, *Österreichs Punzen. Edelmetall-Punzierung in Österreich von 1524 bis 1987*. Vienna, 1987 (2nd ed.).

Rosenan = N. Rosenan, *Das Jüdische Jahr, dargestellt am Ausstellungsgut des Jüdischen Museums der Schweiz in Basel*. Basel 1976.

Roth = C. Roth, ed., *Jewish Art. An Illustrated History*. Tel Aviv, 1971

Rubenovitz = M. L. Rubenovitz, *Altars of My Fathers*, New York, 1963.

Schäfke = Köln, Kölnisches Stadtmuseum, *Goldschmiedearbeiten des Historismus in Köln*, ed. by W. Schäfke, exhibition catalogue, 1980.

Scheffler, *Berlin* = W. Scheffler, *Berlin Goldschmiede*. Berlin, 1968.

————, *Hessen* = W. Scheffler, *Goldschmiede Hessens, Daten, Werke, Zeichen*. Berlin, 1976.

Schliemann = E. Schliemann, ed., *Die Goldschmiede Hamburgs* I–III. Hamburg, 1985.

Seling = H. Seling, *Die Kunst der Augsburger Goldschmiede 1529-1868* I–III. Munich, 1980.

*Sephardic Journey* = New York, Yeshiva University Museum, *The Sephardic Journey 1492-1992*, exhibition catalogue, 5752 (= 1992).

*Shoshanim Le David* = Jerusalem, Center for Jewish Art, *Shoshanim Le David Synagogue. Ritual Objects*. Jerusalem, 1981.

Society of Judaica Collectors = Jerusalem, Society of Judaica Collectors, *Exhibition and Auction. Rare . . . Jewish Works of Art*, sale catalogue, February 5–14, 1989.

Sotheby's Jerusalem 1987 = Jerusalem, Sotheby's, *Judaica . . .*, sale catalogue, May 24, 1987.

———— 1988 = Jerusalem, Sotheby's, *Judaica . . .*, sale catalogue, May 5–6, 1988.

Sotheby's New York 1981 = New York, Sotheby's, *Good Judaica . . .*, sale catalogue, May 13, 1981.

———— 1981a = New York, Sotheby's, *Fine Judaica . . .*, sale catalogue, November 25, 1981.

———— 1982 = New York, Sotheby's, *Fine Judaica . . .*, sale catalogue, November 24, 1982.

———— 1983 = New York, Sotheby's, *Fine Judaica: Works of Art*, sale catalogue, November 9, 1983.

———— 1984 = New York, Sotheby's, *Important Judaica . . .*, sale catalogue, June 27, 1984.

———— 1984a = New York, Sotheby's, *Judaic Books, Manuscripts and Works of Art*, sale catalogue, December 6–7, 1984.

———— 1985 = New York, Sotheby's, *Important Judaica . . .*, sale catalogue, November 25, 1985.

———— 1986 = New York, Sotheby's, *Important Judaica . . .*, sale catalogue, December 18, 1986.

———— 1987 = New York, Sotheby's, *Important Judaica . . .*, sale catalogue, December 14, 1987.

———— 1989 = New York, Sotheby's, *Important Judaica . . .*, sale catalogue, December 18, 1989.

Sotheby's Tel Aviv 1991 = Tel Aviv, Sotheby's, *Important Judaica . . .*, sale catalogue, October 2, 1991.

———— 1992 = Tel Aviv, Sotheby's, *Important Judaica . . .*, sale catalogue, April 28, 1992.

———— 1993 = Tel Aviv, Sotheby's, *Important Judaica . . .*, sale catalogue, October 5, 1993.

———— 1994 = Tel Aviv, Sotheby's, *Important Judaica . . .*, sale catalogue, April 6, 1994.

Stahl = A. Stahl, *The Torah Scroll*. Jerusalem, 1979.

Steinhardt = New York, Hebrew Union College-Jewish Institute of Religion, *The Collector's Room. Selections from the Michael and Judy Steinhardt Collection*, by C. Grossman, exhibition brochure, 1993.

*Stieglitz* = Jerusalem, The Israel Museum, *The Stieglitz Collection . . .*, by C. Benjamin, exhibition catalogue, 1987.

Stone = J. Stone, "English Silver Rimmonim and their Makers," *Quest* 1 (1965), pp. 23ff.

V and A = London, Victoria and Albert Museum, *German Domestic Silver of the Eighteenth Century* (Small Picture Book No. 58). London, 1965.

*Venice* = New York, The Jewish Museum, *The Jewish Patrons of Venice*, by S.J. Makover, exhibition brochure, 1985.

Vienna = Vienna (Hofburg), Museum für Völkerkunde, *Kunstschätze Staatlicher Jüdisches Museum Prag*, by J. Hraský, exhibition catalogue, 1970.

Voet = E. Voet, *Nederlandse Goud- en Zilvermerken*. 's-Gravenhage, 1978.

Warncke = J. Warncke, *Die Edelschmiedekunst in Lübeck....* Lübeck, 1927.

Weinstein = J. Weinstein, *A Collectors' Guide to Judaica*. London, 1985.

Wolpert 1976 = New York, The Jewish Museum, *Ludwig Yehuda Wolpert. A Retrospective*, exhibition catalogue, 1976.

———— 1982 = *In Memoriam Ludwig Y. Wolpert...A Collection of Excerpts ... about ... Wolpert ... October 17, 1982*, n.p., n.d.

*Wüb* = Frankfurt am Main, Jüdischen Museum Frankfurt, *Was übrig bleib. Das Museum jüdischer Altertümer in Frankfurt*, ed. by F. Heimann-Jelinek, exhibition catalogue, 1988.

Yaniv 1982 = B. Yaniv, "The Metalwork of Torah Cases from Iraq in the 19th and 20th Centuries," *Pe'amim. Studies in the Cultural Heritage of Oriental Jewry* 11 (1982), pp. 102– 12 (Hebrew).

Yaniv 1992 = B. Yaniv, "An Attempt to Reconstruct the Design of Moroccan Tower-Form Rimonim according to Spanish Models," *Pe'amim. Studies in the Cultural Heritage of Oriental Jewry* 50 (1992), pp. 69–98 (Hebrew).

Yaniv 1993 = B. Yaniv, "Italian and French Influence on the Design of Torah Cases in Libya and Tunisia," *Pe'amim. Studies in the Cultural Heritage of Oriental Jewry* 59 (1993), pp. 82–113 (Hebrew).

*Yugoslavia* = Zagreb, Museum Gallery Center, *Jews in Yugoslavia*, exhibition catalogue, 1989.

Zagayski 1951 = New York, The Jewish Museum, *Loan Exhibit of Antique Ceremonial Objects and Paintings from the Collection of Mr. M. Zagayski*, exhibition catalogue, 1951.

———— 1963 = New York, The Jewish Museum, *The Silver and Judaica Collection of Mr. and Mrs. Michael M. Zagayski*, by G. Schoenberger and T. Freudenheim, exhibition catalogue, 1963.

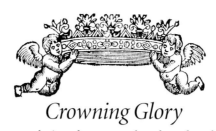

*Crowning Glory*

was designed, composed, and produced

by Scott-Martin Kosofsky at The Philidor Company, Boston.

The text was set in subtly differentiated weights, widths, and optical sizes

of Robert Slimbach's Minion, using Adobe System's invaluable, though all-too-seldomly

used, Multiple Master technology. Minion might be described as an oldstyle typeface with

Venetian tendencies. As such, it's based on Aldus's Bembo type with some characteristics

taken from Jenson's Eusebius face. Perhaps its greatest debt of inspiration is to

Giovanni Mardersteig and Charles Malin's Dante and Griffo types.

The Hebrew typeface is David. Slimbach's Poetica small caps

appear in the running heads; Matthew Carter's Mantinia

is featured in the volume's title; and arrangements

of Giolito's arabesque appear throughout

the book. All the types were modified

to a greater or lesser extent by

Mr. Kosofsky.

The transparencies (most of

which were masterfully shot for this

volume by John Parnell, in New York) and

photographs were scanned by Aurora Graphics

in Portsmouth, New Hampshire, who also generated

the final film. All were edited—some older ones extensively—

by Scott-Martin Kosofsky using Adobe Photoshop 3.0. The pages were

composed in Quark XPress 3.31 (text and pictures) and were output in

four-page spreads on a Scitex Dolev imagesetter. The Nimrod Press,

Westwood, Massachusetts printed the book on Westvaco

Sterling Satin, an acid-free sheet. Acme Bookbinding

of Charlestown, Massachusetts bound the

book in Holliston Record Buckram.